LAW, SOCIETY, AND HISTORY

This book assembles essays on legal sociology and legal history by an international group of distinguished scholars. All of them have been influenced by the eminent and prolific legal historian, legal sociologist, and scholar of comparative law, Lawrence M. Friedman. Not just a Festschrift of essays by colleagues and disciples, this volume presents a sustained examination and application of Friedman's ideas and methods. Some of the writers directly assess and comment on Friedman's vast body of work. Others examine his conclusions to see how well they have stood up over time. Various contributors apply concepts and insights derived from Friedman's work to the study of similar problems in different periods and societies. And others use Friedman's concepts and insights as a foil or contrast to their own approaches to studying law and society from theoretical perspectives very different from his. Together, the essays in this volume show the powerful ripple effects of Friedman's work on American and comparative legal sociology, American and comparative legal history, and the general sociology of law and legal change.

Robert W. Gordon is Chancellor Kent Professor of Law and Legal History at Yale University. He has also taught at the universities of Buffalo, Wisconsin, and Stanford. He is the author of *The Legacy of Oliver Wendell Holmes, Jr.*; *Critical Legal Histories*; and many articles on the history of the legal profession, the uses of history in legal argument, and contract law. He is at work on a history of the American legal profession in the twentieth century.

Morton J. Horwitz is Charles Warren Professor of American Legal History at Harvard University. He is the author of *The Transformation of American Law 1780–1860*, which won the Bancroft Prize in American History; *The Transformation of American Law, 1870–1960*; and *The Warren Court and the Pursuit of Justice*. He is at work on a history of the Supreme Court under Chief Justice Earl Warren, a volume in the Oliver Wendell Holmes Devise History of the Supreme Court.

CAMBRIDGE STUDIES IN LAW AND SOCIETY

Cambridge Studies in Law and Society aims to publish the best scholarly work on legal discourse and practice in its social and institutional contexts, combining theoretical insights and empirical research.

The fields that it covers are: studies of law in action; the sociology of law; the anthropology of law; cultural studies of law, including the role of legal discourses in social formations; law and economics; law and politics; and studies of governance. The books consider all forms of legal discourse across societies, rather than being limited to lawyers' discourses alone.

The series editors come from a range of disciplines: academic law, socio-legal studies, sociology, and anthropology. All have been actively involved in teaching and writing about law in context.

Series Editors

Chris Arup
Monash University, Victoria

Martin Chanock
La Trobe University, Melbourne

Pat O'Malley
University of Sydney

Sally Engle Merry
New York University

Susan Silbey
Massachusetts Institute of Technology

Books in the Series

The World Trade Organization Knowledge Agreements, 2nd Edition
Christopher Arup

Law and Nature
David Delaney

Constitutionalizing Economic Globalization:
Investment Rules and Democracy's Promise
David Schneiderman

Law, Anthropology, and the Constitution of the Social:
Making Persons and Things
Edited by Alain Pottage and Martha Mundy

(continued after Index)

Law, Society, and History

THEMES IN THE LEGAL SOCIOLOGY AND LEGAL HISTORY OF LAWRENCE M. FRIEDMAN

Edited by

ROBERT W. GORDON
Yale University School of Law

MORTON J. HORWITZ
Harvard University School of Law

CAMBRIDGE
UNIVERSITY PRESS

32 Avenue of the Americas, New York NY 10013-2473, USA

Cambridge University Press is part of the University of Cambridge.

It furthers the University's mission by disseminating knowledge in the pursuit of education, learning and research at the highest international levels of excellence.

www.cambridge.org
Information on this title: www.cambridge.org/9781107459496

First published 2011
First paperback edition 2014

A catalogue record for this publication is available from the British Library

Library of Congress Cataloguing in Publication data

Law, society, and history : themes in the legal sociology and legal history of Lawrence M. Friedman / [edited by] Robert W. Gordon, Morton J. Horwitz.
  p. cm. – (Cambridge studies in law and society)
Includes bibliographical references and index.
ISBN 978-0-521-19390-0 (hardback)
1. Friedman, Lawrence Meir, 1930–   2. Sociological jurisprudence.   3. Law – History.
I. Gordon, Robert W. (Robert Watson), 1941–   II. Horwitz, Morton J., 1938–
K376.L388   2011
340'.115 – dc22   2010046417

ISBN 978-0-521-19390-0 Hardback
ISBN 978-1-107-45949-6 Paperback

Contents

Contributors

Erhard Blankenburg is Professor of Law Emeritus at the Free University of Amsterdam.

Jo Carrillo is Professor of Law at the University of California Hastings College of the Law.

Lauren B. Edelman is Agnes Roddy Robb Professor of Law at the University of California, Berkeley.

Malcolm M. Feeley is Claire Sanders Clements Dean's Chair Professor of Law at the University of California, Berkeley.

Vincenzo Ferrari is Professor of Law at the University of Milan.

George Fisher is Judge John Crown Professor of Law at Stanford University.

Marc Galanter is the John and Rylla Bosshard Professor of Law and South Asian Studies at the University of Wisconsin, Madison and LSE Centennial Professor at the London School of Economics and Political Science.

Tom Ginsburg is Professor of Law at the University of Chicago.

Robert W. Gordon is Chancellor Kent Professor of Law and Legal History at Yale University.

Joanna L. Grossman is Professor of Law at Hofstra University.

Morton J. Horwitz is Charles Warren Professor of American Legal History at Harvard University.

Robert A. Kagan is Emanuel S. Heller Professor of Law and Professor of Political Science at the University of California, Berkeley.

Philip Lewis is Senior Research Fellow at the Centre for Socio-Legal Studies, Oxford University.

Stewart Macaulay is Malcolm Pitman Sharp Hilldale Professor and Theodore W. Brazeau Professor of Law at the University of Wisconsin, Madison.

Richard S. Markovits is John B. Connally Professor of Law at the University of Texas, Austin.

Setsuo Miyazawa is Professor of Law at Aoyama Gakuin University Law School (Japan).

Robert V. Percival is Robert F. Stanton Professor of Law and Director of the Environmental Law Program at the University of Maryland.

Rogelio Pérez-Perdomo is Professor of Law at the Universidad Metropolitana in Caracas (Venezuela).

Thomas D. Russell is Professor of Law at the University of Denver.

Harry N. Scheiber is Stefan A. Riesenfeld Professor of Law and History and Director of the Institute for Legal Research at the University of California, Berkeley.

Gunther Teubner is Professor of Private Law and Legal Sociology at the International University College, Torino, Italy and Principal Investigator, Excellence Cluster "Normative Orders," Goethe University, Frankfurt.

José Juan Toharia is Professor of Sociology at the Autonomous University of Madrid.

James Q. Whitman is Ford Foundation Professor of Comparative and Foreign Law at Yale University.

Victoria Saker Woeste is Research Professor at the American Bar Foundation.

Introduction

Robert W. Gordon and Morton J. Horwitz

The chapters in this volume approach and bounce off a common object from many different angles. That object is the set of concepts, themes, methods, and conclusions in the work of one of the most influential and productive scholars of law and society, Lawrence M. Friedman of Stanford University. The authors are an international cast of distinguished scholars of law and society: legal sociologists, legal historians, and students of comparative law. This book is not a Festschrift in the usual sense of a collection of miscellaneous essays by colleagues and disciplines assembled to honor a great scholar. Rather it is a sustained examination and application of the scholar's ideas and methods. Some of the writers directly assess and comment on Friedman's vast body of work. Some examine his conclusions to see how well they have stood up over time. Others apply concepts and insights derived from Friedman's work to the study of similar problems in different periods and societies. Still others use Friedman's concepts and insights as a foil or contrast to their own approaches to studying law and society from theoretical perspectives very different from his.

We should say a few words first about the extraordinary man whose ideas and their applications are the centerpiece of this volume. Lawrence M. Friedman was born in Chicago in 1930. He received a B.A. at the age of 18, a J.D. at 21, and an LL.M. at age 23, all from the University of Chicago. He practiced law briefly in Chicago before becoming a law teacher at St. Louis University (1957–60), University of Wisconsin (1961–8), and ultimately Stanford (1968–present), where he is the Marion Rice Kirkwood Professor. At Wisconsin, James Willard Hurst, the guiding influence on Friedman's life's work, recruited him to the study of the mass of the legal system's ordinary business; Friedman is generally regarded as Hurst's successor as the greatest of American sociolegal historians. He is also preeminent among

All but five chapters were first given in preliminary form at a conference on Lawrence Friedman's work at Stanford University in October 2005. Two chapters were first delivered to a panel on Friedman's work at the American Society for Legal History annual meeting in Cincinnati in November 2005, and three were submitted subsequently.

comparative sociologists of law and has been president of both the American Society for Legal History and the Law and Society Association.

Friedman is extraordinarily prolific. He is the author of 18 books, an editor of 8 more, and has written more than 200 articles. His work falls into four broad categories:

1. Studies of patterns of legal enactments and decisions in particular fields of American legal history: His pioneering study of 500 Wisconsin contract cases in three different periods, *Contract Law in America* (1965), was followed by monographs on government slum housing policy, the political-economic origins of workers' compensation laws, the impact of business cycles on the legal regulation of usury, longitudinal studies of the business of state courts, the rise of personal injury litigation, changes in the law of wills and trusts, the courts' treatment of occupational licensing laws, changing patterns of family and divorce law (e.g., *Private Lives: Families, Individuals and the Law* [2004]), morals regulation (*Guarding Life's Dark Secrets: Legal and Social Controls over Reputation, Propriety, and Privacy* [2007]), and the history of criminal justice policy (e.g., *Crime and Punishment in American History* [1993], a Pulitzer Prize finalist), among many others.

2. Synthetic general works of legal history, such as *A History of American Law* (1973, 3d ed., 2005) and *American Law in the Twentieth Century* (2002), building on the monographs but supplemented by research into hundreds of other topics.

3. Work in legal sociology on the relation between legal enactments and social change, the interpretation of legal texts, and variations in legal cultures, illustrated by comparative and historical examples (e.g., *The Legal System: A Social Science Perspective* [1975]).

4. Reflections on large-scale social trends affecting the design and development of legal systems in the West, particularly in the United States: *Total Justice* (1985), *The Republic of Choice* (1990), and *The Horizontal Society* (1999).

Underlying all of Friedman's work are certain consistent unifying themes:

*   Social conditions create law, and law changes in response to social forces. Friedman treats law "not as a kingdom unto itself, not as a set of rules and concepts, not as the province of lawyers alone, but as the mirror of society. It takes nothing as historical accident, nothing as autonomous, everything as relative and molded by economy and society. . . . The [legal] system works like a blind, insensate machine. It does the bidding of those whose hands are on the controls. . . . [T]he strongest ingredient in American law, at any given time, is the present: current emotions, real economic interests, concrete political groups" (*A History of American Law*, 12).

- Thus law has little autonomy: Law's distinctively legal doctrines, principles, and procedures have little independent importance; legal "traditions" do not by themselves account for much of the current content of law. Law is constantly changing because society changes; when law seems to stand still, it does so not because of the force of precedent, inertia, or "lag," but because powerful background forces have stalemated and current interests are pushing back against pressures for change. Likewise, the forms of law – for example, whether it uses rules or standards, strict or loose interpretations of texts and legal instruments – are usually functions of background demands on legal systems. Change internal to the legal system cannot in itself bring about large social consequences. Law cannot consistently or for long periods remain out of sync with the interests of the powerful in society. The historian or social scientists looking for explanations of legal change will most likely find them in the study of social interests, forces, and demands – not in the doctrines, principles, or internal structures of the legal system. Similarly, legal change is most likely to be effective when it is supported by powerful interests.
- The background demands in modern societies tend to follow broadly convergent patterns of development or modernization. Developed commercial and industrial societies differ from one another in details, but tend to follow similar developmental paths, which produce similar legal doctrines and consequences.
- Although similar in general shape, social demands on legal systems are mediated through variable "legal cultures" – that is, by people's – including legal professionals' – ideas, attitudes, and expectations about law and legal process that help condition what sorts of demands social groups will make on their legal systems.
- Legal cultures also mirror general social trends of modern societies, such as the growth of individual rights-consciousness and the sense of personal entitlement to create and develop selves through choices. These social trends translate into claims on legal systems to provide "total justice" – to play an active role in preventing and compensating violations of rights and to provide security and space for the exercise of personal autonomy.

Along with these general theoretical commitments – and partly as a result of them – Friedman has also developed a distinctive set of working assumptions and methods.

- Friedman is inclined (as we noted earlier) to look for the sources of legal change in external social pressures and interests that generate demands on legal systems. To explain legal change he tends to privilege technological change, social structure, and political movements. He is skeptical of explanations that identify elite theories or ideologies, such as philosophical or juristic movements, legal principles, or the rhetoric of legal opinions, as motors of change. However, he is not any kind of economic determinist: People act out commitments to values as well as interests.

- Like his mentor Willard Hurst, Friedman prefers to study routine rather than exceptional legal phenomena: the output of state legislatures and courts rather than large federal constitutional cases, the commonplace legal problems of ordinary people, the routine dockets of trial and appellate courts. He likes to find his research materials in the courthouse basement. He has written pioneering studies of routine criminal processing in the courts of Alameda County and general court dockets in San Benito County, both in California; of the business of trial courts and appellate courts; and of historical trends in tort and divorce litigation and in morals regulation.
- Although Friedman's general theoretical and methodological commitments are clear, firm, and consistent over a lifetime's work, he is remarkably nondogmatic. His main commitment is openness to being surprised by whatever the data of his research are likely to yield. When he goes on one of his many foraging expeditions into documents in the basement, he has very few preconceived notions about what he is likely to find there – except the general notion that it is *there*, that the truths about law are to be found in the mass of evidence that is collected at the bottom of the system. In the service of that commitment he has made many original discoveries that, where there was previous work, have upended received ideas and, in other cases where he was the first to venture, have laid the foundation for future scholarship.
- Not least important, Friedman has a commitment to an informal and accessible style. Like his preference for studying routine enactments that affect the lives of ordinary people and his privileging of bottom-up social demands as causes of legal change, this is a democratic commitment. Law should not be a mystery; its archaisms are more likely to be affectations than attachments to traditions; and there is no legal doctrine or practice, however technical, that cannot be expounded clearly.

Friedman's prolific output, manifold original historical discoveries, distinctive and forcefully expressed theories of law and society, vast comparative learning, and charming and accessible prose have made him one of the most cited and influential of legal scholars. He is as well known or perhaps even better known internationally as in the United States, and his books have been translated into many languages.

We now introduce the chapters in this volume.

GENERAL OVERVIEWS AND ASSESSMENTS OF LAWRENCE FRIEDMAN'S WORK

Contributors to the first section of this collection treat Friedman's work directly. They give overviews of some of its major themes and provide assessments of its central assumptions and conclusions.

Lauren Edelman's (University of California, Berkeley) "Lawrence Friedman and the Canons of Law and Society" summarizes the basic elements of Friedman's sociology of law. The most important theme is that law is not autonomous, but rather a part of society, a product of social forces; likewise it is dependent on outside social conditions in its effects. Social actors make demands on the legal system and these determine the content of law, but once in place, law has independent feedback effects on social life, affecting the type and shape of future demands. Legal change is most likely to be effective if it reinforces and furthers social changes already in process. Thus to understand the legal system, one has to study it from the outside; its internal doctrines and arguments give little guidance as to how it actually works. And one has to study it in action; the focus is on the grubby detail at the working level of trial courts, bureaucrats' and lawyers' offices, police on the streets, clients, and prisoners.

In "'Then and Now': Lawrence Friedman as an Analyst of Social Change," Vincenzo Ferrari (University of Milan) assesses where Friedman's work places him in the company of sociologists generally and of sociologists of law specifically. Friedman belongs in the rare company of scholars who study law from the outside and develop theories of its functioning as part of a macro-social system, but who also investigate empirically how specific changes within the law are affected by social factors. Friedman is willing to be loose and eclectic in his choices of theory and method. He is a "functionalist" in his concern with analyzing legal institutions such as courts in terms of how they "work," their social purposes and effects, but he does not assume that such functions are benign. The most recurrent theme in his writing is that of social change, law "then and now." Friedman is a particularizer in that his historical work searches out undiscovered and often surprising details. However, he is also a generalizer, who finds large-scale trends and tendencies in (especially) Western legal practices and legal cultures, such as the growing expectation of "total justice," which results in more claims on the legal system for redress, and the growth of "expressive individualism" and tolerance for individual choices.

Victoria Saker Woeste (American Bar Foundation), "Lawrence M. Friedman and the Bane of Functionalism," draws on Friedman's work in legal history to arrive at conclusions similar to those of Ferrari. She addresses the charge made by some of Friedman's critics that he is a "functionalist" or "instrumentalist"; that is, someone who reduces law to an epiphenomenal (or, as Marxists say, "superstructural") effect of material interests and forces. Woeste argues that Friedman is indeed suspicious of the "judicial mind" – intellection by judges, the formal content of legal reasoning, or even judicial psychology – as an important explanatory variable in accounting for legal change, because he believes that change inside the legal system is largely explained by change in outside society as mediated through variable "legal cultures." Yet Friedman is not a crude materialist: He accepts a large variety of social factors as influences on legal change and is pluralist and nondogmatic in attributing influence.

In "Lawrence M. Friedman's Comparative Law," Tom Ginsburg (University of Chicago) examines Friedman's contributions to scholarship on comparative law. Although not a recognized player among scholars of comparative law, Friedman has made important contributions to that field by "asking the right questions." Some law and development writers believe that law does (or should) evolve toward uniform norms of legality; others argue that law is irreducibly culturally specific. Friedman takes a middle ground, asserting that some kinds of law (like commercial law) tend to converge with globalization and modernization, whereas others (like family law), rooted in religion and tradition, are less likely to do so; in any case converging law is a product, not a cause, of social and economic development. He is very critical of the kind of standard comparative law work that compares doctrines across legal cultures or else classifies whole legal systems into families according to their genealogical origins. Both of those approaches treat law as an autonomous system, insulated and independent of social forces. Friedman does not believe law is autonomous, but neither is it reducible to the product of social forces. Societies mediate social demands for law in different ways, depending on variations in social attitudes toward and expectations of legal systems; that is, of "legal cultures." Yet that does not mean that legal cultures are incommensurable: They too are subject to change and tend to converge as societies modernize.

APPLICATIONS OF CONCEPTS, INSIGHTS, AND METHODS IN FRIEDMAN'S WORK

Legal Culture

As Lawrence Friedman defines it, "legal culture" is a broad umbrella concept that includes the whole complex of ideas, attitudes, values, and opinions that people in a society hold about law, lawyers, courts, and the processes of lawmaking. One aspect, and an important one, of legal culture is popular legal culture, which includes the representations of law in mass media, arts and letters, and entertainment. Friedman was one of the first scholars to write extensively about law and lawyers in popular culture. In "To Influence, Shape, and Globalize: Popular Legal Culture and Law," Jo Carrillo (University of California, Hastings College of the Law) explores Friedman's views of how cultural representations both mirror and distort the legal system, and the effects that those reflections and distortions have on the demands that people make on legal systems and on their confidence in outcomes.

José Juan Toharia (Universidad Autónoma de Madrid) has carried out several research projects attempting to operationalize Friedman's concepts of legal culture – both internal (to the legal system) culture and external legal culture. In his chapter here, "Exploring Legal Culture: A Few Cautionary Remarks from Comparative Research," Toharia reports on some of the limitations and difficulties of public opinion research into how ordinary people view and evaluate the legal systems – specifically the courts – in their societies. He notes that survey research on courts tends to be distorted by several common sources of error: "top-of-the-head" responses reflecting superficial commonplace opinions, rather than the results of actual experience or reflection; "clichéd" responses based on stereotypes or prejudices that tend to disappear on more probing questioning; and opinions that are subject to rapid fluctuations or instabilities in public opinion. He concludes that the corrective is the use of sharper and subtler methodological instruments for assessing opinion and cross-checking comparisons across time periods and societies.

Total Justice

Perhaps the best known and the most controversial of Friedman's ideas about legal culture is his theory of "total justice." *Total Justice* (1985) argued that in the early twentieth century Americans began to experience what eventually became a major shift in their demands on the legal system. Generally speaking, nineteenth-century Americans who suffered harm accepted it as the outcome of fate or bad luck or their own fault. By the twentieth century, however, they began to believe that if they were harmed, someone or something else must have caused the harm and could and should be legally blamed for it, made to redress or pay for it, and change their ways to prevent such harms from happening in the future.

In this volume two leading scholars of law and society debate the extent to which the growth of demand for total justice ever was – and if it once was has continued to be – the master trend that Friedman maintained it was. A third scholar then comments on how total justice has become a demand for justice and accountability in international as well as domestic law.

First, Marc Galanter (University of Wisconsin-Madison), in "The Travails of Total Justice," looks at developments since the 1980s to ask whether the total justice thesis may require qualification or abandonment. He cites the campaigns for constriction of tort remedies, the reform of civil justice (managerial judging, diversion to alternative dispute resolution [ADR], fewer trials), the U-turn toward more formalistic contract law, the deregulation of usury, the curtailment of bankruptcy protection, harsher criminal penalties, the collapse of the rehabilitative model, the vast increase in imprisonment, and other changes that can be interpreted as reflecting a turnabout or change of course from the total justice trend. He concludes by asking, Was it truly a master trend or just a local blip?

Robert A. Kagan (University of California, Berkeley) takes up the challenge posed by Galanter. In "'Total Justice' and Political Conservativism" he reexamines the total justice thesis from the roots up. He first points to evidence that tends to qualify the argument that the expectation of total justice was ever sweeping and uniform: In twentieth-century America, plenty of groups continued to believe that people were largely responsible for their own fates and should not look to the legal system to bail them out. Conservative individualism and distrust of government have always been a barrier to the construction of a comprehensive welfare state. Like Galanter, Kagan acknowledges that these counter-tendencies have grown stronger in recent years and have partially rolled back liberal policies promoting security against risk and compensation for harm. Yet he concludes that despite these trends, total justice lives! The norms of security and redress for harm are sturdily embedded in policies and popular expectations.

In a third chapter on total justice, "Failures of War Tribunals from Leipzig, Nuremberg, and Tokyo to Milošević and Saddam Hussein," Erhard Blankenburg (Free University of Amsterdam) argues that total justice is an obsession not only of everyday (American) life but that it also has a grip on international war politics. Although European aristocrats in the nineteeth century still could look at their territorial wars as the ultimate means of politics among family members, modern national leaders have to find legitimacy in morally destroying the enemy regime. Courts and tribunals are new players in the game, and the media have become as important as conventional weapons. With courts defining what is seen as "bellum iustum," a body of law is being built up, with Nuremberg and the Yugoslavia tribunal as the main precedents. Yet this is a risky game that can easily be lost by those playing it. The dilemmas of the Saddam Hussein tribunal demonstrate that a war can be lost not only on the battlefields but also in the courtroom.

THE LEGAL PROFESSION

One of Friedman's abiding preoccupations has been the legal profession. The chapter by Philip Lewis (Oxford University), "Friedman on Lawyers: A Survey," provides a critical survey of Friedman's body of work on lawyers. In *The Legal System: A Social Science Perspective* (1975), lawyers play a significant part, albeit briefly described, in transmitting messages from legal actors to those intended to be affected by them. Friedman touches on their role as advocates and advisers to the latter even more briefly and scarcely mentions the significance of their legal culture, as part of the "internal legal culture." In later, mainly historical work, Friedman portrays lawyers not just as messengers or information brokers but also as a group who would put their legal knowledge to use wherever and in whatever way it might pay them. Relaxed admission requirements worked to promote this internal culture that facilitated, and perhaps encouraged, further demands and an external legal culture of resort to lawyers. Lewis's chapter considers how these historically based observations fit with the more theoretical approach taken in *The Legal System*.

In "Legal Culture and the State in Modern Japan: Continuity and Change," Setsuo Miyazawa (Aoyama Gakuin University Law School) and Malcolm Feeley (University of California, Berkeley) examine an aspect of internal legal culture – recent changes in the Japanese legal profession – in the context of a longer historical background. Pre-Meiji law was not autonomous, but rather was a branch of administration, the instrument of a benevolent paternalism. Meiji-era regimes tried to continue this tradition of state control, but by importing Western models, they unintentionally helped build and strengthen an autonomous profession and the ideal of the "rule of law" as a constraint on the state. Even after World War II, however, the judiciary remained mostly passive; access to justice was limited, and the private bar was small (relative to those of the West), weak, and dependent on the state. Recent reforms – the expansion of the bar, the creation of new independent law schools, the growth of public interest law challenging the state – though modest, may yet help strengthen the profession as an autonomous element of civil society

LAW AND LARGE AREAS OF SOCIAL LIFE

Lawrence Friedman's exceptionally wide-ranging historical and comparative knowledge has enabled him to survey interactions between law and society over long sweeps of time and across many societies. The chapters in this part follow his example and adopt many of his insights and methods to large areas of social life: law and contractual relations, law and the environment, law and religion, and law and the family.

Law and Contractual Relations

In "*The Death of Contract*: Dodos and Unicorns or Sleeping Rattlesnakes?" Stewart Macaulay (University of Wisconsin-Madison) reassesses and updates the argument of Friedman's first major book. *Contract Law in America* (1965) tells a story about legal doctrine. Judges and scholars imagined a contract law that was general, timeless, and wholly abstract, indifferent to context and the situations of parties: such a law, they thought, would be certain and predictable and give effect to free choice. In contrast, Friedman showed that from early on the Supreme Court of Wisconsin bent specific rules and the letter of written contract terms in particular cases. He argued that no economic system could operate with truly abstract contract law, particularly in times of rapid economic development. Notwithstanding the court's undercutting the formality of contract, Wisconsin's economy prospered. In this book Friedman also argued that frequently litigated situations quickly move out of general contract law into specialized statutory and administrative regimes so that the general contract law taught in law schools is a law of leftovers. Macaulay thinks that Friedman's argument was true for its time, but that since then the general abstract and formal law of contracts has undergone a resurgence as a tool used by business interests to impose terms on and to defeat regulation on behalf of workers and consumers.

Law and the Environment

Robert V. Percival (University of Maryland), in "Law, Society, and the Environment," shows how Friedman's ideas about how social forces shape law and how

law, in turn, influences society can help illuminate why we have environmental
laws, why they often seem impossibly ambitious, and why they have been highly
successful in some areas but not in others. Percival traces the history of environmental law from its common law roots to the vast federal regulatory infrastructure
that prevails today. Political theory predicts that federal regulatory legislation to
protect the environment should not exist because it imposes concentrated costs on
politically powerful industries to provide diffuse benefits to the general public. Yet
enduring public support for environmental protection ultimately produced transformative regulatory legislation during the 1970s and 1980s. Although critics of federal
environmental regulation decry the laws' strict directives as inefficient and costly,
they have been largely unsuccessful in efforts to roll back the federal regulatory
infrastructure. Percival's chapter explains why these efforts have failed, focusing on
the symbolic value of the environmental laws and their remarkable tolerance for
innovations that soften their impact. The chapter concludes by examining the limits
of law and the importance of social norms in shaping human behavior that affects
the environment. Public demand to protect human health and the environment is
an important aspect of the "total justice" phenomenon Friedman has described, but
environmental law has been most successful when it has employed approaches that
reinforce preexisting social norms, while failing miserably when it has attempted
to dictate changes in individual lifestyles. Environmental law's promise of comprehensive protection for future generations has helped society feel virtuous, much like
what Friedman has described as the "Victorian compromise" of nineteenth-century
morals legislation, even while tolerating individual behavior inconsistent with some
of its basic premises.

Law and Religion

In "Separating Church and State: The Atlantic Divide," James Whitman (Yale
University) explores what appears to be a strange contradiction. Americans are proud
of the strict separation of church and state mandated by their constitutional law. In
particular, they often compare themselves favorably with continental countries like
France. Yet to outside observers America often looks very much like an aggressively
religious country. In contrast, France may tolerate some intrusions of the state into
religious life, but French religion is kept scrupulously out of French politics. The
United States may have a strong form of the separation of religion and *state*, but
it has at best a weak form of the separation of religion and *politics*. Like other
continental countries, France has a strong form of the separation of religion and
politics. What explains these differences? Whitman proposes an explanation based
on some large claims about the comparative history of church–state relations in
France and the Anglo-American world. In France, he asserts, the state has assumed
many of the historic functions performed by the medieval church. In contrast, in
America, historic church functions have generally either been left to the churches

or else have died out entirely. The aim of Whitman's chapter is to demonstrate that these differences in institutional tradition have played a fundamental role in creating the sharp contrast between the republican traditions we find today on either side of the Atlantic.

Law and the Family

Joanna L. Grossman (Hofstra University) uses Friedman's historical work on family law as a departure point to reflect on "Civil Rites: The Gay Marriage Controversy in Historical Perspective." The legalization of same-sex marriage by one state – and the express condemnation of it by more than forty others – has reintroduced the age-old problem of non-uniform marriage laws and interaction among states with different laws. States historically disagreed about impediments to marriage, and conflicts arose when couples married in one state then sought recognition in the other. These conflicts were resolved by courts, which applied principles of comity to, by and large, grant recognition to disfavored marriages. States also disagreed about the accessibility of divorce. Different standards led to migratory divorce and hard-fought battles among reformers for looser or stricter laws. The "prophets of doom" trotted out easy divorce to signal the moral decay of society; strict laws were the ticket to preserving the institution of marriage. The nineteenth century was thus a time of "national panic" that produced a set of divorce laws that Friedman describes as "an egregious example of a branch of law tortured by contradictions in public opinion, trapped between contending forces of perhaps roughly equal size; trapped, too, in a federal system with freedom of movement back and forth, and beyond the power and grasp of any single state." (Friedman, *A History of American Law* (3d ed. 2005) 381.) The lessons of history – about the legal structures produced in times of panic, the influence of social and economic pressures on the law's development, and the importance of the "separate histories of the law of the fifty states" – cannot be ignored.

FACTS FROM THE UNDERGROUND: DIGGING LEGAL HISTORY OUT OF THE CELLAR

Lawrence Friedman is a major social theorist, but he is also a notable excavator of original historical materials. He follows the archival historians' creed that the dustier and more inaccessible the materials are, the more valuable they must be. His commitment to studying law in action, as it works in the lives of ordinary people, has also driven him to look for records of the most routine cases and transactions – criminal cases, debt collection, divorces, suits for personal injury, and wills. His premier work in this mode is *The Roots of Justice* (1981), the study he wrote with Robert V. Percival about the justice system of Alameda County, California, during the period 1870 to 1910, as evidenced in thousands of nineteenth-century case records kept in a storage room in the basement of the Alameda County Superior Court.

This part exhibits the work of legal historians who have followed Friedman into the basements.

In fact, George Fisher (Stanford University) titles his chapter, "Historian in the Cellar," and he follows Friedman and Percival's footsteps into the archives of Alameda County trial courts. There he finds the record of the murder trial of Hugh Cull. Cull had killed his wife in front of their seven-year-old daughter, but won acquittal when the trial judge deemed the girl incompetent to testify. The case turns out to be much more than just another wrongful acquittal staked in a legal technicality. Driving the case was Hugh Cull's obsessive jealousy of his wife. Cull later claimed he had killed in a fit of madness after being confronted with unanswerable evidence of his wife's unfaithfulness. At the center of the case then is a remarkable set of affidavits sworn months before Jennie Cull's killing and seeming to document an overnight assignation between a neighbor and her at a resort far from town. These affidavits played a critical role in Jennie Cull's death, but not the role Hugh Cull claimed – nor a role that any modern reader would expect without Friedman's tutelage in the family law of the era. The case proves to be an example of the lesson taught by the *Roots of Justice*: The law that matters is not the law as it is written, but the law as it is lived.

Rogelio Pérez-Perdomo (Universidad Metropolitana, Caracas) relies on fresh research into the trial of Venezuelan conspirators against the Spanish crown – leaders of a failed early independence movement – to tell the story of "The Discreet Charm of Inquisitorial Procedure: Judges and Lawyers in a Case of *Lèse Majesté* in Late-Eighteenth-Century Venezuela." Pérez-Perdomo shows how the tribunal (*Audiencia*) that heard the case modified its already draconian procedures to ensure that the conspirators would have no serious defense. The Bishop of Caracas played an important role, interceding to emphasize that disobedience to the king was also disobedience to God, but also to urge mercy for the defendants. Lawyers helped the *Audiencia* collect and analyze evidence, but none helped the defendants, because their careers depended on crown patronage. After independence lawyers would become spokespersons for more liberal procedures and the rule of law, but liberal values were fragile, and inquisitorial procedure tends to return in times of crisis, even today.

Thomas D. Russell (University of Denver) dives into the archives and emerges with "'Keep the Negroes Out of Most Classes Where There Are a Large Number of Girls': The Unseen Power of the Ku Klux Klan and Standardized Testing at The University of Texas, 1899–1999." His chapter intertwines two episodes in the university's history. One episode concerns William Stewart Simkins, a Confederate colonel and founder of the KKK in Florida, who became a UT law professor from 1899 to 1929. After the U.S. Supreme Court ordered the integration of the UT Law School in 1950, portraits and busts of Professor Simkins arrived at the university.

Six weeks after the Supreme Court decision in *Brown v. Board of Education*, the Texas faculty voted to name a law student dormitory after him. The second episode concerns the Supreme Court's decision in *Brown*. Six days after *Brown*, the university registrar outlined a plan that would, he said, "keep the negroes out of the classes with the most girls." One element of this plan was to implement standardized testing, which went into place the very first semester that the university admitted African American students. Archival records show that the university knew about the testing and intended that it have a disparately exclusionary effect on African American applicants.

Harry N. Scheiber (University of California, Berkeley) unearths a movement led by a small group of American scholars and lawyers on the West Coast to advance a new "realist" reformist approach to international law, in "Taking Legal Realism Offshore: The Contributions of Joseph Walter Bingham to American Jurisprudence and to the Reform of Modern Ocean Law." The realists began narrowly by centering on the question of the three-mile rule for offshore jurisdiction, but later expanded their agenda to embrace the entire legal foundation of traditional ocean law. During 1937–45 the debate was inspired by what Canadian and American fishing interests viewed as a threat to their industry posed by the possible entry of Japanese fleets into "their" offshore waters in Bristol Bay and elsewhere on the Pacific coast. Under traditional "freedom of the seas" doctrine, accepted at the core of existing American law of coastal waters, the Japanese fleets had a perfect right to fish within three miles of the U.S. shoreline. Once the debate over legitimacy of the three-mile rule ignited, politicians and industry spokesmen joined with scholars and international lawyers in what became a fascinating confrontation of legal principle and the policy process – especially confrontation of "rule of law" ideals with the perceived imperatives of national self-interest, multilateralism, and, not least, the degree of respect to be given in law to theories generated by scientific research for the structuring of resource management. Among the scholars who pursued a new realism as the touchstone of ocean-law reform were Joseph Walter Bingham, previously an important voice in the legal realist movement, and his young collaborator Stefan Riesenfeld, whose work on coastal fisheries law became a classic statement of the realist position in the literature of law of the sea.

PERSPECTIVES FROM OTHER CONCEPTUAL WORLDS

The final chapters in this collection approach Friedman's work from theoretical perspectives entirely different from – and in some respects rather alien to – his own.

Gunther Teubner (University of Frankfurt) is a legal sociologist, as Friedman is, but he is also a systems theorist. As has been noted here many times, Friedman's view is that law is not autonomous: Although its formal internal structures and doctrines may make it appear so, in fact law is parasitic on its external social context, borrowing and mutating whatever materials from that context it needs to adapt. In contrast, Teubner sees the law, like the economy, as a self-reproducing autonomous system. Law responds to changes in its environment, but only in accordance with its own processing logics. In this chapter, "Sociological Jurisprudence – Impossible but Necessary: The Case of Contractual Networks," Teubner uses the example of legal responses to the emergence of a novel phenomenon in economic relations, the "network." The network is a hybrid of contract and organization. As a hybrid, it perturbs or "irritates" traditional legal categories. The law has to come up with means of dealing with this new economic reality; for example, by attributing legal liability for harms or breaches of obligation. Yet law cannot simply incorporate concepts from economics or sociology – it has to find ways of generating new concepts from within its own categories.

In the second chapter in this section, "How American Legal Academics' Positions on Economic-Efficiency Analysis, Moral Philosophy, and Valid Legal Argument Disserve Law and Society Empirical Research," the lawyer-economist and lawyer-philosopher Richard S. Markovits (University of Texas) identifies the contribution that he believes law-and-society empiricist scholars such as Lawrence Friedman could make to the enrichment of the economic and philosophical analysis of law. At present, economists and philosophers do not make the constructive uses of law-and-society empiricism that they should because they are committed to premises that deny the relevance and utility of such work. For example, law-and-society empiricism would be of service in helping measure "external" preferences (preferences of people for outcomes of interactions that are not directly affected by them) and the types of mistakes that those who cause harms and those who are harmed tend to make about the costs and benefits of their actions and the magnitude of injury. Empirical inquiry could also help answer whether a given society (such as ours) has justice commitments, the type of norms to which it is committed, and the kinds of factors that people conventionally employ to justify or rationalize falling short of those norms in particular situations. Markovits argues for retheorizing basic concepts of economic efficiency and of law as the pursuit of justice, thereby opening them up to sociolegal empiricism.

The chapters in this volume show how broadly and deeply Lawrence Friedman's influence has spread. He has been very prolific, not only in his own prodigious output but also in the many instances of value added to the work of others. Clearly his work has had powerful ripple effects on American and comparative legal sociology, American and comparative legal history, and the general sociology of law and legal change. Intellectual influence, like parenting, is of course a chancy business. Some offspring turn out to be like their parents, others utterly unlike; some rebel and take up opposing stances. Friedman's influence – in part no doubt because of his legendary personal warmth and charm – has always been benign and noninsistent. He seems to welcome the sheer variety of offshoots his example has inspired, even when they head off in different directions from his own. At the age of 80, he still turns out new work that will continue to attract admirers, imitators, and engaged critics wherever scholars seek to understand how law actually works in social life.

ACKNOWLEDGMENTS

In the process of bringing this collection to publication we have piled up several debts. We are particularly grateful to Dean Larry Kramer and Professors Thomas C. Grey and Robert L. Rabin of the Stanford Law School for sponsoring and helping organize the conference at Stanford at which most of these chapters were first presented, and to Jillian del Pozo and Joe Neto for technical support of that conference. Professor Harry N. Scheiber of the University of California, Berkeley organized a panel at an annual conference of the American Society for Legal History that was the occasion for presenting other chapters. Yale Law School students Robin Rotman and Julie Duncan and Stanford Law student William Michael Smith III provided expert help with copyediting and Yale Law students Kari Milligan, Russell Balikian and Kristin Burgess prepared the index. Christopher Tomlins, then of the American Bar Foundation, helped us find a publisher in Cambridge University Press, and John Berger of that press has gracefully facilitated and encouraged the project. We are grateful to Professor Sally Engle Merry, editor of Cambridge Studies in Law and Society, for accepting this volume for inclusion in that series.

Portions of some of the chapters have appeared elsewhere in different form. James Q. Whitman's chapter first appeared in *Historical Reflections/Réflexions Historiques* 34.3 (2008): 86-104 and is reprinted here with the permission of the editors of the journal. Permission to republish is also gratefully acknowledged from the *Stanford Law Review*, for George Fisher's chapter, and the *Law & History Review*, for Harry Scheiber's chapter.

PART I

Overviews and Assessments of Friedman's Work

Lawrence Friedman and the Canons of Law and Society

Lauren B. Edelman

In his witty and usually slightly irreverent way, Lawrence Friedman has provided a set of ideas that serve as the canons for much current work in law and society. Of course, part of the reason for that is that Lawrence himself has written so much of the work in the field. In addition to classic works like *The Legal System: A Social Science Perspective, Total Justice,* and *A History of American Law,* and his reader with Stewart Macaulay and Elizabeth Mertz, *Law in Action: A Socio-Legal Reader,* he has written on topics as diverse as slum housing, contract law, mandatory retirement, crime and punishment, family law, the war on terror, and inheritance. He has even written a movie review of *Legally Blonde.*[1] The rest of us hardly have time to read all of Lawrence's work, much less to write much of our own.

In this brief reflection, I outline a few of the central themes in Friedman's work that have now reached more or less canonical status in the field of law and society. Given his fame and influence, such an exercise may be quite unnecessary, but my goal is to remind readers how very foundational his work is in the field of law and society.

The first and most basic theme that has reached canonical status is that law and the legal system are fundamentally social entities, born of social forces. Building on other important work in law and society,[2] Lawrence Friedman has provided, through his extensive theoretical writings and empirical studies, a rich portrait of the social nature of law. In his 1975 book, *The Legal System: A Social Science Perspective,* as well as in subsequent works – including *Total Justice* (1985) and his textbook, *American*

---

[1] This review was posted at http://www.usfca.edu/pj/blonde_friedman.htm (September 21, 2001).
[2] See, e.g., Durkheim (1949); Weber (1968); Ehrlich (2002); Hurst (1956); Macaulay (1963).

This brief reflection is a revised version of part of a welcoming address to attendees at the conference held in honor of Lawrence M. Friedman at Stanford University in Fall 2005. I thank Howard S. Erlanger, Rosann Greenspan, Stewart Macaulay, Dorit Rubinstein, and Katherine Heard for helpful comments on an earlier draft. I also thank Lawrence Friedman for introducing me to the world of law and society during a graduate seminar at Stanford University in 1978 and for being a wonderful mentor and friend.

Law (1998) – Friedman argues that legal systems are social systems, with social structures and with cultures. Therefore, to understand law, one must understand not only its substantive rules but also the informal social structure of the legal order and, perhaps most important, the ideas, attitudes, and orientations toward law that constitute legal culture. He argues that legal systems are not well-defined entities, and they are not autonomous from the rest of society; rather they are slippery and variable and subject to social definition. Law consists not just of formal rules but also of the interplay between the formal and the informal, the official and the unofficial.

Using specific empirical examples like environmental law, obscenity, criminal law, and inheritance, Friedman shows how the law cannot be understood apart from the social and legal forces that come together to make the law or from the impact of law on social behavior. For example, in *The Legal System*, he wrote the following:

> What gives life and reality to the legal system is the outside, social world. . . . Social forces are constantly at work on the law – destroying here, renewing there; invigorating here, deadening there; choosing what parts of "law" will operate, which parts will not; what substitutes, detours, and bypasses will spring up; what changes will take place openly or secretly.[3]

And in his analysis of law and the family, *Private Lives* (2004), he wrote,

> Social forces shape the legal order. Law is not and never has been an autonomous kingdom. It does not live in a world of its own. The legal system is part of society. . . . What is true of law in general is true for the field of family law as well. It is a product of society, and it reflects, in its general contours, the social structure, social practice, and social debates within its society.[4]

Friedman sees legal culture as a critical intervening variable that affects when, whether, and how social interests produce legal change and how legal change, in turn, affects society. Legal culture, which he defines very broadly as "the climate of social thought and social force that determines how law is used, avoided, or abused,"[5] includes knowledge of law, attitudes toward law, values, professional norms, and behavior patterns, all of which are interrelated. Legal culture then largely determines what social issues become legal issues. The disputes that courts decide are not inherently legal issues, but become legal issues only when social pressures bring them into the legal arena. Moreover, he argues that professionals within the legal system such as judges and lawyers have their own "internal" legal culture, which itself is responsive to the general legal culture. Because social forces flow through legal culture into law, law must be understood as thoroughly a product of society.

[3] Friedman 15 (1975).
[4] Friedman 11 (2004).
[5] Friedman 21 (1998).

Friedman emphasizes not only the social foundations of law but also the social nature of legal impact. Examining the social impact of law is complex: It involves an evaluation not only of compliance but also of deviance and evasion; not only of words of law but also of the multiple intents of lawmakers, of social conditions that may have altered those intents and social understandings of the goals of law, and of the distinction between instrumental and symbolic effects of law. He points out the difficulty of distinguishing the impact of law from the impact of social norms or habits that are consistent with law and of knowing whether social changes result from law directly or instead indirectly through changes in social morality. Finally, he emphasizes the importance of understanding law's legitimacy or why people are motivated to accept and comply with legal rules.

In *The Legal System: A Social Science Perspective*, one finds a comprehensive analysis of why and how law is a social phenomenon. Although Lawrence Friedman is far from the only law and society scholar to emphasize a social or "law-in-action" understanding of law, his work has systematically and eloquently helped institutionalize the law-in-action paradigm as perhaps the central canon in the study of law and society.

The second theme that Friedman stresses, which follows from the social nature of law, is the importance of studying law and legal institutions from "the outside" – stepping outside of the internal methods of law and instead bringing the methods of the social sciences to bear on law. Legal scholarship commonly employs an internal theory of law, which assumes that legal rules can be applied to fact situations in a way that produces a correct legal answer in a rather mechanical manner.[6] Drawing on earlier legal realist scholarship, Friedman articulates the value of social theories of law, which look at law as a product of social forces rather than as an isolated or autonomous subsystem. He suggests that, although internal theories may work in explaining minor or short-term legal events, the long-term direction of law can be explained only in terms of social forces outside of the legal system. Thus social theories look to economic forces[7] or cultural factors[8] to explain legal change.

Friedman's focus on social forces as the primary determinant of legal change has become canonical today in the field of law and society; this position turns on its head the internal perspective of conventional legal scholarship, where the game is to improve doctrine to promote some desirable social end. The nature of inquiry from a law and society perspective is captured in an article Friedman wrote entitled "Taking Law and Society Seriously," which was given at a 1999 symposium, "Taking Legal Argument Seriously":

Suppose we concede that there are "correct" [legal] answers: Why should most of us be interested? . . . Law from the internal perspective is comparable to a system of

[6] Friedman (1977).
[7] Marx (1954); Hurst (1956).
[8] See, e.g., Sumner (1906); Malinowski (1926).

theology. . . . A theologian might argue that "correct" had a concrete, valid meaning within the system of the religion, but an outsider would not particularly care what that "correct" answer was. For those of us who think that law is a political, economic, and cultural subsystem, which varies with, and is determined by, the surrounding society, the "internalist" point of view is perhaps sociologically interesting – but nothing more. . . . [9]

I am, as I said, not very interested in taking legal argument seriously. But social justice through better understanding of the world in which the legal system lives and works – this I would take seriously indeed.[10]

Friedman's comments challenge the very premise of the symposium for which they were written. Although he may have been an outsider at that conference, Friedman's perspective has become canonical within the law and society movement.

The third core theme that Friedman helped institutionalize, which flows directly from the first two themes, is his theory of law and social change. Although it is a dynamic theory, it importantly treats law as a *dependent* variable, one dependent on social institutions, social forces, and social variation. Again, this idea is something that now seems clearly *correct*, but he introduced it at a time when law was generally treated as autonomous from society – something that operated independently and caused social change.[11] The idea of law as a dependent variable is clear in Friedman's suggestion that "[a]ny legal act results from, and is determined by, the preponderance of social force actually brought to bear on the subject,"[12] which he argues flows from the understanding of law as inherently social. In this proposition, social force refers to the exercise of power through demands made on the legal system, which produce new rules, statutes, doctrines, and practices. When, how, and whether that occurs will depend, as discussed earlier, on legal culture.

The interplay of society and law is not unidirectional in Friedman's view. Rather he suggests that, although law results from social forces, it then begins to have its own independent effect on social life.[13] Once in place, law changes social attitudes, expectations, and practices; it channels social development. He described the process in the following way:

[L]aw follows social change and adapts to it. Yet the legal system also crystallizes and channels social change, and plays an important role in community life. After all, it is through law, legal institutions, and legal processes that customs and ideas take on a more permanent, rigid form. . . . The legal system is a structure. It has shape and form. It lasts. It is visible. It sets up fields of force. It affects ways of thinking.

---

[9] Friedman 529 (1999).
[10] Id. at 542.
[11] See, e.g., legal impact studies such as Feest (1968); Ross (1975, 1976).
[12] Friedman 97 (1977).
[13] Friedman (1998).

When practices, habits, and custom turn into law, they tend to become stronger, more fixed, more explicit. They can be imposed on people who do not share these customs and habits or are downright hostile to them.[14]

In other work, Friedman emphasizes that law can act as an important catalyst to social change if it comes along at the right point in the process of social change. In a 1969 article titled "Law Reform in Historical Perspective," Friedman stated the following:

> [F]resh law is a hybrid: half ratification, half real inducement to change. Formal legal change often comes at the middle point in a social process which requires a number of distinct steps for its completion.[15]

Friedman's words suggest that studies that seek to measure the immediate impact of a court decision are misguided: The impact may be indirect or it may be symbolic. Legal change may matter far down the road because of the social change it sets into motion.

The final theme I discuss, consistent with Friedman's emphasis on the social bases of law, is the importance of using empirical data to study law and, in particular, the variation in law across specific social contexts. He cautions against overly general or grand theoretical statements, pointing out that because legal systems vary across social contexts, it usually makes more sense to observe law in specific contexts and to think carefully about the scope of one's conclusions. He advises us to study "the grubby facts of day to day life." Although this advice may seem fairly obvious to today's law and society scholar, it is a radical departure from the law professor's most comfortable turf – the analysis of appellate opinions.

Friedman does not just advocate empirical analyses – he is responsible for conducting some of the best. For example, consider his well-known study with Robert Percival of the criminal justice system of Alameda County, California, from 1870–1910, titled *The Roots of Justice* (1981). Relying on a variety of data sources including arrest blotters, court registers, prison log books, newspaper articles, and appellate court records, Friedman and Percival examined the day-to-day reality of the administration of justice not only in the courts and in the police stations but also in informal settings, such as the hallways of the courts and on the streets. Wading through mountains of data, the authors provided the gritty details of changes in the structure of courts, in court practices over time, and in the social background and roles of judges, lawyers, juries, and police. This is a portrait of the routines of the criminal justice system, far from the elite world of appellate cases. From the same author who offers sweeping theories of the nature of law and society, we see the use

[14] Id at 295.
[15] Friedman 363 (1969).

of detailed examples to give texture to the portrait. For example, consider this 1908 example of property crimes:

> Grace Jones, fresh out of jail, and needing some money, rented a room for 50 cents in a lodging house, and brought in Louis Gee. He took off his clothes, and hung his pants on the wall. At about 1:00 AM (Gee testified), "She go out to take a pee and said she would be back in a few minutes, and she took my money."[16]

Although packed with details that illustrate the world of the Alameda County criminal justice system, the study offers broad conclusions about shifts in the nature of criminal justice over time. We see the interplay of multiple layers of the criminal justice system, a decline in the likelihood of felons going to trial over time, a growing concern with sexual morality, a shift in focus from the crime to the criminal in determining punishment, and an increasing use of professionals at all levels of the criminal justice system.

Law and society scholarship is sometimes criticized for being focused on what might be considered "small" questions or, more charitably, theories of the middle range, rather than the grand style of theorizing of Marx, Durkheim, and Weber. Friedman disagrees with this criticism. In an essay that appeared as the Prefatory to the very first *Annual Review of Law and Social Science*, he wrote,

> What, on the whole, have they [the hundreds, perhaps thousands, of law and society studies] accomplished? Not much, in one sense: no sweeping general laws, no break-through that would make somebody's heart pound, no magic discoveries that change the face of the earth. But in another sense a great deal *has* been accomplished. Small insights, careful studies of particular institutions – there is no reason to look down on these. If two researchers show that there really is plea bargaining in England, despite official denials (Baldwin & McConville 1979), that is no small thing. If a team examines what effect a California tort case had on how psychiatrists and social workers thought and acted, that, too, is important (Givelber et al. 1984). In general, law and society scholars have been like archaeologists, digging patiently into the soil, uncovering bits and pieces of pottery, exposing fragments of buried cities.[17]

Lawrence Friedman has played a major role in encouraging many of us to uncover those buried cities and teaching us how to study them. He deserves an enormous amount of credit not only for the volumes of theoretical and empirical sociolegal work he has produced but also for teaching so many of us to understand the legal system as a part of its social context, to delve beyond the internal logic of law by adopting a broader law and society perspective, to study the social forces that create both law and law's influence on society, and to ground our understanding of the relationship of law and society in the grubby facts of everyday life.

[16] Friedman and Percival 141 (1981).
[17] Friedman 14 (2005a).

REFERENCES

Baldwin, John and Michael McConville (1979). Plea Bargaining and Plea Negotiation in England, 13 *Law & Soc'y Rev.* 287.

Durkheim, Emile (1949). *The Division of Labor in Society*. Glencoe, IL: Free Press.

Ehrlich, Eugen (2002). *Fundamental Principles of the Sociology of Law*. New Brunswick, NJ: Transaction.

Feest, Johannes (1968). Compliance with Legal Regulations: Observation of Stop Sign Behavior, 2 *Law & Soc'y Rev.* 447.

Friedman, Lawrence M. (1969). Law Reform in Historical Perspective, 13 *St. Louis U. L. J.* 351.

———. (1975). *The Legal System: A Social Science Perspective*. New York: Russell Sage Foundation.

———. (1977). *Law and Society: An Introduction*. Englewood Cliffs, NJ: Prentice-Hall.

———. (1985). *Total Justice*. New York: Russell Sage Foundation.

———. (1998). *American Law: An Introduction*. 2nd edition. New York: Norton.

———. (1999). Taking Law and Society Seriously, 74 *Chic.-Kent L. Rev.* 529.

———. (2004). *Private Lives: Families, Individuals, and the Law*. Cambridge, MA: Harvard University Press.

———. (2005a). Coming of Age: Law and Society Enters an Exclusive Club, 1 *Ann. Rev. L. & Social Sci.* 1.

———. (2005b). *A History of American Law*. 3d edition. New York: Simon & Schuster.

Friedman, Lawrence M. and Percival, Robert (1981). *The Roots of Justice: Crime and Punishment in Alameda County, California, 1870–1910*. Chapel Hill: University of North Carolina Press.

Givelber, Daniel J., William J. Bowers, and Caroline L. Blitch. (1984). Tarasoff, Myth and Reality: An Empirical Study of Private Law in Action, 1984 *Wis. L. Rev.* 443.

Hurst, James Willard (1956). *Law and the Conditions of Freedom in the Nineteenth-Century United States*. Madison: University of Wisconsin Press.

———. (1964). *Law and Economic Growth: The Legal History of the Lumber Industry in Wisconsin, 1836–1915*. Cambridge, MA: Belknap Press.

Macaulay, Stewart (1963). Non-Contractual Relations in Business: A Preliminary Study, 28 *Am. Sociol. Rev.* 55.

Macaulay, Stewart, Lawrence M. Friedman, and John Stookey. 1995. *Law & Society: Readings on the Social Study of Law*. New York: W.W. Norton.

Malinowski, Bronislaw (1926). *Crime and Custom in Savage Society*. London: Routledge & K. Paul.

Marx, Karl (1954) trans. *Capital*. Moscow: Foreign Languages Publishing House (first published in 1867).

Ross, Laurence H. (1975). The Scandinavian Myth: The Effectiveness of Drinking-and-Driving Legislation in Sweden and Norway, 4 *J. Legal Stud.* 285.

———. (1976). The Neutralization of Severe Penalties: Some Traffic Law Studies, 10 *Law & Soc'y Rev.* 403.

Sumner, William G. (1906). *Folkways: A Study of the Sociological Importance of Usages, Manners, Customs, Mores, and Morals*. Boston: Ginn.

Weber, Max. (1968) trans. *Economy and Society: An Interpretive Sociology*. 2 vols., ed. Guenther Roth and Claus Wittich. New York: Bedminister Press (first published in 1924).

2

"Then and Now"

Lawrence Friedman as an Analyst of Social and Legal Change

Vincenzo Ferrari

HOW TO CLASSIFY LAWRENCE FRIEDMAN?

A conventional manner of opening an academic discussion about sociology of law often consists in re-proposing a well-known distinction between "the sociology of law of sociologists" and "the sociology of law of jurists." This distinction is a cornerstone in the methodological writings of Renato Treves, for example, who was one of the pioneers of the renaissance of this discipline after World War II; according to Treves, this distinction has solid roots in the different cultural origins, as well as in the diverse methodological choices, of the scholars belonging to the fields of either sociology or law.[1] On the one side, he said that one finds such sociologists as Saint-Simon or Marx, Comte or Durkheim, all builders of complex systems of social thought. On the other, one encounters those jurists, such as Duguit, Pound, Holmes, or Ehrlich, who took an antiformalist stance as opposed to the traditional juristic method. The former aimed at a "macro-sociology" that would describe how the legal system works within the whole social system, whereas the latter aimed at a "micro-sociology," in that they looked at the actual life of legal institutions and observed how nonlegal relations between social actors affected those institutions. Echoing Weber and Kelsen, Treves argued that sociology of law was indisputably part of sociology, not of jurisprudence, but its object (i.e., law) was so peculiar, technically and conceptually, that only well-trained jurists could really grasp it. Therefore, in his view, there would be no true and mature sociology of law until there came to be a community of scholars capable of combining the two approaches – macro and micro. Yet he said that only three scholars – Max Weber, Georges Gurvitch, and Theodor Geiger – had reached this level in the past.[2]

One is tempted to go on playing, placing present-day law and society scholars into these categories. Niklas Luhmann would certainly have fallen into the first one,

---

[1] Treves (1960, 1987, 1992).
[2] Treves 142 ff. (1987).

that of macro-sociology of law. He focused on the construction of a theoretical, all-embracing scheme.[3] Single legal institutions, such as the *Grundrechte* to which he devoted one of his earlier writings,[4] mattered to him as tesserae of a whole theoretical mosaic, as subsystems of the global legal system, not as concrete evidence of societal life: Indeed Luhmann mistrusted empirical investigation in principle. In his turn, Jean Carbonnier fell most probably – though perhaps not entirely – into the second category, that of micro-sociology of law. A great civil law specialist who displayed some impatience toward the exegetic style so typical of his own country, Carbonnier looked at legal rules not only as linguistic utterances but also as products of social action and as a source, in their turn, of subsequent social action. Thus he observed the life of norms through people's deeds or feelings and was rather skeptical of all-embracing theories, to the point of presenting his most brilliant book as "une sociologie du droit sans rigueur."[5]

Into what category can one place Lawrence Friedman? In his wide scientific production, one finds both empirical observation of law's institutions and theoretical constructions. He masters the technicalities of the legal discourse fully, but he is also well aware that a social science approach has its own rules and that these rules lead to a descriptive general view that includes norms and actions in a single and complex whole. He says openly that sociology of law is "a part of the general field of sociology," and even though he also openly rejects grand theorizing,[6] he builds up a theory that goes somewhat beyond the middle range. On these grounds, it would seem quite obvious to conclude that he belongs to the third category singled out by Treves: that of scholars who are capable of combining macro and micro (i.e., general sociological theory and research on single institutions).

This conclusion is probably well grounded, and comes as no surprise, because Lawrence Friedman is universally renowned as one of the leading figures in contemporary sociology of law, not only for his production's width and quality but also for its versatile character. Yet the question is not so simple. Indeed a more careful portraiture will show that classifying this scholar on the basis of predefined criteria, quite mechanically, is no easy task. For this reason, I go into more detail in this chapter, starting with the scholar's method, continuing with his theories, and ending with a more general evaluation of his contributions to the field of law and society.

A RIGOROUS AND IRONICAL WAY OF OBSERVING

Lawrence Friedman is one of the few social scientists who, when they raise a question, may say explicitly that they do so because "they do not know."

---

[3] Luhmann (1972, 1983, 1993).
[4] Luhmann (1992).
[5] Carbonnier (1992).
[6] Friedman 92 ff. (1986).

It might seem a paradox, but the expression "I don't know" is not found frequently in sociological literature. I do not speak of grand theorizing, à la Parsons or à la Luhmann. Such theories are built on the basis of what is previously known or what is thought of as known, not because it has been discovered through research, but because it is part of a background purportedly sufficient to build up a *Weltanschauung*, as is said in the idiom of Kant or Hegel – and it is no coincidence that I refer to them, because this kind of sociology closely resembles the great philosophical systems of nineteenth-century Germany. I intend the middle-range approach, à la Merton, which displays an awareness that reality only reveals itself to our eyes through fragments. Therefore, in a Popperian spirit, this approach proceeds through hypotheses, being ready to discard them when they are proved false and to replace them with other hypotheses, going on and on hypothetically forever. In fact, under the delicate scent of doubt, this kind of sociology often conceals a more resistant smell of solid certainties; perhaps that is because much of what it says has already been diffused within popular culture and is just being re-proposed in academic formulas by empirical researchers, rather than being singled out by rigorous research.

Being confident in middle range observation, Friedman often says that he himself, or also science, does not know, but not so much because he harbors skepticism about the human capacity to know or for a Socratic inclination to doubt – even though he may share such attitudes. Rather he often says he does not know because he believes that, in addition to everything that is known in the field of the social sciences, there is also a lot that is barely known or completely unknown, yet could be revealed to our eyes if we only ventured to seek it with appropriate methods. He does not draw his attention to the "incognizable" – as Herbert Spencer would have said – but just to what escapes us, though lying within our reach, because looking for it would be demanding in terms of costs, labor, and challenges to our ideas and preconceptions. Although the virtues of fallibilism are less widespread among social scientists than one might think, they are of paramount importance, because the value of the social sciences, which is concerned with facts by definition, can be appreciated not only when it helps reconstruct factual realities but also and especially when it leads to the disproving of widely held opinions.

Friedman's writings actually display his anxiety to fill in the empty spaces in the landscapes of social phenomena and, first and foremost, his strong interest in those data that question purported certainties. Among his numerous contributions have been those to the field of litigation. If, as he has said on different occasions, we knew a little more about why, how, and where people litigate, we would avoid taking for granted once for all, for example, the so-called litigation explosion – a topic that, for at least three decades, has inspired many discussions and studies, which often have been misleading because of a lack of information.[7] If we were to agree to make up generalizations on the exclusive basis of a detailed scrutiny of empirical

---

[7] Friedman (1989a, 1989c).

evidence, we might find out that the most reasonable hypotheses can sometimes be deceitful. José Juan Toharia did a detailed analysis successfully in a renowned essay, in which he used statistical data to submit to a critical scrutiny the (reasonable) hypothesis of a direct and linear relationship between the rates of court litigation and economic development[8] – and it is no coincidence that Friedman mentions this work frequently.[9]

The scholar's insistence on the need to look for empirical evidence "by rummaging in cellars," because written legal documents – the main source of knowledge for legal sociologists – can only be found there, may lead one to think that Friedman is a traditional positivist sociologist who sees a "datum" as something objective and self-evident. In fact, in his work, one encounters a number of warnings about the complexity and the limits of field research in all its steps. First, he says that a research topic always implies problems of definition, which concern not only highly abstract concepts, such as law – the joy and pain of all jurists – but also apparently unequivocal legal concepts, such as "court," "tribunal," or "dispute,"[10] or notions that are widespread in general culture, such as "litigation,"[11] "crime,"[12] or "family."[13] One remark he made about disputes is exemplary: If we figured them out on the mere basis of court filings, with no prior definition of the concept, we would not realize that a not-so-negligible quota of cases brought to court are not real litigation. For example, in the majority of divorce cases, "what is presented to her honour is a package of agreements already settled; she merely rubber-stamps these prior agreements."[14]

Then there are problems of measurement and cataloging. As is well known, Friedman recommends – and has a predilection for – quantitative techniques, especially those fitting in with the needs of longitudinal studies, of which he has provided some remarkable examples.[15] Nevertheless he is well aware of the difficulties encountered in the use of quantitative techniques. Apart from phenomena that can be measured through objective indicators (birth, death, or marriage or divorce rates), there are other phenomena whose indicators are far more difficult to construct, because of the multitude of intervening variables or their hardly definable nature; for example, social attitudes that reveal one or another kind of legal culture – a crucial concept in his own visions.[16]

[8]   Toharia (1974).
[9]   Friedman (1985a, 1989a, 1989c, 1995).
[10] Friedman (1976, 1985b, 1989a).
[11] Friedman 18–20 (1985a).
[12] Friedman 3 (1993a).
[13] Friedman 56–7 (1990).
[14] Friedman 18 (1989a).
[15] See, e.g., Friedman (1965); Friedman and Percival (1976, 1981). "Quantitative methods are particularly appropriate, of course, for studies in living law, and explorations in social history: the role of law in the everyday life of the community." Friedman 10 (1989c).
[16] Friedman 33 (1975, 1997).

How should these and other similar problems of field research be solved? It is also well known that Friedman is not fond of excessive methodological rigidity; this stance may be correct in principle, but may channel scientific discourses into too complex footpaths, to the detriment of imagination and creativity. He wishes science to speak, rather than stopping too much to discuss speaking conditions. Thus his solutions are mostly inspired by common sense, but are by no means simplistic. I cite here another telling example. While tackling the meaning of "court" – which, he warned, "are not objects in the real world, but social institutions" – he stressed that arriving at an appropriate definition of the word, be it "functional," starting from the tasks performed, or "structural," starting from actors and their roles, is difficult; it is also dangerous because it can lead to arbitrary exclusions or inclusions and therefore obstruct the significance of empirical data. To solve the puzzle, he recommended relying on the meaning most commonly attributed to the word socially, because "if we stretch too far from the common meaning of the word 'court,' we run the risk of robbing ourselves of any meaningful boundary of the term."[17] Prima facie, one might think that this solution is only too obvious and is just used to sidestep the problem. Yet a good student of the methodology of social description knows very well that this is not so: What the author recommends is actually none other than an explanatory definition that even the most accurate voices of analytical philosophy recommend as the most appropriate one for reasons similar, if not identical, to those advanced by Friedman.[18]

Too much sophistication in the use of words – for example, through highly abstract stipulative definitions – runs the risks of cutting the links between the social science and its object (i.e., society); therefore it jeopardizes the role of the social science itself, which cannot be deprived of concepts that, though hardly definable and measurable, are anyway essential to explanation or to what Friedman seems to consider as the most crucial of the aims of the social science; that is, *comparison*.[19]

To the natural objection that, in this way, the social science suffers a loss of rigor, the counter-objection is also natural: If we want a social science to exist, we must accept its limitations. Defending the concept of "legal culture" at the core of his comparative method against the critiques put forward by Roger Cotterrell, Friedman writes, "There is a lot of room in the house built by law and society scholars. Let a thousand flowers bloom. I do think 'legal culture' ought to be one of these flowers. It is a useful concept, *despite its failings*; and I would hate to have to give it up"[20] (emphasis added). A careful reader will not fail to grasp the author's sense of humor and irony in these words, as in many others one finds in his writings.

[17] Friedman 25–7 (1976).
[18] Scarpelli (1965); Jori (1976). For an attempt to provide an explanatory definition of law see also Ferrari (1987, 2000).
[19] "The essence of scientific method is controlled comparison. Experiment, in or out of the laboratory, includes a control group. Even a 'case study' implies comparison." Friedman 8 (1989c).
[20] Friedman 39 (1997).

AN (ONLY APPARENTLY) ECLECTIC WAY OF THEORIZING

Being aware of the limits that are intrinsic to empirical research, yet without losing sight of the data supplied by that research, Lawrence Friedman has built up a sociolegal theory that is clearly distinct from the majority of similar work in both content and lexicon. Yet that theory is highly solid, so much so that many of his works are still benchmarks for law and society scholars, long after their original appearance.

I speak of "theory" in an open and, to a certain extent, unconventional sense. As already stated, the author distances himself not only from methodological rigidity and from theories devoid of empirical support but also from "strong" theories, meant as sets of assertions that claim to give a full account of a complex reality,[21] once and for all: Even the very word "theory" does not appear very frequently in his writings. Yet his efforts have been often – and increasingly over the years – addressed toward theory, meant not in a "strong" but rather in a "weak" sense as a generalization suggested by experience. Thus theory is something that he sees as specific to the work of sociologists in general and to legal sociologists in particular, as opposed to the work of jurists, lawyers, and even legal historians, at least in the traditional approach.

This kind of theory has developed as part of the author's whole production, but as far as sociology of law (*stricto sensu*) is concerned, it is well known that its more complete expression is to be found in his *The Legal System: A Social Science Perspective* (1975), an internationally renowned book that has been translated into a number of foreign languages. Summarizing it here would be superfluous: For the purposes of this chapter, what matters is to shed light on some of its key points. These key points may be problematic, but they are still considered milestones in the field of sociology of law, more than thirty years after the book's publication, as the influential editor of the Italian edition, Giovanni Tarello, predicted.[22]

The first and perhaps most crucial of such points is expressed in the title and subtitle of the book. When he wrote this book, system theories were just regaining success in the social sciences after the harsh critiques of Parsonian structural functionalism advanced in the late 1960s. Therefore one might have expected that Friedman, who depicted law as a system performing a number of functions, would have involved himself in a field that had already produced some remarkable blossoms, especially the writings of Niklas Luhmann, whose *Legitimation durch Verfahren* (1969), volume one of *Soziologische Aufklärung* (1970), and *Rechtssoziologie* (1972) had already appeared. In fact, such an expectation would have been misplaced. Even though

---

[21] "Ce que j'exclus, alors, c'est une sorte de macro-sociologie du droit, une tentative de grande théorie, qui essaie de prendre chaque petit morceau de matière juridique dans son filet" Friedman 96 (1986).

[22] According to Tarello, "this book is fated to become a classical benchmark in both research and teaching of sociology of law." Before the publication of the Italian edition of the book, another influential Italian legal theorist, Uberto Scarpelli, had commented on the book extensively. Scarpelli (1976).

Friedman knew and occasionally cited Luhmann's works, his construction sprang from and addressed itself elsewhere. Indeed nothing seems farther from the author's interest than system theories in sociology, especially the Parsonian and Luhmannian versions. Had the book not taken serious account of Durkheim and, mainly, Max Weber, one could even say that the author stood fully in the field of the social sciences, but less in the narrower field of sociology, or at least not in its very center, as a reputed Italian reviewer noted with a hint of surprise.[23] The inspiring sources of the volume were in fact different – legal history (Hurst, Holdsworth), jurisprudence (Hart, Hoebel, Llewellyn), and obviously the legal science, in that open and non-formalistic version that had already taken hold in the United States with the birth of a fertile "law and society" field.[24] Friedman's starting point was this rich experience, nurtured on the basis of legal knowledge, field observation, and reflection.

Yet this construction can be traced to sociological structural functionalism, at least partially. Friedman's legal system actually has a "structure," consisting of social institutions – parliaments, governments, courts, and other legal agencies – that receive inputs from the outside world, filter and process them on the basis of a "substance" coinciding with legal rules, and eventually emit outputs that, in their turn, may have a feedback effect on society and the legal institutions themselves. Therefore, at least prima facie, this vision appears to be in good harmony with the (best) tradition of structural functionalism. It comes as no surprise that it was precisely in the framework of functionalism that Treves included it, although he emphasized its "original" features[25] Even Niklas Luhmann, always so alertly monitoring the fortified walls of his system of thought, declared in his *Ausdifferenzierung des Rechts* that Friedman's legal system was "similar" to his own *Rechtssystem*, which he described in this way: "[A] society's legal system consists of all social communications which are formulated with reference to law" (*das Rechtssystem einer Gesellschaft besteht aus allen sozialen Kommunikationen, die mit Bezugnahme auf das Recht formuliert werden*).[26] That this similarity exists is actually rather questionable.[27] What is sure and certainly undeniable is that the portrait painted by Friedman in his writings, of how the legal

---

[23] This is one of the few (but light) critical remarks that Uberto Scarpelli made about the book. Being himself a high-ranking legal theorist, he praised Friedman's frequent references to jurisprudential sources, with special regard to Herbert Hart (although observing that they were hardly compatible with the critiques addressed by Friedman toward normativism). Yet he also wrote that "social grand theory is not really Friedman's vocation." Scarpelli 305 (1976).

[24] Not coincidentally, in his introduction to the Italian edition of *The Legal System*, Giovanni Tarello, a student of American legal realism, stressed the difference between "sociology of law," typical of European culture, and the "law and society" approach that is more indebted to the American tradition of sociological and realistic jurisprudence. Tarello (1978), 7–8, 22.

[25] Treves 304–8 (1987).

[26] Luhmann 35 (1981).

[27] The two conceptions are only partially similar. To make an example, an invitation to perform sent by a creditor to his debtor is *part* of Luhmann's *Rechtssystem*, conceived as a set of social communications inspired by legal rules, whereas it is an *action addressed toward* Friedman's legal system, conceived as a set of structures and rules. For some brief analytical remarks on this point, see Ferrari 6–9 (2000).

system, meant as a functioning machinery,[28] actually works, displays a high degree of explanatory power, precisely in the most classical of sociological perspectives – that of social action, which goes back to Weber and which Friedman himself takes into account. This perspective offers a highly relevant contribution to the understanding of the life of law in society, because it shows how social actors make free decisions, transform them into inputs sent to a system that treats them freely, and produce outputs of *any kind*: predictable or unpredictable, morally acceptable or unacceptable, compatible or incompatible with the existing law, conservative or progressive.

Here, then, a second kernel of the author's theoretical construction comes to light: that of the functions of law. This topic is especially intricate, because it impinges on the terminological and methodological questions that stem from the polysemic concept of "function." Now, Friedman availed himself of the tools of functional analysis without either venturing into the minefield of epistemological discussion or, especially, falling into the traps of sociological functionalism, according to which, traditionally, a function is a *beneficial* contribution offered to a system by an element that affects it from inside or from outside. In this way, law has often been described by sociologists as performing positive functions – "eu-functions," as the most sophisticated functionalist lexicon used to say. Even Niklas Luhmann, who developed the most neutral functionalist explanation of law, did not avoid this destiny. In his view, by selecting and "bringing to congruence" normative social expectations on the basis of the binary code "lawful–unlawful" (*Recht–Unrecht*), the legal system helps reduce social complexity – a fundamental social need in itself. However, his idea, which grasps a part of reality, actually misses another and equally important part: It does not see that law, which depends on subjective decisions from the beginning to the end of any legal process, may bring to the surrounding social system either balance or unbalance, change or stagnation, war or peace. Briefly, the stance adopted by Friedman in his book was compatible with this more open and skeptical portrait of how things go. He actually recorded a number of "functions" of law that are usually described by writers in positive terms, but by causing the functions of the legal system to coincide with its outputs, he paved the way to depicting all possible performances of law in a *wertfrei* way, as Weber would have said. The widest function he envisaged

---

[28] It must be remembered that different authors use this expression – "legal system" – with different meanings. In addition to Luhmann and Friedman, cited earlier, for example, William Evan sees the legal system (and any other social system) as a structure composed of "values, norms, roles and organizations" Evan 47 (1990). I prefer to use it (*"sistema giuridico"*) to signify the system of legal rules in the broad sense (statutes, customs, precedent, etc.), following the example of European jurisprudence. Ferrari 37–41 (2004). Still, it should be stressed that all of these are but *linguistic choices* applied to abstract concepts, not to visible and tangible "objects." Their heuristic value depends on whether their use is consistent with the premises in their respective theoretical contexts. In any case, it is obvious that all the concepts that are described differently as "legal systems" by different authors refer to entities that can be said to operate "systemically."

for law – the allocation of scarce goods and services[29] – is especially value-free. This kind of economic distribution among too many applicants may be applied in general to *any* legal system, while concretely assuming different characters, case by case. It may be equal or unequal, fair or unfair, good or bad: All this concerns individual patterns of allocation and is by all means another question, more typically normative, rather than descriptive, in character.

This open functional vision laid the foundation, explicitly or implicitly, for the subsequent set of theoretical remarks contained in *The Legal System*, such as the distinction between the impact of law and its effectiveness, the description of how negative and positive sanctions work – here such a point as the "deterrence curve"[30] was indeed important – the analysis of how social groups and subgroups act and interact, and, finally, the discussion of the notion of legal culture, a kernel of the author's views and the basis for the analysis of his favorite topic: social change.

It is well known that, in the panoply of Friedman's concepts, that of legal culture was often discussed and criticized for its alleged vagueness.[31] The answer provided by the author, on various occasions, might seem an understatement and may be found originally in the words by which he introduced the notion in *The Legal System* – "*sans rigueur*," as Carbonnier would have said: "The term *legal culture* has been loosely used to describe a number of related phenomena."[32] Certainly the adverb "loosely" looks appropriate if one goes through all such phenomena, which are listed both in the following pages of this book and in later writings, such as in the author's reply to Cotterrell's critiques: "Legal culture, as I have defined the term, refers to ideas, values, expectations and attitudes toward law and legal institutions, which some public or part of the public holds."[33] It is perhaps true that this definition may be taken as analytically too "loose,"[34] as the author himself acknowledges. Still, even forgetting that the same destiny is shared by many other concepts, starting with "law" itself, one can understand Friedman's reluctance to deprive himself of this notion, given its crucial importance for his whole portrait of law in society. Indeed the inputs addressed by social actors toward the legal system do not come from nowhere and are affected by all those factors – not only economic but also cultural – that characterize those actors themselves, their society, and the social groups to which

---

[29] Friedman 20–4 (1975). From an analytical viewpoint, this concept may be considered a sort of "meta-function" of law, as I have noted on two distinct occasions (and with distinct conclusions) in Ferrari (1987) and in my entry ("Functions of Law") in the *Encyclopedia of Law and Society* edited by David Clark. See Ferrari (2007).

[30] Friedman 75–7 (1975).

[31] See, e.g., Cotterrell (1997).

[32] Friedman 193 (1975).

[33] Friedman 34 (1997); see also, Friedman 31 (1985b).

[34] Yet it is worth noting that Uberto Scarpelli, always very demanding with regard to analytical rigor, did not complain about any purported lack of rigor in this notion; instead he said that "Friedman is very careful and thoughtful as to cultural mediation between social forces and law" Scarpelli 305 (1976).

they may belong, or those that may be called on to mediate between society at large and the legal system, such as those professional groups that share what Friedman calls the "internal legal culture."[35] Suffice it to examine the historical evolution of any legal institution – from courts to human rights, from contract to property – to understand that social scientists cannot ignore such factors, however defined, because they contribute, in Weberian terms, precisely to giving a "sense" (*Sinn*) to individual and social action. In a diachronic perspective, they also contribute to institutional change.

This is a theme that accompanies our author's entire production and therefore deserves a separate discussion.

PORTRAITS OF CHANGE

The last chapter of *The Legal System* laid down the guidelines of a general theory of social and legal change by sorting out various different forms of interaction between the legal system and the external society.[36] The discussion that followed was devoted to evolutionist theories, either macro or micro, among others, displaying complete awareness of their epistemological weakness. One point was clearly stated there, however: "Every tool in technique, every new kind of social organization, drags along with it a change in legal norms and that law, even though it is a 'dependent variable,' may either hinder or accelerate social change, especially in a common law culture, in which courts can react promptly and effectively to the new stimuli that come from a society, without the lawgivers' mediation."[37] Therefore, without taking an evolutionist or a neo-evolutionist stance, Friedman has focused his attention throughout his whole production on "then and now" or on "later and earlier," to use his own words.[38] This seems to be, explicitly or implicitly, the most recurrent *Leitmotiv* in his writings.

A number of instances can be produced. They cover an extremely large part of the area of law, which in itself is quite telling if one wishes to evaluate the work of this scholar. I confine myself to some of them that seemed to me especially significant and obviously neglect many others by necessity.

---

[35] Friedman 223ff. (1975). This is a topic that typically can only be tackled successfully by scholars with a specific training in legal education and practice, whose roots can be found in the scholar's earlier writings. See, e.g., Friedman (1965).

[36] Friedman 269 (1975).

[37] Id. at 290. The way in which courts react to external pressures and favor change in the social system and in other legal institutions was the topic of some brilliant lectures given by Lawrence Friedman in Milan University Law Faculty in January 2000.

[38] Friedman 8 (1989c); Friedman 11 (2002a, 2002b). This point has been stressed in a thoughtful Italian essay on multiculturalism and penal law in the United States, which largely relies on Friedman's historical descriptions and uses precisely the words "then and now" to entitle one of the sections. De Maglie 173ff., spec. 182 (2005).

Going back to the author's first writings, we find that, in a long essay published in the *Wisconsin Law Review*, Friedman unraveled the threads of his earlier research and writings on inheritance and succession.[39] This essay offered a number of important remarks, among them the idea that the regime of testamentary freedom is in constant tension with the trend to favor one's own nuclear family, as well as the parallel idea that this tension is the source of the intricacies and technicalities characteristic of inheritance law. Yet what matters most from our viewpoint is the clear distinction he drew between the "property system" and the "non-property system," the latter consisting in that "network of rights and duties in valued objects non governed by rules of buying, selling, giving, and inheriting."[40] Each social class that is privileged not only by wealth, but also by prestige and power develops its own ways to convey its privileges to the next generations, formally or informally. In this light, it is the nonproperty system that seems to achieve increasing importance in our age with respect to the past." This idea placed Friedman at the heart of sociological reflection on this topic internationally.

Jumping to 1985, we find a thoughtful book in which the "then and now" approach is applied to the social trend toward "juridification" or "judicialization," which enjoyed pride of place in sociolegal discussion for at least two decades. The thesis upheld by Friedman is well known: "Legal culture has been moving in a single direction, toward what I called total justice."[41] Technological evolution has rendered society much more complex and plural than in the recent past. All this has brought about profound changes in the field of legal culture and a steady increase in the inputs addressed to the legal system in all its branches: more laws, more administration, more litigation, more (and more diverse) cases brought to court. Social change passes through legal change: It is "juridified" social change, so to say. Whether this is good or bad is an open question, he admitted, that involves the sphere of ethics and politics, but on a descriptive level juridification seems to him to be both undeniable and a distinctive trait of modernity.

Five years later, *The Republic of Choice* took the same direction, even though more emphasis was placed on the kind of change in legal culture and, consequently, in the legal system. In his view, the increase in legal activities between the "liberal" nineteenth century and the twentieth century (i.e., the epoch of state intervention and welfare policies) does not signify that the area of freedom, meant as free choice, has shrunk correspondingly. On the contrary, the dominant and ever-increasing societal trend has favored wider spaces of freedom, in both private and public life. In our times, it is infinitely easier to divorce and remarry, to change jobs, or even to start a new business after going bankrupt. Societies have been increasingly pervaded by a sort of "expressive individualism," as Robert Bellah called it, and law, far from

[39] Friedman (1966).
[40] Id. at 360.
[41] Friedman 147 (1985b).

hindering the rush toward free choice, has favored and accelerated it. In Friedman's words, "Law is the vehicle through which modern notions of choice are translated into living social arrangements."[42]

A little later, *Crime and Punishment in American History* dealt with a subject toward which Friedman felt aversion and attraction at one and the same time.[43] This book appears to be a fully fledged treatise of legal history, more than of sociology of law: It is a history of the American system of criminal law from the colonial period to the present day. Yet, the author used the same theoretical and methodological approach to address the same aim as before (i.e., describing how some variables, especially culture, affect institutional change). Again, Friedman stressed that modern developed societies have been moving toward ever-wider areas of tolerance with respect to individual choices. He observed that in the area of criminal law both process and punishment have changed their social function deeply in the course of the last two centuries. The former, which had been private and secret throughout the Middle Ages, has become (relatively) public and transparent. Inversely, the latter has abandoned the public space and been confined to restricted, isolated spaces, such as modern prisons and death chambers. The mass media question that had captured the author's attention in previous years[44] surfaced in these pages. If "then" it was punishment that turned into a show – the "splendour of torments," of which also Michel Foucault[45] spoke – "now" the show has moved into the courtrooms, as can be easily ascertained by watching a number of TV series, and not only in the United States.[46] He called them "trials as theater" quite recently, while discussing the "vanishing trials" hypothesis with a hint of irony.[47]

The *Horizontal Society* in 1999 followed much the same path, in both aims and approach. Here, as elsewhere,[48] the scholar tackled subjects such as identity, citizenship, migrations, and social integration; that last topic had become perhaps

---

[42] Friedman 37 (1990).

[43] Friedman (1993a).

[44] Friedman (1989b).

[45] Foucault (1975).

[46] See Friedman (2004). Recent experience in Italy confirms Friedman's theses impressively. Not only do criminal trials often occupy center stage in TV broadcasts but they may even be dragged metaphorically out of the courtroom to be remade or even anticipated in TV studios, as if the public, rather than juries or judges, should make the final decision on the defendant's guilt or innocence. In at least two cases (a high-ranking politician and former minister charged with bribery, and a mother charged with murdering her own little child, both convicted), the undeclared though barely concealed purpose of the TV shows was to influence public opinion in favor of the accused and correspondingly convey dissent about the action of both public prosecutors and judges.

[47] See Friedman (2004). This article provides a comment on the (undeniable) fact that trials (either bench or jury) have decreased in number steadily in the United States throughout the past forty years, as is shown in a special issue of the *Journal of Empirical Legal Studies*, whose first article was a highly detailed empirical analysis and theoretical discussion by Marc Galanter (2004). Still, as Friedman observes, "the 'trial' was never the norm, never the modal way of resolving issues and solving problems in the legal system"; therefore, he adds, "There was never much to vanish." Friedman 689 (2004).

[48] Friedman (1998, 2001a, 2001b).

the most popular subject in sociolegal debates at the turn of the millennium. The book looked at these social phenomena in the light of the "rights revolution" that in our times features the characteristic expansion of expressive individualism and free choice. In this world, alongside the erosion of state boundaries, authority (meant in Weberian terms), which for centuries had been vertical (i.e., top down), has become horizontal; this change is a matter of changing choices, although it has not taken place without problems, because the media affect social choices, and with mass migrations from the underdeveloped world to affluent societies, social pluralism also posits the inclusion–exclusion question in acute new ways.

Social pluralism may be taken to involve legal pluralism almost automatically, as many authors have upheld over the last few decades, rediscovering and updating the theories of scholars such as Eugen Ehrlich and Georges Gurvitch. Actually, the question of legal pluralism has long occupied center stage in contemporary discussions about the past, present, and future of legal systems, and Friedman has been taking an active part in such debates. Yet he does not just follow the flow but, once again, looks at this question critically. He sees that there are drastic contradictions at work in the world today, in the field of law as elsewhere. Although there is no denying, on the one hand, that ever more peoples, groups, and subgroups strive for differentiated treatment, often in the name of a different legal system, and legal systems themselves, as an effect, tend to intersect and give way to what has been termed "interlegality,"[49] it is hard to deny, on the other hand, that opposite trends are also visible in the "global world." In a nutshell: are our legal systems deemed to diverge or rather to converge? As long as he reflects on this topic, Friedman seems to opt for the latter alternative. Although he acknowledges that convergence differs from one country, legal culture, or different field of law to another – commercial law obviously tends to uniformity much more than family law – he guesses that the unhindered spread of all kinds of cultural models, whether material or symbolic – from food to music, for example – will ultimately also lead legal systems to converge.[50] To a certain extent, this is a kind of cultural challenge that Lawrence Friedman has issued to both legal sociologists and legal historians who are committed to investigate futures.

These few lines do not do justice to the quantity and quality of the author's descriptions, which avail themselves of a multitude of examples taken not only from field research but also from his rich and direct experience of the world and of cultures quite distinct from his own. Still, I trust that they give enough evidence that Friedman's sociology of law is chiefly, though not exclusively, a sociology of legal and social change.

[49] Santos (1995).
[50] Friedman (1993b, 2001c, 2002c).

A LOOSE CONCLUSION

All this comes as no surprise, because the author, who is more jurist and lawyer than sociologist both by training and by preference, sees law in an essentially historical perspective. If we were to insist on classifying him, perhaps he might be depicted as primarily a legal historian. Indeed, those of his works that are labeled as history, such as *History of American Law*[51] and *American Law in the Twentieth Century*,[52] are of paramount importance in this particular field of studies.[53] Still, these works can be separated from the author's sociological or legal writings only artificially and for the sake of simplicity, but with a large degree of arbitrariness. Reading them, it is easy to perceive the same method, the same threads, and the same direction as are applied in the others. Their key point is always, and firmly, the sharp distinction between what was "then" and what is "now" through the emphasis on the technological, social, and cultural factors of change and the insistence on the speed and the peculiar qualities that social and institutional change has displayed through the age of modernity.

It could be said that comparing "now" and "then" is the typical job of any historian. That is true to a large extent. However, Lawrence Friedman is an historian of a special type. A student and follower of James Willard Hurst, the founder and theorist of the movement of "social history,"[54] he belongs to that (not particularly wide) sphere of historians who do not share the vice of confining themselves to a highly special field and studying it as if it were a "closed world," be it music, literature, art or, obviously, law. As literature affects the arts and vice versa, so technological evolution and cultural expressions, either material or symbolic, are variables that affect any other human activity and, with it, also institutional change. No aspect of the legal system is immune from this impact, even though, recurrently, jurists seek to isolate the world of law and make it "autonomous," as is said in the common law lexicon – or striving for formalism, we would say in the lexicon of continental Europe's legal theory.

Lawrence Friedman is certainly a non-formalist lawyer, as the editors and introducers of the Italian edition of his *History of American Law*, themselves firmly antiformalist, did not fail to observe.[55] This point obviously matters, although to a limited extent only. What is more important is that Friedman looks for the sense of history or, more precisely, for its direction in the interaction between phenomena, rather than in conceptual categories, as happened, for instance, in the great nineteenth-century

---

[51] Friedman (1985a).

[52] Friedman (2002a).

[53] Yet see also the short version of *Law in America* (Friedman 2002b).

[54] It is well known that, according to Friedman, Hurst's *The Growth of American Law: The Lawmakers* (1950) heralded "a new phase of legal history" in the United States. See, e.g., Friedman 8–9 (1989c).

[55] For Giorgio Rebuffa, a disciple of Giovanni Tarello, the founder of a fertile school of legal theory that was to a large extent inspired by American legal realism, "this book is one of the most remarkable outcomes of the anti-formalist stance of American legal culture" Rebuffa (1995).

European philosophy of history. Even such a concept as freedom, which was central to that philosophy and no less crucial in Friedman's own thought, surfaces in his writings as a set of liberties that can be ascertained and measured, rather than as an abstract and comprehensive category of the human spirit. Even more important is the fact that Friedman seeks generalizations through observable phenomena. Even though decades have elapsed since the great methodological battles about the status of the diverse social sciences took place, especially in Germany, many historians on both sides of the Atlantic are still attached to their traditional individualistic and "idiographic" approach and rather mistrust the opposite approach, precisely based on testable generalizations, which they see as typically sociological. Yet, this opposite approach is also typically the approach of Lawrence Friedman: He seems to have felt in a minority because he said that, when legal sociology and legal history happen to meet, they "are treated more or less as two ships that pass in the night."[56] Quite obviously, his choice for a descriptive methodology and controlled generalization pushed him toward empirical sociology, as a science that can disclose the real life of people, past and present, and teach good lessons to historians too. *Vita magistra historiae*, we could say, inverting the terms of the old saying.[57]

That Friedman's generalizations may be debatable is obvious. That they may be biased, as somebody has observed critically, is quite a different matter. Renato Treves said, courageously, that social scientists never succeed in completely shaking off their own cultural and ideological background, so that their honesty consists in admitting that they observe the world from a specific perspective and in declaring their point of view clearly.[58] Friedman usually does that. For example, more than once he has said that he is in favor of those institutional changes that are the most distinctive traits of legal modernity – the due process of law, the rights revolution, the welfare state, social pluralism, protection of minorities, tolerance, and equality in a wide sense of the word.[59] Does this favor affect his interpretation keys? Does he exaggerate in optimism while thinking that the advances that have taken place in the Western world may become universal? Does he neglect, while observing the world from the point of view of affluent societies, the tremendous impact of poverty in the underdeveloped world and of the religious fundamentalism that seems to go hand in hand with it? Indeed many of his pages display full awareness of these and other problems, for modernity itself, in his view, "does have consequences, for good and for evil."[60] However, even admitting that his liberal views may sometimes affect how he interprets reality, one must admit that he produces evidence – and a large amount of it – to uphold his visions. At least as much counter-evidence should be produced to reject them.

---

[56] Friedman 7 (1989c).
[57] It was Helmut Schelsky (1959) who defined sociology as "the historiography of the present."
[58] Treves 222ff. (1987).
[59] See, e.g., Friedman 151 (1985b).
[60] Friedman 190 (1990).

REFERENCES

Carbonnier, Jean (1992). *Flexible droit. Textes pour une sociologie du droit sans rigueur*. Paris: Librairie Générale de Droit et de Jurisprudence.

Cotterrell, Roger (1997). The Concept of Legal Culture, in David Nelken, ed., *Comparing Legal Cultures*. Dartmouth: Aldershot.

De Maglie, Cristina (2005). Multiculturalismo e diritto penale. Il caso americano. XLVIII *Rivista italiana di diritto e procedura penale* 173.

Evan, William M. (1990). *Social Structure and Law. Theoretical and Empirical Perspectives*. Newbury Park, CA: Sage.

Ferrari, Vincenzo (1987). *Funzioni del diritto. Saggio critico-ricostruttivo*. Rome-Bari: Laterza.

———. (2000). Law's Normative Nature as a Sociological Concept, *Associations*. 4 *J. Legal Soc. Theory* 1.

———. (2004). *Diritto e Società. Elementi di sociologia del diritto*. Rome-Bari: Laterza.

———. (2007). Functions of Law, in David S. Clark, ed., *Encyclopedia of Law & Society. American and Global Perspectives*, 2, Thousand Oaks-London-New Delhi-Singapore: Sage, 610 ff.

Foucault, Michel (1975). *Surveiller et punir. Naissance de la prison*. Paris: Gallimard.

Friedman, Lawrence M. (1964). Patterns of Testation in the 19th Century: A Study of Essex County (New Jersey) Wills, 8 *Am. J. Legal Hist*. 34.

———. (1965). Law, Rules, and the Interpretation of Written Documents, 59 *Nw. U. L. Rev*. 751.

———. (1966). The Law of the Living, the Law of the Dead: Property, Succession, and Society. *Wis. L. Rev*. 340.

———. (1975). *The Legal System: A Social Science Perspective*. New York: Russell Sage Foundation. It. edn. *Il sistema giuridico nella prospettiva delle scienze sociali*, 1978, edited and introduced by Giovanni Tarello. Bologna: il Mulino.

———. (1976). Trial Courts and their Work in the Modern World, in Lawrence Friedman and Manfred Rehbinder, eds., *Zur Soziologie des Gerichtsverfahren – Sociology of the Judicial Process*, Bd. IV, Opladen: Westdeutscher Verlag.

———. (1985a). *History of American Law*. New York: Simon & Schuster. Italian edition: (1995) *Storia del diritto americano*, edited by Guido Alpa, Guido Marchesiello, and Giorgio Rebuffa. Milano: Giuffrè.

———. (1985b). *Total Justice*. New York: Russell Sage Foundation.

———. (1986). La sociologie du droit est-elle vraiment une science?, 2 *Droit et Société. Revue internationale de théorie du droit et de sociologie du droit* 91.

———. (1989a). Litigation and Society, 15 *Ann. Rev. Sociol*. 17.

———. (1989b). Law, Lawyers, and Popular Culture, 98 *Yale L.J*. 1579.

———. (1989c). Sociology of Law and Legal History, XVI *Sociologia del diritto* 7.

———. (1990). *The Republic of Choice. Law, Authority, and Culture*. Cambridge, MA: Harvard University Press.

———. (1993a). *Crime and Punishment in American History*. New York: Basic Books.

———. (1993b). Verso una sociologia del diritto transnazionale, XX *Sociologia del diritto*, 1, 39.

———. (1995). Litigios y litigiosidad en los Estados Unidos de América, in María Eugenia Boza and Rogelio Pérez-Perdomo, eds., *Seguridad Jurídica y Competitividad*. Caracas: IESA.

———. (1997). The Concept of Legal Culture: A Reply, in David Nelken, ed., *Comparing Legal Cultures*. Aldershot: Dartmouth.

———. (1998). *Ethnicity and Citizenship*, in Vincenzo Ferrari, Thomas Heller, and Elena de Tullio, eds., *Citizenship and Immigration*. Milano: Giuffrè.

———. (1999). *The Horizontal Society*: New Haven: Yale University Press.

———. (2001a). The Shattered Mirror: Identity, Authority, and Law, 58 *Wash. & Lee L. Rev.* 21.

———. (2001b). Some Comments on "Conflicts and Rights" in Transnational Society, in Vincenzo Ferrari, Paola Ronfani, and Silvia Stabile, eds., *Conflitti e diritti nella società transnazionale*. Milano: Angeli.

———. (2001c). Erewhon: The Coming Global Legal Order, 37 *Stan. J. Int'l L.* 347.

———. (2002a). *American Law in the 20th Century*. New Haven: Yale University Press.

———. (2002b). *Law in America: A Short History*. New York: Modern Library.

———. (2002c). One World: Notes on the Emerging Legal Order, in M. Litowsky, ed., *Transnational Legal Processes: Globalization and Power Disparities*, Oxford: Oxford University Press.

———. (2004). The Day before Trials Vanished, 1 *J. Empir. Legal Stud.* 689.

Friedman, Lawrence, and Robert V. Percival (1976). A Tale of Two Courts. Litigation in Alameda and San Benito Counties, 10 *Law & Soc'y Rev.* 267.

———. (1981). *The Roots of Justice: Crime and Punishment in Alameda County, California, 1870–1910*. Chapel Hill: University of North Carolina Press.

Galanter, Marc (2004). The Vanishing Trial: An Examination of Trials and Related Matters in Federal and States Courts, 1 *J. Empir. Legal Stud.* 459.

Jori, Mario (1976). *Il metodo giuridico tra scienza e politica*. Milan: Giuffrè.

Luhmann, Niklas (1969). *Legitimation durch Verfahren*. Neuwied und Berlin: Luchterhand.

———. (1970). *Soziologische Aufklärung* I. Köln-Opladen: Westdeutscher Verlag.

———. (1972). *Rechtssoziologie*. Reinbek bei Hamburg: Rowohlt.

———. (1981). *Ausdifferenzierung des Rechts. Beiträge zur Rechtssoziologie und Rechtstheorie*. Frankfurt am Main: Suhrkamp.

———. (1992). *Grundrechte als Institution*. Berlin: Duncker und Humblot (originally published in 1965).

———. (1993). *Das Recht der Gesellschaft*. Frankfurt am Main: Suhrkamp.

Rebuffa, Giorgio (1995). Introduction to L. M. Friedman, *Storia del diritto americano*, edited by Guido Alpa, Guido Marchesiello, and Giorgio Rebuffa, Milano: Giuffrè.

Santos, B. de Sousa (1995). *Toward a New Common Sense. Law, Science and Politics in the Paradigmatic Transition*, New York: Routledge.

Scarpelli, Uberto (1965). *Cos'è il positivismo giuridico*. Milano: Comunità.

Scarpelli, Uberto (1976). Lawrence M. Friedman e il sistema giuridico, III *Sociologia del diritto* 299.

Schelsky, Helmut (1959). *Orstbestimmung der deutschen Soziologie*. Düsseldorf: Diederich.

Toharia, José Juan (1974). *Cambio social y vida jurídica en España*. Madrid: Edicusa.

Treves, Renato (1960). Considerazioni intorno alla sociologia giuridica, XIV *Rivista trimestrale di diritto e procedura civile* 169.

———. (1987). *Sociologia del diritto. Origini, ricerche, problemi*. Torino: Einaudi.

———. (1992). Due sociologie del diritto, XIX *Sociologia del diritto* 11.

3

Lawrence Friedman and the Bane of Functionalism

Victoria Saker Woeste

My aims in this chapter are modest. The first is to provide an overview of the corpus of Lawrence Friedman's scholarship. The second is to distill one or two of the essential ideas and themes that in my view emerge from Friedman's work and from his engagement with other historians. One recursive theme is the way that, for Friedman, theory and method are intellectually fused. It is difficult, if not impossible, to separate Friedman's theoretical insights into law and society and legal change from his methodology, his reliance on and analysis of trial court cases, and his use of individual stories to talk about the down-on-the ground meaning of law. This fusion of ideas and method positions Friedman intellectually within the legal history community and within legal scholarship more generally. That observation leads to the second theme I want to identify: the way in which Friedman has come to represent, sometimes all by himself, one clearly demarcated side of an ongoing argument raging among those who seek to get inside the heads of nineteenth-century judges. To explore this theme, I map the interesting fruits of a relatively recent exchange between Friedman and the author of a book with which he took issue, an exchange that both recapitulates and moves forward a dialogue Friedman began more than forty years ago.

MAPPING THE FRIEDMAN RECORD

First, the Friedman corpus. It is enormous! It is profoundly unfair that one person can be so consistently productive for so many years. Friedman's interests are astonishingly broad; his pen flows unceasingly; his tape recorder runs through batteries so fast he puts the Energizer Bunny out of work. If he had written nothing else, Friedman's three editions of *A History of American Law*[1] would cement his contribution to our

[1] Friedman (1973, 1985a, 2005).

field. At the rate he is going, we may expect the fourth edition to appear by the year 2016.

Of course, there is much more to list. Most of today's leading legal historians, social scientists, sociologists, legal theorists, and jurisprudential heavy-weights have cut their teeth on one or more of Friedman's many books. These books include *Contract Law in America* (1965); *Law and the Behavioral Sciences* (1969); *Law and Society: An Introduction* (1977), which has been translated into Japanese, Korean, and Chinese; *The Roots of Justice: Crime and Punishment in Alameda County, California, 1879–1910* (1981), with Robert Percival (they won the Hurst Prize); *American Law* (1984); *Total Justice* (1985b); *Your Time Will Come: The Law of Age Discrimination and Mandatory Retirement* (1985c), a title that manages to be at once prosaic and prophetic; *The Republic of Choice* (1990); *Crime and Punishment in American History* (1993), an ABA Silver Gavel winner and Pulitzer Prize finalist; *The Horizontal Society* (1999a); *American Law in the 20th Century* (2002), another multiple prize winner; *Law in America: A Short History* (2002); and *Private Lives: Families, Individuals, and the Law* (2004). In his abundant free time, Friedman produced a number of important edited anthologies. Even more stunning are his 213 scholarly articles, reviews, presidential remarks, and other occasional publications. Eighty-five of Friedman's 213 articles, or 39 percent, have been written since 1990, the year he turned sixty and when, if there is a natural order to these things, he was supposed to start slowing down.

As this list suggests, the breadth of Friedman's talent and interests is remarkable. He writes in several genres. With deceptive ease he produces the nested, grounded histories of specific times and places that are essential to answer questions about what really happened. He also turns out broad, meta-level, theoretical treatments that relocate the boundaries of the field of inquiry. As Avi Soifer noted in a 1988 review essay, "he's a counter who thinks and a thinker who counts."[2]

Nowhere, I think, is this singular ability put to work more effectively than in my favorite of all Friedman's works, *The Roots of Justice*, coauthored by Robert Percival.[3] In that beautiful study of criminal process in late-nineteenth-century California, we are treated to a classic Friedman act of redirection. He begins by minimizing the significance of the particular place and time he has chosen to study: "What we have here is even less than a slice of life; it is the merest sliver." Yet do not let him fool you. It is in the micro-level data that Friedman finds the lasting echoes of human experience, of human fallibility, of law's forceful authority. Friedman and Percival recovered events that were not particularly noteworthy even as they occurred and found interesting historical patterns and relationships in the mundane and the routine. We need to care about the nameless and faceless who peopled the past, Friedman tells us, because of the intimate relationship between social order and those at the bottom. We should care because law is thoroughly bound up in the

---

[2] Soifer 995 (1988).
[3] Friedman and Percival (1981).

creation and perpetuation of social order. Yet Friedman refuses to overgeneralize, overtheorize, or overargue the historical characterizations he draws: "The world inside [the courtroom] reflected the world outside – *had* to reflect it. . . . The legal system . . . goes hand in glove with its society; it changes as society changes. . . . The criminal justice system of Alameda County, in our period, had no single function, and cannot be summed up in a single, simple formula."[4]

That sort of claim frustrates those looking for theoretical insight – as if that claim were devoid of such insight – and fuels the perception that mere functionalism drives Friedman's legal history. In the *Roots of Justice*, the authors explain their position with some care. Their aim is to study a criminal justice system and how it worked at a particular place and time, not how it should work or should have worked. *The Roots of Justice* captures the essence of the law and society movement's intellectual ecumenism, itself a product of a particular time and a particular intellectual impulse. Precisely because it is so well grounded in its sources, *The Roots of Justice* provides us with what is perhaps the most considered articulation of Friedman's understanding of the relationship between law and society: Law is not autonomous, but is thoroughly interdependent with society; it is not an instrument of passive reflection, like a mirror, but shifts dynamically in response to race, class, gender, corporate power, the buying and selling of public influence, and the institutions and authority of the state. The way Friedman thinks law works begins with its very refusal to be pinned down and categorized. The reification here is mine, not his. Law is about complexity, ambiguity, and the sheer messiness of social life. In *The Roots of Justice*, Friedman puts it this way: The rules of criminal justice, how they were and are enforced, and by whom constituted "a vast tangled system, a network of processes, intertwined like a mass of spaghetti."[5] The image of laws tangled as spaghetti has become metonymic; it is emblematic not just of the thing being described but of Friedman's work as well.

The Roots of Justice epitomizes Friedman's approach to legal history, his uncanny ability to marry method and theory in harmonious congruence, and, above all, his insistence that historians remain true to the requirements of their craft. For him, historical subjects are social creatures, products of their time and place that are not to be marginalized or diminished in the service of grand theory, but worked into theory on their own terms. As a legal historian, he is equally adept whether his subject is Blackstone or Lemuel Shaw or the total number of arrests in Oakland between 1870 and 1910. As an unabashedly enthusiastic empirical scholar, he cautions the reader against drawing easy conclusions while staking out what impressions can be drawn from his sources. As a historian, he is a cautious advocate; as a lawyer, he is a judicious chronicler of the past. He knows that historical records possess chameleon-like qualities; the fact that data will unavoidably look different to different readers

---

[4] Id. at 14.
[5] Id.

is for him less a source of postmodern anxiety than a compelling reminder to read thoughtfully. The historian's goal is to get as full and as accurate a "'feel' for what was happening at the time" as possible while remaining conscious of the interpretive limits of all kinds of source materials.[6] Although law professors resisted the pull of empiricism for decades, they have begun to acknowledge that empirical work does have a legitimate place in legal scholarship. We know this to be true because a law professor analyzed recent law school hiring trends and published her findings in a law review.[7]

MAPPING FRIEDMAN ON THE LEGAL HISTORY TERRAIN

As Friedman knows from hard-fought experience, such advances are hard and long in coming. The battles that have been fought over theory and method and interpretive styles and the place of doctrine versus empiricism have left lasting scars. One of these is the long-standing perception, as Avi Soifer has put it, that Friedman "leads an apocryphal band of reductionist-functionalist-instrumentalists," a phrase I take to mean the belief that Friedman's work is hopelessly sunk into the muck of competing interests fighting it out in the courts.[8] This perception has stuck in spite of Friedman's record of scholarly and intellectual diversity and range. Although I think it is accurate to place Friedman in the Wisconsin school of legal history, it is misleading to consign him to a supporting role, to see him merely as an acolyte of Willard Hurst, who himself became the subject of much revisionist critique beginning in the 1980s. Friedman's legal history does begin with Wisconsin school assumptions: Law and society are interdependent; social, cultural, economic, and political change all influence and are influenced by legal change. Yet he pushes beyond the functionalist concerns that people have long associated with the Wisconsin-school approach.

At the same time, Friedman has done a great deal to rehabilitate functionalism or at least to show that the bad rap he has gotten for being a mere functionalist is not entirely deserved. One legal historian even goes so far as to put Friedman and Morton Horwitz in the same intellectual framework:

> [Neither] Friedman [n]or Horwitz was strictly functional; they had more complex models of change and responded to changing contexts and to historical records. Later critics often relied on provocative statements that the two made in an attempt to shake the older lawyers' legal history autonomous model of change. In other places, the two presented more complex and less functional models of change.[9]

As Ron Harris explains, Friedman's interest in how historical actors understood and used law has helped unpack what law meant in particular times and places; in

[6] Id. at 18.
[7] George (2006).
[8] Soifer 995 (1988).
[9] Harris at n.61 (2003).

doing so, Friedman has explored the very contingency of law and legal authority. Still, the functionalist label sticks. Soifer observes that Friedman continues to figure in a "generational combat" in which his opponents perceive him as one of "the dragons that need killing."[10] Such may have been the case before the rise of critical legal studies (CLS), but CLS turned the debate into a pitched battle.

Soifer has suggested that Friedman was "alienated" from CLS and its legal-historian acolytes.[11] It is true that there was something of a divide between legal scholars who emphasize the power of legal ideas and who see law as working to legitimate structures of power and authority, on the one hand, and social historians who focus on the everyday impact of law, on the other. It is also true that Friedman has frankly assailed others whom he thought were misguided, wrong-headed, or plainly wrong. Still, I wonder if the characterization of Friedman as alienated unintentionally misdirects our attention. In my view, what separates Friedman from the power-and-legitimation scholars and makes him a model for social historians of law is something unrelated to this seemingly implacable divide. It concerns how Friedman, as a historian, views his historical subjects.

DISTINGUISHING BEHAVIORALISM FROM FUNCTIONALISM

Friedman is unwilling to see his subjects as merely ideological actors. Nowhere is this more obvious than in the study of the nineteenth-century common law judge. Friedman sees legal historians' long-standing fascination with the legal mind – their abiding need to try to get inside that legal mind, to figure out its internal systems, and to say something about how it worked – as one of the most fundamental yet vexed tasks of legal history. When done incorrectly, the search for order in judges' thinking, especially when viewed through the imperfect medium of the printed state court report, will lead us, in Friedman's view, to a dark and dangerous result: the romanticization of the judge.

This view surfaced in Friedman's reaction to the work of Peter Karsten, who sought to refute the most influential CLS book ever written, Morton Horwitz's *Transformation of American Law*.[12] Karsten's book, *Heart versus Head: Judge-Made Law in Nineteenth-Century America*[13] drew a sharp, extended critique from Friedman.[14] As Friedman makes clear, his reaction to Karsten's was, in part, personal. After all, he was implicated in the book's revisionist critique, but that critique also lumped him with, as he put it, "a fairly strange collection of bedfellows."[15] In addition, Friedman could not abide a legal-historical approach that considers judges too far out of their

[10] Soifer 996 (1988).
[11] Id. at 997.
[12] Horwitz (1977).
[13] Karsten (1997).
[14] Friedman (1999b).
[15] Id. at 254.

material context. Karsten argues (and here I oversimplify violently) that nineteenth-century judges acted on the basis of a bifurcated value system (the head versus heart framework) that enabled them to issue decisions without making or changing law. Innovation did result when a particularly compelling set of facts tugged at judges' heartstrings: "When they encroached on the principles and doctrines of the past, they did it in response to the impulses of the heart; they made new law, but not for the sake of big business, corporate America, or economic growth. Innovation came in exclusively to help the poor and the weak."[16] For Friedman, such an argument raises profound empirical questions about method and historical causation: "What, after all, *is* an innovation?" he asks. "How would you go about counting them?"[17]

This is not merely a quibble over data or how to count and analyze them. Friedman and Karsten differ honestly and substantively about how to conceptualize the judicial function at any time, not just in the nineteenth century. It is worth reading Friedman's own words on this point:

> Looking at behavior doesn't make one a "behaviorist," which is apparently a terrible thing to be. Behavior is as powerful an indicator of culture and ideology as words are. Often you cannot understand the meaning of behavior without words. But just as often it is the other way around. This is especially true if the words are buried in a judicial opinion. You would learn next to nothing about divorce law in the late nineteenth century if you only read appellate cases. You might learn something about elite opinion, but if you thought this was any guide to the "living law," you would be badly mistaken. And the living law is not just behavior; it is, if you will, ideology translated into action. It is also, of course, the pursuit of money, sex, and power, and all the other things people want.[18]

In short, as Friedman puts it, "I think it is important not to exaggerate the effect of the 'legal mind.'"[19] Why? Because judges and lawyers lived and worked within legal traditions and institutional roles that were themselves undergoing constant change. To focus solely on the intellectual context, which is dynamic and interesting in its own right, will leave the historian blind to the constantly shifting material culture in which judges and lawyers thought and, more importantly, acted. They were creatures of culture, caught between reason and sentiment, constrained by the limits of their humanity and their judicial roles.

This exchange between Friedman and Karsten in the pages of *Law and Social Inquiry* – which I have recapitulated one-sidedly[20] – is not the first time Friedman

---

[16] Id. at 255.
[17] Id.
[18] Id. at 276.
[19] Id. at 277.
[20] Karsten (1999).

has expressed his view of the "judicial mind" approach to the intellectual history of the judiciary. Perry Miller's *The Legal Mind in America, From Independence to the Civil War*[21] got much the same treatment as Karsten's book did in an unforgettable Friedman essay.[22] Whereas Karsten won Friedman's respect for his admirably extensive research and reading, Miller drew a rebuke from Friedman for assuming that the relevant universe of legal ideas was to be found in the formal jurisprudential works, speeches, and treatises of the elite bench and bar.[23] Like Karsten, Miller conceived of the American bar in binary, hearts-and-heads terms, depicting judges as using one at the expense of the other. Unlike the judges in Karsten's moral universe, who kept law in their heads and religion in their hearts, Miller's lawyers substituted law for religion: They were "intellectually committed to the forces of cold reason."[24]

For Friedman, the issue is not how or even whether to resolve the heart-vs.-head dichotomy; it is the nature of evidence on which any such characterizations are (or can possibly be) based. For him, no historical question can be answered until you have figured out *how* you can know what you wish to know. Hearts and heads, however broken or disembodied, do not matter unless you can document their impulses, unless hard evidence can be used to connect inner thoughts and motives to words on a page. We cannot assume, intuit, or infer causal relationships; the historians' job is to make those relationships patent through the marshalling of evidence that can withstand close and critical inspection. What Friedman demands of legal historians is that we always remain aware of context, that we acknowledge the interplay of ideas and events, and that we bring the dense complexity of social and material life to bear in writing about how law was made, how it functioned, and what the people who came under its authority thought it meant. In the end, his theory of legal change transcends functionalism: "As society develops, [the legal system] develops too; like language, it is a tool of culture, and it is static or dynamic when its culture is."[25]

In the end, Friedman's engagement with the contentious definitional issues central to our field in the past twenty-five years has led him to a position that we can now place at the center of the present and future of legal history. In a review of Horwitz's sequel, *The Transformation of American Law, 1870–1960* in 1993, James Kloppenberg identified an approach that he called "pragmatic hermeneutics."[26] This approach, while mediating between the differences that have divided the functionalists and interpretativists, would bring the realm of abstract ideas together with the social and

[21] Miller (1962).
[22] Friedman (1968).
[23] Id. at 245.
[24] Id. at 1246.
[25] Id. at 1259.
[26] Horwitz (1992); Kloppenberg 1333 (1993).

cultural history of law.[27] Kloppenberg, like many others, placed Friedman firmly in the camp of the functionalist combatants. Yet it was Friedman's insistence on the relevance of context and concrete historical developments that helped make possible the merger of law and culture that has now gained acceptance in legal scholarship.

REFERENCES

Friedman, Lawrence M. (1965). *Contract Law in America: A Social and Economic Case Study.* Madison: University of Wisconsin Press.
_____. (1968). Heart against Head: Perry Miller and the Legal Mind, 77 *Yale L.J.* 1244.
_____. (1973). *A History of American Law.* New York: Simon and Schuster.
_____. (1977). *Law and Society: An Introduction.* Englewood Cliffs, NJ: Prentice-Hall.
_____. (1984). *American Law.* New York: W.W. Norton & Co.
_____. (1985a). *A History of American Law.* 2d edition. New York: Simon and Schuster.
_____. (1985b). *Total Justice.* New York: Russell Sage Foundation.
_____. (1985c). *Your Time Will Come: The Law of Age Discrimination and Mandatory Retirement.* New York: Russell Sage Foundation.
_____. (1990). *The Republic of Choice: Law, Authority, and Culture.* Cambridge, MA: Harvard University Press.
_____. (1993). *Crime and Punishment in American History.* New York: Basic Books.
_____. (1999a). *The Horizontal Society.* New Haven: Yale University Press.
_____. (1999b). Losing One's Head: Judges and the Law in Nineteenth-Century American Legal History, 24(1) *L. & Soc. Inquiry* 253.
_____. (2002). *American Law in the 20th Century.* New Haven: Yale University Press.
_____. (2002). *Law in America: A Short History.* New York: Random House.
_____. (2004). *Private Lives: Families, Individuals, and the Law.* Cambridge, MA: Harvard University Press.
_____. (2005). *A History of American Law.* 3d edition. New York: Simon and Schuster.
Friedman, Lawrence M., and Stewart Macaulay, eds. (1969). *Law and the Behavioral Sciences.* Indianapolis: Bobbs-Merrill.
Friedman, Lawrence M., and Robert Percival (1981). *The Roots of Justice: Crime and Punishment in Alameda County, California, 1870–1910.* Chapel Hill: University of North Carolina Press.
George, Tracey (2006). An Empirical Study of Empirical Legal Scholarship: The Top Law Schools, 81 *Ind. L.J.* 141.
Harris, Ron (2003). The Encounters of Economic History and Legal History, 21 *L. & Hist. Rev.* 2. Available at http://www.historycooperative.org/journals/lhr/21.2/harris.htmlhttp:// www.historycooperative.org/journals/lhr/21.2/harris.html, Nov. 2, 2005.
Horwitz, Morton (1977). *The Transformation of American Law, 1780–1860.* Cambridge, MA: Harvard University Press.
_____. (1992). *The Transformation of American Law, 1870–1960: The Crisis of Legal Orthodoxy.* New York: Oxford University Press.
Karsten, Peter (1997). *Heart versus Head: Judge-made Law in Nineteenth-Century America.* Chapel Hill: University of North Carolina Press.

---

[27] Kloppenberg 1335–6 (1993).

————. (1999). Using One's Head: Were Jurists Unconscious Socio-Economic Ciphers or Conscious Agents? A Response to Friedman, 24(1) *L. & Soc. Inquiry* 281.

Kloppenberg, James (1993). The Theory and Practice of American Legal History, 106 *Harv. L. Rev.* 1332.

Miller, Perry (1962). *The Legal Mind in America, From Independence to the Civil War*. Ithaca: Cornell University Press.

Soifer, Avi (1988). Beyond Mirrors, 22(5) *Law and Soc'y Rev.* 995.

4

Lawrence M. Friedman's Comparative Law

Tom Ginsburg

For more than four decades, Lawrence Friedman has been one of the key figures in American law and society studies, as well as the country's leading legal historian. His unique vantage point has brought him into contact with a wide range of subfields in legal studies, including, not least, comparative law. However, Friedman has never published in the leading journals of the comparative law discipline, and he has had only peripheral involvement in the multi-jurisdictional collaborative projects around which comparative lawyers have organized much of their work. Neither does he write about foreign countries. Yet Friedman's series of book chapters and articles commenting on the field of comparative law have articulated a consistent and important methodological challenge to the mainstream of the field.

This chapter elaborates Friedman's comparative jurisprudence and argues that comparative law since the 1960s would have been much more fruitful had it followed Friedman's advice. Friedman's persistent mantra, more often ignored than heeded, has been that comparative law must be integrated with law and society studies. This stance has been rooted in his strong claim that law is not autonomous of other elements of the social system. Only in recent years has the discipline of comparative law begun to come around to Friedman's critique. We have lost more than four decades by ignoring Friedman.

FRIEDMAN ON LAW AND DEVELOPMENT

Friedman and the other grand figures of the law and society movement came of age as scholars in an era, like our own, of optimism about the possibility of transferring legal institutions across borders. Informed by modernization theory, many were

Thanks to Harry Scheiber for encouraging me to undertake the pleasurable task of rereading Friedman's early works in preparation for this chapter. Thanks also to Richard Ross for his helpful discussions and comments.

engaged in the project of intentional legal transfers that became known as the law and development movement.[1] Funded by private American foundations and the U.S. government, and supported by law schools, this movement famously sought to transfer skills, institutions, and ideas from the developed world to the developing world. Leading law schools like Stanford and Yale became major centers of this activity.

The law and development movement ended by the mid-1970s with a sense of frustration, crisis, and "self-estrangement," as the leading epitaph on the movement put it.[2] Reading the early writings of the most sophisticated scholars in the field, including Friedman and Galanter, it seems clear that they recognized early on that the funders' hopes of legal-institutional transformation were naïve. In their view, law was an inherently local technology despite its purported claims to universality. These sociologically informed scholars suggested that efforts to transfer formal law onto very different informal environments would be unsuccessful and possibly even counterproductive.[3] The scholars' own concerns were analytic and positivist rather than technocratic in nature, as they sought to understand the process of social and legal change more than contribute to it. Thus the law and society movement and the law and development movement shared a common genealogy, and the experience of unmet expectations in the Third World no doubt informed the subsequent orientation of many of the major figures in law and society studies.

Friedman's position in this milieu was as a respondent whose role was to keep the others honest and to frame interesting questions, rather than to answer them himself. He did not engage directly in studies of the developing nations, nor did he did tour the world selling the American model of legal education. Instead his role was to critically read the works of those who did tour the world and of those who sought to develop positive theories of law and social change. He has served as an external sounding board, problematizing the frameworks of others.

Consider the contrast between Friedman and figures such as Galanter and Trubek, who traversed some of the theoretical terrain covered by Weber and other modernists.[4] All sought to develop frameworks for understanding modern law that involved wrestling with rationality. In a long and particularly insightful essay entitled "On Legal Development" (1969), Friedman summarizes Galanter's 1966 piece, "The Modernization of Law," which identifies eleven traits that characterize modern law. These familiar traits, including predictability, a transactional character, and uniform and universal application by professionals, are well and good, Friedman seems to say. However, Friedman concludes his summary with a crucial question that went to the core of the law and development movement: Is modern law the cause or product of development? In a typically pointed analogy, he notes that "countries with

[1] Tamanaha (1995).
[2] Galanter and Trubek (1974).
[3] Galanter (1966).
[4] Galanter (1966); Trubek (1972).

high per capita incomes also rank high in the number of neckties worn, low in loin clothes and robes. Yet no one could modernize a country by changing its clothes."[5] Friedman thus suggests that the frameworks that purport to analyze modern law are essentially descriptive in character; they are catalogues or collections of attributes, rather than causal accounts or analyses of the relationships among various attributes.

This point made in 1969 has continuing relevance today, for we are again in an era of optimism regarding intentional legal transfers. International development agencies, human rights groups, and ministries of justice are again trumpeting "law reform." In rereading Friedman's work one has the feeling of déjà vu all over again, leaving one to wonder what lessons have been drawn from the field. We still know very little about the interactions among various legal reforms, issues of timing and sequencing, and the broad issue of causality.[6] The questions have not changed much in forty years, and our answers are not much more insightful either.

One persistent issue in the field is whether institutional transfers are even possible. Comparative law has historically expended the bulk of its energy on tracing the borrowings of legal institutions across borders. Of course, the law and development movements of both the twentieth and twenty-first centuries concerned a subset of these borrowings; namely, ones that are more or less consciously intended. Whether these borrowings can work has been a controversial question: Answers range from the technocratic view that law can move easily and intentionally, to the radical culturalist position that legal transfers are a contradiction in terms and that cultural specificity of the recipient system inexorably transforms the borrowed institution.[7] For these postmodernist scholars, a transplant is a logical impossibility.

Where does Friedman come down on the efficacy of legal transfers? We can best characterize him as a qualified optimist. He frames the question of transferability of law in terms of two competing paradigms. On the one hand, there is a techno-logical view of law that sees it as universal, like an appendectomy procedure that is performed similarly around the world; this view suggests that law involves the same process whether undertaken in California or Kyoto.[8] Presumably this view means that law can be easily transferred across borders. On the other hand, there is a long tradition of seeing law as culturally specific.[9] Friedman's view is that the question of transferability–nontransferability is too general.[10] Transferability is an empirical and sociological question, rather than a conceptual or theoretical one. Although we do have famous examples of legal transplants such as the Turkish adaptation of Swiss law and the legal modernization of Meiji Japan, the number of failed transfers is larger. Some features of law are likely to be more transplantable than others, and the

[5] Friedman 1969b, p. 22.
[6] Stromseth et al. (2006).
[7] Legrand (1907, 2001).
[8] Friedman 28 (1978).
[9] Id.
[10] Id. at 30–1.

key determinant is what might be called the cultural embeddedness of the area of law. Thus, a reasonable hypothesis is that banking law ought to be more amenable to transfer across border than family law.[11] Bankers are business people who respond to relatively universal profit incentives embedded in markets, and banking transactions do not touch on core issues of private or personal behavior. In contrast, family law regulates nonelective choices that are more or less permanent and difficult to exit. It touches on deep questions of religion, culture, and expectation. Therefore legal transfers of family law are less likely to "take" in recipient societies.

Note how this position actually constitutes a hypothesis, amenable in principle to empirical disconfirmation. Are rules that regulate economic behavior more easily transferred than those regulating intimate or personal behavior? Most of us would assume the answer is yes, but one could learn more through careful empirical study. Very few have tried to do so,[12] and Friedman himself did not. His own contributions in this field were conceptual rather than empirical.

Friedman's ability to probe the intellectual underpinnings of legal inquiry has made him a respondent of choice for many organizers of conferences on comparative law. To provide only one example of his technique, he was asked to participate in Cappelletti's high-profile project on access to justice. Friedman argued that access to justice only becomes an issue when one accepts the peculiarly modern notion "that there is, or ought to be, a single, uniform, universal body of norms; that every citizen – every man, woman, and child – regardless of rank, social status or income must be able to enjoy the protection and the privileges of that body of norms."[13] Most law, in most times and places, has been hierarchical, and thus there is little demand for "access" until a liberal regime starts to take hold. Friedman's argument turned the focus back onto the intellectual questions underlying the comparative law inquiry, away from technocratic concerns.

Friedman's questioning stance led him to reflexive consideration not only about the role of law in development but also about the reasons we are interested in law and development. To raise this issue in 1969, as he did, was to foreshadow not only Trubek and Galanter's much more famous 1974 article but also the whole turn to discursive and critical analysis in legal studies.

METHOD IN COMPARATIVE LAW: CRITIQUES

Here we can pivot the discussion away from law and development to broader questions of method in comparative law. Friedman's most sustained critique of traditional comparative law has been methodological. Inasmuch as it possesses a consistent methodology, traditional comparative law uses two techniques: comparative doctrinal analysis and system-level taxonomy. Doctrinal analysis takes law as an

---

[11] Friedman (1969b).
[12] See, e.g., Levmore (1986).
[13] Friedman (1978).

object and examines the relationship between doctrinal developments in different countries, tracing the transfer and spread of specific rules. Taxonomy involves categorizing legal systems according to some dominant characteristic.[14] This approach originates in a scientistic approach to the study of comparative law that was dominant from the time of Montesquieu through the late twentieth century, classifying legal systems according to their genetic characteristics.[15] It is echoed today in the so-called law and finance literature, which postulates long-term effects of legal origins.[16]

Both doctrinal analysis and taxonomy are essentially historical in character, and it may seem ironic that neither method is particularly appealing to an unquestioned giant in legal history. Friedman parts ways from traditional comparative legal historians who focus on the genealogy of particular rules. In a 1990 paper in honor of John Merryman, Friedman diagnoses the ills of comparative law as well as its strengths.[17] In his view comparative law has done a good job of generating information on materials that facilitate cross-border transactions. This is the doctrinal work identified earlier. In a typically succinct analogy, Friedman characterizes comparative law as being preoccupied with the problems of translation across cultures and the corresponding search for functional equivalents. It thus "has the virtues and the faults of a dictionary. A dictionary is an essential reference tool, but nobody can learn a foreign language, or grasp its essential genius, from a dictionary alone. . . . The vital core of a language is not to be found in the dictionary, but in the mouths of real people, using a language in their daily lives." Friedman then notes that understanding a legal system requires more than dictionary-like tools: "A living body of law is not a collection of doctrines, rules, terms and phrases. It is not a dictionary but a culture, and it has to be approached as such."[18]

This stance has strong methodological implications. Both of the traditional methods of the comparativist – doctrinal analysis and taxonomy – implicitly adopt a view of law as highly autonomous. A rule can be divorced from its social context, "transferred" across borders, and then compared; the aggregate of rules forms a legal "system" that exists independent of its society. Yet Friedman rejects this view; he notes that the comparativist's idea of legal tradition, tracing the genealogy of legal rules, is a "fairly arid and formalist affair, divorced from context and the living law."[19]

Taxonomy, which focuses on the aggregate of rules in a system, can fare no better without a sociological approach. It is an essentially genealogical exercise that aggregates the doctrinal development of particular rules into grand statements about the family to which a legal system belongs. For Friedman, one must begin the inquiry with the functioning legal system rather than its historical basis. It takes

---

[14] Mattei (1997).
[15] Marfording (1997).
[16] La Porta et al. (1998).
[17] Friedman (1990).
[18] Id. at 50.
[19] Friedman 20 (1994b).

a certain amount of intellectual courage for a professional historian to reject the dominant historical method in comparative law, and yet Friedman did so because it was the wrong kind of history.

One can summarize his stance in a series of propositions. First, law, however it may be defined, is *not* an autonomous system. It is responsive to needs and demands from society, culture, and the economy, but it is not identical to them. Friedman suggests that law is neither wholly autonomous in the sense of being impervious to social changes, nor is it a mere "mirror" of society.[20] This characterization of law leads to a strong antiformalism:

> Formal change, almost universally, has no power in itself to do more than to act as a tool of strong social forces. Otherwise, we would have to admit that legal words, concepts and propositions have an almost magical power, in themselves, to mold the attitudes, first, of lawyers and judges, then of masses of people and in the long run determine their behavior. There have been many men who believe in such a theory of law – law insulated from and independent of social forces. But it runs counter to the idea which modern social science insists upon – that law is part of the totality of culture; that the part is not master of the whole; that interests and values, pressing in from outside or internalized by those inside the system, make up the law.[21]

Second, law is a culturally specific category whose scope varies across societies.[22] This point poses severe methodological challenges to the comparative enterprise. In the late 1970s, Friedman described comparative sociology of law as a "weak, fledgling branch of legal scholarship,"[23] and it is doubtful whether the recent explosion in research in foreign-focused materials in the law and society journals would lead him to a different conclusion today, as little of this work is truly comparative in scope.

If law, lawyers, and legal systems are defined differently in different societies, comparison may be impossible. Perhaps in response to the paucity of method in traditional comparative law, a number of comparative law scholars have recently begun to follow the interpretive turn in contemporary anthropology.[24] This approach contrasts the *external* study of social phenomena with efforts to capture the *internal* understanding of social meaning. Scholars advocating this perspective call for a new kind of comparative law focused on the diversity and uniqueness of legal systems and legal cultures. By forcing legal phenomena into preexisting and universal categories, it is claimed, the observer loses what is distinctive and meaningful about particular practices. Understanding the meaning of the practices within their cultural contexts is the goal of these comparativists.

[20] See also Tamanaha (2001).
[21] Friedman (1969a).
[22] Friedman (1994a).
[23] Friedman 254 (1978).
[24] Ainsworth (1996).

To some degree, this shift toward an internal perspective was anticipated by Friedman, with his emphasis on culture, but he seems to resist grand postmodernist claims of incommensurability as well. Instead, he moves out to survey the forest rather than the trees and emphasizes surprising similarities rather than particularistic differences. For example, when grappling with Blankenburg's contrast of Dutch and German legal cultures, Friedman questions whether they are really that different.[25] Both systems face many of the same social problems and share methods of attacking them. The difference clearly is one of degree. Although it may be difficult to develop a precise jurisprudential definition of law, it is possible to develop a sociological one.[26] That the borders may be fuzzy, that some things may be difficult to place within the realm of the legal, does not negate the fact that some things clearly are in the category of legal actors and legal behavior. In short, the method implied by this stance requires a lot of reading and hard work. There are no shortcuts other than knowing as much as one can about various societies and how law, as a discrete mode of social ordering, operates in local culture.

Thus Friedman remains optimistic about positive social science. Annelise Riles, in an important critical volume on comparative law as an intellectual discipline, notes that it is normative and modernist in character, seeking "unity through law" and identifying the "common core" of legal systems.[27] Friedman and collaborators made similar points in the late 1970s.[28] They noted that the discipline of comparative law always sought universality and was in this sense a logical extension of continental notions of legal science. Friedman and his collaborators thus identified the same issue that Riles did later, but pushed in the direction of positivist inquiry rather than postmodernist self-reflection.

THE TROPE OF LEGAL CULTURE

Once we move to the behavioral concept of law, comparing two societies is a particularly difficult task. For Friedman, the key point of inquiry is his long-standing trope of legal culture: Culture matters. As he put it in 1969,

> There do seem to be differences between legal systems which cannot be explained as differences in their strictly legal inheritance, cannot be traced to substantive and

---

[25] Friedman (1998a).

[26] Friedman (1969b).

[27] Riles 15–17 (2001). Friedman is not above what Riles calls the modernist notion in comparative law. His contribution, with Teubner, to the Integration through Law exercise is an example, which considered how legal education might be employed for integration. However, his recommendations are predictably interdisciplinary in orientation: European legal education should focus not on norms but on methods, drawing heavily from positivist social science to understand and grapple with national features.

[28] Merryman, Clark et al. (1979). This volume moves toward a quantitative comparative law, collecting statistics on legal activity in many societies; in the end, however, the authors did not take the additional step of testing propositions about modernization.

structural dissimilarities, and cannot be entirely imputed to differences in technology or economy, yet are not purely formal differences either. These differences reside in what we might call the cultural domain. I would like to suggest that what separates modern from premodern and nonmodern law is a critical cultural distinction.[29]

Friedman's concept of legal culture has evolved over time. This quotation makes it sound like it is a residual category, composed of everything not easily explained by other more observable factors. Yet he has in mind something more concrete. In Friedman's sense, legal culture is "values, opinions, attitudes and beliefs about law."[30] It might include (and does include at various points in his corpus of work) ideas about law, propensities to litigate, and customs and habits related to law. Indeed, Cotterrell attacks Friedman as including phenomena too diffuse to fit within a single construct and accuses Friedman of shifting the concept of culture over time.[31]

My reading of his use of culture is as an intervening variable. Social forces make law, but social change does not produce legal change directly. Rather legal culture mediates similar pressures in different ways in different societies.[32] Yet legal culture is not static, but is partially responsive to social, technological, and economic change. For example, as the number and type of economic transactions increase in the developing world, there may be some convergence in attitudes toward law with the developed world. Culture thus represents a kind of lag, though it is hardly predictable in the ways it changes. It is partly a constraint, but also partly a wild card, not capable of mechanistic analysis.

The very notion of culture seems to emphasize the particular and the permanent. Yet Friedman makes the case that legal culture can be studied at a general level: There is a distinctively modern legal culture around which societies converge.[33] The modern legal culture, writes Friedman, shares six traits: (1) rapid legal change, in line with rapid social change; (2) density and ubiquity of law, leading to a juridification of social life; (3) instrumental legitimacy of law as a tool of social engineering; (4) a somewhat paradoxical emphasis on rights and entitlements; (5) a culture of individualism, which explains the shift toward rights; and (6) globalization and convergence of legal cultures.

Here Friedman's angle on globalization becomes apparent. Many argue that globalized efforts to transfer legal institutions are imperialistic and involve crude Westernization. Yet this claim implicitly assumes that the rule of law concept is culturally specific to the West. Friedman argues that it is not so much Western

---

[29] Friedman 27 (1969b).
[30] Friedman 381 (1998a).
[31] Cotterrell (1997).
[32] Friedman (1994b).
[33] Id.

as modern.[34] Modern societies are complex and involve less face-to-face interaction among people who know each other than premodern societies. They also bring about disruption to established social orders, as the adoption of formal equality undermines culturally rooted hierarchies. Again, Friedman has a pithy analogy, likening the historical introduction of modern law in the West to the automobile: "America was the first automobile society, but it does not follow that the streets of Tokyo, Seoul and Bangkok are jammed with traffic because of American influence."[35]

The simple observation that legal culture reflects underlying social forces allows Friedman to emphasize surprising similarities that cut across the traditional "families" of comparative law. Thus, he sees similarities between the legal cultures of Germany and the Netherlands, Japan and the United States,[36] and Belgium and Britain.[37] All of these systems face common problems of industrial societies: auto accidents, bond flotations, social security payments. In contrast, observes Friedman, a British lawyer transported backward in time a century or two would find himself quite unfamiliar with virtually everything about the law. Legal culture is dynamic and responsive, not genetic. This convincingly lays to rest the traditional comparativists' idea that legal families provide much analytic bite in understanding contemporary societies.

Friedman's observation is a good illustration of the liberating power of the concept of legal culture in social explanation. Ross notes that the "alluring ambiguity of legal culture offers a standing invitation to arrange seemingly unconnected bits of the past in new and revealing patterns without dampening enthusiasm or imagination by suggesting in advance what should and should not matter."[38] Indeed the very inclusiveness of the concept "can prod historians to make unexpected connections and stimulate scholarly inventiveness." Friedman has indeed used it to this effect.

Even if one accepts this view of the utility and power of legal culture as a concept, there is still the enormous evidentiary difficulty to overcome in deploying it. How can one know what are the attitudes and ideas about law? Studying living law is difficult and expensive; indeed, one might say that Friedman rejects incommensurability at the theoretical level, only to re-create it at the practical level by using the empirically challenging construct of culture as his key analytic variable. Perhaps then, he means to use the notion of culture as a kind of remonstrance for researchers. Simply because you cannot easily observe it does not mean that culture is not there. Therefore we should at least attempt to read between the lines of what evidence we do have, be it legal documents or litigation rates or judicial decisions, for what it tells us about the

[34] Id.
[35] Friedman 1075–90 (1998b).
[36] Id.
[37] Friedman (1990).
[38] Ross 34 (1993).

real issue of legal culture. Better to focus on the difficult but crucial issues than to bypass them in favor of easier work.

ON BIG THEORIES AND SMALL CASES

Friedman also has what I might call the historian's distaste for grand theory. Ideas produced by legal scholars about law and society no doubt have the potential to shape the legal system. However, Friedman's view is that "great ideas have little or nothing to do with the way the legal system grinds away on a daily basis. . . . Great ideas are distilled from simple, commonplace notions that are part of the fabric of daily life."[39] Of course, this is itself a theoretical statement.

Friedman's concern with bottom-up construction of the legal system, of the details of law in ordinary lives, has led him to participate in a number of exercises in gathering massive amounts of data.[40] Yet at times one wishes for more theoretical integration. For example, the 1979 SLADE volume contains rich time-series data on litigation rates, types of claims, and legal documents in a number of Mediterranean and Latin American jurisdictions. The introduction lays out a critique of law and development, but there is no attempt to analyze the data, to do more. I can picture the other members of the group putting forward suggestions for data analysis, only to have Friedman expose in laser-like fashion the conceptual weakness in their constructs.

It is not that Friedman thinks such analysis is impossible, because as I hope I have made clear, he believes firmly in the possibility of social science. He acknowledges that some comparison is possible, just very difficult. Yet because of his view of culture as *the* key phenomenon for analysis, he has, in a sense, avoided having to *do* the social science work by placing all the weight on the most empirically difficult part of the legal system to study. He has left that difficult work to the rest of us laboring in the trenches of comparative law.

What then might a Friedmanite comparative law look like? First, it would obviously be a branch of and technique for comparative social studies. Friedman's essay with Teubner calls for a shift in legal method "away from doctrine, classification and abstraction, toward a problem-oriented, functional approach."[41] Looking at the operation of law and legal rules in society must be the starting point.

Of course, functionalism has a long tradition in comparative law. However, in general the social science invoked is implicit, not explicit. Classic comparativists recognize that different legal rules can play similar functions in different societies.[42] Yet they do not take the logical next step, which is to identify social, cultural,

---

[39] Friedman 1293 (1994a).
[40] Kagan et al. (1978); Merryman, Clark et al. (1979).
[41] Friedman and Teubner (1986).
[42] See, e.g., Zweigert and Kötz (1998).

and environmental factors as the relevant independent variables worthy of inquiry. Friedman suggests that these factors are not only worthy of study but also are essential to making any progress.

One finds then suggestive hypotheses for empirical testing throughout Friedman's work. For example, "[i]n all societies people avoid activities that impose on them punishments or costs and they perform acts that bring them rewards. What differs from society to society is the perception of benefit or cost."[43] This hypothesis would seem to suggest experimental and empirical projects to isolate the perceptions of costs and benefits, integrating cross-cultural psychology with law and economics. (One might think of this as Lawrence's challenge to his namesake Milton). It also suggests that legal systems are essentially frames or images of social reality. They are epistemologies that guide and orient legal decision makers. These perceptions of legal decision makers are clearly related to, yet autonomous from, the general perceptions of society. As Friedman and Teubner conclude, "The traditional approach to legal doctrine is either dead, or at best ineffective in explaining how legal systems actually behave. The social sciences may not have satisfactory answers; but at least they do sometimes ask the right questions."[44]

CONCLUSION

For comparative lawyers, Friedman is a problematizer and wise critic. Indeed, given the prescience of his articles in the late 1960s, one might even call him prophetic. His consistent concern, too often ignored, has been to push comparative studies to confront the issue of culture and how people understand the law. Yet he consistently rejects claims of incommensurability and in this sense defends the possibility of comparative legal studies.

The challenges faced by a Friedmanite comparative law are enormous because his framework identifies as the key variable something that is very difficult to observe. Indeed, I have suggested that at times his view leans toward a practical incommensurability at the same time that he rejects a theoretical one. Yet we are beginning to see steps in the right direction in comparative legal studies.[45] Much comparative work now relies on very close social science work to grapple with the law in action, taking culture seriously. However, on balance, comparative law and society studies have not come far since Friedman developed his framework in the late 1960s. Had he put on a beret and developed a complex multisyllabic vocabulary, we might think of Friedman as one of the great social theorists of the twentieth century. Instead, he had the simpler virtue of simply asking the right questions, early and often.

---

[43] Friedman (1969b).
[44] Friedman and Teubner (1986).
[45] I hesitate to single out specific studies, but Ross (2004) and Whitman (2004) would likely meet with Friedmanite approval.

REFERENCES

Ainsworth, J. E. (1996). Categories and Culture: On the "Rectification of Names" in Comparative Law, 82 *Cornell L. Rev.* 19.

Cotterrell, R. (1997). The Concept of Legal Culture, in D. Nelken ed., *Comparing Legal Cultures* Aldershot: Dartmouth, 1997, pp. 13–31.

Friedman, L. M. (1969a). Law Reform in Historical Perspective, 13 *St. Louis U. L. Rev.* 351.

———. (1969b). On Legal Development, 24 *Rutgers L. Rev.* 11.

———. (1978). Access to Justice: Social and Historical Context, in N. Capelletti and J. Weisner, eds., *Access to Justice*. Milan: Dott. A. Giuffre Editore II: 3.

———. (1990). Some Thoughts on Comparative Legal Culture, in D. S. Clark, ed., *Comparative and Private International Law: Essays in Honor of John Henry Merryman on his Seventieth Birthday*. Berlin: Duncker and Humblot 49.

———. (1994a). Is There a Modern Legal Culture?, 7(2) *Ratio Juris* 117.

———. (1994b). Law, Legal Institutions and Economic Development, in Philip S. C. Lewis, ed., *Law and Technology in the Pacific Community*. Boulder: Westview Press 7.

———. (1998a). Blankenburg on Legal Culture: Some Comments, in J. Brand and D. Strempel, eds., *Soziologie des Rechts: Festschrift fur Erhard Blankenburg zum 60 Geburtstag*. Baden-Baden: Nomos Verlagsgesellschaft.

———. (1998b). Some Thoughts on the Rule of Law, Legal Culture and Modernity in Comparative Perspective, in *Toward Comparative Law in the 21st Century*. Tokyo: Chuo University Press.

Friedman, Lawrence M. and G. Teubner (1986). Legal Education and Legal Integration: European Hopes and America Experience, in M. Cappelletti, M. Seccombe and J. Weiler, eds., *Integration through Law*. New York: Walter de Gruyter.

Galanter, M. (1966). The Modernization of Law, in M. Weiner, ed., *Modernization: The Dynamics of Growth*. New York, Basic Books.

Galanter, M. and D. Trubek (1974). Scholars in "Self-Estrangement": Some Reflections on the Crisis in Law and Development Studies in the United States, *Wis. L. Rev.* 1062.

Kagan, R., et al. (1978). The Evolution of State Supreme Courts, 76 *Mich. L. Rev.* 961.

La Porta, R., F. Lopez-De-Silanes, A. Shleifer, and R. W. Vishny, (1998). Law and Finance, 106 *J. Polit. Econ.* 1113.

Legrand, P. (1997). The Impossibility of Legal Transplants, 4 *Maastricht J. Eur. & Comp. L.* 111.

———. (2001). What "Legal Transplants?" in D. Nelken and J. Feest, eds., *Adapting Legal Cultures*. Oxford: Hart Publishing.

Levmore, S. (1986). Rethinking Comparative Law: Variety and Uniformity in Ancient and Modern Tort Law, 61 *Tul. L. Rev.* 235.

Marfording, A. (1997). The Fallacy of Classification of Legal Systems: Japan Examined, in V. Taylor. ed., *Asian Laws through Australian Eyes*. Sydney: LBC Information Systems.

Mattei, U. (1997). Three Patterns of Law: Taxonomy and Change in the World's Legal Systems. 45 *Am. J. Comp. L.* 5.

Merryman, J. H., D. S. Clark, et al. (1979). *Law and Social Change in Mediterranean Europe and Latin America*. Stanford: Stanford Studies in Law and Development.

Riles, A. (2001). *Rethinking the Masters of Comparative Law*. Portland, OR: Hart Publishing.

Ross, J. E. (2004). Impediments to Transnational Cooperation in Undercover Policing: A Comparative Study of the United States and Italy, 52 *Am. J. Comp. L.* 569.

Ross, R. J. (1993). The Legal Past of Early New England: Notes for the Study of Law, Legal Culture and Intellectual History, 50 *Wm. & Mary Q.* 28.

Stromseth, J., D. Wippman, and R. Brooks (2006). *Can Might Make Rights?* New York: Cambridge University Press.

Tamanaha, B. (1995). The Lessons of Law and Development Studies, 89 *Am. J. Int'l L.* 470.

———. (2001). *A General Jurisprudence of Law and Society.* New York: Oxford University Press.

Trubek, D. (1972). Max Weber on Law and the Rise of Capitalism, 3 *Wisconsin L. Rev.* 720.

Whitman, J. Q. (2003). *Harsh Justice: Criminal Punishment and the Widening Divide between America and Europe.* New York: Oxford University Press.

———. (2004). Two Western Cultures of Privacy: Dignity versus Liberty, 113 *Yale L.J.* 1151.

Zweigert, R. and H. Kötz (1998). *An Introduction to Comparative Law.* 2nd. edition. New York: Oxford University Press.

PART II

Applications of Concepts, Insights, and Methods in Friedman's Work

Legal Culture

5

To Influence, Shape, and Globalize

Popular Legal Culture and Law

Jo Carrillo

INTRODUCTION: LOOKING FOR LAW

At a law school orientation, a professor of criminal law stood up to introduce himself. A few minutes into his introductory remarks the professor said, "Close your eyes. Count the number of TV shows that you've watched that deal with criminal law. You have ten seconds."

After ten seconds the professor asked, "How many of you can think of at least one program?" All hands went up.

"How many of you can name five programs?" About one-third of the hands in a room of ninety-plus students remained in the air.

"How many of you can think of ten programs?" The students broke into laughter.

The professor conducted this exercise to reassure students about law school. The students might not yet know how to define a tort ("not a fruit pie") or real property ("distinct from fake property"), but they knew something about the criminal justice system because they had seen it represented on TV.

TV, movies, crime novels, popular novels, Web sites, blogs – these are sources of culture. They mediate our experience with the world. They give us the illusion of knowledge about complex systems, the criminal justice system being just one example. Yet their impact stems from more than just the message; it also comes from the medium, as demonstrated by the efforts of trial lawyers to rely more on hypertexting sorts of visual/cultural logic than on the linear textual logic of old.[1] For example, during the O. J. Simpson murder trial, prosecutor Marcia Clark cited the Walt Disney song, "A Dream Is a Wish Your Heart Makes"; Clark wanted the jury to hear that Simpson had once dreamed (as in rapid eye movement [REM] sleep) about killing his wife Nicole.[2] Clark's idea was that a popular song would put the jury at ease about using Simpson's dream as evidence of his state of mind. A *Monk*

---

[1] Sherwin (2000).
[2] Dershowitz (1996).

episode imitates Clark's O.J. Simpson trial move; in that episode a successful rapper named Murderuss (Snoop Dog) complains that he is a suspect in the murder of his rival Extra Large (Marcello Thedford). The evidence against Murderuss is a dream (as in REM sleep) that Murderuss had in which he killed Extra Large.[3]

After attorney Joseph Cotchett won an initial $3.3 billion verdict against Charles H. Keating Jr. on behalf of 23,000 bondholders in the 1980s Lincoln Savings and Loan scandal, Cotchett began coaching big-verdict trial attorneys on how best to sway a jury with visual images.[4] Cotchett explained that he relied on visual images because the general public – the population from which the jury is pooled – watches four to six hours of television a day, meaning that jurors tend to feel more comfortable with visual images than with text.[5]

The criminal law professor's use of popular culture in his law school orientation class stalled in my view – and it stalled for one important reason. The students had been asked to imagine law's connection to culture, but when they opened their eyes the professor reassured them that, despite any talk of TV, he would be the kind of professor who taught "real law" in the form of "real rules." Culture was invoked, but then denied. Culture's connection to law was invoked, but then it too was denied. The end result was that the professor flirted with the idea of law as part of society, but then fell back on tradition when he reassured students that they would learn about an autonomous, textual, logical domain that provides answers to legal questions in the form of rules.[6]

To be sure, it is difficult to link law with culture. To help in this effort, there is a long-standing but still growing body of scholarly literature that challenges the idea of law as an autonomous domain.[7] Lawrence M. Friedman's 1989 article, "Law, Lawyers, and Popular Culture," served as a seed for this literature, because after he published this essay, which is written in his inimitably accessible style, a subdiscipline of scholarship on how law and culture (mostly mass media) influence each other began to take shape.[8]

This chapter explores Friedman's idea of popular legal culture. I start at the present with a look at current arguments in law about popular culture. From there I move on to discuss Hurst's influence on Friedman and the importance of Friedman's "Law, Lawyers, and Popular Culture" article to legal scholarship.

In the spirit of full disclosure, Lawrence M. Friedman was my professor, and his work has had a profound influence on me. Friedman's humor and patience with me as a young and no doubt high-maintenance student, and his many, many kindnesses toward me will always be remembered. Friedman's work ethic remains

---

[3] *Monk* (2007).
[4] Sherwin (2000).
[5] Sherwin (2000, 2001).
[6] Kahn (1999).
[7] Sarat and Simon (2001).
[8] Friedman (1989); Carrillo (2007).

a daily inspiration to me, but in the end it is his written work that continues to shape and inspire me, as it does others. Thus, I dedicate this work, with deep and abiding gratitude, to a writer, scholar, and teacher who has a profound and enduring influence on legal scholarship.

LAW AND POPULAR CULTURE

"Law, Lawyers, and Popular Culture" makes the argument that legal scholars invoke culture, but do not actually take it seriously as a force that shapes law. To do so, legal scholars would have to study how and why popular culture's representation of law is important and how the popular culture–law relationship works. Engaging in this sort of analysis would require that legal scholarship be a different enterprise than it tends to be: It would need to move away from its practical focus on legal reform toward a more intellectual focus on social theory; it would need to shift its view of law as an autonomous – or even partly autonomous – domain and consider more seriously the way in which law is porous and malleable; and its empirical arm would need to become more comfortable with qualitative, interpretive enterprises in legal scholarship. According to Friedman, if this intellectual shift could be made, then legal scholarship could begin to examine *how and why* law and (popular) culture shape and globalize each other.

Friedman's article turns on the idea that culture and law are distinct yet inter-related phenomena.[9] According to Friedman, law has its own culture – a legal culture that can interact with media to transform popular images into "legal dress and shape."[10] For example, film identifies issues with mass appeal, and legal culture responds by delivering a professionally recognized version of these issues to legal professionals (and vice versa). The same is increasingly true of advertising, which responds to pop culture legal news of the day so as to influence mass-market consumers.[11] Legal culture and popular culture become linked – in Friedman's argument – when they translate, transmit, and explain each other's content to different audiences.[12] The important task for scholars who want to move beyond the current boundary of legal scholarship is to explain not just *that* this link happens (an observation about influence) but also *how* it happens.[13]

"Law, Lawyers, and Popular Culture" was published at a time when legal scholarship was viewed by many of its practitioners as a reform-driven discourse whose primary purpose was to clarify legal rules and doctrines for judges and lawyers.[14] In most law schools, legal scholarship was a professional endeavor, not an academic

[9] Friedman (1989).
[10] Id. at 1579.
[11] Sherwin (2000).
[12] Friedman and Rosen-Zvi (2001).
[13] Friedman 1583 (1989).
[14] Id.

discipline. Law scholarship was defined as academic lawyers talking to other academic lawyers about law as an autonomous or partly autonomous domain with impermeable boundaries. Legal scholars developed the law or identified sites in need of reform, but other than that, their disciplinary methods imposed no clear duty to move toward an understanding of why law functions as it does in society.[15] Law and legal scholarship were an insider's game; they were weapons in the greater political battle, not tools with which to expand knowledge. Legal scholarship did little to explain why law moved as it did in the marketplace, or in literature, or in art, or in theology, or in other venues of society.[16]

This meant that traditional legal scholars sought to "mak[e] a claim as to what the law is or should become," not to look to culture for information about how law might intersect with other domains in society.[17] When social norms were cited, as in the criminal law professor's law school orientation lecture, those citations lacked a useful theory for linking law with culture. The assumptions inherent in traditional legal scholarship regarded and still regard law and culture as separate, unrelated domains.[18] Ditto with law and popular culture.

Friedman's argument did not appear in a vacuum. The idea that legal scholars, as academics, should make an effort to understand law rather than to practice it had been around for decades in interdisciplinary legal scholarship.[19] In no sense was Friedman the first to link law and culture, although he was the first to use the phrase *legal culture* in the legal literature to refer to the influence of a social aggregate of individuals on the formation of law.[20] Nevertheless, in 1989, when "Law, Lawyers, and Popular Culture" was published, legal scholarship was a professional pursuit (law reviews published practical, reform-driven, quasi-judicial, normative articles that focused on internal explanations), rather than an intellectual pursuit that engaged in what Friedman called understanding Leviathan.[21] Rather than describe why Leviathan did what it did, legal scholars – having been duly swallowed – were busy describing the strengths and weaknesses of Leviathan's belly. Indeed, articulating these strengths and weaknesses with an eye toward reform was the safe path to tenure.

Thus it was Friedman – with "Law, Lawyers, and Popular Culture" – who argued that law needed a cultural analysis. There was precedent for this claim. In 1969, Friedman had linked legal culture to social development. By 1989, Friedman had expanded his view to link legal culture to popular culture; swimming pools and movie stars. His 1969 article, "Legal Culture and Social Development," gave scholars

[15] Friedman (1994).
[16] Friedman 1605–6 (1989).
[17] Kahn 18 (1999).
[18] Id.
[19] Sarat (2000).
[20] Carrillo (2007); Friedman (1969).
[21] Friedman 1583, 1605 (1989); Friedman 11–18 (1994).

a reason and a way to take culture seriously; in 1989 "Law, Lawyers, and Popular Culture" gave legal scholars a reason and a way to take popular culture seriously. Even more importantly, "Law, Lawyers, and Popular Culture" sidestepped law and literature by speaking to scholars whose exposure to the cultural imagination came in the form of popular films, television shows, and popular fiction (mass media culture), not in the form of classic novels studied in English departments (elite culture).[22]

By the time works such as Paul W. Kahn's (1999) *The Cultural Study of Law: Reconstructing Legal Scholarship* or Richard Sherwin's (2000) *When Law Goes Pop* were published, Friedman's idea had been well integrated into the law and society tradition.[23] Yet Kahn's book argued that "the culture of law's rule," what Kahn also referred to as "the legal imagination," ought to be studied "in the same way as other cultures."[24] For its part, Sherwin's book urged scholars to adopt an epistemological shift that he called, among other things, "affirmative postmodernism."[25] Critical of a "jurisprudence of appearances," Sherwin's work was normative: He worried that the flattened images of popular culture, which were already so enmeshed with law as to be seemingly inseparable by the lay person, posed a direct challenge to law's institutional legitimacy.[26]

Kahn was skeptical about the intellectual possibilities of traditional legal scholarship in a world where "control is exercised through an economy that no single institution or state manages," and thus like Friedman, he advocated an interdisciplinary approach. However, when Kahn's idea to study law as one would study another culture morphed into a set of eight rigid methodological rules, his book boomeranged to the traditional view of law as an autonomous entity.[27] Additionally, rather than acknowledge that he was joining an existing field – had not Friedman already covered this ground? – Kahn fell back on the conventional rhetoric of mainstream legal scholarship to claim invention rights for the idea of "popular legal culture."[28] In contrast, Sherwin's book took seriously the relationship between law and popular culture, but only as a way to urge scholars to study law, culture, and media "from a broadly interdisciplinary perspective" for the instrumentalist purpose of protecting the public.[29] Other than emphasizing an "enhanced awareness of contingency, chance, uncertainty, and multiplicity (of truth and reason and of self and social reality)" – an anthropological approach – Sherwin's approach called for a return to the traditional method in which law-the-autonomous-entity would be

[22] Silbey (2002).
[23] Carrillo (2007).
[24] Kahn 165 (1999).
[25] Sherwin 205, 235 (2000).
[26] Id. at 226, 246–7.
[27] Id. at 91–127.
[28] Id. at 1.
[29] Id. at 235.

shielded from the distorting tendencies of (popular) culture by the work of reform-driven legal scholars.[30]

Friedman's work on legal culture and on popular legal culture appeared first. In addition, in at least three important ways, Friedman's work demonstrated an internal consistency in its approach to culture that neither Kahn's nor Sherwin's works achieved.

First, Friedman used his mid-1990s publications to explore culture as a pervasive force, one that was entirely up for grabs in the definition of local practices and social relations.[31] He repeatedly developed the point that law in modern society was growing increasingly dense and ubiquitous (thus leaving fewer gaps) as it was imagined and reimagined by a legal culture characterized by modern individualism and public opinion.[32] By contrast, Kahn's book, despite a concluding assertion that political life is so fluid that courts cannot command its form, managed to analyze legal scholarship's limits from within a form of law that was sharply bounded by doctrinal perspectives, principles, arguments, calls for reform, and, at the fringes, traditionalist interdisciplinarian critiques of law like those offered by Richard Posner.[33] Sherwin's approach was equally promising at the start, but it too stumbled in its concern about resecuring law's legitimacy, which—for Sherwin meant relabeling the traditional pole—where law was autonomous—as a new (and presumably improved) postmodern pole.[34] Additionally, despite a nod to the importance of finding law "in the multitude of ordinary decisions at the microlevel of everyday transactions" – a comment that could have warranted a citation to any number of law and society scholars including Friedman – Kahn advocated studying law as if one were doing anthropological fieldwork in Washington, D.C.,[35] where the Supreme Court and the U.S. Congress sit, not in the trial courts of Wisconsin[36] or of Alameda County, California,[37] or in the aisles of a grocery store,[38] or in B-list horror movies.[39] Even though Sherwin studied films, he did so mostly as a way of illustrating how flatly they portrayed law and legal institutions.[40]

Second, Friedman's work started from the point of studying law as a sociocultural phenomenon. He spent little time, if any, addressing the traditions or limits of legal scholarship, which (at least to my reading) he took as somewhat obvious, especially to scholars from other fields and to legal scholars with a bent toward other

[30] Id. at 38–9.
[31] Clifford (1986).
[32] Friedman (1999).
[33] Kahn 91–7 (1999).
[34] Sherwin 254 (2000).
[35] Kahn 92 (1999).
[36] Hurst (1982).
[37] Friedman and Percival (1981).
[38] Friedman (1998).
[39] Friedman (1985).
[40] Sherwin 5, 205 (2000).

fields.[41] By contrast, Kahn grounded his discussion in an implicit view of law as an autonomous entity and thus of culture as its equally autonomous but ungovernable twin.[42] Indeed, Kahn's eight methodological rules, although intended to set out the parameters of what he called the culture of law or "the legal imagination," looped back to a traditional model of law as autonomous, independent (or at least mostly so), and self-contained.[43]

Third, for Friedman, the idea of culture was so powerful as to be fixed and anti-essential, agreed on and yet contested, certain and yet ephemeral, total and yet partial.[44] Culture was deeply affected by global forces.[45] Yet at the same time, it was local, situational, contingent, and subject to constant negotiation, as was law.[46] Friedman regarded both culture and law as pervasive and permeable forces, not as bounded or boundable entities. Although Friedman did not follow the vogue of "writing against culture" and he avoided using the word "postmodern," his work was inherently critical of how the idea of culture became polarized, one way or the other, just as it was critical of any model that rested on fixed poles (one way or the other).[47] In a phrase, Friedman's work was distinctively both–and, not either–or.

By contrast, Kahn and Sherwin employed the poles of law and culture with the very fixity that Friedman rejected.[48] Kahn defined culture as social practices.[49] Sherwin defined it as the "symbolic order [that] provides the signs, images, stories, characters, metaphors, and scenarios, among other familiar materials with which we make sense of our lives and the world around us."[50] By dispensing with what one might call the format, traditions, or parameters of traditional legal scholarship and by imagining culture(s) and counterculture(s) as factors that were potentially so fluid and contingent as to be beyond uncontested description, Friedman arrived at a scholarship that was a powerful intellectual tool for understanding law's role in society. Skeptical of the legal scholar's compulsive need to reform or to create reason and order where none might actually exist, Friedman pushed his scholarship toward a social understanding of law. However, it was an understanding with a memory (history), an intellectual/methodological lineage (the law and society movement), and a writer's concern for making scholarship interesting and accessible to general readers.[51]

---

[41] Friedman 28, 206 (1999).
[42] Sarat and Kearns (1993).
[43] Kahn 91–2, 135 (1999).
[44] Friedman 1581 (1989).
[45] Friedman (1990, 1994).
[46] Sarat (2000).
[47] Friedman 1582 (1989).
[48] Id. at 183.
[49] Kahn 35, 92 (1999).
[50] Sherwin 5 (2000).
[51] Friedman 1605 (1989).

Friedman's work stayed consistent in its regard of culture as porous, whereas Kahn's and Sherwin's books treated culture (and law) as autonomous or semi-autonomous domains. Whereas Kahn's book critiqued the assumptions of traditional legal scholarship by using those very same assumptions, Friedman looked to sociological, historical, economic, and cultural data to support his argument that the law is shaped by the culture it serves.[52] Indeed, Friedman devoted at least two books – *The Republic of Choice* (1990) and *The Horizontal Society* (1999) – to the idea that modern individualism, popular opinion, and technology shape and are shaped by law, and to the parallel idea that culture is a fluid, changing, and contestable process of affiliation that shapes and is shaped by law. Finally, Friedman voiced no concern about law's legitimacy. In Friedman's view, serious scholars knew that the past was not necessarily more or less legitimate than the present. Rather, within the parameters of demonstrable fact the past was equally contested, contestable, and thus in constant co-creation with those who would turn their scholarly gaze to any particular moment in time.[53]

In "Law, Lawyers, and Popular Culture," Friedman identified the elements for writing social theory and then expanded on them in *The Republic of Choice* and in *The Horizontal Society*. If Kahn and Sherwin's books implied a world of solid, modernistic givens or universals – culture as an autonomous entity – Friedman's work did not.[54] When it came to describing the ephemeral, Friedman's work was exceptionally practiced and fluid. In it, one could look "at the material structure of law to see it in play and at play, as signs and symbols, fantasies and phantasms."[55] So although legal culture was about attitudes and opinions, it was not a "mysterious, invisible substance"; instead it was measurable by "asking people questions; or indirectly, by watching what people do and inferring their attitudes from what we see."[56]

For Friedman, a social theory of law accomplished three things. It looked for explanations outside of the legal system to explain changes in the system as eagerly as it looked to explanations within the system. It recognized law as its own domain, but it also recognized law as part of society and thus as part of a porous, bounded "kind of network or meshwork through which energy easily flows, rather than a tough, tight skin."[57] It regarded law as a variable domain (system) dependent on other variable domains in society and thus as contingent, negotiable, and subject to the shifting winds of global, national, tribal, local, and other affiliations. As of 1989, this three-pronged approach was Friedman's basic analytic framework – his social theory – for studying the dynamic between legal culture and popular culture.[58]

[52] Id. at 1584–7.
[53] Friedman (1973).
[54] Friedman 1580 (1989); 5 (1990); 1430 (1994).
[55] Sarat 135 (2000).
[56] Friedman 1580 (1999).
[57] Id.
[58] Id. at 1579–87.

TUNE IN, TURN ON, DROP OUT: A SOCIAL THEORY

"Law, Lawyers, and Popular Culture" conveys a method for writing social theory about the intersection of law and culture and provides an early look at what Friedman called "popular legal culture." Despite its brevity, this article gave rise to a new field called law and popular culture, which is concerned with how the legal system is linked to the imaginary life of (American) society.[59] Friedman is cited in well more than one hundred articles on the topic of law and popular culture; where he is not indexed or mentioned in a work on this topic, his absence is a notable error of omission.[60]

James Willard Hurst, Friedman's mentor, might have envisioned an American legal culture too, although when he delivered the Curti Lectures in 1981 he referred to "social order" and "culture" and not to "legal culture." Hurst's concern was with analyzing law's relation to the market, his main point being that law was marginal to the factors that produced the market, even though "law exerted material leverage on [the market's] development and working character."[61] Hurst recognized key elements of the proposals of early theorists who shaped the country's national beginnings. Those early proposals "did not accept the private market as a self-sufficient instrument" and "had no purpose to displace the private market as the principal engine of the economy"; the theorists believed that an expanding market fostered social peace as well as other important social intentions, goals, and innovations.[62]

It appears that Friedman drew from Hurst's work on markets, but then wrote specifically about legal culture and eventually popular legal culture.[63] For Friedman, legal culture, like national culture, had inherent norms. Legal culture could be found in cases and rules, which are the internal sources of opinion about law; however, it could also be found in ideas, attitudes, values, and opinions that people held about law, the external sources of opinion about law.[64] This is why both lawyers and laypeople could form concrete opinions about law even if only the lawyer had access to professional legal culture.

Popular culture could be differentiated from other forms of culture by its source. Friedman defined popular culture as "the norms and values held by ordinary people, or at any rate, by non-intellectuals, as opposed to high culture, the culture of intellectuals and the intelligentsia, or what Robert Gordon has called 'mandarin culture.'"[65] These definitions could expand over time of course, but the basic idea was both clear

[59] Asimow (2001).
[60] Carrillo (2007).
[61] Hurst (1950).
[62] Id.
[63] Friedman (1990).
[64] Friedman (1989).
[65] Id.; Gordon 120 (1984).

and clearly based on Hurst's concept of the interdependent and mutually sustaining relationship between social (aggregated) opinion and social systems (law).[66]

Additionally, Friedman's work echoed the Hurstian view of the individual and society as independent carriers of shared legal values, meaning that the source was also a defining characteristic of popular legal culture. Friedman defined popular legal culture as culture in the sense of "books, songs, movies, plays, television shows which are about law or lawyers and which are aimed at a general audience."[67] Despite their differences, these potentially disparate expressions of culture – general culture, market culture, legal culture, popular culture, and popular legal culture – were useful in the study of the vaporous ephemerals of the legal system.[68] They had the power to provide answers to why the legal system functions as it does. For example, legal culture (people's opinions about law) had the power to shape actual law, but popular legal culture (the way in which consumers of popular culture learned about law from the mass media) had the power to shape opinion about law and lawyers.

For Friedman, national culture and legal culture were connected to norms of commerce and law, both ostensibly rationalizing forces, but so too was popular culture. Popular culture was also connected to emotion, and it drew on powerful, often visual images that could indeed challenge law's legitimacy. Like *American Psycho*'s investment banker Patrick Bateman, popular legal culture was legitimately connected to the pillars of society and especially to commerce, but because popular legal culture also derived from the nonlinear, nontextual recesses of popular culture (the aggregate social imagination), it had the potential to veer toward the insane. Popular culture was trite and fun and entertaining, but it was (potentially) irrational, dangerous, and utterly capable of murdering law's legitimacy (just as some suspected).

Here again, Friedman expanded on Hurst's analysis. Hurst asserted that although the study of law could incorporate an awareness of markets, market awareness was not a requirement of legal study. In Friedman's view, legal scholars could be aware of popular legal culture, but cultural awareness was not required to study law. Yet because popular legal culture was or could be "deeply aware of emotion, opinion, and the fact of consciousness," it could be a powerful force to bear on how law is perceived by ordinary people.[69] Hurst urged scholars to study markets, to see law through the eyes of ordinary people who nonetheless "thought and acted in market terms" based on "shared values."[70] In turn, Friedman argued that legal scholars could study popular legal culture to understand how law is seen from "the minds

---

[66] Hurst 53 (1950).
[67] Friedman 1580 (1989).
[68] Friedman (1973); Sarat (1985).
[69] Friedman 1582 (1989).
[70] Hurst 16–17, 54 (1950).

of its consumers."[71] Both markets and popular legal culture – although apparently unrelated on the surface – melded in Friedman's analysis to the degree that they concerned themselves with ordinary people holding ordinary opinions: opinions that might be right or wrong, safe or dangerous, rational or irrational, but that in the aggregate had the power to influence, shape, and even redefine law.

Friedman's analysis centered on the psyche, the consciousness, or the awareness of the ordinary actor to a greater degree than Hurst's did, and in that sense it was more implicitly ethnographic.[72] In other words, if Friedman started with Hurst's idea that the behavior of ordinary people (in the aggregate) reveals cultural norms, he quickly expanded that idea beyond its original parameters to include the study of the subjective opinions that ordinary people might hold about law. Hurst's everyman was a businessman in a certain industry (like logging) who worked closely with legal realities that required wheeling, dealing, negotiating, and reaping profit in "the shadow of the law."[73]

In contrast, Friedman's everyman was much less explicitly concerned with law or with markets for that matter. He or she was not necessarily important because of personal industry, ability, business habits, or negotiating skills. Friedman's ordinary person did not need direct experience with the law to be affected by it.[74] As far as Friedman was concerned, what made ordinary people worth studying in relation to popular legal culture was not what they did in relation to law, but what they thought, if anything, about law, lawyers, courts, and the other apparatuses of the law after watching them represented in the media. These opinions were outside the legal system, to be sure, and yet – like market behavior – because they were aggregate opinions they could influence, shape, and even redefine the law. When it came to popular legal culture, the link between the individual and the culture was where values were defined as shared and thus as worth sharing.[75]

When popular culture concerned itself with law, it gave rise to popular legal culture. In other words, popular legal culture was created when people dealt with law in art, media, pulp fiction, and other mass media venues. Like popular culture, popular legal culture was and could be everywhere. It could be anything, with one exception: Popular legal culture could not be "mandarin," meaning that it could not be elitist.[76] It was popular – widely shared, usually in the mass media – and easily accessible. Once published, "Law, Lawyers, and Popular Culture" stretched the idea of a unique American legal culture from its Hurstian law, market, social order beginnings to something bigger, something nonquantifiable yet measurable, something popular (non-mandarin) and yet cultural that allows scholars to study

---

[71] Friedman 1583 (1989).
[72] Hurst 178 (1950).
[73] Id. at 90; Macaulay (1963); Mnookin (1979).
[74] Friedman 38–44 (1973).
[75] Hurst 54 (1950).
[76] Gordon 120 (1984).

how expressive and imaginative aspects of society shape and globalize law and legal institutions and, in turn, are shaped by them.[77]

For Friedman, popular legal culture began as an American phenomenon, but it could just as easily originate from any identity context, meaning from any nationalistic, cultural, tribal, ethnic, or racial context within or without any nation-state or time and within or without any virtual media. The key elements in popular legal culture were that it widely shares and it widely disseminates ideas about law as transmitted via music, TV, movies, even sports (which Friedman claimed to vehemently dislike).[78] Popular legal culture had the power to illuminate the porous, permeable boundary between law – a legal domain – and almost every other ostensibly nonlegal domain. In high-church legal culture – meaning the law school, the appellate court, and traditional positivist or historical-jurisprudential scholarship – popular culture was dismissed as a low-brow, nonexplanatory source. If it was even mentioned, it was derided as the opiate of the masses and therefore as not important enough to shape law or the legal system. For Friedman, all that might be true to some degree and in some contexts, but the fact remained that popular culture is a powerful force in the modern world, and when popular culture concerns itself with law, it becomes a potential treasure trove of information about how ordinary people perceive law, lawyers, and legal institutions.

By setting out a methodological primer for writing about popular legal culture in "Law, Lawyers, and Popular Culture," Friedman opened the door to illuminating how scholars might better understand the relationship between law and culture in society. Like Timothy Leary, Friedman's message was tune in, turn on, and drop out, although of course, Friedman did not mean dropping LSD, as Leary had, or waging revolution, as Karl Marx had.[79] Friedman meant that legal scholars should tune in to how law is portrayed in popular culture, turn on to the idea that popular culture can and does shape law, and drop out of the high-church view of law as an autonomous, doctrinally bound domain.

LAW AND MARKETS

"Law, Lawyers, and Popular Culture" encouraged legal scholars to use sources that would not be taken seriously by traditional legal scholars who compile casebooks, treatises, and restatements. The article linked the Hurstian idea of the legal economy (law and markets) to the idea of a cultural economy (law and culture), and it encouraged scholars to pay particular attention to how this link occurs. Moreover, Friedman's article directed scholars to the intangible and qualitative realms of the expressive, imaginary, cultural contexts of society in the study of how culture

[77] Friedman (1973, 1990).
[78] Macaulay (1987–8).
[79] Baur (2006).

(aggregate opinion) shapes opinion about law, lawyers, and the legal system. According to Friedman, it was not enough to say that popular culture influenced law – one had to show *how* it did.[80]

Friedman's work on popular legal culture was a precursor to the now accepted and resolute legal strategy that tries to prove a copycat link between media and action.[81] These strategies are often based on works that tend to take Friedman's idea of the link between law and popular culture literally, something Friedman himself would not advocate.[82] I doubt that Friedman would argue that the social theory he sets out in "Law, Lawyers, and Popular Culture" gives lawyers the insight to direct how and what artists should write. It is doubtful that Friedman would agree with the idea that John Grisham owes it to his public to write a novel that portrays a capable female attorney, although Friedman's theory would regard Grisham's work as a source of popular legal culture, open to a gender critique.[83] Popular legal culture is a powerful lens into law, not because the concept links artists with social problems or otherwise makes artists toe a political line, but because the study of popular legal culture moves legal scholarship toward a deeper, more ethical understanding of the relationship between media and law.

In *Law and Markets in United States History: Different Modes of Bargaining Among Interests*, a book notable for its multiple references to Friedman, Macaulay, Galanter, Horwitz, and other law and society scholars, Hurst wrote a short but stunningly memorable explanation of how the car changed American life and why that change mattered.[84] Friedman expanded on Hurst's car example in "Law, Lawyers, and Popular Culture," driving it around until he sketched how the car gave clear shape to the twentieth-century law of negligence.[85] One could replace the car with the television, or the video game, or the Internet in Hurst's or Friedman's respective accounts and get an analysis of equal force.

For Hurst and later Friedman, the law did not create the car (technology); the car created the law. Stated more generally, one could say that the law does not create markets; markets create the law.[86] Hurst many times noted that the prime function of markets was to allocate material resources to produce and distribute goods and services for sale.[87] He also repeatedly stressed that markets carry out their function on a "great scale" and with such a "pervasive reach" that they affect other sectors of society having to deal with resources, politics, and "the values toward which its people oriented their lives."[88] This was true even in the United States where people

[80] Friedman 1583 (1989).
[81] Friedman and Rosen-Zvi 1430 (2001).
[82] Coffman (1998).
[83] Friedman and Rosen-Zvi 1430 (2001).
[84] Hurst 61 (1950).
[85] Friedman 1584–5 (1989).
[86] 1 Hurst 9–50 (1950).
[87] Id. at 21.
[88] Id. at 32.

were not, in Hurst's view, "much given to philosophizing about their values."[89] Markets allocated goods in a literal sense, but in a broader institutional and cultural sense, they defined shared norms and thus participated in creating society.

For Hurst, a study of markets revealed social norms. Markets maximized the exercise of private will in transactions; they acted as a frame, or a container, or a domain. Even though markets framed issues in predictable ways, they also enhanced individuality. It was people after all – individuals – who exercised what Hurst called private will, because it was people who acted in multiple, unique, idiosyncratic ways, even when making predetermined and standard market choices. So although there was lockstep conformity in the market set by "established structures of power and order" and "shared values," there was also, at the same time, room for individuality and for that something virtually indescribable that individuality brings with it[90] – something called personality or, in the aggregate, culture.[91]

Hurst's economic/historical study of markets was an approach that Friedman adopted when he focused on the interplay between quantifiable and qualitative social orders as the key to understanding the twentieth century. So long as ordinary people believed in freedom of choice, Friedman argued, it did not seem to matter to them if freedom of choice actually existed in any meaningful or deep way.[92] In the twentieth century and certainly by the twenty-first century, especially with the increased prominence of the Internet, the perception of choice was more powerful than was the fact of choice, as Web surfers around the world learned to vote with the unaccountable click of a mouse on everything from presidential popularity to which band should win the music video awards on MTV. In Friedman's view, media allocated opinions with a reach at least as grand and pervasive as that of markets, and both allocations resulted in links between permeable domains that then led to images by which people could understand the choices available to them for the construction of shared meaning.[93]

However, if Friedman was commenting on popular culture, he was also commenting on the "gap" literature that studied the divide between law-on-the-books and law-in-action.[94] Law-on-the-books scholarship did not put ordinary people at ease; indeed most people did not even know that kind of professionalized literature existed, thus making it elitist by definition. In addition, there was too much of it.[95] Nor did law-in-action affect all the people at whom it was directed. Yet scholarship about law and popular legal culture could reveal the link between law-on-the-books and law-in-action and individual, political, and cultural movements. The debate over

---

[89] Id. at 51.
[90] Id. at 51–4.
[91] Id. at 91; Friedman (1969).
[92] Friedman 137–8 (1999).
[93] Id. at 21–7.
[94] Friedman (1973, 1999); Munger (1993); Sarat (2000).
[95] Friedman (1973).

the estate tax offered a good example of this power. In the late 1990s, proponents of the estate tax repeal harnessed the media to spread their message that the estate tax was a tax on middle-class Americans. The idea was that if public opinion could be turned against "the death tax," then the estate tax might come to be regarded as a confiscatory measure of the sort that the middle class should oppose, even if their own (small) estates would transfer untaxed and even though the tax served important public revenue functions.[96]

POPULAR LEGAL CULTURE

"Law, Lawyers, and Popular Culture" offers the first definition of the term "popular legal culture." Drawing on Hurst's general idea of the way in which markets and law interact, as well as on his idea about the role of shared values in the creation of norms, Friedman defined popular legal culture in such a way as to encompass not only cases or reform-minded scholarship (legal culture), not only popular ideas, attitudes, and opinions (popular culture) but also popular ideas, attitudes, and opinions that lay-people (whether day laborers, plumbers, or investment bankers) hold – accurate or not – about law, lawyers, and the legal system.[97]

Friedman introduced the idea of popular legal culture in "Law, Lawyers, and Popular Culture" with examples of how legal scholars could use popular legal culture sources to study law. It was from this framework that Friedman asked where it is that legal rules come from and how the legal system, operating as it does in accordance with free-floating attitudes about law, is shaped. What is the process by which this shaping occurs, given that elitist articulations and popular culture representations of law meld together in every moment of every day in all the most extraordinary and ordinary ways, whether any one of us wants them to or not?[98]

For Friedman an autonomous legal system was an undesirable and impossible myth that legal insiders were taught by professional training to believe in: The myth was as much the first year student's comfort as it was the professor's.[99] Yet although the myth of autonomy, or even of semi-autonomy, plays a central role in legal pedagogy and scholarship, Friedman held that it nevertheless "seem[s] fairly clear . . . that legal systems as a whole cannot be autonomous in the long run . . . [s]ooner or later [the] shape [of a legal system] gets bent in the direction of [its] society (more or less)."[100] Legal scholars can choose to observe and study that shaping/bending process or not. They can choose to acknowledge it or to deny it. However, regardless of the legal academy's collective, traditional, or taught choices about pedagogy or scholarship,

[96] Gates & Collins (2002).
[97] Friedman 1580 (1989).
[98] Friedman 1–35 (1990).
[99] Friedman (1973).
[100] Friedman, Macaulay, and Stookey 10 (1995).

the process wends on: Culture shapes law just as law shapes culture.[101] This process happens with or without anyone bearing witness. Hurst's car example is an example: The car incrementally changed our world without our realizing all that was at stake.[102] On a different scale, so too would TV, or movies, or pulp fiction, or online access and content.[103]

"Law, Lawyers, and Popular Culture" concludes with the idea that legal systems are parochially global, a term I use but that Friedman did not. Legal systems are products of the societies whose disputes they resolve or address or stifle. Yet in a world of global (shared) economies, technologies, values, and beliefs about the rights of the individual in relation to the state, "the legal systems of the world are becoming more and more interconnected."[104] (However, until they actually link up and perhaps even after they do, they remain tribe, nation, and culture bound.[105]) In Friedman's analysis, economic forces can globalize a legal system. So too can technological ones. Yet it was not until "Law, Lawyers, and Popular Culture" that Friedman added popular culture and, more specifically, popular legal culture to the list of powerful globalizing forces that affect law. In Friedman's view, popular legal culture became more than an influencer or a shaper of law. It became a force and a phenomenon with the potential to globalize law – to link up a still parochial American legal system to the rest of the world on the level of values and beliefs about such concepts as authority, identity, fairness, choice, and environmental responsibility.[106]

LINKS AND CHOICES

Friedman's scholarship portends a continuing tension within legal scholarship that is reminiscent of the identity crisis that other disciplines like anthropology, literary studies, and history have faced. On one hand are the legal scholars who clarify doctrine for judges. They assume the role of reformers intent on developing the law.[107] These scholars identify as academic lawyers whose task it is to fix the threadbare places in the mantle of legal reason (those worn places illustrated by the odd example of arguments criticizing the so-called tendency of popular artists like John Grisham to use their work to spread erroneous information about institutions, policies, and even law).[108] To do their work of protecting the law from all that is common, these scholars too often imagine law as an autonomous or partly autonomous domain with a solid (impermeable) skin.

---

[101] Friedman 41 (1999).
[102] Hurst 61 (1950).
[103] Friedman and Rosen-Zvi 1425–30 (2001).
[104] Friedman, Macaulay, and Stookey 10 (1995).
[105] Friedman 206 (1999).
[106] E.g., Moore (2007).
[107] Kahn (1999).
[108] Coffman (1998); Harris (1994).

These scholars, for better or worse (Friedman thought for worse), are in the cathedral with the drapes drawn. That is, it is their *disciplinary bias* to privilege rules over context.[109] It is their *disciplinary bias* to hypothesize that mixing law (rules) with popular culture, or hyphenated masses of people, or any other external force will challenge law's legitimacy. It is their *disciplinary bias* to simplify (state and restate) rules rather than to complicate law with social or cultural context. These legal scholars write from the law professor's disciplinary bias, but – like a first-generation Terminator (from the 1984 movie, *The Terminator*) – they are programmed by the machines of law school or law review or court clerkships or (ironically) by popular culture itself to practice their disciplinary bias, and their disciplinary bias only. When they remain in the cathedral with the drapes drawn, when they write solely from their disciplinary bias no matter what, they choose (whether intentionally or not) to remain isolated and blind to the ways in which law and society are bound and why. The disciplinary bias of the law professor then is like the car in Hurst's analysis or like popular culture in Friedman's analysis, in that it works to bring about a future of a certain affect, effect, and direction.

Then there are the legal scholars who perceive their function as increasing the general fund of knowledge. These scholars tend to consider law as its own intellectual discipline. They accept that law is contextualized in cultural realities. They – for better or worse (Friedman thought for the better) – start in the cathedral but then venture outside into the "often confusing maze" of society, markets, technologies, popular culture, literature, religion, and the like.[110] These scholars think that their mission is not to direct, fix, or reform law, but to observe, analyze, understand, and converse with those whom Friedman called the consumers of the legal system. Their goal is not to shore up the legitimacy of law or its institutions so much as it is to understand why law, lawyers, and legal systems function the way they do in particular moments and circumstances.

In the last two decades, legal scholars have come to realize that popular legal culture – popular culture about law, lawyers, and legal institutions – influences law. Yet because everything potentially influences law, the claim of influence, at least in Friedman's view, is a pedestrian one. The better project for legal scholars – who, after all, know how to "do law" – is to begin to understand how forces – like the car, or the market, or popular film – shape and spread (globalize) views about law, lawyers, and legal systems. According to Friedman, markets, technology, and popular culture have the power to globalize legal systems, which are otherwise parochially tied to their host cultures.[111] Therefore the important work is to expand legal scholarship so that it considers cultural forces.[112] Social theory helps move the legal scholar to that choice.

[109] Cf., Grana, Ollenburger, and Nicolas (2002).
[110] Id. at 2.
[111] Friedman 54 (1999).
[112] Friedman 1606 (1989).

Together, Friedman's three basic propositions hold. First, law (social norms) exists inside and outside of the legal system. Second, the boundaries between law and other systems or domains in society are porous and permeable to exchanged information. Third, law is one, and only one, dependent variable in the greater social system of many other dependent variables, because law, like every other force in society, is subject to the winds and energies of local, national, and global culture and events. Considering these propositions turns popular legal culture from a phenomenon to control, to look down on, to remove, to block, or even to censor into a treasure trove of source material for the study of law.

REFERENCES AND BIBLIOGRAPHY

Alexeeva, Victoria (2003). Images of Women Lawyers: Over-Representation of Their Femininity in Media, 9 *Cardozo Women's L J.* 361.
American Psycho (2000). Edward R. Pressman Film.
Asimow, Michael (2001). Embodiment of Evil: Law Firms in the Movies, 48 *UCLA L. Rev.* 1339.
Baur, Steven (2006). You Say You Want a Revolution: Marx and the Beatles, in Michael Baur and Steven Baur, eds., *The Beatles and Philosophy: Nothing You Can Think That Can't Be Thunk.* Chicago: Open Court.
Brooks, Peter and Paul Gewirtz (1996). *Law's Stories: Narrative and Rhetoric in the Law.* New Haven: Yale University Press.
Calabresi, Guido and A. Douglas Melamed (1972). Property Rules, Liability Rules, and Inalienability: One View of the Cathedral, 85 *Harv. L. Rev.* 1089.
Carrillo, Jo (2007). Links and Choices: Popular Legal Culture in the Work of Lawrence M. Friedman, 17 *S. Cal. Interdisc. L.J.* 1.
Clifford and George E. Marcus (1986). *Writing Culture: The Poetics and Politics of Ethnography.* Berkeley: University of California Press.
Coffman, Carrie S. (1998). Gingerbread Women: Stereotypical Female Attorneys in the Novels of John Grisham, 8 *S. Cal. Rev. L. & Women's Stud.* 73.
Coombe, Rosemary (1998). Contingent Articulations: A Critical Cultural Studies of Law, in Austin Sarat and Thomas R. Kearns, eds., *Law in the Domains of Culture.* Ann Arbor: University of Michigan Press.
Dershowitz, Alan M (1996). Life is Not a Dramatic Narrative, in Peter Brooks and Paul Gewirtz, eds., *Law's Stories: Narrative and Rhetoric in the Law.* New Haven: Yale University Press.
Durkheim, Emile (1984). *The Division of Labor in Society.* New York: Free Press. (Originally published in 1893)
Friedman, Lawrence M. (1969). Legal Culture and Social Development, 4 *Law & Soc'y Rev.* 29.
———. (1973). *A History of American Law.* New York: Simon and Schuster.
———. (1984). *American Law.* New York: W. W. Norton & Co.
———. (1985). *Total Justice: What Americans Want From the Legal System and Why.* New York: Russell Sage Foundation.
———. (1986). The Law and Society Movement, 38 *Stan. L. Rev.* 763.
———. (1989). Law, Lawyers, and Popular Culture, 98 *Yale L. Rev.* 1579.

_____. (1990). *The Republic of Choice: Law, Authority, and Culture.* Cambridge, MA: Harvard University Press.

_____. (1994). Is There a Modern Legal Culture? 7 *Ratio Juris* 117.

_____. (1998). *American Law: An Introduction.* New York: W. W. Norton.

_____. (1999). *The Horizontal Society.* New Haven: Yale University Press.

Friedman, Lawrence M. and Issachar Rosen-Zvi (2001). Illegal Fictions: Mystery Novels and the Popular Image of Crime, 48 *UCLA L. Rev.* 1411.

Friedman, Lawrence M. and Robert Percival (1981). *The Roots of Justice: Crime and Punishment in Alameda County, CA, 1870–1910.* Chapel Hill: University of North Carolina Press.

Friedman, Macaulay, and Stookey (1995). *Law and Society: Readings on the Social Study of Law.* New York: W.W. Norton.

Galanter, Marc (1974). Why the Haves Come Out Ahead: Speculations on the Limits of Legal Change, 9 *Law & Soc'y Rev.* 95.

_____. (1985). The Legal Malaise of Justice Observed, *Law & Soc'y Rev.* 537.

Garcia-Villegas, Mauricio (2003). Symbolic Power Without Symbolic Violence, 55 *Fla. L. Rev.* 157.

Gates, William and Chuck Collins (2002). *Wealth and Our Commonwealth: Why America Should Tax Accumulated Fortunes.* Boston: Beacon Press.

Geertz, Clifford (1983). *Local Knowledge: Further Essays in Interpretive Anthropology.* New York: Basic Books.

_____. (1995). *After the Fact: Two Countries, Four Decades, One Anthropologist.* Cambridge, MA: Harvard University Press.

Gessner, Volkmar (1994). Global Legal Interaction and Legal Cultures, 7 *Ratio Juris* 132.

Gordon, Robert W. (1983). Legal Thought and Legal Practice in the Age of American Enterprise, 1870–1920, in Gerald L. Geison, ed., *Professions and Professional Ideologies in America.* Chapel Hill: University of North Carolina Press.

_____. (1984). Critical Legal Histories, 36 *Stan. L. Rev.* 57.

_____. (1990). New Developments in Legal Theory, in David Kairys, ed., *The Politics of Law: A Progressive Critique.* New York: Pantheon Books.

Grana, Ollenburger, and Nicholas (2002). *The Social Context of Law.* Upper Saddle River, NJ: Prentice Hall.

Grant, Judith (1996). Lawyers as Super Heroes: The Firm, the Client, and the Pelican Brief, 30 *U.S.F. L. Rev.* 1111.

Harris, David A. (1994). The Appearance of Justice: Court TV, Conventional Television, and Public Understanding of the Criminal Justice System, 35 *Ariz. L. Rev.* 785.

Ho, Kevin (2003). 'The Simpsons' and the Law: Revealing Truth and Justice to the Masses, 10 *UCLA Ent. L. Rev.* 275 (2003).

Hurst, James Willard (1950). *The Growth of American Law: The Lawmakers.* Boston: Little-brown.

_____. (1964). *Law and Economic Growth: The Legal History of the Lumber Industry in Wisconsin, 1836–1915.* Madison: University of Wisconsin Press.

_____. (1982). *Law and Markets in United States History: Different Modes of Bargaining among Interests.* Madison: University of Wisconsin Press.

Kahn, Paul (1999). *The Cultural Study of Law: Reconstructing Legal Scholarship.* Chicago: University of Chicago Press.

Kennedy, Duncan (1993). *Sexy Dressing, Etc.: Essays on the Power and Politics of Cultural Identity.* Cambridge, MA: Harvard University Press.

Kessler, Mark (1995). Lawyers and Social Change in the Postmodern World, 29 *Law & Soc'y Rev.* 769.

Lee, Kathryn A. and Elizabeth Morgan (2004). Legal Fictions and the Moral Imagination: Female Fictional Lawyers Encounter Professional Responsibility, 10 *Wm. & Mary J. Women & L.* **569.**

Lemmings, David (2000). *Professors of Law: Barristers and English Legal Culture in the Eighteenth Century.* Oxford: Oxford University Press.

Macaulay, Stewart (1963). Non-Contractual Relations in Business: A Preliminary Study, 28 *Am. Sociol. Rev.* 55.

———. (1984). Law and the Behavioral Sciences: Is There Any There There? 6 *Law & Pol'y* 149.

———. (1987–8). Images of Law in Everyday Life: The Lessons of School, Entertainment, and Spectator Sports, 21 *Law & Soc'y Rev.* 185.

Macaulay, Stewart, Lawrence M. Friedman, and John Stookey (1995). *Law and Society: Readings on the Social Study of Law.* New York: W.W. Norton.

Malinowski, Bronislaw (1926). *Crime and Custom in Savage Society.* New York: Harcourt, Brace.

Masburn, Amy R. and Dabney D. Ware (1996). The Burden of Truth: Reconciling Literary Reality and Professional Mythology, 26 *U. Mem. L. Rev.* 1257.

McLuhan, Marshall (2001). *The Medium is the Message: An Inventory of Effects.* Corte Madera: Gingko Press.

Merry, Sally Engle (1995). Resistance and the Cultural Power of Law, 29 *Law & Soc'y Rev.* 11.

Mezey, Naomi (1994). Legal Radicals in Madonna's Closet: The Influence of Identity Politics, Popular Culture, and a New Generation on Critical Legal Studies, 46 *Stan. L. Rev.* 1835.

Miller, Carolyn Lisa, (1994). "What a Waste. Beautiful. Sexy Gal. Hell of a Lawyer": Film and the Female Attorney, 4 *Colum. J. Gender & Law* 203.

Mnookin, Robert H. (1979). *Bargaining in the Shadow of the Law: The Case of Divorce.* Oxford: Centre for Socio-Economic Studies, Wolfson College.

Monk: Mr. Monk and the Rapper (USA Network television broadcast 2007). Available at http://www.usanetwork.com.

Moore, Michael (2007). *Sicko.* Available at http://www.michaelmoore.com/books-films/index.php (last visited on Aug. 10, 2007).

Munger, Frank (1993). Sociology of Law for a Postliberal Society, 27 *Loy. L.A. L. Rev.* 89.

Posner, Richard A. (1986). Law and Literature: A Relation Reargued, 72 *Va L. Rev.* 1351.

———. (1989). The Depiction of Law in *The Bonfire of the Vanities,* 98 *Yale L.J.* 1653.

———. (1998). *Law and Literature.* Cambridge, MA: Harvard University Press.

Sarat, Austin (1985). Legal Effectiveness and the Social Study of Law: On the Unfortunate Persistence of a Research Tradition, 9 *Legal Stud. Forum* 23.

———. (2000). Book Review: Redirecting Legal Scholarship in Law Schools, 12 *Yale J.L. & Human.* 129.

Sarat, Austin and Thomas Kearns, eds. (1993). *Law In Everday Life.* Ann Arbor: University of Michigan.

Sarat, Austin and Jonathan Simon (2001). Beyond Legal Realism?: Cultural Analysis, Cultural Studies, and the Situation of Legal Scholarship, 13 *Yale J.L. & Human.* **3.**

Sherwin, Richard K. (1992). Lawyering Theory: An Overview: What We Talk about When We Talk about Law, 37 *N.Y.L. Sch. L. Rev.* 9, 10 (1992).

———. (1999–2000). Law/Media/Culture: Legal Meaning in the Age of Images, 43 *N.Y.L. Sch. L. Rev.* 653.

_____. (2000). *When Law Goes Pop: The Vanishing Line between Law and Popular Culture*. Chicago: University of Chicago Press.

_____. (2001). Nomos and Cinema, 48 *UCLA L. Rev.* 1519.

Shiller, Robert (2005). *Irrational Exuberance*. Princeton, NJ: Princeton University Press.

Silbey, Jessica M. (2002). What We Do When We Do Law and Popular Culture, 27 *Law & Soc. Inquiry* 139, 141–2.

Steinbock, Daniel J. (1993). Refuge and Resistance: Casablanca's Lessons for Refugee Law, 7 *Geo. Immigr. L.J.* 649.

Stevens, Robert (1983). *Law School: Legal Education in America from the 1850s to the 1980s*. Chapel Hill: University of North Carolina Press.

The Terminator (1984). Orion Pictures Corp.

Thomas, Jeffrey E. (2005). Harry Potter and the Law, 12 *Tex. Wesleyan L. Rev.* 427.

Trouillot, Michel-Rolph (1995). *Silencing the Past: Power and the Production of History*. Boston: Beacon Press.

Weber, Max (1954). *Max Weber on Law in Economy and Society*. New York: Simon and Schuster.

Williams, Raymond, ed. (1997). *Problems in Materialism and Culture: Selected Essays*. London: Verso Classics.

_____. (2003). *Television: Technology and Cultural Form*. London: Routledge Classics.

6

Exploring Legal Culture

A Few Cautionary Remarks from Comparative Research

José Juan Toharia

Since Lawrence M. Friedman first published his seminal paper on legal culture in 1969,[1] the number of empirical studies on opinions and attitudes with respect to legal and judicial institutions has been constantly growing. Even if, on the whole, the mass of reliable and comparable opinion data now available worldwide is still relatively thin, in some countries the systematic measurement of both the *internal* and *external legal culture*[2] has become a fully consolidated area of research.[3]

It has gradually become accepted that legal culture is an extremely important variable for obtaining a better understanding of how legal systems operate. It is "in a way, the fuel that makes the law machine move and work. It determines the pattern of demands on the legal system. Without the legal culture, 'law' is dead, inert, a skeleton, words on paper."[4]

---

[1] See Friedman (1969); also Friedman (1975).

[2] That is, the aggregate of values, attitudes, and opinions referred to the legal system found among lawyers and jurists (*internal legal culture*) and in the general population (*external legal culture*).

[3] For instance, this is the case for Spain, where over the last thirty years (that is, since the reestablishment of democracy) more than fifty such studies have been carried out, sponsored by institutions such as the Consejo General del Poder Judicial (General Council of the Judicial Power [CGPJ]), the governing body of the judiciary; the National Bar Association (Consejo General de la Abogacía); and several private foundations (such as the Fundación BBVA or the Fundación ICO). The publics studied comprise the general population, court users, judges, public attorneys, lawyers, court clerks, and notaries. For a global summary of most of these studies, see Garcia de la Cruz and Toharia (2005). In addition, for a summary of data referred to Latin European and American countries, see Friedman and Pérez-Perdomo (2003). The last instance I know of survey research carried out on the legal culture of a country (other than Spain) occurred in Belgium and is summarized (with some additional papers providing comparative data) in Parmentier et al. (2004).

[4] Friedman and Pérez-Perdomo 2 (2003).

I first met Lawrence Friedman in 1971 while I was still working on my PhD thesis at Yale University. I have had the privilege of remaining in close contact with him ever since. My intellectual and personal debt to him goes beyond what I could aptly express here. For more than three decades he has been (and will, I hope, still be for a long time to come) both an admired master and a very dear friend, unfailing in his help and support every time I needed it. And this, of course, also refers to Leah.

Legal culture consists basically of values, attitudes, and opinions related to the legal system, and survey research represents a particularly effective operational tool to explore it. Obviously, opinion polls cannot properly and fully capture all the aspects of a legal culture (whether internal or external), but most of its dimensions can only be grasped and measured with the help of surveys. In this sense surveys represent a basic, even if incomplete, instrument in the production of reliable and comparative information.

It is not my intention in this chapter to summarize or even discuss the mass of empirical information already available from research carried out in the United States and in most European Union (EU) countries.[5] Instead my purpose is to explore potential pitfalls that if uncontrolled can blur the adequate perception and interpretation of the attitudes, evaluations, and opinions yielded by survey research on the legal system; this analysis is based on my research experience. I focus on just three significant pitfalls: *top-of-the-head* responses, *clichéd* answers, and sudden and abrupt *switches of opinions*. All three are well-known, standard false friends in public opinion analysis, but they seem somewhat more likely to occur in surveys concerning legal culture, most likely because of the complex, multifaceted, and "mushy"[6] nature of the legal and judicial system as a topic for opinion research.

TOP-OF-THE-HEAD[7] ANSWERS

A glance at the available body of opinion data on courts of justice could easily lead to the conclusion that practically everywhere courts are rather unpopular and basically mistrusted institutions. In the late 1970s, a survey carried out in the United States by the National Center for State Courts found that only 23 percent of the respondents said that they felt extremely or very confident about state and local courts. Twenty years later the situation remained practically unchanged.[8] On the whole, data from EU countries show on the whole a similar pattern: The percentages of European citizens expressing trust and satisfaction with their judicial systems are remarkably low. Satisfaction with the way courts operate ranges from 8 percent in Italy, 13 percent in Portugal, and 14 percent in France to 33 percent in the United Kingdom, 38 percent in Sweden, and 45 percent in the Netherlands. In only three EU

---

[5] Also in Australia, in several ex-Soviet Eastern European countries, in several Latin American countries, and in a few other places in Africa or Asia.

[6] I take the expression from Converse (1987). It well describes the imprecise and vague boundaries that the world of the law seems to have for most lay observers. On the confusing, polysemic nature of the term "justice" for the average citizen, see Toharia (2003).

[7] The term *top-of the-head* is used mainly in advertising research and refers to the most likely word that a person will think of when considering a certain topic. It gives an indication on the relative *salience* of issues (i.e., which are more likely to pop out at the conscious mind when a certain stimulus is activated).

[8] See National Center for State Courts (1999).

countries does that percentage represent an absolute majority: Austria (52%), Denmark (54%), and Finland (61%). As for trust in the judicial system, the percentages expressing positive answers range from 22 percent in Belgium, 35 percent in France, 38 percent in Italy, and 40 percent in Spain to 48 percent in the United Kingdom, 53 percent in Sweden, and 59 percent in the Netherlands.[9] In Canada, in the year 2000, just 13 percent of the population considered that the courts provided justice efficiently.[10] Similar data from several other countries (such as Japan or Argentina, to mention just two quite different cases) have been found as well.

All of these data seem to point in the same direction: When asked to give a first, global appraisal of their system of justice, most citizens in practically all countries tend to produce a blunt, unqualified critical opinion and to express little trust. Yet such a conclusion is unlikely to be a surprise:

> Complaining about courts goes back throughout the 20th century and may go back throughout the history of courts. It is not surprising that courts generate dissatisfaction: they are associated with unpleasant things such as criminals, injuries, divorces and the like. . . . Consequently it is not surprising that when the public is asked to evaluate the courts their evaluations are less than whole-heartedly positive.[11]

Such a generic negative first reaction on the part of the general population seems to make sense given all we know about courts and their history. As a rule, in all times and cultures, courts of justice have striven to inspire respect or awe rather than trust or confidence.[12] The centuries-long iconography for justice mixes scales and sword,[13] a far from reassuring image for the average potential user:

> Although in a general sense the sword symbolizes the role of justice in protecting the innocent, the sword also more precisely represents the rigour of justice. Justice will not hesitate to punish the guilty, neither does it compromise. . . . Though often presented as the judgment of compromise, Solomon's provisional judgment is that justice is not only correct, but also harsh and unyielding.[14]

---

[9] Once more, the best results are found in the same three countries (Denmark, 70%; Finland, 61%; and Austria, 61%). Data refer, respectively, to 1997 and 1999 and come from *Eurobarometer.* See Toharia 62 (2003a).

[10] Roberts 134 (2004).

[11] Kritzer and Voelker 58 (1998).

[12] Only recently "the issue of trust or confidence (in courts) has become one of the most important in the field of public opinion and the administration of justice" (Roberts 131 [2004]), largely as a result of the gradual (and not always easy, at least in continental Europe) acceptance of the idea that courts perform a public service; for instance, in 1989 the French Ministry of Justice published a small booklet with this title, *Le "service public" de la Justice: un concept nouveau* (*Justice as "public service": a new approach*). This new approach has certainly helped encourage empirical research, as a logical consequence of the new prominence granted to "the voice of the people" (i.e., to the "users") in the appraisal of judicial performance. The result has been the already mentioned body of opinion data.

[13] In the words of Loughlin, a "regally-robed, coolly impersonal, blindfolded goddess wielding sword and scales." Loughlin 62 (2000).

[14] Id. at 61.

In addition, as noted by Shapiro,[15] the integration of courts within the state apparatus was intended to protect their activity from potential threats or influences coming from powerful private groups or individuals. To this day the unanticipated side effect of such an institutional arrangement has been that justice risks being perceived as merely the coercive branch of the state – again, an image unlikely to foster a sense of trust and confidence. As pointed out by Packer, the fact that the public usually perceives the operation of the courts as emphasizing more *due process* (and then the protection of the rights of the accused persons) than *crime control* (and consequently the protection of the rights of victims)[16] provides an additional reason for the tendency to express critical evaluations of their overall performance.

Furthermore, in the specific case of continental Europe – and largely as a result of a long-time unchallenged misreading of Montesquieu[17] – over the last two centuries courts of justice have been defined (and have insisted themselves on being so defined) as a *power* on equal grounds with the executive power or the legislative power. Extended and uncritically accepted as this claim has normally been, it has always represented in practice more of a simply rhetorical label than an apt description of actual functions. In fact, in a democracy with a civil law legal system, the role of courts and judges can hardly be described as the implementation of a *power*. Insistence on the concept of "judicial power" has normally resulted both in a consistently dysfunctional performance by courts and an extended popular sentiment of mistrust toward them. It has also probably reinforced in the popular mind the association between the image of justice and that of the State.[18]

All these factors and considerations (and several others that could be added to this short list) certainly create a predisposition among the citizenry to give critical answers when asked about courts. They also tend to predispose the analyst to accept such answers as sensible and reliable. Yet how fair and sound is the conclusion

---

[15] Shapiro 19–20 (1981).

[16] Packer (1968). As multiple survey data, from different countries, over the last two decades amply document.

[17] I refer to his much quoted – but seemingly not so much directly read – text on the "separation of powers" in *De l'esprit des lois* (Book XI, Chapter VI). In fact Montesquieu does not use the term "judicial power": He speaks instead of "*la puissance de juger*," a term that would be more adequately rendered with swords such as "faculty" or "capacity." He describes such a *puissance* as a judicial body of peers (equal try equals), nonprofessional, selected *pro tempore*, and without any capacity whatsoever to interpret the law (the judges he had in mind had to be just "the mouth of the law"). In sum, a variation of a jury trial, but hardly a power in the strictly political sense of the term. See Toharia 38 (2001).

[18] For instance, in those countries (mainly Nordic) that first advocated the idea of the welfare state, public institutions (courts included) are more likely to appear as benign and protective and consequently to be positively evaluated. Contrariwise, in southern European countries, where the state and public institutions (courts included) have usually been perceived by the average citizen more as some kind of threatening predators than as trustworthy guardians or protectors, the image of judicial institutions appears to be particularly negative. The available data would seem to support this hypothetical interpretation.

that there seems to be a stable, practically universal, basic pattern of mistrust and dissatisfaction with courts?

A more careful reading of the data suggests instead that this might be an excessive and hasty interpretation of the existing information. No opinion data "speaks by itself," nor should be accepted at face value, nor is univocal, especially if obtained through simple, direct, and isolated questions (of the type *"How much do you trust your court system?"*).[19] These kinds of generic questions are used in most – if not all – surveys on courts and justice as an introduction to the interview. They allow the respondents to offer a global, unqualified evaluation of the performance of courts and of the degree of trust and confidence they inspire. In this sense such questions represent a good starting point from which to proceed to further and more elaborated questioning. However, they are frequently treated as if they reflect final, balanced and thought-through *resumés* of what the respondents really had in mind. Generic, introductory questions normally elicit what is usually referred to as *top-of-the-head (or top of mind)* answers; that is, the first things that come to the mind of respondents after hearing the question.

Spontaneous, first reactions are unquestionably important to understanding the predominant associations in the collective mind to a given topic, but at the same time they can also hide as much information as they unveil. When asked to evaluate public services, respondents particularly tend to concentrate on the inadequacies, deficiencies, or shortcomings they perceive in them. All that is properly functioning tends to become invisible. And rightly so, it could be argued, because in a well-functioning democracy citizens are entitled to take for granted the best possible service from public institutions. Yet if the purpose of the research is not simply to draw up a list of what goes wrong (or is perceived as going wrong), but rather to gain as complete and detailed an appraisal of the prevailing state of opinion on the global operation of a given institution (the courts, in this case), an attempt has to be made to cover those "invisible" dimensions as well. Otherwise the analysis would be inevitably biased and distorted.

As graphically expressed by Flanagan,

> A single survey of the public represents a "snapshot" of public opinion taken at a specific time (and) there are considerable dangers in drawing inferences about long-term change in the public mood on the basis of cross-sectional single snapshot data.... Any single snapshot represents only one single "pose" ... and there are numerous ways to pose the (same) question.... Methodological details like the question wording, response alternatives, question ordering and many others are consequential in public opinion research.[20]

---

[19] In this respect (but only in this respect!) Robert is correct when he dismisses the validity of "journalistic" public opinion data on courts as a useful tool in the description of legal culture. See Robert 77 (2004).

[20] Flanagan 18 (2004).

Opinions and attitudes with respect to such a complex topic as the system of justice need to be surveyed through continued "snapshots" and from as many different angles – or "poses"– as possible to facilitate the detection of top-of-the-head answers and thereby obtain a sounder and more balanced picture. Analysis of opinion polls can be likened to the contemplation of an impressionistic painting: Each specific detail, when taken in isolation, does not mean much. However, all the strokes complement and qualify each other, and the overall picture they all contribute to emerges clearly only when they are considered globally.

The conclusion that negative perceptions about the performance of courts seem to be widespread becomes less evident when this top-of-the-head factor is corrected. In the case of Spain with which I am particularly familiar (although as far as I know the same could apply to most survey data on courts from other countries), even when only a clear minority of the population initially expresses trust and confidence in courts, large majorities feel that judges are honest, fair, and competent and that courts represent the ultimate and most reliable guardian of civil liberties and democratic institutions. How can such highly positive opinions be reconciled with the poor initial global evaluation? When giving their initial top-of-the-head answers, Spanish respondents seemed to have in mind just two particularly salient features of the overall picture: the slowness they perceive in judicial proceedings and the unintelligible jargon they consider that courts use when addressing them.[21] These two features, and only these two, seem to be behind their first, spontaneous reaction as they temporarily overshadow all other features of the judicial system. Only when offered the opportunity, in the course of the interview, to consider additional aspects and dimensions of the system of justice do the respondents start to express much more qualified and positive evaluations. The final overall diagnosis, which can be constructed by combining all the information gathered, turns out to be quite different from what the first impression might have suggested.[22] In short, top-of-the-head answers provide the researcher with a useful entrance door to prevailing states of opinion, but not with a faithful and reliable summary of them.

CLICHÉS

Clichés are a second possible distorting factor when analyzing public opinion data about courts. They are not always easy to detect: After all, clichés normally express what everybody seems to consider self-evident truths beyond discussion or need of proof. They represent stereotypical ideas based more on deeply rooted and largely pervasive prejudices than on actual personal experiences. They permeate popular culture and in some cases have remained unchanged for centuries and are found practically everywhere: From Greek fables to Roman comedies, from the French

[21] Toharia (2005).
[22] Id.

medieval *Farce de maître Pathelin* to Corneille's *Les Plaideurs*, clichés have stayed with us to this day; they are alive and well and living in plays, novels, cartoons, movies, and jokes.

Clichés are important elements in the analysis of legal culture inasmuch as they represent relatively stable structural components of the collective representations. However, they can be very misleading as descriptors of actual situations. Clichés can be considered to represent the opposite phenomenon to *spirals of silence*:[23] They result from a social predisposition to express a common opinion, whereas the latter represent a socially induced tendency to hide the respondent's own opinion.

Most topics related to the world of the law are tainted with deeply rooted clichés. For instance, when ordinary citizens are asked about the degree of impartiality or independence of courts, their top-of-the-head answers will normally include clichés. In practically all countries for which data exist (be it the United States, the United Kingdom, or Spain[24]), the first reaction of respondents is to strongly question the independence of courts. However, more persistent and detailed questioning on the issue reveals that what most respondents mean is that they perceive courts as being permanently under pressure from the government, or pressure groups, or the media: in sum by practically all relevant social groups and institutions. When offered the possibility of distinguishing between *being under pressure* and *yielding to pressure*, just a small minority of the population perceives courts as being *both* pressured and yielding to pressures. The large majority consider that most of the time courts manage to overcome the generalized attempts to condition their operation.[25] In other words, the initially expressed cliché seriously misrepresents the actual state of opinion.

Recent research data[26] provide a clear example of a cliché about the treatment dispensed by courts that exists in completely similar terms in the legal culture of both Americans and Spaniards. Spain and the United States differ greatly in their social, political, and economic history and have totally unrelated legal institutions and traditions. In both countries, however, strikingly similar percentages of respondents express the belief that some groups receive preferential (or discriminatory) treatment from the courts. In Spain 83 percent of respondents (and 80 percent in the United States) express the conviction that the wealthy are better treated than everyone else. In both countries ethnic and social minorities are perceived to be treated in court worse than everyone else (this view is expressed by 61 percent of the respondents in Spain and by 50 percent in the United States). These data can be taken to prove that the idea that the "haves" always manage to come out ahead of the "have nots" is probably universal. Yet can they also be taken to express actual personal experiences with the way courts operate in Spain and in the United States? How much credibility do they deserve as indicators of the actual prevalence of discriminatory

[23] As defined by Noelle-Neumann (1984).
[24] See Toharia (2003c).
[25] Id.
[26] Id.

practices in both judicial systems? Not much, if any at all: When asked what kind of treatment "*people like you*" could expect from courts, similar percentages in all social groups in both countries give the same answer: the same treatment as all others! In other words, no social group perceives itself as a potential object of preferential or discriminatory treatment by the courts. Yet despite this perception the cliché about unequal treatment is what first comes to mind. Clichés may not be strong enough to fully bias the perception of reality but are prevalent enough to occupy the frontline in spontaneous answers. Clichés are but uncritically held beliefs and as such remain unaffected by real facts. Beliefs are fact-proof, as Proust had already remarked: "Les faits ne pénètrent pas dans le monde où vivent nos croyances, ils n'ont pas fait naître celles-ci, ils ne les détruisent pas."[27]

SWITCHES OF OPINIONS

As noted by Flanagan, public opinion about the legal system shows a remarkable tendency to temporal stability, in the United States and elsewhere.[28] To a certain extent the existence of clichés probably contributes to this stability: Less strongly prejudiced states of opinion probably would prove somewhat more volatile. Yet occasionally, from time to time, substantial and even spectacular changes of opinion seem to take place. The U-turn in Spanish public opinion about jury trials provides a good example.

The current Spanish Constitution, which was enacted in 1978, introduced two basic changes in the realm of criminal law: It abolished the death penalty and reintroduced the jury trial for some specific types of criminal cases. Both measures were meant to symbolize a sharp break from the criminal justice system of the Francoist regime.

In the case of trial by jury, the climate of opinion seemed at first fully supportive of its establishment, with just one qualification: Spaniards declared themselves to be in favor of juries as long as they personally would not be called to sit on one![29] In any case, by 1995 when the law regulating the proceedings in trial was finally passed, the popularity of jury trials seemed quite solid: The dominant idea in Spanish society was that jurors would be more likely than professional judges to make fair decisions, and the majority of Spaniards expressed a preference to be tried, if ever put to trial, by a jury rather than by a professional judge (see Tables 6.1 and 6.2). However, just two years later, in 1997, the climate of opinion experienced a spectacular turnaround: Professional judges came to be clearly preferred over juries. In all likelihood, a single, highly publicized case in 1996 (the Otegui case[30]) undermined the seemingly strong

---

[27] Du côté de chez Swann, 1ère partie, "Combray."
[28] Flanagan 20 (2004).
[29] See Toharia (1987).
[30] In 1996, in the Basque country, a jury found not guilty a militant from the radical separatist group HB (considered to be the political branch of the terrorist ETA band) in the killing in cold blood of two agents of the Basque autonomous police who had approached his home unarmed on a routine

TABLE 6.1. *"In your opinion, who is in a better position to give a fair decision: professional judges or lay jurors?"*

Year	Professional judges (%)	Lay jurors (%)
1987	28	46
1992	30	54
1996	41	48
1997	55	34
2000	50	39
2003	59	28
2005	67	24

TABLE 6.2. *"If you were the defendant in a criminal case, would you rather be tried by professional judges or by lay jurors?"*

Year	Professional judges (%)	Lay jurors (%)
1983	32	44
1985	31	45
1986	32	43
1987	26	47
1990	29	45
1992	29	50
1996	37	49
1997	54	32
2000	38	49
2003	43	41
2005	52	37

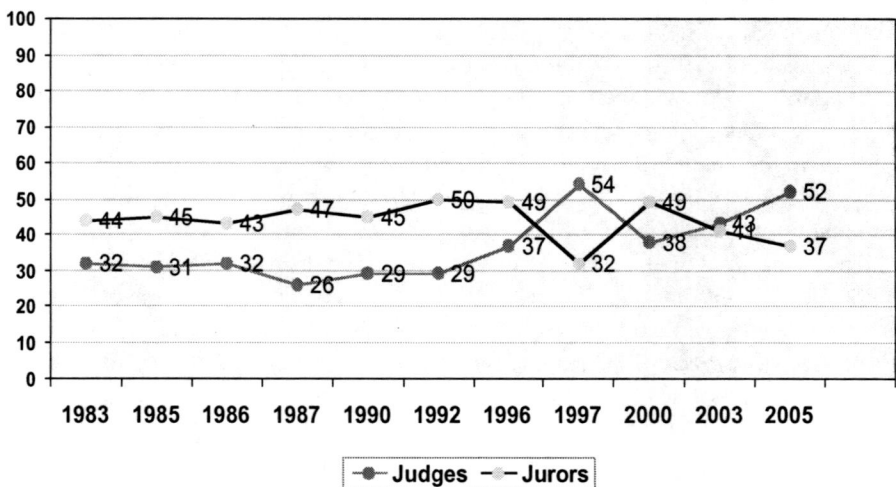

FIGURE 6.1. "If you were the defendant in a criminal case, would you rather be tried by professional judges or by lay jurors?"

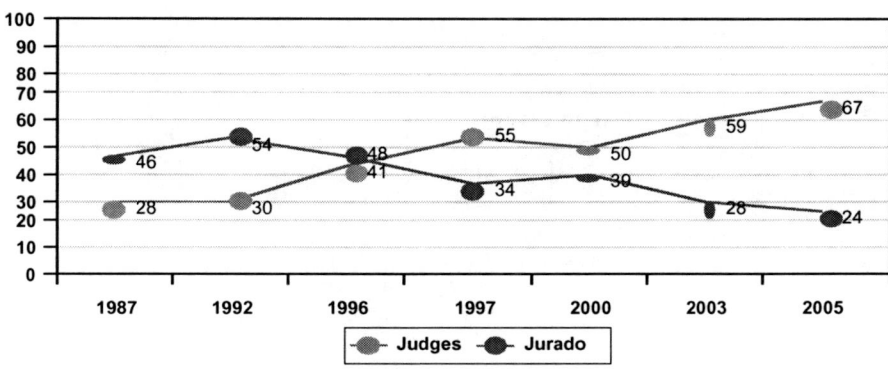

FIGURE 6.2. "In your opinion who is in a better position to give a fair decision: professional judges or lay jurors?"

support for the jury system and sapped its credibility. The question remained if this was just a temporary breach in the two-decades-long public support for jury trials or the beginning of a totally new trend. Data from 2000, 2003, and 2005 clearly show that jury trials do not seem to have recovered their earlier popularity and there is renewed trust and confidence in professional judges[31] (see also Figs. 6.1 and 6.2).

CONCLUSION

What can be done to detect reflexive, top-of-the-head answers or clichés, or to determine if a switch of opinion is just temporary and inconsequential or more permanent and meaningful? There is only one possible remedy: regularly repeated observations allowing for temporal comparisons. As one of sociology's founding fathers, Émile Durkheim, put it, in the realm of social sciences *"on n'explique qu'en comparant."* The depiction of legal culture cannot be done with a single snapshot or from a single *pose*. It requires sequential analyses allowing for comparisons in all possible directions (cross-cultural, cross-temporal, cross-institutional) as well as the use of constantly revised and refined methodological instruments.[32]

---

inspection. The decision of the jury caused an enormous scandal in the Basque country (as well as in the rest of Spain), amid a strong suspicion that ETA had intimidated the jurors. Normally terrorist cases are tried in Madrid in the *Audiencia Nacional*, but the case was originally considered an ordinary case of homicide rather than a terrorist act. The sentence was later annulled by the Basque Higher Court and a retrial ordered. However, by then the accused had gone into hiding where he remains to this day.

[31] In any case, and whatever the symbolic value of the jury trial and its public support, the fact is that its role within the Spanish system of criminal justice is marginal: Only some 300 jury trials are held yearly, on average, in all of Spain.

[32] An attempt to devise a template or basic protocol for the construction of questionnaires to be used in comparative research on legal culture is contained in Toharia (2003c).

REFERENCES

Converse, Philip (1987). Changing Conceptions of Public Opinion in the Political Process, *Public Opinion Quarterly*, 51/Supplement, 12–24.

Flanagan, T. (2004). Public Opinion, Crime and Justice. An American Perspective, in S. Parmentier et al., eds. *Public Opinion and the Administration of Justice*. Brussels: Politeia.

Friedman, L. M. (1969). Legal Culture and Social Development, in H. Kruger, ed., *Verfassung und Recht in Ubersee*. Bielefeld University.

———. (1975). *The Legal System*. New York: Russell Sage Foundation.

Friedman, L. M. and R. Pérez-Perdomo (2003). Latin Legal Cultures in the Age of Globalization, in L. M. Friedman and R. Pérez-Perdomo, eds., *Legal Culture in the Age of Globalization*. Palo Alto, CA: Stanford University Press.

García de la Cruz, J. J. and J. J. Toharia (2005). *La Justicia ante el espejo: veinticinco años de estudios de opinión del CGPJ*. Madrid: CGPJ.

Jensen, E. G., and Th. C. Heller, eds. (2003). *Beyond Common Knowledge. Empirical Approaches to the Rule of Law*. Palo Alto: Stanford University Press.

Kritzer, H. M., and J. Voelker (1998). Familiarity Breeds Respect, 82(2) *Judicature* 58.

Loughlin, M. (2000). *Sword and Scales*. Portland: Hart Publishing.

National Center for State Courts (1999). *How the Public Views the State Courts*. Williamsburg, VA: NCSC.

Noelle-Neumann, E. (1984). *The Spiral of Silence*. Chicago: University of Chicago Press.

Packer, H. (1968). *The Limits of the Penal Sanction*. New York: Oxford University Press.

Parmentier, S. et al., eds. (2004). *Public Opinion and the Administration of Justice*. Brussels: Politeia.

Robert, P. (2004). Opinion publique et administration de la Justice. Recherches françaises, in S. Parmentier et al., eds. *Public Opinion and the Administration of Justice*. Brussels: Politeia.

Roberts, J. V. (2004). Public Opinion and the Administration of Justice in Canada, in S. Parmentier et al., eds. *Public Opinion and the Administration of Justice*. Brussels: Politeia.

Shapiro, M. (1981) *Courts*. Chicago: University of Chicago Press.

Toharia, J. J. (1987). *¡Pleitos tengas! Introducción a la cultura legal española*. Madrid: Centro de Investigaciones Sociológicas.

———. (2001). *Opinión pública y Justicia*. Madrid: Consejo General del Poder Judicial.

———. (2003a). *La imagen ciudadana de la Justicia*. Madrid: Fundación BBVA.

———. (2003b). The Organization, Functioning and Evaluation of the Spanish Judicial System, in L. M. Friedman and R. Pérez-Perdomo, eds., *Legal Culture in the Age of Globalization*. Palo Alto, CA: Stanford University Press.

———. (2003c). Evaluating Systems of Justice through Public Opinion, in E. G. Jensen and Th. C. Heller, eds. *Beyond Common Knowledge: Empirical Approaches to the Rule of Law*. Palo Alto, CA: Stanford University Press.

Total Justice

7

The Travails of Total Justice

Marc Galanter

THE TOTAL JUSTICE EXPLOSION

Among his many gifts, Lawrence Friedman is blessed with a wonderful capacity to detect what he has occasionally called "master trends" in the workings of law and society, discerning the common direction and subterranean connection among diverse phenomena. His observations on "total justice" qualify as a prime example. In his much cited book of that name, published in 1985, he characterizes the advance of remedy and protection for many of life's injuries and troubles and the corresponding elevation of expectations as a master and unidirectional trend in American law and legal culture. The enlargement of justice that he describes includes two components: a general expectation of justice in the sense of fair treatment and recompense for injury and loss.

Total justice is a "super-principle"[1] that has gathered momentum over the past century. Its arrival reflected a sea change in legal culture, that itself reflects profound changes in the organization of society. These changes in society derive from the burgeoning of science and technology that have "made the world over"[2] and increased the social capacity for control and intervention.[3] So this is an Enlightenment story – harsh legal rules give way to a more nurturant sort of law as legal culture changes to reflect humankind's increasing science-based mastery over the troubles and risks of everyday life.

The "total justice" label linked together the expansion of tort accountability (via the relaxation of immunities, the shift to comparative negligence, the rise of new theories of liability, and the emergence of a more proficient plaintiffs' bar), the removal of procedural barriers and the projection of due process into many settings, the softening of contract law, the accessibility of legal services, and above all the

[1] Friedman 43, 75 (1985).
[2] Id. at 51.
[3] Id. at 70.

disinterment of civil rights for blacks and the extension of rights for many sorts
of subordinates and outsiders, from students to consumers to women to prisoners.
Dynamic minority, consumer, environmental, and women's movements institutionalized the claims of these constituencies and made them a presence on the legal
scene.[4] Whether or not total justice is a happy name for this bundle, it certainly captured the radical heightening of expectations that drove and in turn were bolstered
by these changes.

Friedman was well aware that this "deep and powerful trend" toward total justice
contended with dogged resistance and robust countertrends, but he concluded that
"they were insufficient to affect the main line of the story."[5] He anticipated little
potential for a major reversal and offered the (highly qualified) prediction that "[t]he
new legal culture – the general expectation of justice and its corollaries – may buck
and bend, but it will not go away. . . . It is fundamental to modern society, and in
essence, for the short run at least, it seems to be here to stay."[6] He has since reaffirmed
this optimistic reading: Acknowledging that "[t]here is no denying the backlash and
movements against 'total justice,'" he remains "convinced of the central point– the
evolution of an enhanced sense of legality, a growing, vibrant consciousness of right,
and a genuine strain toward total justice."[7]

RECOIL

When *Total Justice* was published in 1985, the great wave of expansion of remedy
in the civil rights movements and its companion consumer, environmental, and
women's movements had crested, although the flow of entitlements and expectations
generated by these initiatives continued to swirl through the legal system. By then,
that system was assailed by a fusillade of "countertrends" that became ever noisier
and more corrosive.

The expansion of protection and remedy that Friedman describes was not celebrated in all quarters. Resistance to desegregation was massive and included sustained campaigns against the Warren Court.[8] The less dramatic and visible expansion of tort remedies provoked more specialized animosities. By 1960 occasional
newspaper editorials groused at the mounting number of unjustified lawsuits, the
reckless generosity of juries, and the "lawsuit-happy" public.[9] By 1965 insurance
defense lawyers warned of a "law explosion."[10]

---

[4] Epp (1998).
[5] Friedman 148, 151 (1985).
[6] Id. at 152.
[7] Friedman 145, 146 (2002).
[8] Lytle (1968); Hyneman Ch. 2 (1963).
[9] "We're Suing Ourselves to Death," *St. Petersburg Times*, Mar. 5, 1960, reprinted in *For the Defense*
     1(3), 19 (May 1960).
[10] Defense Research Institute 1965: 3. The "law explosion" was seen as a problem largely specific to
     tort cases and one for which "[m]uch of the responsibility . . . must be charged against the national

In August, 1971, soon to be Supreme Court Justice Lewis F. Powell Jr., then a lawyer in Richmond, prepared a "Confidential Memorandum" at the invitation of the chairman of the Education Committee of the U.S. Chamber of Commerce that addresses a "broad-based and consistently pursued" assault on the American free enterprise system that was "gaining momentum and converts."[11] Powell bemoans the "impotency of business" in policy arenas and its default in intellectual and scholarly forums: "[F]ew elements of American society today have as little influence in government as the American businessman, the corporation, or even the millions of corporate stockholders."[12] Powell advises the Chamber of Commerce to mount an aggressive campaign to cultivate and support scholars "who do believe in the system," to critique textbooks, to promote a "steady flow" of scholarly and popular articles, and to intervene in the courts. This document foreshadows the pronounced increase in business spending on politics,[13] an increase facilitated by judicial recognition of corporate campaign contributions as protected free speech.[14] It anticipates the arrival of right-wing think tanks, institutes, and foundations and the establishment of conservative public-interest law firms (starting with the Pacific Legal Foundation in 1973).[15] Although Powell is critical of the use of law by liberal and left groups to produce unfavorable doctrine, he does not point to litigation per se as a threat to business. The enemy is not the Association of Trial Lawyers of America (ATLA), but Ralph Nader, the ACLU, and Charles Reich.[16]

Yet litigation, and especially tort liability, was what aroused and alarmed others. *Business Week* reported that "[a]lmost to a man insurance executives think that the tort system is running amok."[17] A medical malpractice insurance crisis in 1972–4 led many state legislatures to curtail remedies; a crisis in product liability insurance in 1974–6 aroused wide sections of the business and insurance communities. The *Journal of Insurance* devoted its entire September–October 1978 issue to litigation; it consisted of reprints of opinion pieces from newspapers and magazines with titles like "Lawsuit Fever," "The Sue-Syndrome is Spreading," "A Surfeit of Lawsuits,"

organization of attorneys who represent claimants in personal injury cases and receive their remuneration from 'contingent fees.'" The organization referred to is the Association of Trial Lawyers of America (ATLA), founded in 1946 as the National Association of Claimants Compensation Attorneys and renamed the American Association for Justice in 2006.

[11] Powell (1971).

[12] Id.

[13] Pertschuk (1982); Shapiro (1984); Ackard (1992); Su et al. (1995); Kerr (2002).

[14] *Buckley v. Valeo*, 424 U.S. 1 (1976). The role of corporate wealth in elections has been given further protection and encouragement by Citizens United v. Federal Election Commission, 130 S. Ct. 876 (2010)

[15] Aron 75 (1989); Southworth (2005).

[16] Reich's "The New Property" (1964), proposing that entitlements be regarded as property, was immensely influential. By 1978 it had been cited in more than forty cases in the U.S. Supreme Court. Donahue 59 (1980). In the mid-1990s it was the fourth most cited law review article of all time. Shapiro 767 (1996).

[17] "The Overload on the Nation's Insurance System" 46 (1976).

"The Law Gone Crazy," and "The Mugging of American Industry."[18] Schemes for cutting back on remedies abounded. Insurers sponsored full-page advertisements in national publications warning the public about the infirmities and the dangers of the law.[19]

A large section of the legal elite, including Chief Justice Warren Burger, identified litigation as an ominous threat. The Chief Justice decried a "litigation explosion" and denounced "legal activism" by judges and lawyers.[20] In 1973 a *Fortune* article, titled "The 'Legal Explosion' Has Left Business Shell-Shocked"[21] described a "new era in corporate law [that] began in 1966," an era in which the "big problem" is "the enormously increased legal exposure."[22] The arrival of "consumerism, environmentalism, and other forms of Naderism" and the increasing litigiousness of Americans[23] threaten to bring about "a society in which business is endlessly besieged by legal problems."[24] Critics accused the courts of overreaching and constituting an "imperial judiciary."[25]

In 1976, Chief Justice Burger organized a conference on "The Causes of Popular Dissatisfaction with the Administration of Justice," held on the seventieth anniversary of Roscoe Pound's celebrated address on that topic.[26] It was attended by the attorney general and solicitor general, prominent judges, distinguished practitioners, and influential legal academics. Speakers emphasized the burden placed on the courts, especially federal courts, by the increased caseload and ever expanding demands for intervention to address social problems. There was a general consensus that the courts should scale back their excursions into problem solving. Various speakers proposed to reduce the quantitative burdens by eliminating the diversity jurisdiction of the federal courts, abandoning the use of the jury in civil cases, and, in what proved to be the conference's truly influential paper, promoting the use of alternative dispute resolution.[27]

[18] *Journal of Insurance* (1978).
[19] The impact of these ads on juries is examined in Loftus (1979).
[20] Carruth 65 (1973).
[21] Id. at 166.
[22] Id. at 65.
[23] Id. at 157. The "five areas" that the author finds "matters of serious and widespread concern" are "antitrust, securities and stockholder matters, consumerism, environment, and fair employment practices." Surprisingly to one looking over her shoulder from thirty years later, her list does not include torts (except to the extent that topic may be represented by consumerism, environment, or fair employment).
[24] Id. at 157.
[25] Glazer (1975); van den Haag (1978); American Enterprise Institute (1978). Cf. Taylor (1981).
[26] Pound Conference (1976); Levin and Wheeler (1979). Needless to say there was little to connect the criticisms voiced there with "popular dissatisfaction." Unlike more recent meetings by legal establishment groups, which have tried to consult public opinion by surveys, focus groups, or representation of various stakeholder groups, the conferees ascertained public opinion by consulting their own experience and insights.
[27] Sander (1976) and its reception are widely regarded as a watershed for the subsequent flourishing of ADR.

By late 1970s, expansive legal remedies were seen as a problem not just for courts or for particular industries but as a systemic social problem. Laurence H. Silberman, later to become a federal judge, asking "Will Lawyering Strangle Democratic Capitalism?" recounts "the harmful impact of an ever expanding legal process on our society."[28] He details how "the legal process, because of its unbridled growth, has become a cancer which threatens the vitality of our forms of capitalism and democracy."[29] The profligate creation of new individual rights was weakening the "intermediate institutions [families, churches, schools, corporations, labor unions, and political parties] . . . that are indispensable pillars of a pluralistic democracy."[30] In addition "litigation of all kinds [was] becoming a major structural impediment to our economy."[31] Silberman declares that the bloated lawyer population "may confer a competitive advantage on our economic rivals in Japan and Europe."[32] In this view, the claiming, rights, and expectations that together constitute total justice are symptoms of pathology – a cancer that threatens vast social damage.

THE TURNABOUT

The apprehensions of Burger and Silverman are emblematic of a larger set of related changes in elite ideology, institutional practice, and popular culture that transformed the legal environment starting in the 1970s.[33] By the time *Total Justice* was published in 1985, the prevailing critique of the legal system was no longer "not enough justice" but "too much law."[34] In one sector after another, the expansion of remedies and protections for ordinary people slowed, halted, or even was reversed.

In the civil rights area, the enlargement of remedy came to an end and enforcement for existing rights diminished.[35] Although arguments against inclusion of African Americans in the nation's life remained taboo, courts, citing the virtues of color-blindness, became increasingly reluctant to countenance remedies for their past and present exclusion.

While opposition to civil rights was uneven and unproclaimed, resistance to enlarged tort accountability was massive and growing. In 1976 the term "tort reform" acquired its current sense of curtailing corporate accountability, reducing the scope of remedies, and making access to them more difficult.[36] At first tort reform was

---

[28] Silberman 44 (1978).
[29] Id. at 44.
[30] Id. at 18.
[31] Id. at 21.
[32] Id. at 21.
[33] Galanter (2002).
[34] Galanter (1994).
[35] Detlefsen (1991); Shull (1993).
[36] "The Overload on the Nation's Insurance System" (1976); "Generous Juries Cost You a Bundle" (1976). Earlier it was a shorthand expression for "reform of the tort system" in the sense of expanding remedies and accountability.

largely a response by insurers, but by the late 1980s, after the second product liability crisis, it gained a wider corporate constituency who bankrolled well-funded campaigns to depict American civil justice as a pathological system that was systematically victimizing businesses, local governments, scout troops, and expectant mothers.[37] This "litigation as social pathology" theme came to full flower with the appearance of the canonical anti-litigation texts, Peter Huber's *Liability* in 1988 and Walter Olson's *The Litigation Explosion* in 1991, both funded by the Manhattan Institute. Along the way, it animated tendentious reports from the Department of Justice and from the first President Bush's Council on Competitiveness.[38] Although the best available evidence overwhelmingly discredited the assertions of this literature, they were supported by folklore and powerfully reinforced by skewed media coverage.[39]

State legislatures adopted caps on recovery of noneconomic damages and punitive damages and a variety of other impediments to recovery. Judicial innovation in favor of tort claimants tapered off.[40] The lawyers who represented those claimants were demonized. Jurors became less generous, awards were smaller, and fewer claims were brought.[41] It was the end of what Rustad and Koenig call the "democratic expansionary era" of tort law, which they date from 1945 to 1980.[42]

Charles Knapp describes a comparable turn in contract law: "American contract law underwent a major evolution during roughly the middle half of the [twentieth] century" from classical "Dominance-of-the-Document formalism" to a law based on a "transactional and social perspective" that embodied "concepts of commercial reasonableness, good faith and fair dealing, and unconscionability."[43] The promulgation of the Restatement (Second) of Contracts in 1979, which was the high-water mark of the greening of contract law, was soon followed by a U-turn to a "New Conceptualism" that "embraced with fervor all the earlier-disdained incidents of classical formalism – the duty to read, the 'plain meaning' rule, a vigorous parol evidence rule, a high tolerance for 'puffing,' etc. – with the effect, intended or not, of reducing or eliminating any constraints on the activities of the drafters of form contracts."[44] With encouragement from the courts, those drafters soon discovered that adhesion contracts could be used to strong-arm claims into arbitration forums congenial to the drafting party. Mandatory arbitration clauses moved many claims of employees, customers, and other "little people" (in Leona Helmsley's famous phrase) out of the realm of accountability to

---

[37] Daniels and Martin (1995).
[38] United States Department of Justice (1986); President's Council on Competitiveness (1991).
[39] Haltom and McCann (2004); Galanter (1998).
[40] Henderson and Eisenberg (1990); Eisenberg and Henderson (1992).
[41] Daniels and Martin (2000, 2006).
[42] Rustad and Koenig 5 (2002).
[43] Knapp 766, 767, 772, 773 (2002). See also Hillman (1999); Mooney (1995).
[44] Knapp 774 (2002).

public standards in visible proceedings and in many cases entirely out of reach of remedy.[45]

The judicial blessing of arbitration was part of a broader endorsement of "alternative dispute resolution" (ADR) that accompanied a set of changes that redefined the role of the judge. In the period since *Total Justice* was published, judges have embraced "managerial judging," shifting their efforts to case management and promotion of settlements; hailed outsourcing to ADR forums; and multiplied summary judgments and other nontrial adjudication, contributing to the displacement of trials and the corresponding displacement of the jury.[46]

Other parts of the safety net have also become more abrasive rather than more protective. The consumer credit industry, freed by the deregulation of usury (with an assist from the Supreme Court's disallowance of state controls on out-of-state lenders)[47], promoted a vast increase in consumer debt: "Credit card debt . . . increased . . . from less than $10 billion in 1968 (inflation adjusted) to more than $600 billion in 2000."[48] Resort to bankruptcy likewise increased: "The U.S. personal bankruptcy rate . . . [rose] to a historically high level, from less than one per thousand population annually in the early 1970s to almost five per thousand population for the year ending September 30, 1997."[49] Warren and Tyagi report that "[n]early 90% [of bankrupt families] had been felled by a job loss, a medical problem, or a family breakup, or by some combination of all three."[50] Nevertheless the credit card industry conducted a sustained campaign, based on ersatz claims about the cost of bankruptcy, to reduce the protections for debtors.[51] In 2005 its efforts were crowned by passage of the ironically named Bankruptcy Abuse Prevention and Consumer Protection Act that bid fair to accomplish that reduction.[52] For those who turn to welfare rather than bankruptcy, another fancifully named act, The Personal Opportunity and Work Opportunity Reconciliation Act, reduces the protections afforded by public aid. [53] According to that act, welfare is no longer an "entitlement," but is limited by work requirements and a lifetime cap on the benefits an individual may receive.[54]

These developments on the civil side were paralleled by a major turn in criminal law, starting in the 1970s, away from rehabilitative principles and in the direction of harsh punishment and control.[55] David Garland describes the "sudden and

---

[45] Sternlight (2005).
[46] Resnik (1995, 2004); Burbank (2004); Hadfield (2004); Cohen and Smith (2004).
[47] *Marquette National Bank of Minneapolis v First of Omaha Service Corp.*, 439 U.S. 299 (1978).
[48] Warren and Tyagi 130 (2003).
[49] Ellis (1998).
[50] Warren and Tyagi 132 (2003).
[51] Warren (2002).
[52] Pub. L. 109-8, 118 Stat. 23 (2005)
[53] Pub. L. 104-193, 110 Stat. 2105 (1996).
[54] Handler and Hasenfeld (2007).
[55] Garland 8 (2001).

startling reversal" during the 1970s, a "sharp discontinuity" marked by an "accelerating movement away from the assumptions that shaped crime control and criminal justice for most of the twentieth century."[56] This new dispensation was manifested in harsher criminal penalties, mandatory sentencing, reduction of judicial discretion, and a shift of discretion from judges to prosecutors.[57] A massive increase in the prison population has been accompanied by curtailment of prisoners' legal recourse and increased judicial deference to the alleged administrative needs of prison officials.[58]

What were once seen as issues of a professional and technical character are now highly politicized.[59] The political discourse pivots on a "sense of crisis" that entails a "narrative of moral decline"[60] in which the virtuous and workable law of the good old days has been usurped and corrupted by activist judges, greedy lawyers, and self-pitying claimants. In each case the turnabout reveals a loss of confidence in government to promote and supply justice, a preference for retrenchment to modest aims that eschew promotion of solidarity or investment in public goods, and more reliance on markets and private providers.

By the end of the twentieth century, provision of legal services for the poor was a shadow of the vigorous and innovative lawyering of the years before publication of *Total Justice*. Funding of the Legal Services Corporation reached its high point (in constant dollars) in 1979 and fell by more than half by 2003.[61] Not only was funding cut, but Congress also imposed a long list of restrictions designed to confine representation to clients' day-to-day legal problems, rather than the "more general systemic problems of the client community."[62] Some of the cuts have been offset by increased pro bono efforts of the private bar, but overall disparities in legal services have widened rather than narrowed. The private bar devotes an increasing share of its effort to serving organizations rather than natural persons.[63] Lawyers who provide services to individuals enjoy lower prestige than their corporate counterparts.[64] Lawyers like those who helped deliver the advances in tort law and civil rights that Friedman commemorates have been demonized by the Right and are widely distrusted by the general public. The widening disparity in the provision of legal services mirrors the growth of inequality in American society, as income disparities have widened, the progressivity of taxation has declined,[65] and the safety net has frayed.[66]

---

[56] Id. at 3.
[57] Zlotnick (2004).
[58] Schlanger (2003); Sinema (2004); Bussert and Sickler (2005).
[59] Garland 13 (2001).
[60] Id. at 19, 195.
[61] Houseman and Perle 36 (2003).
[62] Id. at 34–7; Brennan Center for Justice (2001).
[63] Heinz et al. 41–4 (2005); Galanter 1381–7 (2006).
[64] Heinz et al. 85–6 (2005).
[65] Zelenak (2006).
[66] Phillips (2002).

TOTAL JUSTICE UN-DONE OR UNDONE

Some twenty-five years after the publication of *Total Justice* we may wonder whether we have crossed into a different world where total justice appears not as the pulse of history but as a now embattled legacy. In 1985 one could look back on a vista of a half-century of expanding nurturant law or at least the promise of it. Since then there has been a turn if not a reversal. Surely there have been several conspicuous extensions of the total justice principle, notably the flourishing of disability rights and the ascendant (although still controverted) gay rights. There has also been an expansion of concern with righting old wrongs[67] – at least for individual victims and for some groups, in particular Native Americans, but only grudgingly and fractionally for African Americans. Overall our more abundant law seems more hospitable to the claims and interests of organizations and less forgiving to individuals, particularly those in disfavored categories and without substantial resources like prisoners, welfare recipients, immigrants, and bankrupt debtors.

Like Friedman I prefer to believe that we are moving inexorably toward more ample justice. There is no evident slackening of the features that Friedman mentions as positively associated with total justice – mobility, interdependence, new technology, and a more ample capacity for control. All of these have continued their upward trajectory, so we have to look elsewhere to account for the faltering of total justice as an animating principle. There are many trends that are an uncomfortable fit with the ampler justice story.

In 1985 Friedman assumed that legalization was inescapable and would proceed in tandem with total justice and its equalizing redistributive thrust.[68] Legalization has certainly continued unabated.[69] The output of regulation has remained high,[70] the number of lawyers has continued to grow,[71] and the portion of the Gross Domestic Product spent on legal services has doubled since *Total Justice* was written.[72] Yet it is not evident that total justice has advanced at a similar pace.

If the faltering of total justice is not attributable to a slackening of the factors that Friedman views as its sources or companions, how can we account for it? First, there is the gathering strength of a competing super-principle that has a long and honored presence in our legal culture – individual responsibility/self-reliance. Even as total justice flourished, the individual responsibility theme remained a powerful limiting force. In his portrait of the legal culture of a rural Illinois county in the late 1970s, David Engel describes the way that individual responsibility attenuated expression of

---

[67] Galanter 2002.
[68] Friedman 148 (1985).
[69] Galanter (1992).
[70] Crews (2006).
[71] The lawyer population of the United States grew by 70% from 655,191 in 1985 (Carson 1 [2004]) to 1,116,967 in 2006 (American Bar Association, National Lawyer Population by State, http://www.abanet .org/marketresearch/2006_national%20lawyer_population_survey.pdf).
[72] Galanter 29 (2006).

the total justice theme.[73] The penetration of total justice norms was uneven and very thin. Individual responsibility themes animate the vast outpouring of criticism of contemporary law, from the McDonald's coffee case to bankruptcy reform. William Haltom and Michael McCann explain how ideas about individual responsibility "have been invoked . . . to stigmatize certain types of legally authorized rights claims by citizens."[74] They describe a "moral crusade" based on the "unabashed defense of core American values of individual responsibility and moral discipline," that has reinforced the "reigning common sense."[75]

Second, there is the increasing dominance of corporate entities in the legal/ political arena. They are more proficient legal actors than natural persons. As corporate actors populate the legal arena, "both popular news accounts and prominent pundits have reinforced inherited inclinations to blame social problems on pathologies of individual irresponsibility, negligence, and greed among plaintiffs or their attorneys obsessed with rights claiming rather than on incidents of corporate irresponsibility or the deficiencies of our public regulatory and insurance systems."[76] In the cultural residue of the McDonald's coffee case, Haltom and McCann find that "the interpretive narrative extolling individual responsibility has obliterated the narrative about defective products liability that motivated the plaintiff and persuaded the jury."[77]

The same heightened expectations of protection, remedy, and insulation from risk that Friedman celebrates as total justice are manifested not only by "have-not" victims but also by corporations, millionaires, and doctors who define themselves as the victims of excessive regulation, confiscatory taxes, and frivolous lawsuits. As total justice moves the frontier of remedy, it violates the sense of entitlement to previously enjoyed leeways and immunities. Those who resent enlarged accountability view themselves as "victims" entitled to relief. Paradoxically, the advance of total justice inspires a new set of actors to employ its rhetoric to impede or even roll back its extension.

On another level, we must appreciate how unsteady total justice is as an ideal. At one disarming point, Friedman observes that as a destination, "total justice is a mirage."[78] The mirage image is apt. Total justice is a direction, not a destination; it is indeed a mirage that shimmers and recedes before us.

The justice afforded by the measures that Friedman describes as total justice is often not "total" but embarrassingly partial. The tort system and law generally are rough instruments or vehicles for achieving justice. For example, the tort system only affords remedy against solvent injurers, it has high transaction costs, and it

---

[73] Engel (1983). See also Sanders (1987).
[74] Haltom and McCann (2004).
[75] Id. at 22, 108.
[76] Id. at 22–3.
[77] Id. at 214.
[78] Friedman 148 (1985).

overcompensates small losses and undercompensates catastrophic losses. The thrust for remedy is frequently diverted because of the presence of competing principles of responsibility and fault.

Even this limited total justice does not flow automatically from enhancement of the popular appetite for justice. Melvin Lerner points out that the psychological need to imagine a just world leads people to underperceive injustice; that is, to acquiesce in and maintain distinctions that violate fairness and equality. Insistence that it is a just world drives extensive rationalization of accepted practices and widespread resistance to enlarging the share of those who have least.[79]

Finally, even when there is advance toward total justice, it does not necessarily bring us to a condition of less injustice, for the same forces that fuel higher expectations of justice enlarge the realm of injustice as they amplify the human capacity for control and intervention. A group of bioethicists recently observed that

> [t]he boundary between the natural and the social, and between the realm of fortune and that of justice, is not static. What we have taken to be moral progress has often consisted in pushing back the frontiers of the natural, in bringing within the sphere of social control, and thereby within the domain of justice, what was previously regarded as the natural, and as merely a matter of good or ill fortune.[80]

As the scope of possible interventions broadens, the presence of avoidable bad things or the absence of achievable good things gives rise to new perceptions of injustice. So technology enlarges the supply of injustices as well as the capability to assuage them. Claims for the intervention of legal institutions are antithetical and compete for limited resources. Which injustices will be addressed and how effectively will depend on the ability of democratic politics to control the corporations and governmental bodies that manage the advances in human capability that drive the moving frontier of injustice.

Total justice is the view in our rear-view mirror. Looking back between the narrow walls of the canyon, we can see how high we have climbed from the valley floor. But surrounded by sheer cliffs hidden in the mists of the impenetrable future, we cannot be so certain that what lies ahead is an ascent to a still higher elevation.

REFERENCES

Ackard, Patrick J. (1992). Corporate Mobilization and Political Power: The Transformation of U.S. Economic Policy in the 1970s, 57 *Am. Sociol. Rev.* 597.

American Enterprise Institute (1978). *An Imperial Judiciary: Fact or Myth.* Transcript of a forum held December 12, 1978.

Aron, Nan (1989). *Liberty and Justice for All: PIL in the 1980s and Beyond.* Boulder: Westview Press.

---

[79] Lerner (1980); Dharmapapa et al. (2006).
[80] Buchanan et al. 83 (2000); cf. Shklar 5, 51–82 (1990).

Brennan Center for Justice (2001). *Hidden Agendas: What is Really behind Attacks on Legal Aid Lawyers.* New York: Brennan Center for Justice, NYU Law School.

Buchanan, Allen, Dan W. Brock, Norman Daniels, and Dan Wickler (2000). *From Chance to Choice: Genetics and Justice.* Cambridge: Cambridge University Press.

Burbank, Stephen B. (2004). Vanishing Trials and Summary Judgment in Federal Civil Cases: Drifting toward Bethlehem or Gomorrah? 1 *J. Empir. Legal Stud.* 591.

Bussert, Todd and Joel Sickler (2005). Grin and Bear It: Bureau of Prisons Update: More Beds, Less Rehabilitation, 29 *Champion* 42.

Carruth, Eleanore (1973). The "Legal Explosion" Has Left Business Shell-Shocked, 87(4) *Fortune* 65.

Carson, Clara N. (2004). *The Lawyer Statistical Report: The U.S. Legal Profession in 2000* Chicago: American Bar Foundation.

Cohen, Thomas H. and Steven K. Smith (2004). *Civil Trial Cases and Verdicts in Large Counties, 2001.* Washington, DC: Bureau of Justice Statistics Bulletin, April 2004.

Crews, Clyde W., Jr. (2006). *Ten Thousand Commandments: An Annual Snapshot of the Federal Regulatory State.* Washington, DC: Competitive Enterprise Institute.

Daniels, Stephen and Joanne Martin (1995). *Civil Justice and the Politics of Reform.* Evanston, IL: Northwestern University Press.

———— (2000). "The Impact That It Has Is between People's Ears:" Tort Reform, Mass Culture, and Plaintiffs' Lawyers, 50 *DePaul L. Rev.* 453.

———— (2006). Texas Plaintiffs' Practice in the Age of Tort Reform: Survival of the Fittest – It's Even More True Now, 51 *N.Y.L. Sch. L. Rev.* 285–320.

Defense Research Institute (1995). *The Injury Industry and Law Explosion.* Milwaukee: Defense Research Institue.

Detlefsen, Robert (1991). *Civil Rights under Reagan.* San Francisco: ICS Press.

Dharmapapa, Dhammika, Nuno Garoupa, and Richard H. McAdams (2006). *The Just World Bias and Hate Crimes Statutes.* University of Illinois College of Law, Illinois Law and Economics Working Papers Series, No. LE06-011.

Donahue, Charles (1980). The Future of the Concept of Property Predicted from Its Past, in J. R. Pennock and J. W. Chapman, eds., *Property: Nomos,* vol. XXII. New York: New York University Press.

Eisenberg, Theodore, and James A. Henderson, Jr. (1992). Inside the Quiet Revolution in Products Liability, 39 *UCLA L. Rev.* 731.

Ellis, Diane (1998). The Effect of Consumer Interest Rate Deregulation on Credit Card Volumes, Charge-Offs, and the Personal Bankruptcy Rate, 98-05 *Bank Trends.* Available at http://www.fdic.gov/bank/analytical/bank/bt_9805.html.

Engel, David (1983). The Oven Bird's Song: Insiders, Outsiders, and Personal Injuries in an American Community, 18 *Law & Soc'y Rev.* 551.

Epp, Charles (1998). *The Rights Revolution.* Chicago: University of Chicago Press.

Friedman, Lawrence M. (1985). *Total Justice.* New York: Russell Sage Foundation.

———— (2002). Legality and Its Discontents, in R. A. Kagan, M. Krygier, and K. Winston, eds., *Legality and Community: On the Intellectual Legacy of Philip Selznick.* Lanham, MD: Rowman & Littlefield.

Galanter, Marc (1992) . Law Abounding: Legalisation Around the North Atlantic, 55 Modern L. Rev. 1 (1992).

———— (1994). Predators and Parasites: Lawyer-Bashing and Civil Justice, 28 *Ga. L. Rev.* 633.

———— (1998). An Oil Strike in Hell: Contemporary Legends about the Civil Justice System, 40 *Ariz. L. Rev.* 717.

―――― (2002). Righting Old Wrongs, in Martha Minow, *Breaking the Cycles of Hatred: Memory, Law and Repair*, edited by Nancy Rosenblum. Princeton, NJ: Princeton University Press.

―――― (2004). The Vanishing Trial: An Examination of Trials and Related Matters in Federal and State Courts, 1 *J. Empir. Legal Stud.* 459.

―――― (2006). Planet of the APs: Reflections on the Scale of Law and Its Users, 53 *Buff. L. Rev.* 1369.

Garland, David (2001). *The Culture of Control: Crime and Social Order in Contemporary Society*. Chicago: University of Chicago Press.

Generous Juries Cost You a Bundle (1976). *Chemical Week*, Nov. 24, 1976, at 21.

Glazer, Nathan. (1975). Towards an Imperial Judiciary, 41 *Pub. Int.* 104 (Fall).

Hadfield, Gillian (2004). Where Have All the Trials Gone? Settlements, Nontrial Adjudications, and Statistical Artifacts in the Changing Disposition of Federal Civil Cases, 1 *J. Empir. Legal Stud.* 703.

Haltom, William and Michael McCann (2004). *Distorting the Law: Politics, Media and the Litigation Crisis*. Chicago: University of Chicago Press.

Handler, Joel F. and Yeheskel Hasenfeld (2007). *Blame Welfare, Ignore Poverty and Inequality*. New York: Cambridge University Press.

Heinz, John P., Robert L. Nelson, Rebecca L. Sandefur, and Edward O. Laumann (2005). *Urban Lawyers: The New Social Structure of the Bar*. Chicago: University of Chicago Press.

Henderson, James A., Jr. and Theodore Eisenberg (1990). The Quiet Revolution in Products Liability: An Empirical Study of Legal Change, 37 *UCLA L. Rev.* 479.

Hillman, Robert A. (1999). The "New Conservatism" in Contract Law and the Process of Legal Change, 40 *B.C. L. Rev.* 879.

Houseman, Alan W. and Linda E. Perle (2003). *Securing Equal Justice for All: A Brief History of Civil Legal Assistance in the United States*. Washington, DC: Center for Law and Social Policy.

Huber, Peter (1988). *Liability: The Legal Revolution and Its Consequences*. New York: Basic Books.

Hyneman, Charles S. (1962). *The Supreme Court on Trial*. New York: Atherton Press.

Journal of Insurance (1978). Special Issue on Litigation, 39(5).

Insurance Information Institute (1977). *The Product Liability Problem: Proposals for Solutions through Tort Reform*. New York: Insurance Information Institute.

Kerr, Robert L. (2002). Reasserting the Voice of Big Business in the Marketplace of Ideas: Analysis of Legal and Media Discourse Significant to the 1970s Empowerment of the Right and Practice of Corporate Speech, PhD diss., University of North Carolina.

Knapp, Charles L. (2002). Taking Contracts Private: The Quiet Revolution in Contract Law, 71 *Fordham L. Rev.* 761.

Lerner, Melvin J. (1980). *The Belief in a Just World: A Fundamental Delusion*. New York: Plenum Press.

Levin, A. Leo and Russell R. Wheeler, eds. (1979). *The Pound Conference: Perspectives on Justice in the Future*. St. Paul, MN: West Publishing.

Loftus, Elizabeth (1979). Insurance Advertising and Jury Awards, 65 *A.B.A. J.* 68.

Lytle, Clifford M. (1968). *The Warren Court and Its Critics*. Tucson: University of Arizona Press.

Mooney, Ralph James (1995). The New Conceptualism in Contract Law, 74 *Or. L. Rev.* 1131.

Olson, Walter K. (1991). *The Litigation Explosion: What Happened When America Unleashed the Lawsuit*. New York: Dutton.

The Overload on the Nation's Insurance System (1976). *Business Week*, Sep. 6, at 46.

Pertschuk, Michael (1982). *Revolt against Regulation: The Rise and Pause of the Consumer Movement*. Berkeley: University of California Press.

Phillips, Kevin (2002). *Wealth and Democracy: A Political History of the American Rich*. New York: Broadway Books.

Pound Conference (1976). National Conference on the Causes of Popular Dissatisfaction with the Administration of Justice, 70 *Federal Rules Decisions* 79.

Powell, Lewis F., Jr. (1971). Confidential Memorandum/Attack on American Free Enterprise System, addressed to Mr. Eugene B. Sydnor, Jr., Chairman, Education Committee, U.S. Chamber of Commerce, dated Aug. 23, 1971. Available at http://64.233.167.104/search?q=cache:cA-SjDqQEIAJ:reclaimdemocracy.org/corporate_accountability/powell_memo_lewis.html+Powell+Sydnor+1971&hl=en&ct=clnk&cd=1&gl=us&client=netscape-pp

President's Council on Competitiveness (1991). *Agenda for Civil Justice Reform in America*. Washington, DC: President's Council on Competitiveness.

Reich, Charles (1964). The New Property, 73 *Yale L.J.* 733.

Resnik, Judith (1995). Many Doors? Closing Doors? Alternative Dispute Resolution and Adjudication, 10 *Ohio St. J. of Disp. Resol.* 211.

———— (2004). Migrating, Morphing, and Vanishing: The Empirical and Normative Puzzles of Declining Trial Rates in Courts, 1 *J. Empir. Legal Stud.* 783.

Rustad, Michael L. and Thomas H. Koenig (2002), Taming the Tort Monster: The American Civil Justice System as a Battleground of Social Theory, 68 *Brooklyn L. Rev.* 1.

Sander, Frank (1976). Varieties of Dispute Processing, 70 *Federal Rules Decisions* 111.

Sanders, Joseph (1987). The Meaning of the Law Explosion: On Friedman's *Total Justice*, *Am. B. Found. Res. J.* 601–15.

Schlanger, Margo (2003). Inmate Litigation, 116 *Harv. L. Rev.* 1555.

Shapiro, Fred R. (1996). The Most Cited Law Review Articles Revisited, 71 *Chi.-Kent L. Rev.* 751.

Shapiro, Irving S. with Carl B. Kaufmann (1984). *America's Third Revolution: Public Interest and the Private Role*. New York: Harper & Row.

Shklar, Judith N. (1990). *The Faces of Injustice*. New Haven: Yale University Press.

Shull, Steven A. (1993). *A Kinder, Gentler Racism? The Reagan-Bush Civil Rights Legacy*. Armonk, NY: M. E. Sharpe.

Silberman. Laurence (1978). Will Lawyering Strangle Democratic Capitalism? *Regulation* March–April, 15.

Sinema, Kyrsten (2004). Overton v. Bazzetta: How the Supreme Court Used Turner to Sound the Death Knell for Prisoner Rehabilitation, 36 *Ariz. St. L.J.* 471.

Southworth, Ann (2005). Conservative Lawyers and the Contest over the Meaning of "Public Interest Law," 52 *UCLA L. Rev.* 1223.

Sternlight, Jean R. (2005). Creeping Mandatory Arbitration: Is it Just? 57 *Stan. L. Rev.* 1631.

Su, Tie-ting, Alan Neustadtl, and Dan Clawson (1995). Business and the Conservative Shift: Corporate PAC Contributions, 1976–1986, 76 *Soc. Sci. Q.* 20.

Taylor, Stuart, Jr. (1981). Attorney General Outlines Campaign to Rein in Courts, *New York Times*, Oct. 30.

Top of the News: Red Light on Litigation (1971). *Trial*, July-Aug. at 50.

United States Department of Justice (1986). *Report of the Tort Policy Working Group on the Causes, Extent and Policy Implications of the Current Crisis in Insurance Availability and Affordability* (Richard K. Willard, Chairman, Feb. 1986). Washington, DC: U.S. Department of Justice.

Van Den Haag, Ernest (1978). The Growth of the Imperial Judiciary, 4 *Pol'y Rev.* 57.

Warren, Elizabeth (2002). The Market for Data: The Changing Role of Social Sciences in Shaping the Law, 2002 *Wis. L. Rev.* 1.

Warren, Elizabeth and Amelia Warren Tyagi (2003). *The Two-Income Trap: Why Middle Class Mothers and Fathers Are Going Broke*. New York: Basic Books.

Zelenak, Lawrence A. (2006). The Declining Progressivity of the Federal Income Tax, in Paul Carrington and Trina Jones, eds. *Law and Class in America: Trends since the Cold War*. New York: New York University Press.

Zlotnick, David M. (2004). Shouting into the Wind: District Court Judges and Federal Sentencing Policy, 9 *Roger Williams L. Rev.* 645.

8

"Total Justice" and Political Conservatism

Robert A. Kagan

In *Total Justice* (1985), Lawrence M. Friedman describes a dramatic change in American legal culture. Friedman defines legal culture as ordinary people's views about what law is, should be, and should provide. Over the last century or so, he contends, American legal culture has come to include a widespread demand for "total justice." In turn that demand has generated thoroughgoing change in the law and legal life of the country. One strand in the legal culture of total justice is "a general expectation of recompense" for arbitrarily inflicted devastating losses, particularly accidentally imposed personal injuries. A second strand is the "expectation of fair treatment." Friedman argues that Americans increasingly expect nondiscriminatory treatment and some version of "due process of law" when institutions deny them some important benefit. They expect fair treatment not only in courts and government agencies but also "in all settings: in hospitals and prisons, in schools, on the job, in apartment buildings."[1]

In its focus on popular legal culture, *Total Justice* reiterates a theme that runs through the entire library of Friedman's books and articles: At least in the United States, developments in popular legal culture, much more than the theorizing of legal scholars and judges, are the primary drivers of legal change. In turn, the evolution of legal culture is driven primarily by social changes that affect the day-to-day texture of life. Thus the most powerful insights in the book concern the social changes that have engendered a popular legal culture attuned to total justice.

The first of these social changes has been the ongoing march of scientific and technological change. By the end of the nineteenth century, Friedman writes,

> A new kind of society had developed in the West: the society of technology, industry, science, machines. Science and machines gave people tremendous control over

[1] Friedman 43 (1985).

time, distance, and destiny. . . . Each advance in science and technology seemed to increase the possibility of control – over nature, over the conditions of life.[2]

Scientific and technological changes could hardly help but influence legal culture:

People came to feel that it was possible to control situations of peril or need – that government inspectors, for example, could make sure canned meat was not rancid or poisonous. This was followed by a concrete demand that the state should exercise that control. . . . More important perhaps, they changed the very definition of "legal" in people's minds, changed ideas about . . . what was feasible through law. This in turn encouraged a fresh round of demands. The process spiraled in the direction of more law, more state intervention.[3]

Throughout the twentieth century, businesses, hospitals, and governments increasingly were perceived to have access to technologies, research methods, and organizational capabilities that would enable them to identify and minimize sources of harm at reasonable expense. Because they *could* prevent and compensate harm, it made sense for the law to *require* them to do so.[4]

Friedman points out that another enormously important social change was the diffusion of casualty insurance, a remarkable social invention that enables the fortunate, through relatively small policy payments, to compensate the unfortunate. The widespread availability of liability insurance, *Total Justice* tells us, revolutionized the tort law system.[5] It freed judges and juries to compel businesses, hospitals, professionals, and government bodies to fully compensate victims of negligently inflicted personal injury without being driven into bankruptcy. It made the pursuit of compensation the central focus of twentieth-century tort law, reinforcing a "general expectation of recompense."

Thus in the first half of the twentieth century, every state enacted workers' compensation acts, which required employers to subscribe to insurance policies that

---

[2] Id. at 42.

[3] Id. at 42–3.

[4] Relating this idea to the rise of the regulatory state, I wrote:

Protect us, O Government, from harm! Protect us, surrounded as we are by the side effects of capitalist production and modern technologies. For we dwell in fear that we and our children will ingest or inhale invisible chemical toxins. Agricultural chemicals, mechanized logging, industrial pollutants, and massive construction projects threaten our remaining forests, marshes, and streams. We are vulnerable to dangerous machines and products, deceitful promoters, and all kinds of human error. In the name of human decency, O Government, protect us from harm! Kagan 181 (2001).

Versions of this fervent prayer are voiced every month in legislative hearing rooms, television programs, and the newsletters of environmental organizations. In democracies, governments take those prayers seriously. They commission studies which analyze risks and they enact additional regulatory obligations into law.

[5] Friedman 59–63 (1985).

would compensate workers for injuries "arising out of employment," regardless of fault. In the 1960s, courts drastically curtailed the defenses of contributory negligence and assumption of risk and abandoned long-standing doctrines of charitable and governmental immunity from tort liability. Courts changed evidentiary rules to facilitate medical malpractice claims, imposed "strict liability" for product defects, expanded property owners' liability to those injured in their facilities, and expanded the right to recover compensation for accident-related emotional distress and loss of consortium.[6] State judicial systems adopted the lawyer-driven pretrial discovery rules embodied in the Federal Rules of Civil Procedure, which strengthened the ability of plaintiffs' lawyers to gather evidence concerning the defendant's liability. Other rulings made it easier for entrepreneurial lawyers to aggregate the claims of large numbers of accident or defective-product victims into massive class action suits.[7] The Supreme Court held that laws and regulations that barred advertising by lawyers amounted to unconstitutional restrictions on freedom of speech. Ads for tort lawyers blossomed on bus-stop benches and late-night television. Plaintiffs' lawyers developed sophisticated methods of "ambulance chasing," such as holding press conferences near the sites of large accidents and chemical spills and deploying representatives to advertise for and sign up potential claimants for product liability suits.

Casualty insurance also provided the model for governmentally provided social insurance programs, which Friedman sees as another manifestation of the expectation of total justice.[8] The parallel is clear. Governments' enhanced capacity to raise and distribute money via taxation means that government *can* alleviate the plight of those threatened with impoverishment by bank failures, unemployment, physical inability to work, crop failures, natural disasters, and huge medical bills. Hence it is not unreasonable to demand that government *should* enact laws establishing social insurance programs that do just that. And so government has, profoundly changing both law and politics in the twentieth century, indeed blurring the line between the two, as law came to be viewed as a mode of social engineering and policy implementation. Legal scholars, educators, lawyers, and judges gradually came to accept what Philippe Nonet and Philip Selznick[9] later labeled a transition from "autonomous law" to "responsive law" – a mode of legal thought that demands attention to the social consequences of law and legal procedures. Indeed, Nonet and Selznick view the shift to responsive law as a "strategy of legitimation" in dealing with a legal culture that expects something like total justice, not merely formal legal rights that are too expensive or difficult to actually enjoy.

---

[6] Ursin 243–4 (1981); Priest (1985); Sugarman 456–70 (1999).
[7] Coffee 1356–8 (1995); Priest 461 (1985).
[8] Friedman 76 (1985).
[9] Nonet and Selznick (2002).

THE CRITIQUE OF *TOTAL JUSTICE*:
HOW PERVASIVE, HOW ENDURING?

Two related but analytically separate critiques of *Total Justice* might be made. The first would question whether there really was such widespread acceptance of the idea of total justice and the general expectation of compensation – in 1985, when the book was published, or even in the 1960s and '70s, a high point for expansion of constitutional rights, regulatory protections, liability law, and social benefit programs. The second critique, assuming that Friedman's assumptions about the breadth of support for total justice were correct, would question how deep, solid, or enduring that support has been, particularly in light of the shift toward conservatism in American politics and American law in the last two decades. This section and the next examine those critiques and assess the extent to which *Total Justice* transcends them, focusing primarily on the "general expectation of compensation" strand of total justice and the related politics of tort law in the United States.

How Pervasive? Who Does and Does Not Believe in Total Justice?

Reviewing Friedman's book, Joseph Sanders wrote,

> On the day I began to read . . . *Total Justice*, the newspapers reported that the widow of Challenger astronaut Michael Smith had brought a $15 million suit against NASA under the Federal Tort Claims Act, alleging negligence in the launching of the rocket. Two days later we had some friends over, and the story came up. Our guests, Mr. and Mrs. Bell, are in their eighties. . . . They have spent much of their lives in the Far East, where Mr. Bell has worked for oil companies. They both opposed the Smith claim. They agreed that NASA had not performed as it ought, but to paraphrase them, when one gets on top of a machine like the shuttle one knows one's life is at risk. . . .

> Approximately two years ago Sue Titus Reid, a law professor at the University of Tulsa, gave a talk . . . [that suggested that] the law, recognizing that certain people are relatively undeterrable, was seeking out individuals and organizations whose behavior might be altered by sanctions. One key example was the movement to extend liability to social hosts who continue to serve obviously intoxicated guests when they know the guest may later operate an automobile. . . .

> Reid spoke to an audience primarily of faculty and graduate students in sociology, a group collectively far removed from the Bells in terms of their age, ethnicity, socioeconomic status, and politics. Their response to this trend in tort law, however, was not much different. The reactions ran from neutrality to outrage.[10]

[10] Sanders 601–2 (1987).

These reactions led Sanders to argue that Friedman's account of the rise of attitudes of total justice in American legal culture – a claim that Friedman cited no opinion poll data to bolster – was, at a minimum, overstated. Clearly, other attitudes were widespread.

The divergence might be viewed in terms of political scientist Aaron Wildavsky's typology of competing political cultures. Wildavsky contended that all political cultures, rooted in basic forms of social interaction, can be viewed in terms of four ideal types – fatalism, competitive individualism, egalitarianism, and "hierarchy" (orderly governance by informed rulers).[11] He argued that most modern polities include adherents of each of those contending political cultures – and of course many who intuitively subscribe to a mix or balance of those preferences.

Applying the typology to the doctrinal expansion of American tort law in the 1960s and '70s, Polisar and Wildavsky noted that, from the standpoint of power politics, this transformation seems puzzling.[12] There was no organized political movement to change tort law throughout the nation, and the state supreme judges who forged the new doctrines generally were not very susceptible to direct political pressure. Thus legal scholars' accounts of those developments concentrate on the theories and influence of particular legal scholars (such as Robert Keeton, Fleming James, William Prosser, and Guido Calabresi) and of certain creative judges (such as Roger Traynor of the California Supreme Court). These scholars and judges theorized that imposing strict liability for harmful products on manufacturers would be more effective and economically efficient than the traditional negligence standard in reducing the sum of accident costs and accident prevention costs, while spreading the cost of prevention and compensation to all users of those products.[13] That rationale exemplifies Wildavsky's category of "hierarchical" governance – a belief system, one might imagine, that would be congenial to highly educated law professors who are committed to rationalizing the law for social betterment.

Yet how can one explain the acceptance of those theories by the politically and educationally diverse ex-politicians who served as state court judges and by the politicians who acquiesced in the judicial expansion of tort liability? Wildavsky's answer is that in the 1960s, as the civil rights, environmental, and anti-Vietnam War movements attacked both government and capitalism, adherents of the egalitarian, populist strain in American culture gained influence,[14] attacking inequalities of many kinds. The judges, lawyers, and law professors who led the revolution in American tort law, Wildavsky argued, were members of the same class of educated,

---

[11] Wildavsky (1990).
[12] Polisar and Wildavsky (1989).
[13] Ursin (1981); Priest (1985).
[14] Interestingly, Friedman relates the growth of a legal culture of total justice to a decline in fatalism – one of Wildavsky's categories – as insurance, technological change, scientific change, and the growth in the organizational capacity and wealth of corporations and governments seem to make the causes of accidents and illnesses more understandable and preventable, and the harms more affordably compensable.

elite activists that produced a simultaneous, equality-tinged revolution in civil rights law, constitutional law (criminal defendants' rights, electoral redistricting, abortion rights), regulatory law (environmental regulation, consumer protection regulation), and administrative law. From this standpoint, the revolution in American tort law was not the product of the spread of popular demands for total justice. Rather, it reflected the political agenda of adherents of a particular political and legal culture, one that endorsed notions of legal responsibility favored by egalitarians rather than by individualists.

Still, in Wildavsky's analysis, the United States remained a *mix* of political cultures. At the level of private morality and popular culture, he suggested that a traditional individualistic vision of responsibility retained a substantial hold, as exemplified by Joseph Sanders' friends, the Bells, and the Midwestern sociology students who opposed tort liability for social hosts. From that perspective, the intensification of tort law in the 1960s and '70s, pushed by professional elites, moved tort doctrine and practice toward an egalitarian ethos with which a great many Americans were not comfortable.

More generally, Wildavsky might argue, Friedman's picture of American legal culture, although not untrue, is only a partial view. It neglects other widely held political attitudes, such as distrust of government regulatory bureaucracies, opposition to tax increases, and a preference for policies and laws that favor economic freedom and growth rather than governmental control and redistribution. Consequently, it could be argued that conservative individualism in the American electorate has been a strong brake on any legal train that sought to speed toward total justice. Indeed most of the big legal changes mentioned by Friedman occurred only in three short historical bursts of political activity – the workers' compensation laws generated by the Progressive Movement, the social insurance and labor legislation of the New Deal, and the extraordinary outpouring in 1960s and early 1970s of civil rights and regulatory legislation and of judicial activism in constitutional and tort law. It might be argued that this pattern suggests the causal importance not of a broadly endorsed legal culture of total justice but of particular moments of elite-led political activism.

The brake of conservative values also seems evident in the huge gaps, delays, and resistances to converting total justice ideas into law. Even in 1964, after a Democratic landslide, Congress mustered only a bare majority to pass the Medicare bill – which, since President Truman proposed it in 1949, had been blocked by objections that it represented a dangerous step toward socialism.[15] Compared to the welfare states of Western Europe, for example, the entitlements that American governments – state and federal – guarantee for the elderly, for impecunious unwed mothers and children, for the unemployed, for the disabled, and for the sick are significantly less comprehensive and less generous, as are workers' rights to a decent minimum wage, maternal leave, paid holidays, severance pay, child care, and protections

[15] Blumenthal and Morone (2005).

against arbitrary dismissal.[16] For all its liberal activism in the 1960s and '70s, the Supreme Court declined the invitation when reformers asked for rulings establishing a constitutional right to "subsistence"[17] or decent housing.[18]

In terms of "the general expectation of compensation" for personal injury, American law has fallen far short of the idea of enterprise liability that inspired the workers' compensation acts, in which any injury arising out of an enterprise's activity is compensable without proof of the enterprise's fault. In the United States, unlike some European countries, the workers' compensation model has not been extended to cover motor accidents on the way to and from work or to injuries from medical procedures and pharmaceuticals.[19] Notwithstanding some movement toward "strict liability," American tort plaintiffs still must present evidence indicating that the defendant company or governmental body was in some sense at fault.[20] That means that lawsuits are contentious, costly, and risky to pursue, which in turn means that most victims of medical malpractice or product injuries or parking lot muggings do not file claims and do not recover any compensation from their injurors.[21] Total justice indeed!

How Enduring? Where Is Total Justice in a Conservative Era?

In 1985, when *Total Justice* was published, Ronald Reagan was president, having been elected in 1980 after a campaign attacking "overregulation" of American business. A majority of the justices on the U.S. Supreme Court were Republicans; liberal justices Brennan and Marshall soon would be replaced by more conservative judges. In the 1990s, Democratic president Bill Clinton, presumably addressing the median voter, proclaimed that the "era of big government was over," a point underlined by the defeat of his plan for universal health care coverage. The 1994 election inaugurated 14 years of Republican control of Congress and led to a 1996 federal law limiting welfare rights for poor families. From 2001 to 2008, a stridently conservative Republican administration dominated congressional and regulatory agency agendas as well as the nomination of federal judges, employing rhetoric that showed little fear of being punished at the polls for failing to advance the agenda of total justice. Nor in that period did national political leaders feel compelled by popular attitudes to respond meaningfully to the sharp decline in federal employer-paid health insurance for workers[22] or to the reduced certainty of employer-provided pension guarantees.[23]

---

[16] Wilensky (2002); McFate et al. (1995).
[17] *Dandridge v Williams*, 397 U.S. 471 (1970).
[18] *Lindsey v Normet*, 405 U.S. 56 (1972).
[19] Kagan 129 (2001).
[20] Bell and O'Connell 32 (1997).
[21] Saks 1147 (1992); Abel 448–51 (1987).
[22] Hacker (2002).
[23] Id.

All this could be interpreted to mean that the expectations of total justice discerned by Friedman had only shallow roots in American legal and political culture and were devoid of influence when the political winds began to blow in a conservative direction. In *Distorting the Law*, William Haltom and Michael McCann go a step further, arguing that in recent decades political conservatives have effectively transformed the culture of total justice.[24] They show how conservative activists generated scholarship and communication networks that emphasize often-distorted tales of a tort system run amok (e.g., the McDonald's hot coffee spill case). The news media spread these anti-tort tales, while neglecting sociolegal scholars' more realistic portrait of the tort system. The upshot, Haltom and McCann contend, is that the conservative tort reformers have dominated the social construction of the tort law system in the mass media, mass culture, and political debate. Hence, they argue, far from emphasizing the plight of the injured, corporate heedlessness, and the right to compensation, popular legal culture now emphasizes the importance of individual responsibility and the irresponsibility of the tort law system.

The anti-tort campaign has had an impact on law. Since the mid-1980s, a majority of state legislatures have enacted "tort reform" laws that impose limits on large money damage awards, curtail joint and several liability, and in general seek to discourage tort litigation. Business interests made sizable contributions supporting a 1986 ballot measure that resulted in the ouster of liberal California Supreme Court justice Rose Bird, even though plaintiffs' lawyers had contributed $400,000 to her retention campaign.[25] In subsequent years, the California Supreme Court issued a number of rulings that chipped away at the 1960s doctrinal reforms that sought to impose liability on the entities that could most efficiently prevent accidents.[26] Here, too, the voice of total justice has scarcely been heard from, as if it has faded from prominence in both law and politics.

The conservative tort reform campaign described in *Distorting the Law* probably has reduced the pursuit of total justice in practice. In Franklin County, Ohio, with a population of more than 1 million (including Ohio's capital city, Columbus), the number of product liability and medical malpractice cases declined through the 1990s to hardly a trickle each year; defendants won most jury verdicts in such cases, and when plaintiffs won, the amounts awarded declined.[27] Daniels and Martin's study of plaintiffs' lawyers in Texas indicates that the conservative media campaign has made jurors more skeptical about lawsuits and stingier in their awards for pain and suffering – and hence has led insurance companies to be tougher and compelled plaintiffs lawyers to eschew personal injury cases in which an accident victim's injuries are not so serious.[28] Valerie Hans, after interviewing civil case jurors,

[24] Haltom and McCann (2004).
[25] Wold and Culver (1987).
[26] Sugarman 472 (1999).
[27] Merritt and Barry (1999).
[28] Daniels and Martin (2004).

concludes that news media and conservative politicians' denunciations of the "out of control" tort law system have made them more skeptical of injured plaintiffs' claims and more reluctant to make generous damage awards[29] – another bit of evidence that inclinations toward total justice, assuming they once were prevalent, have faded.

TOTAL JUSTICE LIVES!

Deep vs. Surface Change

In *Total Justice*, Friedman pays little attention to the particular political moments, electoral shifts, judicial appointments, or interest groups that trigger legal change. His causal model is (a) social change → (b) change in legal culture → (c) change in law and legal practices. The long-term social and attitudinal changes laid out in *Total Justice* are akin to the deep oceanic currents and temperature changes produced by an El Nino or by global warming, whereas the conservative critiques are more like storms that create turbulence at the surface the sea: They focus on short-term political influences on movement from (b) to (c) and are about the pace and constancy of change. In contrast, *Total Justice* is not precise about the pace of change or about the timing and mechanisms of (b)'s influence on (c). Friedman simply assumes that those linkages will be made, sooner or later. That might indeed be seen as an omission in his account, as is his limited attention to the power of competing values in American legal culture. Yet such omissions are not fatal to *Total Justice*'s larger point about the long-term, if wavering, trend toward total justice in both culture and law.

Friedman acknowledges that the spread of the total justice culture is neither complete nor constant. He notes that there are "many holes and gaps in these 'general' expectations, and certainly in the state of the law."[30] Friedman also points out that significant changes in social attitudes and law often trigger resistance and backlash. The legal system's steps toward meeting the general expectation of justice and recompense have occurred "not without protest, not without countermovement."[31] He would not expect people like Joseph Sanders' elderly friends to abandon their ideas about "assumption of the risk" as soon as the courts abandoned that defense. From Friedman's perspective, a "lean" toward total justice in the general legal culture does not guarantee a verdict for the plaintiff in every personal injury case that goes to trial. He could agree with Wildavsky that the law professors and reformist judges who wrought the great changes in tort law in the 1960s and '70s were leaping ahead of the ideas of the median voter. Yet Friedman also could point out that American law professors and judges did not advocate those changes in the late nineteenth century

---

[29] Hans (2000).
[30] Friedman 75–6 (1985).
[31] Id. at 5.

and he could explain why not: The legal elite's 1960s idea that tort law should be reformulated to encourage socially efficient risk reduction and cost spreading reflects the twentieth century social changes underscored in *Total Justice* – the ready availability of insurance, the faith in organizational and technical capacities to identify and control hazards, and the idea that law can and should be wielded as a tool of social engineering.

Nor does Friedman suggest that law has *constantly* moved toward total justice. In his model of legal change, such moves would likely come in bursts, when the tensions between social expectations and current law are greatest – such as during the Great Depression and the sociopolitical turmoil of the 1960s. Again, the key point in *Total Justice* is that the groundwork for those sudden, sweeping legal changes had been laid by the two great social changes discussed in the book – the growing capacity of governments to undertake such programs when the need for them is viewed as great and the growing tendency in legal and political discourse to define governmental and legal failure to respond to such needs as unjust. Those changes cause legal culture, law, and legal practice to "bend toward the norm [of total justice] like plants bending and growing toward the light."[32] Conservative wind gusts can periodically bend the plant in the other direction, but they cannot reverse the fundamental social and attitudinal changes discussed in *Total Justice*.

How Total Justice Limits Conservative Politics

There is validity to the critique that *Total Justice* neglects other values that are tightly woven into American legal culture – such as a preference for entrepreneurial liberty and low taxes, mistrust of government, and an emphasis on individual as well as collective responsibility – preferences that restrain the extent to which the law institutionalizes total justice ideals. Yet it is equally important to note the persistence of a total justice element in American political and legal culture that operates as a brake on politically *conservative* law reforms and sometimes pushes Republican politicians to *endorse* legal protections of the kind discussed in *Total Justice*.

Thus, notwithstanding the recent conservative trend in American politics and law, American presidents and governors, Democrat or Republican, still hasten to proclaim official disaster areas in the wake of hurricanes and floods, rushing compensatory payments and loans to devastated communities, families, and businesses. Responding to arguments keyed to the themes of total justice, Republican president George H. W. Bush signed two major pieces of legislation that deliberately *expanded* the role of litigation in policy implementation in the United States – the Americans with Disabilities Act (1990), which is structured to rely primarily on private lawsuits, not administrative regulation, to bring about compliance,[33] and

[32] Id. at 67.
[33] Burke (2002).

the Civil Rights Reform Act of 1991, which, by authorizing larger damage awards, was expressly designed to make it more profitable for plaintiffs' lawyers to take on and litigate discrimination cases.[34] In 1994, newly victorious congressional Republicans were unable to enact the sweeping environmental regulation reforms promised in their "Contract with America," and since that unpleasant political experience, Republican Congresses have not enacted any significant revisions of major federal environmental protection laws. Political support for major governmental programs to aid families threatened with income loss – Social Security, Medicare, and Medicaid – has remained strong.[35] Thus a conservative George W. Bush administration felt politically compelled to add prescription drug coverage (however inadequate) to Medicare and, in the face of broad public opposition, backed away from proposals to replace Social Security, in part, with private savings accounts. The machinery of due process that, beginning in the 1960s, was built into local criminal justice systems, social benefit administrations, schools, corporate personnel systems, and land use permitting processes continues to operate unabated and basically unchallenged.

Of course Republicans have pushed for more conservative policies on many fronts and, except in some especially liberal states, have declined to enact laws that would better fulfill expectations for social justice[36] while foreclosing movement in that direction by cutting tax rates. Yet political conservatives have not directly challenged the core ideas discussed in *Total Justice*. In the realm of social insurance and regulation, they have sought primarily to increase efficiencies or limit rising costs of existing programs, rather than modify the programs' basic goals. The 1996 federal welfare reform law, endorsed by Democratic president Bill Clinton, basically sought to restructure aid to poor families to reduce the incidence of "moral hazard" and encourage employment, not to eliminate all welfare rights. Those efforts are not inconsistent with Friedman's explication of the idea of total justice, which he does not define as systematically egalitarian. He does not contend that the desire for total justice will always and in all cases trump other values, such as efficiency or liberty

---

[34] Farhang (2010).

[35] According to 2000 poll data, more than 90% of respondents, even in "red states" (that voted for George W. Bush in the 2000 election), favored expanding Medicare to cover prescription drugs, and two-thirds (including 64% in "red states") answered "yes" to a question asking if the United States should 'do whatever it takes to protect the environment.' Fiorina 20 (2005). More than twice as many respondents thought the then-existing federal government budgetary surplus should be used to bolster Social Security and Medicare than felt that it should be given back to the public in the form of reduced taxes. Id. The burden of Fiorina's persuasive book is that "[t]here is little evidence that Americans' ideological or policy *positions* are more polarized today than they were two or three decades ago, although their *choices* often seem to be. The explanation is that the political figures American evaluate are more polarized." Id. at 8.

[36] In terms of welfare state policies, conservatives mostly have sought to reduce program costs and some forms of medical coverage through low-visibility budget decisions, rather than taking the political risk of seeking substantial legislative revision. Pierson (1994, 2000); Hacker (2002, 2004). New legal protections have not been enacted to deal with job loss caused by downsizing and outsourcing. Nor, as this is written, have governments (except in Massachusetts) mandated employer-provided health insurance, even as coverage, previously brought about by market pressures, has been eroding.

or the desire for lower taxes. If an average American believes in total justice, she still could (and should) rationally want laws that deter those who unjustifiably exploit government benefit-providing programs.

Presumably our average American would think the same of those who file legally unfounded or exaggerated cases in the courts. She could simultaneously believe in total justice and believe that the current American tort system is a terrible way of fulfilling the "general expectation of compensation" because its costliness and uncertainty prevent most injured people from suing or obtaining compensation, encourage many others to file padded claims,[37] produce shockingly large awards in other cases, and allow lawyers to extract extraordinary transaction costs.[38] Yet she probably would oppose any "reforms" that threaten to undermine the tort system's ability to punish and deter clearly negligent or heedless businesses or governmental bodies or to compensate those who suffered serious injury as a result of such negligence or indifference.[39]

Conservative tort reformers certainly have acted as if a majority of voters shared a Jones-like belief in the "general expectation of compensation." The scores of tort reform bills enacted by state legislatures and the handful enacted by Congress have not *significantly* weakened the tort system. Rather, the conservative reforms have focused primarily on measures that might be acceptable to believers in total justice – such as reducing the incidence of "frivolous" or "unnecessary" claims (e.g., by imposing costs on plaintiffs who turn down settlement offers that turn out to have been reasonable or changing the collateral source rule to prevent "double" recovery), and imposing caps on nonmonetary damages and punitive damages to introduce more predictability into an erratic system. Conservative tort reformers generally have not sought to change core tort liability principles.[40]

---

[37] A careful study by the RAND Institute for Civil Justice Institute led the authors to the astonishing estimate that "about one-third of the automobile industry medical costs submitted to insurers appear to be excess." RAND Institute 1 1995; Carroll et al. (1995).

[38] Kagan (2001).

[39] Hans (2000). Thus in her extensive interviews with jurors in civil cases, Valerie Hans (2000) found them to be both skeptical toward tort plaintiffs' efforts to shift responsibility to business corporations and inclined to hold business corporations to higher standards of care, because of their greater capacity for organized risk management.

[40] Congress and state legislatures have enacted statutes granting business corporations in particular industries qualified immunity from lawsuits. Generally, they have done so only when (1) litigation has plausibly threatened the continued provision of valued goods and services, such as the production of small airplanes, vaccines, or (in the immediate aftermath of the 2001 World Trade Center terrorist attack) commercial air traffic; and (2) litigation campaigns are widely regarded as shifting tort liability from the individuals primarily at fault for causing harm to businesses that are providing a legal product, as in the case of suits against gun manufacturers for injuries or deaths intentionally or negligently caused by gun users, or against fast food restaurants for contributing to claimants' adverse health effects from eating too much of those foods. In contrast, in 1998, state attorney generals proposed to settle their suits against major tobacco companies for $368 *billion*, in return for a congressional law granting tobacco companies immunity from future liability suits. However, Congress failed to pass that bill, despite pressure from virtually every state government to endorse the deal. Haltom and McCann 339 n. 20 (2004); Kagan & Nelson (2001).

The Path Dependency of Total Justice

Laws are shaped by institutional arrangements and the play of interests as well as by ideas and beliefs. In recent decades, students of the politics of public policy have explored the power of "path dependence" – the idea that laws and institutional arrangements created at one point in time generate patterns of activity that continuously reinforce the attitudes and interests of those who benefit from those laws and arrangements, producing an institutional "stickiness" that deflects or resists pressures for institutional or policy change.[41]

From this perspective, each time the legal culture of total justice is manifested in a concrete change in law, legal practices, or institutions, it generates self-reinforcing attitudes and patterns of activity, which in turn become difficult to undo. Once legal precedents, social insurance, or due process rights are established, they henceforth strengthen expectations of total justice and the incentives of lawyers and politicians who see profit in vindicating those rights. Thus Barnes observes that the intensified American tort system created in the 1960s and '70s, by making tort litigation more remunerative, encouraged the development of a larger, more legally sophisticated, and better financed plaintiffs' bar.[42] Plaintiffs' lawyers learned to litigate to establish legal precedents that make future cases easier to win. They organized to influence judicial appointments and legislative policymaking.[43] Their higher earnings and organizational capacities led to the dissemination of techniques for identifying and proving malfeasance and making the case for higher damages.

Consequently, despite the tort system's negative press, steady and substantial funding from the American Trial Lawyers Association (ATLA) has succeeded, by and large, in lining up Democratic politicians on the anti-conservative-tort-reform side[44] and in blocking,[45] watering down, circumventing, or overturning a great many conservative tort reform laws. Left intact and operating at high speed are the basic engines that make the American tort system uniquely powerful – (1) an entrepreneurial contingency-fee-driven bar, (2) armed with extensive tools of pretrial

---

[41] Pierson (1994); Hacker (2002); Stone Sweet 112 (2002).

[42] Barnes (2005).

[43] Parikh and Garth (2005).

[44] Burke (2002).

[45] At the federal level, year after year, beginning in the mid-1980s, ATLA and its allies in the Democratic Party blocked conservative product liability reform bills in Congress. Heymann and Liebman (1988). Even after Republicans swept into control of both houses in 1994 after offering a "Contract with America" that included a promise to restrict tort law, President Clinton successfully vetoed a Republican bill that would have capped punitive damage awards and eliminated joint and several liability in product liability cases. Schmitt, (1996); Lewis, (1996). In 2005, Congress enacted a law that seeks to restrict lawyers who assemble huge class actions from "forum shopping", that is, filing the case in those particular county courts they think will be most pro-plaintiff; the law channels class actions seeking $5 million or more into U.S. district courts. Analysts speculate, however, that there are numerous ways for plaintiffs' lawyers to continue to use the most favorable courts, at least for strong claims. Stern (2005).

discovery, (3) motivated by the prospect of monetary damages much larger (even with newly legislated "caps") than damages awarded by tort systems in other rich democracies, and (4) in some cases, motivated by the huge money damages made possible by the aggregation of individual claims into large class action suits. Nor have conservative legislatures sought to change core features of tort *adjudication* in the United States – trial by lay juries, with wide discretion (even after the enactment of caps in many states) to assess the amount of noneconomic damages.

Incentives to block revision also arise from regulatory and social insurance statutes that reflect total justice norms. Those incentives have persisted long after the political movements that created the laws during the New Deal or the 1964–72 period have faded away. Year by year, the political constituencies that demand undiminished Social Security and Medicare benefits continue to grow, represented by large, influential organizations like the American Association of Retired Persons. Civil rights groups stand ready to battle change in antidiscrimination legislation. Dominant corporations that have invested heavily in regulatory compliance become advocates for the regulatory status quo or even for moderate increases in regulatory stringency, because tough laws help them ward off cut-rate competitors.[46] More generally, the distinctive institutional fragmentation of power in American government – separation of powers, bicameralism, multiple legislative committees, candidate-based campaign financing – creates multiple legislative veto points that make it far easier to block or modify (than to enact) reforms that would eviscerate existing laws that reflect total justice norms.

Thus in legislation, as in judicial decisions, a one-way ratchet tends to operate, whereby once a law or precedent embodying total justice norms comes into effect, it is not impossible but politically difficult for subsequent legislatures or courts to take away or dilute those rights and protections. For advocates of expanded legal recognition of total justice norms, the logic of the law – treat equal cases alike – is ever present as an argument for the extension of rights and protections to analogous groups, situations, losses, and risks.

THE FUTURE OF TOTAL JUSTICE

In 1910, a century ago, the United States was a democracy only for white males. Millions of African Americans were excluded from the protections of the rule of law, especially but not exclusively in southern states. In 1900, there were no public defenders' offices, providing representation for criminal defendants. The federal Bill of Rights did not impose restrictions on interrogations by municipal police or on state prison conditions. There were no public-interest law firms, no class actions to threaten huge monetary damages against corporations that violated antidiscrimination or tort law. There was no income tax law, no bank deposit insurance law,

---

[46] Vogel (1995).

no Social Security law. There were no laws regulating the filling in of wetlands, industrial air pollution, the safety of new medicines, or the accuracy of corporate financial statements.

By the end of the twentieth century, thousands of American citizens each day were making free telephone calls to police departments, workplace safety inspectorates, and environmental agencies, whose officials fanned out into the community to enforce legal rights and duties. By the end of the twentieth century, the threat of legal liability permeated the operations of investment banks, hospitals, universities, public school systems, land developers, municipal governments, motor vehicle manufacturers, and police departments. Tens of millions of ordinary individuals had come to think of themselves as rights-bearing citizens for whom "the law" signifies not only official constraints and demands but also a universally available set of entitlements.[47]

This quick "then and now" comparison makes it hard to dispute the essential correctness of the cultural legal transformation that Friedman laid out. There surely have been contrary pulls and periods of retrenchment, but the overall trend clearly has been toward more accessible and comprehensive legal protection, embodying the values of total justice.

The causal analysis in *Total Justice* also suggests that the trend will continue. The key social changes identified by Friedman – the growing social, organizational, and governmental *capacity* to compensate the unfortunate; to investigate and address the sources of injury and injustice; and to instill antidiscrimination norms into both public and private bureaucracies – are entrenched features of modern society. Just as important, and just as entrenched, is competitive democratic politics, which gives lawyers, journalists, and opposition politicians ongoing incentives to criticize governments and legal institutions for failure to *use* existing capacities to remedy obvious gaps in the fabric of total justice.

It is true that *Total Justice* pays only scant attention to competing American political values and to competing strains in popular legal culture. Nor does it focus on the periodic mini-rebellions, led by conservative politicians, against the particular legal mechanisms chosen to implement demands for total justice. It seems likely that these will continue to come and go. Yet, as argued earlier, those efforts are not inconsistent with the legal culture of total justice that, in Friedman's analysis, has always been sensitive to economic limitations. Tort law, the welfare state, and environmental regulation expanded only as the society became capable of absorbing and spreading the *costs* of total justice – through affordable insurance, rising incomes and profits, fluid markets, and increasing governmental revenues.

Thus the ideal of total justice, as Friedman describes it, rests on a utilitarian morality, not a justice-at-all costs Kantian imperative. Most believers in total justice also care about job growth, affordable tax rates, and economic efficiency. They might

---

[47] Ewick and Silbey (1998).

well be unhappy about the inefficiency and unpredictability of the American tort system, the transaction costs imposed by complex, constantly changing regulatory regimes, and the soaring costs and cheating associated with huge social and health benefit programs. They might support legal reforms aimed at trimming those costs when they seem too high. Thus in the future, as in the past, the pace at which the desire for total justice will be translated into new laws and rights is likely to be contested and variable. The path of the law will be shaped in part by variation in economic conditions and the availability of good policy ideas for vindicating total justice expectations in relatively efficient, only moderately costly ways.

Some observers might see a threat to the gradual but ongoing march of total justice in the rapid pace of globalization – a fundamental economic and social trend that is not explicitly discussed in the pages of *Total Justice*. The revolutions in cargo transportation, the mobility of capital, communications, and the opening of national markets conceivably could push legal culture in a different direction, producing a race to the bottom in national legal protections as rich, high-wage nations strive to remain competitive through deregulation and ever more laissez-faire policies. In the United States, it could be noted, working-class wage levels have stagnated, private-sector union membership has shrunk, employers have cut funding for employee health care and pension funds, and huge national trade and budget deficits limit expansion of governmental benefit programs. One might speculate that these trends will shove aside the culture of total justice in favor of a legal culture that cares *primarily* about limiting costs to individual taxpayers, business, and government.

The evidence thus far suggests that such fears are exaggerated. Consider the experience of Western Europe, where welfare state and labor laws have gone further in institutionalizing ideas of total justice than similar laws in the United States. In the 1980s and 1990s, European countries responded to pressures for greater economic efficiency by privatizing public utilities. However, they simultaneously expanded regulatory protections for the public; the title of a major book on the subject is *Freer Markets, More Rules*.[48] In the last decade, Western European environmental and consumer protection regulation has become in many spheres more risk averse, more stringent than American regulation, reversing the relationship that had prevailed from the 1960s through the 1980s.[49] Although Western Europeans talk about the passing of the "golden age" of the welfare state and the arrival of the "age of austerity," most academic analyses have characterized the last decade's legal changes in most countries as efficiency-enhancing reforms, rather than as massive retrenchment.[50]

---

[48] S. Vogel (1996).

[49] D. Vogel (2003).

[50] Pierson (2001). In a study of labor market regimes in several Western European countries, Stewart Wood (2001) concluded that despite pressures for more flexible labor markets and some legal changes in workers' rights, there has been no convergence on a 'liberal, market-oriented model' and that labor law regimes in the three models of European welfare state approaches – Scandinavian, Christian-Democratic, and liberal – "remain distinct in ways that demonstrate profound continuities with their

More generally, studies of environmental and other types of labor market regulation indicate that globalization generally has not resulted in significant cutbacks in the stringency of regulation in richer countries.[51]

The resilience of total justice norms, despite pressures for global economic competitiveness, stems partly from the dynamic of path dependency. The powerful political constituencies that form around legally established rights continue to demand the protections they have come to value. As political scientists Myles and Pierson put it, "no government wants to pass legislation that will lead to its demise."[52]

In addition, globalization itself, by causing economic and social disruption, generates new and *stronger* demands for security, for *expansion* of legal protections. Intensified global competition drives less nimble firms in rich countries into bankruptcy and makes employment less secure. It stimulates immigration, which leads to new ethnic tensions. Rapid technological and economic change constantly generates new opportunities for fraud, new kinds of inequalities, new kinds of environmental degradation, new sources of personal injury. Yet at least in rich democracies, all these social disruptions and threats also seem to generate new demands for legal protection, more aggressive enforcement of antidiscrimination laws, more legal guarantees to protect families from impoverishment by economic change.

The reason, *Total Justice* suggests, lies in the higher expectations generated by modernization itself, which continuously and visibly demonstrates that prodigies of technological, financial, organizational, and social inventiveness are possible. For all its disruptiveness, globalization also is likely to help rich countries like the United States become even richer – making it more possible, not less, to combine the drive for economic efficiency with legal attempts to fulfill the ideals of total justice.

REFERENCES

Abel, Richard (1987). The Real Tort Crisis: Too Few Claims, 48 *Ohio St. L J.* 443.
Barnes, Jeb (2005). Is Adversarial Legalism Path Dependent? Congressional Inertia and Court-Based Tort Reform during the Asbestos Crisis. Paper Prepared for the 2005 Annual American Political Science Association Conference, Washington, DC.
Bell, Peter and Jeffrey O'Connell (1997). *Accidental Justice: The Dilemmas of Tort Law.* New Haven: Yale University Press.
Blumenthal, David and James Morone (2005). Waiting for Another L.B.J., *New York Times*, July 30.
Burke, Thomas (2002). *Lawyers, Lawsuits, and Legal Rights: The Battle over Litigation in American Society.* Berkeley: University of California Press.

'golden age' incarnations" (p 369). See also Gitterman (2004). The same conclusions emerge from comparative studies of health care expenditures (Giamo [2001]) and pension reform. Myles and Pierson (2001). Recently, of course, severe far-reaching austerity measures have been reviewed in several European countries. On the other hand, the powerful political reactions against those measures suggest considerable uncertainty about how enduring and stringent those cutbacks will be once economic growth revives.

[51] D. Vogel (1995); Vogel and Kagan (2004).
[52] Myles and Pierson 322 (2001).

Carroll, Stephen, Allan Abrahamse, and Mary Vaiana (1995). *The Costs of Excess Medical Claims for Automobile Personal Injuries.* Santa Monica, CA: RAND Institue for Civil Justice.

Coffee, John C, Jr. (1995). Class Wars: The Dilemma of the Mass Tort Class Action, 95 *Colum. L. Rev.* 95.

Daniels, Stephen and Joanne Martin (2004). The Strange Success of Tort Reform, 53 *Emory L.J.* 1225.

Ewick, Patricia and Susan Silbey (1998). *The Common Place of Law: Stories from Everyday Life.* Chicago: University of Chicago Press.

Farhang, Sean (2010). *The Litigation State: Public Regulation and Private Lawsuits in the U.S.* Princeton: Princeton University Press.

Fiorina, Morris P. (2005). *Culture War? The Myth of a Polarized America.* New York: Pearson/Longman.

Friedman, Lawrence M. (1985). *Total Justice.* New York: Russell Sage Foundation.

Giaimo, Susan (2001). Who Pays for Health Care Reform? in Paul Pierson, ed., *The New Politics of the Welfare State.* Oxford: Oxford University Press.

Gitterman, Daniel (2004). A Race to the Bottom, a Race to the Top or the March to a Minimum Floor? in D. Vogel and R. A. Kagan, eds. (2004). *Dynamics of Regulatory Change: How Globalization Affects National Regulatory Policies.* Berkeley: University of California Press.

Hacker, Jacob (2002). *The Divided Welfare State: The Battle over Public and Private Social Benefits in the United States.* Cambridge: Cambridge University Press.

―――. (2004). Privatizing Risk without Privatizing the Welfare State: The Hidden Politics of Social Policy Retrenchment in the United Stats. 98 *Am. Pol. Sci. Rev.*

Haltom, William and Michael McCann (2004). *Distorting the Law: Politics, Media and the Litigation Crisis.* Chicago: University of Chicago Press.

Hans, Valerie P. (2000). *Business on Trial: The Civil Jury and Corporate Responsibility.* New Haven: Yale University Press.

Heymann, Philip and Lance Liebman (1988). No Fault, No Fee: The Legal Profession and Federal No-Fault Insurance Legislation, in P. Heymann and L. Liebman, eds., *The Social Responsibilities of Lawyers.* Westbury, NY: Foundation Press.

Kagan, Robert A. (2001). *Adversarial Legalism: The American Way of Law.* Cambridge, MA: Harvard University Press.

Kagan, Robert A. and William Nelson (2000). The Politics of Tobacco Regulation in the United States, in Robert Rabin and Stephen Sugarman, eds., *Regulating Tobacco.* New York: Oxford University Press.

Lewis, Neil (1996). A Compromise on Restricting Liability Suits, *New York Times,* March 14.

McFate, Katherine, Roger Lawson, and William Julius Wilson, eds. (1995). *Poverty, Inequality, and the Future of Social Policy: Western States in the New World Order.* New York: Russell Sage Foundation.

Merritt, Deborah and Kathryn Barry (1999). Is the Tort System in Crisis? New Empirical Evidence, 60 *Ohio State L.J.* 315.

Myles, John and Paul Pierson (2001). The Comparative Political Economy of Pension Reform, in Paul Pierson, ed., *The New Politics of the Welfare State.* Oxford: Oxford University Press.

Nonet, Philippe and Philip Selznick (2002). *Law and Society in Transition: Toward Responsive Law.* New Brunswick, NJ: Transaction Books.

Parikh, Sara and Bryant Garth (2005). Philip Corboy and the Construction of the Plaintiff's Personal Injury Bar, 30 *Law & Soc. Inquiry* 269.

Pierson, Paul (1994). *Dismantling the Welfare State? Reagan, Thatcher, and the Politics of Retrenchment.* New York: Cambridge University Press.

_____ ed. (2001). *The New Politics of the Welfare State*. Oxford: Oxford University Press.

Polisar, Daniel and Aaron Wildavsky (1989). From Individual to System Blame: A Cultural Analysis of Historical Change in the Law of Torts, 1 *J. Pol'y Hist.* 129.

Priest, George L. (1985). The Invention of Enterprise Liability: A Critical History of the Intellectual Foundations of Modern Tort Law, 14 *J. Legal Stud.* 461.

Saks, Michael J. (1992) "Do We Really Know Anything About the Behavior of the Tort Litigation System – And Why Not?" 140 *Pa. L. Rev.* 1147.

Sanders, Joseph (1987). The Meaning of the Law Explosion: On Friedman's *Total Justice*, 1987 *Am. B. Found. Res. J.* 601.

Schmitt, Richard (1996). As Clinton Vows to Veto Products Liability Bill, Some Ask if He's Too Close to Trial Lawyers, *Wall Street Journal*, March 22.

Stern, Seth (2005). Lawyers Seek Loopholes in Class Action Overhaul, *CQ Weekly*, Feb. 28.

Stone Sweet, Alec (2002). Path Dependence, Precedent, and Judicial Power, in Martin Shapiro and Alec Stone Sweet, eds., *On Law, Politics, and Judicialization*. London: Oxford University Press.

Sugarman, Stephen D. (1999). Judges as Tort Law Un-Makers: Recent California Experience with "New" Torts, 49 *DePaul L. Rev.* 455.

_____. (2005). A Comparative Look at Pain and Suffering Awards. Presentation at Clifford Symposium on Pain and Suffering, DePaul Law School, April.

Ursin, Edmund (1981). Judicial Creativity and Tort Law, 49 *Geo. Wash. L. Rev.* 229.

Vogel, David (2003). The Hare and the Tortoise Revisited: The New Politics of Consumer and Environmental Regulation in Europe, 33 *Br. J. Pol. Sci.* 557.

_____. (1995). *Trading Up: Consumer and Environmental Regulation in a Global Economy*. Cambridge, MA: Harvard University Press.

Vogel, David and Robert A. Kagan, eds. (2004). *Dynamics of Regulatory Change: How Globalization Affects National Regulatory Policies*. Berkeley: University of California Press.

Vogel, Stephen (1996). *Freer Markets, More Rules: Regulatory Reform in Advanced Industrial Countries*. Ithaca, NY: Cornell University Press.

Wildavsky, Aaron (1990). A World of Difference – The Public Philosophies and Political Behaviors of Rival American Cultures, in Anthony King, ed. *The New American Political System*, Washington, DC: AEI Press.

Wilensky, Harold (2002). *Rich Democracies*. Berkeley: University of California Press.

Wold, Jon and John Culver (1987). The Defeat of the California Justices, *Judicature* April/May.

Wood, Stewart (2001). Labour Market Regimes under Threat: Sources of Continuity in Germany, Britain and Sweden, in Paul Pierson, ed., *The New Politics of the Welfare State*. Oxford: Oxford University Press.

9

Failures of War Tribunals

From Leipzig, Nuremberg, and Tokyo to Milošević and Saddam Hussein

Erhard Blankenburg

Total justice is an obsession not only of everyday (American) life, but has its grip on the politics of war too. Although European aristocrats in the nineteenth century still could look at their territorial wars as the ultimate means of political distribution among family members, modern national leaders have to find legitimacy in morally destroying the enemy regime. The media are as important as conventional weapons, and courts or tribunals have become new players in the game. With courts defining what is seen as *bellum iustum*, a body of law is being built up, with Nuremberg and the Yugoslavia tribunals as the main precedents. These tribunals show that the courtroom does not often reveal moral victory. The dilemmas of the Saddam Hussein tribunal also demonstrated that a war may be lost not only on the battlefields but also in the courtroom.

It is a modern custom for victors of war to try the losers before a tribunal, charging them with moral guilt for crimes of war, genocide, and violations of human rights. The aim is to expose the obscene crime of a few selected culprits so as to evoke total moral condemnation of the defeated regime. The most eager helpers are incriminated, but the mass of fellow travelers may be excused for their opportunism. Drawing borderlines between these groups is a political decision made with a view to the future. The time and complexity of legal procedures help move the political purge to some historical distance. More urgent is the destruction of support for the defeated regime. Cleansing true believers in the old regime from state institutions has to be supported by means other than criminal law: Certainly money and denying them future positions will be central, but moral whitewashing might also help. Thus, the task of dispensing rather quick justice is vital for turning the military triumph into a permanent victory.

Yet there are obvious dangers involved in the rule of law: Usually the victors have been somewhat responsible for not preventing the war. *Unavoidably, they committed some pretty ugly crimes themselves, and despite careful procedural scrutiny they will fail to keep the legal showdown as following process as they might want.* Any fair procedure will invite the defense to stage counterattacks.

It therefore seems wise to give some advice to the triumphant victors on how *not* to use war tribunals.

FIRST RULE: IF TRIBUNALS ARE TO ESTABLISH MORAL "GUILT," BE AWARE OF MOCKERY AND OF COUNTERATTACKS

When the Milošević trial before the Yugoslavia tribunal was broadcast live on Serbian TV for weeks beginning on November 17, 1992, the popularity and general support for the incriminated leader actually increased.[1] The nightmare of any tribunal seemed to come true: that the main accused would turn around the moral message by presenting himself as a martyr of victor's justice and threatening to counterattack the victors. Delivering Milošević to the court was made possible only by paying off the Serbian government and by putting him on a plane before the Serbian president was able to prevent the government from delivering him. However, the Western media largely ignored the protests in Serbia, and by showing the gray appearance of the accused (who had refused any defense lawyers and wanted to defend himself) opposite the flamboyant robes of judges and prosecutors, it managed to portray the event as a triumph of justice.

The Yugoslavia tribunal has a mandate: *individual* indictment of war crimes, genocide and crimes against humanity. As such, it is more restricted than the Nuremberg and Tokyo tribunals, which combined indicting individual war actions with the condemnation of collective war guilt. The moral message is similar, to fix individual responsibility as well as collective guilt. Besides creating a public podium for scandalizing, these tribunals also had to translate the moral accusation into indictment under legal doctrine. The Nuremberg trials were taken as precedents in the efforts to form a body of international penal law.

The first such court was the Leipzig tribunal in 1924. It was a last attempt to blame World War I guilt on the German Kaiserreich. Articles 228 to 230 of the Treaty of Versailles in 1919 had already tried to establish a court for the purpose of demonstrating both collective guilt and individual responsibility for war crimes to the moral public, particularly that of the defeated country. However, the treaty was immediately ignored, with the Netherlands (which had not been party to the war and had not signed the Versailles treaty) refusing to extradite the German Kaiser, who had gone into exile at the small country place of Doorn; then the German government refused to extradite 900 suspects whom the allied countries had put on a list of alleged war criminals.[2] The German government avoided an allied tribunal by establishing its own special war tribunal, but the German judicial authorities made a mockery of it by only charging a few low-ranking soldiers who had been looting

---

[1]   Cf. Dimitrijević 59 (2002).
[2]   Cf. Schwengler (1982).

and mistreating prisoners while dismissing charges against officers on the grounds that they had only been following orders. The furious reaction of the international and German press and public led to the conviction of the commander and two officers of a submarine for not saving two British shipwrecked marines. Then the German military got upset, and when the case was appealed in 1928, it ended with an acquittal. Only eleven cases were tried before the war tribunal at the Reichsgericht in Leipzig. The attempt to hold the German Kaiserreich responsible for World War I and to assign individual responsibility for the war had failed.

The Nuremberg tribunal was more successful as it was not restricted to questions about war guilt, but instead presented ample evidence of civic and professional crimes of collaboration with the racist Nazis: It was a tribunal on the wrongs of an entire culture, which had capitulated at the end of a total war. More so than later tribunals, the tribunal at Nuremberg conducted trials of various social groups; for example, political as well as military leaders, doctors as well as jurists. The overpowering evidence of concentration camps and planned mass murder opened the eyes of even the true believers who had refused to realize the anti-Semitic fury. Only a minority of Germans reproached the international tribunal for delivering "victors' justice" until the 1950s. However, the purge of former Nazis from public office, which was initiated under allied control, soon became a Cold War propaganda issue as communist East Germany charged the West German government of rehabilitating the Nazi elites. It was not until the 1960s that a younger generation took seriously the procedures for purging the surviving Nazi elites.[3]

The 1946 Tokyo trial directed war crimes charges at seventy members of the military and government elite, although only twenty-eight military, political, and diplomatic leaders stood trial. The tribunal issued seven death sentences, seven life sentences, and two shorter prison sentences. The twelve other defendants, including industrial leaders, were released in 1948. Before the trials began, General Douglas MacArthur, the allied commander, struck a deal that left the Tenno sacrosanct and spared some groups such as medical doctors, who were responsible for biological warfare. A number of the allied judges dissented from individual sentences, and Judge R. M. Pal from India dissented from the entire trial in protest against the dropping of the atomic bomb. The victors were interested in demilitarization and at the same time were counting on Japan to serve as a bloc against communist hegemony in Southeast Asia. The overhasty conclusion of the trial left victim countries and victim groups up to our own day pressuring Japanese leaders to admit to war crimes.[4]

---

[3] The German public was already alerted of war criminals in their midst when the Eichmann trial took place in Jerusalem 1961, but it took the "Auschwitz trial" against former camp guards in Frankfurt, held from 1963 until 1965, for Germans to fully grasp the horror of the concentration camps.

[4] From the end of the war until 1951, many individual Japanese soldiers stood trial all over southeast Asia. However, it was only after atrocities against women were classified as a war crime by the Yugoslavia tribunal that the issue of the so-called comfort women was charged by an NGO tribunal in 2000.

The tribunals of Leipzig, Nuremberg, and Tokyo took place after capitulation of the defeated war party, and they were aimed at the home population – to lead them back into the international community and to legitimize reparation payments. In contrast, in the former Yugoslavia, such victor's logic was neutralized by the fact that the war was not yet over. Neither Croatian, Bosnian, nor Serbian authorities fully cooperated with the investigations of the The Hague prosecutors, and the court had to issue repeated subpoenas to help the investigations out of an impasse. The indictment of two of the main suspects, Mladić and Karadžić, had been well prepared since 1995, but despite extreme political pressure by the United Nations and the European Union, Karadžić's trial only started in July 2008 and Mladić is still in hiding at the time of this writing. Absentee indictment is possible; trial by default is not.

The Yugoslavia tribunal has a mandate to deliver only *individual* indictments of war crimes, genocide, and crimes against humanity. As such, it is more restricted than the Nuremberg and Tokyo tribunals, which combined the indictments of individual actions with the condemnation of collective guilt. However, the Yugoslav tribunal's moral aims are similar: to find both individual responsibility and collective guilt and to translate the moral accusation into an indictment under legal doctrine.

The Baghdad tribunal faced a different dilemma from the Yugloslav court: The crimes of the main villain Saddam Hussein had been identified for a long time. An indictment dossier of some thousand pages had been prepared by the American administration by the year 2000, but it took a controversial war to enable his arrest. Actually, even though the American occupation forces had already transferred sovereignty to a domestic government, the tribunal remained dependent on external military protection. Instead of transferring the villain to an international tribunal where the captive suspect might be kept more safely, Saddam Hussein remained in Baghdad, officially awaiting trial under national law, but effectively guarded by the victorious American army. For fear that he might achieve status as a martyr, he might have been the only person whose life was truly protected in a city beleaguered by war. Nevertheless, the little information that trickled out of his high-security prison could not convince the media that his treatment satisfied criteria of preparations for a fair trial.

The embarrassment was obvious and difficult to mitigate. Teams of defense lawyers operated from outside of the country with free access to the media, while prosecutors and even potential judges(!) had to be prepared for the trial by the victors' law professionals. A spokesperson for the Iraqi government was more optimistic when he gave a press conference on February 9, 2005:

> He would not say which of Saddam's 11 lieutenants were likely to face the Iraqi Special Tribunal first and it was unclear when Saddam would stand trial.

In December 2004, investigative judges summoned Saddam's cousin, Ali Hassan al-Majid, better known as Chemical Ali, for his role in poison gas attacks against

Iraq's Kurdish minority and former Defense Minister Gen. Sultan Hashim Ahmad to appear before them in closed-door preliminary hearings.

Saddam and many former Baath Party members have been jailed for more than a year. U.S. military officials transferred the 12 defendants to Iraqi custody in June 2004 with the transfer of sovereignty.

In July, a judge told the group they were under investigation for war crimes. In Saddam's case, he was informed that court officials were investigating him in the killings of rival politicians, the gassing of the Kurds in 1988, invading Kuwait in 1990 and brutally suppressing Kurdish and Shiite uprisings in 1991.

Formal charges will not come until the investigating judges refer the cases to the trial chamber. The first dossiers are expected to be delivered to trial judges within several weeks, the legal expert said.

"I can't give you an exact timeframe, but I'm talking weeks for this to begin," he said. "I would say a few weeks, give or take."

Video cameras and reporters will be allowed into the courtroom, and there will be a limited number of seats for the public in a viewing gallery behind bullet proof glass.

Unlike the common-law court system in the United States, the Iraqi tribunal will have no jury, and the verdicts and sentencing will be handed down through a majority decision of the five-judge panel.

The court will hear from victims, witnesses, a state prosecutor, defence witnesses and, in some cases, the defendants themselves. Defendants have the right to appeal the verdict to a nine-judge appellate chamber.

The first press conference given by the Special Tribunal on June 5, 2005, refuted all pronouncements of Iraqi government officials and announced that the indictment of Saddam Hussein would be reduced to indictment on 12 charges (out of about 500 possible charges). Contrary to American advice, they would put Saddam Hussein on trial first, trusting that evidence would be sufficient for pleading the death penalty.

Their task was not easy: Their lives were threatened, and they could not operate openly. In addition, the law they had to apply was a combination of the Iraqi pre-Hussein codes (formulated in 1951 by Abd al-Razzaq-al-Sanhuri as an Arab adaptation of Italian law), filled in by precedents of international law as developed by the tribunals of The Hague and Arusha, and it had to be credible with the local Sunni and Shi'ite religious leaders and their idea of justice. The degree of malleability of this "law" can be seen from the changes in the maximum penalty in recent years: After the defeat of the Baath regime the provisional government passed a law prohibiting the death penalty in accordance with the law of international war tribunals. The victorious president of the United States nevertheless announced his imminent use of the death penalty, and with the regaining of Iraqi sovereignty in 2004 it was reintroduced.

SECOND RULE: DO NOT CHARGE A MAIN VILLAIN FROM THE BEGINNING, BUT START WITH INDICTING SOME OF THE ASSOCIATES OF THE REGIME

When the Yugoslavia tribunal started in May 1993, its prospects did not look hopeful. There soon were some thirty indictments, but few of the suspects appeared, and once accused, they regularly pleaded "not guilty." Only one "guilty" plea came without the prosecution having asked for it: Erdemović, a former volunteer soldier who had appeared in 1996 as a witness for the prosecution against Tadić,[5] burst into tears during his testimony and confessed to participating in the shooting of prisoners. The prosecution and court, eager to present even a small case, grasped the opportunity to put him on trial. The first sentence of the tribunal came within a half-year; it amounted to ten years' imprisonment. "It was in the interest of jurisprudence that Erdemović has to be sentenced,"[6] was the comment of his defense lawyer when he lodged an appeal. Two years later, after a few more cases had been tried, the appeal court reduced his sentence to five years.[7]

Twelve years after it had taken up its work, the tribunal could present a rather proud record: with 162 indictments, the appearance of 128 of the accused, 56 judgments, and 37 final sentences (including appeal) the court had proven its efficacy.[8] In 2004 the prosecution announced that it would not prepare any new indictments, as the UN Security Council would terminate the tribunal's mandate in 2008. Certainly, the tribunal did not rule on more than a tiny fraction of all suspects, but it had left its mark on the doctrine and law of warfare.

More even than in everyday justice, it is evident that the goal of *preventing war crimes* by tribunals is illusory. War tribunals can only serve as symbolic institutions. They can establish definitions of what may legitimately be considered a "just" war. The conventions of The Hague in 1907 and of Geneva in 1949 have been attempts to establish substantive rules of the manners and customs of a "decent" war. They pose norms, but do not devise any institutions to implement them. They oblige parties in war to submit violations committed by their troops to military tribunals, but this obligation is largely neglected. They try to limit war actions to fighting among troops, but cannot prevent the civil population from becoming victimized nor their suffering being used as a means of war. The presence of live media encourages the age-old custom of taking hostages from among the civil population.

Violating the norms of a just war has been long-standing practice, but modern wars do so much more systematically. That is why world opinion plays such an important role. Politicians in far-away countries have to do at least *something*; the stream of refugees alone does not allow them to remain passive. Thus, the idea of

---

[5] IT 94–1.
[6] *NRC Handelsblad*, December 23, 1997.
[7] IT 96-22.
[8] See the excellent Web site, http://www.icty.org.

using the symbolic power of a tribunal to express moral indignation arose. Resolution 808 of the Security Council of the United Nations cites individual responsibility for violations of the "norms and customs of war, genocide and violations of human rights of the civil population." Public opinion regards these violations as accusations of war guilt, even though formally the crime of *conspiracy*[9] is limited to "responsibility for military command not preventing the violations."

THIRD RULE: DO NOT HESITATE TO USE THE DISCRETION OF PROSECUTORS. AS NO TRIBUNAL CAN CHARGE MORE THAN A SMALL FRACTION OF ALL SUSPECTS, SELECTION IS A PRACTICAL NECESSITY. BUT THE POLITICAL SUCCESS OF A TRIAL DEPENDS ON CHARGING CRIMES AGAINST ALL MAJOR VICTIM GROUPS

Of course, thousands of victims and many, many conflict groups all over the world might try to use a political tribunal for propaganda purposes. Expatriates and people in refugee camps are natural breeding grounds for denunciations. Political groups and numerous NGOs compete in gathering evidence materials. Guided by their own interests and perception biases, they mislead as often as they provide useful information. Tryng to investigate all incoming reports would drown any prosecution office. Yet even if most of these reports fade away because of insufficient evidence, there might still be reason enough not to charge those accused because prosecutors do not want to be embarrassed by witnesses with vague memories or by confused witnesses.

The danger of instrumentalizing the tribunal frivolously can be controlled, however. Prosecutions in war tribunals enjoy practically unlimited discretion over whom to indict and whom to ignore. As indicated, the Nuremberg and Tokyo trials used their forums to make clear political and moral indictments of group responsibility, whereas the Yugoslavia and Rwanda tribunals picked their individual charges purposively with an eye on public acceptance. More than 120,000 individuals suspected of war crimes and genocide had been taken prisoner in Rwanda, but only 25 have been accused so far before the tribunal.[10] It took nine years after the genocide attacks in 1994 to provisionally release some 25,000 prisoners. The special reconciliation proceedings (*gacaca*) had a hard time getting started. Operating largely on the basis of guilty pleas, they were harshly criticized for not guaranteeing an adequate defense to the suspects. Another strategy to relieve the burden on the tribunal and to free the masses of detainees would be referral of cases to national courts. Since 1997,

---

[9] Defining the charge of *conspiracy* or *joint criminal enterprise* in doctrinal terms is very difficult for war tribunals. Even though the definition that Judge Cassese gave in the Tadić appeal case IT 94–1 will lead to future decisions, the prosecution was struggling with the exact wording of the accusation in the Milošević case.

[10] See the very informative Web site, http://www.ictr.org.

however, Rwandan national courts have tried only a few suspects for crimes under Rwandan law. As the Rwandan national system of justice is not capable of trying the masses of ordinary perpetrators, the ambition of restoring (*total*) justice remains unfulfilled.[11]

Yet not only the prosecution of ordinary war criminals but also the indictment of the most prominent leaders allow for outright opportunism. If the definition of "courts" entails compulsive jurisdiction (which within its mandate would oblige a court to pass judgment on any case brought before it), war tribunals would not satisfy this definition because of their close relation with prosecution. Selective indictments tend to be oriented to *policy*, not *law*. Arrest warrants for the Yugoslavia tribunal had to be balanced carefully among Serbian, Croatian, and Bosnian suspects, and their enforcement was subject to political pressure, including paying the countries for cooperation. When the hiding tactics of those indicted became obvious, the prosecution even resorted to clandestine indictments.

There is no need to make the prosecution policy transparent: Selectivity of indictment is absolute and accounting to media or to the defense not necessary. Even equality claims of some of the accused are restricted: The appeal courts of both the Yugoslavia and Rwanda tribunals decided that defendants' pointing at others who had committed the same crime without being prosecuted would be unavailing unless they could give evidence of discrimination in their own verdict.[12] Thus, legally, total discretion of the prosecution allows for selecting the cases with the best and easiest to obtain evidence. Yet politically, the charges have to be morally convincing to the different victim groups that expect retribution from the tribunal.

FOURTH RULE: THE AIMS OF WAR TRIBUNALS ARE HYBRID: RETRIBUTION OR RECONCILIATION OF THE CONFLICTING PARTIES MIGHT BE TOO MUCH TO PROMISE, AND TRIUMPH OF THE VICTORS CANNOT BE ENOUGH

If ongoing conflicts render it impossible to maintain due process and equality under the law, it would be better not to convene a tribunal at all. The legitimacy of a tribunal can only be achieved by relating to and contributing to an established body of law.

It is no wonder that victors of modern wars try to charge the defeated enemy before tribunals. Next to the military victory the art of warfare seeks a win in the media and in the sphere of morality. These days, legitimacy does not come from above, nor could it be maintained by mere self-pretension of vital interests. In the open forum of global credibility there are few authorities left besides the law.

---

[11] Herik 49–57 (2005).
[12] Čelebići case IT 96–21A; Akayesu case ICTR 96–4 A; cf. Cote 165, 172–7 (2005) and Jallow 154–60 (2004).

Unavoidably, however, the greater its involvement in power and conflict, the more a moral institution will be attacked as being part of the warfare. The Saddam Hussein tribunal in the middle of Baghdad had to be kept under high security, and the judges had to be guarded day and night, for as soon as their faces were shown on TV or their names became known, they received death threats. A prosecutor and a designated judge were shot even before the trial started. The Kurds in the north of Iraq hoped for a death sentence, and the Shi'ites in the south supported the trial. The Sunnis around Baghdad, however, used the occasion of the trial to heat up their guerrilla war, even if they did not necessarily want the return of the Baathist regime.

Of course, it would have been better to hold the trial outside Iraq as had been announced and prepared by the Clinton administration before the war.[13] Under President Bush, however, it had become impossible to invoke an international tribunal. The Iraq government (certainly with approval of the White House) saw it as an impediment that an international tribunal would not allow for a death penalty. This also made it impossible to call upon the International Criminal Court at The Hague[14], which the American government had boycotted out of principle. Rejecting the existing institutional bodies, the Saddam Hussein tribunal had to remake its procedure and to pretend public transparency under adverse security conditions.

REFERENCES

Cote, Luc (2004). Reflections on the Exercise of Prosecutorial Discretion in International Criminal Law, 3 *J. Int'l Crim. Just.* 162.

Jallow, H. B. (2004). Prosecutorial Discretion and International Criminal Justice, 3 *J. Int'l Crim. Just.* 46.

Dimitrijević, Vojin (2002). Milošević on Trial, *E. Eur. Const. Rev.* 11.

Herik, Larissa van (2005). *The Contribution of the Rwanda Tribunal to the Development of International Law.* Leiden: Nijhoff.

NRC Handelsblad, December 23, 1997.

Schwengler, Walter (1982). *Völkerrecht, Versailler Vertrag und Auslieferungsfrage*, München.

[13] A 2,000-page indictment document was prepared by the Office for War Crimes Issues.

[14] The International Criminal Court (ICC) is set up to investigate and prosecute individuals accused of crimes against humanity, genocide, and crimes of war. It will step in only if national courts are unwilling or unable to investigate or prosecute such crimes. The ICC Statute was advocated by a coalition of NGOs and adopted at an international conference in Rome on July 17, 1998: 120 countries voted to adopt the treaty, only 7 countries voted against it (including China, Israel, Iraq, and the United States), and 21 abstained. As of October 2010, 114 countries are members of the Court.

PART III

The Legal Profession

10

Friedman on Lawyers

A Survey

Philip Lewis

INTRODUCTION

This chapter is about Lawrence Friedman's writing on lawyers. I am sorry not to have known the 29-year-old who wrote the extremely funny note on lawyers and law reviews in 1959,[1] but I was getting to know the author of *The Legal System* (LS) when it was published in 1975.[2] Concepts in LS, above all that of legal culture (originally introduced in 1969 in his article, "Legal Culture and Social Development" [LCSD]), continue to inform and provoke discussion. My own research interests have been in lawyers. I have described[3] as a "legal system approach" to the study of lawyers one that asks questions about them that are based on the part they play or may possibly

[1] Friedman (1959).
[2] In addition to giving me the personal support from which I, like so many others, have benefited, Lawrence has, in many conversations, filled my mind with apparent minutiae of unexpected significance from zoology and linguistics. This breadth of mind has enriched his general approach to the social and historical study of law and served us all well. See, for example, Friedman 57 (1975), comparing communication by the general broadcasting of messages to the sex life of fish.
[3] Lewis 31ff. (1989).

For convenience (I hope) the following abbreviations (placed in chronological order) are used for books or articles by Friedman referred to in the text.

CLA	*Contract Law in America* (Friedman 1965)
LCSD	"Legal Culture and Social Development" (Friedman 1969)
LS	*The Legal System* (Friedman 1975)
HAL	*A History of American Law*, 3d edition (Friedman 2005)
TJ	*Total Justice* (Friedman 1985, 1987)
LLLP	"Law, Lawyers and Legal Practice in Silicon Valley" (Friedman et al. 1988–9)
LCCP	"Lawyers in Cross-Cultural Perspective" (Friedman 1989)
RC	*The Republic of Choice* (Friedman 1990)
LLIED	"Law, Legal Institutions, and Economic Development" (Friedman 1994a)
AWLP	"Are We a Litigious People?" (Friedman 1996)
HS	*The Horizontal Society* (Friedman 1999)
ALTC	American Law in the 20th Century (Friedman 2002)

play in forwarding the purposes of the legal system, whether these purposes are seen in normative or sociological terms. LS is still one of the few attempts to provide a general account of legal systems from a social science perspective, and thus it gives us an unusual opportunity to consider this kind of question about lawyers and Friedman's suggested answers. Yet Friedman, the historian and social analyst, has written many other works in which lawyers also appear, some of which I review here to discuss how they fit into or perhaps enrich the points made in LS.[4]

THE LEGAL SYSTEM

In LS, lawyers, along with their advisory work, are recognized as part of the legal system.[5] They appear in three main contexts: legal impact,[6] the origin of law and laws,[7] and internal legal culture.[8] Yet what is said about them needs to be read in the light of Friedman's strongly argued general points – that the legal system should be approached, both in general and in particular, as if it were the product (perhaps even the arena[9]) of social forces and that this approach is for the most part correct. In consequence, in more than one place he downplays the significance, in a social science account of the legal system, of judges and lawyers and moves them away from the central role, which he sees them as unjustifiably playing in more traditional accounts. He downplays their role not only because he systematically doubts their autonomy but also because he sees much of what they do as having no effects outside the legal system and so their activities are tolerable to the social forces pressing on the system.

Lawyers and Impact

It is novel, but in this context it should not be surprising, that lawyers appear first only as part of a subhead of the chapter on the impact of law. Friedman is considering first the impact and afterward the effectiveness of law. Before a rule or norm can have an impact, he says, the rule or norm must be communicated;[10] he uses the metaphor of "messages." After discussing the type of message best suited for communication, he points out that there must be a track or path along which the message can travel. Messages may not be clear, or they may be too complex for anyone but a specialist to cope with. In Western societies these specialists are lawyers.

---

[4] There are two issues I have tried to avoid going into here. One is more than a passing mention of the relationship of social forces and demands to the legal system, a question too wide to discuss just in terms of lawyers. The other is discussion by other scholars of matters raised by Friedman; examples would be Kagan (1994), on lawyers as an interest group, and McBarnet (1988), on lawyers' manipulation of messages. This is intended as an examination of Friedman's own work.

[5] Friedman 10 (1975).

[6] Id. at 60.

[7] Id. at 160.

[8] Id. at 246–7, 271–2.

[9] Friedman (1994a).

[10] Emphasis in quotations is from Friedman's original text.

Friedman describes the role of lawyers in two ways: In one they are concerned with the content of the message, but in the other (the "track" aspect) they act as "brokers or middlemen" of information. They translate the content of messages into terms and behaviors the client understands; receive rules and regulations, which are diffuse messages broadcast into the air; and store those messages until the client needs them. The government needs lawyers to ensure compliance, and the client needs them as advocate and counselor and also, on occasion, as carriers of feedback information. Later in the same section the lawyer (and Friedman also includes "underground lawyers" from other societies) knows not only the rules but also the ways through the corridors of power, which will ensure that the messages from below get to the right people.[11] The lawyer has "unconscious" power; he or she can "knowingly or not" bend the messages going each way.

Friedman might have developed a more complex picture had research on the legal profession been more advanced when he wrote LS,[12] but he simplifies his picture to ensure its clarity. For instance, in describing the lawyer's role in the communication net, he refers to Blumberg's characterization of the law as confidence game,[13] which is now usually seen as an example of lawyers preferring their own interests – in this case in not impeding the smooth running of an organization of which they are continuing members – to those of their clients. However, Friedman is concerned with effects, the impact of the legal system on society, and the part lawyers play in mediating it, not, here at least, with lawyer-client relations.

He explores the idea of messages coming from the legal system and going back to it, using the expressions "downwards" and "upwards" in doing so, although he points out that these directional words are only metaphors.[14] They take their force, as he might have indicated, from the trappings of authority with which legal actors seeking to influence others dress themselves; he also uses the metaphor of a pyramid to suggest how limited the upward path is.[15]

The significance of Friedman's approach has not been appreciated. He draws attention to the part that lawyers (and other intermediaries) play in the space between governmental, particularly normative, acts and the citizen. The significance of the concept of messages is too little recognized because they are so pervasive and various, and the concept is overlaid by an emphasis on the distinction between laws and judicial decisions, on the one hand, and other governmental acts. His approach

[11] Friedman seems to be hinting that lawyers and their networks act as communicators in ways that are not accounted for by their formal place in the legal system. His whole framework is perhaps even less traditionally legal than one might have thought.

[12] He was able to use a much more apt example in Friedman (1996); see later discussion.

[13] Blumberg (1967).

[14] A parallel thought juxtaposes "penetration," the imposition of government, and "participation" in government: Friedman 44 (1969).

[15] Although Friedman does not emphasize the point in this context, these "upward" flowing messages are part of the "demands" or "social forces" that, in his view, press on and, at least in the long run, shape the legal system.

also opens up the possible equivalence, in a wide-ranging social concept of a legal system, of messages that go downward and upward, and he raises fruitful inquiries into possible directional symmetry. His approach is the best candidate I know of for useful explanation of the role of lawyers in a socially oriented account of a legal system.

Interests, Demands, and Culture

Friedman's approach in LS is to distinguish in general between long-term changes in the legal system and changes in particular laws.[16] It is the latter changes that are relevant here. For all the importance of social forces and interests, they do not make law until they make demands on the system: Legal culture presides over the conversion of interests into demands. The system's response depends on the "structural variable" (the structure of the legal system) and the distribution of power and influence in the outside society. Friedman's argument being for the primacy of social forces, he is against giving any very substantial weight to the structural variable: In particular, he argues against theories of "lag," which suggest that something about the legal system itself can delay change. Instead what does delay change are "real forces, real people – the concrete opposition of interest groups expressed through or in the legal system."[17]

His second point on lawyers is that that they and judges (and government too) are an interest group in their own right;[18] he mentions the profession's values, traditions and habits, strong economic interests, and political strength (including their disproportionate membership in legislatures).

Internal Legal Culture

The third context in which LS discusses lawyers is that of legal culture, the most influential concept in the book. Attitudes toward lawyers, part of what Friedman calls "external legal culture," do not seem to be discussed in LS. However, he does write on the internal legal culture of legal professionals. He recognizes that this internal

---

[16] Friedman uses changes over centuries as a powerful demonstration of the primacy of social forces. At the other end of the scale he accepts that minor and short-term events may well call for minor short-run explanations. "If the question is, why Congress did not enact a national health law *yesterday*, it is a fair answer to point out that yesterday was Sunday, and Congress did not sit. There is no need to drag in big business, doctors' groups or even legal doctrine." Friedman 154 (1975). We now know that this particular answer is insufficient: "The Schiavo case: The Overview; Congress Passes and Bush Signs Schiavo measure," *New York Times*, March 21, 2005. Nevertheless, his general point – that the time-scales of events and explanations should have some correspondence to each other – is a good one.

[17] Friedman 155 (1975).

[18] Id. at 160.

legal culture has a degree of autonomy and that it can affect the pattern of demands made on the legal system. In an exceptionally interesting passage, Friedman indicates some of the difficulties in harmonizing these facts with an approach based on the primacy of society over law:[19]

> A specially important kind of group legal culture is that of legal professionals – the values, ideologies, and principles of lawyers, judges, and others who work within the magical circle of the legal system. The behavior and attitudes of professionals have a great effect on the pattern of demands on the system. To this extent, the legal system does seem more than a conduit, the rope in our metaphor; but the actions of professionals, too, have their explanation. A judge will decide in such a way as to satisfy demands made upon him when it is in his interest to do so or when his peers or his values so demand. The values, however, as we have suggested, are the long-term residue of social structure, representing old power and influence; and peer pressure depends on who the peers are – on patterns of recruitment into the profession, for example, a factor which is far from politically neutral. Hence the complex behavior of professionals, the legal culture of the insiders, is by no means an autonomous growth and by no means an exception to the general proposition about the primacy of society over law.

In the discussion of internal legal culture,[20] lawyers are legal actors, like judges or legislators. "Social pressure" or needs and interests have to be converted into demands that fit the requirements of the internal legal culture, the legal culture of "those members of society who perform specialized legal tasks."[21] Later in LS[22] he describes how "closed" legal systems (those in which reasoning can only be based on a closed set of premises) need a "professional class of law-men," who conversely "have an economic and social interest in keeping a system closed."[23] The relevance of this point is that an internal legal culture favoring a closed system (particularly one that rules out innovation – another of Friedman's categories) will limit the kind of demand that can be made on the system or at least on that limited part of the system in which rules are applied by specialists in law, rather than "specialists in non-legal disciplines, or by lawyers not acting as such or by outright amateurs."[24] The interests of lawyers recur later in a discussion of legal language,[25] which, in addition to being the kind of shorthand useful to any group with shared experiences, marks members of the group who use it off from the ordinary world, giving them status and bonding them together.

[19] Id. at 194.
[20] Id. at Ch. IX.
[21] Id. at 223.
[22] Id. at 246.
[23] As we shall see, Friedman's accounts of the U.S. legal profession suggest that there can be a professional class of "law-men" who see their social and economic interests very differently.
[24] Friedman 247 (1975).
[25] Id. at 262–3.

"Social Change and Legal Change"

Finally, lawyers appear in the chapter entitled "Social Change and Legal Change"; they engage in "law reform," an activity that satisfies a professional need for a "posture of concern for the public good" and also may be a way of asserting their claim to a monopoly of practice, but is of little social significance.[26] However, activist lawyers, in the presence of an activist judiciary and a genuine social movement whose values are shared by at least some judges and power holders who accept the results of disruptive litigation, can upset many old and established arrangements by the use of judicial review.[27] We may see this last passage as written while memories of decisions on desegregation and poverty were still fresh, and it illustrates the conditions under which actors within the legal system may have effects on the legal system and on society if social forces are on their side.

Summary

The intention of this chapter is to see how the points made about lawyers in LS are worked out or supplemented in Friedman's other works. To recapitulate, these points are as follows:

(1) (a) Lawyers play a part in the way the legal system has effects on society by communicating messages about legal norms or rules or other legal acts to citizens.
   (b) Lawyers also pass messages "upwards" to the government or perhaps other legal actors.
   (c) Lawyers can bend the messages each way.
(2) The legal system responds to the social demands made on it, and lawyers are one of the interest groups (like government itself) asserting demands.
(3) The legal culture of lawyers is an internal legal culture and, apparently, a structural element in the legal system. It can affect the demands made on the legal system, but is itself a residue of previous social forces and demands.
(4) Lawyers can have effects on the legal system and society when other social forces assist them.

Although this listing is presented here as a framework for looking at Friedman's other work on lawyers, it should be remembered that he was not himself intending any such explicit analysis of a group that, in his conceptual and descriptive scheme, might almost be thought marginal. Therefore it should not be surprising that he does not use any such framework when he comes to describe lawyers in his other work.

[26] Id. at 271–2.
[27] Id. at 277–8.

HISTORY

I pick out arbitrarily (completeness would be impossible) mentions of lawyers in Friedman's other work to see how they fit in with the picture in LS. This section considers some of his historical work.

Contract Law in America: A Social and Economic Case Study (CLA)

In CLA, there is little description of what lawyers do. There is one apparently large claim: "Lawyers who draft documents and invent new forms of doing business create law in a real and important way."[28] However, this claim is made in the context of the recognition by commercial law of "custom and usage" and "business practice," which "makes possible the free evolution of living patterns of behavior into law." It is thus a comparatively narrow (by Friedman's standards) kind of "law" that they make. Otherwise lawyers mainly appear as an occupation facilitating the transfer of land, an activity they share with land agents (many of whom might also be lawyers). It is this activity, which Friedman will later (in 1989 in "Lawyers in Cross-Cultural Perspective"[29]) use as a basis for his explanation of the nature of the U.S legal profession, that makes law an expansive occupation with few formal limits. Yet he also mentions that the majority of some lawyers' work (in his Period I: 1836–61) was handling debt collection, which they apparently engaged in quite frequently for Eastern investors in or financers of land purchase.

A History of American Law (HAL)

The latest (2005) edition of HAL[30] describes itself as rejecting any notion that law is autonomous. Law is a mirror of society. Perhaps it is a distorted mirror, and perhaps in some regards society mirrors law, but surely law and society interact. The central point remains: Law is the product of social forces, working in society. If it has a life of its own, it is a narrow and restricted life.[31]

Lawyers are discussed in the context of the book's three main chronological sections, the Colonial period,[32] the period from 1776–1850,[33] and the period from

---

[28] Friedman 206 (1965).
[29] Friedman 7–8 (1989).
[30] Friedman (2005). All page references in HAL are to the third paperback edition.
[31] Id. at ix. This seems to replace a less qualified statement in the second edition (12):

"This book treats American law, then, not as a kingdom unto itself, not as a set of rules and concepts, not as the province of lawyers alone, but as a mirror of society. It takes nothing as historical accident, nothing as autonomous, everything as relative and molded by economy and society."

[32] Friedman 53–9 (2005).
[33] Id. at 226–49.

1850 to the end of the nineteenth century.[34] Although HAL contains a chapter entitled "Internal Legal Culture in the Twentieth Century,"[35] for the purposes of our discussion, it does not seem to add to what Friedman said in 2002 in *American Law in the 20th Century* (discussed later).

The Colonial Period

Friedman's description of lawyers in the Colonial period draws a contrast[36] between the continuing unpopularity of lawyers in the seventeenth and well into the eighteenth century and the fact that "a competent, professional bar, dominated by brilliant and successful lawyers . . . existed in all major communities by 1750." Attitudes to lawyers might be seen as aspects of society's external legal culture, but American legal culture before the twentieth century is not explored under that heading in this book. Friedman's discussion of the opposition to lawyers is of interest because of the wide general issues he raises with such a light touch. The range covered in one paragraph[37] on the seventeenth century is extraordinary. He mentions the hostility of revolutionary or utopian regimes to lawyers without the necessary new habits,[38] the dislike of servants of the government among those wishing to run their own affairs, and the inconsistency of a profession that has "special privileges and principles" and a "private, esoteric language" with a theocratic social order, directed from the top. Finally, the Quakers opposed the adversary system in principle and saw lawyers as contentious and unnecessary. Two of these concerns are associated with the legal system, and the others with the position of lawyers in the social order. Friedman describes the latter kind of concern persisting into the eighteenth century, because the lower classes identified lawyers with the upper class, and governors and royal parties were not sure of lawyers' loyalty and afraid of their power. Yet the first kind of concern also comes up in his account, because changes to a more "rational" and "professional" law made it more confusing and remote to merchants and businessmen.

Yet as mentioned, lawyers prospered, and Friedman's account partly shifts from perceptions. Lawyers were a "necessary evil," and "no colony could even try to make do without lawyers."[39] They thrived as "soon as a settled society posed problems for which lawyers had an answer or at least a skill . . . the skill of the lawyer had a definite market value."[40]

The other main topics with which Friedman deals for this period are education and competition, which are obviously not separate in view of the role that the

---

[34] Id. at 463–500.
[35] Id. at 538–53.
[36] Id. at 53–5.
[37] Id. at 53–4.
[38] Cf. Friedman 243, 246 (1975).
[39] Friedman 54 (2005).
[40] Id. at 55.

attempted imposition of educational requirements has historically played in competition in the legal profession. He also discusses[41] the evidence for the degree to which lawyers were "professional" or were only part-time or "amateur." For instance, Friedman sees the statistics for the number of lawyers taking part in the Constitutional Convention or signing the Declaration of Independence as representing a group of people who "identified themselves as lawyers" with a "pride of profession," rather than as members of any other occupation. He cites Boorstin as having seen "the pervasiveness of legal competence and the vagueness of the boundary between legal and other knowledge," but himself sees a less indistinct line than in earlier years between lawyers, who saw themselves as having a "common fund of experience and training,", and laymen.[42] This difference in emphases raises the question[43] whether it makes a difference that functions are assigned to lawyers. Friedman's preference may also show an interest group in formation.[44]

The Revolution to 1850

As far as lawyers are concerned, the period from the Revolution to 1850 is mainly dealt with in a single chapter, "The Bar and its Works" (the same subject for the period from 1850 to 1900 takes two chapters). It touches on a number of themes. The most significant are the growth of numbers at the bar, its attractions to the ambitious (particularly in the West), differences in social background and the divisions between rich and poor lawyers, the significance of litigation both in successful lawyers' practices and generally as a means of establishing a reputation, and the move from itinerant to more settled forms of practice.

Although it was highly unusual, he also describes[45] the practice of R. M. Blatchford, whom his source[46] describes as doing collections, but for city merchants and English exporters. Among the legal documents he drafted "affecting industry, trade and finance" were pledges or conveyances of a security to a trustee where a group of lenders were needed – "the forerunner of the modern corporate trust" and a form of "investment security . . . of the same general nature as the modern investment trust."

He also describes the organization of the bar, emphasizing its inability to control admission to it, because of generally weak governmental control of occupations and high geographical and social mobility. He also describes how mass ownership of land resulted in a society in which many people, not just the noble or the lucky few, needed some rudiments of law, some forms or form books, some know-how about

[41] Id. at 58–9.
[42] Boorstin seems to have run together two ideas: Legal competence might be pervasive in sections of society without any vagueness in the boundary between legal and other knowledge, unless, of course, legal knowledge is defined as that held by lawyers. Friedman's description is neutral on these points.
[43] Friedman 4–5 (1989).
[44] Cf. the mention of language and the interests of lawyers in Friedman 262–3 (1975), cited earlier.
[45] Friedman 232–3 (2005).
[46] Swaine (1946).

the mysterious ways of courts and governments. In short, it was a society that needed a large, amorphous, open-ended profession. The rest of the chapter describes legal education and the literature of the law, going into particular detail on Kent and Story.

On the whole, in A *History of American Law*, Friedman outlines, but does not explore closely, the substance of what lawyers did for their clients. In this period too, he emphasizes the significance of litigation, both quantitatively as part of the lawyer's practice and also for its significance in establishing and spreading the lawyer's reputation. Yet in another chapter ("Outposts of the Law") he had described[47] the opportunities for ambitious young men in the new states and territories:

> The economic base was land, town land and country land. Who had the skill to decipher titles to land? Who could master the maze of rules on land grants, or on the sale and transfer of land? Only the lawyers.

The Period from 1850–1900
In his description of lawyers in the second half of the nineteenth century, Friedman still describes practice in general terms. He emphasizes the general growth in numbers and also the rise of the Wall Street bar as "a servant and advisor to big business, an architect of financial structures; it did not feed on law-suits, rather it avoided them."[48]

The picture of the rest of the bar is inevitably less clear. On the one hand, the New York Code of Civil Procedure symbolized "in a way, the end of the hegemony of the court-room"; that the "work of the lawyer became less centered on litigation and court-room work . . . was an outstanding fact of the practice in the second half of the century." Yet "[m]ost lawyers still went to court."[47] Later he says that "[s]mall-town and small-city practice changed less in this period than big city practice"; the "gap between Wall Street and Main Street was very wide."[48] For these other lawyers, litigation, and principally collections, was a major part of their practice.[49] He suggests[50] that "The Nimble Profession" was responding to competition and social invention elsewhere,[51] which had affected their work in title searches and, by the end of the century, in debt collection and estate work.

A *History of American Law*: A Summary
As mentioned, Friedman notes in *The Legal System* (LS) that the government needs lawyers to ensure compliance and that clients need them as an advocate and counselor. Some of the activities lawyers perform as advocates and counselors

---

[47] Friedman 110 (2005). See the reference above to the significance of land-holding.
[48] Id. at 490.
[49] Id. at 491.
[50] Id. at 483.
[51] Friedman points out that they might have chosen something smaller and narrower, restricting themselves to specialist activities in the manner of barristers or brain surgeons.

may be sending messages upward, and others may be the interpretation of messages coming downwards. What is described in HAL allows us to look at these activities more carefully.

The role of the lawyer in the frontier conditions described in HAL[52] in mastering the maze of rules on land grants or on the sale and transfer of land illustrates perfectly the interpretation of messages, as does Friedman's description of them as "fuzzy or complex."[53] This description also bypasses any need to discuss the messages' exact origin and legal status. Yet the "messages" approach seems hard to fit in even to land transfers or to acting on behalf of Eastern investors; in these roles the lawyer may be using a knowledge of the messages, along with a possibly wide knowledge of local affairs and the commercial environment, to achieve the clients' aims. Again, Blatchford's activities in drafting documents for trade and finance, or the innovations in corporate and investment trusts in which he took part, require a knowledge of governmental messages, but go far beyond their interpretation to the construction of new legal institutions.

At one level Friedman's description does no more than to point out the difference between duty-imposing and power-conferring rules or facilitative rules, but in this context we are concerned not so much with the rules as with the (socially sanctioned) roles of lawyers in the legal system. Just as in relation to duty-imposing rules they pass on the messages of government about what citizens must do, lawyers might be seen as just passing on the messages about the powers that citizens may exercise. However, if we are looking at the working legal system that Friedman describes in HAL, rather than at a jurisprudentially analyzed set of rules, the practical role of lawyers clearly goes further than merely explaining the rules about land title and transfer or lending on security.

Similarly, if we bear in mind the points made about lawyers in LS, as set out earlier, and look broadly at the rich historical description in HAL, we are reading on the whole about internal legal culture, which much of Friedman's other writings might lead us to suppose is without great social significance. However, if we think in terms of the external legal culture that causes society to use or turn away from law, he is describing a profession on the receiving end of many demands, with an internal culture of willing reception of them. What HAL suggests is a wider vision of the legal system than appears in LS. The legal system contains not only messengers or information brokers but also a group of lawyers who would put their legal knowledge to use wherever and in whatever way it might pay them, with few boundaries imposed by legal rules or their own culture. In this context, the relaxed educational and admission requirements, which allowed the entry of hungry and ambitious practitioners, worked to promote this internal culture, which at least did not discourage but facilitated and perhaps encouraged further demands and an

[52] Id. at 110 (2005).
[53] Friedman 60 (1975).

external legal culture of resort to lawyers. This connection between internal legal culture and external legal culture and demands illustrates Friedman's statement in LS that the "behavior and attitudes of professionals have a great effect on the pattern of demands on the system."[54] Here, however, it is intended to point out, too, that the internal legal culture may result in actors who are more than messengers or information brokers.[55]

American Law in the 20th Century (*ALTC*; 2002)

Although this recent work of Friedman's is historical in approach, it might in fact have been grouped with the works in the following section on social analysis, whose findings are incorporated into its narrative. Like his other historical work (perhaps like all his other work), ALTC is not intended to test or even illustrate the theses of LS, although it shares the same general attitude toward the primacy of society.[56]

Although ALTC marks the explosion in the number of lawyers, particularly after World War II, in its introduction,[57] it deals with the legal profession in only one chapter, on internal legal culture. This heading deemphasizes what might correspond to the message-transmission aspects of LS – what lawyers do – but the text is somewhat more fruitful. Lawyers are not courtroom warriors; instead they service business. In doing so, "they maneuver through tangles of red tape; they cope with federal, state, and local government"; here the messenger and information-broking functions are obviously significant. Yet they also "help form corporations; they advise on corporate affairs . . . they help put deals together."[58]

Although the chapter describes summarily nonbusiness matters – criminal defense work, divorce and family law, civil rights, and personal injury law for plaintiffs – its main emphasis is on forms of practice, size of firms, and competition. Declining client loyalties toward transactionalist lawyers and the rise of the billable hour[59] are also of interest, because they tackle the difficult problem of the value of what lawyers do. The sheer number of lawyers and their ability to make money suggest that they serve some function. The truth is that the legal system is so complex and so ubiquitous that lawyers have become indispensable. People in trouble obviously need a lawyer. Other people need lawyers to stay out of trouble. Similarly, he concludes, Silicon Valley lawyers must have been doing something beneficial while they got rich; the

---

[54] Id. at 194.

[55] The phrasing of this account runs somewhat counter to Friedman's view that internal legal culture is by no means an exception to the general proposition about the primacy of society over law. Friedman 194 (1975). A full discussion of that point even in this context would go far outside the intended scope of the chapter.

[56] Cf. Friedman 7 (2002), where he describes the growth of "legal stuff." "Changes in legal culture account for a lot of the growth. The supply of law is bigger because the demand is bigger." Technology, too, has a part to play.

[57] Id. at 9.

[58] Id. at 461.

[59] Id. at 469 ff.

lawyers were undoubtedly guiding their clients across dangerous legal minefields.[60] Here the references to staying out of trouble and "legal minefields" suggest the activity of information broking, although as we see later, elsewhere he describes a much more facilitative and constructive role for Silicon Valley lawyers. People in trouble may need lawyers for more than information and passing messages to the government; they may need suggestions for courses of action, such as negotiating with creditors or selling their business, that will get them out of it.

On the growth of the welfare state, he comments, "the mobilization of hundreds of eager, reform-minded, talented lawyers and other who flocked to Washington, was crucial."[61] Yet there are limits to what even motivated lawyers can do: "[W]hite, middle-class America's deep distaste for the urban poor was too great a barrier" for poverty lawyers and welfare litigation. . . . Public interest lawyers can huff and puff, but they can blow down only houses made of straw."[62]

SOCIAL ANALYSIS

In three wide-ranging books, *Total Justice* (TJ; 1985), *The Republic of Choice: Law, Authority, and Culture* (RC; 1990), and *The Horizontal Society* (HS; 1990), Friedman describes some broad changes in attitudes, mainly in U.S. society, although he discusses parallel movements elsewhere and HS has a more general approach. All three books have relevance to what he would describe as the external legal culture of a society. The goal here is not to consider any of them as a whole, as Kagan does in Chapter 8 in this volume on Total Justice, but to pick out their mentions of lawyers.

It is relevant here that TJ reads as a broad response to perceptions that there is too much "something" in U.S. society – too many lawyers, too much law, or too much litigation. More narrowly, in setting out the first complaint of too many lawyers, Friedman suggests that demand is responsible. To those who argue that lawyers create demand, his answer is that the evidence in favor of that argument is hard to find, and if lawyers have a monopoly on certain activities they keep the demand for lawyers artificially high. Yet this is not the same as creating the demand for what lawyers do.

To the argument that they are too powerful, he suggests that there is no clear evidence of their effects.[63] An earlier comment, in a characteristic tone, had been even more skeptical:

> it is wholly erroneous to assume that, had the legal profession not mobilized itself to serve the needs of industrial corporations, modern big business would have been strangled in infancy and the United States would have stayed in the era of cottage handicrafts and subsistence agriculture.[64]

[60] Id. at 470.
[61] Id. at 176.
[62] Id. at 471–2.
[63] Friedman 10 (1985).
[64] Friedman 1540 (1963).

In a section in TJ, "The Case against the Case against the Law,"[65] he reiterates the significance of demand[66] and argues that "on the whole, lawyers do not lead; they follow. The demand for their services comes from outside the legal system."[67] He cites ambulance chasing as the example of a much criticized practice that was a response to a social demand. However, when the book moves on to the more general discussion of the changes in culture, which are its main focus, there is little or nothing on the part that lawyers or segments of the legal profession may have contributed to them. Very much the same is true in RC and HS, although one could imagine descriptions of lawyers' contributions, for instance, to a culture of free, open choice or to judicial review.[68] This is in line with the general approach of LS and of Friedman's work generally in treating internal legal culture, where significant, as dependent on external social forces.

However, in HS there is a suggestion that the global practice of law is an element, along with banks and big corporations, in the construction of a shared global culture.[69] This suggestion may be related to an idea that appears in "Lawyers in Cross-Cultural Perspective" (LCCP)[70] that lawyers can create a "working rationality," although in HS this role is not confined to lawyers. Law's role in the creation of a global culture seems to be another instance of the nonlegal involvement of lawyers, which was suggested in his original LS passage on messages and information broking.[71]

ARTICLES AND ESSAYS

Of Friedman's many articles and essays, I pick three that bear on the subject of this chapter: "Lawyers in Cross-Cultural Perspective" (LCCP; 1989); "Law, Lawyers and Legal Practice in Silicon Valley" (Friedman et al.; 1989); and "Are We a Litigious People?" (AWLP; 1996). These papers were originally written for meetings and a symposium between 1984 and 1993. The first two are explicitly about lawyers.

"Lawyers in Cross-Cultural Perspective" (LCCP)

In the period between LS (1975) and LCCP (written in 1984 and published in 1989), the growth in the size of legal professions had, if anything, accelerated not only in the

---

[65] Friedman 23 ff. (1985).

[66] Id. at 25.

[67] See also Friedman 13–14 (1990).

[68] Friedman 67–9 (1999).

[69] Id. at 13.

[70] Friedman 17–18 (1989).

[71] See note 11. These are also apparent examples of the effects of lawyers' work, touched on in LS in the context of social change and legal change and only occasionally in Friedman's other work. A difficulty with this topic is touched on later.

United States but also in other countries, and scholarly interest in the legal profession had increased, giving Friedman more materials on which to draw. However, serious interest in globalization and global legal practice was still to come.

LCCP takes off from a description of a functional approach to the generation and answering of questions about lawyers, an approach that was not present, in this particular context, in LS. This description includes an important section on reasons why the legal profession originally expanded so greatly in the United States and continued to expand; even if there are necessary social functions in most modern societies of a kind that could be performed by occupations other than lawyers, the early development of a middle class in the United States with needs for advice on landholding had given rise to a legal profession ready to take on any opportunities that might come its way.[72] The argument from the American experience suggests "that the precise role of the legal profession is historically contingent."[73] In his discussion of the functional approach, Friedman had returned to the information-broking activity he set out in LS in the context of communication, which was the prerequisite for law's having any effect in society. However, in LCCP, he makes no reference to the upward communication touched on in the earlier work.[74] Yet information brokers are a necessity, because no "citizen, no entrepreneur can know or understand everything about law or government regulation; the system has become too complicated." He points out that information broking is not inherently a "lawyer-job" and is shared, on what may be a contentious basis, with thousands of other people who are "paid to know about certain rules and regulations, where to find them, and what to do about them."[75] Nevertheless he is reluctant to accept that it makes no difference whether functions are performed by lawyers or by some other group.[76]

The majority of the essay is devoted to the effects that lawyers have on society, a topic absent in LS, and to suggesting a possible gloss on the principal message in LS – that lawyers are on the same footing as the legal system generally, subject to the forces and demands of society in general. He picks out several fields for evaluation of the part they play in the reduction of legal pluralism, in the rise of capitalism, and in the maintenance of the status quo, as well as their ideological or symbolic role in society. One of the most interesting observations is that lawyers can produce "a *working* rationality in place of indigestible legal forms" by the use of their general know-how and experience in addition to their expertise in law.[77]

---

[72] Friedman 7–8 (1989). In LLIED he sums this up: "Millions of people had a stake in the economy; they needed basic legal services and skills. This produced a large, active legal profession; and it generated a *concept* of lawyers as factotums, do-it-alls, general advisers, people who knew their way around in business and government." Friedman 21 (1994a).

[73] Friedman 8 (1989).

[74] He does, however, discuss upward communication in AWLP. Friedman 54 (1996).

[75] Friedman 3 (1989). See also Friedman 8 (1994a).

[76] Friedman 4–5 (1989).

[77] Id. at 17–18.

"Law, Lawyers and Legal Practice in Silicon Valley" (LLLP)

LLLP (written with Robert Gordon and others) addressed a region close to Friedman's home. Although it is a study triggered by the increasing importance of the local industrial district and the enormous local growth in the population of lawyers, it nevertheless is not confined to the best known technology-oriented law firms, but shows how the local bar had its roots in an ordinary and continuing small-town practice. After a general survey (based on other literature) of the role of lawyers in typical growing companies, the article describes the specific Silicon Valley experience.[78] Even as the industries grew, some lawyers were "busy at their usual jobs – as pervasive facilitators in society."[79]

Of the rapidly growing high-tech law firms the authors write,

> In one sense they were merely riding the waves. Or did the firms help to make the waves? Did they make the boom possible by clearing away legal obstacles, by finding and broking the union of brains and money, and by structuring arrangements?[80]

The authors suggest that it is probably best to accept both views as reasonably accurate. Yet they give not their own accounts, but those of some leading local lawyers of the practice roles and styles that in their view distinguish Silicon Valley lawyers from New York lawyers – general business advice based on local knowledge, access to local finance, a facilitative approach to client problems, and a style of practice matched to the local business culture.[81] The authors expand on these roles and relate them to their previous account of business phases.[82] Ultimately, however, they regard questions about effects as too hard to answer, resting on thought experiments or quasi-experiments with only limited comparability.

"Are We a Litigious People?" (AWLP)

In AWLP Friedman considers the evidence for the existence and causes of adversarial legalism. Among the possible causes, he considers the numbers and activities of lawyers. He points out that many lawyers engage in activities that cannot be described as part of adversarial legalism. Some of the examples are court related, whereas others

---

[78] Friedman et al. 554 ff. (1989).

[79] Id. at 561.

[80] Id. at 561. What is the relationship between the proposition that the legal system (as a living organism) is shaped by the demands made on it by society, and the proposition that what lawyers do can affect society? Are the effects of lawyers' activities also predictable by the balance of social forces? Recall the comment that public-interest lawyers could only blow down "houses made of straw." Is it true that Indian casinos in the United States (an $18bn+ business) were the result of a suggestion by a legal services lawyer? If so, what social forces were at work?

[81] In these accounts by lawyers, culture, demands, and outputs seem very close, and "legal obstacles" and the "dangerous legal minefields" mentioned in ALTC 470 are less emphasized.

[82] Interesting discussions on changes over time and the rise of in-house counsel in the area do not seem relevant to the point of this chapter.

are best described as "facilitating": Many lawyers mediate, negotiate, help businesses and individuals reach goals, and clear away obstacles from their path. They develop innovations, help clients "manage uncertainty," and act as middle-men between investors and entrepreneurs.[83] Although he concedes that some adversarial legalism is contributed to or caused by lawyers (as Kagan had argued[84]), he feels that, if we have to choose, "adversarial legalism is the *cause* of the huge size of the legal profession, rather than the effect of it."[85] What is significant for the present discussion is not the conclusion about adversarial legalism, but that so much of what he describes does not fit comfortably into even a broad conception of "message passing," which in AWLP seems to be concerned with representatives and lobbyists,[86] though he is able, very aptly, to cite Edelman et al. (1992) for lawyers' power to "distort the message and modify the rule."[87]

WHAT LAWYERS KNOW AND DO

I have summarized a number of passages in which Friedman describes what lawyers do: some activities fit into the message passing discussed in LS and others, such as litigation and institution making, do so uneasily, if at all. I have perhaps missed the article in which Friedman described what lawyers do in one place in English, and I have not been able to read his 1994 article, "What Do Lawyers Know? Toward a Sociology of Legal Practice" (Friedman 1994b), as it is in Japanese. Some clues may be found in what he wrote about lawyers' knowledge in a 1997 NSF grant application (quoted with his permission), in which he categorizes the main types of knowledge possessed by lawyers (the numbers are added for ease of reference):

(1) "a body of knowledge of 'the law'" and how to find the relevant law
(2) "translation skills" – the ability to transform raw "facts" or the stories and demands of clients into "legal" facts; to know what elements of a situation are or are not legally relevant
(3) transaction-experiences and skills, ways of handling situations, a sense of what is typical and what is unusual in situations, knowledge of how to proceed in certain modal situations – the steps to take and in what order, the forms to fill out, transaction-traditions and local customs
(4) problem-solving, creative, or innovative skills; inventions of legal structures and forms for new and difficult situations or better ways to handle old situations that go beyond customary ways of structuring transactions

[83] Friedman 54 (1996).
[84] See Kagan (1994).
[85] Friedman 55 (1996).
[86] Id. at 54. This would be true even if message passing were extended to messages between citizens; however, that would not fit tidily into the LS picture of "upwards" and "downwards."
[87] Id. at 74, n. 9. The article cited suggests that other professions may go even further.

(5) documentary sense: skill in reading and in reading between the lines, drafting skills, ways of verbally structuring transactions

(6) advocacy, litigation, and bargaining skills, including modes of arguing, negotiating, mediating, dealing with lawyers for the "other side," and counseling and "cooling out" clients

(7) networking and corridor skills; knowledge of the ins and outs of court, business, or governmental bureaucracies; knowing the right people to call, the right doors to open; the right names, places, and times; reciprocity building and cultivation of contacts

(8) interdisciplinary knowledge: economics, statistics, medicine, engineering, computer science, psychiatry, chemistry, social work –where relevant to particular transactions or aspects of practice

To what extent do these fall within the message transmission account? (1) does, and (2) can be seen as passing messages "from below"; (3), (4), (5), and (6) for the most part seem to go appreciably beyond it, although "cooling out" clients is a quintessential "message" function; (7) may be a prerequisite for passing messages "from below," although business and governmental bureaucracies are dealt with together; and (8) seems a more general background to whatever they do.

CONCLUSION

The trigger for this chapter was the fact that Friedman has been one of the few people to present a social science account of legal systems, with a description of the place of lawyers within them. One of the most striking and successful elements in that account is the part played in the effects and effectiveness of law by the communication of its messages and the role played by lawyers in that communication. A second is the legal culture of actors, including lawyers, in the legal system: the "internal legal culture." A third is the part played by the demands made on the legal system by interest groups, of whom lawyers are one.

The work of the legal historian and social analyst does not develop these points directly. The first element is almost totally passed over, except perhaps in ALTC, which discusses the part played by lawyers in the communication of messages. Instead, the emphasis is on the active part they play in litigation, the drawing up of documents, and the development of institutions. On the whole, what is described is a much more active response to the demands of clients, which seem to go far beyond a need for information about messages.[88] One should remember Friedman's points that not all functions that lawyers perform necessarily have to be performed by lawyers[89] and that even the message-transmission function is often performed by

---

[88] See, e.g., Friedman et al. 562–3 (1989).
[89] Friedman 9 (1989).

others.[90] Nevertheless, a summary of Friedman's work in legal history and social analysis suggests that a more complete social science account of legal systems would have a place for a group of people with a more or less specialized knowledge of legal rules using it actively (probably along with other knowledge) to achieve a range of public and private purposes.[91]

In contrast, Friedman's other work has quite a lot to say about internal legal culture in the United States (although it is not usually identified as such). In particular, what is variously described as a "nimble" profession (HAL), a "jack-of-all-trades" (LCCP),[92] or "factotums" (LLIED)[93] because of its readiness to respond to all kinds of demands,[94] not just those framed narrowly within preexisting categories, contributed to an external legal culture that favored resort to law. On the whole, LS downplays the independent significance of that part of internal legal culture that previous legal writers had emphasized – modes of legal thought and perhaps internal legal culture generally (see the earlier discussion).

On the whole the other writing also adds little to the description in LS of lawyers as an interest group. HAL cites concern for the power of lawyers as a reason for their unpopularity in the colonial period,[95] and the passing reference to the part played by reform-minded lawyers in the New Deal in ALTC may also be relevant,[96] although it might also indicate the significance of legal expertise as a resource in social contests, which does not fit into the LS framework at all well. In TJ he rather plays down the power of lawyers.[97]

It will always be hard to lay down strict criteria for the part played in a social science account of legal systems by elements that can be seen as marginal or historically contingent. In my view, Friedman's other work suggests that such an account should include a place for the constructive and institutional work pervasive in modern legal systems (characteristically but not invariably carried out by lawyers), and allow more specifically for the likelihood that internal legal culture can have effects on external legal culture, even if (and this has not been discussed in this chapter) both are ultimately determined by wider social forces. There can be no doubt whose clarity of thought and direct but elegant prose would be best suited to the task.

[90] Id. at 3.
[91] Much modern Anglo-American legislation seems to take for granted the existence of such groups. It will be recalled that Friedman points out that lawyers may "bend" the messages as they go in either direction: Friedman 62 (1975). A more radical development of this idea might be that there are no messages, only texts, which legal actors can manipulate or use as resources in their own interests or those of their clients. I have found no support for this kind of approach in any of the works of Friedman discussed here.
[92] Friedman 6 (1989).
[93] Friedman 21 (1994a).
[94] "Every major social development turns into an opportunity for lawyers." Friedman 8 (1989).
[95] Friedman 54 (2005).
[96] Friedman 176 (2002).
[97] Friedman 10 (1985).

REFERENCES

Blumberg, Abraham (1967). The Practice of Law as Confidence Game, 1 *Law & Soc'y Rev.* 15.

Edelman, Lauren B., Steven E. Abraham, and Howard S. Erlanger (1992). Professional Construction of Law: The Inflated Threat of Wrongful Discharge, 26 *Law & Soc'y Rev.* 47.

Friedman, Lawrence (1959). A Comment on "Bar Reactions to Legal Periodicals: The West Virginia Survey," 11 *J. Legal Educ.* 384.

———. (1963). Review, Levy, Corporation Lawyer: Saint or Sinner? 63 *Colum. L. Rev.* 1537.

———. (1965). *Contract Law in America: A Social and Economic Case Study.* Madison: University of Wisconsin Press.

———. (1969). Legal Culture and Social Development, 4 *Law & Soc'y Rev.* 29.

———. (1975). *The Legal System: A Social Science Perspective.* New York: Russell Sage Foundation.

———. (1977). The Social and Political Context of the War on Poverty: An Overview, in Robert Haveman, ed., A *Decade of Federal Antipoverty Programs: Achievements, Failures, and Lessons.* New York: Academic Press.

———. (1985). *Total Justice.* New York: Russell Sage Foundation.

———. (1989). Lawyers in Cross-Cultural Perspective, in Richard L. Abel and Philip S. C. Lewis, eds., *Lawyers in Society, vol. III, Comparative Theories.* Berkeley: University of California Press.

———. (1990). *The Republic of Choice: Law, Authority and Culture.* Cambridge, MA: Harvard University Press.

———. (1994a). Law, Legal Institutions, and Economic Development, in Philip S. C. Lewis, ed., *Law and Technology in the Pacific Community.* Boulder: Westview Press.

———. (1994b). What Do Lawyers Know? Toward a Sociology of Legal Practice, (in Japanese), 44(1) *Kobe Hogaku Zasshi (Kobe L.J.)* 172.

———. (1996). Are We a Litigious People? in Lawrence M. Friedman and Harry N. Scheiber, eds., *Legal Culture and the Legal Profession.* Boulder: Westview Press.

———. (1999). *The Horizontal Society.* New Haven: Yale University Press.

———. (2002). *American Law in the 20th Century.* New Haven: Yale University Press.

———. (2005). *A History of American Law.* 3d. edition. New York: Simon & Schuster.

Friedman, Lawrence, Robert Gordon, Sophie Pirie, and Edwin Whatley (1989). Law, Lawyers, and Legal Practice in Silicon Valley: A Preliminary Report, 64 *Ind. L.J.* 555.

Kagan, Robert A. (1994). Do Lawyers Cause Adversarial Legalism? A Preliminary Inquiry, 19 *Law & Soc. Inquiry* 1.

Lewis, Philip S.C. (1989). Comparison and Change in the Study of Legal Professions, in Richard L. Abel and Philip S. C. Lewis, eds., *Lawyers in Society, vol. III, Comparative Theories.* Berkeley: University of California Press.

McBarnet, Doreen (1988). Law, Policy, and Legal Avoidance: Can Law Effectively Implement Egalitarian Policies?, 15 *J. Law Soc'y* 113.

Swaine, Robert (1946). *The Cravath Firm and its Predecessors, 1819–1948*, vol. 1. New York: Ad Press.

11

Legal Culture and the State in Modern Japan

Continuity and Change

Malcolm M. Feeley and Setsuo Miyazawa

INTRODUCTION

Thirty years ago Lawrence Friedman introduced the concept of "legal culture," and it quickly became a major organizing concept in sociolegal studies.[1] Inspired by the work of Willard Hurst, Gabriel Almond, and Sidney Verba, he argued that law is best understood as a system of social forces, one that both produces and responds to these forces. He invited scholars to embrace the concept of "legal culture," move beyond their traditional concern with doctrine, and instead explore the social forces that give rise to law and legal change. He was particularly interested in forces that give rise to legal change and, in turn, the impact law has on society. It was broadly an appeal for empirical inquiry sources and the effects of the law.

To facilitate systematic inquiry Friedman distinguished between external legal culture and internal legal culture. The former includes those social factors "constantly at work on the law" and those "parts of general culture – customs, opinions, ways of doing and thinking – that bend social forces toward or away from the law."[2] Internal legal culture includes the distinct culture of legal professionals and allied actors who work within the legal system. According to Friedman, although law is far from an autonomous self-regulating system, nevertheless those few specialists who administer it and possess expert knowledge of it are far from passive actors responding to uncontrollable social forces. In reacting to these forces, they have, within limits, the capacity to shape and refine them.

Since adapting the term "legal culture" from Almond and Verba's classic work, *The Civic Culture*, and setting out his own general framework, Friedman's work

---

[1] Friedman (1975).
[2] Id. at 15.

This is a slightly revised and shortened version of a paper presented at the Symposium in Honor of Lawrence M. Friedman at Stanford Law School on October 1, 2005. The text was revised as of August 2007, and footnotes were added in January 2010.

has been picked up and used by vast numbers of scholars. It is perhaps the most influential framework within sociolegal studies in the world. Most of those who employ this framework (either explicitly or implicitly) emphasize "external" legal culture and seek to account for law, legal practice, and legal change as a function of this larger legal culture. Much less attention has been directed at his idea of "internal" legal culture. Furthermore, most of those who employ his framework have applied it to Western legal systems where perhaps it is most compatible with the pluralist analysis that characterizes so much Western sociopolitical scholarship.

In this chapter we apply his concept of external and internal legal cultures in a non-Western setting, Japan. In particular we examine the emerging features of the internal legal culture over time and connect this development to broader changes in Japanese society and its external legal culture. This is part of a larger project that explores the relationship of the "legal complex" to the rise of the moderate, liberal state.[3]

We argue that there is substantial continuity in Japanese legal culture from the Tokugawa era to today. The legal system in Japan has not developed a robust and wholly independent "internal" culture. Traditionally law in Japan has been indistinguishable from public administration, and to a considerable extent it remains so today. Despite this continuity, however, the legal system has gradually become more developed and distinct, yielding something of a separate and robust "internal" culture of legal professionals. Yet, the state still tries to influence the shape of the legal complex, and the bar often depends on the state to promote its interests and ideals, in much the same way that the state's domination of civil society has been maintained throughout modern Japanese history.[4]

THE STATE AND THE LEGAL COMPLEX BEFORE WORLD WAR II

Outline of the Pre–World War II Situation

The history of Japanese law is largely a history of Japanese public administration. Until the modern era, there was no meaningful distinct or autonomous legal system or even the "myth" of one.[5] Law was widely understood to be a feature of administration and not a distinct sphere, let alone an autonomous system. In pre-Meiji Japan, the Japanese government forbade the establishment of a separate legal profession. Despite various efforts to skirt this prohibition, the state was largely successful in insisting that litigants appear before its administrators without aid of attorneys. Indeed laws governing behavior in many walks of life were not even published or circulated, but were invoked after the fact by administrators who thought of them as but

---

3 See Halliday and Karpik (1997); Halliday, Karpik, and Feeley (2007); Feeley and Miyazawa (2007).
4 Garon (2003).
5 Shapiro (1981).

one of many sanctions they had at their disposal to assure order. The consequence was of course to concentrate power into the hands of state bureaucrats.

Even when Western-style law and legal training were introduced in Japan during the Meiji era, they were imposed for purposes of state. Western-style law was adopted to head off Western imperialism, and law schools were created to train government bureaucrats in its intricacies. Although these plans did not unfold precisely as planned – support for the rule of law and a desire to be part of an independent legal profession grew dramatically – Meiji officials were vigorous in trying to stamp out the emergence of any idea of autonomous law or a distinct internal legal culture shared by the bench and the bar. In the next sections of this chapter, we describe the long-standing connection between law and state administration and then chart the painfully slow but steady rise of a separate and distinct internal legal culture through the post–World War II period.

The State and the Legal Complex in Tokugawa Japan

It is conventional to start a historical analysis of modern Japan from the Meiji Restoration in 1868, contrasting Meiji-era Japan with the two and a half centuries of Tokugawa rule that preceded it. However, this chapter emphasizes the continuities between the two periods to show that many developments that are associated with the Meiji era were in fact extensions of characteristics of the earlier era. An excellent example of recent scholarship that demonstrates these continuities is Herman Ooms' study of civic life and power struggles in Tokugawa villages.[6]

Ooms describes vibrant communities rife with conflict, whose residents seethed with envy and resentment, were possessed of a refined legal consciousness, and were quick to name and blame and claim: "To change unwanted situations, the peasants relied far more frequently on suits and petitions than on mass protests or uprisings."[7] However, he goes on to show how the distinction between law "suits" and personal "petitions" was blurred. The village judge and headman were one and the same person. Both petitions and lawsuits used a suppicatory form of address that appealed to the "good will" of the official decision maker, and outcomes were routinely "not verdicts but conciliations or compromises without clear-cut winners or losers."[8] In addition, the types of petitions and their solutions were affected by the status of the parties involved. Still, Ooms observes, "One cannot avoid the impression that lawyerless Tokugawa Japan was far more litigious than the Japan of today."[9]

At the national level the Tokugawa shogunate developed a sophisticated form of commercial law to facilitate a robust commercial economy. Codes were developed,

---

6 Ooms (1996).
7 Id. at 8.
8 Id. at 8–9.
9 Id. at 8.

judges handed down decisions, and rulings were written down and used as precedents. A complicated legal order capable of dealing with problems arising from an advanced commercial life – bills of exchange, banks, clearinghouses and produce exchange, promissory notes and checks, and chain stores – was created. There was an elaborate judicial system, with national courts in Edo, the capital, under the direct control of the central authorities, and a far-flung system of local courts staffed by members of the leading *daimyos* (feudal lords). Village headmen and other officials handled local disputes. However, all the courts ultimately derived their authority from the shogunate. "Going to Edo" was a common phrase of the Tokugawa period.

Although it was sophisticated, the legal system was thoroughly paternalistic. In Weberian terms, Tokugawa justice was more like a system of substantive irrational justice, not of formal rational legal justice. The closing article of the Code of 1615 symbolizes this spirit. Quoting Confucius, it states, "Let the people abide by the law, but not be instructed in it." One well-known Tokugawa dictum holds, "Unreason is less than Reason; Reason is less than Law; Law is less than Authority; and Authority is less than Heaven."[10] Accordingly, many codes and judicial decisions were never published.[11] Furthermore, law was not universally available. "Whether they were family or feudal, the rule was that suits brought by inferiors were not accepted."[12] Still at the village level, regulations admonishing residents to fulfill their civic duties were required to be read aloud annually to assembled villagers. Criminal punishments were specified in detail and elaborately graded by the status of both the offender and the victim.[13] Yet within these strictures, people could and did complain to authorities, and in theory everyone – men and women – had a voice.[14]

For all this sophistication, law in Tokugawa Japan was not autonomous. Legal professionals had not developed their own distinct legal culture. Its judiciary is best understood in terms of division of labor and specialization within the well-developed bureaucracy, not as a separate or distinct "branch" in Montesquieu's sense. Law may have been formal in a great many ways, and it possessed a high degree of consistency and regularity. Certainly judges were celebrated for their wisdom and lack of bias. However, there was never any doubt that at some level law was an instrument, a tool used by officials to foster order.

In the Tokugawa era, there was no position that could conventionally be understood as the functional equivalent of today's lawyer. The judicial process was inquisitorial; wise and knowledgeable judges were expected to investigate matters, and affected parties were expected to cooperate in the quest for substantive justice. Officials believed that there was no need to have agents speak in lieu of the parties themselves: Administrators, like wise parents, were capable of sorting out conflicts,

---

[10] Id. at 312.
[11] Hiramatsu (1981).
[12] Henderson 118 (1965).
[13] Ooms 39 (1996).
[14] Id. at 34.

imposing responsibilities, and acting decisively but fairly. To suggest otherwise was to insult their capacities.

Still, as a matter of practice in a great many areas regulated by the law, there were those who came to act in behalf of others and even receive fees for doing so. Known as *kujishi*, they were proprietors of inns at which parties to litigation stayed while awaiting a hearing before a judge.[15] However, the role of *kujishi* did not evolve into that of a professional advocate. *Kujishi* were not required to have legal training, and they never gained official recognition. The popular literature of the times portrays them as shysters; there is no counter-narrative that portrays even a tiny fraction of them as champions of the rights of the underdog. In contrast, there is a large and robust popular literature that celebrates the wise administrator-judge who capably investigates matters and crafts Solomon-like judgments.

The moral is clear: Justice flows from rulers who have the wisdom to ferret out truth and the insight to discover true character. Law was "administration," and the extent to which it was moderate had more to do with benevolent paternalism[16] than with limits imposed by a rule of law. Law had no anchor in civil society. Indeed civil society may not even have existed in Japan in any meaningful form at the time.[17] In the next section, we describe how Meiji Japan inherited and built on this association between state and law and the extent to which this relationship was slowly transformed and the two separated, as a distinct internal legal culture associated with legal specialists and somewhat separate from state administration emerged.

Meiji Restoration

Although the Meiji Restoration of 1868 did restore the symbolic importance of the emperor, it restored little else. Rather it ushered in a period of unprecedented change. In an effort to fend off Western imperialist powers, Meiji leaders adopted Western institutions with a vengeance – although, as they emphasized, on Japan's own terms and not at the end of a gun barrel.

The effects of this effort were staggering. Within twenty-five years Japan was transformed from a feudal society whose economy was based on agriculture and light manufacturing into one of the world's major economic and colonial powers. By the early twentieth century its industrial output ranked fourth in the world, behind only the United States, Great Britain, and Germany.[18] Its colonial holdings on mainland Asia and throughout the Pacific islands made it one of the world's great imperial powers. This rapid change condensed into a quarter-century a process that had taken well over one hundred years in England: the displacement of the feudal, land-based aristocracy by the rising new commercial and industrial elite.

---

[15] See, e.g., Ooms (1996); Matsui 3 (1990); and Ch'en 73 (1981).
[16] Foote (1992).
[17] Garon (2003).
[18] Holt and Turner (1966).

To consolidate this change, the leaders began to establish many of the features of modern Western governments – popular elections, a parliamentary system, and a judicial system. However, the new Meiji constitution adopted in 1889 (many of its provisions had been put into place some years earlier) maintained the tradition of rule by oligarchy. Sovereignty continued to reside in the emperor, not the people,[19] although the emperor was "little more than [a] legitimating façade."[20] Real authority resided with the prime minister and his cabinet of ministers, all drawn from the new elites associated with the new economy. Unlike modern parliamentary democracies, the prime minister was named by and responsible to the emperor and not the legislature. In effect this meant rule by a self-perpetuating oligarchy. Oligarchs selected the prime minister, who would then be named by the emperor. The function of the legislature was to ratify – and occasionally modify – proposals originating from the cabinet members and the ministries they led.

Still the new constitution did provide for elected representatives and anticipated a modern bureaucracy whose staff was selected by competition, advanced by merit, and protected by civil service. For the first time in Japan's history, it established a specialized and legally trained if not independent judiciary.[21] As we shall see, this development slowly took on a life of its own.

The State and the Legal Complex in the Meiji-Taisho Periods

To keep the Great Powers at bay and to facilitate international commerce, Japan needed modern Western business law and legal experts. Accordingly, the government set about acquiring this expertise. In 1869, it established the Kaisei School (later Tokyo Imperial University) for the express purpose of assessing the applicability of Western ideas and technology for use in Japan, including the establishment of a Western-oriented law faculty.[22] Two years later, a Ministry of Justice was established, and in turn it promptly established its own legal training school.[23] Law was to be taught and used as a branch of public administration. The expectation was that these new law-trained specialists would join the Ministry of Justice, draft laws, serve as administrators, and work as judges and prosecutors.

Yet those who received the new Western-style legal education at the Tokyo Imperial University received more lessons than officials bargained for. Three prominent professors had been trained in England and the United States and came back not only to teach law but also to extol the virtues of an independent legal profession and the nobility of private practice. Students in droves followed their advice and

---

[19] Abe, Shindo, and Kawato 7–8 (1994).
[20] Id. at 7.
[21] McClain 182 (2002).
[22] For a history of legal education in Japan see Miyazawa and Otsuka (2002).
[23] Matsui 66 (1990).

pursued private practice rather than public service.[24] In the 1870s and 1880s, this development was facilitated by the establishment of a number of private law schools, some freestanding and others eventually developing into large universities (such as Waseda and Chuo) whose faculties were recruited from among the newly licensed lawyers.[25]

The government responded by severely restricting the roles of lawyers and by trying to seize control of the legal profession. It enacted a statute in 1872 specifying the roles of judges and prosecutors and prescribing a very limited role for private lawyers, who were initially called *daigennin* until they obtained the new title of *bengoshi* in 1893. Yet even as it sought to restrict the roles of these new lawyers, the government's actions had the effect of helping legitimate the new legal profession. Indeed, the 1872 statute was revolutionary. For the first time, the Japanese government recognized a distinct legal profession complete with law-trained judges and prosecutors and a private bar. The genie was out of the bottle. Unwittingly a legal profession had been established.

However, the government resisted this unexpected development at the Tokyo Imperial University. In 1895, after finding that up to two-thirds of law graduates preferred private practice, the government changed the content of legal education there: German law replaced Anglo-American law. Subsequently new graduates' defections to the private bar declined.[26]

On the other hand, in 1880, the Ministry of Justice enacted new regulations that established higher barriers for access to the profession, restricted activities of lawyers (they could initially address courts only on behalf of clients in civil but not criminal cases that had been initiated by the government),[27] and placed the emerging profession under progressively tighter state supervision (attorneys were initially disciplined by the court on request from the local prosecutor).[28]

Not withstanding these restrictions, the bar continued to grow. To keep them under its thumb, the state required *daigennin* to form local associations (*kumiai*),[29] which they did with a vengeance. The *daigennin* then used these associations to advance their professional interests. Although by Western standards, the number of lawyers in Japan was tiny, the number continued to grow and the bar continued to organize into local and national groupings and exercise limited but growing influence in public affairs. The number of lawyers per capita in the 1930s was higher than it would be in the 1970s.[30] In 1928 the bar was even powerful enough to convince the government to introduce a limited form of jury trial along Anglo-American lines

[24] Hattori 127 (1963).
[25] Matsui 6 (1990).
[26] Hattori 127 (1963).
[27] Matsui 7 (1990).
[28] Id. at 7–8.
[29] Id. at 9.
[30] Haley 97 (1991).

for criminal defendants. Although militaristic government in 1943 suspended this
innovation, nevertheless it does reveal the power of the bar before militarization took
firm root in the mid-1930s.

The government's vigorous efforts to control the bar also helped define the bar's
ethos, perversely strengthening it as an oppositional force to government. Throughout the Meiji and Taisho periods (from 1868 to 1925), the government regularly used
criminal prosecutions to intimidate labor union and political activists who opposed
its policies. Lawyers instinctively sympathized with those who experienced the heavy
hand of the state. Throughout the 1880s and 1890s, lawyers played leading roles in
the formation of new political parties. They regularly provided *group* legal defenses
in politically motivated prosecutions and were at the forefront of challenging land
seizures. In turn the Ministry of Justice continued to try to dominate the bar. It took
control of the administration of bar exams, reduced the number who were admitted
to the bar, and sought to exercise ever greater control over lawyer discipline. For
instance, an ordinance in 1888 banned 250 lawyers from Tokyo.[31]

In 1990, Yasuhiro Matsui wrote that the "origins of the anti-government sprit
('*zaiya seishin*') which is the spiritual basis of present day practicing attorneys" can
be found "in the anti-establishment spirit of *daigennin* who defended activists of the
Freedom and Popular Rights movements."[32] Although Matsui clearly romanticizes
the idealism of the Meiji-era lawyers, many attorneys and legal scholars would agree
with his basic point.

The State and the Legal Complex in the War Period

Japan's governmental response to the Great Depression of 1929 took two forms. In
the 1930s, the government accelerated colonial expansion in Korea, Manchuria,
and the Pacific islands, and it asserted greater control over the Japanese economy.
These programs reinforced each other; they responded both to right-wing populists
and military officers who felt that Japan had not done enough to assume its rightful
place in the world and to workers and farmers who were clamoring for protection
against unbridled capitalism. As the crisis deepened, the government reverted to
an increasingly traditional Japanese form. *Jushin*, "senior statesmen," consisting of
former ministers and prime ministers, and other leading public figures embraced the
idea of replacing the emerging party government with a national unity government
that was "above politics" – a return to oligarchy. Once established, this national unity
government cracked down on dissent, and as the international crisis deepened,
opposition to the new government withered and most former dissidents fell into
line.[33]

---

[31] Matsui 19 (1990).
[32] Id. at 31.
[33] McClain 429 (2002).

Neither the organized bar nor the bench distinguished themselves during this "emergency" that continued up to and through World War II. Although the Japan Attorneys Association (*Nippon Bengoshi Kyokai*) formally protested the decline of respect for civil rights and liberties throughout the 1930s,[34] its efforts diminished markedly toward the end of that decade and all but disappeared during the war. Some lawyers' associations even became champions of the government's policy.[35] For instance, in 1940 the Japan Attorneys Association established the National Federation of Attorneys for the New System, whose mission was to cooperate with the government in furthering the war effort.

The judiciary fared no better. For instance, chief judges of the highest court, the Great Court of Cassation, often urged at judicial conferences that the judiciary should cooperate with the government to win the war and apply severe punishments to those who jeopardize the war, while lower court judges who were in charge of thought crimes worked closely with prosecutors and some of them argued that judges should accept prosecutor's opinion in such cases.[36] Some judges resisted this situation. For instance, when Prime Minister Hideki Tojo addressed a judicial conference in 1944 and told judges that they should not care too much about details of law and that the government would take proper measures if they decide cases in such a way that hinders war, a high court judge tried to send a protesting letter to the Prime Minister through the chief judge of the Great Court of Cassation. However, the chief judge ignored it, and this high court judge was criticized by other leading judges.[37]

Comparing Tokugawa Japan and Pre–World War II Japan

Japan's emerging new legal system failed in the years before and during World War II, as the rule of law was abandoned in the name of security and safety. Yet it would be wrong to conclude that this return to oligarchic rule and the substitution of administration for law meant essentially a return to Tokugawa-era practices. Despite these problems in the 1930s and throughout the war, there was a distinct difference between the rule of law in pre-Meiji Japan and pre–World War II Japan.

A constitution had been enacted in 1889, and a series of statutes on the judicial system were adopted the following year. Courts then began deciding cases and publishing opinions; legal procedures were transparent and adhered to. Although these laws granted vast powers to the state, offered only limited protections against arbitrary government, and made no provisions for judicial review, nevertheless the *public* nature of the law and adjudication forced the government to follow prescribed procedures and be subject to judicial oversight, something that was alien to officials in the Tokugawa era. In this sense pre–World War II Japan clearly had embraced

---

[34] Matsui 198–210 (1990).
[35] Id. at 211–25.
[36] Id. at 172–179.
[37] Id. at 175–176.

"the rule of law" – that governmental action must be based on law – and this in turn had led to a more moderate state.[38] A quasi-autonomous internal legal culture had been established and institutionalized.

Furthermore the division of labor that is implied by law-trained officials and a separate Ministry of Justice reinforced the rule of law. Law could no longer be so casually and so completely associated with "administration." Despite the continued heavy-handedness of the government, a functioning legal profession had emerged. The fact that it was only occasionally successful when challenging the state does not negate its role in helping secure the rudimentary features of the rule of law.

In sum, the emergence of an internal legal culture in the early twentieth century transformed the legal system; adjudication was now distinct from state administration as it had been during the Tokugawa era.

However, the Japanese legal system had to wait until the end of World War II before substantial change occurred. Even today, whether the Japanese legal system has developed a distinct and autonomous internal legal culture is questionable. We deal with this issue in the next section.

THE STATE AND INTERNAL LEGAL CULTURE IN POSTWAR JAPAN

Judiciary in Postwar Japan

In his history of the postwar judicial system, Takaaki Hattori, a Tokyo District Court judge who later became Chief Justice of the Supreme Court from 1979–82, wrote, "[T]he Judge has been completely freed from the supervisory power of the Minister of Justice, who had exerted an undesirable influence over the prewar judiciary. Now the judiciary is subject only to the general supervision of the Supreme Court, a group of their own professional seniors."[39] Hattori went to describe how the courts were granted the power of judicial review and gained independence from the legislative and executive branches, citing the Supreme Court's powers to manage such matters as judicial recruitment, promotion, and assignment.

Not everyone agrees with Hattori's argument that this system of self-management overseen by the Supreme Court has led to a robustly independent judiciary. It has clearly facilitated establishment of career judges who are selected from among the best and the brightest of the graduates from the Legal Training and Research Institute (LTRI), an educational program that everyone who passes the bar exam and wishes to practice law must complete. The Supreme Court also controls the initial selection process for "assistant judges," as well as their placement, rotation, promotion, and subsequent reappointment every ten years thereafter. Indeed it oversees a large and well-developed judicial bureaucracy that encompasses all aspects of judicial

---

[38] See Halliday and Karpik (1997).
[39] Hattori 131 (1963); see also Oppler Ch. 8 (1976).

administration and judicial assignments. Needless to say from the outset of their careers, individual judges are highly dependent on this bureaucracy, and at its top, this bureaucracy is highly sensitive to governmental prerogatives.

Critics maintain that this arrangement has led to a judiciary that is inward-looking, being far removed from the real-world concerns of both the practicing bar and their clients; is conformist; and is both conservative and biased toward the government. Considerable evidence has been offered to support this view. Miyazawa has documented many instances of lower court judges being discriminated against by the General Secretariat of the Supreme Court because of their political views and memberships in some outside organizations.[40] Such practices are frequent enough to show up as distinct patterns in statistical studies of the career patterns of large numbers of judges. Judicial rotation and promotion are dependent on conforming to the judicial philosophy and legal interpretations of judicial bureaucrats on the staff of the General Secretariat.[41] Even John Haley,[42] who is a vigorous defender of the Japanese judiciary, concedes this point, although he argues that such internal oversight is far preferable to the alternative, which would likely be direct intervention in the judicial affairs by conservative politicians.[43]

Even when the Supreme Court has been accorded more power, it has been loath to use it. The Constitution of 1946 provided for judicial review, but the Supreme Court has used this power sparingly. Between 1947 and 2005, it held laws unconstitutional only seven times, and in the two cases of malapportionment of voting districts the Supreme Court refrained from nullifying the election results.[44]

The passivity of the judiciary – and by extension the limited effects of litigation and lawyers – is seen in many other ways as well.[45] One important measure of judicial independence is the frequency with which citizens turn to the courts to challenge governmental agencies. Japan lags far behind other democratic, industrialized countries on this measure. According to the judiciary's own statistics, in Japan in 1999, when the Justice System Reform Council was established, only 1,790 cases

[40] Miyazawa (1994). One of those outside organizations is the Young Lawyers Association (YLA), which was established in 1954 to protect the Constitution of 1946 from the conservative movement to amend it. It included scholars, attorneys, as well as judges. The YLA still exists, but its judicial section was closed in 1984 after the persecution of its members by the Supreme Court. The other organization was the Friendly Meeting of Judges. It was established in 1971 when judicial members of the YLA were persecuted and consisted only of judges. This group was disbanded in 2007.

[41] Ramseyer and Rasmusen (2003).

[42] Haley (1998, 2007).

[43] For the most recent and comprehensive study of the Japanese judiciary, including interviews of retired and sitting judges, see Law (2009). He concludes, "The Japanese judiciary may be a bureaucracy, but it is also a highly disciplined one in which power is concentrated to an unusual degree in the hands of one person [Chief Justice]. It is, as a result, neither resistant nor unresponsive to political influence." Law 1593 (2009).

[44] The Supreme Court held a law unconstitutional for the eighth time in 2008.

[45] Daniel Foote (2006) argues that Japanese judges have been active in creating new policies in a variety of areas. However, his examples do not include areas where the court directly challenged governmental policies. One area (traffic accidents) is an organized effort to reduce courts' caseload.

were filed against administrative agencies, and among these, plaintiffs prevailed in only 15.6% of the cases. These figures are low by almost any criteria. For instance in the United States in 1999, 34,376 claims against the federal government were filed in the federal district courts, and plaintiffs prevailed at a much higher rate. In Germany in 1998, 201,543 cases were filed in administrative courts, and in France, in 1997, 106,985 such cases were filed.[46]

The postwar Japanese Supreme Court and the judicial hierarchy have consistently and successfully opposed increasing the size of the judiciary in spite of the heavy and increasing caseload of individual judges. Indeed, there are far fewer judges per capita in Japan today than there were one hundred years ago. (In 1890 there were 1,531 judges nationwide compared to only 2,896 in 1998, despite more than a threefold increase in population and an explosion of commercial and administrative law in the interim.[47])

Throughout the postwar era, and particularly since the activism of the 1960s, the bar has been at the forefront of the criticism of a passive judiciary that is all too willing to bend to the interests of the government. However, the most effective initiative for judicial reform has come from the business community.[48] Beginning in the mid-1990s, businesses began pressing for less administrative oversight of business, on the one hand, and an expansion of access to the justice system, on the other. The increasingly neoliberal government under the Liberal Democratic Party (LDP) that had been pursuing a policy of deregulation and less government was sympathetic to these requests, and in June 1999, it established the Justice System Reform Council (JSRC) to consider ways to implement these policies. Seeing this as a rare political opportunity, other groups who had long campaigned for related reforms joined the bandwagon for judicial and legal reform and sought to influence the JSRC, which had been given a broad mandate to consider changes in the size, recruitment, and training of the judiciary, as well as the size and structure of the bar.[49]

The JSRC's central question was, Do the bench and the bar provide sufficient access to justice? Its answer was an unequivocal "no." In its final report of June 2001 which was presented to Prime Minister Jun-Ichiro Koizumi at the end of its term, the JSRC was forthright in observing that something must be done to transform both the spirit of law and the rule of law into "the flesh and blood of this country."[50] In uncharacteristically forthright language for a Japanese government-sponsored report, it acknowledged that in a very real sense the rule of law had not taken root in Japan, despite a 130-year experience with a modern legal system and a 50-year history with its liberal postwar constitution. According to the JSRC, the law has remained an instrument of the government and not an autonomous system that

[46] CD-Rom, *Jurisuto* [Jurist], No. 1208, 2001.
[47] Hattori (1963); Justice System Reform Council (2001).
[48] Miyazawa (2001, 2007a, 2007b); Kingston Ch. 3 (2004).
[49] Justice System Reform Council (1999).
[50] Justice System Reform Council (2001).

could be used by members of the public as a means of holding the government legally accountable for its actions. Furthermore, the number of lawyers and judges per capita in postwar Japan had declined. Considering that disputes have become enormously more complex in recent years, the JSRC concluded this decline was all the more remarkable. Accordingly, it recommended that the government triple the number of new lawyers by 2010, add a minimum of five hundred new judges over the next ten years, and add still more if caseloads continued to increase.[51]

Throughout this process, the Supreme Court's General Secretariat steadfastly frustrated the JSRC's efforts. It resisted its investigation, denied its findings, and opposed its recommendations. The Secretariat argued that the courts are not over-burdened and that there are ample opportunities for citizens to gain access to justice through the courts or other government-sponsored dispute resolution programs. When the dust settled in this confrontation over the JCRS report, most informed observers concluded that the Supreme Court had won the bureaucratic battle. The Court acceded to some modest changes, but was successful in opposing all propos-als for major innovations. It reluctantly agreed to modest increases in the size of the judiciary,[52] but successfully resisted recommendations to fundamentally change the ways new judges are appointed and sitting judges evaluated. It agreed to the reestablishment of a jury system, but succeeded in transforming the proposal for an Anglo-American style jury system (which Japan in fact had from 1928 to 1943, albeit in a very restricted form) into a mixed panel of three professional and six lay judges that could possibly be dominated by the professional judge members.[53] Other changes included the following: national and regional boards were established under the Secretariat to review qualifications of judicial candidates nominated by the Secre-tariat; new judges were to spend two years during their ten-year tenure as assistant judges working in law firms or some other organizations outside the judiciary; the Secretariat was to cooperate more closely with the Japan Federation of Bar Associa-tions to increase the numbers of private attorneys who apply for judicial positions; and the Secretariat agreed to establish and publicize standards and procedures for evaluating sitting judges. None of these reforms constitute a major break with past practices.[54] Even the most seemingly innovative reform, the new jury system, is limited: It can be used only in the most serious criminal cases.[55] Furthermore all of these new arrangements will be overseen by the Secretariat, so that it and it alone continues to maintain near-total control over judicial administration.

[51] Id. at 45.
[52] Since 2001 the legally authorized number of judges has increased gradually as a result of justice system reform. There were 3,566 judges in April 2009, including 15 Supreme Court Justices, and 806 summary court judges who need not be a qualified lawyer (Article 1, Law on the Authorized Number of Judicial Employees [*Saibansho Shokuin Teiinho*]).
[53] Miyazawa (2002).
[54] For reforms of judicial appointment and judicial evaluation, see Miyazawa 86–8 (2007b).
[55] The lay judge system has been implemented since May 2009. For an observation based on the first two cases, see Johnson (2009).

However there are indications that sitting lower court judges are taking note of these reforms and have been emboldened to assert their independence in individual cases, although they remain cautious and timid in doing so.[56] Still, one should probably not read too much in such developments. Since the reforms have gone into effect, judges promoted to the Supreme Court General Secretariat and the Supreme Court itself still continue to be drawn exclusively from the conservative old guard who have steadfastly opposed the reforms and resisted their implementation. Certainly the judiciary in the 2010s is more insulated from political pressures than the judiciary in prewar Japan, but it is not yet likely to fully exercise its institutional power. In this sense, the judiciary itself chooses to remain in the shadow of the state by default, and the internal legal culture remains stunted and underdeveloped.[57]

The Bar in Post–World War II Japan

In the postwar era, the Japanese bar has regained and even expanded the autonomy and sense of independence it had briefly held in the interwar period. Article 1 of the Practicing Attorney Law [*Bengoshi Ho*] of 1949 proclaims, "A practicing attorney is entrusted with a mission to protect fundamental human rights and to realize social justice." Follow-up legislation made good on this pledge. Attorneys were required to join local bar associations (*bengoshikai*) as well as a national organization, the Japan Federation of Bar Associations (JFBA; *Nihon Bengoshi Rengokai*). The bar was established as autonomous; local bar associations and the JFBA rather than the Justice Ministry were given the power to discipline attorneys. Furthermore, training of future attorneys was combined with that of future assistant judges and prosecutors; all take the same national bar examination (*Shiho Shiken*), and all those who pass spend a total of two years (as of 2006 this has been reduced to one year) as judicial trainees at the Legal Training and Research Institute (LTRI) and in field placements in local courts, prosecutors' offices, and attorneys' offices.[58] All trainees were paid salaries by the state until they were changed to loans provided by the state in 2010. From the outset, despite the fact that this arrangement meant that new attorneys are subjected to the stricture of supervision by the Supreme Court, attorneys welcomed this joint training, believing that symbolically it equalized the status of judges, prosecutors, and private attorneys. As of this writing, with minor modification this arrangement still holds.

[56] In December 2009, the Osaka High Court held the general election of the more powerful Lower House of the Diet in August 2009 unconstitutional for the reason of malapportionment. However, it refrained from nullifying the election.

[57] The Democratic Party of Japan won in the general election of the Lower House of the Diet in August 2009. The new cabinet has appointed six new Supreme Court justices as of October 2010. It has so far maintained the practice of the Liberal Democratic Party of replacing a retiring justice with a new justice from a similar background.

[58] Hattori 137 (1963).

These postwar reforms must be considered in light of still more developments that have occurred under the Practicing Attorney Law of 1949. In 1952, the JFBA sponsored the establishment of the Japan Legal Aid Society to provide legal aid in civil cases[59] and continued to sponsor it for nearly fifty years until the enactment in 2000 of a new Civil Legal Aid Law that provided government funding (at substantially greater levels than were provided by the bar) for civil legal aid. In 1990 local bar associations instituted a British-like duty solicitor system to provide pretrial detainees with counsel at an early stage of the criminal process where a publicly supported defense system did not yet operate.[60] Increasingly since the 1970s, members of the bar have banded together as "cause lawyers" to pursue a variety of public-interest concerns, especially those involving environmental protection or constitutional issues.[61] Still other lawyers, again through the auspices of the organized bar, have pursued human rights protection work and lobbied UN committees to counter the government's official reports on conditions in Japan. Lawyers, again with the blessings of the organized bar, also work in a variety of nonprofit and nongovernmental organizations.[62]

Minor as they are from the perspective of those members of the bar who had hoped for more far-reaching changes, this list of reforms and activities nevertheless illustrates the continuity of the long-standing ethos of the bar as an autonomous and something of an oppositional force to the government.[63]

Still the Japanese bar continues to be small and weak in comparison to most Western bars. Indeed, it has not (yet) obtained full power to manage its own affairs. Several recent developments reveal this continued dependence on the state. The Practicing Attorney Law that establishes basic provisions about the profession is a state law, even though it was introduced into the Diet as a member bill by practicing attorneys who were members of the Diet.[64] Even when the government amended it in 2002 in the wake of the Justice System Reform Council's proposals, the JFBA was only consulted and the new provisions were ultimately introduced by the government.

Although most attorneys approve of the joint training arrangement at the LTRI because it provides private attorneys symbolically equal status with judges and prosecutors, it also places a crucial phase of legal education in the hands of state officials. The fact that trainees are financially supported by the government only reinforces this dependency. In short, the bar continues to depend on the state to manage many of its own affairs that in other countries are matters that the state has delegated to the bar itself. Indeed, the bar remains deeply divided on this relationship with the Supreme Court. For instance, many members of the bar opposed the JSRC's

---

[59] Ichiki and Ohishi (1999).
[60] Murayama (2002).
[61] See Kidder and Miyazawa (1993); O'Brien and Okoshi (1993); Miyazawa 27–38 (1999).
[62] Tsujinaka (2003).
[63] Miyazawa (1999).
[64] Oppler 108 (1976).

recommendation for a new system of legal training that would have graduate professional law schools at its core. They were concerned that the law schools would threaten the Supreme-Court-run LTRI, and hence their status as equals to judges and prosecutors. Similarly, many members of the bar resisted the JSRC's recommendation to triple the number of new lawyers by 2010.[65]

Finally, the bar accepted state rather than bar control of the Japan Legal Assistance Center (*Nihon Shiho Shien Senta*) that was established in 2006 as a national network of law offices that administer publicly funded criminal defense and civil legal aid to people of limited means.[66] This organization is a public corporation supervised by the Justice Minister. Thus many of the functions long performed by the bar-controlled Legal Aid Society and the JFBA are now handled by the new ministry-controlled Center. Although the bar initially opposed this arrangement, it eventually agreed to it in exchange for government rather than bar-association funding for the enterprise.

Some steps have been taken to ensure independence of the Japan Legal Assistance Center (JLAC), but they may not be sufficient. For instance, recently retired judges and prosecutors cannot be appointed as the board members for the new organization, and complaints against contracting attorneys must be reviewed by an "independent" review board. However, the JLAC's first Secretary General (director) is a JFBA member (as opposed to a retired judge, which many had feared),[67] and to date the JLAC has operated without interference from the judicial bureaucracy. Still, fearful of their autonomy, young attorneys hesitate to join the Center as staff attorneys, and it remains seriously understaffed.[68] Furthermore, if the fate of legal services providers in the United States is any lesson, dependence on state funding should remain a serious concern.

Yet to the extent that members of the bar accept such arrangements and continue to resist radical expansion of the bar, there is little chance that the bar will gain full autonomy and the independent stature it enjoys in many other industrialized nations. Although the government continues to exert controls over the profession, many of its most serious problems stem from its own actions. As long as the bar accepts the training institute for new lawyers run by the Sepreme Court and resists expanding the bar much beyond its current size,[69] it is unlikely that the bar can

---

[65] They appear to have succeeded. See note 70 below.

[66] About the Japan Legal Assistance Center, see Miyazawa 84–6 (2007b).

[67] He has since been promoted to the chairman of the board.

[68] The Japan Legal Assistance Center has more than seventy law offices all over Japan, but most office are staffed with only one or two full-time lawyers. Most civil and criminal legal aid cases are handled by private attorneys who have contracted with the center.

[69] Although the Justice System Reform Council proposed to license 3,000 new lawyers by around 2010, the bar examination passed 2,074 in 2010, and the JFBA proposed to freeze the number of new lawyers at that level so it could examine the quality of and job market for new lawyers. The new postgraduate professional law schools established in 2004 and 2005 according to the recommendation of the Justice System Reform Council now face an unexpectedly low and rapidly declining bar passage rate. See Miyazawa, Chan, and Lee (2008). The bar passage rate in 2010 was merely 25%.

gain greater autonomy and influence in the legal complex. Indeed, the dependency on government funding for the legal assistance center may create still another dependent relationship.

CONCLUSION

This chapter has surveyed salient features of the legal system in Japan since the late Tokugawa period. Our purpose has been to describe the relation of the legal system to the state and to offer some observations about the autonomy of the internal legal culture of Japan.

A strong state once did not differentiate law from administration and exercised firm control of the legal system, thereby prohibiting the emergence of a separate and distinct internal "legal culture." This domination of the legal process by the state in the Tokugawa period was unwittingly weakened early in the Meiji period as the state sought to situate itself more securely on the world stage. Once legality took root, the drive for autonomy of the law emerged as something of an independent force doggedly pursued by the emerging new legal profession. Slowly and steadily both the bench and the bar gained greater degrees of independence.

Yet the bench and the bar did not unite, as they have in some countries, to produce their own autonomous and "internal" legal culture distinct from the state. A conservative judiciary has emerged. Although it has been able to gain a degree of bureaucratic independence from other branches of the government, the judiciary has neither sought to align itself nor help foster a more robust legal profession or idea of an autonomous rule of law. In contrast, the bar has consistently sought to set itself apart from the state and minimize governmental control. This effort has been only partially successful, and by deciding to support the idea of a small (tiny, by Western standards) bar, the bar has so far failed to become a political force that might be mobilized to generate a more robust and autonomous legal profession and a more robust internal legal culture distinguished and distinguishable from the state.

Thus, we found fundamental continuity between Tokugawa Japan and postwar Japan. It remains to be seen whether the increase in size of the bar, removal of the main part of professional legal education from the LTRI to university-based law schools, expanded opportunities for lawyers to work as in-house counsels of business corporations and government agencies, and other changes introduced by the present judicial reform will produce further transformations of the relationship between the state and the bar, resulting in a more assertive internal legal culture.

REFERENCES

Abe, Hitoshi, Muneyuki Shindo, and Sadafumi Kawato (1994). *The Government and Politics of Japan*. Tokyo: University of Tokyo Press. Translated and with an introduction by James W. White.

Ch'en, Pauyal Heng-Chao (1981). *The Formation of the Early Meiji Legal Order*. Oxford: Oxford University Press.

Feeley, Malcolm M. and Setsuo Miyazawa (2007). The State, Civil Society, and the Legal Complex in Modern Japan: Continuity and Change, in Terence C. Halliday, Lucien Karpik, and Malcolm M. Feeley, eds., *Fighting for Political Freedom: Comparative Studies of the Legal Complex and Political Change*. Oxford: Hart Publishing.

Foote, Daniel H. (1992). The Benevolent Paternalism of Japanese Criminal Justice, 80 *Cal. L. Rev.* 317.

———. (2006). *The Judiciary and Society: Reconsidering the "Myth" about the Judiciary [Saiban to Shakai: Shiho no "Joshiki" Saiko]*. Tokyo: NTT Shuppan. Translated by Masayuki Tamaruya.

Friedman, Lawrence M. (1975). *The Legal System*. New York: Russell Sage Foundation.

Garon, Sheldon. (2003). From Meiji to Heisei: The State and Civil Society in Japan, in Frank J. Schwartz and Susan J. Pharr, eds., *The State of Civil Society in Japan*. New York: Cambridge University Press, 42–62.

Haley, John O. (1991). *Authority without Power: Law and the Japanese Paradox*. New York: Oxford University Press.

———. (1998). *The Spirit of Japanese Law*. Athens: University of Georgia Press.

———. (2007). The Japanese Judiciary: Maintaining Integrity, Autonomy and the Public Trust, in Daniel H. Foote, ed., *Law in Japan: A Turning Point*. Seattle: University of Washington Press.

Halliday, Terence C. and Lucien Karpik (1997). Politics Matter: A Comparative Theory of Lawyers in the Making of Political Liberalism, in Terence C. Halliday and Lucien Karpik, eds., *Lawyers and the Rise of Western Political Liberalism*. Oxford: Clarendon Press.

Halliday, Terence C., Lucien Karpik, and Malcolm M. Feeley, eds. (2007). *Fighting for Political Freedom: Comparative Studies of the Legal Complex and Political Change*. Oxford: Hart Publishing.

Hattori, Takaaki (1963). The Legal Profession in Japan: Its Historical Development and Present State, in Arthur Taylor von Mehren, ed., *Law in Japan: The Legal Order in a Changing Society*. Cambridge, MA: Harvard University Press, 111–152.

Henderson, Dan Fenno (1965). *Conciliation and Japanese Law: Tokugawa and Modern*, vol I. Seattle: University of Washington Press.

Hiramatsu, Yoshiro, (1981). Tokugawa Law, 14 *Law in Japan* 1.

Holt, Robert T. and John E. Turner (1966). *The Political Basis of Economic Development: An Exploration in Comparative Political Analysis*. Princeton, NJ: D. Van Nostrand Co.

Ichiki, Gotaro and Tetsuo Ohishi (1999). Current Issues for Legal Aid in Japan: Reform Perspective, in Louise G. Tribe and Jeremy Cooper, eds., *Educating for Justice around the World: Legal Education, Legal Practice, and the Community*. Aldershot: Ashgate.

Johnson, David T. (2009). *Early Returns from Japan's New Criminal Trials*. Available at http://www.japanfocus.org/-David_T_-Johnson/3212

Justice System Reform Council (1999). *The Points at Issue in the Justice Reform*. Available at http://www.kantei.go.jp/foreign/policy/sihou/singikai/991221_e.html

———. (2001). *Recommendations of the Justice System Reform Council: For a Justice System to Support Japan in the 21st Century*. Available at http://www.kantei.go.jp/foreign/policy/sihou/singikai/990612_e.html

Kidder, Robert L. and Setsuo Miyazawa (1993). Long Term Strategies in Japanese Environmental Litigation, 18 *Law & Inquiry* 605.

Kingston, Jeff (2004). *Japan's Quiet Transformation: Social Change and Civil Society in the Twenty-First Century*. London: Routledge Curzon.

Law, David S. (2009). The Anatomy of a Conservative Court: Judicial Review in Japan, 87 *Tex. L. Rev.* 1545.

Matsui, Yasuhiro (1990). *A Study of Japanese Practicing Attorneys [Nihon Bengoshi Ron]*. Tokyo: Nippon Hyoronsha.

McClain, James L. (2002). *Japan: A Modern History*. New York: W.W. Norton.

Miyazawa, Setsuo (1994). Administrative Control of Japanese Judges, in Philip S. C. Lewis, ed., *Law and Technology in the Pacific Community*. Boulder: Westview Press.

———. (1999). Lawyering for the Underrepresented in the Context of Legal, Social, and National Institutions: The Case of Japan, in Louise G. Trubek and Jeremy Cooper, eds., *Educating for Justice around the World: Legal Education, Legal Practice, and the Community*. Aldershot: Ashgate.

———. (2001). The Politics of Judicial Reform in Japan: The Rule of Law at Last?, 2 *Asian-Pac. L. & Pol'y J.* 89.

———. (2002). Summary of and Comments on Recommendations of the Japanese Judicial Reform Council (2001), in Malcolm M. Feeley and Setsuo Miyazawa, eds., *The Japanese Adversary System in Context*. London: Palgrave Macmillan.

———. (2007a). The Politics of Judicial Reform in Japan: The Rule of Law at Last?, in William P. Alford, ed., *Raising the Bar: The Emerging Legal Profession in East Asia*. Cambridge, MA: Harvard University Press.

———. (2007b). Law Reform, Lawyers, and Access to Justice, in Gerald Paul McAlinn, ed., *Japanese Business Law*. The Netherlands: Kluwer Law.

Miyazawa, Setsuo, Kay-Wah Chan, and Ilhyung Lee (2008). The Reform of Legal Education in East Asia, 4 *Ann. Rev. L. & Soc. Sci.* 333.

Miyazawa, Setsuo and Hiroshi Otsuka (2002). Legal Education and the Reproduction of the Elite in Japan, in Yves Deale and Bryant Garth, eds., *Global Prescriptions: The Production, Exportation, and Importation of a New Legal Orthodoxy*. Ann Arbor: University of Michigan Press.

Murayama, Masayuki (2002). The Role of the Defense Attorney in the Japanese Criminal Process, in Malcolm M. Feeley and Setsuo Miyazawa, eds., *The Japanese Adversary System in Context*. London: Palgrave Macmillan.

O'Brien, David M. and Yasou Okoshi (1993). *To Dream of Dreams: Religious Freedom and Constitutional Politics in Postwar Japan*. Honolulu: University of Hawaii Press.

Ooms, Herman (1996). *Tokugawa Village Practice: Class, Status, Power, Law*. Berkeley: University of California Press.

Oppler, Robert (1976). *Legal Reform in Occupied Japan*. Princeton, NJ: Princeton University Press.

Ramseyer, J. Mark and Eric B. Rasmusen (2003). *Measuring Judicial Independence: The Political Economy of Judging in Japan*. Chicago: University of Chicago Press.

Shapiro, Martin (1981). *Courts: A Comparative and Political Analysis*. Chicago: University of Chicago Press.

Tsujinaka, Yutaka (2003). From Developmentalism to Maturity: Japan's Civil Society Organizations in Comparative Perspectives, in Frank J. Schwartz and Susan J. Pharr, eds., *The State of Civil Society in Japan*, New York: Cambridge University Press.

PART IV

Law and Large Areas of Social Life

Law and Contractual Relations

12

The Death of Contract

Dodos and Unicorns or Sleeping Rattlesnakes?

Stewart Macaulay

Just because we are amazed by Beethoven's Ninth Symphony, we should not over-look the charm of his First. In something of the same spirit, I have been charged with commenting on Lawrence Friedman's first book, *Contract Law in America*, which was published in 1965. Friedman now has composed many more "symphonies" than even Beethoven since this first effort, but it is instructive to turn back to the beginning.

In the interest of full disclosure, I must note that I am not a neutral detached observer. I am thanked in the preface of *Contract Law in America*, and two years after its publication we mixed some of the ideas in Friedman's book with some of mine and made a presentation at the Association of American Law Schools annual meeting.[1] Furthermore, one of my scholarly roles seems to be writing favorable blurbs for the back of jackets for Friedman's books, and the Friedman and Macaulay families have been close friends for more than forty-five years. Indeed, I can point to places where ideas from *Contract Law in America* have influenced my work.[2] Nonetheless, even an unbiased observer should conclude that the book has had some real influence in the contracts world, and it stands up very well after forty-five years.

In *Contract Law in America*, Friedman looks at the contracts opinions of the Supreme Court of Wisconsin for three periods: (1) the organization of the Wisconsin Territory to the Civil War (1836–61); (2) the Progressive era in the first two decades

---

[1] Friedman and Macaulay (1967). Harvard's Lon Fuller was one of the discussants at the AALS panel. He was not happy with our presentation. I remember him saying, "Frequency of occurrence is not the only indicator of importance." True enough, but frequency is one indicator of importance.

[2] See, e.g., Macaulay (1989).

I want to thank my corporate-lawyer daughter, Laura Macaulay, for suggestions about this chapter. She, too, has long been a great admirer of Leah and Lawrence Friedman. I also want to thank Bonnie Shucha, Reference and Electronic Services Librarian at the University of Wisconsin Law Library, for finding all of the reviews of *Contract Law in America*.

of the twentieth century (1905–15); and (3) a time ten years after World War II (1955–58). He considers the kinds of contracts cases brought before the highest court in the state, and he analyzes the contracts doctrines that the court used. He also examines the ever growing quantity of legislation that removed transactions from the domain of pure common law contract doctrine.

Friedman finds that the court moved from the application of "abstract" rules of contract law in the early period to later seeking justice based on the particular facts of the cases brought before it. He notes, "The heavy use of such malleable concepts as waiver and estoppel shows how the court, faced with inherited rules, but with facts which looked the other way, was inclined to use these formulae of escape from the rigors of abstraction."[3] The court was free to turn from abstraction because more and more of the contracts cases that it faced did not reflect the major economic issues of the state.[4] People did not bring these issues to the court for several reasons: Contract was robbed of its subject matter by legislation that removed whole categories of cases or particular issues from its domain. In addition, those drafting contracts could avoid some problems just by changing the language that they used. People also no longer brought major economic issues to the court because of increasing cost barriers to litigation and appeals. Reputational norms and sanctions made litigation unnecessary and punished those who would sue rather than working out matters. There was a growing social distance between business people and the judges. Friedman notes, "Two generations was longer than most contract type-problems survived. Either social change 'solved' the problem,[5] or a business cured its sickness itself, without the need for litigation."[6]

As a result of these developments, contract law became a residual category – the law of leftovers, of areas too new or not important enough to have their own statute. In Friedman's words,

> In part, the activism of government in Period III was a judgment that the market was a failure; in another sense, it was a judgment that the economy consisted not of a market, but of many markets, each with its appropriate modality of control. In such a context, the law of contract remained alive, not, however, as the organic law of the state's economic system – a kind of constitution for business transactions – but

---

[3] Friedman 190 (1965).

[4] Steve Hedley looks at what we know about British commercial people in the middle-to-late Victorian period and questions whether courts ever frequently applied contract law to important commercial transactions: "So, to discuss the history of the relations between contract theory and contract practice, we really have two histories: one of how legal discourse managed to avoid much contact with business, the other of business' attempts to evade the clutches of the law." Hedley 91 (1997).

[5] Professor Maggs argues, in a fashion anticipated by Friedman, that "the recent growth of electronic commerce actually tends to diminish the importance of [Uniform Commercial Code] Article 2's present contract formation rules because it removes many sales transactions from the coverage of those rules." Maggs 598 (2003). He continues, "The formation provisions in Article 2 were designed to handle contracts formed in the traditional manner of exchanging phone calls and written purchase orders and confirmations. For the most part, these specialized rules have no application in the context of electronic commerce." Id. at 611.

[6] Friedman 201 (1965).

as one among many. It was the system of rules applicable to marginal, novel, as yet unregulated, residual, and peripheral business, and quasi-business transactions, transactions which might, in exceptional cases, call for problem-solving and dispute-settling. "Contract" stepped in where no other body of law and no agency of law other than the court was appropriate or available.[7]

Contract Law in America also contains some harsh words about law school teaching of contracts: "[T]he traditional course-work in contracts was outmoded. The subject-matter had long since flown away. Instructor and student were grappling with trivia."[8] Friedman continues in a manner almost sure to offend traditional contracts teachers: "Carried into modern times by treatise writers and the Restatements, the common-law approach to law in the schools and in legal literature at its worst could be compared to a zoology course which confined its study to dodos and unicorns, to beasts rare or long dead and beasts that never lived."[9]

Friedman's key concept is contract law as *abstraction* as distinguished from particularity. Some of his readers, both those who have praised and those who have criticized the book, do not seem to grasp this idea. We must understand Friedman's use of the term "abstraction" to understand his argument. In a sense, "unconscionability" and "substantial performance" are abstract concepts. However, Friedman uses the term "abstract" in another way. He tells us, "Contract law is abstraction – what is left in the law relating to agreements when all the particularities of person and subject-matter are removed."[10] A judge cannot apply ideas such as unconscionability or substantial performance without looking at all of the details of the case before the court; thus, they are not abstraction as Friedman uses the term. Writers have long assumed that abstract contract law served the free market and laissez-faire: Within broad boundaries, the courts should enforce the bargains that the parties made just as they had made them. Doing so facilitates planning and risk assumption and lowers transaction costs as well.

Professor Speidel, when he reviewed the book in *The Wisconsin Law Review*, pulled together the following explanation from its text:

> Abstraction [for Friedman] is a bundle of at least three things: (1) private agreements that are not "subject, in whole or in part, to special legal treatment, by virtue of some special statute or legal rule (the tax law, the statute on union membership clauses, the anti-trust law)"; (2) contract doctrine from which all particulars of person and subject matter are removed; and (3) a judicial approach that deliberately renounces the particular in favor of the general – "a deliberate relinquishment of the temptation to restrict untrammeled individual autonomy or the completely free market in the name of social policy."[11]

---

[7]   Id. at 193.
[8]   Id. at viii.
[9]   Id. at 25.
[10] Id. at 20.
[11] Speidel 303 (1967).

I have argued that, viewed empirically, the law of contract and restitution contains four inconsistent approaches – the contradictions of contract.[12] For example, the classic contract law reflects *market functioning policy*. It purports to set out clear boundaries within which people can make agreements, knowing that the law will enforce them. This is what Friedman labels "abstraction." These rules tend to be formal and quantitative.[13] However, *transactional policy* seeks to carry out the expectations of the parties in the particular case. What did I lead you to believe was the deal? To answer this question, we must look at language in its full particular context. Indeed, sometimes courts must ignore the written language in a document called a contract and seek the real deal made by the parties. Transactional legal standards are qualitative, calling for a judgment by judges and jurors. Contract and restitution also, at times, seek to blunt or offset the market. Courts can follow *social planning policy*. Here they seek to decide cases by general rules that aim to protect society from harmful deals. They also can follow *relief of hardship policy* by seeking a fair result on a case-by-case basis. Rather than a consistent approach, we find cycles of emphasizing one or another of these approaches, but all four are always there ready to be mobilized in the right case.[14]

Wood v. Boynton,[15] an 1885 law school classic, can serve as an example of a policy conflict. The briefs and record on appeal show that Mrs. Wood went to Boynton's jewelry store to have a pin repaired. While in the store she showed Boynton an unusual stone that she had found near Eagle, Wisconsin. She asked him what it was. He said that he thought that it was a semiprecious stone, "maybe a topaz." He offered her $1 for the stone, but she did not want to sell it. Later she brought the stone back to the store and asked if he would buy it for $1. He did. The stone was an uncut diamond of great value ($1,000 in 1885 money). She sued to rescind the sale. Her lawyer argued that Mrs. Wood and Boynton had assumed a zone of risk. The stone might have been worthless, or it might have been worth the value of a semiprecious jewel such as a topaz. What no one could have foreseen was that anyone had found a diamond in Wisconsin. (As far as I know, this was the only diamond ever found in Wisconsin. Probably, the glaciers that formed the Great Lakes had pushed it to Eagle). A diamond in Wisconsin thus was outside of the zone of risk assumed by Mrs. Wood and paid for by Boynton. This was a transactional argument: It asked the court to find the real deal made by the parties. There was also a relief-of-hardship claim in Mrs. Wood's brief. Her lawyer painted her as a poor woman who had dealt with a businessman of superior bargaining skill, knowledge, and power. She

---

[12] Macaulay (1966).
[13] See Friedman (1967) for a discussion of the functions of quantitative and qualitative rules.
[14] Shamir (1993). Often there is, as Duncan Kennedy has pointed out, what seems to be a hard rule, but it is encircled by a periphery of soft exceptions. For example, consideration is offset to some extent by the reliance doctrine, but contract law is extremely uncertain about when this exception applies. Kennedy 1700–1, 1737 (1976).
[15] 64 Wis. 265, 25 N.W. 42 (1885).

asked him for his expert judgment, and she claimed that she had a right to rely on his response. The Supreme Court of Wisconsin brushed aside her arguments. The parties had made a bargain: Money was exchanged for a stone. There was no fraud or mutual mistake – the parties knew that they did not know what they were buying and selling. The jeweler was not a fiduciary. The abstract market functioning policy said that a deal was a deal. The court did not want to upset sales by getting into the particular facts of the case. Mrs. Wood lost.

Friedman finds the Wisconsin court later abandoning this kind of abstraction. He tells us,

> The law likes to frame its rules, whenever possible, as if they were homely truths; or even as statements of fact about the physical world. . . . But under cover of simple truths, the courts set standards of fair dealing; in extreme cases they sat in judgment on the wisdom of private contracts. Expansion of the concepts of fraud and mistake was one way in which the law of contract changed in fact, if not in theory. In this way much of what a later day regarded as the "harshness" of the classical law was mitigated; this "harshness" was nothing more than the prevailing abstraction of nineteenth-century contract law.[16]

What can we say about the argument of *Contract Law in America*? Are the contracts that come before American courts trivial? Has the subject matter dried up? To what extent have the courts abandoned the application of contract rules and turned to a case-by-case quest for fairness on the particular facts? Finally, to what extent, if at all, has this book influenced modern contracts teaching and scholarship? Are contracts courses and scholarly articles still focused on dodos and unicorns?

Contracts teachers probably would assert that we can find many important commercial contracts cases that have come before American appellate courts in the last quarter of the twentieth century. These scholars would defend their turf and claim that, instead of Friedman's dodos and unicorns, grizzly bears and great white sharks roamed and swam in their world. Without replicating Friedman's study or perhaps expanding it to sample many states and the federal courts, we can only speculate. My colleague at Wisconsin, Marc Galanter, looked at the available data about litigation, and he found that there was a "trough" in all American litigation from roughly 1930 to 1960.[17] However, there was a great surge of contract litigation from 1960 to 1990. This comeback came to an end in 1990: "[I]n the early 1990s several years of substantial decline reduced the volume of contract cases by about one third; this was followed by a period of little change year to year."[18]

Of course, these are statistics about cases filed, whereas Friedman studied cases appealed that produced opinions. Not all cases filed go to trial, not all trials are

---

[16] Friedman 99 (1965).
[17] Galanter (2001). Vincent-Jones reports somewhat similar findings from a study of England and Wales. Vincent-Jones (1993).
[18] Galanter 586 (2001).

appealed, and not all cases appealed produce opinions.[19] If we replicated Friedman's study today, we might find a surge of reported appellate contract opinions beginning in the 1960s, but we might not. We know that we can fill casebooks with appellate opinions about matters of some economic significance if we draw from all fifty states and the federal courts and pay no attention to economic context or to what decade or what century the cases come from. Yet doing so would probably yield a most misleading picture. Casebooks do not present a random sample of the business of courts, disputes, or business practices related to the topic.

Those of us eccentric enough to read appellate reports in this area regularly can speculate about a possible resurrection of contract litigation and published appellate opinions in the field, and our speculations can be backed by a little empirical grounding.[20] Over the past fifty years, the world and the economy have changed in ways that were hard to foresee. More and more accepted business patterns have been disrupted and provoked contract litigation: For example, war closed the Suez Canal,[21] the Vietnam conflict strained the ability of firms that supplied the military to perform their civilian contracts,[22] and the oil-producing states formed OPEC to raise prices, succeeding in provoking a drastic sudden increase in the price of oil. These actions upset assumptions about costs of energy for those who had made long-term bargains.[23] Globalization caused firms to downsize in the United States, and employees who had assumed that they had tenure during good behavior found that they were but employees at will.[24] Technological change produced disruption too. Computers were sold as the solution to all kinds of business and manufacturing problems before the computer manufacturers could make reliable machines.[25] The peaceful atom was going to solve both the problems of energy and environmental protection. The actual construction and operation of nuclear power plants provoked

---

[19] Hadfield 733 (2004): "[The data] show an even sharper decline in bench trials as opposed to jury trials, emphasizing that the shift we may be observing is a shift in the way *judges* decide cases, away from full-scale trial adjudication toward more piecemeal nontrial adjudication." [Emphasis in original.]

[20] See Marc Galanter and Rogers (1991). The two paragraphs in the text that follow are taken largely from my comment on Galanter's article cited in the preceding note. See Macaulay (2001).

[21] See *Transatlantic Fin. Corp. v. United States*, 363 F.2d 312 (D.C. Cir. 1966).

[22] See *Eastern Airlines, Inc. v. McDonnell Douglas Corp.*, 532 F.2d 957 (5th Cir. 1976).

[23] See, e.g., *Nanakuli Paving and Rock Co. v. Shell Oil Co.*, 664 F.2d 772 (9th Cir. 1982); *Aluminum Co. of America v. Essex Group, Inc.*, 499 F.Supp. 53 (W.D.Pa. 1980).

[24] See Kim (1999). In note 230, she comments: "[T]he interests of the frontline manager who makes the decision to fire may not align with the interests of the firm, resulting in the discharge of productive workers for personal rather than profit-based reasons. If the potential for opportunistic behavior or agency problems did not exist, then not only the law, but the norm forbidding discharge without cause as well, would be unimportant." See also Nielsen (1999).

[25] See, e.g., *AMF, Inc. v. McDonald's Corp.*, 536 F.2d 1167 (7th Cir. 1976); *Burroughs Corp. v. United States*, 634 F.2d 516 (Ct.Cl. 1980); *Badger Bearing Co. v. Burroughs Corp.*, 444 F.Supp. 919 (E.D.Wis. 1977), aff'd mem., 588 F.2d 838 (7th Cir. 1978).

disputes involving large sums of money.[26] All of these many disruptions of what was expected may have caused the relational glue that was holding bargains together to come unstuck.[27] Plaintiffs may find contract law flawed, but they have few, if any, other tools. I once analogized attempting to deal with these problems of disrupted contracts through classic contract law as trying to drive nails with a wrench. Marc Galanter responded, "But it is better than trying to drive nails with a banana."

Years after Friedman wrote his book, contract law in the hands of business lawyers became a powerful tool for gutting many statutes.[28] During the 1960s and 1970s, Congress and the state legislatures passed many statutes attempting to empower employees who might be the victims of discrimination; consumers who faced conduct on the borders, if not in the middle, of fraud; and franchisees subject to the power of franchisors. The business lawyers' solution? Sneak an arbitration clause into something that you could call a contract. The clause would send the parties to a kangaroo court sitting as an arbitration panel. It would be located in as inconvenient a place as was possible. Then, if challenged in court, the business lawyers would find sympathetic judges who would sing the praises of ADR while applying the Federal Arbitration Act to what they called contracts and ignoring any requirement of communication.[29] However, the business lawyers got greedy, and they created what looked like a license for their clients' sales and advertising people to lie. Many of the mandatory arbitration clauses provided in substance that major corporations would run almost no risk of liability when they failed to comply with their contracts or with regulation. We have seen a wave of challenges to these pretend contracts on very particular grounds such as unconscionability.[30] Some plaintiffs overturn the

---

[26] See, e.g., Eagan (1980); Joskow (1977). See also *Florida Power and Light Co. v. Westinghouse Electric Corp.*, 517 F.Supp. 440 (E.D. Va. 1983), 597 F.Supp. 1456 (E.D. Va. 1984), reversed, 826 F.2d 239 (4th Cir. 1987).

[27] William Glaberson, The Recession Begins Flooding into the Courts, *New York Times*, Dec. 28, 2009 at A1, suggests that the economic crisis that began in 2008 will bring many contracts disputes to the courts. Contracts disputes throughout New York were projected to be up 9% from 2008, and contracts disputes in Arizona were up 77% over the last two years. Only a small percentage of these cases will be appealed and provoke appellate opinions. The defendant must have assets so that there is a good chance that any judgment would be paid, and the appellant's chances of winning on appeal have to be good enough to warrant investing in all of the costs of lawyers' fees and the like. Moreover, even the few cases that provoke appellate opinions may be ones where the facts will suggest to the courts that they are free to seek substantive justice rather than attempting to fashion predictable rules to guide business lawyers and their clients.

[28] Compare McBarnet (1988, 1991), where she discusses analogous evasion strategies.

[29] See, e.g., *Circuit City Stores, Inc. v. Adams*, 532 U.S. 105 (2001). See also Speidel (1989). For related but slightly different adaptation to individual rights of employees, see Edelman, Abraham, and Erlanger (1992); Edelman (1990).

[30] Stephan Brooem (2006), An Unconscionable Application of the Unconscionability Doctrine: How the California Judiciary is Circumventing the Federal Arbitration Act, 3 *Hastings Bus. L.J.* 29, reports a study of 114 cases involving arbitration of consumer disputes decided by the California Court of Appeals between 1982 and 2006. He found that in 53 cases, the arbitration agreement was found to be unconscionable; in an additional 13 cases a particular aspect of the arbitration agreement was

arbitration clause; others lose. The law of leftovers that we saw as a dead rattlesnake turned out to be a very alive one that was only sitting very still while sunning itself.[31]

This story of the resurgence of contract, however, is not inconsistent with Friedman's tale. In *Contract Law in America*, he writes,

> So long as social change remained possible, so long as new kinds of business, new products, new techniques kept emerging, the court retained a small but vital role. Between the time when new business practices evolve and the time when the kinks have been smoothed out of forms and documents relating to the emerging practice, some agency of law must be ready to solve unforeseen problems. When continuing relations break down, or in cases of novel business problems or fluid business hierarchical arrangements, the court performed this role.[32]

Moreover, Friedman would predict that these problems would disappear over time as people solved them using tools other than litigation. Lane Kenworthy, Joel Rogers, and I looked at litigation in the automobile industry in the late twentieth century.[33] We discovered data indicating an upsurge in contracts cases in this industry in the early 1980s. Yet the data also indicated that contracts cases involving the automobile manufacturers dropped off rapidly after that period. Our interviews with officials in the industry suggested that experience with litigating and appealing contracts cases pushed them to search for other ways to solve their problems. My impression is that people in areas other than automobiles are also searching for solutions to problems other than litigation and appeals.[34] Contracts litigation and appeals do not produce satisfied customers. The rattlesnake is likely to go back to sunning itself and looking dead.

Let me be clear: Contract ideas in the broader legal culture are alive and well. People try to perform their promises and at least apologize when they cannot.

---

found unconscionable; and in 46 cases the arbitration agreements were enforced because the court found them not to be unconscionable. Anthony Niblett (2006), Inconsistent Contract Enforcement, 3 *Hastings Bus. L.J.* 1, looked at 174 decisions of the California Courts of Appeal involving consumer and employment arbitration that were decided between 1977 and February 2006. He reports that 91 of these cases found the arbitration clause unconscionable. Both of these studies criticize the courts' decisions. See Vail and Osborne 22 (2005): "These days a fight over termination at will is as likely to happen in a nearby Holiday Inn meeting room as in the local courthouse."

[31] I was eight and nine years old in 1939 and 1940, and I lived in Laguna Beach, California. This was before California became one continuous housing tract, and there was still open land in places such as Laguna Beach. Rattlesnakes still lived in the cliffs overlooking the ocean. I still remember the important advice given to a little boy by a neighbor: "Never pick up a dead rattlesnake."

[32] Friedman 201 (1965).

[33] Kenworthy et al. (1996). Daimler-Chrysler graded its approximately 900 suppliers' performances, and the grades were posted on a Web site accessible to all suppliers. Those in the top 15% were given rewards, including preferences in gaining new contracts in the future. The underperformers did not get such new contracts. See *Financial Times*, Aug. 5, 2005, at 18. This system seems to have been far more effective than even threats of suits for breach of contract, let alone actual litigation.

[34] This is the pattern found by a Spanish scholar, José Juan Toharia (1974). Economically developed societies tend to have litigation rates that stabilize or decline. After a disruption that provokes increased litigation, the rate tends to return to the trend line or decline again.

Settlements of disputes reflect many factors, but one is the original deal. In some subset of all contracts and contracts disputes, perceptions about contract law itself may play a role in creating and reinforcing expectations. Even misperceptions about contract law itself can have this effect. Sometimes, however, a settlement requires parties to put aside ideas about legal rights and fault to seek the best solution to the existing problem that they face.

Yet what of the style of judicial opinions in those contract cases that do come before the courts? What of abstraction and particularity? To a great extent, the increasingly particularistic approach described in *Contract Law in America* has continued. Article Two of the Uniform Commercial Code (UCC) became the law in most states about ten years after the last period Friedman examines in his book. This statute is filled with qualitative standards that can be applied only by focusing on all the particular facts of the case. For example, all contracts for the sale of goods are subject to a requirement of "good faith" (§1–203), which the statute defines as "honesty in fact" plus "the observance of reasonable commercial standards of fair dealing in the trade" (§2–103(b)). Courts are given power to avoid "unconscionable" provisions in contracts, (§2–302), but this term is not defined.[35] One of the judiciary's favorite wild cards – waiver – is recognized (§§1–107; 2–209(4)(5)). A party to a contract can be excused "if performance as agreed has been made impracticable by the occurrence of a contingency the non-occurrence of which was a basic assumption on which the contract was made" (§2–615). Article Two of the Code applies only to transactions in goods (§2–102); however, the American Law Institute, one of the organizations that created the UCC, published its Restatement (2d) Contracts a little more than a decade after the UCC became law in almost all states. In many situations, the Restatement takes the particularistic approach of Article Two and applies it to all contracts. Many courts have accepted this invitation to avoid quantitative more-or-less certain rules and to turn to qualitative standards that call for judgment based on the circumstances of the case before them.

Professor Robert Scott of the Columbia University Law School has studied appellate cases that raise contracts issues governed by Article Two, particularly

---

[35] The term is not defined in the statute. The citation found in the Official Comment to Sec. 2–302 sends us to Judge Herbert Goodrich telling us intuitively that Campbell Soup's lengthy one-sided form contract with its suppliers of vegetables was just "carrying a good joke too far." *Campbell Soup Co. v. Wentz*, 172 F.2d 80, 83 (3d Cir. 1948) ("This is the kind of provision which the late Francis H. Bohlen would call 'carrying a good joke too far.'") Francis H. Bohlen was a professor at the University of Pennsylvania Law School from 1898 to 1938. He was the reporter for the American Law Institute's first Restatement of Torts. Judge Goodrich had been the dean of the University of Pennsylvania Law School and the head of the American Law Institute. He also was an upper class gentleman, and I have always thought that he was telling us that a well brought-up person would not have committed the one-sided form contract that Campbell imposed on its suppliers of vegetables. A gentleman would know that it just was not proper. Campbell's executives cannot have been pleased when the case was discussed in *Fortune*, Mar. 1949, at 142, and Campbell quickly revised its form contract so that it at least looked fair. The new contract was upheld in *Campbell Soup Co. v. Diehm*, 111 F. Supp. 211 (E.D.Pa. 1952).

those calling for contracts to be interpreted according to the norm of commercial reasonableness.[36] In Friedman's terms, Scott found that courts have not sought to create abstract rules. Scott complains, "[C]ourts have consistently interpreted these statutory instructions not as inductive directions to incorporate commercial norms and prototypes, but rather as invitations to make deductive speculations according to 'Code policy' or other noncontextual criteria."[37] Scott is highly critical of this particularistic approach; it fails to produce "default terms suitable for other contracting parties." Yet particularistic approaches, even when appellate judges are far removed from experience in commercial matters, may serve to provoke settlements by the parties. One who would pursue an appeal must take the risk that the judges will just get it wrong.[38] Often it would be better to avoid this risk by striking a deal.[39] Even if events at the end of the twentieth century provoked more contracts opinions than Friedman found in Wisconsin during the periods he studied, the judicial function in this area continued to be one where "[f]reed of the necessity to pay great attention to matters of . . . principle . . . the court is the more apt to turn to the particular situation before it, and to seek an adjustment which accords with current notions of fairness in the particular situation, untroubled by considerations of grand generality."[40] In addition, those involved in important commercial transactions have many ways to avoid this process if they see it as imposing undue risks. In many areas, mediation and arbitration replace going to court to solve disputes, and even when complaints are filed, cases almost always settle – often after the summary judgment stage.

Finally, to what extent, if at all, has *Contract Law in America* influenced modern contracts teaching and scholarship? Is such scholarship still focused on dodos and unicorns? Friedman's book was widely reviewed after its publication, and most reviews were highly favorable. For example, "he blends common sense, insight and shrewd judgment so that the over all impression of the reader is one of admiration for his scholarship."[41] "Professor Friedman has made a contribution to the literature on the law of contracts, and his book belongs in every law library."[42] "Professor Friedman . . . [is] doing the only work in contracts of which I know that has in it the breath of new life."[43] "When all else is said, Professor Friedman's uncanny ability to stimulate new thinking in conceptualized area makes *Contract Law in America* must reading for serious students of the law."[44]

---

[36] Scott (2000a).
[37] Scott (2000b). See also Scott (2009); Kraus and Scott (2009).
[38] As Hedley says, "It is hard to predict precisely what will happen if one side invokes the law, but it is likely to be inconvenient and expensive, and is for that reason a powerful motivation to respect what that person takes to be legal entitlements." Hedley 88 (1997).
[39] See Macaulay (2003).
[40] Friedman 194 (1965).
[41] Jones 886 (1965–6).
[42] Hamilton 130 (1966).
[43] Sharp 416 (1966).
[44] Speidel 311 (1967).

Of course, Friedman probably expected that the contract traditionalists would respond to his attack on their field. They did, and they counterattacked. Here is one example:

> This reviewer has grown weary of much of the talk about the deficiencies of contract law and teaching, especially that which proceeds on the assumption that the thing we presently palm off in the classroom is some spruced-up, rearranged version – in content and spirit – of what occupied the minds of Langdell and Williston. . . . That each beginning law course carries a designated title confirms the existence of an established body of learning, organized and subdivided into fields. In presenting one of these fields to students we are space-bound by received classifications; there is a language to be learned and a culture to be passed on.[45]

Yet the most negative review attacked what the reviewer called Friedman's "tote 'em up" method of counting the frequency with which doctrines were used by the Wisconsin court. Moreover, this reviewer was offended by the claim that contract law was in decline or decay:

> A comparative study of the American law of contracts, 100 years ago, 50 years ago, and today, might be a valuable book. . . . It can neither ignore nor distort the fact of an increasingly complicated and fragmented law of contracts. It cannot restrict itself to one provincial state, and it must enjoy a reasonable quotient of scholarly neutrality; it cannot require us to describe the shift from, say, Williston to Corbin as "decay" or "decline" of any sort. . . .

> We must, obviously, strive for the relevant, and many or all of us need often to be reminded of the fact, but if put to the choice I should prefer teaching dodos in their full contexts to "toting up" instances of their invocation.[46]

---

[45] Henderson 1468, 1475 (1975).

[46] Childres 484 (1966). Childres was a professor at New York University. The reference to Wisconsin as "one provincial state" reminds me of the classic *The New Yorker* cover picturing the New Yorker's view of the world. Saul Steinberg's "A View of the World from Ninth Avenue," was *The New Yorker* cover of March 29, 1976. It shows a bird's-eye view of the city from Ninth Avenue looking westward, with space becoming ever more condensed, and leading to Asia. Most of the middle of the country simply does not exist in this drawing. Without doing the work, Childres could not assert that a study of New York appellate opinions would produce significantly different results than those produced by Friedman's trip through the wilds of Wisconsin. Professor William C. Jones, in a mixed review of the book, said, "If Mr. Friedman really considered the English law, for example, to say nothing of the continental, it seems to me that he would not be quite so confident of equating the market economy with contract law, nor would it be so clear that its importance had disappeared with its decline in the utterances of the Wisconsin Supreme Court." W. Jones 242 (1967). Of course, Friedman wrote about a particular kind of contract law – abstraction – and saw such fields as labor law, insurance law, employment law, and consumer protection as something else. We cannot tell what one would find in Professor Jones' proposed study of "actions of Dutch courts over the 350 years," but my guess is that insofar as the Dutch courts pursued abstraction, they would be seeking to serve the market. For another largely negative review of Friedman's book, based on Friedman's acceptance of the court's particularistic approach, see Treitel (1965).

The many thoughtful and largely positive reviews meant that scholars could learn about the book. Yet did it have any influence? At the outset, we must note that Grant Gilmore both quoted at length and highly praised Friedman's book in Gilmore's *The Death of Contract*. Friedman deserves some credit for the great reappraisal that Gilmore's challenge to the field provoked. Gilmore tells a story of a bargain theory of contract fashioned by Holmes, Langdell, and Williston that fell apart with the large shift in the legal culture during the first half of the twentieth century. *The Death of Contract* prompted a great outpouring of articles defending the field. Jay Feinman noted, "Gilmore's work engendered such an extraordinary critical reaction that the reviews quickly exceeded the book in length."[47] He continued, "This scholarship sometimes seems desperately justificatory rather than celebratory, and such justifications generally occur when those involved sense that something has gone wrong in their subject."[48]

However, we cannot blame any of Gilmore's excesses on Friedman. Several authors have argued that, despite his praise for *Contract Law in America*, Gilmore did not seem to understand Friedman's book.[49] Jean Braucher wrote,

> Gilmore quoted a long passage from Friedman, part of which referred to Friedman's central point about the marginalization of contract law, but Gilmore did not engage with this point. Rather, Gilmore gave loving attention to the beautiful trees (the reasoning of cases in his account of the rise and fall of classical contract doctrine), while Friedman kept his eye on the big picture, seeing that much of the forest had been chopped down.[50]

Robert Gordon said that Gilmore was a case-law realist, whereas Friedman was a behavioral realist.[51] A case lawyer, Gordon asserted, sees the study of deciding appeals as the "master process whose study reveals the rest, as the microscopic study of a beetle was believed in the 18th century to unlock the pattern of the mind of God."[52] Behavioral realists "refuse to limit their universe of investigation to cases. . . . Behaviorists . . . ask not only what social functions are performed by courts but also who else in society, official agencies or private parties, performs those same functions. Once the focus of study is thus shifted, they assert, the work of courts is seen to shrink to near insignificance."[53]

Has the behavioral realist part of *Contract Law in America* had any impact on the teaching and writing about the field? A search of WestLaw's law review database

---

[47] Feinman 669 (1989).

[48] Id. at 670.

[49] Friedman himself seems to disagree with Gilmore's idea that contract has died: "One could argue the very opposite case: that is, the 'values involved in individual freedom of choice' has gotten more robust over the years." See Friedman 81 (1990).

[50] Braucher 76–7 (1995).

[51] Gordon (1974).

[52] Id. at 1222.

[53] Id. at 1223.

that goes back to the early 1980s yields 159 hits, and we know that the book still is being cited. As recently as 1999, Ian Ayres looked at what he called "Friedman's path breaking 1965 book," but he argued that the domain of contract was not waning but rather waxing.[54] He reached this conclusion by offering a new definition of "contract," one that was very different from the classic view of the field that Friedman challenged. Ayres suggested that any field could be viewed as contractual "if the parties have substantial freedom to reorder their legal relationship privately." Ayres' move is to plug back into contract all of the specialized fields that legislation and case law had "removed" during the first part of the twentieth century. We can accept this redefinition, but then we can ask these questions: How many of the disputes in these areas go to court, and what do the courts do with them? I would be surprised if we found a litigation explosion and a great deal of abstraction. After all, insurance was one of the first areas "removed from the domain of contract," and it was the home of waiver, estoppel, construction of language against the drafter, and the modern "reasonable expectations" doctrine that calls for courts to seek what insurance buyers likely assumed rather than the literal text of the policy.[55]

The contracts field has changed over the course of the more than forty-five years since *Contract Law in America* was published in ways that I think might please Friedman. As is so often the case, we have little evidence about causation. I cannot show that anyone read the book, saw the light, and converted to the true path. Nonetheless, we can point to changes consistent with Friedman's position. Some schools have trimmed their required contracts course down to a quick-and-dirty three unit once-over-lightly. This change seems consistent with Friedman's views about teaching abstract contract doctrine as being analogous to teaching a "zoology course which confined its study to dodos and unicorns, to beasts rare or long dead and beasts that never lived."[56] Perhaps zoologists need to learn just a little about extinct and mythical beasts, and perhaps beginning law students need to absorb just a little of this part of the classic legal culture even if it is totally misleading. Maybe one has to master the ritual to join the fraternity, and perhaps it is a better initiation rite if it is contradictory and impossible to understand fully. (I suspect that some professors manage to make a silk purse out of the sow's ear of a three-credit contracts course, but it cannot be easy.)

Another approach, the one that I favor, takes just the opposite tack.[57] Some schools offer more hours to broaden the subject of the contracts course so that it covers such

[54] Ayres (1999).
[55] See, e.g., *C & J Fertilizer, Inc. v. Allied Mut. Ins. Co.*, 227 N.W.2d 169 (S.Ct. Iowa 1975). For a discussion of the doctrine, see Korobkin 1270–3 (2003); Lim 613–15 (2003).
[56] Friedman 25 (1965).
[57] See Stewart Macaulay et al., (2003). "Et al." conceals the fact that the editors are Stewart Macaulay, John Kidwell, and William Whitford. Marc Galanter joined us for the first but not the second edition. The project that produced the book was such a partnership that I have always regretted the citation form that reduces real contributors to "et al." The authors' favorite title of a review of our book is Woodward (1997). His title was "Contracts for Grown-ups."

elements as the contracts part of Article 2 of the Uniform Commercial Code, the doctrine and the politics involved in employment at will, franchise protection laws, and an introduction to consumer protection statutes and regulation. For example, the expanded course considers the doctrine of "reasonable expectations" in insurance law, and students are asked whether this attack on the literal language of complex printed form contracts might be expanded to other areas where fine print is used to confuse rather than inform. More and more contextual material has become available, and it can be used to make such points as the limited utility of individual causes of action in consumer transactions and the great push toward settling disputes rather than litigating them. Thus pure contract law – abstraction – becomes only one of several strands of contract thought. Those in the field have begun to ask when this approach is appropriate, what are its costs, and who benefits and who loses when we turn to formalism. In sum, since the publication of *Contract Law in America*, much of the field has lost its major focus on dodos and unicorns. I am sure, although I cannot prove, that Friedman's book had a great deal to do with this change for the better. As I said at the outset, we should not forget Friedman's First.

REFERENCES

Ayres, Ian (1999). Empire or Residue: Competing Visions of the Contractual Canon, 26 *Fla. St. U. L. Rev.* 897.

Braucher, Jean (1995). The Afterlife of Contract, 90 NW. *U. L. Rev.* 49.

Childres, Robert (1966). Book Review, 18 *J. Legal Educ.* 478.

Eagan, William (1980). The Westinghouse Uranium Contracts: Commercial Impracticability and Related Matters, 18 *Am. Bus. L.J.* 281.

Edelman, Lauren B. (1990). Legal Environments and Organizational Governance: The Expansion of Due Process in the American Workplace, 95 *Am. Sociol. Rev.* 1401.

Edelman, Lauren B., Steven E. Abraham, and Howard Erlanger (1992). Professional Construction of Law: The Inflated Threat of Wrongful Discharge, 26 *Law & Soc'y Rev.* 47.

Feinman, Jay M. (1989). The Jurisprudence of Classification, 41 *Stan. L. Rev.* 661.

Friedman, Lawrence M. (1965). *Contract Law in America*. Madison, WI: University of Wisconsin Press.

———. (1967). Legal Rules and the Process of Social Change, 19 *Stan. L. Rev.* 786.

———. (1990). *The Republic of Choice, Authority, and Culture*. Cambridge, MA: Harvard University Press.

Friedman, Lawrence M. and Stewart Macaulay (1967). Contract Law and Contract Teaching: Past, Present and Future, 1967 *Wis. L. Rev.* 805.

Galanter, Marc (2001). Contract in Court; Or Almost Everything You May or May Not Want to Know about Contract Litigation, 2001 *Wis. L. Rev.* 577.

Galanter, Marc and Joel Rogers (1991). *A Transformation of American Business Disputing? Some Preliminary Observations*. Madison: University of Wisconsin Institute for Legal Studies.

Gordon, Robert W. (1974). Book Review, 1974 *Wis. L. Rev.* 1216.

Hadfield, Gillian K. (2004). Where Have All the Trials Gone? Settlements, Nontrial Adjudications, and Statistical Artifacts in the Changing Disposition of Federal Civil Cases, 1 *J. Empir. Legal Stud.* 705.

Hamilton, Robert W. (1966). Book Review, 59 *Law Libr. J.* 129.

Hedley, Steve (1997). The "Needs of Commercial Litigants" in Nineteenth and Twentieth Century Contract Law, 18 *Legal Hist.* 85.

Henderson, Stanley D. (1975). Book Review, 124 *U. Pa. L. Rev.* 1466.

Jones, Ernest M. (1965–6). Book Review, 13 *UCLA L. Rev.* 897.

Jones, William C. (1967). Book Review, 1967 *Wash. U. L.Q.* 238.

Joskow, Paul L. (1977). Commercial Impossibility, the Uranium Market and the Westinghouse Case, 6 *J. Legal Stud.* 119.

Kennedy, Duncan (1976). Form and Substance in Private Law Adjudication, 89 *Harv. L. Rev.* 1685.

Kenworthy, Lane, Stewart Macaulay, and Joel Rogers (1996). The More Things Change, the More They Stay the Same: Business Litigation and Governance in the American Automobile Industry, 21 *Law & Soc. Inquiry* 631.

Kim, Pauline T. (1999). Norms, Learning, and Law: Exploring the Influences on Workers' Legal Knowledge, 1999 *U. Ill. L. Rev.* 447.

Korobkin, Russell (2003). Bounded Rationality, Standard Form Contracts, and Unconscionability, 70 *U. Chi. L. Rev.* 1203.

Kraus, Jody S. and Robert E. Scott (2009). Contract Design and the Structure of Contractual Intent, 84 *N.Y.U. L. Rev.* 1023.

Lim, Julian S. (2003). Tongue-tied in the Market: The Relevance of Contract Law to Racial-Language Minorities, 91 *Cal. L. Rev.* 579.

Macaulay, Stewart (1966). Private Legislation and the Duty to Read – Business by IBM Machine, the Law of Contracts and Credit Cards, 19 *Vand. L. Rev.* 1051.

———. (1989). Bambi Meets Godzilla: Contracts Scholarship and Teaching vs. State Unfair and Deceptive Trade Practices and Consumer Protection Statutes, 26 *Hous. L. Rev.* 575.

———. (2001). Almost Everything That I Did Want to Know About Contract Litigation: A Comment on Galanter, 2001 *Wis. L. Rev.* 629.

———. (2003). The Real and the Paper Deal: Empirical Pictures of Relationships, Complexity and the Urge for Transparent Simple Rules, 66 *Mod. L. Rev.* 44. This paper is also included in Campbell, David, Hugh Collins, and John Wightman, eds. (2003). *Implicit Dimensions of Contract: Discrete, Relational & Network Contracts*. Oxford: Hart Publishing.

Macaulay, Stewart et al. (2003). *Contracts: Law in Action*. 2nd edition. Newark, NJ: LexisNexis.

Maggs, Gregory E. (2003). The Waning Importance of Revisions to U.C.C. Article 2, 78 *Notre Dame L. Rev.* 595.

McBarnet, Doreen (1988). Law, Policy and Legal Avoidance: Can Law Effectively Implement Egalitarian Policies? 15 *J. Law & Soc'y* 113.

———. (1991). Whiter than White Collar Crime: Tax, Fraud Insurance and the Management of Stigma, 42 *Br. J. Sociol.* 323.

Nielsen, Laura Beth (1999). Paying Workers or Paying Lawyers: Employee Termination Practices in the United States and Canada, 21 *Law & Pol'y* 247.

Scott, Robert E. (2000a). The Uniformity Norm in Commercial Law: A Comparative Analysis of Common Law and Code Methodologies, in Jody S. Kraus and Steven D. Walt, eds., *The Jurisprudential Foundations of Corporate and Commercial Law*. Cambridge: Cambridge University Press.

———. (2000b). The Case for Formalism in Relational Contract, 94 *NW. U. L. Rev.* 847.

———. (2009). In (Partial) Defense of Strict Liability in Contract, 107 *Mich. L. Rev.* 1381.

Shamir, Ronen (1993). Formal and Substantive Rationality in American Law: A Weberian Perspective, 2 *Soc. & Legal Stud.* 45.

Sharp, Malcolm P. (1966). Book Review, 28 *Rutgers L. Rev.* 415.

Speidel, Richard E. (1967). Book Review, 1967 *Wis. L. Rev.* 301.

———. (1989). Arbitration of Statutory Rights under the Federal Arbitration Act: The Case for Reform, 4 *Ohio St. J. on Disp. Resol.* 157.

Toharia, José Juan (1974). *Cambio Social y Vida Jurídica en España, 1900–1970.* Madrid: EDICUSA.

Treitel, Guenter H. (1965). Book Review, 33 *U. Chi. L. Rev.* 418.

Vail, John and Tom Osborne (2005). The Menace of Mandatory Arbitration, *Trial*, Aug. 2005, at 22.

Vincent-Jones, Peter (1993). Contract Litigation in England and Wales 1975–1991: A Transformation in Business Disputing?, 12 *Civ. Just. Q.* 337.

Woodward, William J., Jr. (1997). Contracts for Grown-ups, 47 *J. Legal Educ.* 139.

Law and the Environment

13

Law, Society, and the Environment

Robert V. Percival

Throughout his remarkable career, Lawrence Friedman has explored how social forces shape law and how law, in turn, influences society. Although he has not written extensively about environmental law, his work provides valuable insights for understanding issues that have puzzled scholars in the environmental law field. This chapter explores how Friedman's work can help illuminate why we have environmental laws, how they have evolved over time, and why they have been highly successful in solving some problems but not others.

The chapter begins by discussing the evolution of environmental law from its common law roots to the vast federal regulatory infrastructure that prevails today. Reflecting Friedman's conviction that appellate case law often provides a distorted lens for viewing the development of law, it examines how common law principles of liability for environmental harm were adapted in practice to preserve the economic vitality of economically important polluters, while ultimately encouraging the development of pollution-control technology. Mindful of Friedman's emphasis on empirical historiography, it presents some previously unpublished data concerning an early-twentieth-century effort to supplement nuisance law with an alternative system of administrative compensation for environmental harm.

Political theory predicts that federal regulatory legislation to protect the environment should not exist because it imposes concentrated costs on politically powerful industries to provide diffuse benefits to the general public.[1] Yet during the 1970s Congress adopted transformative environmental legislation, which it expanded and strengthened during the 1980s. Although these laws seek to prevent harm before it occurs by authorizing expert administrative agencies to adopt precautionary regulations, in practice regulation usually is reactive, responding only after harm has become visible enough to create public demand for action.

[1] Olson (1965); Farber 60 (1992).

Critics of federal environmental regulation decry the laws' impossibly strict directives as inefficient and excessively costly, yet efforts to roll back the federal regulatory
infrastructure have been largely unsuccessful. This chapter discusses why federal
environmental regulation has proven to be so durable, focusing on the symbolic
value of the environmental laws and their remarkable capacity for innovation. Public demand to protect human health and the environment has been an important
aspect of what Friedman has labeled the "total justice" movement. Environmental
law generally has avoided clashes with what Friedman calls the "profoundly indi-
vidualist culture" of the United States by refusing to regulate individual behavior
even when it contributes to environmental harm. Environmental law has been most
successful when it reinforced preexisting social norms, while failing miserably in the
few cases when it tried to dictate changes in individual lifestyles.

The chapter concludes by arguing that the environmental statutes' promise of
comprehensive, preventive regulation has been tempered by the influence of some
of the common law norms it sought to displace. Courts hearing challenges to environmental regulations have created their own brand of "regulatory common law"
by requiring more detailed evidence that regulatory targets are responsible for causing substantial harm. The shadow cast by common law concepts also is evident in
judicial efforts to restrict the standing of environmental litigants and to revive doctrines of regulatory takings and constitutional limits on federal power. Despite these
obstacles, environmental law has emerged as a global imperative with an impres-
sive record of accomplishments in the developed world. Like what Friedman has
described as the "Victorian compromise" of nineteenth-century morals legislation,
environmental law's promise of comprehensive protection for future generations
has promoted social norms of environmental responsibility, even while tolerating
individual behavior inconsistent with its goals.

THE COMMON LAW ROOTS OF U.S. ENVIRONMENTAL LAW

Environmental law has a much longer and richer history than most people realize.
Conventional accounts of the history of U.S. environmental law generally trace its
emergence to the early 1970s when Congress enacted regulatory legislation to protect
the environment.[2] Yet the roots of environmental law run much deeper. Long before
the enactment of federal regulatory programs to protect the environment, states
engaged in fierce disputes over transboundary pollution that were heard by the U.S.
Supreme Court, exercising its original jurisdiction over disputes between states.
Early in the twentieth century, the Court actually issued injunctions restricting
emissions of air pollution from a copper smelter,[3] requiring the city of Chicago to

---

[2] Lazarus (2004).
[3] *Georgia v. Tennessee Copper Co.*, 237 U.S. 678 (1915).

build a sewage treatment plant,[4] and ordering New York City to build a garbage incinerator to stop ocean dumping of its garbage.[5]

The Court decided these cases by applying principles of the common law of nuisance, which by then had been under development for nearly 400 years. These principles provide that even nontrespassory interferences with one's quiet use and enjoyment of land can be actionable as nuisances[6] and that no one has the right to use his or her property in a manner that causes significant, foreseeable harm to others.[7] These have become foundational principles for the field of environmental law, but they do not resolve vexing questions concerning how significant harm must be before it is legally actionable and what remedies should be applied to redress it. When polluters are important economic enterprises, courts face difficult choices in fashioning remedies. Before the development of modern pollution-control technology, courts were reluctant to mandate abatement of pollution for fear of causing economic harm to the community.

This reluctance is well illustrated by the history of nuisance litigation against copper smelters. Before pollution-control technology for smelters was developed in the early twentieth century, pollution from smelters usually destroyed all vegetation for miles around. In nineteenth-century Britain, farmers and owners of country estates brought several nuisance cases against companies operating copper smelters. Despite the visible damage that their smelters caused, the companies usually escaped significant liability because their enterprises were viewed as too important to the local economy.

In response to complaints about their pollution, British copper companies initially sought to control their emissions by building taller smokestacks to disperse the pollution away from the immediate vicinity of their plants. Although some owners of copper works claimed that smoke from their tallest smokestacks never reached the ground, the tall stacks actually served to spread the damage over a much wider area.[8] Whenever local economies were heavily dependent on copper production, victims of the smelter pollution faced an uphill fight in convincing courts to stop it. The few landowners who did pursue legal action against British smelters had the odds stacked against them because their lawsuits were viewed as threats to the economic health of their communities.[9] Although more than twenty lawsuits were brought against smelters in Britain during the eighteenth and nineteenth centuries, plaintiffs clearly prevailed in only five reported cases.[10]

---

[4] *Wisconsin v. Illinois*, 281 U.S. 179 (1930).
[5] *New Jersey v. New York City*, 284 U.S. 237 (1931).
[6] Aldred's Case, 77 Eng. Rep. 816 (1611).
[7] *Tenant v. Goldwin*, 92 Eng. Rep. 222 (1702).
[8] Rees 40 (1993).
[9] Brenner (1974).
[10] Newell 670 (1997).

Uncontrolled pollution from copper smelters produced similar environmental devastation in the United States where it appeared to spawn even more litigation. The most famous U.S. judgment against the copper industry occurred in *Georgia v. Tennessee Copper*, in which the U.S. Supreme Court upheld Georgia's right to stop harmful emissions from copper smelters located just across the Tennessee border.[11] Detailed examination of the record compiled in this litigation reveals some important features of early nuisance litigation in the United States.

First, it appears that U.S. copper smelters were the targets of far more private nuisance actions than would be expected based on the British experience. Although the *Tennessee Copper* case involved a *public* nuisance claim brought by the state of Georgia, a document in the case file revealed that a total of 44 *private* lawsuits concerning pollution were pending in state or federal court against one of the smelter companies as of November 1, 1913.[12] A local historian reports that the first private nuisance suits against the smelters had been filed in 1895.[13] Some succeeded in obtaining modest damages. In *Ducktown Sulphur, Copper and Iron Co. v. Barnes*, 60 S.W. 593 (1900), the Tennessee Supreme Court upheld the right of plaintiffs in private nuisance actions to recover damages against the Ducktown Company. Although there is no reported decision documenting what happened on remand, a letter in the files of the Ducktown Company, dated January 14, 1903, reports that a check had been sent that day to the plaintiffs' attorney, Judge James G. Parks, to cover payment of the damages awarded in the case: Plaintiff William Madison received $100.00 in damages, Margaret Madison $1.00, and John A. Fortner $92.50.[14] When three cases seeking injunctions to stop the smelter emissions reached the Tennessee Supreme Court, the court refused to issue an injunction.[15] Noting that there was no alternative method of roasting copper ore nor any more remote place for the companies to locate their operations, the court concluded that an injunction would "blot out two great mining and manufacturing enterprises, destroy half of the taxable values of a county, and drive more than 10,000 people from their homes."

In a subsequent public nuisance action filed by the state of Georgia, the U.S. Supreme Court, exercising its original jurisdiction over suits between states, upheld Georgia's right to an injunction to control emissions from the smelters because they had caused significant transboundary harm.[16] This decision has served as an important precedent for the development of both national and international law governing transboundary pollution. It has been cited by other courts in more than 130 cases, and it was the centerpiece of the U.S. Supreme Court's decision in April 2007 upholding the right of states to sue the U.S. Environmental Protection Agency for

---

[11]   206 U.S. 230 (1907).

[12]   List of Smoke Suits Pending 1 (1913).

[13]   Barclay 9 (1977).

[14]   Id. at 73.

[15]   *Madison v. Ducktown Sulphur, Copper & Iron Co.*, 83 S.W. 658 (1904).

[16]   *Georgia v. Tennessee Copper Co.*, 206 U.S. 230 (1907).

refusing to regulate emissions of greenhouse gases (*Massachusetts v. EPA*, 127 S.Ct. 1438 (2007)). Yet even though the Supreme Court ultimately granted an injunction to limit emissions from one of the smelters (*Georgia v. Tennessee Copper Co.*, 237 U.S. 678 (1915)), the case confirms the wisdom of Lawrence Friedman's admonition to look beyond the decisions of appellate tribunals in seeking to understand the impact of law on social behavior. Close examination of the subsequent history of *Georgia v. Tennessee Copper* reveals that the Court's rhetoric concerning the right of Georgia to prevent harm to its people and lands was tempered by the economic importance of copper production.

The Tennessee Copper Company reached a settlement with the state of Georgia that allowed it to continue its smelting operations substantially as before, in return for agreeing to pay claims of property damage to be decided by a board of arbitrators. The board consisted of two arbitrators, one appointed by Georgia and the other by the company with an umpire appointed by Georgia to resolve any disagreements between the two. Those who filed claims with the arbitration board were barred from seeking redress in court, even if their claims were denied by the board. Awards were to be made to citizens of north Georgia who convinced the arbitrators that their property had been damaged by emissions from the smelter. The company posted a bond in the amount of $16,500 per year (the equivalent of more than $300,000 in today's dollars) to ensure payment of arbitral awards.

After the Ducktown Company refused to settle, the Supreme Court issued an injunction limiting its emissions to no more than 20 tons of sulphur per day during the growing season (from April 10 until October 1) and to no more than 40 tons per day during the rest of the year.[17] This represented a level of total permissible emissions of 11,140 tons, merely a 13.4% reduction from the 13,000 tons the company previously had emitted. The Court conceded that "[i]t is impossible from the record to ascertain with certainty the reduction in the sulphur content of emitted gases necessary to render the territory of Georgia immune from injury."

The Court apparently was seeking to reduce the damage caused by the smelter's emissions without significantly curtailing the company's production of copper. Its injunction represented what has been described as "a best available technology (BAT) injunction."[18] Yet the company fought successfully to relax the injunction. On April 3, 1916, the Court modified the injunction to increase allowable sulphur emissions from 20 to 25 tons per day from April 10 until October 1 and from 40 to 50 tons per day at other times. As modified, the injunction actually allowed the company to emit nearly 14,000 tons of sulphur per year, more than 7 percent more than it emitted in 1913.

A year later, when the United States entered World War I, the state of Tennessee and the U.S. Secretary of the Navy urged the Supreme Court to relax the injunction

[17] *Georgia v. Tennessee Copper*, 237 U.S. 678 (1915).
[18] Morag-Levine (2003).

TABLE 13.1. *Arbitration claims and awards, 1921–8*

Year	Claims	Awards	Total Claimed	Total Awarded
1921	61	39	$1,841.50	$240.00
1922	19	13	$1,142.00	$75.00
1923	7	0	$467.00	$0.00
1924	89	69	$6,998.40	$940.00
1925	2	0	Unknown	$0.00
1926	4	1	$211.00	$10.00
1927	2	0	$150.00	$0.00
1928	19	18	$2,342.00	$245.00

even more. The Ducktown Company agreed to participate in the arbitration system for providing compensation to property owners in return for Georgia's agreement to relax the injunction substantially. Georgia agreed to allow emissions of 40 tons of sulphur per day, rather than the 25 tons specified in the injunction. The company posted a bond of $8,500 per year to ensure that it could pay its share of arbitration awards.

The arbitration system required that any citizen claiming damages from smelter pollution had to file a claim with the state's arbitrator within five days of the occurrence of damage. Claims were made by filling out a form listing the type of crops for which damage was claimed, the number of acres of each damaged crop, and the dollar value of the damage. Awards could only be made for damage actually verified by the arbitrators by visiting the claimant's property. Examination of the claim forms in the Georgia State Archives reveals that they contained a preprinted space on the back for the arbitrators to record the date of their visit, whether they found any damage, and its estimated value. The claim forms indicate that these visits usually occurred within a few weeks after the crops or timber were alleged to have been damaged.

This system of administrative compensation proved very disappointing to farmers who filed claims for damages from smelter pollution. A union of Georgia farmers passed a resolution in 1917 claiming that the arbitral board "has arbitrarily ignored the just claims of the citizens for their damages." It stated that because the arbitrators "have repeatedly ignored all claims from Gilmer County," refusing even to investigate them, the citizens of Gilmer County "have become disgusted and say it is all a farce and that they will not file any more claims with it."

Despite relaxation of the emissions limits, the board of arbitrators was not very generous in awarding compensation to those who claimed damage from the smelter pollution. The original records of the board for the years from 1921 to 1928, which are located in the Georgia State Archives, provide the data shown in Table 13.1.

These data indicate that the pattern of very small awards protested by the farmers' union before the Ducktown Company joined the arbitration system persisted during the 1920s. The amounts of compensation actually awarded were so small that more money was paid to the arbitrators (who received a salary of $100 per month and $30 per month for expenses) than to the farmers who claimed damage from the pollution. Because the total damages awarded were less than the administrative costs of the arbitration system, the Georgia Legislature in 1921 abolished the standing office of the third arbitrator and provided that such an umpire would be appointed only if the two other arbitrators disagreed, which apparently never happened.

As courts struggled to fashion remedies to protect victims of pollution without shutting down valuable enterprises, the common law's most significant contribution may have been to create incentives for companies to develop improved pollution-control technology. Although the U.S. Supreme Court's decision in *Georgia v. Tennessee Copper* ultimately resulted in an injunction that limited emissions from a copper smelter, the initial emissions limits were set at a level that did not threaten the economic viability of the company. Yet the threat of future liability and particularly the uncertainty concerning the ultimate remedy to be applied by courts in abating nuisances helped encourage the companies to develop new technology. They ultimately developed the lead acid chamber method for removing sulphur from their emissions. This process allowed them to use the reclaimed sulphur to produce sulphuric acid, which eventually proved to be even more valuable than the copper they produced.

The battle between Georgia and the Tennessee copper companies was part of a larger pattern of environmental conflicts that arose in other areas where smelters operated. In Butte, Montana, lawsuits against the Anaconda copper smelter ultimately were settled by the company agreeing to pay damages and by the appointment of a commission of experts to ensure that the smelter was using the best available pollution-control technology. The company also agreed to land swaps with the federal government, which enabled it to acquire the property most affected by the pollution.[19] Cross-border damage caused by a lead and zinc smelter in Trail, British Columbia, produced a major international environmental dispute, which culminated in 1941 in a decision by an international arbitral panel established pursuant to a treaty between Canada and the United States. Relying on the precedent of *Georgia v. Tennessee Copper*, the tribunal awarded modest damages and required the smelter to adopt pollution-control measures similar to those employed by the Tennessee smelters. However, it did not accept the U.S. demand that all pollution causing cross-border damage must cease.[20]

Each of these conflicts illustrates the difficulty of proving precisely what damages were caused by pollution even when such damage is highly visible and traceable to large, single sources of uncontrolled emissions. Despite intensive study and thousands of pages of affidavits from experts, the courts and tribunal acknowledged that it was not possible to determine what levels of emissions would adequately control

[19] Macmillan (2000).
[20] Wirth (2000).

the damage caused from the smelters. When the Supreme Court did limit emissions from the Ducktown copper smelter, the initial limits were set at a level that did not threaten the economic viability of the company, and they ultimately were adjusted upward to accommodate increased production demands. In light of this experience, it is not surprising that the U.S. Supreme Court ultimately embraced federal regulatory legislation as a justification for retiring from the task of adjudicating interstate pollution controversies under the federal common law of nuisance.

THE RISE OF THE REGULATORY STATE

The common law proved to be a crude vehicle for responding to environmental problems, particularly those whose causes could not be traced to large, single sources of pollution that visibly damaged their surroundings. Its requirement that plaintiffs demonstrate individualized proof of causal injury was a significant obstacle to its ability to respond to multiple-source, multiple-pollutant problems that expanding industrial activity generated. Even a deadly substance like asbestos, which killed hundreds of thousands of workers, escaped the common law's grasp for decades in part because of the long latency period between exposure and the onset of diseases uniquely linked to it. During the 1970s Congress sought to overcome the deficiencies of the common law by enacting comprehensive federal regulatory legislation that mandated preventive regulation to protect human health and the environment.

Lawrence Friedman has argued that legal systems reflect the societies in which they are embedded and that as society changes so does its law.[21] This is well illustrated by the dramatic growth of federal regulatory legislation to protect the environment in the 1970s. Beginning with the signing into law of the National Environmental Policy Act (NEPA) on New Year's Day 1970, the entire federal regulatory infrastructure to protect the environment was adopted by Congress in the span of a few short years. This remarkable burst of legislative activity was the product of a social movement fueled in part by growing warnings from scientists concerning the long-term environmental damage that could be caused by a buildup of toxic chemicals in the environment. Even before Rachel Carson's *Silent Spring* was published in 1962, scientific warnings concerning a buildup of radioactive byproducts from atmospheric nuclear testing had alarmed the public. The discovery of strontium-90 in the teeth of children around the world helped provide the impetus for the 1963 Test Ban Treaty, which banned above-ground testing of nuclear weapons.

With the enactment of the Clean Air Act Amendments of 1970, the Federal Water Pollution Control Act Amendments of 1972, and the Safe Drinking Water Act in 1974, Congress made federal agencies the nation's guarantors of clean air, clean lakes and rivers, and safe drinking water. This legislation dramatically expanded the federal role in environmental protection matters, which had long been considered the

---

[21] Friedman 10 (2002).

responsibility of state and local governments. To be sure, Congress had intervened before when particularly visible problems, such as exploding steamship boilers in the 1830s, had commanded national attention. Its response then was to appoint a national commission to regulate steamship safety, a subject clearly within what then was a more limited understanding of federal power to regulate interstate commerce. In 1912, Congress used its power to impose excise taxes to effectively ban the use of white phosphorus in match manufacturing because it caused a particularly visible and gruesome disease called "phossy jaw" in which the jaws of its victims dissolved into a horrible pus.[22] Rather than joining the Bern Convention of 1906, an international treaty to ban the use of white phosphorus, the U.S. Congress acted after President William Howard Taft, describing phossy jaw as "frightful," called for "imposition of a heavy federal tax" on white phosphorus in his State of the Union Message in December 1910.[23]

Before the enactment of comprehensive federal regulatory legislation, when threats to public health attracted national attention, conferences of experts would be convened to examine how to respond. After the highly publicized deaths of thirteen workers in tetraethyl lead (TEL) manufacturing plants in October 1924, several cities banned the sale of tetraethyl lead.[24] At the urging of public health advocates, the Surgeon General convened a conference in May 1925 to consider the health risks of TEL. The conference commissioned a quick study that concluded in January 1926 that TEL posed no health risks to the general public; it was deemed dangerous only when used in concentrated form during manufacturing and processing.[25] The TEL bans were rescinded, and for nearly sixty years the combustion of leaded gasoline resulted in elevated levels of lead, a potent neurotoxin, in the bodies of millions of Americans.

The environmental laws adopted during the 1970s sought to prevent harm before it occurred by authorizing expert administrative agencies to issue precautionary regulations. This approach represented a departure from common law norms that required detailed proof of causal injury before the government could intervene. The environmental statutes helped spawn a revolution in administrative law by dramatically expanding the regulatory responsibilities of federal agencies. In an effort to ensure that the general public – the intended beneficiaries of this legislation – enjoyed its fruits, Congress provided for citizen suits, not only to enforce the new laws against polluters but also to force agencies to carry out their responsibilities under the acts. These suits proved critical to the implementation of the new regulatory statutes as time and time again regulations were issued only after successful citizen suits were brought against EPA and other agencies.[26]

[22] Lee 3 (1966).
[23] Congressional Record, 1910: 3629 (House Comm. on Ways and Means, 1912: 9).
[24] Machle 578 (1935).
[25] Cagin and Dray 54 (1993); Rosner and Markowitz 344 (1985).
[26] May (2003).

The National Environmental Policy Act sought to transform the culture of the federal bureaucracy from within by making environmental protection an integral part of every agency's mission. The requirement that agencies prepare and consider detailed environmental impact statements before taking any major action that would significantly affect the environment has become a model for the world. Nearly every country on the globe now requires some form of environmental assessment, and some make it the centerpiece of their system of environmental regulation.

During the 1980s Congress reauthorized and amended the environmental laws it had adopted during the 1970s. When it did so it almost invariably strengthened their requirements and increased their penalties for noncompliance. It also embraced new strategies for influencing corporate behavior by imposing strict, joint, and several liability for the costs of cleaning up releases of hazardous substances and by adopting right-to-know provisions that require companies to inform the public annually of the types and amounts of toxins they discharge into the environment.

The federal environmental laws now aspire to provide comprehensive protection against environmental risks in all media. They promise to provide the public with an "ample margin of safety" against the most dangerous air pollutants and an "adequate margin of safety" against all others.[27] They establish a "national goal that the discharge of pollutants into the navigable waters be eliminated by 1985,"[28] and they seek to ensure proper management of waste from "cradle to grave" (Resource Conservation and Recovery Act). Their ambitious goals are consistent with Lawrence Friedman's notion that popular legal culture in the United States now demands "total justice."[29] Friedman notes that, as science and technology have advanced, the public has come to expect that government will protect them against all controllable risks and that it will ensure that they are compensated when harm befalls them.

Some scholars have criticized the environmental laws for being too ambitious in their goals without providing adequate means for attaining them.[30] They argue that some aspects of the environmental laws are "symbolic legislation," designed to reap political benefits for Congress while avoiding the difficult policy choices that would be necessary actually to achieve their ambitious ends. Although some of the laws' goals undoubtedly are overly ambitious, the insertion of citizen suit provisions into most of the federal environmental laws has helped overcome bureaucratic inertia by providing a vehicle for judicial oversight of their implementation and enforcement.[31] The federal environmental laws have helped stimulate the development of improved technology to control pollution at lower cost, even as they have fallen short of achieving many of their ambitious promises. As Oliver Houck observes, "[O]ft-criticized for its 'impossible' goals (e.g. zero discharge), 'unrealistic' deadlines and

[27] Clean Air Act §§112 & 109.
[28] Clean Water Act §101(a)(1).
[29] Friedman (1985).
[30] Dwyer (1990); Pederson (2004).
[31] May (2003).

'command and control' mechanisms, the ineludible fact is that the [the Clean Water] Act's fixed deadlines, technology standards, permits, and enforcement mechanisms have stimulated measurable compliance, new and improved technologies, source reduction, waste recycling, and a growing number of voluntary, quasi-voluntary, and alternative abatement schemes."[32]

THE LIMITS OF LAW: SOCIAL NORMS AND REGULATORY TARGETS

As Lawrence Friedman has noted, law is the product of social culture, and social norms give law its legitimacy. Law "expresses values and ideals as well as power," and "these values and ideals seep into the consciousness of citizens, high and low, and affect the way they behave, the policies they pursue, the candidates they vote for."[33] The environmental laws adopted by Congress during the 1970s and 1980s have survived repeated efforts by a hostile Congress to relax them in recent years because they articulate enduring values that have become an indelible part of public consciousness. This is reflected in the results of a detailed survey of public opinion conducted in 2005, which found that eight in ten voters support "stronger national standards to protect our land, air and water," with 40 percent strongly supporting it.[34] How then to explain the election in 2004 of a Congress controlled by a political party hostile toward environmental protection? The survey found that "the environment is low on voters' priorities," ranking "last among nine issues tested" with just 10 percent of voters identifying it as "the most important issue to them personally."

Public demand for comprehensive protection of human health and the environment is an important aspect of the total justice phenomenon Friedman has described, but environmental regulation has been most successful when it has employed approaches that reinforce preexisting social norms. It has failed miserably when it has attempted to dictate changes in individual behavior. What Friedman has described as the "profoundly individualistic culture" of the United States[35] is reflected in the fact that U.S. environmental law generally has refrained from making individuals the targets of environmental regulation, despite the fact that they contribute substantially to many serious environmental problems.[36] In the few cases where regulators have deviated from this pattern, the laws have been rather quickly amended to bar regulation of individual behavior.

The most dramatic illustration of this point is EPA's ill-fated effort to impose a transportation control plan on Los Angeles in 1973. After EPA proposed regulations that would restrict automobile use and require federal approval for new parking lots,

---

[32] Houck (1999).
[33] Friedman 17–18 (2002).
[34] Public Opinion Strategies 3 (2005).
[35] Friedman 177–8 (2002).
[36] Vandenbergh 537–84 (2004).

Congress responded to public outrage by removing EPA authority to impose such plans. Reflecting on the lessons from this experience, former EPA administrator Russell Train noted,

> The most important was that EPA could possess undoubted statutory authority, backed up by federal court orders, but such authority availed us very little when we were confronted by broad-scale public opposition. . . .
>
> In a democratic system, ultimate power resides in the people. The exercise of authority, whether derived from statute or from judicial decision, unless accompanied by persuasion and the agreement of the public, will never achieve a given goal.[37]

Another example involves the fate of a provision in the 1990 Clean Air Act Amendments that required major employers to persuade a portion of their employees not to drive to work alone. This program was quickly repealed before it was implemented. The provision, known as the employee trip reduction program, applied to an estimated 30,000 employers with 11 million employees.[38] It required these employers to develop plans to ensure that within two years their employees would have a vehicle occupancy rate 25 percent greater than the average in the area. After several states refused to implement the program, EPA announced that it would not take enforcement action against employers covered by the program.[39] At the end of its 1995 legislative session, the House of Representatives voted unanimously to repeal the mandate. The House bill was passed by the Senate the following day by unanimous consent and signed into law by President Clinton a few days later.[40]

Although the employee trip reduction mandate did not directly apply to individuals, the difficulty of getting employers to change the commuting behavior of their employers was its ultimate downfall. The Clean Air Act's requirements for vehicle inspection and maintenance of pollution-control equipment also have been particularly problematic because they require individuals to bring in their vehicles for periodic testing.[41] When unleaded gasoline was first introduced to protect the catalytic converters that are used to control vehicle emissions, there was widespread misfueling that damaged these pollution-control devices. Consumers continued to use leaded gas because it was several cents per gallon cheaper than unleaded gasoline.[42] This problem ultimately was eliminated by EPA's decision to phase out the use of lead additives in gasoline to protect public health.

The public's antipathy to being a target of environmental regulation is so well understood by EPA that the agency even has exempted individuals from laws that do

---

[37] Train 176–7 (2003).
[38] Oren 142 (1998b).
[39] Oren 371 (1998a).
[40] Oren 144 (1998b).
[41] McGarity (1996).
[42] McGarity (1994).

not require such exemptions. For example, EPA has excluded household waste from regulation under federal hazardous law, even though it may contain very hazardous substances.[43] EPA also has announced an enforcement policy that removes the threat of Superfund cost recovery actions from residential homeowners.[44] Reluctance to regulate individuals directly also provides a powerful explanation for the failure of Congress to enact federal land use legislation, despite recognition that non-point-source pollution has become the most serious unregulated contributor to water pollution problems.[45] During the environmental frenzy that prevailed in Congress in the early 1970s, the U.S. Senate twice passed federal land use legislation supported by the Nixon administration, but it ultimately failed in the face of fierce opposition in the House.[46]

In recent years, environmental regulation increasingly has emphasized informational approaches that can harness the power of informed consumer choice to stimulate environmental improvements. Informed consumers can be a powerful weapon for change, as illustrated by consumer response to the discovery that chlorofluorocarbons (CFCs) could be destroying Earth's protective ozone layer. In 1974, two scientists – Sherwood Rowland and Mario Molina – who were working on an environmental impact statement for the space shuttle, announced their belief that chlorine loading in the stratosphere from the decomposition of CFCs could significantly deplete the stratospheric ozone layer that protects the planet from harmful ultraviolet radiation.[47] At the time the United States accounted for nearly half of the world's production and consumption of CFCs. U.S. consumers simply stopped buying products containing the substances after learning that they could contribute to destruction of the ozone layer. Sales of aerosol spray products using CFCs, which accounted for half of all CFC use, plummeted so rapidly that companies quickly began advertising CFC-free products.[48] As a result, EPA had little difficulty imposing a regulatory prohibition on CFC use in 1978. The United States took the lead in overcoming European resistance to a global phase-out of CFCs that eventually was mandated in the Montreal Protocol on Substances That Deplete the Ozone Layer. The CFC ban represents one of the very few instances in which environmental policy has imposed stiff regulatory measures on the basis of scientific theory alone. The wisdom of this precautionary approach was later confirmed with the discovery of a large hole in the ozone layer.

Although the common law could respond to localized environmental hazards when they became obvious and egregious, the public law of environmental protection seeks to promote a more precautionary approach that can prevent even widely

---

[43] Vandenbergh 565 (2004).
[44] Id. at 566.
[45] Vergura and Jones (2001).
[46] Train 109 (2003).
[47] Schreurs and Economy (1997).
[48] Cagin and Dray 205 (1993).

dispersed harm before it occurs. To accomplish this end, the environmental statutes generally authorize preventive regulation predicated on certain threshold showings of risk, thereby relaxing the common law's traditional reliance on individualized proof of causal injury. Yet as a practical matter the CFC phase-out is virtually the only instance in which purely precautionary regulation has been undertaken. This reflects the fact that it is easier for scientists to identify hazards and to predict harm *after* it occurs and that regulation is most politically salient when it responds to hazards that have become highly visible to the public. As a result, environmental policy often is saddled with the far more difficult task of remediating environmental contamination after it has occurred.

JUDICIAL REVIEW AND THE RISE OF "REGULATORY COMMON LAW"

Among the most distinctive features of American legal culture identified by Lawrence Friedman are judicial review, rights-consciousness, individualism, and fear of concentrated power.[49] Each of these elements has played a role in efforts to rein in environmental regulation through litigation challenging regulatory decisions. With Congress in gridlock over environmental legislation, the judiciary has become the focus of efforts to change environmental law. The result has been the development of a kind of "regulatory common law," as reviewing courts have prescribed additional requirements for agencies to validate regulatory decisions and to ensure that regulations comport with statutory and constitutional limits.

The most dramatic judicial endorsement of precautionary regulation was a product of EPA's initial effort to use the regulatory authority provided to it in the 1970 Clean Air Act Amendments to limit levels of lead in gasoline to protect public health. Rejecting the claims of tetraethyl lead manufacturers that EPA needed to produce a "dispositive study" proving that lead emissions had caused specific harm, the U.S. Court of Appeals, sitting en banc in 1976, upheld the regulations by a 5–4 vote. The court ruled that there was sufficient evidence to regulate lead additives, even though it could not be proven with certainty that they endangered public health. In a majority opinion by Judge J. Skelly Wright, the court noted the precautionary nature of the Clean Air Act's regulatory mandate: "Regulatory action may be taken before the threatened harm occurs; indeed the very existence of . . . precautionary legislation would seem to demand that regulatory action precede, and, optimally, prevent, the perceived threat."[50] The court expressed its clear understanding that the environmental statutes departed sharply from the common law by authorizing precautionary regulation:

> Where a statute is precautionary in nature, the evidence difficult to come by, uncertain, or conflicting because it is on the frontiers of scientific knowledge, the

[49] Friedman 13 (2002).
[50] *Ethyl Corp. v. EPA*, 541 F.2d 1, 13 (D.C. Cir. 1976).

regulations designed to protect public health, and the decision that of an expert administrator, we will not demand rigorous step-by-step proof of cause and effect. Such proof may be impossible to obtain if the precautionary purpose of the statute is to be served.[51]

Concerns that regulation could be too precautionary led the U.S. Supreme Court in 1980 to articulate limits on the ability of the Occupational Safety and Health Administration (OSHA) to regulate workplace toxins. In its "Benzene decision," a plurality of the Court held that OSHA must first conduct a risk assessment to determine that a substance it seeks to regulate poses a "significant risk" that can be appreciably reduced by regulation.[52] As a result of this decision, agencies now routinely perform risk assessments to validate environmental and occupational safety regulations. However, the *Benzene* Court declined the petroleum industry's invitation to require cost-benefit analysis as a precondition for regulatory action, and it endorsed the use of conservative assumptions in risk assessment when supported by a reputable body of scientific thought.

Although the Supreme Court continues to resist industry efforts to establish cost-benefit analysis as a precondition for regulatory action,[53] it has sought to revitalize constitutional doctrines limiting federal power,[54] restricting citizen access to the courts,[55] and requiring compensation for property owners disadvantaged by regulatory action.[56] In each area, the legal impact of the Court's decisions has been decidedly more modest than initially expected. Subsequent decisions by the Court have tempered limits on federal power,[57] restrictions on citizen access to the courts, and requirements to compensate property owners.[58] As a result, the Court's efforts to reign in governmental power seem to have spawned considerable litigation challenging regulatory decisions on grounds that ultimately are unsuccessful.

Empirical data gathered by the author on the impact of the *Lopez* decision[59] reveal that during the first decade after the decision it spawned nearly 1,000 published federal court decisions responding to claims that Congress had exceeded its authority under the commerce clause. These decisions included thirty-five cases in which *Lopez* challenges were made to environmental regulations. In only one environmental case, which was reversed on appeal (*United States v. Olin Corp.*, 107 F.3d 1506 (11th Cir. 1997)), was an environmental regulation struck down as exceeding federal power under the commerce clause. *Lopez* challenges were raised to attack

---

[51] 541 F.2d at 38.
[52] Industrial Union Dept., AFL-CIO v. *American Petroleum Institute*, 448 U.S. 607 (1980).
[53] *Whitman v. American Trucking Associations*, 531 U.S. 457 (2001).
[54] *United States v. Lopez*, 514 U.S. 549 (1995).
[55] *Lujan v. Defenders of Wildlife*, 504 U.S. 555 (1992).
[56] *Lucas v. South Carolina Coastal Council*, 505 U.S. 1003 (1992).
[57] *Gonzales v. Raich*, 125 S.Ct. 2195 (2005).
[58] *Palazzolo v. Rhode Island*, 533 U.S. 606 (2001).
[59] Percival and Madea (2005).

1,026 convictions under various federal criminal statutes. Courts upheld 97% of the convictions challenged under *Lopez*, while only reversing 3% of them. Thus, one clear impact of the Supreme Court's effort to establish new constitutional limits on federal authority has been to routinize the raising and rejection of challenges to federal authority in litigation. The few beneficiaries of successful *Lopez* challenges during this period were ten arsonists who were set free, along with four people who possessed a handgun within a school zone, three people convicted under the Violence Against Women Act, two child pornographers, two people convicted for violating the Hobbs Act, one money launderer, one person convicted of bribery, and one person who violated the murder-for-hire statute.

This is not to suggest that *Lopez*, *Lujan*, and *Lucas* have had no impact beyond generating additional constitutional arguments that ultimately prove fruitless in the vast majority of cases. By articulating the notions that there has to be some judicially enforceable limit on federal power and citizen access to the courts, and that regulation that totally destroys the value of real estate requires compensation, the Court has signaled regulators to be careful to avoid overreaching. This is likely to have some effect on regulatory decisions, even though the Court seems unable ultimately to articulate clear lines that regulators should not cross. By making the contours of those lines turn on showings that regulatory targets have a substantial effect on interstate commerce, that plaintiffs are directly harmed by environmental violations, and that regulation is necessary to prevent common law nuisances, the Court has required plaintiffs to make factual showings similar to what the common law required, but now as a precondition for insulating regulatory action from constitutional challenges.

CONCLUSION

Although the common law tolerated considerable environmental damage in the name of economic progress, it also helped stimulate the development of pollution-control technology, and it established some of the legal foundations of environmental law today. These include the principle that no one has the right to cause significant harm to others, the "polluter pays" principle that seeks to require actors to bear the full social costs of their actions, and the "look before you leap" principle embodied in NEPA's environmental impact assessment requirement. Taken together, these principles do not in themselves establish a coherent field of "transformative nature-centered rules" that will "tame the drive to exploit and modify all planetary life support systems."[60] Thus, as Dan Tarlock has argued, "environment law will for the foreseeable future be a messy process of adapting the contingencies and limitations of science to 'wicked' problems informed by rebuttable principles."[61]

---

[60] Tarlock 253–4 (2004).
[61] Id.

Building on its common law roots, the regulatory infrastructure created by the federal environmental statutes has been a considerable success. Despite failing to prevent the asbestos tragedy and widespread lead poisoning, the United States today enjoys an environment that is cleaner, safer, and healthier than ever before. The nation is far better off because it invested in environmental protection long before other countries where environmental concerns were neglected until their toxic legacy became highly visible.

The history of U.S. environmental law also provides some important policy lessons. It now is well understood that it is better to prevent environmental harm in advance, rather than to attempt to remediate it once it has occurred, but that it is rare that truly precautionary regulation will command sufficient public support without some dramatic development that makes it politically salient. The importance of public participation to the implementation and enforcement of regulatory schemes also is well known, as are the limits of law in the face of concerted public opposition to regulating individual behavior.

Despite an occasional stumble, U.S. environmental law generally has been successful because it has not tried to defy social norms by regulating individual behavior directly. Although it is now understood that land use regulation and environmental taxes could be enormously useful in preventing non-point-source pollution and stimulating environmentally beneficial consumption patterns, these options remain off the table in the current U.S. political climate. As Lawrence Friedman has reminded us, law is constrained by social norms, even though it has some capacity to shape how those norms evolve. Environmental law's promise of comprehensive protection for present and future generations, like what Lawrence Friedman has described as the "Victorian compromise" of nineteenth-century morals legislation, has helped reinforce social norms of environmental responsibility, even while tolerating considerable behavior inconsistent with such aims.

REFERENCES

Barclay, R. E. (1997). *The Copper Basin – 1890 to 1963.* Knoxville, TN.
Brenner, J. (1974). Nuisance Law and the Industrial Revolution, 3 *J. Legal Stud.* 403.
Cagin, Seth and Philip Dray (1993). *Between Earth and Sky.* New York: Pantheon Books
Cong. Rec. 46: 3629 (1910).
Dwyer, John P. (1990). The Pathology of Symbolic Legislation, 17 *Ecology L.Q.* 233.
Farber, Daniel A. (1992). Politics and Procedure in Environmental Law, 9 *J. L. Econ. & Org.* 59.
Friedman, Lawrence M. (1985). *Total Justice.* New York: Russell Sage Foundation.
———. (2002). *Law in America.* New York: Modern Library.
Houck, Oliver (1999). Recent Developments in the Clean Water Act, 1998–1999. *ALI-ABA Continuing Legal Education Course of Study,* Feb. 10, 1999.
Lazarus, Richard J. (2004). *The Making of Environmental Law.* Chicago: University of Chicago Press.

Lee, R. Alton (1966). The Eradication of Phossy Jaw: A Unique Development of Federal Police Power, 29 *Historian* 1.

List of Smoke Suits Pending against the Ducktown Sulphur Copper & Iron Co., Ltd. in the Circuit Court of Polk County, Tennessee, at Benton; in the Chancery Court Polk County, Tennessee, at Benton, and in the Circuit Court of the United States for the Southern Division of the Eastern District of Tennessee, at Chatanooga, November 1, 1913 (Box 5, File 89, files of Dr. John T. McGill in the Special Collections of the Jean and Alexander Heard Library, Vanderbilt University).

Machle, Willard F. (1935). Tetra Ethyl Lead Intoxication and Poisoning by Related Compounds of Lead, 105 *J. Am. Med. Ass'n* 578.

Macmillan, D. (2000). *Smoke Wars: Anaconda Copper, Montana Air Pollution, and the Courts, 1890–1920*. Helena, Montana Historical Society.

May, James R. (2003). Environmental Citizen Suits at Thirtysomething: A Celebration & Summit, Part I, 10 *Widener L. Rev.* 1.

McGarity, Thomas O. (1996). Regulating Commuters to Clear the Air: Some Difficulties in Implementing a National Program at the Local Level, 27 *Pac. L.J.* 1521.

———. (1994). Radical Technology-Forcing in Environmental Regulation, 22 *Loy. L.A. L. Rev.* 943.

Morag-Levine, N. (2003). *Chasing the Wind: Regulating Air Pollution in the Common Law State*. Princeton, NJ: Princeton University Press.

Newell, E. (1997). Atmospheric Pollution and the British Copper Industry, 1690–1920, 38 *Tech. Culture* 655.

Newell, E. and S. Watts (1996). The Environmental Impact of Industrialization in South Wales in the Nineteenth Century: "Copper Smoke" and the Lianelli Copper Company, 2 *Env't & Hist.* 309.

Olson, Mancur, (1965). *The Logic of Collective Action: Public Goods and the Theory of Groups*. Cambridge, MA: Harvard University Press.

Oren, Craig N. (1998a). How a Mandate Came from Hell: The Making of the Federal Employee Trip Reduction Program, 28 *Envtl. L.* 267 (1998).

———. (1998b). Getting Commuters out of their Cars: What Went Wrong?, 17 *Stan. Envtl. L.J.* 141.

Pederson, William (2004). Using Federal Environmental Regulations to Bargain for Private Land Use Control, 21 *Yale L.J.*

Percival, Robert V. and Cortney Madea (2005). The Impact of Lopez, unpublished paper on file with author.

Public Opinion Strategies & Hart Research (2005). *Report of Key Findings and Analysis from Research Conducted on Behalf of the Nicholas Institute*.

Rees, R. (1993). The Great Copper Trials, 43 *Hist. Today* 38.

Report of The House Comm. on Ways And Means, (1912). Taxing White Phosphorous Matches, 62nd Cong., 2d Sess. 9.

Rosner, David and Gerald Markowitz (1985). A Gift of God?: The Public Health Controversy over Leaded Gasoline During the 1920s, 75 *Am. J. Pub. Health* 344.

Schreurs, Miranda A. and Elizabeth C. Economy, eds. (1997). *The Internationalization of Environmental Protection*. New York: Cambridge University Press.

Tarlock, A. Dan (2004). Is There a There There in Environmental Law? 19 *J. Land Use & Env'tl L.* 213.

Train, Russell E., (2003). *Politics, Pollution and Pandas: An Environmental Memoir*. Washington, DC: Island Press.

Vandenbergh, Michael P. (2004). From Smokestack to SUV: The Individual as Regulated Entity in the New Era of Environmental Law, 57 *Vand. L. Rev.* 515.

Vergura, Jim and Ron Jones (2001). The TMDL Program: Land Use and Other Implications, 6 *Drake J. Agric. L.* 317.

Wirth, J. D. (2000). *Smelter Smoke in North America: the Politics of Transborder Pollution.* Lawrence: University of Kansas Press.

Law and Religion

14

Separating Church and State

The Atlantic Divide

James Q. Whitman

TWO MODELS OF SEPARATION OF CHURCH AND STATE

If you go to the U.S. State Department Web site, you will find a 2004 posting entitled "Separation of Church and State in the U.S." It includes the following proposition about comparative law: "The government of the United States – unlike Great Britain and other European countries – may not declare one religion as the national religion nor support one religion over another."[1] The implication is that the United States is unique among Western countries in its commitment to the separation of church and state. There is certainly some truth in this claim. American law is in fact unusually strict about maintaining an institutional separation of church and state. As a result, we Americans are not likely to embrace German or Scandinavian practices like paying pastors from state funds.[2] Nor are we likely to permit the state to subsidize religious schools, as it does in France.[3]

It is also true that our constitutional tradition of "free exercise" guarantees liberties that are not guaranteed elsewhere. This means that American law will never tolerate anything like the much denounced 2004 French headscarf law, which led the State Department to list France, along with numerous Third World dictatorships, as a country guilty of "abuses of religious freedom."[4] Nor has that particular "abuse," if that is what it is, vanished since 2004. On the contrary, efforts to ban headscarves and burkas have been spreading across Western Europe for several years. In recent years, the campaign has been particularly vigorous in the Netherlands, for example.[5] Other parts of Western Europe too have seen significant efforts and movements of the same kind. Most Americans undoubtedly see this gathering European campaign against

---

[1] Abboud (2004).
[2] See, e.g., Eberle 74–5 (2006); Constitution of Denmark § 4.
[3] Custos 356–8 (2006).
[4] Id.
[5] "The Netherlands" (2008).

Islamic dress as stark evidence that Europeans will never succeed in accommodating their Muslim minorities. Most of them are undoubtedly proud of America's more uncompromising commitment to religious liberty. However, when it comes to matters like the toleration of Islamic dress, America *is* more uncompromising.

We can all recognize that the problem is more complicated than the State Department Web site is prepared to allow. Yes, America has a strong tradition of formal nonestablishment and deep-seated norms of tolerance. Yet it defies common sense to claim that we have a full-scale separation of religion from government. After all, religion, especially Christianity, plays a far more prominent role in American government than it does in northern continental Europe. In most parts of the United States, no politician can be elected without loudly proclaiming his or her religious faith. This was notably true even among the Democrats in the presidential election of 2008. To many Europeans, this American style of religious electioneering is every bit as bizarre and disturbing as headscarf laws are to Americans: How can Americans boast about their separation of church and state when their political leaders routinely present themselves to the electorate as persons of faith?

Nor does it end with elections. Sessions of Congress in the United States are opened with a prayer – a practice firmly rejected by France as long ago as 1884.[6] Moreover, invocations of Christ, the Christian faith, and the Bible remain constant in the American legislative process. Just try doing a word search in the *Congressional Record* for "Bible." The hits are by no means limited to Republicans, and they did not end with the last election. For example, here is how Democratic Congressman Rush of Illinois speaks in support of a higher minimum wage in January 2007, after the Democratic triumph in the 2006 elections: "Mr. Speaker, the Bible tells us that our servant is worthy of his hire. Well, the American people are certainly worth more than the current $5.15 minimum wage that they are receiving."[7] This bit of biblical fluff might seem innocent enough to many of my American readers, but it represents a symbolic acceptance of Christian rhetoric in lawmaking that would be wholly unacceptable – even a bit shocking – to many people in northern continental Europe. Why are such things being said in the legislature of a modern secular country?

So does America really have a strict separation of church and state? We do find ways to be uniquely tolerant toward religious minorities within our borders. At the same time, prominent American officials, from the president on down, use Christian language and biblical arguments in ways unheard of across the Atlantic. As a result, to outside observers, our country can sometimes look like a crudely Christian, or Judeo-Christian, power – a perception that threatens to cause major foreign policy problems as we deal with Islam abroad. Just remember what happened when President Bush made his clumsy reference to a "crusade" after 9/11. We have a certain form of

[6] Boussinesq (1994).
[7] Rush (2007).

the institutional separation of church and state, but unlike the French, we have no separation of *religion from politics*. Are the French clearly wrong to be puzzled or indeed troubled by this situation?

Nor is it just that there is no separation of religion from *politics* in America. In important ways, there is also no separation of religion from *law*. Biblical authority is frequently cited not only in Congress but also in American courtrooms, and not just in the Bible Belt. It is cited particularly frequently in death penalty cases. For example, in the sentencing phase of one California death penalty case, a convicted murderer's defense attorney made the following argument, which deserves to be quoted at length:

> [The convicted man] will die in prison. That is no longer an issue.... The only remaining question is who will decide when he dies, you or the Almighty.... When I contemplated the awesome responsibility that you will soon face, I thought about the punishment that God gave to Cain for the murder of his brother Abel. In chapter 4 of Genesis, the Lord said to Cain, "[Y]our brother's blood cries out to me. You shall be banished from the land on which you spilled your brother's blood. You shall become a restless wanderer in the wilderness."... Today there is hardly a place we call a wilderness. Instead we have to build our wildernesses. We call them maximum security prisons. The mark we put on people who have committed such crimes is a sentence of life in prison without the possibility of parole. Our banishment.

The prosecution responded in kind, with the following speech:

> Defense brought up Cain and Abel, and what it said in the Bible about Cain and Abel, and I want to give you other ideas about the way the Bible feels about the death penalty. It seems that through the ages and the Ten Commandments when they talked about thou shalt not kill that is a misnomer and not true. It's the King James mistranslation of what should have been thou shalt not do murder.... As you know from what we've talked about murder is not killing. Killing is one thing, and when I talked to you with the jury instructions and told you what murder was, it's the unlawful killing with malice. That's murder.... [I]n the book of Deuteronomy, chapter 22, it teaches that the death penalty was required for rape and adultery back in those biblical times. In chapter 21 of Deuteronomy as well, hanging was the method for carrying out that sentence. So they had the death penalty way back then.... So I don't want this appeal to religion to dissuade any of you, because the Bible does not say thou shalt not kill. It says thou shalt not murder. And you have already decided we have had a murder here.

After listening to these exercises in pop biblical exegesis, the jury sentenced the defendant to death. The California Supreme Court upheld the sentence, despite the heavy use of biblical arguments by both sides.[8] The use of biblical authority

[8] *People v. Bradford*, 14 Cal. 4th 1005 (1997).

might be particularly common in death penalty litigation,[9] but a full study of the topic would include many other kinds of cases as well.[10] American textbooks nowhere declare that the Bible is a source of law. Nevertheless, it sometimes functions exactly that way in American litigation. Maybe one can defend citations to the Bible in Congress by invoking the value of free speech. It is harder to see what could justify telling jurors to draw their wisdom from the Bible while deciding on the death penalty. In a modern secular country, should people be sentenced to death on the strength of biblical authority?

Well, of course America *is* a modern secular country, by many sociological measures. However, it is a striking fact that, unlike other modern secular countries, it has no strict separation of religion from politics and no strict separation of religion from law. Here I must express my disagreement (fondly) with my friend and inspiring colleague Lawrence Friedman, who believes deeply that modern legal systems are converging. Not so, at least when it comes to church and state.

To be sure, we should not exaggerate. It is silly to claim, as foreign journalists sometimes do, that the entire American government is driven by a fundamentalist Christian agenda. Christianity is certainly not the only ideological competitor for influence on American politics and law. It remains true that the Supreme Court would likely strike down American legislation that too obviously lacked a "secular purpose."[11] Christian influence ebbs and flows in American law, and it is possible that we are now simply at a momentary crest. Yet the point is not that America is utterly Christianized. The point is that Christianity is permitted to function as an ideological competitor in American politics, at times a very successful one, and that the Bible *is* cited as a de facto source of law in litigation involving matters as important as the death penalty. By these measures, Christianity is by no means kept separate from the state in the United States. By contrast, European countries maintain a far stricter separation.

The State Department Web site thus has it wrong or, rather, only half-right. It is simply not the case that the United States is alone in its commitment to separating church and state. The comparative law of church and state is considerably more complicated than that. There are two different Western models of the separation of church and state. The American model aims at an *institutional* separation of church and state. It demands that the state take a studiously hands-off approach to churches, while at the same time permitting the nearly unlimited expression of religious views in all contexts, including the courtroom. This has the paradoxical consequence that religion sometimes has a powerful impact on the substance of the law and often receives vocal endorsement from American legislators.

---

[9] Egland 337 (2004).
[10] E.g., *Ex parte* Melof, 735 So. 2d 1172, 1187 (Ala. 1999), (Chief Justice Hooper, concurring specially, invoking Deuteronomy and Leviticus in a case involving the constitutionality of tax apportionment).
[11] *Lemon v. Kurtzman*, 403 U.S. 602, 612–13 (1971).

By contrast, the continental European model aims at a separation of religion from politics. It also insists on a separation of religion from law, holding in particular that biblical authority has no place either in the making of legislation or in the decisions of courts. At the same time, the continental model countenances what seem to Americans to be gross governmental interferences in the institutions of daily religious life and in freedom of religious expression. Neither model is enforced without exception. There are cases in which American government does arguably slip into institutional "entanglements,"[12] just as there are French politicians, like Nicolas Sarkozy, who sometimes flirt with religious rhetoric.[13] Nevertheless, the two models, imperfectly realized as they are, do broadly dominate the countries on either side of the Atlantic.

Both represent forms of the separation of church and state. Both belong to a venerable tradition in Western Christendom: With rare exceptions, the Western Christian tradition has always demanded that church and state be separated in *some* way. Muslims are not wrong when they insist that the idea of the separation of church and state is a distinctly Christian idea. Yet the remarkable fact is that contemporary America and contemporary northern continental Europe have arrived at two different means of pursuing this common, ancient, Christian ambition to mark church off from state. What our State Department ought properly to declare is that America has its way of separating church and state, whereas "European countries" have theirs.

HISTORICAL ROOTS OF SEPARATION OF CHURCH AND STATE IN CONTINENTAL EUROPE

My purpose in beginning with these observations is not to disparage American constitutional law. Rather it is to set the stage for a larger discussion of the historical roots and contemporary forms of these differences between the United States and continental Europe. It is wrong to suppose that there is some single way of separating church and state, wrong to suppose that we can condemn this or that Western country for failing to respect "the" separation of church and state. The two halves of the Atlantic world have simply arrived at different ways of separating church and state, and as I aim to show in this chapter, these two halves of the Atlantic world are the products of two differing religious histories. Moreover, their differing religious histories have had large consequences for the shape of state and society on either side of the Atlantic – consequences that extend beyond problems of religious freedom to cover other questions of fundamental importance, such as why the continental countries have such comparatively vigorous social welfare states.

[12] Most controversially, recently, *Van Orden v. Perry*, 545 U.S. 677 (2005), which declared constitutional a display of the Ten Commandments on the Texas State Capitol grounds.
[13] See, e.g., Garraud (2008).

The idea that America and continental Europe are the products of different religious traditions is not new. Many observers have argued exactly that. Yet the claim that most of them have offered cannot be correct. What scholars most frequently argue is that America takes the shape it does because it is Protestant rather than Catholic. A distinguished lineup of scholars has backed this argument: to name only some of them, Alberto Alesina and Edward Glaeser of the Harvard Economics Department,[14] Reformation historian Diarmuid MacCulloch,[15] and French legal scholars Antoine Garapon and Ioannis Papadopoulos.[16] These authors identify different aspects of Protestantism as crucial. For example, MacCulloch describes America as a child of the visionary traditions of the Reformation: Like sixteenth-century Protestants, Americans believe in religious revival and the reform of a fallen world.[17] For Garapon and Papadopoulos, the key point is that the American Revolution was shaped by a Protestant "distrust of power."[18] All of them see America as distinctively Protestant, however.

So is that it? Is it that America is Protestant? The answer has to be no. For starters, continental countries with dominant Protestant traditions, such as the Netherlands, northern Germany, and the Scandinavian countries, do not resemble the United States at all. Conversely, there are Catholic European countries, like Italy and especially Poland, in which religion and politics mix much as they do in America. (It was this difference, let us remember, that produced the bitter controversy a few years ago over whether to declare the Christian roots of Europe in the proposed Constitution of the European Union.) It is just not the case that Protestantism inevitably fosters religiosity in politics and law, whereas Catholicism keeps its politics religion-free. In any case, Catholics make up the largest single religious grouping in the United States, and they are quite active in politics. Christian sects of *all* stripes are more powerful political actors in the United States than they are in the countries of continental Europe, as Tocqueville long ago insisted.[19] The contrast is not between Catholicism and Protestantism. Rather it is between northern continental Europe and the United States.

So what explains that contrast? The right answer has nothing to do with confessional differences, and if we do not get the answer right, we will not comprehend the policy challenges we face on either side of the Atlantic. The right answer has to do with a simple but telling difference in historical sociology: On the one hand, we have northern continental countries (like France, Germany, and the Scandinavian countries) in which *the state, over many centuries, has gradually assumed many of the historic functions performed by the medieval church.* This has happened

---

[14] Alesina and Glaeser (2004).
[15] MacCulloch (2003).
[16] Garapon and Papadopoulos (2003).
[17] MacCulloch 700–1, 704 (2003).
[18] Garapon and Papadopoulos 177 (2003).
[19] For a survey of the literature making this familiar observation, see Lipset 60–7 (1996).

differently in different parts of the northern continent, but in one way or another it has happened in all of the countries that lie north of the Alps, east of the Pyrenees, and west of the Elbe. There is nothing peculiarly Catholic about this pattern: It marks the Lutheran and Calvinist North as clearly as it does the Catholic South. In contrast, American law is the product of a very different Anglo-American history. In the Anglo-American tradition, medieval church functions have, by and large, never been assumed by the state: *In America, historic church functions have generally either been left to the churches, or else they have died out entirely.* The result is a very different pattern of church–state relations down to this day. Even beyond that, in the result is a very different pattern of government activity and very different patterns of religious belief and activity.

This is obviously a large historical proposition. For the sake of economy I concentrate on the example of France to make the point. Many aspects of French society have been shaped by the long-term state absorption of activities historically associated with the medieval Catholic Church – including some of the aspects of French society that President Sarkozy has declared himself most eager to change.

Some of this involves matters of little contemporary policy importance, but of great significance for the texture of everyday life. To take one example of symbolic importance, marriage is now solemnized by the French state, not by the church.[20] Indeed, this principle is so important in France that it is a matter of criminal law. French people are permitted to have a church bless their unions after the state has formalized their union. However it is nothing less than a criminal offense in France for a religious official habitually to hold a church ceremony before the state has solemnized the marriage (Code Pénal art. 433–21). This prohibition appears, remarkably enough, in Book IV of the Penal Code, "Crimes against the Nation, the State and the Public Peace," along with such offenses as treason and espionage.

In my experience, the notion that performing marriages is a task for the state seems entirely natural to the French. In fact, French people are baffled to discover that clergy still have the legal power to perform valid marriages in the United States – a fact that deserves a place in the ethnography of comparative law. The French make tacit assumptions about the role of the state in everyday life that are quite different from our own. Another prime everyday example of how the French state has displaced the church is a particularly entertaining variety of law: the law of baby names. The church historically maintained a baptismal register and kept a careful watch over the names parents gave their children. It has long since lost this power – while the modern French state (like the German and Scandinavian states) has taken it over, although today it wields its authority with a light hand.[21]

---

[20] Cornu 278 (2003).
[21] I discuss the comparative law of baby names in Whitman 1151–221 (2004). For the longer French history, see Lefebvre-Teillard (1990).

Marriage and baby names may seem to be minor issues in the law. Let me emphasize that there are also other issues of more obvious policy importance. Education, on all levels, is dominated by the state. Perhaps most importantly, charitable giving is organized by the French state, which has accepted a wide-ranging responsibility for the care of the poor and infirm: It is manifest that the French social welfare state is the child not only of a secular socialist tradition but also of an older and deeper Christian tradition. In all of these respects, the French state has taken over historic church functions.

There are also telling aspects of French life that reflect the long-term influence of canon law. Take the treatment of minors in criminal law. Canon criminal law insisted on shielding minors from criminal liability, and that remains the rule in France much more than in America.[22] Something similar is true of canon contract law: French law is much more willing to engage in price regulation than American law. In this willingness, I would argue, we can see the lasting legitimacy of very old Christian just price doctrines.[23] In these respects (and others), the French legal system looks unmistakably like a descendant of the legal system of the medieval church.

Where did this French pattern come from? The answer takes us much farther back in French history than most French people realize. The French generally imagine that their separation of church and state dates to the Revolution in 1789 and to the law on the separation of church and state passed in 1905, during the Third Republic.[24] In fact, the French pattern reaches as far back as the fifteenth century.[25] The large story is one of continuity, as Tocqueville famously insisted. This is not the place for a detailed exploration. Let me simply focus on one special issue: the headscarf controversy. The modern French principle of *laïcité* holds that there must be a public sphere from which religion is banned. This "laic" public sphere includes the world of politics, and it also includes the world of public education, which must be dedicated to the inculcation of a common French identity independent

[22] Readers should be aware that this is an assertion that other scholars might contest and that would require fuller argument than I give it here. The basic differences in doctrine are traced in my book *Harsh Justice: Criminal Punishment and the Widening Divide between America and Europe* (Oxford, 2003).

[23] Here again I make an admittedly contestable assertion that would require more detailed proof. The influence of canon law on ancien régime contract law can be seen most conveniently in Robert-Joseph Pothier, as the title of his *Traité des Obligations, Selon les Règles tant du For de la Conscience que du For Extérieur* indicates. See, for example, Part. 1, Ch. 1, § 8 (partial reception of canon doctrine on contracts reinforced by oath); Robert-Joseph Pothier, *Traité du Contrat de Vente, Selon les Règles tant du For de la Conscience que du For Extérieur* (2nd edition, Paris, 1781), Ch. II (good faith and just price). Although there is no just price norm in the Code Civil itself, French law (like European law more generally) remains much more hospitable to price regulation than does American law. For a brief discussion, see James Gordley, "Is Comparative Law a Distinct Discipline?," Am. J. Comp. L. 46 (1998): 610–11. I discuss much of the current law of price regulation in James Q. Whitman, "Consumerism versus Producerism: A Study in Comparative Law," Yale L.J. 117 (2007): 340.

[24] See, e.g., among many, Boussinesq 15–16 (1994); Barbier 23–66 (1995).

[25] I refer to the rise of French Gallicanism. This chapter is not the place to discuss that history in detail.

of religion. It is the notion that public education must be "laic" that underlies the 2004 law banning "ostentatious" religious garb like the veil. Ordinary French people think of *laïcité* as a principle that dates to 1905, when the Third Republic brought the Revolution to its modern culmination, but they are simply wrong. *Laïcité* has deep historical roots, and it too can be thought of as the product of the government takeover of an historic church function.

The function in question is the creation of a common culture, shared by all and permeating daily life – the creation of a kind of homogeneous cultural identity. Of course this function was historically a church business: It was once the Catholic Church that inculcated a common culture that permeated every aspect of daily life. In part, the premodern church tried to inculcate this single common culture in the same way that the French state does today, through schooling. However schooling was not available to most members of society before the nineteenth century, and other means were also employed. Thus the common culture was inculcated through the calendar of holy days, which gathered the community together for shared, moralized ritual experience. It was further inculcated through the confessional. By the sixteenth century, the common culture was also maintained through the parish registry, which recorded births and deaths, tying the whole community to its church.[26] The parish registry marked all the major events of daily life for the individual. Here again, the law of baby names deserves mention. Part of the power associated with the parish registry was its authority to choose names for newborn children. The church insisted on saints' names, thus tying individual identity to the daily ritual calendar.

The French state was already beginning to claim this historic church function for itself well before 1905 and indeed well before the 1780s, and in ways that prefigured the *laïcité* of today. Consider one of the key moments in the history of prerevolutionary religious intolerance: the revocation of the Edict of Nantes in 1685. Students of French history will remember that in 1598 Henri IV issued the Edict of Nantes, guaranteeing toleration to Protestants. The Edict of Nantes permitted Protestants to engage in public worship within certain geographical confines. In 1685, however, Henri's grandson Louis XIV revoked the edict, establishing a model of absolutist religious intolerance that lasted until Protestants were accorded formal toleration in 1788, shortly before the Revolution.

The revocation of the Edict of Nantes is generally thought of as a high point in the prerevolutionary history of state-enforced religious conformity, but the story is more complicated than that. The revocation, which I quote in a contemporary translation, was announced in "An edict of the French king prohibiting all *publick* exercise of the pretended reformed religion in his kingdom."[27] Indeed. Technically, the revocation of the Edict of Nantes did not ban Protestantism in France. As the leading French jurist Jean Carbonnier explains, what it did was to "forbid public

---

[26] Lefebvre-Teillard 92 ff. (1990).
[27] "An Edict" (1686). Italics in original.

worship of any faith except that of the Prince."[28] In fact, its closing article declared a form of toleration:

> Those of the said *Pretended Reformed Religion* . . . till it shall Please God to enlighten them . . . may abide in the several respective Cities and Places of our Kingdoms, Countries, and Territories under our Obedience, and there continue their Commerce, and enjoy their Goods and Estates, without being any way molested upon account of the said *Pretended Reformed Religion*; upon condition nevertheless . . . that they do not use any public Religious exercise, nor assemble themselves upon the account of Prayer or Worship of the said Religion, of what kind soever the same may be, upon forfeiture . . . of Body and Goods.[29]

To be sure, the supposed toleration announced in this article meant little in practice. The revocation was a draconian measure that effectively forbade Protestant worship, brought with it severe and violent state persecution, and of course drove Protestants out of France in vast numbers.[30] Moreover, it was a measure presented in a spirit of ugly triumphalism, perhaps most colorfully represented by Jean Hardy's bombastic 1688 relief "La Religion Terrassant l'Hérésie," now in the sculpture galleries of the Louvre.[31] The aims and spirit of the Revocation of the Edict of Nantes bore no resemblance whatsoever to the aims and spirit of modern-day French legislation.

Nevertheless, it is important that we attend to the justificatory language offered for Louis XIV's momentous revocation. That justification was precisely that France had to have a single religious culture in the "public" sphere. What we would now call "private" religious belief was to remain "unmolested."[32] This is of course little different from what French legislation proclaims today. Louis XIV certainly did not share the aims of the Third Republic or the Fifth Republic, but he conceived of the field of battle in exactly the same way his successors would. He believed that there was a "public" arena that had to be swept clean of improper religion so that a common French identity could be proclaimed and maintained. *His* aim was to guarantee that the French monarchy would impose its brand of Catholicism on the country, not to create a secular France, but his methods foreshadowed the

---

[28] Carbonnier 55 (1986).

[29] "An Edict" (1686).

[30] See, e.g., Garrisson (1985).

[31] Available at http://cartelfr.louvre.fr/cartelfr/visite?srv=obj_view_obj&objet=cartel_4219_5162_s0001620 .001.jpg_obj.html&flag=true

[32] Or so at least the Revocation has always been understood. The text of the edict itself does not use the word "public," oddly enough. Yet contemporary accounts did understand it that way, just as Carbonnier (cited in n.28) still did. For example, the *Gazette de France* reported the revocation as a measure by which the king forbade the "exercice public de la Religion Prétendue Réformée." Text available at http://hypo.ge-dip.etat-ge.ch/www/cliotexte/html/france.revocation.1685.html. It is worth remembering that this French measure was not unparalleled elsewhere. Public worship was controlled in precisely the same way – although to be sure not in the same spirit of oppression – in the Netherlands.

methods still pursued today in the name of *laïcité*. Like so much of modern French governmental practice, *laïcité* thus has a history that begins in the reign of Louis XIV. As Marcel Gauchet rightly observes, the history of "republican separation" in France must be seen as only one chapter in the evolution of church–state relations – one preceded by the chapter of "absolutist subordination."[33]

The pattern of development we see in this is not a Catholic pattern: France is simply typical of northern continental countries, which all show variants on the same long-standing tendency of the state to constitute itself as a kind of updated, secularized church. Lutheran Germany and Scandinavia are no different in this respect; neither is the historically Calvinist Netherlands. The process began later in the German, Dutch, and Scandinavian worlds. At the beginning, it coincided with the spread of Lutheranism, whose appeal to princes lay partly in the fact that it gave them control over the church. The state takeover of church functions that began in the sixteenth century in these countries has assumed forms different from the French form. For example, state domination of the educational system has a different history in parts of Germany from its history in France, and it takes a different shape today. In Germany pastors are still on the state payroll, which is no longer the case in most of France. Moreover, as a consequence of long-term conflict between Protestants and Catholics, Germany has seen self-defined "Christian" parties – both Christian Democrats and Christian Socialists. To that extent, the separation of religion from politics is certainly less marked in Germany than it is in France. Each of the northern continental countries has its own distinctive tradition. Nevertheless, the broad pattern is much the same: All over northern continental Europe, the historic functions of the church have, since the later Middle Ages, slowly been gathered into the bosom of the state.

This continental pattern helps explain much about the two disparate halves of the Atlantic world – and much that goes well beyond the familiar problems of religious expression. It helps us understand why the social welfare state has so much more vigor in continental Europe than in America, while private charitable giving is so much more limited in Europe than in the United States. Not least, the continental pattern of church–state relations may help explain the high rates of European secularization.

Why indeed has religious belief become so weak in continental Europe? If we look at the map of rates of secularization in the world, we discover that the highest rates of secularization in the West are to be found precisely in the northern continental countries that I have described. It would be foolish to argue that the pattern I trace in this chapter offers anything like a full explanation for continental secularization, but it does provide part of the answer. I suggest that the key is to be found in the sociology of Max Weber. In France as in other northern continental European countries, the old charismatic functions of the church have now become routinized,

---

[33] Gauchet 8 (1998). For royal domination of the Church in the seventeenth century, see also Bergin 8 ff. (1996).

bureaucratized governmental functions. In northern Europe, church functions are just another governmental activity. For most northern Europeans, the encounter with church officials is just another bureaucratic event, little different from the encounter with a bored desk sergeant at a police substation or with any other officer of government. Correspondingly, the government takeover of church functions has not created a theocratic state in France – or Germany or Sweden. Far from it. Instead, the government's assumption of church functions has tended to rob the church of much of its moral force and political energy. A church that has surrendered most of its mission to the state is a church that retains little independent political influence. To put it a little differently, when church functions become government functions, they become denatured; they lose their charismatic character. This is once again just as true of continental Protestant countries as it is of continental Catholic ones.

THE AMERICAN CASE

It will be obvious to my American readers that the United States followed a very different course of development. The range of historic church functions that have become the province of the French state remain largely outside state hands in America. Marriages are still commonly solemnized by religious officials in America. Private charitable giving remains vigorous, and the state has never assumed real responsibility for the care of the poor and infirm. Indeed, there is a substantial body of opinion on the American Right that holds that charitable activity ought to be a private function and not a government function at all. Here again it is impossible to resist citing some of the biblical rhetoric to be heard in the halls of Congress, in this case from a Seventh-Day Adventist congressman from Maryland who explains the imperative of dismantling the social welfare state as follows:

> [T]he Bible says, "It is more blessed to give than to receive." . . . Has not the government usurped the role of philanthropist and denied our citizens the reward that the Bible promises, that it is more blessed to give than to receive? A whole bunch of the money that the government forcibly takes from us on April 15 [the date on which federal tax payments are due] goes to philanthropy, a totally inappropriate function of the Federal Government, a constitutionally denied function of the Federal Government.[34]

This kind of political rhetoric is not mere fluff. It is shaping the agenda of an important wing of the American Right and in ways that go far beyond the sort of "puritanical" legislation that Europeans like to highlight when they talk about the Christian character of American law.

The other examples that I offered above are also worth mentioning. Historic canon law doctrines of contract law and criminal law have far less impact on modern secular legal practice. American constitutional law remains viscerally hostile to the idea that

---

[34] Bartlett (2004).

church functions might be performed by the state. It is one of the core teachings of American law that any effort by the state to introduce itself into church functions is to be condemned as an "entanglement." It hardly needs to be said that American society has experienced nothing like the far-reaching secularization of northern continental Europe.

What are the reasons for this American pattern? Why do Americans behave differently from continental Europeans? Protestantism has nothing to do with it. The core reason is a negative one: Like most of the world, we have not experienced the peculiar pattern of state development characteristic of northern continental Europe. The historic functions of the church have not been sucked up by the state.

That does not mean that there are no parallels between Anglo-American and continental history. There certainly have been moments and periods during which Anglo-American government made efforts like those we find on the continent. The English Reformation was like Lutheran Reformations to some extent – although only to some extent.[35] Massachusetts Puritans tried to institute something like the same enforced public orthodoxy that the monarchy of Louis XIV tried to institute.[36] So did the Stuart monarchs.[37] Anglo-American history, like all histories, is not without its ambiguities and complexities, not without peaks and troughs in the graph of its development. Nevertheless, the broad pattern is clear enough, and the historical bottom-line is manifest when we scrutinize contemporary practices of government, especially in America. The state assumption of church functions that characterized the northern continent, whether Catholic or Protestant, has never taken place in the United States.

Partly in consequence, American churches, unlike the French church, have never lost their charismatic force or their political energy. Precisely because the American churches have never surrendered their mission to the state, they have never become denatured, they have never lost their charismatic character. The encounter with church personnel in America often remains charged with sacredness, and the churches have survived as independent political actors, capable of exercising significant influence on government and of serving as ideological competitors on the American stage. This American pattern has nothing to do with Protestantism as such. It applies broadly across all American denominations and faiths.

As with France, the roots of this American attitude reach well back into the Middle Ages, but the key moments in the development date to the end of the seventeenth century – to the Glorious Revolution that was contemporaneous with the great governmental experiments of Louis XIV and that was indeed intended as a forceful rejection of Louis' practices.

---

[35] The Anglican Church was subjected to the monarch as its "governor," but remained a distinct institution from the state. However, the key point for my purposes is the failure of the common law to absorb the norms of canon law. Detailed comparison with the continental reformation is obviously out of place here, however.

[36] See, e.g., Feldman 363–8 (2002).

[37] Notably through the Conventicles Acts, 16 Car. II c. 4 (1664); 22 Car. II. c. 1 (1670).

SOME CONCLUSIONS

We are the heirs of a very long tradition of state noninterference with religious life, a tradition that has become much stronger in America than it ever was in England itself. Neither the continental nor the American model is perfectly realized in practice. Nevertheless, these contrasting histories have resulted in a sharp divergence in the West. Over the past several centuries, transalpine Western Christendom has split into two schools when it comes to the separation of church and state. Those schools are not Catholicism and Protestantism. In the one school – that of northern continental Europe – the social mission of the church has been transformed into a social mission of the state; and more broadly, the legal remit of the church has become the legal remit of the state. A "public sphere" has been defined in which the state reigns alone and religious expression is, to one degree or another, excluded. At the same time, popular religious belief has largely evaporated. In the other school – our own American tradition – the social mission of the church has remained largely the social mission of the church, and the law of the church has never become the law of the state. There is no "public sphere" from which religious expression is excluded, and popular religious fervor has survived and often flourished. One consequence is that the historic mission of the church has been taken over by the social welfare states of Europe, while private charity has survived in the United States.

Both of these patterns, let us frankly admit, are recognizably Christian. They simply represent two different occidental efforts to give institutional reality to the ancient Christian ambition of maintaining a separation of church and state. The real difference is that the continental model is close to the Christian model of the government of Louis XIV, whereas the American model is closer to that of the Glorious Revolution.

So what should we say, as a policy matter, about these two models? Does either one of them represent the right way of separating church and state? The short answer is no. As a practical matter, it is pointless to declare that either model sets the "correct" standard for the separation of church and state. Both belong to very old and deeply entrenched traditions. Continental Europeans are not going to embrace the American way of doing things. On the contrary, the spread of anti-headscarf laws suggests that Europeans are moving steadily away from the American approach. Americans are certainly not going to convert to Europeanism.

Nevertheless, if we understand the two traditions rightly, we can recognize that they pose distinct policy problems in the world today, in both domestic and foreign affairs. The best lesson we can draw from comparative study is not that we have it right and they have it wrong, or vice versa. The best lesson we can draw is that Europeans and Americans, having pursued different paths to the separation of church and state, now find themselves enjoying different advantages and confronting different dangers.

Some of those differences have to do with a great, and indeed elemental, contrast between continental Europe and the United States: the contrast between a

Europe in which the social welfare states are relatively strong and a United States in which private charity is relatively strong. This contrast has many consequences. For example, American universities benefit prodigiously from the American tradition of private charity, whereas French universities languish. American foreign aid also passes largely through private hands, where European foreign aid mostly comes from government coffers. Of course, much more could be said.

In the current climate, though, it is especially worthwhile to focus on the dangers our different traditions carry in the encounter with Islam. First, the continental model does indeed display a dangerous tendency toward a certain kind of intolerance – a kind of intolerance that might pose a threat to social stability in Europe. The danger has become evident in the controversy over anti-headscarf laws. The continental approach, as exemplified by French *laïcité*, depends on a distinction between "public" and "private." That distinction is at least as old as the revocation of the Edict of Nantes, and it carries some of the same dangers that that terrible measure carried. Let us remember that the revocation led to serious oppression, and indeed quasi-pogroms, in seventeenth-century France, despite its guarantee of an "unmolested" private life for Huguenots.[38] This was no accident. Any state measure that targets a particular religious group, no matter how avowedly tolerant, may stir up public attacks against the group in question – and everybody recognizes that the veil laws are targeted against Muslims. In that sense, these laws may well threaten the basic legal requirement of the *ordre public*.

Moreover, the very idea of "private" belief was problematic for the Protestants of 1685, and it is even more problematic for Muslims today. Here the issues have to do with some features peculiar to Christianity. Distinguishing between the public and private spheres makes some sense within Christian tradition. Dating back to antiquity, there have been dominant strains of Christianity that concentrated ritual within the church building. Unlike Judaism and other ancient religions, Christianity puts comparatively little emphasis on the performance of rituals within the family or in other everyday doings. For Westerners accustomed to this ancient Christian pattern of worship, it is easy to imagine that there can be a "private" sphere of religion and a "public" sphere from which ritual is banished. Christianity itself has already divided the world into two spheres – the ritual sphere within the church building and the relatively nonritualized sphere outside. By contrast, for adherents to other major religions, the division is not so easy. For observant Muslims, or Hindus, or Sikhs, or Jews, *every* corner of life is governed by ritual prescriptions. There is no way of delineating a "public" area in which religion does not apply. In this sense too, the solution to the church–state problem offered by *laïcité* is an unmistakably Christian solution. Moreover, it is a formula for social tension – tension that can only grow as Muslim populations multiply.

All this makes it unwise, in my view as in the view of many observers, for Europeans to push bans on Islamic dress too hard. It is understandable that some Europeans feel

---

[38] See the account in, e.g., Négroni 78 (1996).

disconcerted and even fearful when they encounter "ostentatious" Islamic symbols. They have long since grown used to a secularized "public" sphere. Their uneasiness is also inevitably deepened by the undeniable political tensions between Islam and the West. Nevertheless, the risk of exacerbating the current conflict is great, and it is better to put off full secularization of Europe's Muslim populations until some future date. Europeans have the right to hope that Muslims might accept basic European norms at some time in the future – just as Jews have mostly done. Yet that process will take generations, and the right counsel at the moment is the counsel of patience. Absolutism in the pursuit of the continental tradition of separation of church and state is foolish.

The United States does not face the same problem. We are much less inclined to require anybody to put off religious garb when entering the "public" sphere. Our state does not aim to chase religion out of public life. Adherents to non-Christian faiths are thus likely to experience daily life in the United States as more tolerant; indeed survey evidence suggests that is the case.[39] In that sense, there is no doubt that the United States is more tolerant – at least within its own borders.

But that does not mean that the American model cannot go too far. We have the same tendency as Europeans do: the tendency to believe that our model represents the true form of the separation of church and state and that we must remain absolutely obedient to it. Like the Europeans, we tend to an absolutism – although ours is primarily an absolutism of free expression.

Yet free expression can go too far. First and foremost, our model of free expression goes too far when we fail to keep religion out of the courtroom. Citations to biblical authority have no place in court. In particular, they have no place in death penalty cases. As one – but only one! – of our fifty state supreme courts has persuasively argued, "reliance in any manner upon the Bible or any other religious writing in support of the imposition of a penalty of death" should be "reversible error per se and . . . subject violators to disciplinary action."[40] Even outside the context of death penalty cases, the Bible has no role to play when American citizens judge each other. American lawyers do have a defense of the use of biblical citations to offer: They typically insist that biblical texts are cited simply as evidence of larger, non-Christian, moral truths. As Justice Breyer put it, religious texts like the Ten Commandments may simply communicate "a secular moral message (about proper standards of social conduct)."[41] But this is specious. It is fatuous to imagine that Christian jurors respond to the Bible as though it were some sort of ecumenical piece of moral philosophizing. Christian jurors will inevitably treat Scripture as an authority that commands obedience, not as a compendium of admirable bromides. Yet our social compact commits us to submit to democratically enacted laws. No

---

[39] See, e.g., "Muslims Largely Assimilated in U.S., Survey Shows," *Detroit News*, May 23, 2007.
[40] *Commonwealth v. Chambers*, 599 A.2d 630, 644 (Pa. 1991). See the fuller discussion in Simson and Garvey 1110–13 (2001).
[41] *Van Orden v. Perry*, 545 U.S. 677, 701 (2005).

source of authority should be determining our rights and liabilities in court unless it is the product of the proper forms of democratic deliberation. The Bible simply does not satisfy that standard.

But what about that process of democratic deliberation? Is it wrong for legislators to cite the Bible? Here I must admit that my sympathies are continental. I am put off and even mildly scandalized by the invocation of the Bible in our legislatures, Nevertheless, I think it would be entirely unrealistic to demand a separation of religion from politics of the continental type. Separating religion from politics would run much too strongly contrary to American traditions and sensibilities. We are stuck with the legislative practices we have.

Nevertheless, there is one special danger in our promiscuous mixing of religion and politics that needs to be brought home. Vigorous expression of religious belief creates real difficulties in international relations. Christians remain the overwhelming majority in the United States, and when religious expression is tolerated in the public sphere, the impression inevitably arises that the United States is a paladin in the Christian cause. To some extent, the same is true of Jewish expression, which is also very vocal in the United States. Indeed, our refusal to separate religion from politics arguably has something to do with the surface plausibility of the insinuation that the "Jewish lobby" has captured Congress. It is difficult for the United States to make the case that it is acting strictly in the secular national interest in the Middle East precisely because we talk so loudly and so often in religious terms.

Such indeed is the bottom-line, or one bottom-line, of the split between our two occidental approaches to the separation of church and state. America may seem more tolerant domestically, but its traditions tend to foster conflict on the international plane. Continental Europe shows more or less the reverse pattern. We can see the results in the rhetoric on both sides of the Atlantic. French officials often try to defuse tensions at home by observing that France is tolerant and indeed friendly toward Islam abroad.[42] American officials for their part, try to defuse tensions abroad by insisting that America is tolerant at home.[43] Both are right in some sense, but neither has found a path to religious peace.

REFERENCES

Abboud, A. (2004). Separation of Church and State in the U.S.: Courts, Politicians, Continue to Debate Meaning. Available at http://www.america.gov/st/washfile-english/2004/June/20040616151919maduobbao.4806024.html

Alesina, A. and Glaeser, E. (2004). *Fighting Poverty in the US and Europe: A World of Difference*. New York: Oxford.

Barbier, M. (1995). *La Laïcité*. Paris: L'Harmattan.

---

[42] For a typical effort by former President Chirac, see "L'Efcacité de la Politique Arabe de la France à l'Épreuve," *Le Nouvel Économiste*, September 17, 2004.
[43] See, e.g., Doder (2003).

Bartlett, R. (2004). Remarks on Appropriating Money. 150 *Congr. Rec.* H2247–02, H2253.

Bergin, J. (1996). *The Making of the French Episcopate, 1589–1661.* New Haven: Yale.

Boussinesq, J. (1994). *La Laïcité Française: Mémento Juridique.* Paris: Editions du Seuil.

Carbonnier, J. (1986). Sociologie et Psychologie Juridiques de l'Edit de Révocation, in R. Zuber and L. Theiss, eds., *La Révocation de l'Édit de Nantes et le Protestantisme Français en 1685.* Paris: BSHPF.

Code Pénal art. 433–21 (Fr.). English translation available at http://www.legifrance.gouv.fr/html/codes_traduits/code_penal_textan.htm

Cornu, G. (2003). *Droit Civil: La Famille.* Paris: Montchrestien.

Custos, D. (2006). Secularism in French Public Schools: Back to War? *American Journal of Comparative Law* 54: 337–399.

Doder, D. (2003) Selling America like Shampoo. *Baltimore Sun,* 5 January.

Eberle, E. (2006). Religion in the Classroom in Germany and the United States. *Tulane Law Review* 81: 67–122.

An *Edict of the French King Prohibiting All Publick Exercise of the Pretended Reformed Religion in His Kingdom* (1686). England. Available at http://books.google.com/books?id=cepbAAAAQAAJ&ots=v9oRWzj8YW&dq=An%20Edict%20of%20the%20French%20King%20Prohibiting%20All%20Publick%20Exercise%20of%20the%20Pretended%20Reformed%20Religion%20in%20His%20Kingdom&pg=PP1#v=onepage&q=&f=false

Egland, T. (2004). Prejudiced by the Presence of God: Keeping Religious Material out of Death Penalty Deliberations. *Capital Defense Journal* 16: 337.

Feldman (2002). Intellectual Origins of the Establishment Clause. *New York University Law Review* 77: 346–428.

Garapon, A. and Papadopoulos, I. (2003). *Juger en Amérique et en France.* Paris: Odile Jacob.

Garraud, D. (2008). Laïcité: Les professions de foi contradictoires de Sarkozy. *Charente Libre,* 8 February.

Garrisson, J. (1985). *L'Édit de Nantes et sa Révocation.* Paris: Éditions Labor.

Gauchet, M. (1998). *La Religion dans la Démocratie: Parcours de la Laïcité.* Paris: Gallimard.

Lefebvre-Teillard, A. (1990). *Le Nom: Droit et Histoire.* Paris: Presses Universitaires de France.

Lipset, S. M. (1996). *American Exceptionalism: A Double-Edged Sword.* New York: Norton.

MacCulloch, D. (2003). *The Reformation.* New York: Allen Lane.

Négroni, B. (1996). *Intolérances. Catholiques et Protestants en France 1560–1787.* Paris: Hachette.

The Netherlands: Government Said to Back Off Burqa Ban. (2008, January 24). *Reuters.* Available at http://www.nytimes.com/2008/01/24/world/europe/24briefs-burqa.html

Rush, B. L. (2007). Remarks on the Fair Minimum Wage Act of 2007, 153 *Congr. Rec.* H260, 287.

Simson, G. and Garvey, S. (2001). Knockin' on Heaven's Door: Rethinking the Role of Religion in Death Penalty Cases. *Cornell Law Review* 86: 1090–1130.

Whitman, J. (2004). The Two Western Cultures of Privacy: Dignity versus Liberty. *Yale Law Journal* 113: 1151–1221.

Law and the Family

15

Civil Rites

The Gay Marriage Controversy in Historical Perspective

Joanna L. Grossman

Family law throughout American history has developed amidst controversy. Although the work of many family lawyers today is routine – uncontested divorces and formulaic claims for child support are the "bread and butter for thousands of lawyers"[1] – family law, writ large, has been the locus of hard-fought battles over morality, privacy, state control over private life, civil rights, and federalism.

The most trenchant battle in family law today is over the ability of same-sex couples to marry. This chapter considers the modern same-sex marriage controversy through the lens of history. As researcher, shrewd observer, and storyteller, Lawrence Friedman is one of the original and best contributors to our collective understanding of family law history. His work provides both overarching themes and ground-level observations that are useful for reflecting on the ongoing controversy about same-sex marriage.

THE MODERN PROBLEM

The legalization of same-sex marriage by first one state and then four more and the District of Columbia – and the express condemnation of it by more than forty others – has reintroduced the age-old problem of non-uniform marriage laws and interaction among states with different laws regulating family creation and dissolution. Massachusetts launched the same-sex marriage revolution with the landmark ruling of its highest court in *Goodridge v. Department of Public Health* in 2003. The state's highest court held that a ban on same-sex marriages "works a deep and scarring hardship on a very real segment of the community for no rational reason" and violates the state constitution's guarantees of both equality and due process.[2]

---

[1] Friedman 18 (2004).
[2] *Goodridge v. Department of Public Health*, 798 N.E.2d 941, 968 (Mass. 2003).

After a rash of recent rulings and enactments, same-sex couples can now also marry in Connecticut, Iowa, Vermont, New Hampshire, and the District of Columbia, as well as in a growing handful of foreign countries, so far including Argentina, Belgium, Canada, the Netherlands, Norway, South Africa, Spain, and Sweden. Although the granting of full marriage rights for same-sex couples *anywhere* was a striking development, the anti-same-sex marriage developments in other jurisdictions are even more remarkable.

In anticipation that Hawaii might (although it never did) legalize same-sex marriage in the 1990s, Congress enacted the Defense of Marriage Act to absolve states of any potential obligation under full faith and credit principles to recognize same-sex marriages from sister states. A significant majority of states responded to their absolution with historically unprecedented statutory and constitutional reforms that both ban the celebration of same-sex marriage within their borders and preclude their courts from recognizing same-sex marriages validly celebrated elsewhere. Efforts to amend the federal constitution to bar same-sex marriage nationwide were also undertaken, albeit unsuccessfully.

Even the state of Massachusetts, the first (and, for four years, the only) state to legalize same-sex marriage, took steps to restrict the right by refusing to issue licenses to nonresident couples. (This tactic was not entirely surprising because the legalization of same-sex marriages came via a judicial decision rather than as a result of political will.) The state temporarily closed its doors to nonresident same-sex couples seeking to marry, because as then-governor Mitt Romney warned, "Massachusetts should not become the Las Vegas of same-sex marriage."

This story – a challenge to traditional marriage, a divisive moral debate, and the emergence of strong oppositional forces that are stuck, at least temporarily but perhaps indefinitely, in a kind of stalemate – is not a new one. American states have never been of one mind about the appropriate level of state control over domestic relations, and the federal government has for the most part steered clear of regulating families. Although most conflicts involving state regulation of marriage and divorce had been resolved by the middle of the twentieth century, the battles were long and hard fought and left an indelible imprint on family law history.

Take, for example, historical disagreements among states about prohibitions on marriage. Although all states banned marriages that were polygamous, closely incestuous, or involved an "imbecile" or "lunatic," they differed in the imposition of other restrictions. States disagreed about interracial marriage, marriage between first cousins or between individuals related by affinity, the minimum age for marriage with and without parental consent, and marriage by those with a communicable or hereditary disease. Despite the broad agreement about some restrictions, disagreements about others led to moralistic fights, jurisdictional wars, the erection of statutory blocks to interstate recognition, and lobbying for federal control over marriage law.

The battle within and among states over accessible divorce was even starker and more hard fought. Although the story is by now familiar, the path by which we traveled from a country without judicial divorce in the eighteenth century to a country with almost universal divorce on demand in the twenty-first was by no means peaceful. Instead it was marked by the ebb and flow of legal reform and retrenchment, depending on the momentary sway of the moral tides, strident wars among states for control over their own residents' marital status, and a "seedy underbelly" of abandonment, perjury, and corruption that developed as the law failed to respond quickly enough to the rising social demand for divorce.

In these historical battles over marriage and divorce, there are lessons to be learned: that a moral stalemate often produces a nonsensical patchwork of laws, that a profound gap between formal law and its working reality often arises in the wake of such compromises, and that the competitive market for the law of domestic relations in the federalist system can wreak real havoc on laws and lives – and, above all else, that social forces eventually "shape the legal order."[3]

THE MORAL STALEMATE

Throughout American history, states, and factions within states, have had long-standing disagreements about the accessibility of divorce. Colonial America, following England's "divorceless" tradition (which lasted until 1857), did not permit judicial divorce. Although states began to enact laws to provide for judicial divorce after the Revolutionary War, the trajectory from those strict early laws to the no-fault, divorce-on-demand laws of today was neither smooth nor continuously arced in one direction. The early laws reflected a general consensus that divorce was a remedy for an innocent spouse who had been wronged by a partner who breached the legally established obligations of marriage. What made these early laws strict were the narrowness of permissible grounds for divorce (adultery and abandonment, for example), the requirement that the plaintiff be innocent, and, to avoid trespass by more lenient laws elsewhere, lengthy residency requirements.

Toward the middle of the nineteenth century, several states experimented with broader, general grounds for divorce. For example, Rhode Island permitted divorce for "gross misbehavior and wickedness in either of the parties, repugnant to and in violation of the marriage covenant."[4] Yet broader laws like this one fell between the 1870s and the 1890s under pressure from the anti-divorce moralists who warned of the dire consequences to society of more accessible divorce.[5] Connecticut's first divorce law permitted dissolution on grounds of "misconduct," but it too eventually reverted to narrower, more traditional grounds like adultery and abandonment.

Easy divorce was hauled out by the "prophets of doom" to signal the moral decay of society; strict laws were proffered as the key to preserving the institution of marriage. For many religious and more moderate moralists, divorce was "at best

---

3 Id. at 11.
4 Blake 50 (1977).
5 May 4 (1980).

a necessary evil."[6] Lenient laws were defended and pushed for by feminists and free lovers, but also by pragmatists like Joel Prentiss Bishop, author of the first treatise on marriage and divorce, who thought divorce law should be "adapted to the general needs of society."[7] Social demand and moral ideology thus warred, and the resulting laws at any particular time were a reflection of the relative strengths of these forces. As Friedman notes, "Small or large shifts in moral climate, or in the strength of contending groups, are reflected in the living law, which is a thermometer measuring the current moral climate of society."[8]

The nineteenth century was a time of "national panic" that produced a set of divorce laws that Friedman describes as "an egregious example of a branch of law tortured by contradictions in public opinion, trapped between contending forces of perhaps roughly equal size; trapped, too, in a federal system with freedom of movement back and forth, and beyond the power and grasp of any single state."[9] By the close of the nineteenth century, the moralists had more or less won. Most states only permitted divorce for traditional, well-defined grounds such as adultery, abandonment, and imprisonment for a felony. Some also permitted divorce based on cruelty, although many judges clung to an interpretation that required proof of physical abuse.[10] South Carolina continued to ban divorce altogether, and New York permitted it only on grounds of adultery.[11] Yet, the social demand for divorce was higher than it had ever been, reflecting both the increasing expectations associated with companionate marriage and the needs of the newly propertied middle class for legal papers to reflect broken marriages.[12] After all, demand for divorce is "a demand for legal status; nobody needs a formal divorce or a court order to skip out of a marriage, to pack one's bags and move out, or to move in with somebody else."[13]

The moral stalemate over the formal law coupled with rising demand to create "a classic case of a dual system" in which the law on the books was entirely unreflective of its subterranean life. Yet the formal law was entrenched; "[t]here was no way to reform the law, or to move it in either direction."[14]

The concept of a "moral stalemate," which so aptly characterizes divorce law in the second half of the nineteenth and first half of the twentieth centuries, holds some force in the modern same-sex marriage controversy as we begin to see some evidence of an emerging compromise between moralists on the one hand and pragmatists and advocates on the other. When the Vermont Supreme Court concluded that the existing ban violated the state constitution's guarantee of "common benefits"

[6] Friedman 33 (2004).
[7] Bishop 22 (1851).
[8] Friedman 16 (1984).
[9] Friedman 381 (2005).
[10] Griswold (1982).
[11] Grossman 90–2 (2001).
[12] Friedman 378–89 (2005); Griswold (1982).
[13] Friedman 32 (2004).
[14] Id. at 38.

to all citizens, it gave the legislature the choice between opening civil marriage to same-sex couples or fashioning a legal equivalent.[15] The legislature chose the latter option, creating a new status called a "civil union." Several years later and without the pressure of a court ultimatum, Connecticut also adopted a civil union law, as did, eventually, New Jersey and New Hampshire. (England has recently adopted a "civil partnership" law that significantly resembles the American civil union.) The "civil union" is a nonmarriage marriage that preserves, at least symbolically, the tradition of heterosexual marriage, while permitting its rights and obligations to be shared by those who could not, historically, lay claim to the tradition.

These alternative status laws, like the strict nineteenth-century divorce laws, represent a triumph of symbolism over functional meaning. Yet the symbolism comes at a price – reflected in a second theme developed in Lawrence Friedman's work and discussed later: the dual system. A civil union is a marriage, except in name. Yet through the work of Friedman and others in family law, we know that such symbols as marriage are not easily discarded – and the symbol of traditional marriage remains steadfast, while its hold on human behavior has steadily declined.

Politically, the "civil union" status has become a marriage alternative that is acceptable, surprisingly, even to many conservatives. (It has also proven a gateway to full marriage rights, because both Connecticut and New Hampshire moved there from civil unions.) Pragmatically, within a single state, civil unions are easy to administer because they replicate marriage, legally, in all but name. Yet, as with divorce, the same-sex marriage stalemate has produced some pretty unworkable results, inconsistencies within individual states, and problems of portability across state lines. For example, California adopted both an expansive domestic partnership law (at the hands of the legislature) and an anti-same-sex marriage law (by voter initiative). With the benefit of the state supreme court's view about how these two laws might coexist,[16] registered same-sex partners in California are rightfully considered "spouses," but their union is not a "marriage." Then, in the midst of this chaos, the state legislature twice passed a bill to permit same-sex marriage, only to be rebuked by the state's governor, Arnold Schwarzenegger, who vetoed the bills because the legality of same-sex unions is a "matter for the courts." (This statement is particularly ironic for a Republican governor, because the main voiced objection to same-sex marriage in Massachusetts has been that it was undemocratically foisted on the people by the courts.) The state's highest court then weighed in – ruling the state's ban on same-sex marriage unconstitutional, thereby giving same-sex couples the right to marry.[17] More than fourteen thousand couples made it to the altar before voters amended the state constitution by referendum to once again prohibit

[15] *Baker v. State*, 744 A.2d 864 (Vt. 1999).
[16] *Knight v. Schwarzenegger*, 128 Cal. App. 4th 14 (2005); *Koebke v. Bernardo Heights Country Club*, 115 P.3d 1212 (Cal. 2005).
[17] *In re Marriage Cases*, 183 P.3d 384 (Cal. 2008).

same-sex marriage and to return to a domestic partnership regime.[18] The referendum was upheld by the state's highest court, although the already solemnized marriages were grandfathered in.[19] The same referendum was recently struck down, however, by a federal district court as a violation of the federal constitution's guarantees of equal protection and due process.[20] The ruling, however, was stayed pending appeal. Same-sex couples in California thus continue to live in a legally ambiguous landscape.

Although the moral stalemate has resulted in some compromises and led to the emergence of alternative status laws in some jurisdictions, the scale is still weighted heavily against same-sex marriage. In the vast majority of states, proponents of same-sex marriage have not mustered enough force to demand even a compromise position. In Maine, the legislature passed a law legalizing same-sex marriage, only to have the law wiped off the books by a "People's Veto" in an election six months later in November 2009. Forty-one states have enacted either a statute or constitutional amendment or both banning same-sex marriage, and most of those also refuse to recognize a same-sex marriage validly celebrated elsewhere (whether from a sister state or one of the several foreign countries that have legalized the practice in recent years). The only states without such provisions are the five states that expressly permit same-sex marriage and New Jersey, New Mexico, New York, and Rhode Island.[21]

At the federal level, opponents have prevailed strongly enough that no real compromise can be detected. With enactment of the Defense of Marriage Act in 1996, marriage became defined, for all federal purposes, as a union between a man and a woman. Thus, a same-sex marriage validly celebrated in an American state does not qualify for important federal rights like Social Security survivor benefits, immigration rights, or joint tax status.

In contrast, even in staunchly anti-same-sex-marriage states, there is still the potential for compromise. Efforts to enact a federal constitutional ban on same-sex marriage were stalemated in part by a dispute among same-sex marriage opponents about whether to leave room for or perhaps even endorse a marriage alternative like civil unions. Without George W. Bush in the White House to champion the effort to enact a federal constitutional ban, it has effectively died. Efforts to amend the Massachusetts constitution and thus override the judicial authorization of same-sex marriage also failed because the leading opponents refused to leave room for something like civil unions.

Moreover, to the extent social forces really drive the legal order, the dramatically increased social acceptance of same-sex relationships would suggest that compromise or even full acceptance will be an inevitable byproduct of the passage of time. One need only look at the portrayal of same-sex relationships in television and

---

[18] Proposition 8 § 2 (2008).
[19] *Strauss v. Horton*, 207 P.3d 48 (Cal. 2008).
[20] *Perry v. Schwarzenegger*, 704 F. Supp. 2d 921 (2010).
[21] Grossman and Stein (2009).

movies, the results of polls showing fairly significant acceptance of such relationships (particularly if you take the word "marriage" out of the question), and the marked inverse relationship between disapproval of homosexuality and voter age to see the potential effect of this social force on the near-term horizon. Yet, of course, the interrelationship between changing public opinion and the legal order is complex, and although the growing support is reinforced by greater constitutional protection for intimate relationships, including same-sex ones (*Lawrence v. Texas*, 2003), it is dampened by more deeply entrenched negative views and greater polarization of public opinion. For example, the decision by the most recently anointed pope to drum out and banish homosexual priests could have the effect of reminding Catholics that they are supposed to actively oppose homosexual relationships.

In family-law years, the stalemate is still young. The moral pendulum will no doubt continue to swing on same-sex marriage for many years before coming to a rest. In the meantime, the stalemate means living with an inconsistent and sometimes irrational legal order.

THE DUAL SYSTEM

A second recurring theme in family law history is the concept of a dual system, what Friedman describes as the "two faces of law."[22] These two faces – the moralistic surface and the "working realities" – have been present in many contexts over the course of American legal history. For example, prostitution was almost universally criminalized, yet hardly ever prosecuted. Through this unstated compromise, the "moralists wanted, and got, symbolic affirmation of their standards, and this was valuable to them."[23]

Historically, divorce provides the best example of a true "dual system." The official rules at the end of the nineteenth century made divorce accessible, but not "routine or automatic."[24] As mentioned earlier, the law imposed substantive and procedural roadblocks to easy, consensual divorce. Yet, the divorce rate rose steadily throughout that period, and spouses from all walks of life managed to get their judicially approved walking papers. The demand for divorce clearly rose even beyond the increases reflected in the actual divorce rate. Scholars have found that, as expectations for marriage gradually increased during the Victorian era, spouses were more likely to experience disappointment with their unions.[25] Equality for women and increasing pressure on the family to carry out society's missions were among the forces driving higher expectations for marriage and a more pressing need for an escape valve.[26]

[22] Friedman (1984).
[23] Id. at 24.
[24] Friedman 145, 377–81 (2005).
[25] Griswold (1982); May (1980).
[26] Degler 168 (1980); O'Neill (1967); Grossman and McClain (2006).

Divorce is the obvious remedy for alleviating increasing marital dissatisfaction, but the formal law and the moral stalemate it resulted from refused to budge. The dual system thus emerged with two main escape valves that allowed the moralistic laws to survive amid increasing demand for divorce and greater marital unhappiness: collusive divorce – husbands' and wives' conspiring to obtain a decree of dissolution to which neither was entitled – and simple abandonment. No scholar has been more insistent about the prevalence of collusion in divorce practice than Lawrence Friedman, and the evidence he cites is convincing. Although most state divorce laws expressly prohibited collusion – and required judges to deny a petition for divorce if they suspected it – it was obviously common. From the "unknown blonde" who confessed to participating in mock adultery for more than one hundred divorces, to the boilerplate and often obviously perjured testimony in divorce trials around the country, to the overwhelming percentage of female plaintiffs (who had more to lose in terms of custody, spousal support, and reputation in the community by being found "at fault" for a marriage's breakup), couples routinely made a mockery of the moralistic laws designed to constrain exit from marriage.[27] Indeed it was primarily a clamoring for a more "honest" system of divorce, rather than a shift in underlying morals, that led to the widespread adoption of no-fault laws in the 1970s.[28]

For unhappy couples who could not manage to obtain a divorce, collusive or otherwise, the solution was to simply act as if they were no longer married. As Friedman describes England in its pre-1857 divorceless era, the "most common 'solutions' when a marriage broke down were adultery and desertion."[29] Strict American laws encouraged those pragmatic remedies as well, and American mobility and westward expansion facilitated them. In Friedman's words, a prototypical bigamist might be a "man who found his marriage unsatisfying or stifling; he decamped, without the bother of a divorce, and started over again, usually in some other city."[30] Consensual separation, often without court approval, was another remedy for unhappiness: "When unhappy nineteenth-century couples lacked the legal grounds or the financial means or the moral or religious support to seek a divorce, many separated."[31]

The demand for divorce, coupled with dismay over the integrity of the broken system, was sufficient to finally overcome the opposition to accessible divorce. There has always been pressure for the law to accord formal recognition to the social reality of failed marriages, but as Friedman reminds us, "[s]ocial change leads to legal change; but never automatically."[32] The dual system ultimately came to an end in the second half of the twentieth century, when the law finally conceded its strict stance.

[27] Friedman 380–1 (2005).
[28] Jacob 66–9 (1988).
[29] Friedman 142 (2005).
[30] Friedman 642 (1991).
[31] Hartog 29 (2000).
[32] Friedman 589 (2002).

Has the moral stalemate in the same-sex marriage context produced the same sort of dual system that history has taught us to expect? Yes and no. One historically typical reaction to non-universal marriage prohibitions is evasive marriage. Yet, with respect to same-sex marriage, that avenue was initially foreclosed by a reverse marriage evasion law in Massachusetts, which forbids clerks from issuing marriage licenses to same-sex couples from out of state unless their home states would permit them to marry. Notwithstanding a few wedding announcements in the *New York Times* that suggested imperfect enforcement of the law, Massachusetts enforced its law excluding nonresident couples from the right of same-sex marriage until it was repealed in 2007.

However, there are opportunities now for same-sex couples to evade their own states' prohibitions by marrying in another state or country that permits it. The problem lies in gaining recognition by their home states that makes such a marriage legally meaningful. So-called Metro-North marriages have made headlines, as New Yorkers travel to neighboring Connecticut to marry, precisely because New York, unlike most other states, seems inclined to grant full recognition to same-sex marriages validly celebrated elsewhere.[33] Even without full recognition, however, anecdotal evidence reveals small-ticket ways around the anti-same-sex marriage regime, such as subversively filing joint federal tax returns (which do not, it turns out, ask the gender of the filer or filer's spouse), notwithstanding the federal law's refusal to recognize same-sex unions. However, again, this practice does not amount to a dual system as history might understand it.

Evidence of the dual system, to the extent it exists, lies in two places: (1) census data that reflect same-sex couples replicating spousal lives and (2) the patchwork of laws and judicial decisions that permit them to form, maintain, and dissolve families in ways that often significantly resemble marriage. One way of looking at marriage is by its "incidents": cohabitation, procreation, child rearing, inheritance and other economic rights, and the like. When the 2000 census was conducted, same-sex couples could not legally marry anywhere in the United States. Yet, data show gays and lesbians are partaking of the incidents of marriage in large numbers. Nearly 600,000 American households were anchored by a same-sex couple, comprising more than 10 percent of all unmarried-partner households. Same-sex couples were present in 99 percent of all U.S. counties, and nearly a quarter of them were reportedly raising children.[34]

Laws other than those governing marriage often permit same-sex couples to formalize these incidents; they can thus establish significant legal ties to one another that in some cases mimic those between married couples. The national landscape reveals a sliding scale of rights for same-sex couples. In addition to the five states (plus the District of Columbia) providing full marriage rights, New Jersey offers

---

[33] Foderaro (2009).
[34] Simmons and O'Connell (2003).

civil unions, which gives couples access to all marital rights and responsibilities. California, Oregon, Washington, and Nevada offer a robust domestic partnership status that grants most of the rights of marriage. Further down the scale, Colorado, Hawaii, and Maryland offer a more limited type of domestic partnership, and a handful of states provide limited benefits to same-sex partners of state employees. In addition to rights at the state level, many localities also grant same-sex couples the ability to register as domestic partners, entitling them to some, usually very limited, benefits. The willingness of state legislatures to express support for "all families," while simultaneously affirming traditional marriage through anti-same-sex marriage initiatives, reinforces this dual system.[35]

Court decisions in many jurisdictions have upheld different marriage-like incidents for same-sex partners, even as the voters or legislators within the same jurisdiction have formally condemned same-sex marriage. These decisions, which are often motivated by the injustice that would result from excluding committed same-sex couples from legal protections that married heterosexuals take for granted, contribute to a real and identifiable dual system of laws.

The ability of gays and lesbians to reproduce – a prime "incident" of traditional marriage – has become much easier because of advances in reproductive technology. Alternative reproductive technologies like artificial insemination and in vitro fertilization have facilitated biological parenthood for lesbian women, and gay men are increasingly using surrogacy as a gateway to biological fatherhood. It has also become easier for same-sex couples to raise children together, with legal protections as parents.

Despite the widespread prohibitions of same-sex marriage, same-sex parenting has eked out legal protections in many states. One core issue is whether lesbians and gays possess the ability to legally adopt children – either as individuals or as part of a same-sex couple. At one end of the legal spectrum is a state like New York, which permits both so-called second-parent adoptions (where an individual adopts the legal or biological children of a same-sex partner) and joint adoptions by same-sex couples. Along the middle of the spectrum lie states that permit second-parent adoptions, but not joint adoptions, or vice versa. There also seem to be states in which same-sex couples are permitted, in practice, to adopt, despite the lack of a statute or judicial ruling on the subject. In addition, a few states apply the traditional rules of "legal" parentage to same-sex couples – potentially deeming a person the legal parent of a child based on his or her relationship to the child's other parent or his or her functional parentage, regardless of whether an adoption has occurred.[36]

Some states do prohibit gay and lesbian couples from adopting. Florida has a law banning all homosexuals from becoming adoptive parents, a product of a vocal anti-gay campaign by celebrity Anita Bryant in the 1970s, which sought, among other

35　McClain (2008).
36　*K.M. v. E.G.*, 117 P.3d 673 (Cal. 2005).

things, to "Save Our Children" from gay parents. A federal appellate court upheld this law against a constitutional challenge, but a state appellate court recently struck it down.[37] Mississippi and Utah bar same-sex couples from jointly adopting children, and Arkansas voters recently passed a referendum to prevent all unmarried couples from adopting.[38] However, the marked trend is toward permitting same-sex couples and gay and lesbian individuals to adopt on the same terms as other couples and individuals. This trend is not entirely surprising, given the significant number of studies suggesting that children with gay parents fare as well in all relevant respects as children raised by heterosexuals.

Other incidents of marriage can sometimes be replicated through contractual and other private mechanisms. Couples in many states have successfully used parenting agreements to regulate the co-parenting relationship between biological and nonbiological lesbian mothers. There are lawyers in many jurisdictions who devote their entire practice to assisting same-sex couples in creating partnerships and co-parenting arrangements that are enforceable within the existing legal framework. Same-sex couples can enter into reciprocal wills and durable powers of attorney that mimic the health care decision-making and inheritance rights of spouses. Except for a handful of states like Virginia that expressly negate the legal force of contracts between same-sex couples that purport to replicate marriage-like rights, same-sex couples can enter into binding agreements to obligate themselves financially to one another. Regardless of a state's law, same-sex couples can partake in commitment ceremonies in which they publicly vow love and fidelity toward one another: These celebrations are often indistinguishable (in content, appearance, *and* cost) from heterosexual weddings. Finally, since the Supreme Court's 2003 decision in *Lawrence v. Texas*, which invalidated Texas's same-sex sodomy ban as unconstitutional, they can freely engage in intimate sexual conduct without fear of government interference.

However, the emerging dual system for same-sex marriage is not yet a complete replication of the past dual system for divorce. At least some same-sex couples have contracted evasive same-sex marriages in Massachusetts or elsewhere that have only symbolic effect at home. Couples thus act "married" in the same way that unhappy couples sometimes pretended to be "divorced." Yet it turns out that marriage is harder to fake than divorce, because the piece of paper – the marriage certificate – itself is what entitles the bearer to commonly availed benefits of the status, such as dependent health insurance coverage, hospital visitation rights, joint tax filing status, and the spousal elective share. After all, one can pretend to be divorced by simply moving out and moving on. One can even remarry – although not legally – without first obtaining a divorce by simply checking "single" on the marriage license

---

[37] *Lofton v. Sec'y Dep't of Children & Family Servs.*, 377 F.3d 1275 (11th Cir. 2004) (en banc); *In re Adoption of X.X.G. and N.R.G.*, 2010 Fla. App. LEXIS 14014 (2010).

[38] Grossman (2009).

application form. Although the chances of eventually being caught in this day and age are high, bigamous remarriages are undoubtedly still celebrated.

Yet in both cases we see real limits on the law's ability to shape culture and human behavior. Refusing to allow unhappily married couples to divorce did not make them happily married, and refusing to permit same-sex couples to marry does not lead them to either marry someone of the opposite sex or remain single. However, history teaches that a long-standing social practice often forces the law to take account of it. With cohabitation, for example, courts have had to "face the fact that living in sin is now a recognized legal category."[39] In so many cases, it is not only financial or economic needs that drive the push for recognition but moral ones as well. Existing realities tend to gain acceptance over time, and the deprivation of formal recognition itself becomes an unacceptable slight. Language in those judicial decisions that have struck down bans on same-sex marriage have emphasized the stigmatic effect of exclusionary marriage laws.[40]

THE BATTLE AMONG STATES: THE PRICE OF MOBILITY AND FEDERALISM

Although the moral stalemate over divorce fed an unsatisfactory dual system within almost every state, the history of marriage and divorce is actually far more complicated than that. The formal law differed not only from the social reality but also differed, sometimes profoundly, from state to state. Because American states did not (and do not) exist in isolation, differences in the laws of marriage and divorce engendered legal conflicts when couples married or divorced in one state and sought recognition in another. For marriage, the practice of intentionally crossing state lines to contract a marriage prohibited at home became known as "evasive marriage" and was banned by statute in a small number of states and made ineffectual in a few others through judicial application of a common law anti-evasion principle. Yet not all evasive marriages were ignored, and when couples simply married in one place and later migrated elsewhere, the traditional approach in most states was staunchly weighted in favor of recognition. Under common law principles of comity, recognition was often, but not always, granted to disfavored marriages that were validly celebrated elsewhere.

States thus warred with each other about the restrictive laws, fearing that laxer standards would always trump stricter ones, particularly as American mobility increased. Several uniform marriage laws were proposed near the beginning of the twentieth century, although none were widely adopted by states. Some attempts were made to federalize marriage law, either generally through a grant of jurisdiction to

---

[39] Friedman 581 (2005).
[40] *Goodridge v. Dep't of Public Health* (2003); *Kerrigan v. Commissioner of Public Health* (2008).

Congress or specifically by constitutionalizing bans on, say, polygamy and interracial marriage.[41] None of these efforts were successful, however, and states eventually learned to coexist and show each other tolerance despite significant differences in marriage laws.[42]

The states' wars over divorce laws were always more tumultuous and drawn out than those over marriage. From the early-eighteenth-century advent of judicial divorce through the widespread adoption of no-fault divorce laws in the 1970s, states clashed over the accessibility of divorce. Some of the differences were regional. The South was always more hostile to divorce than other areas of the country, but so-called divorce mills sometimes popped up in surprising places. For the most part, these mills were intentionally created and, because of their appeal to out-of-staters, "pitted state against state."[43] States competed for divorce business by shortening residency requirements (which were otherwise typically at least one year) and adding broader or more flexible grounds for divorce.

For example, Indiana lured divorce-seekers with the combination of an "omnibus" ground for divorce and a requirement only that the plaintiff be a state resident at the time the petition for divorce was filed.[44] It closed the door in 1873, only to be replaced in popularity by first Utah, then North and South Dakota, and then Nevada, which retained its divorce-haven status for many decades. Nevada's unusually short residency requirement – six weeks – enabled nightclub singer Eddie Fisher to use a forty-four-night gig at *The Tropicana* to stage his divorce from Debbie Reynolds and virtually simultaneous remarriage to Elizabeth Taylor.[45]

The lack of uniform divorce laws and the ability of an opportunistic state like Nevada to facilitate migratory divorce were sources of significant conflict among states. Efforts to promote uniform divorce laws were more pronounced than in the marriage context, although they were equally unsuccessful. The National Divorce Reform League did bring about the repeal of broad grounds of divorce in some individual states, but was never able to secure true uniformity. Congress appropriated money for a national study of marriage and divorce, in large part to determine the migratory divorce rate and fuel efforts to combat it. Yet it turned out that the strictness of laws had very little to do with the divorce rate in any particular state or nationally. Only drastic changes in law affected the divorce rate, and even then, the effects were generally short term.

Both collusion and the possibility of migratory divorce left states impotent in the battle to control marital exit, and the long-standing relegation of control over domestic relations to the states made a federal mandate unpalatable. States were

[41] Stein (2004).
[42] Grossman (2005).
[43] Friedman 436 (2005).
[44] Blake 119 (1977).
[45] Blake 1–4 (1977).

generally unwilling to conform their laws voluntarily on controversial issues, including divorce.[46] Thus, in addition to collusion and perjury, the federal system itself
provided a "prominent door" around strict divorce laws.[47] A natural outgrowth of
this situation was an effort in many states to refuse recognition to obviously migratory
divorces. Uniform laws for the first three decades of the twentieth century endorsed
this approach by laying out rules of jurisdiction, residency, and full faith and credit
designed to maximize the ability of each state to enforce its own standards against
its own domiciliaries.[48] The Supreme Court had given the green light for many of
the refusals of recognition in a 1906 case, *Haddock v. Haddock*, in which it held
that states could ignore out-of-state decrees if only one party was domiciled in the
granting state and the other did not receive personal service of court papers or make
an appearance. This enabled a fragile compromise, whereby states had the ability
to draw the line at so-called quickie divorces, while generally giving effect to each
other's decrees.

The unstated compromise among states was undone by the Supreme Court in
1942, when it reversed itself in interpreting the recognition requirements under the
Full Faith and Credit Clause. In *Williams v. North Carolina*, the Court held that
states must give effect to out-of-state divorce decrees as long as the granting state
properly exercised jurisdiction under its own rules.[49] Although the force of that
ruling was diminished by two later decisions,[50] it nonetheless put a stop to most
state efforts to refuse recognition to out-of-state divorces. By judicial force, states
thus learned to coexist amidst a non-uniform set of divorce laws and despite stark
disagreements about the moral implications of easy divorce. This, the Supreme
Court observed, was simply "part of the price of our federal system."[51]

Same-sex marriage is once again putting to the test our federalism and commitment to state control over domestic relations. What had been a period of relative
calm in the state marriage wars was upended by the decision of the Massachusetts
Supreme Judicial Court in *Goodridge*. The non-uniformity the ruling created is a significant one, particularly given the prominence of gay rights and same-sex marriage
in the national debate.[52]

---

[46] Friedman 305 (2005).

[47] Friedman 36 (2004).

[48] Grossman (2004).

[49] *Williams v. North Carolina*, 317 U.S. 287 (1942).

[50] In a second review of the same case, the Supreme Court ruled that North Carolina could make its
own determination on collateral review as to whether Nevada's jurisdictional requirements had been
met. See *Williams v. North Carolina*, 325 U.S. 226, 239 (1945) (*Williams II*). Then, in *Estin v. Estin*,
334 U.S. 541 (1948), the Court held that while a New York court had to honor a Nevada divorce with
respect to determining the marital status of the parties, it did not have to relieve the plaintiff-husband
from the incidental obligations of separation previously adjudicated by a New York court. Though
neither of these cases overruled the core holding of *Williams I*, both undermined its practical effect.

[51] 325 U.S. 239 (1945).

[52] *Goodridge v. Department of Public Health* (2003).

Massachusetts' legalization of same-sex marriage, and the decade-earlier anticipation that Hawaii would permit it, triggered many responses. In rushing to respond, states and the federal government largely ignored the long history of state conflicts over marriage and the fragile, but workable compromise that states had reached. Congress sought to assert national control over marriage law through constitutional amendment, much as it had done in the first half of the twentieth century to combat, at various times, polygamy, interracial marriage, and the quickie divorce. Although separated by generations, these efforts all failed.

At the state level, the modern response to same-sex marriage has been both a replication and an extension of our historical experience. Although states have long taken steps to shore up their virtual borders against the transgressions of other states with more lenient marriage and divorce laws, the lengths to which they have gone to protect against same-sex marriage are unprecedented. (Massachusetts even tried to prevent its *own* marriages from having extraterritorial effect – not something we have seen before – by strictly enforcing until its recent repeal its reverse marriage evasion law.)

States historically retained the right to refuse recognition to a marriage under the common law rules of marriage recognition, but ultimately the decision whether to exercise that right fell mostly to courts. On a case-by-case basis, courts thus determined whether to grant full, or perhaps just single-purpose, recognition to an out-of-state marriage that the forum state would not itself have permitted. Although the outcomes turned on a number of variables, courts categorically refused recognition only to polygamous or closely incestuous marriages. Even then courts sometimes recognized particular incidents of those marriages, especially if the parties would not have the opportunity to cohabitate within the states' borders. For example, a court might recognize the validity of a marriage – effectively ended by the death of one party – for inheritance purposes. Courts routinely granted recognition to marriages that would have been prohibited because of age, race, and relationships of affinity, unless the marriages were obviously evasive. The rules of recognition were driven by principles of comity – the idea of courtesy among political entities – and concerns about the havoc that would be wreaked by nonportable marital statuses.[53]

The modern landscape looks quite different from the historical one. Except for a handful of states that have not taken any action to stop same-sex marriage at the border, the decision whether to recognize a same-sex marriage from elsewhere has been removed from the courts. Instead states have enacted sweeping statutes or constitutional amendments to prevent both the celebration and recognition of same-sex marriages. These laws, patterned after the federal Defense of Marriage Act, admit of no exceptions and do not, in many cases, permit even incidental recognition of same-sex marriage. Courts, for example, have refused to grant divorces to same-sex couples because doing so would require them to first "recognize" the marriage and

---

[53] Grossman (2005).

then dissolve it.[54] A handful of state laws go even further. They prevent courts or the state's legislature from granting any formal recognition to same-sex unions, whether it is a marriage, a domestic partnership, a civil union, or some as-of-yet-undefined intermediate status. Unprecedented in scope, these laws threaten to undermine the orderly creation and dissolution of intimate unions, a goal states have worked toward over the centuries.

In the few states that have not erected such obstacles, the historical patterns of recognition may emerge. Courts have shown themselves hesitant but not totally unwilling to recognize same-sex marriages or civil unions, even though their own laws do not permit them to be celebrated. A handful of trial courts have quietly granted civil union partners a "divorce" without necessarily recognizing the under-lying union. In addition, as discussed earlier, the California Supreme Court has granted domestic partners protection against "marital status" discrimination.[55] More directly, New York has upheld recognition of same-sex marriages in a variety of cases and governmental orders.[56]

The conflicts among states with respect to same-sex marriage are relatively young, since such unions have been legally celebrated in the United States for only seven years. However, with the recent expansion in the number of states and foreign countries that authorize same-sex marriage and the potential for a few others to do so in the near future, these conflicts will multiply. Whether same-sex marriage survives in only the current five or is extended to a small block of states, the country as a whole will have to learn to coexist.

As more same-sex marriages occur and more state-to-state conflicts arise, the harsh-ness of the modern anti-same-sex marriage landscape may reveal itself more starkly. The unintended consequences of a nonrecognition regime – legalized polygamy when states lines are crossed, uncertainty about marital status, risks to children whose parents' obligations to them might be unenforceable outside of the state of creation, and public dependencies created by the displacement of private, reciprocal obligations of care – may prove sufficient to cause a retrenchment.

CONCLUSION

Of what predictive value are the parallels between the history of marriage and divorce and the modern controversy over same-sex marriage? When considering what a legal historian of the twenty-first century might write in 2100, Friedman cautions, "There is no crystal ball."[57] Yet the lessons of history – about the unsustainable legal structures produced in times of panic, the influence of social and economic pressures on law's

---

[54] *Chambers v. Ormiston*, 935 A.2d 956 (R.I. 2007); *In re Marriage of J.B. and H.B.*, 2010 Tex. App. LEXIS 7127.
[55] *Koebke v. Bernardo Heights Country Club* (2005).
[56] *Godfrey v. Spano*, 892 N.Y.S.2d 272 (2009).
[57] Friedman 603 (2002).

development, and the importance of the "separate histories of the law of the fifty states" – still offer us wise counsel. Had modern states paid more attention to those lessons, particularly to the reasons why states historically managed to peaceably coexist despite stark disagreements about morality, eugenics, and state control over marriage, reproduction, and divorce, our modern landscape might be less troubled.

The vast changes to the law of marriage and, even more so, to the law of divorce between the nineteenth and twenty-first centuries notwithstanding, marriage remains a robust institution and a central part of our society. Many insisted that the rising demand for divorce in the nineteenth century was a symptom of society's decline, and yet marital exit also paved the way for remarriage.[58] A shift in underlying morals caused divorce to be viewed as better than adultery, and a happy remarriage as at least arguably better than a miserable first marriage. Indeed, the very challenges to marriage themselves are a testament, in some ways, to its strength as an institution; divorce was "a sign that people valued marriage highly."[59]

Here is how Friedman closes the third edition of his famous compendium, *A History of American Law*:

> Marriage and family have changed enormously; but they have also survived, and will continue to survive. They are simply in the process of changing their definitions. Some sort of essential core of marriage remains – and remains vital. This core is commitment. Even the idea of gay marriage, which so horrifies traditional people, is a kind of homage to commitment, to stability, monogamy, and to a kind of old-fashioned nuclear family. Traditional marriage has lost its monopoly of legitimacy. But one of its key ideas: long-lasting, unselfish love, is very much still alive.[60]

REFERENCES

Baker v. State (1999). 744 A.2d 864 (Vt.).
Bishop, Joel Prentiss (1851). *Commentaries on the Law of Marriage and Divorce*. Boston: Little, Brown, and Company.
Blake, Nelson Manfred (1977). *The Road to Reno: A History of Divorce in the United States*. New York: MacMillan.
Chambers v. Ormiston (2007) 935 A. 2d (R.I.).
Degler, Carl N. (1980). *At Odds: Women and the Family in America from the Revolution to the Present*. New York: Oxford University Press.
Estin v. Estin (1948) 334 U.S. 541.
Foderaro, Lisa W. (2009). Gay New Yorkers Head to Greenwich for Weddings. *New York Times*, June 10.
Friedman, Lawrence M. (1984). Two Faces of Law, 1984 *Wis. L. Rev.* 13.
———. (1991). Crimes of Mobility, 43 *Stan. L. Rev.* 637.
———. (2002). *American Law in the 20th Century*. New Haven: Yale University Press.

[58] Hartog (2000); Grossman (2005).
[59] Friedman 39 (2004).
[60] Friedman 582 (2005).

_____. (2004). *Private Lives*. Cambridge, MA: Harvard University Press.

_____. (2005). *A History of American Law*. 3d edition. New York: Simon & Schuster.

Godfrey v. Spano (2009). 892 N.Y.S.2d 272.

Goodridge v. Department of Public Health (2003). 798 N.E.2d 941 (Mass.).

Griswold, Robert (1982). *Family and Divorce in California, 1850–1890: Victorian Illusions and Everyday Realities*. Albany: State University of New York Press.

Grossman, Joanna L. (2001). Separated Spouses, 53 *Stan. L. Rev.* 1613.

_____. (2004). Fear and Loathing in Massachusetts: Some Lessons from the History of Marriage and Divorce, 14 *Bost. Pub. Int. L.J.* 88.

_____. (2005). Resurrecting Comity: Revisiting the Problem of Non-Uniform Marriage Laws, *Or. L. Rev.* 101.

_____. (2009). *When Same-Sex Couples Adopt: Problems of Interstate Recognition*. Available at http://writ.news.findlaw.com/grossman/20090609.html.

Grossman, Joanna and McClain, Linda (2006). *"Desperate Feminist Wives": Does the Quest for Marital Equality Doom Marital Happiness*. Available at http://writ.findlaw.com/commentary/20060404_mcclain.html

Grossman, Joanna L. and Edward Stein (2009). *The State of the Same-Sex Union*. Available at http://writ.findlaw.com/grossman/20090721.html

Haddock v. Haddock (1906). 201 U.S. 581.

Hartog, Hendrik (2000). *Man and Wife in America: A History*. Cambridge, MA: Harvard University Press.

In re Adoption of X.X.G. and N.R.G. (2010). Fla. App. LEXIS 14014.

In re Marriage of J.B. and H.B. (2010) Tex. App. LEXIS 7127.

In re Marriage Cases (2008). 183 P.3d 384 (Cal.).

Jacob, Herbert (1988). *Silent Revolution: The Transformation of Divorce Law in the United States*. Chicago: University of Chicago Press.

Kerrigan v. Comm'r of Public Health (2008). 957 A.2d 407 (Conn.).

K.M. v. E.G. (2005). 117 P.3d 673 (Cal.).

Knight v. Schwarzenegger (2005). 128 Cal. App. 4th 14.

Koebke v. Bernardo Heights Country Club (2005). 115 P.3d 1212 (Cal.).

Lofton v. Sec'y Dep't of Children & Family Servs. (2004). 377 F.3d 1275 (11th Cir.) (en banc).

May, Elaine Tyler (1980). *Great Expectations: Marriage and Divorce in Post-Victorian America*. Chicago: University of Chicago Press.

McClain, Linda C. (2008). Red versus Blue (and Purple) States and the Same-Sex Marriage Debate: From Values Polarization to Common Ground, 77 *U.K. L. Rev.* 415.

O'Neill, William L. (1967). *Divorce in the Progressive Era*. New Haven: Yale University Press.

Perry v. Schwarzenegger (2010). 704 F. Supp. 2d. 921.

Proposition 8, § 2 (effective Nov. 5, 2008), codified in Cal. Const., Art. I § 7.5 (2009).

Simmons, Tavis and O'Connell, Martin (2003). *Married-Couple and Unmarried-Partner Households: 2000 (Census 2000 Special Reports)*. Washington, D.C.: U.S. Census Bureau.

Stein, Edward (2004). Past and Present Proposed Amendments to the United States Constitution Regarding Marriage, 82 *Wash. U. L Q.* 611.

Strauss v. Horton (2008). 207 P.3d 48 (Cal.).

Williams v. North Carolina (1942). 317 U.S. 287.

PART V

Facts from the Underground: Digging Legal History out of the Cellar

16

Historian in the Cellar

George Fisher

HISTORY FROM THE BOTTOM

Get out of the light, Lawrence Friedman has told legions of legal historians – *and go down to the cellar.* Upstairs you will find only the history of appellate law. There, in floodlit reading rooms, celestial metaphors take flight – those judicial luminaries and penumbral rights, that omnipresence in the sky. Yet the *law of society* – the law as we live it – is not the work of common law judges or even elected lawmakers, who leave their tracks above ground. It is instead the shadow of that law, cast across the streets and shops and tenements of town. The stuff of the law, and especially the criminal law, concerns those dredged up from the bottom of society. And they leave their tracks in the cellar.

So down he went. Three decades ago Lawrence Friedman and his student Robert Percival followed those tracks to the basements of Oakland. In that grubby port town, squatting across San Francisco Bay from its shimmering big sister, they started to dig. From precinct to courthouse to prison to press, they unearthed the shards of a whole system of criminal justice. Then they rebuilt it in living detail – the entire anatomy of crime detection and punishment in Alameda County between 1870 and 1910. They called their work *The Roots of Justice* – for it was in every sense a history from the bottom.

From the bottom, quite literally, it came. The richest among the authors' many sources were the Alameda Superior Court records they found moldering away in a basement storage room two floors beneath stately vaulted courtrooms. The basement room was untended, unkempt, alluring in its disarray. Lining its shelves and

I am grateful to Kate Wilko and Sonia Moss of Stanford's Crown Law Library for their diligence in hunting down many far-flung sources. Aidan McGlaze added research support and a steady editorial hand. Bob Percival kindly offered memories and guidance. An earlier version of this chapter appeared in the *Stanford Law Review* in 2006 and benefited from the meticulous editorial work of Daniel Korn, Alice Yuan, and many others.

cramming its drawers were thousands of case records. Within each was a story – a bundle of folded stock, bound with ribbon, hardened with time. Here Friedman and Percival spent long weeks, sometimes searching systematically, sometimes simply browsing – rooting around for justice's roots.

Of course there is no point in rooting around if you cannot smell a truffle. In dreary records of rote proceedings, the authors found the mushrooms amid the mold. They uncovered in one old drawer a group of bail bonds dating from 1898 to 1910. In their hands, the forgettable matter of bail threw light on the entire trial process. Defendants held for trial proved almost four times as likely to plead guilty and almost twice as likely to be convicted after trial as those released on bail, suggesting perhaps that defendants with bail money could hire better lawyers or, once released, could better aid their defense or that judges set lower bail when the state's case seemed weak. In another drawer they found a report on a judge's probation statistics for 1909 to 1910. Of forty-two defendants granted probation, forty-one had pled guilty – stark evidence that probation had morphed from a reforming regimen for young offenders into a bargaining chip in plea negotiations. Elsewhere the authors found the trial records of Clara Fallmer, a young woman charged with murdering a man who promised her marriage, but abandoned her pregnant. She killed in public view and had no defense at law. Yet her lawyers adorned her with a veil and violet bouquet and then rose in defense of injured womanhood, defining a genre in which the law played a small supporting role to the moral drama onstage.[1]

Such flash lit show trials, in which richly funded lawyers deployed all the stagecraft of justice, defined the third and highest tier of the Alameda County justice system. Yet for every full-dress morality play that drew throngs to one of the oak-paneled courtrooms of the upper tier, dozens or hundreds of unwatched proceedings clotted the lesser courts below. Friedman and Percival broke custom by lingering longer on these lower levels. In the middle tier, they found the routine felony courts – the scene of hasty trials, humdrum pleas, and harsh punishments – where the business of crime control was done. Still lower, in the first tier of the county's justice system, they uncovered the mechanisms of order and discipline. Here police rustled drunks and brawlers and raided brothels and opium dens.[2] Here the authors found the figures who interested them most – those who inhabited the nether regions near justice's roots. This then was the second way in which *Roots of Justice* was history from the bottom. For here were society's losers, the luckless and landless, social misfits who held neither jobs nor liquor well, caught in the system's maw.[3]

Roots of Justice was history from the bottom in yet a third way. Friedman and Percival spurned all pretense of grand overview: "Our study deals with what is, after all, one remote corner of civilization, a dot of land in the ocean of history."[4]

[1] Friedman and Percival 164–66; 180–1 & n. 79; 239–44 (1981).
[2] Id. at 311–15.
[3] Id. at 3, 113, 235, 317–18.
[4] Id. at 3.

They were working at the foundation level of historiography, contributing one brick among hundreds to the structure of an era. Such scholarly humility at the cost of massive effort deserves notice, yet somehow shuns it.

Here then is a tribute to a rare great work of legal history. But how to honor the humility of history from the bottom? Only one answer came to mind.

I went to Oakland.

THE OAKLAND COURTHOUSE

The Alameda County Courthouse sits at the flat edge of a windswept cityscape. Overly broad streets hint that planners foresaw a bustling business district choked with traffic. Yet the businesses never came, so the traffic never followed. Waiting at a corner for the light to halt streams of imaginary cars, visitors sense they have stumbled onto the deserted set of *War of the Worlds*.

The courthouse has the same sense of Soviet overbreadth. Anticipating the era of truck bombs by some sixty years, its Public Works Administration (PWA) engineers hoisted the whole structure atop a granite pedestal rising a floor above street level. Massive steps face down visitors on three sides, a solid wall on the fourth. Those who venture further find the main entrance locked, its granite portico deserted. In a genuine concession to terror threats, all visitors are funneled through a narrow side door into the metal detector beyond.

So the lobby comes as a shock – for if PWA had a grand style, this was it. Suddenly the ceiling flares up, and floor-to-sky windows cast glare onto tricolor terrazzo parquetry. Full brass crowns frame the elevators' lapis-blue doors. Their deco exuberance announces that *these* elevators *lead someplace*. On either side of the deserted main entrance rise wall murals in marble mosaic. One mural depicts the missionary settlement of America, the other its secular settlement by explorers and other Europeans. The murals supply a second reason to bar the front doors: Locking them against terrorists spared the county an ideological attack on its art.

Slipping through one of the brass and lapis doorways, I descended to the basement. Here the grandeur is happily gone. Along an empty concrete hallway haloed in fluorescence, only the stylized wall signs hint at the gaudy brilliance above. This was a place an archival digger could love. Yet where were the records? I had read and heard of their clammy storage room and knew where to look – but it was gone. A door advertises instead the offices of the courtroom interpreters, who appear some years since to have evicted Friedman's and Percival's finds.

The records turned out to be close by. They had been moved a flight higher to the office of the criminal court clerk, which abuts the gleaming lobby. I knew Lawrence Friedman would disapprove of the change. Today a visiting historian works not alone, but under the clerk's watchful eye; not in dim basement recesses, but in full natural light; and not with century-old paper that stains hands as proof of an honest day's work, but in a medium Friedman hates – microfilm.

I had come to Oakland hoping to untie one of Friedman's and Percival's old case records – to honor their book by continuing their work. Although I missed the chance to unravel old ribbon, I confess relief at finding the records on film. Technology has its virtues, and there is something to be said for push-button copying.

UNEARTHING A CASE

I decided to reopen the murder case of H. C. Cull. Friedman and Percival mentioned the case in a brief footnote when surveying the region's violent crime:

> Another alleged wife-killer, Hugh Cull (no. 634, 1885), was found not guilty. The main witness was the defendant's seven-year-old daughter; in Superior Court, on defense motion, the judge excluded her testimony.[5]

The outrage of disqualifying a seven-year-old who no doubt was competent to tell the horror of her mother's murder caught my eye. As an evidence teacher, I hoped to learn something of old competency notions. Yet the *Cull* case's lessons proved to have nothing to do with my fields of study and all to do with Friedman's.

The case began in Livermore. There Hugh Cull and his young wife, Jennie, moved with their four children at the beginning of September 1885.[6] We never learn why they moved. Newspaper reports describe Cull as a farmer or rancher and never say why, at age thirty-eight, this "ruddy and much tanned man" who "looks every inch a rancher" abandoned his ranch and took his family to town. Nor do they say why the Culls chose the district called Laddsville. Cull was reportedly "well to do," but Laddsville was not a place for the better sort.[7]

Nor was the Culls' new residence an elegant affair. A day after the killing, a prying reporter took an unauthorized tour. Worsening the home's location, deemed "gruesome in the extreme," was abundant proof of penury. The "one-story cottage of four rooms only" was "covered with worm-eaten paint." The reporter entered into "the sitting-room, so called," where a washstand stood on a threadbare rug. In one bedroom the three boys had slept. In a second, measuring just ten feet by twelve, the Culls had crammed two beds.[8] On one slept the parents. On the other slept their

---

[5] Id. at 137 n.1.

[6] Trial: 58–60 (Moore); Trial: 92 (Weymouth). I cite to the trial transcript in this way, with the witness's name in parentheses. One of the mysteries of this case is why there is a trial transcript at all. Because transcripts were expensive to produce, they typically exist only if a case was appealed and never if the defendant was acquitted, as was Hugh Cull. It is also a mystery why the transcript of Cull's trial ends, mid-page, in the middle of a witness's testimony on the second day of trial. The trial concluded at the end of the second day, so it appears that the transcript covers about 80% of the testimony. It also omits opening statements.

[7] *Tribune*, Sept. 14, 1885: 3; Sept. 15, 1885: 3.

[8] *Tribune*, Sept. 15, 1885: 3; Trial: 10 (Samuel Cull).

youngest child, Carrie, who lay awake on the night of September 13 to 14, two weeks after the move, when her father flew in a rage and strangled her mother to death.[9]

Carrie testified twice about her mother's death – first at the coroner's inquest on the day of the crime and again at the preliminary hearing almost two weeks later. Surviving sources suggest little variance between these accounts, although it appears Carrie spoke with less reserve and in more detail at the coroner's inquest. I begin here with the preliminary hearing, for the transcript of this courtroom proceeding supplies the best evidence of the girl's competency to testify at trial.

Her testimony began rockily. To the DA's opening question, "How old are you, little girl?" Carrie answered she was six, although all other sources, including her own aborted trial testimony the next summer, suggest she was seven at her mother's death.[10] Worse, Carrie denied knowing "what it is to take an oath, to swear in Court." Yet she did not hesitate again. She said she had been in school more than six months and could read. Then she recounted the horror of that Sunday night with astonishing composure:

Q. What was it that waked you?
A. They commenced to fight and that woke me up. . . .
Q. Now just tell what happened after you heard them fighting. . . .
A. Mamma got up and ran and sat down on a box of apples; and then Papa jumped up and ran right after her. She jumped on my bed then, and Papa was right on top of her.
Q. Now what did he do to her when she was on your bed?
A. He was choking her.
Q. What did she do?
A. She just went awful. She went like she was choking awful; made an awful noise. . . . Then she went and lay down on her own bed and hollered for me: "Oh Carry, oh Carry;" Kind of sadly, awful.
Q. Was that before he choked her?
A. No, that was after he choked her, and then he got her back on the bed and she never said another word. . . .
Q. After your fat[h]er let go your mother, did she speak or say any word after that?
A. No, I told him to "stop, stop" and he said "that is all right, that is all right, that is all right" three times right straight along.
Q. Well, did your mother ever speak or say anything after that?
A. No, not another word.[11]

---

[9] Prelim.: 3 (Carry Cull). The reporter who transcribed the preliminary hearing rendered the girl's name "Carry." Other sources, including the trial transcript, call her "Carrie."
[10] Prelim.: 2 (Carry Cull); *Tribune*, Sept. 14, 1885: 3; Trial: 2 (Carrie Cull).
[11] Prelim: 2–5 (Carry Cull).

When Carrie had finished, the defense counsel objected to her testimony "on the ground that she . . . did not understand the nature of an oath." The prosecutor's response – "[t]he witness is competent [if] she can note occurrences properly and relate them truly afterwards" – tracked the relevant statute, which excluded witnesses under age ten only when they "appear incapable of receiving just impressions of the facts respecting which they are examined, or of relating them truly."[12] The prosecutor could have added that although the leading case required that child witnesses have "sufficient instruction to appreciate the nature and obligation of an oath," the case also suggested that the trial judge could instruct witnesses on the subject.[13] In any event the magistrate overruled the defendant's objection without comment. Then, after hearing from Carrie's oldest brother, who told how their father raced off after the murder, and from a neighbor who described abrasions he saw on Mrs. Cull's lifeless neck, the magistrate duly held the defendant to answer for murder.[14]

At this juncture, the story of Jennie Cull's death seemed brutally clear: Hugh Cull had murdered his wife in a rage. He was not merely a murderer but a monster, for he had killed his little girl's mother before her eyes. Jennie Cull was a tragic victim – young (just twenty-eight), pretty (the papers said), and faultless but for her choice of mate.[15] She deserved better than this brooding tyrant who housed her in squalor and snuffed out her life.

The press eagerly reported this tidy version of events with its clean moral fault lines. Explaining that Cull had killed his wife "in the Presence of a Child," the *Oakland Tribune* ran the story under large block letters: "A LIVERMORE THUG." The sobriquet stuck. The next day the paper reported that "crowds assembled to get a look at the 'Thug.'" A few days later it referred to "the Livermore thug, who strangled his wife to death."[16] Nor did the *Tribune* shrink from rendering legal judgment. Cull was from the very start "The Murderer," the term unhedged by a squeamish "alleged."[17] Public sentiment readily followed the *Tribune*'s lead. The paper hinted that a Livermore lynch mob had been gathering until the sheriff moved the prisoner to Oakland. Even then, one of the spectators who met Cull's train after his preliminary hearing "carried a coil of rope, with a suggestive noose dangling from the end of it."[18]

Had the press and public maintained this flat-hued moral outrage throughout the case, they might have responded more indignantly when, almost a year after the crime, the trial judge deemed Carrie Cull incompetent to testify about the killing

---

[12] Prelim.: 5; Calif. Civ. Pro. Code § 1880(2) (1883); Cal. Pen. Code § 1321 (1885).
[13] *People v. Bernal*, 10 Cal. 66, 67 (1858).
[14] Prelim.: 5–7 (Sammy Cull); Prelim.: 8–9 (Allen).
[15] *Call*, Sept. 15, 1885: 1; *Examiner*, Sept. 15, 1885: 2.
[16] *Tribune*, Sept. 14, 1885: 3; Sept. 15, 1885: 3; Sept. 19, 1885: 4.
[17] *Tribune*, Sept. 14, 1885: 3.
[18] *Tribune*, Sept. 15, 1885: 3; Sept. 28, 1885: 3.

only she had seen.[19] Carrie arrived at trial "a sweet, sad-faced little thing," the *Tribune* wrote, whose "wee fingers twisted a tiny handkerchief with which she occasionally wiped the tears from her eyes." She was then eight and had been living since the crime with her father's brother Curgus.[20] We never learn whether Carrie's memory of the fateful night had faded in the intervening year, for the trial judge cut off her testimony before she got that far.

Unmistakably there were signs she had slipped. She no longer attended school, she said, and no longer could read. She still could not say "what it is to be sworn," nor did she know the number of minutes in an hour, hours in a day, or months in a year. Evidently her Uncle Curgus had neglected her education. The *Tribune* may have been right that to Carrie, "all these solemn proceedings are an enigma."[21]

Or perhaps *no* witness could have survived the trial judge's peculiar test of Carrie's competency. On learning that Carrie had gone to live with her uncle after her mother's death, the judge tested her memory of the trip to her new home:

Q. Who drove the buggy?
A. My uncle. . . .
Q. Was anybody else with you?
A. My aunt Lizzie.
Q. What did she say to you?
A. She didn't say much of anything.
Q. Do you know what she said?
A. No sir.
Q. Don't you remember what she said?
A. No sir.
Q. Do you remember what your uncle said?
A. No sir. He didn't say anything. . . .
Q. Whom did you meet [on the road]?
A. I don't know.
Q. Don't you remember whom you met?
A. No sir.[22]

This was a cheap lawyer's trick. It traded on the absurdity of testing a child's memory of a singularly memorable event by quizzing her about pointless adult blather on the day after the horror.

The upshot of the trial judge's refusal to let Carrie testify was this: The defendant won acquittal in part because of the trauma his crime inflicted. He did not merely strangle his wife, but did so in front of his young daughter, scarring her mind and abandoning her to her uncle's indifferent care. Carrie predictably failed to thrive in

[19] Trial: 38.
[20] *Tribune*, Aug. 10, 1886: 3; Trial: 2 (Carrie Cull); Prelim.: 3 (Carry Cull).
[21] Trial: 2–5 (Carrie Cull); *Tribune*, Aug. 10, 1886: 3.
[22] Trial: 6–7 (Carrie Cull).

the year after her mother's death; perhaps she even regressed. So the awful events
that tore apart her life denied her a role in bringing her mother's killer to justice.

All this should have spurred outrage. Yet by the time the *Cull* case reached trial
in August 1886, the press's (and maybe the public's) moral measure of the matter
had changed.

SHIFTING MORAL SANDS

Rumors of Jennie Cull's Unfaithfulness

Even early on there were hints the case was not so simple. First was the question
of motive. Viewed close up, the killing appears entirely unforewarned. On Saturday
the Culls had gone to a skating rink. On Sunday evening the parents attended
church, where Cull, considered "a devout religious man," was a regular attendant
and substantial giver. After returning home with his wife, Cull led the family in
prayer – reportedly his custom – and they retired.[23] Between that moment and the
killing several hours later, all is silence. Neither Carrie nor her older brothers could
say what drove their father over the edge. Perhaps the parents fell to quarreling. Or
perhaps Cull killed without quarreling, being suddenly overcome with resentment
at past injuries.

News accounts speculated about the nature of such past injuries. "The cause of
the trouble seems to be that Cull has thought for a long time that his wife was untrue
to him," the *Tribune* wrote the day of the crime. Even the defendant's brother called
him "unordinarily jealous of his wife." Yet having aired these rumors, the *Tribune*
demurely withheld judgment: "Whether there was any ground for the jealousy is
not known here."[24] The next day, the paper again first teased and then primly
retreated: "Rumors thick and fast are flying about Livermore in regard to alleged
stories of infidelity upon the part of the woman." Yet from "good authority . . . it is
now understood that the report grew out of" a misunderstanding. A strange man *had*
been visiting the old Cull ranch, but he "was visiting a servant girl in the employ of
Cull, and not Mrs. Cull."[25]

Alongside rumors of Jennie Cull's infidelity was speculation about Hugh Cull's
deep mental instability. One day after the killing, the *Tribune* reported townspeople's
view "that Cull had for years been insane, owing to a belief that his wife was untrue
to him." Indeed Cull seemed to be playing the lunatic's part. "From melancholy
he returns to mania," the paper wrote of his behavior in the hours and days after
his arrest. "It was during one of his fits of despondency that he made the remark
that he did not care to live." Then there were the slash marks across Cull's chest,

---

[23] *Call*, Sept. 15, 1885: 1; *Tribune*, Sept. 15, 1885: 3; Trial: 95 (Winning).
[24] *Tribune*, Sept. 14, 1885: 3.
[25] *Tribune*, Sept. 15, 1885: 3.

penetrating to his ribs and still bleeding the day after the crime. If Cull carved the marks himself, as he claimed, it was not his last suicide attempt. In jail shortly after his arrest, when the constable left him briefly alone, Cull "tried to beat his brains out by hitting his head against the door."[26]

None of this would surprise Lawrence Friedman. Rumors of a wife's infidelity were common features of mid- and late-nineteenth-century murder cases, as were contrived symptoms of a husband's insanity. As Friedman explains in his 2004 book, *Private Lives*, men charged with killing their wives' paramours often appealed to the "unwritten law" of the age, which deemed a man's defense of the sexual purity of his home sufficient cause for murder. Jurors, almost always male, understood the unwritten law and needed little coaching to apply it. Because defense counsel could not openly invoke this lawless doctrine, they instead claimed temporary insanity as the legal "fig leaf covering . . . nakedly biased" appeals to chivalric honor.[27] Victorian norms of sexual morality sometimes also forgave women accused of murdering the men who stole their honor. Recall Friedman's and Percival's account of young Clara Fallmer, charged in 1897 with killing her lover. Fallmer's claim that the man promised her marriage and then left her with child was not a legal excuse for murder. "But the case was tried in front of a jury, not the draftsmen of the code."[28]

Clara Fallmer's prosecutor, A. A. Moore Jr., should not have been surprised at her playing a woman betrayed. Moore's own father, Albert A. Moore, had represented Hugh Cull eleven years earlier and had appealed to the same Victorian moral code in Cull's defense. At that time, as Friedman and Percival reported, the elder Moore was one of the most prominent lawyers in the county. The announcement days after the killing that Cull had hired him was itself news.[29] Nor did Albert A. Moore come cheap. One paper grumbled that the Cull family had paid a huge $900 retainer (at a time when superior court judges earned $4,000 per year) "for the purpose of giving the people unequal justice in the case of H. C. Cull."[30]

In his opening statement at Cull's trial, Moore appealed as directly as he could to the unwritten law. As the *Tribune* recalled the scene, he neatly channeled rumors of Jennie Cull's infidelity – otherwise both irrelevant and hearsay – through Hugh Cull's claim of insanity:

> Mr. Moore earnestly disclaimed all approval of insanity pleas as a general rule, considering them simply cloaks for crime, but in this case the facts were plain and the circumstances so conclusive that he felt no hesitation in presenting the evidence as he found it. . . . As a matter of course, Mrs. Cull's fidelity or infidelity to her husband did not enter into the question, [yet] it was proper to show if her conduct produced such an effect upon his mind as to cause the commission of the

[26] *Tribune*, Sept. 15, 1885: 3; Sept. 18, 1885: 3; Trial: 39, 42 (Fitzgerald).
[27] (Friedman 30–1 (2004).
[28] Friedman and Percival 240 (1981).
[29] Id. at 65, 243; Shuck 899–900 (1901); *Tribune*, Sept. 18, 1885: 3.
[30] *Argus*, Oct. 10, 1885: 2 (citing Livermore *Review*); Friedman and Percival 48 (1981).

act with which he stands charged. They proposed to show that Cull loved his wife; that rumors of

HER UNFAITHFULNESS

To him were current.... These things drove him to such a frenzy that he even attempted his own life, and he still bears the wounds on his breast where he tried to kill himself with a knife. It was certainly his intention to end his life with hers.[31]

Eloquent – and sly – as Moore's statement may have been, a hard road lay ahead. Cull's case was not after all a classic application of the unwritten law. For Cull had killed not his wife's paramour, but his wife – a response to adultery that fit less comfortably within Victorian notions of chivalry. Still, Moore had better material than did most lawyers who appealed to the unwritten law. *His* client could claim evidence of insanity from *before* the alleged murder. Moreover, his client had unusually good evidence of his wife's infidelity.

Hugh Cull's Insanity

It is not certain how long before the crime Cull first showed signs of instability. Newspaper accounts suggest a trigger was Jennie Cull's departure from their home about three months before her death. For reasons never explained, she and two of her four children went to her father's home in Kentucky, only to return about three weeks before the killing.[32] At trial Moore offered a train of witnesses to tell of Cull's conduct in his wife's long absence. Almost all described a man obsessed – with either his consuming love for his wife or his suspicions of her or his dread of a vaporous "conspiracy." Cull assured one witness that "he was haunted by a mob that was to take his life" and another that "there was a conspiracy on the part of some fifty or a hundred residents of the valley to take his life." The latter witness added the telling detail, significant later, that Cull's conspiracy was "headed, as I understood him to say, by this man Donnelly."[33]

Obsessive jealousy, however, was not insanity, even when mixed with paranoia. Yet Attorney Moore had better evidence. He proceeded to offer three markers of Cull's insanity that might have moved even ardent skeptics. First was Cull's brief commitment. Several weeks before the killing, Cull's brother William had brought him to see a physician often consulted for sanity determinations in court proceedings. The doctor testified that on examining Cull, he judged "that it was not safe to allow the man to go by himself.... [H]e was of unsound mind, most decidedly so." The doctor recommended a week's confinement at the county jail for treatment and safekeeping. When, at the end of the week's stay, the doctor advised asylum

[31] *Tribune*, Aug. 11, 1886: 3.
[32] *Tribune*, Sept. 14, 1885: 3; *Call*, Sept. 15, 1885: 1; *Examiner*, Sept. 15, 1885: 2.
[33] Trial: 85, 88 (Weymouth); Trial: 45, 54 (Bellamy).

confinement, Cull's family balked. Apparently believing "there was some stigma attached to going to the Asylum," they took Cull home.[34]

Second was the bizarre evidence offered by Cull's pastor of an overnight visit the defendant made to the pastor's home during Jennie Cull's absence. Although the surviving trial transcript unfortunately ends before the minister's testimony, the *Tribune* captured his account vividly:

> One night Cull stayed at witness' house and slept in a room with witness' three boys. During the night witness was disturbed by one of the most
>
> HIDEOUS SCREAMS
>
> He ever heard from a human being, and when [the pastor] rushed into the room he found Cull holding one of the boys down in bed and choking him. When he was torn from his victim, he said he thought the conspirators were after him to kill him.

Naturally distressed, the minister wrote Jennie Cull in Kentucky and warned her not to come home. When she returned anyway, he told her "it would be dangerous for her to live with [Cull] alone."[35]

Finally there was little Carrie Cull's description of her father's acts immediately after he strangled his wife. At the preliminary hearing Carrie testified that Cull "tried to hang himself with a rope on the bedstead." At the coroner's inquest, as reported in the *Tribune*, she spoke in more detail: "Papa then tied a rope around his neck and fastened it to the bed-post, and lay down and pulled back. I told him to stop or he would hurt himself. He then got up."[36] True, Carrie offered no such testimony at trial, for Attorney Moore had succeeded in excluding her evidence. Moore nonetheless sought testimony about the rope from at least two other witnesses, one of whom – the acting coroner – saw it on the morning of the crime hanging from Cull's bedpost. "There was a kind of slip-noose in one end," he said, "and this other end was hung over the bedpost."[37]

The capstone of Moore's case was evidence not of Hugh Cull's insanity, but of Jennie Cull's infidelity. Moore withheld it almost until the end. Under the heading, "THE AFFIDAVITS," the *Tribune* recounted the dramatic moment:

> H. S. Cull, the brother of the prisoner, then took the stand and told how he had read a certain paper to his brother, and from that time on Cull exhibited signs of insanity. The paper was the affidavit of several persons at Brentwood in regard to the infidelity of Mrs. Cull.[38]

---

[34] Trial: 77–9 (Barber).
[35] *Tribune*, Aug. 11, 1886: 3.
[36] Prelim.: 4 (Carry Cull); *Tribune*, Sept. 14, 1885: 3.
[37] Trial: 31, 33 (Graham); *see also* Trial: 23–4 (Allen); *Tribune*, Sept. 15, 1885: 3.
[38] *Tribune*, Aug. 11, 1886: 3.

Although the surviving trial transcript ends before this testimony, the Brentwood affidavits themselves survive full-form in the microfilmed trial record. They bear close study.

All three affidavits are dated June 9, 1885 – about three months before Jennie Cull's death. All were notarized, all written in the same apparently professional hand, and all signed in Brentwood, a community about thirty miles north of Pleasanton, where Cull and his family then lived on his ranch. All three bore on the events of April 21 or 22, 1885, when two guests arrived at John Jones's Brentwood hotel. According to Mary Jones, the visitors "engaged a room for the night – and they occupied together room No 11 – and in the morning following they left together" (Jones Aff.). A Brentwood butcher who boarded in the adjoining room and eyed the newcomers suspiciously – for there seemed "something wrong about them" – was "considerably annoyed" during the night "by their apparently being upon a kind of a Lark" (Marble Aff.). A neighboring blacksmith who stabled the couple's horse and buggy for the night complained that the man called in the morning for the horse and buggy "and left town – the Stable Bill unpaid" (Graber Aff.).

Who were these rambunctious scofflaws? Although she did not say how she knew, Mary Jones identified them as "Mrs Jennie Cull of Pleasanton" and "a Gentleman." The butcher ventured no identification. The blacksmith dealt only with the man, who identified himself as "Mike Donelly" of Pleasanton. Five days later the blacksmith saw the couple's horse and buggy about seven miles away at the Odd Fellows Picnic in Stewartville. On inquiry, he learned "it belonged to *Mrs Cull*."

How these affidavits came to be is hardly clear. The *Tribune*'s summary of Cull's brother's testimony reported only that "[t]hese three affidavits were obtained by H. S. Cull, who went [to Brentwood] especially for that purpose."[39] Nothing suggests how H. S. Cull learned of the Brentwood events. Yet it seems likely his meddlesome errand explains the *Tribune*'s remark a day after the killing: "it is hinted that one of the brothers of the strangler gave material aid in fomenting the fatal trouble between the man and his wife."[40]

Whatever their provenance, the affidavits had the effect Attorney Moore desired. So confident was Moore of their force that he sat down without making a closing argument. After ten minutes' deliberation, the jury acquitted.[41] Although at least one newspaper reported that the acquittal was "on the ground that [Cull] was mentally irresponsible," the actual verdict slip, signed by the jury foreman, reads simply "not guilty."[42] The consequence in either event was Cull's freedom. Even before trial began, he had been discharged as cured by the Stockton Insane Asylum, where

39 *Tribune*, Aug. 11, 1886: 3.
40 *Tribune*, Sept. 15, 1885: 3.
41 *Chronicle*, Aug. 12, 1886: 8; *Examiner*, Aug. 12, 1886: 2.
42 *Examiner*, Aug. 12, 1886: 2; Verdict Slip.

he was committed after killing his wife. Barely two weeks after his acquittal, the Livermore *Herald* noted Cull's return to town.[43]

And so the moral tables of the trial had turned. Hugh C. Cull, the "Livermore Thug," who murdered a good and patient wife before their child's eyes, now was the victim of her infidelity. Here was a man "CRAZED BY LOVE," declared the *Tribune*'s closing headline on the case. Here were "The Vagaries of a Diseased Mind."[44]

LOOK TO THE LAW

Somehow the pieces of Moore's morality tale did not fit. Consider first the Brentwood couple's stable bill. Here was a woman married to a high-strung and highly possessive man on an escapade with someone else. Discretion surely was their watchword. Why would such a couple *assure* the blacksmith's notice by absconding on their stable keep? Had they been traveling in the man's buggy, they might have taken that chance. Yet they were traveling in the lady's, and apparently it was quite recognizable.

For that matter, they might have kept quieter at night. That is, they acted as if *trying* to be noticed. If *that* was true, the whole Brentwood sex frolic was a fraud.

Yet whose fraud? At first the suspicion arises that Hugh Cull was more deeply evil than first imagined – that one brother took him to a doctor and arranged for his token jail commitment to lay the stonework for an insanity defense, and another brother went to Brentwood to collect affidavits after paying Donnelly and a friend to pass themselves off as Jennie Cull and a beau on a tear.

That cannot be right. Nobody *plots* an insanity defense. First of all, even in Cull's day, there was no guarantee a jury would look kindly on a man who killed his wife, however unhinged he was and however unfaithful she may have been. Then there is the year in custody that Hugh Cull presumably spent waiting to mount his insanity defense – not to mention the small fortune his family paid for that defense. And think of the little girl. Even if a man were so deranged as to plan to kill his wife before their daughter's eyes, why would he risk it? Carrie was a plucky little girl and would have cut quite a figure as a witness, with her wee fingers twisting her tiny handkerchief and wiping tears from her eyes. What if the trial judge had not so pliantly found, against the evidence, that she could not perceive facts justly or relate them truly? Then the jury might have heard Carrie say how she "told him to 'stop, stop,' and he said 'that is all right, that is all right, that is all right'" and went right on choking her mother to death. A lot of good Cull's insanity defense would have done him then.

No. The sexcapade in Brentwood *was* a fraud. Yet it was not Hugh Cull's fraud: It was Jennie's.

[43] *Call*, Aug. 12, 1886: 3; *Tribune*, Sept. 3, 1886: 1 (citing Livermore *Herald*, Aug. 26, 1886).
[44] *Tribune*, Aug. 11, 1886: 3.

Only scattered hints of the truth intrude into the trial record. That is not surprising. Albert Moore knew his best trial strategy was to paint Cull as a man driven to distraction by his wife's infidelity. Arguing that Cull was driven to distraction by his wife's *feigned* infidelity would have been a far more complicated matter. Still, here and there a witness's stray remark unsettled Moore's carefully cropped picture of a man betrayed.

Among the many witnesses Moore called to describe Cull's altered behavior in the weeks and months before the killing was G. W. Langon, a Livermore lawyer. According to the *Tribune*, Langon testified that "Cull had acted strangely different during the last few times that [Langon] had seen him." Langon elaborated: "*[I]t seemed that Cull was afraid that his wife was trying to obtain a divorce from him and that she was working with a man named Donnelly and a girl that was working for him*"[45] (emphasis added).

Out of nowhere and for the first time came this word *divorce*. The possibility that Jennie Cull planned to sue for divorce could explain why Hugh Cull consulted Attorney Langon in the first place. Cull's distress about a possible divorce also could explain a second stray remark in the trial record, uttered by Samuel Sellers, a Livermore merchant whom Moore called on the matter of Cull's insanity. The *Tribune* supplied the only surviving record of this testimony:

> [Sellers] testified that one day Cull, about three weeks before the killing, came to him and asked to have an attachment issued against him as he wished to pay his honest debts, and that some enemies were going to burn his house that night.[46]

Moore surely hoped the jury would attend to the last part of these remarks, for Cull's fear of a violent conspiracy was one component of his insanity defense. The former statement was less helpful – and harder to explain. Why would a man who hoped to pay his honest debts not simply pay them? Why would *any* man ask that a creditor attach his property?

One possibility is that Cull, fearing a divorce action and a claim for community property, aimed to shrink his wife's take by draining the common pool. The same motive may have lain behind Cull's otherwise unexplained move from his ranch to the little house in Laddsville. The family left the ranch about two weeks before the killing. Sellers said he spoke with Cull about three weeks before the killing – or about the time Jennie Cull returned home from her long stint in Kentucky.

Yet how could a woman's feigned adultery help win her a divorce? Surely the law of divorce was not then so liberal as to grant a woman a divorce on evidence of her own unfaithfulness. On the contrary, the California Civil Code required the party

---

[45] *Tribune*, Aug. 11, 1886: 3. It appears that the *Tribune* misspelled attorney George W. Langan's name. Drummond 4 (2008).

[46] *Tribune*, Aug. 11, 1886: 3.

suing for divorce to show the other spouse's fault – his adultery, extreme cruelty, desertion, neglect, intemperance, or crime.[47] So what was Jennie Cull up to?

Once again, Lawrence Friedman's writings supply essential clues. Starting with a 1976 collaboration with Robert Percival and extending through his more recent *Private Lives*, Friedman often has explored the use of sham liaisons in divorce actions. His prototypical fraud, in which a hapless bellhop invariably interrupted the red-handed husband and his red-faced date, bore one resemblance to Donnelly's charade in Brentwood: In each case the participants took pains to assure discovery.[48] In other ways, the imagined case of *Cull v. Cull* would have looked quite unlike the far larger contingent of contrived divorces that Friedman helped expose to the world.

For Friedman has told of *collusive* divorces. They worked because one spouse faked sex while the other filed suit – a tactic many used to win amicable splits in days before no-fault divorce. Yet one cannot collude alone, and there is no evidence that Hugh Cull sought to divorce Jennie. On the contrary, he obsessed about his slipping control over her and perhaps worried about his reputation at church. Even when partners did collude, Friedman reports it was almost never the woman who shammed the tryst, but almost always the man.[49] For as a Missouri court wrote in 1895, "What destroys the standing of the one in all the walks of life has no effect whatever on the standing for truth of the other."[50] Even men apparently preferred other accusations to adultery. Friedman writes that although wives often alleged adultery in New York, where adultery was the sole ground for divorce, they rarely did so in California, where extreme cruelty, desertion, and neglect also sufficed and proved far more popular.[51]

Here Friedman offers a fundamental insight: When seeking to explain the behavior of spouses seeking divorce, look first to the governing law. Indeed the missing link in the *Cull* case lies in the reporters of the California Supreme Court. Consider first *Powelson v. Powelson*, decided in 1863. Seeking divorce on grounds of cruel treatment, Mrs. Powelson alleged that her husband "was in the habit of using toward [her] the vilest and most abusive language, *falsely charging her with adulterous intercourse*" (emphasis added).[52] The lower court rejected her claim, concluding that only physical violence constituted extreme cruelty. "The better opinion, however, is opposed to this view," the California Supreme Court wrote, "and we think that any conduct sufficiently aggravated to produce ill-health or bodily pain, though operating primarily upon the mind only, should be regarded as legal cruelty." As for Mr. Powelson's specific conduct, the court declared in notably strong terms that "if

[47] Calif. Civ. Code §§ 92, 94, 130 (1885).
[48] Friedman 1512–15 (2000); Friedman and Percival 78–80 (1976).
[49] Friedman 1528–9 (2000).
[50] *State v. Sibley*, 131 Mo. 519, 532 (1895).
[51] Friedman 36 (2004); Friedman 1518–19 (2000).
[52] *Powelson v. Powelson*, 22 Cal. 359, 360–1 (1863).

any treatment short of physical violence can amount to legal cruelty, we regard [this] case as fully made out."[53] Seven years later, in 1870, the California legislature broadened the high court's holding by redefining "extreme cruelty" to include infliction of either "grievous bodily *or mental* suffering" (emphasis added).[54]

Now advance to *Haley v. Haley*, decided by the California Supreme Court on May 14, 1885, just a few weeks after Jennie Cull's supposed indiscretion in Brentwood and a few weeks before its apparent discovery by her brother-in-law H. S. Cull. The trial court had deemed Mr. Haley guilty of extreme cruelty based on his wife's claim "that *he had accused her of having committed adultery*, and that in consequence of such accusations her mental suffering was so great that . . . *she was obliged to leave his home and seek shelter elsewhere*" (emphasis added).[55] The California Supreme Court reversed this judgment – not, however, because it thought the wife's allegations insufficient. Rather the court held that the trial judge had acted on insufficient proof. Mr. Haley had accused his wife of adultery only in "conversations of a friendly and confidential character, sought by plaintiff's attorney with her knowledge, and with a view to settle matters between the parties." That is, Mrs. Haley's suit failed because she and her husband were colluding, arranging things so that "a divorce could be got with little expense, scandal, and notoriety." The California Supreme Court complained that there was no evidence Mr. Haley had spoken "with any wanton or cruel intent" and no evidence other than Mrs. Haley's say-so "of any accusations made by defendant before she left his house, nor that she left his house, or underwent any suffering in consequence of any such accusations."[56]

Mrs. Cull was not so negligent in her proof. Having heard this warning from the California Supreme Court, she (and presumably her lawyer) knew what they needed to prove extreme cruelty. They had to show that the defendant accused his wife falsely of adultery, that he did so in conversations that risked public notoriety, and that his accusations so pained Mrs. Cull that she left his house. Let us take these points in turn.

If indeed Mr. Donnelly "and a girl that was working for him" made the overnight ruckus in Brentwood, any accusation of adultery based on this episode was false. It is even possible that the young woman in question was Cull's own employee. Recall the *Tribune*'s report on the day after the killing that despite "thick and fast" rumors of Jennie Cull's infidelity, it was all a misunderstanding, for the strange man seen visiting the Cull ranch "was visiting a servant girl in the employ of Cull, and not Mrs. Cull." If Donnelly was working with Cull's servant, they may have made

---

[53] *Powelson*, 22 Cal. at 360–1 (1863). Robert Griswold reports that some lower California courts recognized false accusations of adultery as a species of cruelty in a husband as early as 1857. He describes many divorce actions between 1863 and 1888 in which women sued for divorce on this basis. Griswold 19, 72–4 (1982). Elsewhere Griswold addresses development of the doctrine nationally. 1 Griswold 136–38 (1986a); 2 Griswold 721, 724–31 (1986b).

[54] Act of March 12, 1870: 291.

[55] *Haley v. Haley*, 67 Cal. 24, 24 (1885).

[56] Id. at 25.

the trip to Brentwood in Jennie Cull's buggy – which would explain the Brentwood blacksmith's claim that when he next saw the buggy he had boarded for the night, he learned "it belonged to *Mrs Cull*." The servant's involvement in the scheme against Cull also could explain why Cull fantasized killing her. For among the witnesses produced by Attorney Moore to prove Cull's insanity was one who testified that Cull "didn't dare to go alone" to his ranch after he'd moved out because Cull "had an idea that the hired girl was dead in the house, and if he went alone, if he found her dead, it would be laid to him."[57]

Surely Jennie Cull could prove that her husband had made her alleged affair notorious. *Someone* started those "thick and fast" rumors the *Tribune* so piously debunked. H. S. Cull said at trial that he had collected the infamous Brentwood affidavits and read them to his brother. The defendant then helped spread the news. His doctor testified that about two months before the killing he met with Cull and the pastor of the church they both attended. Cull spoke (albeit doubtfully) of the rumors of his wife's infidelity. Then "he exhibited the proof spoken of here, I think, by some – some papers – affidavits, perhaps."[58] The pastor confirmed that while Jennie Cull was in Kentucky Cull "appeared to be trying to think his wife was true to him, but . . . named various instances where he believed [her] unfaithful to him."[59] A handyman who helped the Culls move into their Livermore home two weeks before the killing testified that the defendant fretted about his wife's fidelity: "[H]e said there was lots of talk about her, and so on, and talked about Mike Donnelly and her."[60] Cull even disclosed his suspicions to the press. On the day after the killing, a *Tribune* reporter asked Cull about his earlier, week-long stint in jail for psychiatric observation, which had commenced about six weeks before the crime: "'You know, Cull, when you was in here before you said your wife had gone off with another man.'" Perhaps regretting having spread such tales, Cull now backtracked: "'If I said she was off with another man before I don't remember it, and it was a mistake.'"[61]

Finally Jennie Cull could prove she fled her husband's home shortly after he began smearing her good name. H. S. Cull secured the Brentwood affidavits on June 9, 1885. He likely showed them immediately to his brother, and Hugh Cull likely raised a prompt (and perhaps violent) accusation against his wife. No source states precisely when Mrs. Cull fled for Kentucky with two of her four children. Yet on the day of the crime – September 14, 1885 – the *Tribune* reported she had left "[a]bout three months ago."[62] A natural inference from the evidence is that Jennie Cull left rather swiftly after her husband hurled his accusation and began spreading

---

[57] Trial: 85–6 (Weymouth).
[58] Trial: 44, 48–9, 51 (Bellamy).
[59] *Tribune*, Aug. 11, 1886: 3.
[60] Trial: 74 (Moore).
[61] *Tribune*, Sept. 15, 1885: 3.
[62] *Tribune*, Sept. 14, 1885: 3.

the slander. Even without knowledge of the affidavits, the San Francisco *Examiner* retold the story of Jennie Cull's departure in these terms on the day after the killing:

> Cull is an excitable, reckless man, given to brooding on alleged wrongs, and he some time since gained an idea that his wife was untrue to him. Despite her protestations he kept constantly abusing her, and about three months ago the woman left him and returned to her father . . . [in] Kentucky.[63]

For a moment one is tempted to wipe away all evidence of Jennie Cull's scheme and dismiss the all-too-clever notion that she plotted the Brentwood affair. Maybe Donnelly really *did* have an affair with the Culls' domestic helper. Perhaps they borrowed Jennie Cull's buggy on an overnight errand and took the chance for a romp. Perhaps H. S. Cull just happened to hear the rumors from Brentwood and was ready to think the worst. He collected the affidavits, his brother leveled the accusation, and Jennie, genuinely injured, fled their home, consulted a lawyer, and threatened divorce under the fortuitous doctrine of *Powelson* and *Haley*.

Perhaps so, but there is one decisive reason to think not. The trial witness who delivered the critical evidence of Jennie Cull's plot – "it seemed that Cull was afraid that his wife was trying to obtain a divorce from him and that she was working with a man named Donnelly and a girl that was working for him" – was a lawyer. It is possible that Cull consulted this lawyer seeking an escape from Jennie's trap, but the lawyer knew a good trap when he saw one. After all, Jennie Cull was not the first California woman who wished to divorce a man who wanted to stay married. Given the liberal terms of *Powelson* and *Haley*, other women (and their lawyers) may have lured their husbands into similar traps, prompting them to broadcast false allegations of adultery.

The kicker was this: Armed with what the California Supreme Court had declared in *Powelson* in 1863 to be virtually a prima facie case of mental cruelty, Jennie Cull was entitled not just to divorce. By taking her bait and spreading false news of her outing to Brentwood, Hugh Cull had made himself the offender under California divorce law. The code set out the consequences: "Where a divorce is granted for an offence of the husband, the court may compel him to provide for the maintenance of the children . . . and to make such suitable allowance to the wife for her support . . . as the court may deem just."[64] What is more, Cull was destined to lose more than half the couple's community property. For although courts typically split community property equally between divorcing spouses, when a divorce was on grounds of extreme cruelty, the code provided that "community property shall be assigned to the respective parties in such proportions as the court, from all the facts of the case, and the condition of the parties may deem just."[65] The California Supreme Court had ruled that the natural inference of this provision "is that . . . the injured party is to receive, as a general rule, more than one half of the property, and as much more

---

[63] *Examiner*, Sept. 15, 1885: 2.
[64] Calif. Civ. Code § 139 (1885).
[65] Calif. Civ. Code § 146 (1, 2) (1885).

as the Court shall deem just."[66] Still worse, even if Cull's ranch was his "separate property," its status as the family "homestead" empowered a court "to assign it for a limited period to the innocent party."[67]

Little wonder, then, that Cull asked a local merchant "to have an attachment issued against him as he wished to pay his honest debts" – for Cull preferred to pay money he owed over money the court wrung from him. Little wonder that he quit his ranch in favor of the probably rented shack in Laddsville – for he wished to shield the ranch from homestead status. And little wonder that his townspeople concluded Cull was deranged – for Cull, always unstable, had grown delirious with rage at having his jealousy turned against him, at being played for a chump.

A MULTILAYERED TALE

And so we have a morality tale in many layers. An obsessive and controlling husband drove his wife to seek divorce; a rigid, uncompassionate law demanded that she first prove his fault; and so she contrived a trap into which his own demons drove him. There followed his brooding and his rage – at his wife for deceiving him and at himself for being so easily deceived – and then his crime, her death, and their orphaned daughter's imposed silence.

Many-layered tales can make good history but bad trials. After telling of Clara Fallmer, whose lawyers displayed her with veil and violet bouquet but whom prosecutors painted a perjuring harlot, Friedman and Percival wrote that neither side could afford the simple truth – that Clara was neither waif nor wench, "but essentially a woman, with ordinary feelings and passions."[68] At Cull's trial, too, where the truth was not so simple, neither side could afford it. The prosecutor preferred a helpless Jennie who fled to her father over the true Jennie, however injured, who plotted for her freedom. Attorney Moore preferred a cuckolded Cull crazed by love over the true Cull, however crazed, who killed the wife who duped him. Seizing on the fortuitous affidavits, Moore converted faked adultery into fact and won for Cull his freedom.

And so we have a story, but not a moral. That is what we find amid the mold.

REFERENCES

Books and Articles

Drummond, Gary (2008). Livermore's Historic Legacy to Be Displayed, 39 (3) *Livermore Heritage Guild* 1.

Friedman, Lawrence M. (2000). A Dead Language: Divorce Law and Practice before No-Fault, 86 *Va. L. Rev.* 1497.

[66] *Eslinger v. Eslinger*, 47 Cal. 62, 64 (1873).
[67] Calif. Civ. Code § 146(4) (1885).
[68] Friedman and Percival 242 (1981).

_____. (2004). *Private Lives: Families, Individuals, and the Law*. Cambridge, MA: Harvard University Press.

Friedman, Lawrence M. and Robert V. Percival (1976). Who Sues for Divorce? From Fault through Fiction to Freedom, 5 *J.Legal Stud.* 61.

_____. (1981). *The Roots of Justice: Crime and Punishment in Alameda County, California 1870–1910*. Chapel Hill: University of North Carolina Press.

Griswold, Robert L. (1982). *Family and Divorce in California, 1850–1890*. Albany: State University of New York Press.

_____. (1986a). The Evolution of the Doctrine of Mental Cruelty in Victorian American Divorce, 1890–1900, 20 *J. Soc. Hist.* 127.

_____. (1986b). Law, Sex, Cruelty, and Divorce in Victorian America, 1840–1900, 38 *Am. Q.* 721.

Shuck, Oscar T, ed. (1901). *History of the Bench and Bar of California*. Los Angeles: Commercial Printing House.

Newspapers

Alameda Argus (Oct. 10, 1885): 2.

Oakland Tribune, "A Livermore Thug" (Sept. 14, 1885): 3.

Oakland Tribune, "The Livermore Horror" (Sept. 15, 1885): 3.

Oakland Tribune, "He Wants to Die" (Sept. 18, 1885): 3.

Oakland Tribune, "At the County Jail" (Sept. 19, 1885): 4.

Oakland Tribune, "Cull's Examination" (Sept. 28, 1885): 3.

Oakland Tribune, "Cull on Trial" (Aug. 10, 1886): 3.

Oakland Tribune, "Crazed by Love" (Aug. 11, 1886): 3.

Oakland Tribune, "The County: Livermore" (Sept. 3, 1886): 1.

San Francisco Morning Call, "Strangled to Death" (Sept. 15, 1885): 1.

San Francisco Morning Call, "Oakland News" (Aug. 12, 1886): 3.

San Francisco Chronicle, "Acquitted of Murder" (Aug. 12, 1886): 8.

San Francisco Daily Examiner, "A Farmer in Alameda County Murders His Wife" (Sept. 15, 1885): 2.

San Francisco Daily Examiner, "Oakland Items" (Aug. 12, 1886): 2.

Cases

People v. Bernal, 10 Cal. 66 (1858).

People v. H. C. Cull (Alameda County Superior Court, 1885, No. 634) (Trial Record & Transcript); *People v. H. C. Cull* (Murray Township Justice's Court, 1885, No. 1399) (Preliminary Hearing Transcript).

Eslinger v. Eslinger, 47 Cal. 62 (1873).

Haley v. Haley, 67 Cal. 24 (1885).

Powelson v. Powelson, 22 Cal. 359 (1863).

State v. Sibley, 131 Mo. 519 (1895).

Statutes

Act of March 12, 1870, ch. 188, 1869–70, Calif. Stat.: 291.

California Civil Code (1885): Chapter 2 (Divorce)

California Civil Procedure Code (1883): Chapter 2 (Witnesses).

California Penal Code (1885): Chapter 2 (Who May Be Witnesses in Criminal Actions)

17

The Discreet Charm of Inquisitorial Procedure

Judges and Lawyers in a Case of Lèse Majesté *in Late-Eighteenth-Century Venezuela*

Rogelio Pérez-Perdomo

On July, 13, 1797, the *regente* (presiding officer) of the *Real Audiencia de Caracas* (the highest court in the province and most important government council), Antonio López de Quintana, acting on a tip, apprehended the prosperous businessman Manuel Montesinos Rico, searched his house, and discovered the existence of a conspiracy meant to repudiate the power of the Spanish monarchy and to establish an independent republic in what is today Venezuela. By so doing, the *Audiencia* initiated the most politically significant judicial case in the history of colonial Venezuela.

Soon the *Audiencia* discovered that the conspiracy was quite broad in scope, especially in the cities of La Guaira and its surroundings, including Caracas. Its leaders were Manuel Gual and José María España, which is why this episode is known as *La Conspiración de Gual y España*. Both men were prosperous landlords. Gual was a retired army captain; España was the administrator of one of the church's estates and the judge (*corregidor*) of Macuto, a small city near La Guaira. Other important figures in the conspiracy were businessmen José and Manuel Montesinos Rico, engineer Patricio Ronán, the priests Tomás Sandoval and Juan Agustín González, and the lawyer Luis Tomás Peraza. Like Ronán and the Montesinos Rico brothers, several conspirators were peninsular Spaniards; others were "creoles," the term used for whites born and established in the province. There were also whites from lower social strata (*blancos de orilla*) and a good number of *pardos* (free, mixed-blood people). A large number of those involved were part of the ordinary militia and a specially well-trained militia, the veteran corps.

Among the plotters were also three peninsular Spaniards who had conspired earlier against the king in Madrid in 1796 and had been condemned and sent as prisoners to La Guaira fortress. One of them, Juan Bautista Picornell, seems to have

I thank Sonne Lemke for the English version and the comments to the text.

been one of the most important ideologists of the conspiracy,[1] even though Gual and España were also very knowledgeable about political ideas of the time and current with the situation in France and the United States, where there had been recent revolutions. The existence of these "prisoners of the state," as they were officially known, seems to have been important in giving additional strength to a preexisting conspiracy. The plotters helped these prisoners escape, and consequently in the judicial case, the investigations of the prisoners' escape and of the conspiracy are often intermingled.

The case's documents show the influence of current liberal and enlightened ideas on the plot's leaders and presumably on a good portion of their fellow conspirators and the people of the province. That is why the conspiracy's documents are of such interest for Venezuelan historians, who have given them due attention.[2] Unfortunately historians have not focused on the actions of the Bishop of Caracas whose help and intervention in the *Audiencia*'s investigation were very important. The criminal procedure and the actions of the lawyers also have not been analyzed. The purpose of this chapter is to examine these neglected topics and materials.

The first important element of this case is the extreme gravity of the crime. Conspiring against the king was a crime of *lesa majestad* (*lèse majesté*), as it is called in *Las Siete Partidas*, the great law book of the Spanish tradition that was still much read at that time.[3] This type of felony was later called treason and today is best known as a crime against state security. This translation into modern language does not capture the crime's enormous gravity. The king's power was believed to have come directly from God. Thus the crime of *lèse majesté* was a crime not only against the king but also against the divine order and religion.[4] Any participation in a crime of this sort was punishable by death and confiscation of one's property and placed a stigma on all male descendants.[5]

The procedural rules also were very different from those of the present. We call the procedure of that time "inquisitorial" because theoretically the role of the judge was to search for the truth. Actually, the judge was involved more in a search for evidence of guilt, and to this end, he was the chief protagonist in conducting the legal proceedings and reaching a verdict. Because the judge's role was so active, the prosecution and the defense had diminished importance compared to today. This chapter analyzes the role of the lawyers in the proceedings.

This case had a large number of defendants, adding to its importance. At the outset of the proceedings, twenty defendants were sent to Spain so that authorities there could decide what to do with them. In addition, fifty people were tried and thirty-three of them were found guilty, of whom six were given the death penalty.

---

[1] López (1997).
[2] García Chuecos (1949); López (1997); Grases (1997).
[3] The *Siete Partidas* are generally attributed to King Alfonso X of Castile, called "The Wise," who lived in the thirteenth century. The book was much read and used until the nineteenth century.
[4] Sbriccoli (1974).
[5] *Siete Partidas*, Partida 7a, Titles 1 and 2.

Their verdicts were pronounced in May and June 1799, less than two years after the proceedings began. Given the importance and the complexity of the crime and the number of people involved, this can be considered a very brief time. How was the justice system able to act so quickly despite the fact that there were no police at the time to pursue the investigation of the conspiracy? The entire state's apparatus was thin, to say the least, and it could not have provided strong support to the judicial investigation. Public power in general and the justice system in particular counted on the support and cooperation of social institutions. In this chapter, I analyze the political and social institutions that played a role in the proceedings and the principles and the rules guiding how they functioned.

This chapter places a legal case in specific historical circumstances, looking for the social and political context that can explain it. It was written in honor of Lawrence Friedman who has excelled in this approach to legal history. The work has benefited from access to the voluminous files of the proceedings, but its interest is not to narrate the incidents but rather to explain how justice was served in a case of such magnitude. For this purpose the chapter is divided into several sections. In the introduction I analyze the inquisitorial procedure both in terms of its principles and its application to this case. The central sections explore the role of the principal institutional actors: the judges, the bishop, and the lawyers. In the conclusion I address the theme of inquisitorial procedure and its various incarnations in Venezuelan history.

THE INQUISITORIAL PROCEDURE

Venezuelan judicial procedure has a very ancient foundation. *Las Siete Partidas*, especially in the third and seventh *partidas*, which regulated legal proceedings, was written in the thirteenth century. The *Novísima Recopilación de las Leyes de España* of 1805 (Book XIII, Title XXXII) retained the central features of these regulations.[6] Nevertheless, the procedure is better described in the works for professional practice, such as those of Fernández de Herrera Villarroel (1704), Villadiego Vascuñana y Montoya (1766), Castillo de Bovadilla (1704), and Miguel Sanz (1774), which surely were the most immediate sources of information for the *Audiencia* judges.

According to this traditional literature there were two ways in which to initiate a judicial criminal procedure: (1) by accusation or denunciation by a party or (2) by investigation or inquisition by a judge. As expected, the role of the judge varied depending on how a case was initiated. In *Las Siete Partidas* the primary way was by means of an accusation, with very limited power granted to the judge. The inquisition was restricted to certain kinds of cases. Beginning in the sixteenth century, the situation reversed, and the inquisition became the principal form of criminal

---

[6] The *Novísima Recopilación de las Leyes de España* was published after the conspiracy and trial, but it did not intend to innovate but rather to compile the existing legislation. It is thus a good indication on what was considered officially in force in Spain and the colonies in the early nineteenth century.

procedure. Once a crime was committed, a judge would take over the investigation, given total discretion in how he obtained information about the crime, and then reached a verdict.[7]

In the inquisitorial trial the judge searched for the truth of what actually happened. For that purpose he might use several methods of collecting evidence, most commonly through witnesses and the confession of the presumed perpetrator. The relative weight of these sources of evidence was regulated. The preference was clearly for the confession, which was considered a more reliable proof than witness testimony.[8]

Once a judge had the suspect's name, he would detain and interrogate him. As a general rule, the suspect was kept in prison, so he could be at the judge's disposal for interrogation as frequently as he wished. To obtain the confession of those under suspicion, the judge could use torture. The kind, the occasion, and the intensity of the torture were regulated, but for some very serious crimes, such as those of *lèse majesté*, the judge could use torture that went beyond the regulations (or "exquisite" torture).[9]

The inquisitorial procedure underwent significant development in the ecclesiastic courts, especially in those of the *Santo Oficio*, which were known for that reason as the Inquisition Courts. Yet the procedures in the regular criminal courts were very similar.[10] More than the always elusive truth, the judges looked for evidence of guilt that allowed the suspect to be condemned.

The proceedings were written down so that there would be a record of everything that had occurred.[11] In the initial investigation phase, the reason the suspect had been detained was kept from him. Therefore his lawyer had no chance of knowing the reasons for his client's detention, nor did he have access to the records of the proceedings. In the second phase, called plenary, the suspect was informed of the crime for which he was being investigated and was allowed to defend himself, eventually with the representation or counseling of a lawyer. Nevertheless, during this phase, the judge's role remained the same; he continued his inquiry and could very well condemn the suspect for a crime other than that signaled by the prosecutor, if evidence surfaced during his investigation.

The *fiscal* (a law-trained officer and member of the court) represented the king's interests and was supposed to keep him informed of what went on. He could make specific charges asking for specific punishments, if he deemed it useful, but doing so did not limit the power of the judge to continue his investigation. The *fiscal* also could participate in the judge's deliberations.

---

[7] Alonso Romero (1979); Tomás y Valiente (1969); Heras Santos (1991).
[8] Gacto Fernández (1997); Esmein (1882).
[9] Gacto Fernández (1997); Tomás y Valiente (1973).
[10] Tomás y Valiente, (1982); Alonso Romero (1979).
[11] *Novísima*, book XII, title XXXII, Law III (1805).

For many crimes the penalty was death, but in practice there were not many executions because judges had considerable discretion in imposing penalties. For common crimes, justice was lenient.[12] The condemned person's property was confiscated, or in cases in which he was deemed to be only partially responsible for the crime, he could pay the cost of the judicial proceedings. By the eighteenth century the inquisitorial system was already subject to criticism in Spain as well as the rest of Europe. Among these criticisms were that the remuneration of the judges depended partially on the conviction rate, which served as an obvious incentive to find suspects guilty.

The investigation of the rebellion plot began on July 13, 1797, and the *Audiencia* soon developed a very intense level of activity. By January 1798, all of the suspects had been interrogated, and the ministers of the *Audiencia* felt that they had acquired a complete understanding of the case; thus the investigative phase was concluded. The files do not show any use of torture, but those implicated in the crime had to swear on a cross under God to tell the truth. They were frequently reminded of that oath and pressured to confess in the terms desired by the *Audiencia*.

On January 12, 1798, the *Audiencia* formally addressed the issue of procedure and the opening of the plenary phase. In contrast to other decisions, for which no legal justification appears, for this issue the *Audiencia* extensively quoted the applicable law. *La Real Pragmática* of 04–17-1770 prescribed that for crimes that caused popular disorder, ordinary criminal procedure should be followed and evidence from the accused should be admitted. This *Pragmática* (Articles 17 and 19) established that judges would not be allowed any discretion in these cases.[13] It was applicable in America under the *Real Cédula* of 02–19-1775, which established that "the loyal vassals were to be treated with the softness and benignancy usual in the royal government."[14]

Rather than following the procedures thus prescribed, the *Audiencia* improvised special procedures for these cases. The prescribed procedure required the designation of lawyers to defend the prisoners. The lawyers would then study the proceedings and be allowed time to formulate their defenses. At that point, each defendant would be allowed to call witnesses or present other pieces of evidence, and this process would likely take more than the 180 days that were legally allowed. The *Audiencia* felt that this delay would give the impression that the detainees were innocent and that they were being held out of the judges' cruelty. Therefore the *Audiencia* decided that the *relator*, the judge or clerk who analyzed the evidence and wrote a draft of the decision), should begin an overview of the case assisted by three lawyers (Francisco Espejo, Antonio Martínez de Fuentes, and José Bernabé Díaz) who had been present for the defendants' confessions and statements. These three lawyers

---

[12] Pérez-Perdomo (1987; 1994).
[13] *Pragmática*, quoted in Archivo General de Indias (AGI), Legajo 432, page 315.
[14] *Real Cédula* quoted in AGI, Legajo 432, page 316.

were to report whatever evidence they had found in favor of those prisoners within the limits of the law. This procedure had the advantage of simultaneously informing the *fiscal* and the judges, and it was consistent with the spirit of the law and the best interest of the monarchy and the state.[15] The *fiscal* agreed to this way of proceeding, with the exception of reducing his time for reviewing the case.

In sum, the only time that the *Audiencia* cited the applicable law, it decided not to follow the rules. It argued that acting according to the simplified procedure, as it was known at the time, was more consonant with the spirit of the law and provided a better service to the king than would following the applicable law.

It is interesting to see how the judges separated themselves so expressly from the established procedure. They were probably correct that doing so would better serve the king, and they could consequently expect recognition from him and the *Consejo de Indias*, the highest court and government council for the American territories. They did not adopt formalist legalism; on the contrary, they opted for a material rationality.

Depriving the defendants of their right to a defense was not seen as a problem. It is notable that the judges considered it appropriate for the lawyers who had previously performed prosecutorial roles to shift to the defense role, without even consulting with the defendants. This is conceivable only if the judges believed that they were collectively searching for the truth. In this conception of criminal procedure, the lawyers' defense and the accusation roles are superfluous.

The *fiscal* took some months to read the files. The documents show that on April 1798 the *vista* – the revision of the dossier – was initiated. The documents do not include information on which charges were filed by the *fiscal* or what was discussed. It does not appear that the three lawyers supposedly in charge of the defense actually provided any defense. A letter from the priest José Agustín González could be considered a defense argument or brief. Ramón Peraza, brother of the lawyer Dr. Luis Tomás Peraza, also wrote a letter that could be viewed as a brief, in which he pointed out the good character and career prospects of the defendant. Of course, as the accusations were not known, these defense arguments were shots in the dark.

It is likely that the departure from the case of *Capitán General* Carbonell and the deaths of *fiscal* Julián Díaz de Saravia (on December 30, 1797) and judge Juan Nepomuceno de Pedrosa (on June 7, 1798) delayed the process. The *vista* lasted another year when, at the end of April 1799, information provided by the slave Rafael España permitted the capture of his owner, José María España. After his capture, España was transferred to Caracas to be intensively interrogated over several days. He was then condemned to be drawn and quartered, and his head and dismembered body were put on display in the public places that he had frequented.[16] On June 1, 1799, a decision was made regarding the other defendants. Five were

---

[15] *Acta del Acuerdo* of January 12, 1798, AGI, Legajo 432, 319.
[16] Decision of May 6, 1799, AGI Sevilla, *Audiencia de Caracas*, Legajo 433.

condemned to a death similar to that of España; thirty-three were condemned to various punishments, which included perpetual exile and confiscation of assets, or fines and payment for procedural costs. The most frequent punishment was six to eight years of hard labor, in ankle chains, to be served in fortresses in Havana or in Florida.

Who were these judges who so readily discovered the threads of the conspiracy? How did they arrive at such harsh decisions?

La Audiencia

At that time, the *Real Audiencia de Caracas* was the highest court in Venezuela and was also the most powerful government institution. Only the king and the council through which he acted for his American colonies, the *Consejo de Indias*, ranked higher. The *Audiencia* was headed by the highest ranking political authority, in this case, the governor of the province of Caracas and *capitán general* of Venezuela. Thus the governor, *capitán general*, and president of the *Audiencia* held all the power, with the exception of ecclesiastical power, which was in the hands of the bishop of Caracas.

The president of the *Audiencia* had no legal training, but rather had a military career. For this reason, when the *Audiencia* acted as a law court it had to be presided over by the *regente*. Because of its political importance, however, the two *capitanes generales* who were successively involved in this conspiracy case presided over meetings of the *Audiencia*. Even Capitán General Guevara Vasconcelos was present at the interrogation of José María España, one of the principal leaders of the conspiracy.

Responsibility for daily management of the *Audiencia* was given to the *regente*. The other judges were called *oidores*. The *regente*, *oidores*, and *fiscal* were required to have a law degree. There were very detailed rules for their conduct. They could not be "sons of the country," which meant that they could not have been born in the territory under the jurisdiction of the *Audiencia*. They could not marry or acquire real estate in this territory, nor could their sons marry a woman from this territory. They could not attend funerals or marriages, unless they were accompanied by the entire membership of the *Audiencia*. These rules were intended to keep these functionaries of the crown as distant as possible from local life and to prevent their involvement with possible litigants. In practice these rules resulted in a preference for the selection of peninsular Spaniards. The *Audiencia* of Caracas functioned from 1786 to 1810, when the independence movement began. During this twenty-four-year period a total of sixteen ministers were appointed, of whom eleven were peninsular Spaniards and five were from other countries of Spanish America. Among the five, only two had significant service; the rest were appointed late in the life of the *Audiencia*, when Spain was losing control of the country.[17]

---

[17] López Bohórquez 86 (1998).

Although there is no doubt that the members of the *Audiencia* were part of the Spanish Empire's bureaucratic elite, as López Bohórquez points out, the role of *oidor* or *regente* in Caracas was not the ending point of a career.[18] The prohibition against marriage and acquiring properties in the territory of the *Audiencia* also served the purpose of ensuring that these individuals would be available to serve the king anywhere. Caracas was very far from being an important city. The ministers of the *Audiencia* surely hoped to keep moving upward in their careers. For example, they expected to go on to the *Audiencia* of Mexico or of Lima or, finally, to the *Consejo de Indias* in Madrid.

A typical case is that of *Regente* Antonio López de Quintana, a key character in the repression of the conspiracy. He was born in Spain in 1741 and was licensed in law in Salamanca in 1761. In his early years he taught in Salamanca and pursued an intellectual vocation. He became a lawyer, then an *oidor honorario* and provisional *fiscal* in the Canary Islands, and then *fiscal* in the *Audiencia de la Contratación* in Seville (1779) and *fiscal* in the *Audiencia* of Guadalajara (1783). He was the first *regente* of the *Audiencia* of Caracas (1786–1809), and later he became a minister in the *Consejo de Indias* (1809). He died in 1814.

Another example is that of Francisco Ignacio Cortines, born in Seville where he completed his studies and taught in the university. First he served as lieutenant governor and *Auditor de Guerra* in Venezuela (1779), and then he was named *oidor* in 1786. He was promoted to *regente* of the *Audiencia de Quito* (1801) and then *Consejero de Indias* (1809), but he died before knowing about this latter appointment.

The *Audiencia* could also have *oidores honorarios*, who were designated by the *Audiencia* itself and who were not subject to the same restrictions that applied to regular members. The *Audiencia* of Caracas had two *oidores honorarios*: Antonio Fernández de León, named Marqués de Casa León in 1810, and Francisco Espejo. The first was born and graduated in law in Spain, but had considerable properties in Venezuela as a result of marriage. He was already an *oidor honorario* by the time of the conspiracy. Espejo was promoted later, mostly because of his contribution to the completion of the plotters' files. The *oidores honorarios* did not receive a salary and did not have specific obligations, but they could be present at deliberations. They had to be treated as regular *oidores* in ceremonial acts. Their designation also ensured that they would be named as interim members in case of a vacancy on the *Audiencia*. Espejo was interim *fiscal* from 1808 until independence.

The *Audiencia* was especially active in this conspiracy case. As soon as he learned from an informant that there were plans to replace the monarchy with a republic in which all would be equal, *Regente* López de Quintana decided to apprehend the accused, Manuel Montesinos Rico. He did so at 11:30 at night after having waited for hours for Montesinos to return home. Once Montesinos was apprehended, the *regente* and his team proceeded to search his home, where they found subversive

[18] Id.

documents. In the morning, during the meeting of the *Audiencia*, it was decided that the *oidor* Juan Nepomuceno de Pedrosa was to complete the case investigation. Pedrosa was also the *Alcalde del Crimen*, the criminal judge of Caracas. As the initial interrogations indicated that there were participants in the plot in La Guaira and several other places, the *Audiencia* also agreed to name commissioners who would take charge of the investigation in those locations. The lawyer Francisco Espejo and the *oidor honorario* Antonio Fernández de León were the first to be commissioned. It is notable that the *Audiencia* preferred to send lawyers from Caracas as opposed to using local judges.

In spite of the regulations, the ministers of the *Audiencia* of Caracas had developed strong ties with local families and engaged in behavior that would still today be a matter of scandal.[19] Research has provided evidence of the various internal conflicts. In January 1796, one and a half years before the conspiracy case, the *capitán general* wrote a confidential letter to the king concerning the *Audiencia*. According to this letter, the *regente* López de Quintana was an intimate friend of the brothers Esteban and Antonio Fernández de León. They were both very rich landowners, and Esteban was *Intendente del Ejército y Real Hacienda*, which means he managed the country's finances. Antonio, an *oidor honorario*, was married to Josefa Carrera, a member of a wealthy and powerful family. This group had managed to control the other ministers of the *Audiencia* and other centers of power in the country.[20]

To investigate the complaints of the *capitán general* and of other prominent residents of Caracas, the *Consejo de Indias* ordered a *visita* (site visit), which exposed delays, irregularities, and corruption.[21] The relevant point here is that these delays of the *Audiencia* and the division among the ministers and the *capitán general* were not evident in the conspiracy case that is the subject of this chapter.

THE BISHOP: IDEOLOGY, POLICING, AND INDULGENCE

The bishop of the Diocese of Caracas, Don Fray Juan Antonio de la Virgen María y Viana, was the most important church authority of the diocese, a religious jurisdiction that coincided with the jurisdiction of the *Audiencia* and the military jurisdiction of the *capitán general*. The bishops were appointed by the pope, at the suggestion of the king. Because there was no separation between church and state, the role was as political as it was religious: The bishop was politically important and independent from the *Audiencia* and the *capitán general*. In July 1797, Bishop Viana was spending some time in La Guaira (which offered warmer weather) and almost immediately received news of the conspiracy. He provided his complete cooperation. For example, in his letter to the *capitán general* of July 19, 1797, he indicated that he, "with

[19] Albornoz de López (1987).
[20] López Bohórquez 174 (1984).
[21] Albornoz de López (1987).

prudence and caution, has exercised the most intense effort in order to find whatever might lead to the discovery of the plot and the men involved in it" and immediately notified *Comisionado* Espejo concerning the people he should interrogate.[22]

The bishop's actions also had an important ideological dimension. The pastoral letter dated July 28, 1797, is a long document on the origins of the king's divine power. It argued that because God was the creator of humankind and supreme author of political power, the enemies of the king were also enemies of God and of religion. The letter contained many quotes from the Bible, St. Paul, St. Peter, St. John, St. Augustine, St. Ambrose, and Tertullian. Only human weakness, inspired by the devil, could deny those truths. Clearly, it was the hand of God, with the intercession of the Virgin of Carmen (the plot was discovered on her feast day) that allowed for the plot to be discovered. The letter ends by encouraging collaboration with the authorities in any possible way, including sacrificing one's life, to overcome this terrible evil.[23]

The bishop also suggested to the *Audiencia* that it should pardon those who spontaneously presented themselves to confess their participation and name their accomplices. The *Audiencia* did so on August 8, 1797,[24] and many of the plotters heeded the call and confessed. Alarmed at the size of the conspiracy, the *Audiencia* subsequently reneged on its offer. The first plotters who responded to the call were imprisoned and sent to Spain to be dealt with by the *Consejo de Indias*. Their properties were confiscated. Those who came forward later were arrested and handled in the same manner as other implicated in the plot.

On April 7, 1798, the bishop wrote to the king, on behalf of the Prince of Peace, asking for clemency for the defendants, acknowledging that they had committed a terrible crime and deserved the harshest punishments. The bishop informed the *Audiencia* of his letter, in which he wrote,

> They have presented to us as repentant men, crying and sobbing profusely. Their sweet sons, their wives and families, who have nothing to do with the crime, lament their disgraces, sob their unhappiness and their grief over their inability to erase the stain of infamy from their distinguished birth. The public come to me asking pity and compassion because they see the misery and the degradation these men suffer in their prisons; and along with them, their sons, wives and families. The accomplices are related by blood to distinguished families. A carefully considered pardon, far from opening the door to other similar or worse crimes, would provide opportunities for virtue, and those pardoned will give unequivocal proof of loyalty and fidelity to the King and country, blessing the benignity of the government. It appears that the public good, which is the supreme law of the State, demands the

---

[22] AGI Sevilla, Legajo 427, folio 17.
[23] AGI, Legajo 427, n 2, folio 42.
[24] AGI, Legajo 434, n 1, folio 1.

beneficence and mercy of the Sovereign. As father of the country and of his vassals and with his infinite power, he could use clemency, overlook the just rigor of his laws and sign with his sweet hands the pardon of so many unhappy people.[25]

The bishop's actions show the close relationship between religion and politics, the church and the *Audiencia*. There is no doubt that the church's apparatus was at the service of the *Audiencia* and that the bishop was an important contributor to the suppression of the plot. Yet his actions reflected a different ethos from that of the judges. The bishop was inclined toward forgiveness, in accordance with the moral theology of Catholicism, which emphasizes the importance of acknowledging guilt and of repentance as the path to forgiveness. The dynamics of the judicial process were entirely different because the judicial process was developed with the goal of punishing misbehavior.

THE LAWYERS

The local lawyers had a college education that was available only to white men of "old Catholic" families, thus excluding women and those of African, Jewish, and Moorish origin; Indians; and mixed-race people. Their university studies were complemented by an internship and a very elaborate ritual to become a lawyer. Lawyers worked with very significant limitations: Most cases could be litigated without their participation. In the courts of commerce and mining, lawyers' presence was forbidden, and any material that appeared to be written by a lawyer was immediately discarded. In criminal cases, in which the judges were supposed to search for the truth, the presence of the lawyers was considered unnecessary, as we have seen. With the exception of the members of the *Audiencia*, one was not required to be a lawyer to become a judge (*corregidor* or *teniente de justicia*). Because they lacked legal training but were required to decide according to law, judges and other public officials, such as *intendentes* (financial officials), consuls, and mayors, required the assistance of lawyers.[26] By performing important public functions or providing advice to high-ranking officials, the lawyers often gained honor, power, and income.[27]

In this case, acting as advisors and *comisionados* of the *Audiencia* were lawyers Francisco Espejo, Antonio Fernández de León, José Bernabé Díaz, José Antonio Felipe Borges, Tomás Hernández de Sanabria, José María Ramirez, Domingo Gómez de Rus, Ignacio Javier Uzelay, Antonio Martínez de Fuentes, and José Gimón. Miguel José Sanz and Juan Germán Roscio also collaborated to a lesser extent. The lawyers played an important part in detaining suspects, visiting and searching houses, and interrogating suspects and witnesses. However, there were

---

[25] AGI, Legajo 432, n 86, folio 57.
[26] Pérez-Perdomo (1981, 2003).
[27] Uribe-Urán (2000); Pérez-Perdomo (2003).

no lawyers defending suspects in the case. It would likely not have been easy for the defendants to find any lawyer. Soon after the plot was discovered, the *Colegio de Abogados* (bar association) issued a statement that lawyers as "vassals of honor, and with vehemence, courage and activity in these critical times, in the city, the countryside, the forests, ports and other places where they could be destined, were ready to fight until victory and until the last drop of blood" was spilled.[28] The lawyers went out to patrol the city in armed groups.

Because of their distinguished status in the eyes of the king and the *Audiencia*, it was natural that the lawyers had no inclination to act as defenders of those who were presumably implicated in crimes of *lèse majesté*. Their honor, their career, and their eventual incomes depended too much on their loyalty to the monarch to be risked on defending a rebel or conspirator against the king. Even in a less serious case, the Nueva Grenadian (Columbian) Antonio Nariño did not find any lawyers willing to defend him after he printed a Spanish translation of the French *Declaration of the Rights of Man*.[29]

Only one lawyer, Luis Tomás Peraza, participated as a conspirator. The documentation shows that he had a close relationship to Manuel Gual, with whom he shared a place in Caracas, and he probably had knowledge of the conspiracy without being one of its leaders. Various historians have expressed surprise that lawyers collaborated so actively in the repression of the plot given that they would subsequently support autonomy, independence, and the constitution of a republic in 1810.[30] Antonio Fernández de León was one of the leaders of what has been known as the *Conspiración de los Mantuanos* in 1808.[31] In 1810 and 1811 he, Espejo, Sanz, Roscio, and other lawyers who collaborated with the repression were among the leaders of the republican movement.

Some of these lawyers were clearly opportunists. Fernández de León is known in Venezuelan history for his ability to hold important positions on both sides of the independence conflict, until his luck ran out in 1821 and he ended up in exile, with his properties confiscated.[32] In constrast, Espejo, Sanz, and Roscio were very important and loyal leaders of the republican side. They greatly influenced the drafting of the constitution and of fundamental documents justifying independence. Espejo and Sanz died in 1814 and Roscio in 1821.

There is no reason to think that the lawyers were not sincerely monarchical in 1797. They considered themselves and were considered part of the *Audiencia*. As we have seen, their most important ideological and occupational connection was with the state and the *Audiencia*. They were educated in the principles of inquisitorial procedure. The enormous cruelty of the system may have shocked them, but they

---

[28] Public statement of the Colegio's board, quoted in Parra Márquez 132 (1973).
[29] Hernández de Alba (1958); Uribe-Urán (2000).
[30] García Chuecos (1949); Parra Márquez (1952; 1973).
[31] Quintero (2002).
[32] Briceño Iragorry (1954).

probably accepted it as a part of life. In 1808, the terrible political mistakes made by Carlos IV and Fernando VII resulted in Spain's falling into Napoleon's hands and set in motion the crisis leading to the independence movement. Venezuelan lawyers were likely familiar with the liberal and enlightened ideas of the late eighteenth century, but these ideas were surely perceived as too far from Spanish American realities. Spain's fall into the hands of Bonaparte in 1808 gave that literature a different significance.

The lawyers also had a personal interest in the autonomy of the provinces, which would provide them opportunities for more important roles in the control of their own country. José Bonaparte's lack of legitimacy as the king of Spain and the collaboration of the *Consejo de Indias* with the French provided the opportunity to declare this autonomy. The colonial authorities' rigidity in times of serious crisis fueled the movement toward independence. In the king's absence, the lawyers were forced to invent the Republic. However, acceptance of liberal and modern ideas was surely a slow process. The subtitle of Roscio's great book (1817), *Confessions of a Repentant Sinner*, was not simply a rhetorical artifice.

Francisco Espejo was perhaps the most obvious case of a lawyer whose position shifted in favor of independence. His able service as a representative of the *Audiencia* in 1797 and 1798 led him to become *oidor honorario* and, after that, provisory *fiscal*. In 1809, in his accusation against the French military men involved in a rebellion case, he showed a significant transformation by presenting his case with modern arguments,[33] but he clearly was on the monarchical side. He also opposed the *conspiración de los mantuanos* in 1808, but probably because he was on bad personal terms with the plotters, especially the Fernández de León brothers. By that time he had shifted to a policy favoring more autonomy. When the Spanish monarchy seemed lost, it is probable that giving the choice between accepting José Bonaparte as king or forming an independent state, he preferred the latter. In his defense in 1812 he alleged this.[34] Based on his behavior, we can conclude that his republicanism of 1810 was sincere and that he was surely still a republican in 1814 when the monarchical forces under Boves executed him. He was surely a repentant inquisitor, to paraphrase Roscio (1996).

Let us see what happened to the inquisitorial procedure after independence.

AFTER THE PAST

With independence came the enactment of a national or federal constitution as well as the constitutions of several of the states or provinces that make up Venezuela. These constitutions did not take effect at the time because war broke out relatively soon after, but they are very important as a means of understanding how the country's

---

[33] Parra Márquez (1954).
[34] Id.

founding fathers conceived the basis of state organization. Among these founders were a number of lawyers. The signers of the 1811 constitution included Juan Germán Roscio y José María Ramírez, who participated in the case of Gual and España. Francisco Espejo did not have a role in the federal constituent congress but had very important roles in the First Republic: He was part of the first triumvirate that held executive power. Espejo is credited as the primary drafter of the *Código Constitucional del Pueblo Soberano de Barcelona Colombiana* (Constitution of Barcelona Province, 1812).

Both the 1811 federal constitution and the 1812 Barcelona constitution closely followed the French declaration of rights and in general are based on liberal republican concepts of law and rights, in clear reaction against the inquisitorial system. Both declared the principle of equality before the law (article 3 of the Barcelona constitution and 154 of the federal), which was anathema to the Spanish regime. In addition to this and other general principles, the constitutions included very specific statements about criminal judicial procedure. Both constitutions established the principle of the presumption of innocence (articles 14 and 159, respectively). The federal constitution, in particular, spelled out these principles in detail. It decreed that all persons have the

> right to be informed of the reasons for the accusation made against them and to know its nature by confronting their accusers and witnesses again them and by producing other witnesses in their favor and whatever evidence is favorable to them . . . and none shall be compelled, nor forced in any circumstance to give testimony against themselves, nor their ancestors children, or relatives, up to the fourth degree by birth and second by marriage.[35]

Article 160 is in clear opposition to inquisitorial justice. Moreover, the federal constitution established trial by jury (161), the prohibition of cruel and unusual punishments (171), and the perpetual abolition of torture (173). Not even a sentence for treason against the state or other such crimes could bring infamy on the children and descendants of the criminal (175). The same articles were repeated in the Constitution of the Republic of Venezuela in 1830, which had a long life.

When we read these words we envision lawyers ready to dramatically shift the principles of judicial process from those in which they themselves had participated. Sadly, these statements did not extend beyond good intentions. During the great upheavals that shook Venezuela and nearly all the countries of Latin America in the nineteenth century, the inquisitorial process returned, although in a more moderate form, in the codes of criminal procedure that were developed in the region. There was too much fear of social disorder, too much preoccupation with state security for the judiciary to function in any other way.[36]

---

[35] Article 160. *Constitución Federal de los Estados Unidos de Venezuela*, 1811.
[36] Duce and Pérez-Perdomo (1999).

In today's Venezuela, the well-established regime's control over judges and prosecutors has resulted in a resurgence of inquisitorial forms in spite of the fact that the 1998 Code of Criminal Procedure removed all vestiges of inquisitorial procedure. Unfortunately this resurgence comes as no surprise: Even in countries with well-established rule of law and with long experience of accusatorial criminal procedures that guarantee the defense of the indicted, such as the United States, England, and France, the inquisitorial procedure has enjoyed a perverse resurgence. These developments raise the question of what forces sustain the inquisitorial procedure. The fight for rule of law and human rights has not ended.

REFERENCES

Albornoz de López, Teresa (1987). *La visita de Joaquín Mosquera y Figueroa a la Real Audiencia de Caracas (1804–1809): conflictos internos y corrupción en la administración de justicia.* Caracas: Academia Nacional de la Historia.

Alonso Romero, María Paz (1979). *Historia del proceso penal en Castilla (siglos XIII–XVIII).* Salamanca: Ediciones Universidad de Salamanca.

Briceño Iragorry (1954). *Casa León y su tiempo.* Caracas: Edime.

Castillo de Bovadilla, Jerónimo (1704). *Política para corregidores, y señores de vasallos, en tiempos de paz y de guerra, y para juezes eclesiásticos y seglares.* Amberes.

Duce, Mauricio and R. Pérez-Perdomo (1999). Seguridad ciudadana y reforma de la justicia penal en América Latina, *Boletín Mexicano de Derecho Comparado*, 102.

Esmein, Adhémar (1882). *Histoire de la procédure criminelle en France et spécialement de la procédure inquisitoire: depuis le XIIIe siècle a nos jours.* Paris: Larose et Forcel.

Fernández de Herrera Villarroel, Gerónimo (1719). *Práctica criminal.* Madrid.

Gacto Fernández, Enrique (1997). Observaciones jurídicas sobre el proceso inquisitorial, en A. Levaggi (coordinador), *La inquisición en Hispanoamérica. Estudios.* Buenos Aires: Universidad del Museo Social Argentino y Ediciones Ciudad Argentina.

García Chuecos, Héctor (1949). Estudio histórico crítico. Instituto Panamericano de Geografía e Historia: *Documentos relativos a la revolución de Gual y España, precedidos de un estudio histórico crítico del doctor Héctor García Chuecos.* Caracas.

Grases, Pedro (1997). *La conspiración de Gual y España y el ideario de la independencia.* Caracas: Academia Nacional de la Historia (Tercera edición).

Heras Santos, José Luís de las (1991). *La justicia penal de los Austrias en la Corona de Castilla.* Salamanca: Ediciones Universidad de Salamanca.

Hernández de Alba, Guillermo (1958). *El proceso de Nariño a la luz de documentos inéditos.* Bogatá: Editorial ABC.

Las Siete Partidas del muy noble Rey Don Alfonso el Sabio. Glosadas por Gregorio López (1844). Madrid: Compañía General de Impresores y Libreros del Reyno.

López, Casto Fulgencio (1997). *Juan Picornell y la conspiración de Gual y España.* Caracas: Academia Nacional de la Historia. (Segunda edición).

López Bohórquez, Alí Enrique (1984). *Los ministros de la Audiencia de Caracas, 1786–1810: caracterización de una elite burocrática del poder español en Venezuela.* Caracas: Academia Nacional de la Historia.

_____. (presentación y selección de textos) (1986). *La Real Audiencia de Caracas en la historiografía venezolana.* Caracas: Academia Nacional de la Historia.

_____. (1998). *La Real Audiencia de Caracas / Estudios*. Mérida: Universidad de los Andes.

Novísima Recopilación de las Leyes de España (1805). Madrid.

Parra Márquez, Héctor (1952). *Historia del Colegio de Abogados de Caracas*. Tomo Primero. Caracas: Imprenta Nacional.

_____. (1954). *El doctor Francisco Espejo. Ensayo biográfico*. Segunda edición. Caracas: Presidentes de Venezuela.

_____. (1973). *Historia del Colegio de Abogados de Caracas*. Tomo Segundo. Caracas: Colegio de Abogados del Distrito Federal.

Pérez-Perdomo, Rogelio (1981). *Los abogados en Venezuela*. Caracas: Monte Ávila.

_____. (1987). Teoria y práctica de la legislación en la temprana República (1821–1870). In A. Giuliana and N. Picardi (eds.): *Modelli di legislatore e scienza della legislatione*. Perugia: Edizione Scientifiche Italiane.

_____. (1994). Proceso penal y castigo. Tradición hispánica y cambios republicanos en Venezuela en la primera mitad del siglo XIX. In A. Giuliani and N. Picardi (eds.): *Modelli storici della procedura continentale*. Edizione Scientifiche Italiane. Perugia.

_____. (2003). *Los abogados de América Latina. Una introducción histórica*. Bogotá: Universidad Externado de Colombia.

Quintero, Inés (2002). *La conjura de los mantuanos: último acto de fidelidad a la monarquía española*. Caracas: Universidad Católica Andrés Bello.

Roscio, Juan Germán (1996). *El triunfo de la libertad sobre el despotismo o confesiones de un pecador arrepentido*. Caracas. Biblioteca Ayacucho (edición original 1817).

Sanz, Miguel C. (1774). *Modo y forma de instruir y sustanciar las causas criminales*. Valladolid.

Sbriccoli, Mario (1974). *Crimen laese maiestatis. Il problema del reato politico alle soglie della scienza penalistica moderna*. Milano: Giuffrè.

Tomás y Valiente, Francisco (1969). *El derecho penal de la monarquía absoluta (siglos XVI–XVII–XVIII)*. Madrid: Tecnos.

_____. (1973). *La tortura en España*. Barcelona: Estudios históricos.

_____. (1982). *Gobierno e instituciones de la España del Antiguo Régimen*. Madrid: Alianza.

Uribe-Urán, Víctor (2000). *Honorable lives: Lawyers, family, and politics in Colombia, 1780–1850*. Pittsburgh: University of Pittsburgh Press.

Villadiego Vascuñana y Montoya, Alonso de (1766). *Instrucción política y práctica judicial, conforme al estilo de los consejos, audiencias, tribunales de corte*. Madrid.

18

"Keep Negroes Out of Most Classes Where There Are a Large Number of Girls"

The Unseen Power of the Ku Klux Klan and Standardized Testing at The University of Texas, 1899–1999

Thomas D. Russell

I. ADMISSIONS

Nine days after Chief Justice Earl Warren issued the U.S. Supreme Court's 1954 opinion in *Brown v. Board of Education,* The University of Texas's Registrar and Dean of Admissions – a man named Henry Y. McCown – wrote to President Logan Wilson with a plan to "keep Negroes out of most classes where there are a large number of girls."[1]

II. SIMKINS

William Stewart Simkins – a University of Texas (UT) law professor from 1899 until his death in 1929 – and his brother Eldred James Simkins, a regent of The University of Texas from 1882 to 1896, organized the Ku Klux Klan in several Florida counties after the American Civil War.[2] The brothers Simkins were natives of

---

[1] *Brown v. Board of Education of Topeka,* 347 U.S. 483 (May 17, 1954); H[enry] Y. McCown, Registrar and Dean of Admissions, to President Logan Wilson, May 26, 1954, Chancellor's Office Records, Box 9, folder "Negroes," Dolph Briscoe Center for American History, The University of Texas at Austin (hereafter DBCAH).

[2] *The Handbook of Texas Online,* s.v. "Simkins, Eldred James," http://www.tshaonline.org/handbook/online/articles/SS/fsi11.html; s.v. "Simkins, William Stewart," http://www.tshaonline.org/handbook/online/articles/SS/fsi12.html (accessed March 22, 2010).

I thank Lawrence Friedman for being an excellent teacher, a great example, and a warm human being. It is a privilege to have been asked to participate in this volume.

I would also like to dedicate this work to the memory of two great scholars. John Hope Franklin (1915–2009), a teacher of mine for one semester at Stanford Law School, was a great historian and great American. I cherish the memory of visits to his home in North Carolina, where we talked about history and he gave me advice about orchids, among other things. Not quite a year before Professor Franklin's death, the world lost the greatest law librarian ever, Professor Roy M. Mersky (1925–2008). Professor Mersky was a good friend and supporter of my historical research during the decade that I was a member of the Texas faculty. Professors Franklin and Mersky were staunch advocates of civil rights, history, and scholarship throughout their lives.

South Carolina's Edgefield District, which also claims James Henry Hammond, "Pitchfork" Ben Tillman, and Strom Thurmond as native sons.[3] William Stewart Simkins attended the Citadel in Charleston, and he helped start the Civil War by relaying the order to fire on the "Star of the West," a vessel carrying provisions to Ft. Sumter. He entered the Confederate army as a lieutenant and by war's end held the rank of colonel. Until the end of his life, he was known as Colonel Simkins.[4]

When the war ended, Colonel Simkins and his brother Eldred traveled to Monticello, Florida, which is in Jefferson County about thirty miles east of Tallahassee.[5] In an article that he would later publish in the 1916 commencement edition of UT's alumni magazine, Colonel/Professor Simkins recounted that when he arrived in Florida in May 1865, he "found the negroes on the plantations, and while there was some suppressed excitement, there was no indication that they were going to assert their freedom by abandoning the plantations; there was no particular evidence of unrest."[6] He continued, "Our political peace lasted until the meeting of Congress in December, 1865, which was dominated by such men as Stephens, Sumner, and Wilson, all apostles of hate and one of whom at least had declared the Constitution of the United States 'a league with hell.'" With the transition to radical Reconstruction and "with the enforcement of their theory," Simkins related, "our troubles began."[7]

Colonel Simkins revealed to his readers that although the Freedman's Bureau "met under the guise of protecting the negroes from their former masters; it was in fact, a method of organizing the negroes as pliant tools of the Republican party." Simkins explained that the Freedman's Bureau "was also armed with powers that were intended to humiliate the South, enforce the anticipated Civil Rights laws, the germ of which was social equality." He complained that United States soldiers obeyed the orders of the Bureau to "assist in crushing the pride of the South by the elevation of the negro to political control." Simkins commented that General Sherman's incendiary march through the South was "not more blighting in its effect upon the people of the South."[8]

By 1868 – the year that the states ratified the Fourteenth Amendment – Colonel Simkins saw that "the negroes became bolder, incendiary harangues were heard everywhere, white women could not appear on the streets without escort, and

[3] *Id.* Orville Vernon Burton, *In My Father's House are Many Mansions: Family and Community in Edgefield, South Carolina* (Chapel Hill: University of North Carolina Press, 1985); Carol Bleser, ed., *The Hammonds of Redcliffe* (New York: Oxford University Press, 1981).

[4] "Simkins, William Stewart," vertical file, DBCAH. "Statement of Judge W.S. Simpkins, [*sic*] Univ. of Texas, Austin, Tex. In RE: FIRING OF THE FIRST GUN OF THE CIVIL WAR," (TS, May 24, 1920), William Stewart Simkins Collection, The Citadel Archives & Museum, Charleston, South Carolina.

[5] "Simkins, Eldred James" and "Simkins, William Stewart," *Handbook of Texas Online*; Robert Jones, "William Stewart Simkins," (TS, 1958) Rare Books and Special Collections, Tarlton Law Library, The University of Texas.

[6] W[illiam] S[tewart] Simkins, "Why the Ku Klux," 4 *The Alcalde* (June 1916): 735–48, 736.

[7] *Id.*

[8] *Id.*

domestic duties were performed with a ready pistol at hand."[9] He also observed, "Equal rights began to assume the form on insistence on social equality."[10] In his 6,700-word article for the alumni magazine – titled "Why the Ku Klux" – Professor Simkins explained that "to meet this saturnalia of crime and insolence; to suppress this volcano on which our women and children were nightly sleeping; . . . arose the "Invisible Empire."[11] He noted that "the Klan was composed of the best young men of the land, soldiers of the Southern army, many of them heroes in battle, and now as fearless in their duty as they had been in war." "Our mission," the Klansman said succinctly, "was the protection of our women and children."[12]

III. ADMISSIONS

The Texas Constitution of 1876 excluded African Americans from the educational institutions that whites attended. Article VII, Section 7 specified that "[s]eparate schools shall be provided for the white and colored children, and impartial provision shall be made for both."[13] Twenty years after the adoption of Texas's 1876 constitution, the U.S. Supreme Court ratified "equal but separate" accommodations for whites and African Americans aboard trains in Louisiana.[14] With the opinion in *Plessy v. Ferguson,* the Supreme Court endorsed cultural practices of racial segregation that had developed since the conclusion of the Civil War.[15]

The University of Texas opened in 1883.[16] Although the Texas Constitution specified separate education for "children," there seems to have been no question that at the university level, there would be no African American students in either the undergraduate or graduate schools.[17] However, Mexican American students – not

[9] *Id.*
[10] *Id.* at 740.
[11] *Id.*
[12] *Id.* at 741.
[13] Section 7, Article VI, Texas Constitution of 1876.
[14] *Plessy v. Ferguson,* 163 U.S. 537 (1896).
[15] C. Vann Woodward, *The Strange Career of Jim Crow,* 3d revised edition (New York: Oxford University Press, 1974); Michael J. Klarman, *From Jim Crow to Civil Rights: The Supreme Court and the Struggle for Racial Equality* (New York: Oxford University Press, 2004); Barbara Young Welke, *Recasting American Liberty: Gender, Race, Law, and the Railroad Revolution, 1865–1920* (New York: Cambridge University Press, 2001).
[16] Margaret Catherine Berry, *UT History 101: Highlights in the History of The University of Texas at Austin* (Austin: Eakin Press, 1997), 9.
[17] Section 14, Article 7, Texas Constitution of 1876 specified that "The Legislature shall also when deemed practicable, establish and provide for the maintenance of a College or Branch University for the instruction of the colored youths of the State, to be located by a vote of the people; provided, that no tax shall be levied, and no money appropriated out of the general revenue, either for this purpose or for the establishment and erection of the buildings of the University of Texas." Chancellor James P. Hart received from university attorney Scott Gaines in 1951 an analysis of the legal authorities supporting segregation in Texas education. Gaines concluded that "In so far [*sic*] as the public higher educational institutions of this state are concerned, there does not seem to be any express but only an implied requirement of law that separate education of negro students should be provided from those

considered "colored" for purposes of constitutional exclusion – were able to enroll at the university, and the first Mexican American student graduated in 1894.[18]

IV. SIMKINS

Colonel Simkins joined the UT faculty in 1899. In the early 1870s, the Simkins brothers had gone to Texas to practice law together, first in Corsicana and later in Dallas.[19] Two years before Colonel Simkins left his law practice to become Professor Simkins, both houses of the state legislature had passed a resolution concerning the political sympathies of the Texas faculty. The resolution, which originated in the House, first complained that

> there has been employed and included in the faculty of said University those who are out of touch and not in sympathy with the traditions of the South, but hold our traditions and our institutions in contempt and circulate and teach political heresies in place of the system of political economy that is cherished by our people.[20]

The Texas House of Representatives sent a committee over to investigate the heresies of the university professors. The committee questioned the president and two historians, George F. Garrison and David F. Houston. Professor Houston had apparently excited the controversy, and the legislative committee reported that it had "not had the time to make a critical examination of the book written by Professor Houston entitled 'A Study of Nullification in South Carolina,' but from a casual reading would pronounce it to be unacceptable from a Southern standpoint as setting forth principles contrary to Southern teachings." The committee members carefully questioned Professor Houston, a South Carolinian, who assured the members that he wrote the book before coming to Texas, did not use the book while teaching at Texas, and never referred to it.[21]

---

provided for white students." Scott Gaines to Chancellor James P. Hart, April 20, 1951, Chancellor's Office Records, Box 9, "Negroes," DBCAH.

[18] *Handbook of Texas Online*, s.v. "García, Manuel Marius," http:www.tshaonline.orghandbook onlinearticlesGGfga84.html (accessed March 22, 2010).

[19] The *Handbook of Texas Online* entry for Eldred James Simkins, *supra*, indicates that he and his brother went to Texas in 1871, and the entry for William Stewart Simkins says that he went to Texas in 1873.

[20] Resolution by Mr. Hensley, June 9, 1897, H.J., p. 110, 118 in *A Source Book Relating to the History of The University of Texas: Legislative, Legal, Bibliographical, and Statistical*, comp. H. Y. Benedict, University of Texas Bulletin, No. 1757: October 10, 1917 (Austin, 1917), 406.

[21] Committee Report of June 17, 1897, H.J., p. 191–2 in *A Source Book Relating to the History of The University of Texas*, 406–7; David F. Houston, *A Critical Study of Nullification in South Carolina* (New York: Longmans, Green, and Co., 1896). Professor Houston received a master's degree at Harvard, which may have been the problem. He never published another academic book and instead became an academic administrator serving first as the president of Texas Agricultural and Mechanical College (now Texas A&M University) and later, remarkably, as president of The University of Texas. *Handbook of Texas Online*, s.v. "Houston, David Franklin," http://www.tshaonline.org/handbook/online/articles/HH/fho70.html (accessed March 22, 2010).

Concerned about the propriety of the teaching at the university, the legislature solved the problem of the influence of anti-Southern heresies by

> requesting the regents of the University to exercise great care hereafter in selecting as members of the faculty only those who are known to be in sympathy with Southern political institutions, and further request them to cancel as soon as possible any existing contract with members of the faculty not so in sympathy.[22]

By hiring Colonel Simkins, the regents complied perfectly with the legislators' directive.

V. ADMISSIONS

Beginning in the 1930s, the National Association for the Advancement of Colored People (NAACP) and its Legal Defense Fund began a concerted attack on the constitutional support for Jim Crow segregation in the United States. In higher education, Charles Hamilton Houston, Thurgood Marshall, and other NAACP lawyers targeted the segregative practices of Texas and other states. For example, although states provided education in separate schools for their young white and African American students, at the level of university education – particularly graduate school – states might have nothing to offer African American students. Rather than allow African American graduate students to attend schools with white graduate students, and in place of establishing separate graduate schools for African Americans, some states shipped their African American students out of state to educate them.[23]

The NAACP's Legal Defense Fund lawyers challenged this interstate commerce in Negro students – and won. In 1938, with *Missouri ex rel Gaines v. Canada*, Charles Hamilton Houston was successful in convincing the U.S. Supreme Court to hold that states could not ship their African American students out of state for education. With a Supreme Court decision that said the states had to provide in-state education to African American students, Houston and Marshall then started bending the *equal* prong of the constitutional standard of separate but equal.[24]

Houston and Marshall focused their incremental strategy on graduate and professional schools – as opposed to elementary or secondary education. The Legal Defense Fund brought a series of important cases that historians would later see as stepping-stones to *Brown*. In Oklahoma, Marshall successfully fought the University

---

[22] Resolution by Mr. Hensley, in *A Source Book Relating to the History of The University of Texas*, 406. See also Joe B. Frantz, *The Forty-Acre Follies* (Austin: Texas Monthly Press, 1983), 3, 27–40.

[23] Jack Greenberg, *Crusaders in the Courts: How a Dedicated Band of Lawyers Fought for the Civil Rights Revolution* (New York: Basic Books, 1994); Mark V. Tushnet, *The NAACP's Legal Strategy against Segregated Education, 1925–1950* (Chapel Hill: University of North Carolina Press, 1987); Idem, *Making Civil Rights Law: Thurgood Marshall and the Supreme Court, 1936–1961* (New York: Oxford University Press, 1994).

[24] *State of Missouri ex rel Gaines v. Canada et al.*, 305 U.S. 337(1938); Tushnet, *The NAACP's Legal Strategy*, 70–81; Idem., *Thurgood Marshall*, 116–49.

of Oklahoma's refusal to admit Ida Sipuel to its law school because of her race. The university offered her no opportunity at all for legal education, not even education at a "separate but equal" facility. In a per curiam opinion, the Supreme Court held in 1948 that Oklahoma's refusal violated the Fourteenth Amendment.[25]

The Legal Defense Fund lawyers fought another battle in Oklahoma even as they started one in Texas. Two years after the *Sipuel* decision, the Supreme Court sustained the NAACP's challenge to the University of Oklahoma's decision to admit an African American student and then segregate him by seating him in a separate-though-connected anteroom during class. By educating him together with but separate from the white students, the university and state's lawyers argued that he was receiving education consistent with the constitutional requirements of separate but equal.[26] Chief Justice Vinson disagreed and held that McLaurin, "having been admitted to a state-supported graduate school, must receive the same treatment at the hands of the state as students of other races."[27]

On February 26, 1946, with the support of the NAACP, Heman Marion Sweatt applied for admission to The University of Texas School of Law. He was thirty-three years old at the time and worked for the Post Office. Sweatt, a Houston native, was the fourth of seven children.[28]

Sweatt's application to the university and subsequent litigation were part of the long-term strategy of the Legal Defense Fund. Sweatt had a strong, activist family background, and he himself had been involved with the NAACP for decades. Since early in 1945, the NAACP had been looking for the right plaintiff to file an application to The University of Texas. Although initially reluctant, Sweatt stepped into that position, applied, and later litigated, with the NAACP handling the legal work. As with Sipuel, Sweatt's struggle for admission to the university was not the fight of one person versus a single institution but instead was a struggle between institutions and communities.[29]

On the day that he applied to the university, Sweatt first met with an NAACP delegation at Samuel Huston College, a historically black college that is now part of Huston-Tillotson College. Together, they all went to the university, where they met with President Theophilus Painter and other university officials, including the registrar, E. J. Mathews. Sweatt and the NAACP group asked President Painter what the university was doing for African American Texans. Like other southern schools, UT had exported its African Americans for graduate education. Notwithstanding

---

[25] *Sipuel v. Board of Regents of University of Oklahoma*, 332 U.S. 631 (1948); Tushnet, *The NAACP's Legal Strategy*, 120–2; Lawrence M. Friedman, *American Law in the 20th Century* (New Haven: Yale University Press, 2002), 287.

[26] *McLaurin v. Oklahoma State Regents for Higher Education et al.*, 339 U.S. 637 (1950); Friedman, *American Law in the 20th Century*, 288.

[27] 339 U.S. at 642.

[28] See Gary M. Lavergne, *Before Brown: Heman Sweatt, Thurgood Marshall and the Long Road To Justice* (Austin: The University of Texas Press, 2010), 5–6, 10–11.

[29] Tushnet, *The NAACP's Legal Strategy*, 125–32.

the 1938 decision declaring this practice to be unconstitutional, President Painter explained to Sweatt and the NAACP delegation that exportation for education was all that was available for African Americans who were interested in graduate or professional school.[30]

However, Sweatt and his NAACP supporters were uninterested in this interstate transshipment of African American students: Sweatt insisted on applying to the university. The registrar, E. J. Mathews, boasted that he had no more "than the normal amount of prejudice against Negroes" and tried to talk Sweatt out of applying. However, Sweatt insisted and filed his application to the school of law.[31]

UT's President Painter then geared up the legal process. Painter asked for an opinion from the attorney general, Grover Sellers. In this request Painter noted that Sweatt was "duly qualified for admission into the Law School at The University of Texas, save and except for the fact that he is a negro."[32] Painter also noted that he could see that Sweatt's application was to be a test case, even though the NAACP representatives had denied this.

Attorney General Sellers advised that the university refuse to admit Sweatt. In his opinion, Sellers referred to "the wise and long-continued policy of segregation of races in educational institutions of this state."[33] Sellers noted that Sweatt could go to Prairie View University, an all-black school. At the time, there was no law school at Prairie View, but even so, Sellers suggested that Prairie View could provide legal instruction.

Next came the filing of a lawsuit.[34] W. J. Durham, the great Dallas lawyer, filed suit on Sweatt's behalf in Travis County; like many other African American lawyers, Durham used his initials to avoid having judges disrespect him by calling him by his first name.[35] A month after filing, Judge Archer held a hearing. The judge agreed that the denial of admission to Sweatt violated Sweatt's constitutional rights, but he gave the state six months to create a substantially equal course of instruction. After six months, although there was still no law school, Archer said that a resolution by the Texas A&M Board to provide legal education when an African American

[30] Dwonna Goldstone, *Integrating the 40 Acres: The Fifty-Year Struggle for Racial Equality at the University of Texas* (Athens: University of Georgia Press, 2006), 17–21.

[31] Id., 21; Amilcar Shabazz, *Advancing Democracy: African Americans and the Struggle for Access and Equity in Higher Education in Texas* (Chapel Hill: University of North Carolina Press, 2004), 67–8.

[32] President Theophilus S. Painter to Attorney General Grover Sellers, February 26, 1946, in Charles T. McCormick Papers, Box I115, *Sweatt v. Painter* & TSUN files, Rare Books & Special Collections, Tarlton Law Library, The University of Texas at Austin.

[33] Attorney General Grover Sellers to President Theophilus S. Painter, March 16, 1946, Chancellor's Office Records, Box 9, folder "Opinions–Attorney General's Office," DBCAH.

[34] For primary sources connected with *Sweatt v. Painter*, including trial court pleadings and transcripts, newspaper accounts, and oral histories, see Thomas D. Russell, ed., *Sweatt v. Painter Archive* http://www.houseofrussell.com/legalhistory/sweatt/ (accessed March 22, 2010).

[35] *Handbook of Texas Online*, s.v. "Durham, William J.," http://www.tshaonline.org/handbook/online/articles/DD/fdu46.html (accessed March 22, 2010); Greenberg, *Crusaders in the Courts*, 40; See also *Hamilton v. Alabama*, 376 U.S. 650 (1964) ("Miss Mary" case).

applicant demanded access to law school was good enough. This case then bounced up to the Court of Civil Appeals, which sent the case back down on remand. During this time, the state legislature enhanced the status of Prairie View and attempted to create a law school connected with Prairie View and Texas A&M in Houston.[36]

State of Texas officials and university administrators chose a different path than did the state of Oklahoma. Rather than segregating Sweatt within its white law school, Texans chose to create a separate law school for African Americans. In March 1947, the state legislature passed Senate Bill 140, which created the Texas State University for Negroes – now Texas Southern University. The campus would be in Houston, on land already set aside for the Houston College for Negroes. However, the law school would be in Austin for the first year.[37]

The idea behind the "separate but equal" law school was that the state could thereby satisfy the federal constitutional requirements established in 1896 with *Plessy v. Ferguson*. Until this time, the Supreme Court had not looked too closely at the "equal" part of that standard. Charles McCormick, the great evidence scholar who was then the dean of The University of Texas School of Law, worked hard with staff from the attorney general's office to create the separate school. They leased part of a building that was immediately north of the capitol on East 13th Street in Austin. They outfitted the facility with desks and books and sent some of the regular UT faculty there to teach.[38]

Texas offered Sweatt admission to the Texas State University for Negroes School of Law, something that Oklahoma – lacking a separate school – could not have done with Ida Sipuel. The separate law school opened in March 1947, but the NAACP had worked hard to discourage the application of students to this school and no students had applied. In the fall of 1947, the separate but equal law school enrolled three students, two men and one woman. Within a few weeks, the woman dropped out, but Heaullan Lott and Henry Doyle remained. One of the teachers at the separate school was Corwin Johnson, who was just starting his teaching career. He taught at UT for more than fifty years, all the while worried that because he had taught at the separate school, he might be viewed as having supported segregation.[39] After the 1947–8 academic year, the law school moved to Houston and is now the Thurgood Marshall School of Law at Texas Southern University.[40]

[36] *Sweatt v. Painter Archive*; Goldstone, *Integrating the 40 Acres*, 21–2.

[37] Goldstone, *Integrating the 40 Acres*, 22.

[38] See *Sweatt v. Painter Archive* for letter files and other papers of Dean McCormick in setting up the Texas State University of Negroes School of Law. One often hears that it was a basement law school; ground floor or "garden level" is more accurate, but this, of course, is a quibble.

[39] Sheree Scarborough, *Corwin W. Johnson: An Oral History Interview* (Austin: Jamail Center for Legal Research, The University of Texas at Austin, 2003) (excerpt available at *Sweatt v. Painter Archive*).

[40] For an interesting – and bitter – view of the founding of the Texas State University for Negroes by the dean of its law school, see Ozie Harold Johnson, *The Price of Freedom* (TS, 1954).

By 1947, the NAACP lawyers had shifted to a frontal assault on segregation, deny-ing that separate could ever be equal. Durham, Marshall, and James M. Nabrit Jr. handled most of Sweatt's case. In May 1947, they tried the case in Austin. Attorney General Price Daniel, who would later be governor, and his assistant, Joe Green-hill, who would later be Chief Justice, defended segregation for the state and the university. Greenhill and Daniel argued that the two law schools, although separate, were equal. The litigation attracted a good bit of publicity. To no one's surprise, Greenhill and Daniel won in the state's trial courts, but in early June 1950, the U.S. States Supreme Court ruled unanimously that The University of Texas must admit Sweatt and that it had to start admitting African Americans to its law school and graduate school.[41]

The NAACP lawyers had focused on a law-school case, because they believed that the justices of the Supreme Court would understand that a separate, black school like the Texas State University for Negroes could never be equal to a white school, neither in tangible qualities nor in intangibles such as the reputation of the alumni. Marshall, Durham, Nabrit, and their colleagues knew that if a mighty state like Texas could not marshal the resources to create a separate school that was equal, then less wealthy southern states like Alabama, Mississippi, or Georgia would never be able to meet the *Plessy* standard. The Supreme Court justices might have chosen to rely in the *Sweatt* opinion on tangible differences between The University of Texas and the Texas State University for Negroes, but the justices instead decided to rely on intangibles that could never be equal between two racially segregated schools. In 1950, Thurgood Marshall understood that the *Sweatt* opinion signaled the end of the Supreme Court's support for segregation. The final steps to *Brown v. Board of Education* lay before him.[42]

VI. SIMKINS

As Professor Simkins explained in his Klan speech before the university community and in his Klan article in the alumni magazine, he and his brother both participated in Klan violence against African Americans during Reconstruction. Like the Spanish inquisitors who claimed *ecclesia non novit sanguine*, Simkins denied that he and his fellow Klansmen ever drew any blood.[43] Yet Professor Simkins readily admitted assaulting freed people of color. He recounted that, during Reconstruction, he "was staying at the hotel in my town when one morning a lady came in apparently quite

---

[41] *Sweatt v. Painter et al.*, 339 U.S. 629 (1950). The Supreme Court issued its opinion in *McLaurin*, 339 U.S. 637, on the very same day.

[42] Friedman, *American Law in the 20th Century*, 288; Tushnet, *The NAACP's Legal Strategy Against Segregation*, 136–7; Greenberg, *Crusaders in the Courts*, 85–7.

[43] Simkins, "Why the Ku Klux," 748.

FIGURE 18.1. Photograph of a portrait of William Stewart Simkins. Copyright 2010, Thomas D. Russell. Photograph by Wyatt McSpadden.

frightened and in tears. I asked her what troubled her. She said she had been insulted by a negro. Ascertaining the name of the negro," Colonel Simkins "seized a barrel stave lying near the hotel door and whipped that darkey down the street and into the Freedman's Bureau."[44]

Professor Simkins also proudly described to the undergraduates and alumni his attempted ambush of Robert Meacham, a freed person who was an African Methodist Episcopal minister serving as a Florida state senator.[45] Colonel Simkins planned to beat Senator Meacham with a stick that he had hidden in his desk, but the senator suspected trouble and ran from Simkins' office. Colonel Simkins "grabbed the stick and made for him." Known by the townspeople to be a Klansman, Simkins "pursued [Meacham] up to the postoffice door and through a street filled with negroes and yet not a hand was raised or word said in his defense, nor was the incident ever

---

44 Id. at 741.
45 Id. at 742. Larry Eugene Rivers, *Laborers in the Vineyard of the Lord: The Beginnings of the AME Church in Florida, 1865–1895* (Gainesville: University Press of Florida, 2001).

noticed by the authorities. The unseen power was behind me,"[46] Colonel Simkins commented with satisfaction.

VII. ADMISSIONS

During the summer of 1950, following the Supreme Court's *Sweatt* decision, the first African American graduate students enrolled at the university. Sweatt himself was one of six African American students to enroll at the law school in the fall of 1950. The reaction to the presence of African American law students was mixed, with some students in favor, some indifferent, and some opposed.[47] At an alumni gathering at the law school during the years that I taught at UT, one alumnus told me that one faculty member, Judge Stayton, stopped using honorific titles when calling on students so that he could avoid having to say "Mr. Sweatt."[48] Sweatt did have some friends among the faculty and students, but not surprisingly, he was under continuing pressure.

Within two years, Sweatt flunked out of law school.[49] Yet lasting that long demonstrated his great fortitude. On the morning of his first semester's exams, his wife left him. On October 17, 1950, during Sweatt's first semester at the law school, a wooden cross covered with kerosene-soaked rags burned on the law school grounds. The student newspaper reported that "Austin firemen Tuesday night doused a 'fiery cross' that burned for more than fifteen minutes near the southern corner of the Law Building." In the lead paragraph, the student reporter noted, "The letters 'KKK' were found painted on the building's steps nearest the fire."[50]

VIII. SIMKINS

In a portrait that his brother Eldred's daughter Martha painted before 1927, Colonel Simkins resembled Mark Twain, particularly his unkempt white hair and bushy

[46] Simkins, "Why the Ku Klux," 742.

[47] Sheree Scarborough, *Oscar H. Mauzy: An Oral History Interview* (Austin: Jamail Center for Legal Research, The University of Texas at Austin, 2007) (excerpt available at *Sweatt v. Painter Archive*).

[48] For corroboration, see Goldstone, *Integrating the 40 Acres*, 28–9. (Professor Goldstone misidentifies Stayton as Stanton.) See also Dean Paul Carrington to Professor Roy M. Mersky, December 1, 1992 (TS on file with the author.) (Professor Mersky's papers, when processed, will be available at the Tarlton Law Library.) Dean Carrington reports on conversations with his uncle Dean Charles McCormick and others in his family. He notes, "My informants all report that McCormick, like most of the Texas faculty, was very supportive of black students when they came in 1951. (The exceptions were Bailey and Stayton.)"

[49] Professor Goldstone suggests that Sweatt may not have flunked out, but instead was kicked out unfairly. Goldstone, *Integrating the 40 Acres*, 163 n136. See also Heman Sweatt to Thurgood Marshall, October 28, 1950, image 23190, Reel 15, NAACP Papers. ("McCormick called me in his office to discuss with me the submitted assignment mailed with this letter. He informed me of his respect for my ability to analize [sic] contracts, and freely pointed out the error in conclusion, – in fact he told me that my discussion was the most able one submitted.")

[50] Charlie Lewis, "Cross Is Burned Near Law School," *The Daily Texan*, October 18, 1950.

mustache.[51] Simkins was wild and grumpy at the same time. He smoked and chewed tobacco. He drank whiskey. When the temperance advocate (and vandal) Carrie Nation visited in 1903, Professor Simkins got into a famous quarrel with her. The professor initiated several law school traditions, including the creation of a mythical animal called the Peregrinus, which later became the name of the yearbook. The law school's greatest dean, Page Keeton, went to his grave with a Peregrinus on his left lapel. Simkins also began the practice of calling first-year students J. A.'s, which stands for Jack Asses. The law school faculty has since discontinued that practice.[52]

During the entire time that Klansman Colonel Simkins was a law professor at The University of Texas, there were no African American students, of course. Before about 1915, there were no Mexican American students.[53] There was one woman student in 1905–6, but she dropped out; no woman graduated from the law department before 1914 or 1915. After that, there was a trickle of women and of Mexican Americans. So, for the first fifteen years of his teaching here, Professor Simkins taught no African Americans, no Mexican Americans, and, at most, one woman. Colonel Simkins taught civil procedure and equity. Although he wrote several books on contracts, equity, and federal practice, he was neither an important scholar nor an especially original thinker.[54]

The students – that is, the white male students – loved Colonel Simkins. The students loved Colonel Simkins's flamboyant wildness and his common abuse of them. More importantly, they loved him as a supporter of Southern traditions and institutions, just as the legislators and regents intended.

The first record of Professor Simkins' wildly popular public lecture about the Ku Klux Klan comes from 1914. That year, a student government leader organized a Dixie Day celebration for campus. The day was also called Confederate Day. At that time, Memorial Day was still an exclusively northern holiday, and Dixie Day was to be a southern alternative or response to Memorial Day. The first such observance of Confederate or Dixie Day at the university took place on May 29, 1914. Benjamin Dudley Tarlton, who was a law professor from 1904 to 1920 and for whom the law school's library is now named, spoke first on behalf of the faculty. Professor Tarlton

---

[51] Martha Simkins exhibited the portrait in a Dallas exhibition in May 1926. *Exhibition by Martha Simkins and Pupils, May 15 to 22, 1926, Highland Park Art Gallery*, Eldred J. Simkins Collection, Huntington Library.

[52] I had the honor of being a colleague of Dean Keeton for the last years of his life, and I took note of the Peregrinus lapel pin that he wore in his casket. On Simkins, see Charles S. Potts, "Old Simp and his Jackasses," 31(1) *Southwest Review* (Fall 1945): 23–7; Simkins Vertical File, DBCAH.

[53] Mike Widener, Archivist/Rare Books Librarian, "Hispanic Students at the University of Texas School of Law, 1884–1959," (TS in possession of the author, November 27, 1996). The first Mexican American graduate of the law school was Miguel Cardenas, who graduated in 1917.

[54] W.S. Simkins, *Contracts and Sales* (Austin: Von Boeckmann-Jones Co., 1905); *Equity as Applied in the State and Federal Courts in Texas* (Austin: Von Boeckmann-Jones Co., 1903); *Federal Practice and the Jurisdiction of all Federal Court at Law in Equity Including Removal of Causes* (Rochester: Lawyers Co-operative Publishing Co., 1923).

gave a speech on the confederacy. Colonel Simkins, who was a platform guest, was so moved by the occasion that he gave an extemporaneous account of Reconstruction and his involvement in organizing the Florida Klan. The thrilled students willingly stayed well past the scheduled end of the event to listen to Simkins.[55]

During the next academic year, Colonel Simkins's speech was the main event on the most important American day for feasting and prayerful reflection. His speech, titled "The Ku Klux Klan," was the centerpiece of the first-ever celebration of Thanksgiving Day on campus. Well over three hundred students crowded into the campus auditorium to hear him. In the student newspaper report of his speech, the headline was "Simkins Gives Famous Lecture on 'Ku Klux.'" To his appreciative student audience, Simkins explained, "We had to protect the women and children of the State against the ignorance and lust of the negro office-holders." He concluded his address, the *Daily Texan* reported, "with eloquent praise of the South, and urged the young men present to be loyal to their homeland and their Nation."[56]

That Simkins gave his speech in 1914 is a datum of importance. Simkins and others first formed the Klan during Reconstruction, but the organization went into remission during the 1870s. The Klan resumed operation in the twentieth century, and the accepted date for the birth of the twentieth-century Klan is Thanksgiving night of 1915, when Alabamian William Joseph Simmons called the Klan back into existence on top of Stone Mountain in Georgia.[57] By the 1920s, the Klan was again strong in Texas and elsewhere in the United States. In 1921, more than 500 Klansmen marched up Austin's Congress Avenue in a daylight parade. The following year, Klan candidates won a number of important elective offices in Texas. Whether Simkins was active in Klan affairs in Austin is unknown, but he does deserve to be credited with having a hand in the twentieth-century renaissance of the Klan. His exhortatory speeches about the Klan predate by at least one year the 1915 reinvention of the Klan in Georgia; Texas might compete with Georgia as to which state deserves credit for the rebirth of the Klan.

In the early twentieth century, white supremacy and segregation were dominant elements of Texan and southern culture. Extralegal violence, including lynching, facilitated white southern maintenance of the regime of white supremacy. Actually historians argue that lynching was central to the New South.[58]

In a brilliant 1998 book called *Making Whiteness*, a University of Virginia historian named Grace Elizabeth Hale describes the history of southern lynching. In a

[55] "Heroes of South will be Honored by Special Day," *Daily Texan*, May 29, 1914, p. 1; "Meeting of Student Body in Main Auditorium," *Daily Texan*, May 30, 1914, p. 1; Simkins Vertical File, DBCAH.
[56] "Meeting of Student Body in Main Auditorium," *Daily Texan*.
[57] Alabama Department of Archives and History, Alabama Moments in American History, "The 20th Century Ku Klux Klan in Alabama," http://www.alabamamoments.state.al.us/sec46det.html (accessed March 22, 2010).
[58] Fitzhugh Brundage, *Lynching in the New South, Georgia and Virginia, 1880–1930* (Urbana: University of Illinois Press, 1993), 15; Edward L. Ayers, *The Promise of the New South: Life after Reconstruction* (New York: Oxford University Press, 1993), 155–9.

chapter entitled "Deadly Amusements," Professor Hale focuses on a public variant of lynching, which she terms "spectacle lynching." Public lynchings possessed a very different sort of power than did private lynchings, which accounted for most lynchings. Public or spectacle lynchings were murders for which entire towns would turn out. Special trains would run to bring spectators to the scene. Schools would close so that the schoolchildren could watch. News of lynchings passed by telegraph, telephone, and even newspaper.[59]

Spectacle lynchings came to include scripted elements, which Professor Hale identifies: "[L]ike all cultural forms, over time lynching spectacles evolved a well-known structure, a sequence and pace of events that southerners came to understand as standard." She explains this sequence: "The well-choreographed spectacle opened with a chase or a jail attack, followed rapidly by the public identification of the captured African American by the alleged white victim or the victim's relatives, announcement of the upcoming event to draw the crowd, the selection and preparation of the site." Next, she describes the truly grisly spectacle: "The main event then began with a period of mutilation – often including emasculation – and torture to extract confessions and entertain the crowd, and built to a climax of slow burning, hanging, and/or shooting to complete the killing. The finale consisted of frenzied gathering and display of the body and the collected parts."[60]

Texans invented spectacle lynching. Hale describes "the 1893 lynching of Henry Smith in Paris, Texas, for the alleged rape and murder of three-year-old Myrtle Vance" as "[t]he founding event in the history of spectacle lynchings." By this she means that it "was the first blatantly public, actively promoted lynching of a southern black by a large crowd of southern whites." This lynching event included a specially chartered train, publicly sold photographs of the lynching, and the wide, unabashed retelling of the tale by the lynchers. This murder also yielded a widely distributed pamphlet that detailed the lynching.[61]

Pamphlets and photographs allowed wide distribution of the unmistakable message of white supremacy supported by violence and murder. In his book *Trouble in Mind*, the historian Leon Litwack includes a chilling chapter on lynching. In 1908, the Harkrider Drug Company, in Center, Sabine County, in Texas published a picture postcard of five African American men hanging from a tree.[62] Beneath the

[59] Grace Elizabeth Hale, *Making Whiteness: The Culture of Segregation in the South, 1890–1940* (New York: Pantheon Books, 1998), 199–239. See also Christopher Waldrep, *African Americans Confront Lynching: Strategies of Resistance from the Civil War to the Civil Rights Era* (Lanham: Rowman & Littlefield Publishers, 2009); James Allen and John Littlefield, *Without Sanctuary* (Photographs and Postcards of Lynching in America) http://www.withoutsanctuary.org/main.html (accessed March 22, 2010).

[60] Hale, *Making Whiteness*, 204.

[61] Id. at 207; [Anonymous], *The facts in the case of the horrible murder of little Myrtle Vance and its fearful expiation at Paris, Texas, February 1st, 1893* (Paris, Texas, P.I. James: 1893).

[62] An image of the postcard is at http://nationalhumanitiescenter.org/pds/maai2/politics/text5/dogwoodtree.pdf (accessed March 22, 2010).

photograph, the lynchers included a poem about white supremacy as a warning to all the state's blacks:

THE DOGWOOD TREE
This is only the branch of a dogwood tree;
An Emblem of White Supremacy.
A lesson once taught in the pioneer's School,
That this is a land of White Man's Rule.
The Red Man once in an early day,
Was told by the Whites to mend his way.
The negro, now, by eternal grace,
Must learn to stay in the negro's place.
In the sunny South, the land of the free,
Let the White Supreme forever be.
Let this a warning to all negroes be,
Or they'll suffer the fate of the dogwood tree.

The popularity of Simkins as an orator and as a teacher stemmed not from his Twain-like grumpiness or great intellect, nor from his abuse of the students. As the legislature and regents intended, Simkins was a supporter of southern institutions and culture. When they were children or young adults, his students may have witnessed or participated in the 1893 lynching of Henry Smith in Texas. If they did not, then they may well have read about the murder in the pamphlet edition. Or, perhaps they viewed the postcards of the 1908 lynching about which Leon Litwack has written. Simkins' description of his own youth – he was in his mid-20s when he and his brother organized the Florida Klan – served as an inspiration to the young UT students.

Perhaps some of the University of Texas students who listened to Professor Simkins' Thanksgiving Klan lecture of 1914 were among those 15,000 Waco residents – women, men, and children – who watched or performed the 1916 public lynching of Jesse Washington.[63] Some of these Wacoans may also have enjoyed the spectacle of lynching in D. W. Griffith's film, *Birth of a Nation*, released the year before Washington was burned alive. Before burning him, the murderers cut off Washington's penis; before his burned body had cooled, the frenzied crowd cut off fingers, toes, and other burned body parts as souvenirs – all of this typical of spectacle lynchings, as the historian Hale has noted. As with the 1908 lynching in Sabine County, commercial photographs of Washington's lynching circulated for ten cents apiece, much less than the five dollars that each of his teeth commanded at the end of his last day.[64]

[63] See Patricia Bernstein, *The First Waco Horror: The Lynching of Jesse Washington and the Rise of the NAACP* (College Station, TX: Texas A&M University Press, 2005).
[64] Hale, *Making Whiteness*, 218.

To understand what Simkins meant to university students while he was teaching, one must think of him in relationship to Texas culture in the early twentieth century. This culture rested on a *Grundnorm* of white supremacy, supported by extralegal violence and most forcefully reinforced through the medium of spectacle lynchings. There was more to Simkins than whiskey and tobacco. With his vivid recollections in speeches and writing of his own life as a terrorist supporter of white supremacy as a Florida Ku Klux Klansman when he was in his mid-20s, Simkins was a perfect role model for young Texans being educated in the violent culture of Jim Crow segregation and white supremacy.

IX. ADMISSIONS

Beginning in the 1940s, Henry Y. McCown was the largely unseen central actor in The University of Texas's effort to exclude African Americans from admission. McCown, who had commanded a naval vessel during World War II,[65] served variously as registrar, dean of admissions, and dean of students. He was the registrar when Heman Sweatt applied to the university in 1946. Before the *Brown* decision in 1954, McCown had admitted no African American undergraduates to the university.

However, beginning in 1950, McCown had admitted African American graduate students to master's and PhD programs, and of course he had admitted some law students. As was common at the time, applicants to the law school did not require an undergraduate degree to apply, and McCown considered law to be an undergraduate professional degree program. In the months immediately after the Supreme Court's decision in *Brown*, McCown first advocated a very restrictive policy regarding any expansion in the admission of African American students. By the end of the summer, he had decided to be slightly less restrictive and to admit a very few African American students as undergraduates in certain professional fields – mostly engineering. In this decision, though, the Board of Regents overruled him, instituting instead the very restrictive plan that McCown suggested in May.[66]

The very restrictive plan for admissions that McCown suggested on May 26, 1954 – nine days after the *Brown* decision – required that African American students seeking admission to undergraduate professional programs first spend a year taking required courses at either Prairie View University or Texas Southern University. McCown explained to President Wilson that the "procedures for handling admissions for the Graduate School are well established as we have had many applicants for graduate work. In the undergraduate area, we have not accepted any Negro applicants for work in the professional fields except in Law." Because of *Brown*, he predicted – correctly as it turned out – there will be "added interest in [African-American] undergraduates

[65] "McCown, H.Y.,' Vertical File, DBCAH.
[66] *Id.*

gaining admission." McCown suggested that "we should give some consideration to the procedures for admission of undergraduates." Here, he explicitly expressed his goal and suggested a plan: "If we want to exclude as many Negro undergraduates as possible, we could require applicants for professional work not offered at Texas Southern University or Prairie View to first enroll in one of the Negro schools and take at least one year of the academic work required for all degrees." McCown then revealed the fear that he sought to allay: "This will keep Negroes out of most classes where there are a large number of girls." If McCown could force African American students in undergraduate professional degree programs to take all required coursework at black universities, then the young white women in classes such as freshmen English would not have to share classroom space with African American men, nor would white men have to compete with the African American men.[67]

When he wrote to President Wilson on May 26, 1954, McCown attached a letter that the state's Commissioner of Education, J. W. Edgar, had written two days before. Commissioner Edgar had sent his letter to all the state's school superintendents, all members of the legislature, Governor Shivers, Attorney General John Ben Shepperd, and the members of the State Board of Education. With his letter, Edgar sent a one-page attachment that included the entire last paragraph of Chief Justice Warren's opinion in *Brown*. Warren began the final paragraph by noting, "Because these are class actions, because of the wide applicability of this decision, and because of the great variety of local conditions, the formulation of decrees in these cases presents problems of considerable complexity."[68] In his letter, the Commissioner of Education advised that "[s]ince the present action of the Court is not final[,]" the superintendents should make no changes in response to *Brown* for the 1954–5 academic year. As he reminded the superintendents, "The Texas public school system is administered under the Texas constitution and the statutes passed by the Texas legislature, and no change should be contemplated until further action has been taken by the United States Supreme Court and until the Texas Legislature points the way for such changes." He directed all the state's superintendents that "[e]very local board should plan its budget, program, and policies for 1954–55 pursuant to Texas law and should make no changes until directed to do so."[69]

During the summer of 1954, McCown gave up his restrictive plan to protect the university's white women and offered admission to seven African American men as undergraduates. Two of the seven students were admitted to bachelor's

[67] McCown to Wilson, Chancellor's Office Records, Box 9, folder "Negroes," DBCAH. For a discussion of McCown's concerns, see also Goldstone, *Integrating the 40 Acres*, 38–9.

[68] *Brown v. Board of Ed. of Topeka, Shawnee County, Kan.*, 347 U.S. 483, 495–6 (May 17, 1954).

[69] J. W. Edgar, Commissioner of Education, Texas Education Agency to All Superintendents of Schools, May 24, 1954, attachment to McCown to Wilson, May 26, 1954, Chancellor's Office Records, Box 9, folder "Negroes," DBCAH.

degree programs in architecture with the other five admitted to differing engineering programs. One of the engineering students was Marion George Ford Jr.[70]

Marion Ford encountered McCown's officiousness when he applied. Ford apparently first applied for a bachelor of science degree program without specifying his major field. Registrar McCown then wrote to him asking for his field of study. Ford wrote back: chemistry. McCown wrote again with the news that Ford could go to Texas Southern University to study chemistry. According to a summary that W. B. Shipp, who worked for McCown in the registrar's office, provided to President Wilson on August 25, 1954, Ford wrote back and complained that he was "a victim of 'Southern Discrimination'" and that "the course of study he actually wished to pursue was Chemical Engineering."[71]

After learning that Marion Ford wanted to be a chemical engineer, McCown wrote to him again on July 23. In this letter, McCown recounted the story of their correspondence and explained the admissions policy:

> The University of Texas' policy on admission of Negro students is as follows: we will admit Negroes to our Graduate School or to professional schools provided that the course of study which they wish to pursue is not offered in one of the Negro state-supported schools (Texas Southern University or Prairie View). This policy will continue in effect for the academic year 1954–55 as the method of implementing the recent Supreme Court decision has not yet been determined.[72]

After explaining the policy to Ford, McCown blasted him. "I have admitted hundreds of Negro students to the University, and you are the first applicant to claim discrimination[,]" he lectured. In the final paragraph, McCown wrote, "I am pleased to advise you that we will accept you for admission to pursue a course of study in the field of Chemical Engineering." Then, for good measure, he completed the paragraph by writing: "I hope that you will do well in the University and that you will get over your inferiority complex and the idea that you are being discriminated against."[73]

However, a little more than a month later, at the direction of the Board of Regents and President Wilson, McCown rescinded Ford's admission.

After Registrar McCown offered Ford admission, President Logan Wilson had become involved. McCown had written his insulting letter of admission on July 23; on August 25, President Wilson learned of Ford's admission and telephoned Tom Sealy, the chair of the Board of Regents. At the same time, Regent Leroy Jeffers

---

[70] Shabazz, *Advancing Democracy*, 156. W. B. Shipp to President Logan Wilson, August 25, 1954, UT President's Office Records, VF20/B.a, General Files, Folder "Negroes in Colleges, 1939–54," DBCAH.

[71] *Id.* Shipp also noted that Ford's "letter further states, 'I am not interested in living in your dormitories or becoming socially prominent with the Caucasians, but I do want a chance to get the best formal training in my state, Texas.'"

[72] H. Y. McCown, Registrar and Dean of Admissions, to Marion George Ford, Jr., July 23, 1954, UT President's Office Records, VF20/B.a, General Files, Folder "Negroes in Colleges, 1939–54," DBCAH.

[73] *Id.*

wrote from Houston to Sealy in Midland to let him know that "a Sports Writer for The Houston Chronicle called me at home and advised me that Marion Ford, a Houston negro high school football star and an honor graduate of Wheatley High School, had been accepted as a freshman student in chemical engineering at The University of Texas, and that he desired to try out for the freshman football team this fall at the University."[74] Regent Jeffers sent his letter to the entire Board of Regents and enclosed a copy of the newspaper story, which was titled "Houston Negro Seeks Grid Tryout at Texas."[75] Sealy replied on August 28 and let Jeffers know that Logan Wilson had already telephoned him to alert him of the matter.[76] Sealy then noted that he would bring the matter before the regents' executive committee and ask for opinions from the university's lawyers, Scott Gaines and Rupert Harkrider.[77]

With the regents buzzing about the admission of the university's first African American undergraduates, McCown met with President Wilson and then wrote a three-page letter to Wilson in which he "review[ed] in detail policies and procedures for admission of Negro students."[78] McCown's letter to President Wilson served three purposes. First, although unstated in the letter, McCown must have written it for President Wilson's use at the next meeting of the Board of Regents. Second, having admitted the first African American undergraduates, McCown may have doubted his job security; he wanted to retain his bureaucratic authority concerning race and admissions. McCown reminded his boss that he had been in charge of the rejection or admission of African American applicants for a number of years. McCown noted that, after the Supreme Court's decision in *Sweatt*, he, along with President Theophilus Painter and dean of the Graduate School, A. P. Brogan, "passed on each individual Negro application. To be completely covered in the case of Negro students not eligible for admission, we consulted with the Attorney General on the exact wording of each letter of rejection."[79] McCown let President Wilson know that "[a]s time passed, and the admission of Negro students became somewhat routine, President Painter and Dean Brogan turned the matter over entirely to me unless I considered that the case was unusual and should seek their advice."[80] McCown emphasized to Wilson that "I have personally handled the admission of all Negro students and endeavored to adhere strictly to the policy agreed on."[81] A

[74] Leroy Jeffers to Tom Sealy, August 25, 1954, UT President's Office Records, VF20/B.a, General Files, Folder "Negroes in Colleges, 1939–54," DBCAH.
[75] Id. There were no African American football players at Texas through the 1960s. The Texas team that won the football national championship in 1969 was the last all-white team to do so. Goldstone, *Integrating the 40 Acres*, 130.
[76] Tom Sealy to Leroy Jeffers, August 28, 1954, UT President's Office Records, VF20/B.a, General Files, Folder "Negroes in Colleges, 1939–54," DBCAH.
[77] Id.
[78] H. Y. McCown to President Logan Wilson, August 30, 1954, UT President's Office Records, VF20/B.a, General Files, Folder "Negroes in Colleges, 1939–54," DBCAH.
[79] Id.
[80] Id. at 1–2.
[81] Id.

paragraph later, McCown circled back to protect himself: "After you superseded Dr. Painter as President, I discussed the matter of Negro admissions with you on at least two occasions and gained the impression each time that it was your desire to adhere to the previously established admission policy."[82]

The third purpose of McCown's August 1954 letter to Wilson was to make clear that he did not want the university's admissions policies concerning African Americans to change. The *Brown* decision was hardly self-executing at The University of Texas. McCown explained to President Wilson that, notwithstanding the Supreme Court opinion in *Brown*, *Sweatt v. Painter* remained the relevant case for admissions policy. Since 1950, McCown and others at the university understood Sweatt to mean that the university could exclude African American applicants for graduate and professional degree programs if one of the state's black universities offered the intended program. For this purpose, professional programs included undergraduate degrees in engineering. The seven African American students to whom McCown had offered admission were to be engineering students, and McCown emphasized that, consistent with *Sweatt v. Painter* – not *Brown* – he had offered to admit these students. Even after the *Brown* decision, McCown stuck with separate but equal as a guide to admissions.[83]

McCown explained to Wilson that back in 1950, after the *Sweatt* decision, he, President Painter, and Vice President Dolley had met with Attorney General Price Daniel to receive instruction. He recounted that "the Attorney General advised orally that we had no course open to us except to accept Negro students for graduate and professional work provided that the program of study was not offered in a state-supported Negro School."[84] The Attorney General's advice meant that McCown could turn away an African American applicant when the program to which he or she sought admission was available at one of the state's black universities. "If in doubt as to whether a program or study was offered at one of the Negro schools," McCown explained to Wilson, "I have written or telephoned to Prairie View or Texas Southern University to determine the facts in the case."[85]

By the end of the summer of 1954, McCown had taken *Brown* into account by not changing admissions practices at all. With his letter to Wilson, McCown sought to protect his administration of admissions policy. Well before the Supreme Court signaled with the *Brown II* opinion of May 1955 that states could slow down their implementation of integration, McCown had his own sturdy bureaucratic plan of resistance, which was unseen outside the university administration. Notwithstanding *Brown*, he noted, "There has been no change whatever in our admission policy."[86]

[82] Id.
[83] Id. at 2.
[84] Id. at 1.
[85] Id. at 2.
[86] Id.

Before making that point, he explained to Wilson that "[t]he added interest of the recent Supreme Court decision has caused undergraduate students to take a more calculated approach. They are now carefully advised and are constantly probing for programs of work not offered at one of the Negro institutions."[87] Consequently, the university "accepted six Negro freshman for professional fields (all Engineering)."[88] Overall, McCown perceived that African American applicants were becoming more crafty regarding the criteria for admission under *Sweatt*, but by August 1954, he showed no signs of yielding to the more expansive implications of *Brown*.

On the same day that McCown wrote his long letter to Wilson, Board of Regents chair Tom Sealy wrote to the attorney general asking "whether under existing law The University of Texas is required to admit negro students for professional courses at the undergraduate level in such fields as aeronautical, architectural, petroleum, chemical, electrical, and mechanical engineering, etc., where such courses are not offered or given at any State of Texas institution of higher learning for negroes." These majors were of course the very programs into which seven African American men had been admitted. Sealy also asked the attorney general "whether The University of Texas is required to permit such negro students upon admission to participate in such extracurricular activities as band and football or other intercollegiate activities."[89]

On the very next day, President Wilson wrote to Dean McCown and directed him to rescind the admission of all seven African American men.[90] The president of the university first noted that in the afternoon, he and two staff members had combed through the schedules of Prairie View University and Texas Southern University as well as UT's schedule. They determined that the African American students could do their coursework at one of the state's black universities. Wilson noted that he had telephoned Sealy, who had in turn conferred with the Board of Regents executive committee. Wilson included a draft of the letter that McCown was to send to each student when he rescinded his admission.[91] McCown executed his assignment immediately. Within seven days of President Wilson learning of Marion Ford's admission, the Board of Regents, their executive committee, the university's lawyers, the attorney general, and McCown undid the admission of what would have been UT's first African American undergraduates. Two weeks later, President Wilson received a memo from the university's News and Information Service with

[87] *Id.*

[88] *Id.*

[89] Tom Sealy to Honorable John Ben Shepperd, August 30, 1954, UT President's Office Records, VF20/B.a, General Files, Folder "Negroes in Colleges, 1939–54," DBCAH.

[90] Logan Wilson to H. Y. McCown, August 31, 1954, UT President's Office Records, VF20/B.a, General Files, Folder "Negroes in Colleges, 1939–54," DBCAH.

[91] *Id.*

a clipping of a small nine-line news story that the memo indicated "seems to be the only mention by the Negro press of the Ford matter."[92]

X. SIMKINS

After the law school moved to a new building in the fall of 1953, Chancellor James P. Hart toyed with the idea of renaming the old law building "Simkins Hall."[93] (This was the building in which Heman Sweatt had been a student.) "If it were not for the fact that the Law School is no longer there," Hart wrote to the Buildings and Grounds Committee of the Board of Regents, "I would suggest Simkins Hall, since Judge Simkins' memories certainly pervade the atmosphere of the Building."[94] Ultimately, the Board of Regents chose a different name: Pearce Hall.

At the dedication of the new law building – called Townes Hall after the first law school dean – Simkins reappeared. Herbert Brownell, the U.S. attorney general, was the featured speaker at its dedication on December 5, 1953.[95] He delivered a boring address in which he announced a new program to hire law graduates at the Department of Justice. Late in the program – which lasted three hours – members of the class of 1911 returned to donate portraits to adorn the walls of the new building. Thomas S. Taliaferro, of Houston, represented the class of 1911. Taliaferro was a native of Houston, who earned an undergraduate degree at Princeton before enrolling at The University of Texas School of Law. A biographical booklet about the class of 1911 notes that, when Taliaferro went to Princeton, "he must have taken along with him the old Southern traditions, for he was known there as 'Nig' Taliaferro."[96] On behalf of his class, Taliaferro donated five portraits, including one of Colonel William Stewart Simkins.[97] This was three years after the Supreme Court's decision in Sweatt and six months before *Brown*.

In addition to the two portraits of Professor Simkins, the law school also has a brass bust of him. The provenance of this sculpture is unknown. For most of the 1990s when I taught at UT, the bust adorned the reference desk of the Tarlton Law Library. Students used to pat Simkins' head and rub his nose for good luck, just as visitors to Florence rub the snout of the boar sculpture *Il Porcellino* to guarantee a return visit to that great Renaissance city. The law students generally had no idea

---

[92] WEK to Dr. Wilson, September 13, 1954, UT President's Office Records, VF20/B.a, General Files, Folder "Negroes in Colleges, 1939–54," DBCAH.
[93] Chancellor James P. Hart to Mrs. Edgar Tobin, Mr. Lee Lockwood, and Mr. D. A. Woodward, Jr., November 20, 1953, UT President's Office Records, VF22/B.a., folder "Buildings," DBCAH.
[94] Id.
[95] "Brownell Urges Faith in Justice Department," *The Daily Texan*, December 6, 1953, p. 1.
[96] *The 1911 Law Class of The University of Texas*, (n.p., n.d.), 167–8.
[97] I have not been able to determine who painted this portrait of Simkins. Through the 1990s, when I taught at The University of Texas and during the pendency of the *Hopwood v. Texas*, 78 F.3d 932 (5th Cir. 1996) litigation – a suit by a white plaintiff that challenged the law school's affirmative action practices – Simkins' portrait hung next to the doorway of the registrar's office.

FIGURE 18.2. Photograph of a portrait of William Stewart Simkins. Copyright 2010, Thomas D. Russell. Photograph by Wyatt McSpadden.

who Professor Simkins was, and the bust remained on the reference desk until a newly hired librarian of color with a sense of history insisted on its removal.

XI. ADMISSIONS

After World War II, enrollment at The University of Texas jumped, partly because of population growth but in very large part because of the return of veterans eager to attend the university on the GI Bill. At the end of World War II, enrollment had been around 7,000, and it climbed to around 18,000 by 1960.[98] From its inception and through the *Sweatt* and *Brown* years, the university admissions policy was one of open enrollment for Texans – except, of course, black Texans. This meant that high

[98] Berry, *UT History 101*, 33.

FIGURE 18.3. A brass bust of William Stewart Simkins. Copyright 2010, Thomas D. Russell. Photograph by Wyatt McSpadden.

school graduates who wanted to go to the university could enroll. Indeed after World War II, they enrolled in droves, which created for the university's administrators a legitimate need to find some way to limit enrollment.

At the start of July 1955 – more than a year after the first Supreme Court decision in *Brown* – the Board of Regents announced the desegregation of the university. At the same time, they announced the end of the policy of open admissions; thereafter, applicants would have to take an entrance exam to be admitted to the university. *The Daily Texan* reported that "[p]resent University policies of refusing Negroes undergraduate work will be retained until UT has a chance to work out long-considered enrollment problems"[99]; "beginning in 1956–67, a form of entrance exams, based on merit, will be given to all persons who want to enter the University, regardless of racial origin."[100]

Although the crush of students who sought enrollment after World War II served as an independent justification for the institution of standardized testing as way to limit enrollment, the regents' decision to start using standardized testing in the very

[99] *Daily Texan*, July 12, 1955.
[100] *Id.*

same semester that they first admitted African American undergraduates was no coincidence. President Wilson had been looking into the permissibility of limiting enrollment at least as early as February 1955.[101] By June 1955, President Wilson knew that instituting standardized testing would be an effective way to limit disproportionately the enrollment of African Americans as undergraduates.

A four-person committee consisting of Professor Harry Ransom, Herschel Manuel, W. B. Shipp, and Dean of Students McCown met as the "Committee on Selective Admissions" for the first time on June 15, 1955. In advance of that meeting, Professor Harry Ransom, the committee chair, provided to President Wilson a draft statistical report on high school graduates and their test scores. The report, which is marked *"Not for publication"* at the top, estimated that in the spring of 1954, there had been a total of 56,363 high school graduates in Texas, of whom 11 percent were African American and 89 percent were white. Based on these figures, the report noted parenthetically that "[i]f 2,700 freshmen were distributed according to these percentages, 300 of them would be Negroes." The fifth page of the report consisted of a typed table comparing the aptitude test scores of UT freshmen in one column with scores labeled "Three Colleges for Negroes" in the other column. This column was labeled with double asterisks and a footnote that said "[t]hese figures from confidential reports to the Texas Commission on Coordination in Education cannot be made public." Almost certainly, committee member Herschel Manuel – an education researcher who worked with the Commission on Coordination in Education – was the source of these confidential data. The data showed lower scores for the African American students – a median of 54 – compared with the median of 102 for University of Texas freshmen.[102]

A footnote to the statistical chart made the committee's intention and analysis clear. After highlighting the confidentiality of the data about African Americans' test scores, the note indicates that a "[c]utting point of 72 would eliminate about 10% of UT freshmen and about 74% of Negroes." Returning to the earlier prediction of 300 African Americans in a class of 2,700, the note continues, "Assuming the distributions are representative, this cutting point would tend to result in a maximum of 70 Negroes in a class of 2,700 – one-fourth of one-ninth of the class."[103] The committee members understood and reported to President Wilson that the implementation of standardized testing would reduce the size of the incoming class and, at the same time, reduce the number of enrolled African Americans by three-quarters. The committee understood the disparate racial impact of implementing standardized testing and that testing would eliminate only about 10 percent of the white applicants.

[101] Scott Gaines to President Logan Wilson, February 3, 1955, UT President's Office Records, VF20/B.a, General Files, Folder "Negroes in Colleges, 1939–54," DBCAH.
[102] H[arry] H. Ransom to President Logan Wilson, June 13, 1955, UT Chancellor's Office Records, Box 34, Folder "Committees–Standing, Admissions Committee," DBCAH.
[103] *Id.*

Ten days after its meeting, the special committee on admissions provided a formal report to President Wilson. It dropped any reference to the disparate impact of testing on African-American applicants to the university.[104] The disproportionate racial impact of testing – laid bare in the draft – was unseen in the final, facially neutral report.

The testing's disproportionate impact on African-American applicants made the general question of limiting admissions more palatable. As a general matter, President Wilson and the regents were reluctant to limit admissions to the university. The openness of enrollment at The University of Texas was important to the university, its officials, and to the state's white people. Limiting admissions, Wilson knew, was not going to be popular. An editorial in the *Austin American* noted, "It is a matter of regret that the doors of the Main University no longer will remain open to all Texas youths who would prefer to attend it."[105]

When the university announced the implementation of entrance exams, William D. Bryce, a newly minted alumnus from the class of 1955, wrote to President Wilson to complain. Bryce was concerned, apparently, about elitism. He wrote,

> As to the entrance examination let me respectfully remind you that the State of Texas need not be governed as is Great Britain. This entrance examination business is one more step toward state-sponsored scholarships and the insidious approach of socialism. Enlarge the facilities, but do not limit the number of students acceptable because of lack of physical space; please base your administrative ideals on firmer grounds then cramped quarters.[106]

President Wilson responded patiently to Bryce, noting that "I am somewhat at a loss to see any connection between the use of entrance examinations and anything remotely connected to socialism."[107] Perhaps Bryce imagined that he would not have been able to pass the entrance examination had it been in place when he graduated from high school.

President Wilson discussed the relationship between desegregation and standardized testing in a speech that he gave to the Houston Rotary Club on August 11, 1955. His third topic was the "De-segregation action of the UT Regents," which had been announced by the regents the month before. In his typed notes for the speech, Wilson first reassured his Rotary Club audience that desegregation is "*not* prompted by missionary or reformist motives. Merely a realistic acceptance of inevitable to avoid legal hassles." He further explained that desegregation is a "[s]ensible compliance with Supreme Court decision." He also predicted the following: "Do not

[104] H[arry] H. Ransom *et al.* to Logan Wilson, June 22, 1955, UT Chancellor's Office Records, Box 34, Folder "Committees–Standing, Admissions Committee," DBCAH.

[105] "University Makes 2 Historic Decisions," *Austin American*, July 9, 1955.

[106] William D. Bryce to Logan Wilson, n.d., rec'd July 12, 1955, UT Chancellor's Office Records, Box 34, Folder "Desegregation," DBCAH.

[107] Logan Wilson to William D. Bryce, July 13, 1955, UT Chancellor's Office Records, Box 34, Folder "Desegregation," DBCAH.

anticipate any great numbers of N's, but to avoid appearing to discriminate against unqualified have tied it in with a selective admissions policy for all students without ref. to racial origin, etc."[108]

In an August 1956 letter from the Board of Regents chair Tom Sealy to a Houston attorney named Fred Moore, the linkage between admissions testing and the exclusion of African Americans is even clearer. Moore had written to Governor Allen Shivers, who forwarded his letter to Sealy. Sealy explained the recent history of the university's admissions policies to Moore. After the *Brown* decision, the regents anticipated "that unless it made some good faith effort to comply with the decision, suits would be instituted in 1955 by negroes seeking to enter as freshman in the fall semester of 1955." He further explained that, given the university's policy of open admissions, "[w]e felt it was a foregone conclusion the Federal courts would rule such negroes were entitled to enter the University as undergraduate students and the University probably would be enjoined from preventing the admission of any negro high school graduate student as an undergraduate at the University, regardless of the applicant's scholastic record."[109]

Sealy next explained to Moore the pressure that the university was experiencing in enrolling the increased numbers of white students. He tried to make clear to Moore that the combination of selective admissions with desegregation allowed the university to limit the number of African American students: "You may be sure that if we had not done what we did last July, there would have been filed in the immediate future a similar suit for the admission of students at the undergraduate level and we would have been forced to admit all negro students seeking undergraduate work regardless of their qualifications."[110] The Board of Regents, like President Wilson, Dean McCown, and others who worked on the issue of selective admissions, knew that by instituting standardized testing they would substantially limit the number of African American students at The University of Texas. They addressed the need to limit the total number of students and met their desire to limit the number of African American students.

XII. SIMKINS

In 1954 – a year after the opening of the new law school building, Townes Hall – the regents planned a new dormitory for law students and graduate students just down the street from the law school at the intersection of San Jacinto and what was then East 26th Street. In a February 1954 letter, Dean Keeton suggested calling the building Simkins Hall because "[m]any law school traditions center around Colonel

---

[108] "Notes for August 12, 1955 speech by Logan Wilson," UT Chancellor's Office Records, Box 30, folder "Addresses and Papers, Vol. II, 1954–55," DBCAH.

[109] Tom Sealy to Fred W. Moore, August 16, 1956, UT Chancellor's Office Records, Box 34, Folder "Desegregation," DBCAH.

[110] *Id.*

W.S. Simkins" and "[h]e was a man of fine character and is well respected by all the lawyers throughout the State who went to Law School during the time that he was on the faculty."[111] The university's Faculty Council assigned the naming issue to a special naming committee.

For the Faculty Council discussion of the matter, the naming committee presented some biographical information regarding Simkins, which they found in the then-new *Handbook of Texas*. In their recommendation, they cited the *Handbook*, which included a three-paragraph entry for Colonel Simkins. The faculty committee mentioned his birth in South Carolina, his participation in the Civil War, the years that he taught at the law school, and the donation of his law books to the university after his death. However, it failed to mention his Klan activity, even though it is described in the *Handbook of Texas* entry.[112] The second paragraph of that entry noted that "[s]oon after the war Simkins went to Monticello, Florida, where he and his brother E. J. Simkins, organized the Florida Ku Klux Klan." The next paragraph referred to "[t]he judge's [sic] long white hair, his love of applause, his traditional lecture on the Ku Klux Klan, his encounter with Carrie Nation in 1903, his tobacco, all became part of the university tradition."

Five weeks after Chief Justice Earl Warren issued the Supreme Court's 1954 opinion in *Brown v. Board of Education*, the Faculty Council of The University of Texas at Austin – advised by a bureaucratic committee that ensured that Simkins' Klan past would be unseen – voted to name the new dormitory for law and graduate students after law professor and Ku Klux Klansman William Stewart Simkins. Simkins Hall carried his name until July 2010, when UT's Regents renamed the building Creekside Residence Hall in response to an early draft of this essay.

---

[111] Page Keeton to Logan Wilson, February 25, 1954, UT President's Office Records, VF22/B.a., folder "Buildings – Suggested Names for Building Committee–Board of Regents," DBCAH.

[112] "Report of the Special Committee to Suggest Names for Certain New Buildings," in F. L. Cox, Sec'y, Minutes with Index of the General Faculty, The University of Texas (September 1953–August 1954), p. 6332; Walter Prescott Webb, ed., *The Handbook of Texas*, Vol. 2, (Austin: Texas State Historical Association, 1952), 612.

19

Taking Legal Realism Offshore

The Contributions of Joseph Walter Bingham to American Jurisprudence and to the Reform of Modern Ocean Law

Harry N. Scheiber

A conscientious reading of the rich historical literature on the American legal realist movement would provide no suggestion that any of the academic writers and other commentators in that movement ever gave the slightest attention to international law.[1] It is entirely understandable that the realists should be remembered as having been concerned exclusively with the analysis and reform of domestic jurisprudence and legal process, because there was only one exception in this regard: the Stanford Law professor Joseph Walter Bingham (1878–1973). Bingham is a figure who has

[1] Among the numerous important studies of legal realism, one may mention in particular Wilfred E. Rumble, *American Legal Realism: Skepticism, Reform, and the Judicial Process* (Ithaca: Cornell University Press, 1968); William Twining, *Karl Llewellyn and the Realist Movement* (London: Wiedenfeld and Nicolson, 1973); Edward A. Purcell, Jr., "American Jurisprudence between the Wars," *American Historical Review* 75 (1969): 424–46, reprinted in *American Law and the Constitutional Order*, ed. Lawrence M. Friedman & Harry N. Scheiber (expanded edition, Cambridge, MA: Harvard University Press, 1988), 359–74; Laura Kalman, *Legal Realism at Yale 1927–1960* (Chapel Hill: University of North Carolina Press, 1986); Morton Horwitz, *The Transformation of American Law, 1870–1960* (New York: Oxford University Press, 1992); John Henry Schlegel, *American Legal Realism and Empirical Social Science* (Chapel Hill: University of North Carolina Press, 1995); N. E. H. Hull, *Roscoe Pound and Karl Llewellyn: Searching for an American Jurisprudence* (Chicago: University of Chicago Press, 1997); and Dalia Tsuk Mitchell, *Architect of Justice: Felix S. Cohen and the Founding of American Legal Pluralism* (Ithaca: Cornell University Press, 2007). For excerpts from the writings of the best remembered legal realists, with insightful scholarly commentary, see *American Legal Realism*, eds. William W. Fisher III, Morton J. Horwitz, and Thomas A. Reed (New York: Oxford University Press, 1993).

This chapter is dedicated, in friendship, to my colleague Lawrence M. Friedman. A preliminary version was presented to a conference at Stanford University in his honor, and it was first published in revised form in *Law and History Review*, the journal of the American Society for Legal History; the present study incorporates some further minor revisions. I am grateful to my colleague Professor David D. Caron (UC Berkeley Law School), to Professor Stewart Macaulay (Wisconsin Law School) and other participants in the Friedman conference at Stanford, and to Professor David Tanenhaus and two anonymous reviewers for *Law and History Review* for valuable editorial and substantive suggestions. The law librarians at UC Berkeley, the Harvard Law School, and The University of Texas all extended themselves greatly to accommodate my requests for materials.

been almost entirely neglected by historians of legal thought,[2] and yet he was one of the earliest American legal commentators to promote an iconoclastic, reformist approach to the common law and American constitutional law. As discussed in this chapter, his writings in the 1910s and 1920s were important early contributions to the iconoclastic, reformist approach to the law that would become a central canon of legal realism. His uniqueness among the realists rests in the fact that he would go on in later decades to play a prominent part in contending for basic doctrinal reforms in international law.

Bingham's career is also of interest in regard to Lawrence Friedman's central place in the scholarship on law as related to historic social, political, and economic processes that have reshaped the landscape of law and society studies (the derivative, successor approach to legal realism). I refer here to the Stanford Law dimension of Bingham's story.

The now abundant historical literature on legal realism centers attention on Chicago, Yale, and Columbia, with Pennsylvania and Berkeley as peripheral players in the drama of the realists' challenge to the Langdellian tradition. Stanford is never mentioned as being of any importance in this regard before the 1960s. Today, of course, the academic landscape of law and society studies is very different, with prominent centers especially active at the University of California at Berkeley, Northwestern University, New York University, and several other institutions (including the three "original" centers of legal realism). Stanford's law faculty, too, has now become a major locus of innovative work in sociolegal scholarship, largely reflecting Lawrence Friedman's influence. As this chapter shows, however, Stanford should not be regarded only as a contributor to the second wave in the twentieth-century development of legal realist/law and society studies. There actually were two very active scholarly outposts on the West Coast in the earlier years: One was UC Berkeley (where Max Radin, Barbara Armstrong, and Roger Traynor, among others, were teaching and writing by the 1940s). The other, which was of major importance in the earlier ("founding") period, was Stanford Law School – as evidenced by the work that Joseph Walter Bingham was publishing at the time.

In this chapter, I first lay out the reasons why we should locate Bingham historically as a figure of considerable significance in the history of American legal realism. Not

---

[2] Exceptions with regard to recognizing Bingham's early contributions to realism are the references to his early writings some forty years ago, in Rumble, *American Legal Realism*, 32, 82–3, 104, 140–1; and brief mentions in Hull, *Roscoe Pound and Karl Llewellyn*, 75 n.122, 204–5. Bingham himself left a 110-page informal commentary on his own writings and a partial memoir, *List of Writings of Joseph Bingham* (1965), on deposit with the Stanford Law School Library. The provenance of this document is documented in George Torzsay-Biber, "A Preliminary Bibliography," 17 *Stanford Law Review* (1964–5): 1017–18. An informative appreciation of Bingham as a teacher and as a scholar is provided in an unpublished memorial statement by Moffatt Hancock et al., "Memorial Resolution: Joseph Walter Bingham (1878–1973)," http://histsoc.stanford.edu/pdfmem/BinghamJ.pdf. Twining notes that when Llewellyn first entered law studies as a young man, the published writings of Bingham and Pound were already laying the groundwork for legal realism. (Twining, *Karl Llewellyn and the Realist Movement*, 366.)

that I want to contend that Bingham had the degree of influence exerted over the long haul by Roscoe Pound, say, or Karl Llewellyn or Jerome Frank; but I do argue that he clearly deserves a place among the other notables in the pantheon of the movement's founders.

Second, I show that Bingham's career was important historically because of his prominent role in carrying both the reformist zeal and the critical intellectual posture of realism into a prominent area of controversy in international law, starting in the late 1930s. In this area of legal discourse and polemics, he was a central figure in a debate over "offshore jurisdiction" that animated lawyers and diplomats both in America and internationally, beginning at a time of deeply troubled international relations that would soon bring on World War II. The debate centered on the sensitive question – one that was of immediate concern to the United States and other naval powers that were then building up for war – of the distance out into ocean waters to which the prerogatives of sovereignty of coastal states could legitimately be exercised offshore.

In this debate over offshore jurisdiction, Bingham stridently challenged the inherited precepts and the prevailing national policies regarding this highly sensitive aspect of the law of the sea. Legal realism – as an approach to the law that he had helped launch in the 1910s – thereby became an intellectual platform from which Bingham argued for a fundamental departure from customary law, contending for the adoption of new principles for the law of the sea. Bingham's ideas on jurisprudence of ocean law and on the need for explicit reforms were influential in their day – just as his writings in the earliest days of the realist movement had been important for the way they challenged the legacy of classical legal formalism. He not only functioned as academic gadfly and challenger to classical legal formalism; he also exerted an immediate impact in establishing the terms of the policy debate and in influencing actual policy outcomes.[3] Indeed, in recognition of his influence on the formation of American foreign policy during the late 1930s, specifically with regard to ocean law doctrines, diplomats would later routinely refer to his developed position on the law of offshore waters and jurisdiction over fisheries – important questions then in controversy in international law and foreign relations – as the "Bingham doctrine."[4]

In the field of international law, Bingham's theories on ocean law proved to be not only boldly reformist but also remarkably prescient. This was so because his

---

[3] There were other legal scholars who joined with Bingham to pursue the realist approach in debates of international law, most prominently Stefan Riesenfeld and William W. Bishop. Yet in any event they were not of sufficient reputation as of 1938 to be identified as members of the realist school; their major contributions to international law would come later. On Riesenfeld's collaboration with Bingham, see text at notes 51–7. Bingham is referred to in one respected scholarly study as being in 1950 among "the most eminent authorities in the field of international law"; Ernest R. Bartley, *The Tidelands Oil Controversy* (Austin: University of Texas Press, 1953), 208–9.

[4] For example, the phrase was used frequently in the internal correspondence and minutes of the British Foreign Office, as will be discussed in my book, in progress, on the development of modern ocean law, 1937–58.

arguments for reform were in the cause of legitimizing on a "realistic" jurisprudential basis claims of extended offshore jurisdiction by coastal states beyond the limits that then prevailed as customary law. (For most nations, including the great naval power Great Britain, the limit was three miles; for a few states, it was as far offshore as twelve miles.) Indeed when the 1982 United Nations Convention on the Law of the Sea (UNCLOS) incorporated as a key provision agreement on authorization for jurisdictional claims out to 200 miles or more, under the rubric "Exclusive Economic Zone," it reflected in a basic sense the rationale that Bingham had advanced in his arguments for ocean-law reform some forty-five years earlier.[5]

The extension of national authority out onto ocean waters far beyond historic limits was a radical proposal at the time Bingham first espoused it; many colleagues in the academy admonished him for advocating claims that would escalate controversy among nations that were already on the verge of war. Yet Bingham's ideas are now integral to the new "constitution for the oceans" that UNCLOS has provided and that serves today as the basic framework for the regime of the global oceans.[6]

Given his innovative role both with regard to legal realism and to the reform debates that led to this dramatic redrawing of the map of ocean jurisdictions, Bingham's ideas and activist record deserve a fresh reconsideration by the historians of American and of international law.

---

[5] I use the phrase "in a basic sense" because the essential question in the debate from 1935 to 1982 was whether the old rule in customary ocean law – predominantly a three-mile claim for sovereignty (the territorial sea) with only a few exceptions such as for the hot pursuit of smugglers or protection against pollution out to twelve miles – should yield to a rule that a coastal nation's jurisdiction should be extended out as far as a realistic assessment of practical need for special purposes (e.g., for protection of coastal fisheries resources) would warrant it. The Exclusive Economic Zone (EEZ) as provided for by the UN 1982 Convention authorized the 200-mile limit for purposes of regulating economic activity; it did not authorize full sovereignty, and in that sense too it was fully consistent with Bingham's basic idea that specified types of activity should be covered by offshore jurisdiction to the distance that was warranted by their character and their effect on interests of the coastal state.

An important aspect of the controversy – one that was not explicitly considered by Bingham until after World War II – has to do with the distance to which a contiguous continental shelf may extend, for a particular state, beyond the 200-mile EEZ limit and thus (as the 1982 Convention permits) authorize a claim to economic use of the seabed in the shelf area in question. This potentially dangerous issue is in play, as of this writing, especially in the Arctic area, as Russia (which has planted a flag on the seabed under the North Pole, to highlight its claim of a continental shelf extension to that distance), Denmark, and Canada have all become committed to claims to shelf distances in the Arctic far beyond 200 miles offshore. See the papers in a special symposium issue on international law relating to the continental shelf and offshore jurisdiction of coastal states, in the *International Journal of Marine and Coastal Law* 21 (Sept. 2006): 263–373; Daniel Kressey, "Russia at Forefront of Arctic Land Grab," *Nature* 448 (Aug. 2, 2007).

Assertive continental shelf claims by the Soviet Union have generated international tensions in the Barents Sea region of the Arctic dating back to the 1960s.

[6] In this legal context, the term "the oceans" is invoked as including the regimes for use of airspace and economic exploitation of the seabed in the jurisdictional area in question, not only fishing, scientific activity, and maritime and naval operations or other activities on the surface or in the water column. See generally the essays in Davor Vidas and Willy Østreng, eds., *Order for the Oceans at the Turn of the Century* (The Hague: Kluwer Law International, 1998); and Harry N. Scheiber, ed., *The Law of the Sea: The Common Heritage and Emerging Challenges* (The Hague: Martinus Nijhoff Publishers, 2000).

BINGHAM AS A FOUNDER OF AMERICAN LEGAL REALISM

The obscurity to which Bingham has been largely relegated in the historical studies of realism is surprising – and certainly is unjustified – if for no other reason than because his role in scholarly debates of legal theory during 1909–15 was explicitly acknowledged in later years by the realist giants Karl Llewellyn, Roscoe Pound, and Jerome Frank, among others, as having had a formative influence in the articulation of the movement's premises, analytical methodology, and objectives.[7] Granted, as Rumble wrote years ago, "there is no infallible method to determine who is a legal realist."[8] Yet it is indisputable that any description of the genus would be deficient if it excluded Bingham.

Bingham joined the Stanford faculty in 1907 after earning his law degree at the University of Chicago in 1904, devoting a year to practice, and then teaching law at Cornell University during 1905–7.[9] He wrote his most influential works in the formative realist period (perhaps better termed the "pre-realist era") soon after joining the Stanford law faculty. As previously noted, Bingham's work at Stanford provides ample reason for recognizing that institution's law faculty as being important in this early history of realist thought – especially because when Bingham's first important realist writings were being published, Wesley Hohfeld was a colleague of his on the faculty there. Hohfeld too was influential in shaping both early realist jurisprudence and the pragmatic reformist posture of legal realism in later years.[10] However, unlike Bingham, Hohfeld has received from legal historians the attention he amply merits. However, such attention has been without reference to his being a contemporary and a colleague of Bingham's at a time when Hohfeld's own position on consequentialism and pragmatism was taking shape.[11]

---

[7] See text at note 14. The objectives of the later realists varied, of course, with some of them mainly concerned to advance empirical research (and teaching of empirical legal process) and others with more theoretical or policy-reform preoccupations. See Schlegel, *American Legal Realism, passim.* Bingham's early writing anticipated all these variants, although he made no pretense of pursuing empirical research himself and merely advocated bringing social science and psychology into the analysis of law.

[8] Wilfrid E. Rumble, Jr., "Legal Realism, Sociological Jurisprudence, and Mr. Justice Holmes," *Journal of the History of Ideas* 26 (1965): 547–66 at 547 n.1.

[9] Marion R. Kirkwood and William B. Owens, "A Brief History of the Stanford Law School, 1893–1946," http://www.law.stanford.edu/school/history/historysls.pdf – 2003–05-22. See also Hancock et al., "Memorial Resolution."

[10] In her important studies of the subject, N. E. H. Hull uses the term "Progressive-Pragmatic, anti-Formalist movement" to describe the contributions of Pound and others in what I call here the "pre-realist" period; and she distinguishes it from the later legal realism in the jurisprudence associated with Llewellyn and the other major figures (see text at note 13) who were writing in the late 1920s and the 1930s. Hull, "Reconstructing the Origins of Realistic Jurisprudence: A Prequel to the Llewellyn-Pound Exchange over Legal Realism," *Duke Law Journal,* 1989 (1989): 1334. See also note 39.

[11] Twining describes Hohfeld as of 1913, when he submitted his first article for editorial consideration, as a "hitherto unknown professor at Stanford." (Twining, *Karl Llewellyn,* 34.) Hohfeld is the subject of much attention in the standard histories and in studies of legal theory. See, e.g., N. E. H. Hull, "Vital Schools of Jurisprudence: Roscoe Pound, Wesley Newcomb Hohfeld, and the Promotion of an Academic Jurisprudential Agenda, 1910 to 1919," 45 *Journal of Legal Education* (1995): 235–81;

Let us return to the question of how to locate Bingham properly in the intellectual history of legal realism. A key indication of his prominence as it was seen by the most relevant contemporaries is to be found in the famous lists that Llewellyn and Frank put together in 1931 when preparing to respond to Roscoe Pound's withering attack on the realists.[12] In those lists, the giants who are best remembered today all appear: Oliphant, Clark, Cook, Powell, Radin, Douglas, Yntema, Patterson, and the rest of the familiar suspects.[13] (Of course, none of these scholars had given attention in their writings to problems of international law, except perhaps Max Radin insofar as he was concerned with comparative jurisprudence.) One additional name that Llewellyn and Frank placed at the very top of that list – a name that was included "as of course," Llewellyn stated – was that of Joseph Walter Bingham.[14]

For his part, Pound concurred in acknowledging Bingham's place in the first ranks of the realists: When Llewellyn and Frank challenged him to identify the authors of some specific writings that he deemed exemplary of realist thought, as portrayed in his critique, Pound came forth with only three names, one of which was Bingham's.[15] Pound linked Bingham with Lorenzen as having been "particularly insistent upon the unreality of supposed rules, principles, and doctrines."[16] In refining his own list, Llewellyn placed Bingham in a small subgroup that he categorized as "those who may have taken extreme positions on one point or another."[17] Meanwhile, in 1930

and Joseph William Singer, "The Legal Rights Debate in Analytical Jurisprudence from Bentham to Hohfeld," *Wisconsin Law Review*, 1982 (1982): 975–1059. Hohfeld was appointed at Stanford in 1905 and remained on the faculty there until taking a sabbatical leave in 1914–15, when he accepted the position at Yale. A Stanford Class of 1913 alumnus later recalled that the influence of Bingham and Hohfeld in the classroom "stimulate[d] deep thought that pierced far below any superficial crust which rested lightly on vague legal terminology." Homer R. Spence, "Joseph Walter Bingham," *Stanford Law Review* 17 (1964–5): 1009, 1016.

    Unfortunately little documentation seems to have been discovered that can yield robust information regarding the intellectual or personal relationship of the two men. In a letter to Roscoe Pound, written when Hohfeld was at Stanford and ardently seeking Pound's support in his career, Hohfeld referred rather sarcastically to Bingham's recently published article "What is Law?" and omitted to mention Bingham by name. One is left with the impression, taking this letter as a whole, that Hohfeld felt obliged to refer to the article – but that certainly he was not going out of his way to give marquee recognition to his colleague and that he was distancing himself from what he characterized as excessiveness in Bingham's wholesale critique of previous jurisprudential scholarship. (Hohfeld to Pound, Feb. 25, 1913, Roscoe Pound Papers, Harvard University Law Library, microfilm, Reel 7). In one of Bingham's later writings (see text at note 38), Bingham was explicitly uncomplimentary with regard to Hohfeld's intellectual style. Withal, one sees no sign of cordial colleagueship between the two men in these glimpses from what scant evidence is apparently available.

[12] See "Llewellyn's 'Sample' of Realists," in Twining, *Karl Llewellyn and the Realist Movement*, 76; the successive lists are reproduced in Hull, *Roscoe Pound and Karl Llewellyn*, 343–6; and the published version in the footnotes of Llewellyn's article, Karl Llewellyn, "Some Realism about Realism," *Harvard Law Review* 44 (1931): 1222, 1227 n.18.

[13] See the full account in Hull, *Roscoe Pound and Karl Llewellyn*, 202–19.

[14] Quoted in Twining, *Karl Llewellyn*, 76; see also Hull, *Roscoe Pound and Karl Llewellyn*, 204.

[15] Hull, *Roscoe Pound and Karl Llewellyn*, 204.

[16] Pound to Llewellyn, March 21, 1931, quoted in ibid., 204.

[17] The list sent by Llewellyn to Pound, April 6, 1931, reproduced in ibid., 344.

Jerome Frank devoted six pages of his book, *Law and the Modern Mind*, to a full summary of Bingham's 1912 article entitled "What Is the Law?" – although Frank resorted heavily to paraphrasing because of Bingham's "forbidding Austinian style." Frank parenthetically suggested that this difficult prose style was the reason that Bingham had not been given the full recognition that he merited.[18]

Late in his life, Bingham himself reflected ruefully that his early works had been seen by colleagues as "reconditely interesting but practically useless." He said that his viewpoint on legal philosophy had been too far ahead of his time – "twenty years . . . [before] the cult of realists was formed with headquarters at Yale and Columbia."[19] How had Bingham come to be recognized, then, at the time two decades afterward when giants in the fields of jurisprudence and legal realism such as Pound and Llewellyn were exchanging those famous volleys?[20]

Bingham's earliest writings, published in the Michigan and Columbia law journals, were critical analyses of inherited procedural norms in the common law of property and of torts.[21] These first efforts, in a retrospective view, firmly establish his credentials as a key figure in the intellectual movement that would later set legal realism on its course.[22] Bingham declared that his main purpose in writing these early set of articles was to establish that law should be viewed "as a field of study analogous to that of any science" and that its subject matter be subject to objective "scientific investigation" rather than being studied by a methodology that was distorted by its reliance on the perpetuation of "stereotyped rules and principles." He also contended that judges and scholars seeking to formulate the proper applications of the law must depend on concrete realities of particular cases.[23]

In a stab at Langdell and at the concept of immutable rules underlying a comprehensive jurisprudence, Bingham deplored "the vague current idea that the purpose of scientific investigation is the extraction from their hiding places and the domestication of certain wild beasts of the jungle of ignorance known as principles and

[18] Jerome Frank, *Law and the Modern Mind* (New York: Brentano's, 1930), 275n. and 274–9. Frank stated that Bingham's work had not come to his attention until after the book had actually been sent to editors for consideration. (ibid., 275n.). When Llewellyn sought advice on his list of realists, in preparation for his response to Pound, he had some correspondence with Bingham, who recommended that Pound himself should be included in that list! (Hull, "Reconstructing the Origins," 1317.) See also Moffatt Hancock, "Joseph Walter Bingham," *Stanford Law Review* 17 (1964–5): 1111.

[19] Bingham, *List of Writings*, 7.

[20] As Twining has noted, when Llewellyn was still a student in 1919, papers were already in print by Bingham, along with others by Corbin and by Hohfeld, that "foreshadowed the growth of the Realist movement." (Twining, *Karl Llewellyn*, 366.)

[21] Joseph Walter Bingham, "Some Suggestions Concerning the Law of Fixtures," *Columbia Law Review* 7 (1907): 1; "Some Suggestions Concerning 'Legal Cause' at Common Law," Parts 1 and 2, *Columbia Law Review* 9 (1909): 16, 136; "What Is the Law?" Parts 1 and 2, *Michigan Law Review* (1912): 1, 109, with a "Supplementary Note" entitled "The Nature of Legal Rights and Duties," ibid., 12 (1913): 1; "Some Suggestions Concerning 'Legal Cause' at Common Law," Parts 1 and 2, *Columbia Law Review* 9 (1909): 16, 136.

[22] See quotations in text at notes 15–18.

[23] Bingham, "What Is the Law?" 9–11, 13–14.

rules."[24] He insisted that the very concept of what one calls a "legal principle" must be understood as "a psychological phenomenon"; it should not be conceived of as an idea with "an existence independent of the human mind," and when legal principles or rules "pass[ed] the limits of utility, they should be discarded."[25] Thus did Bingham give new expression to an idea fundamental to Holmes's jurisprudence – an idea carried forward in the contemporaneous writings of Roscoe Pound to the effect that "the social value of a rule" rather than inherited obeisance to it should be the "test" of its legitimacy.[26]

One of the basic postulates of legal realism, in its assault on what Bingham termed "befogging superstitions, mystifying dogmas, and the treadmills of inadequate generalities and sophistical reasoning,"[27] was that "rights" or the essential terms of "causes" in torts were formulated in response to specific situations. In these situations, "duties" were inferred from the terms of specific agreements and the factual nature of the objects to which duty and claims referred. This idea was a major theme also of Hohfeld's early work, on which Llewellyn depended heavily; it was also a key element of the attack on the foundation of constitutional formalism and its "rights discourse" based on a concept of natural and universal rights.[28] Given Hohfeld's association with Bingham at Stanford, it is reasonable to see the work of the two on this theme as part of a certainly parallel, although not demonstrably shared, intellectual enterprise. Indeed, in its broad outlines and the major thrust of argument, as well as in its more technical aspects, Hohfeld's famous analysis in 1913 of "fundamental legal conceptions" of duties and rights expressed many of the same ideas that Bingham had been expounding in the years immediately before.[29]

Also strikingly manifested in Bingham's "pre-realist" scholarship was a view of the judicial process and of judges' mental processes that foreshadowed some of the later realists' emphasis on psychology and law, especially as expressed in Frank's extreme

[24] Ibid., 4.

[25] Ibid., 11.

[26] Pound, as quoted approvingly in Cardozo, *Nature of the Judicial Process* (New Haven: Yale University Press, 1921); see discussion in Horwitz, *Transformation of American Law*, 190.

[27] Bingham, "What Is the Law?" 119. See also note 29.

[28] Horwitz, *Transformation*, 154 and passim.

[29] Hohfeld, "Fundamental Legal Conceptions as Applied in Judicial Reasoning," *Yale Law Journal* 26 (1917): 711–70. However, Horwitz points out that Hohfeld essentially "reintroduced a theme highlighted by Holmes forty years earlier" – the theme that "duties precede rights, logically and chronologically" – a comment that certainly applies with equal accuracy to the way in which Bingham advanced his arguments on duties and rights. Bingham in his early studies gave explicit credit to Austin, Holmes, and Pound, as well as to J. B. Thayer and others (e.g., in text and footnotes in Bingham, "What Is the Law?" 112–13, 120).

A Stanford law student recalled as follows the impact of Hohfeld and Bingham on teaching in his day: "With the zeal of crusaders, these men, each in his own way, started to do some pioneering in the field of attempted clarification of legal concepts and reasoning . . . " and that this attribute could leave "[an] indelible imprint upon the mind of every law student who is fortunate enough to experience its influence." Homer R. Spence, "Joseph Walter Bingham," *Stanford Law Review* 17 (1964–65): 1016.

view of the force of subjectivity in judging.[30] In Bingham's formulation, judges make decisions "not . . . by reference to some mysteriously and anciently evolved system of rules and principles of inherent authority," but rather by "processes of intelligent reasoning" that reflect personal experience and knowledge of the individual judge. Thus "impressions, beliefs, and conclusions concerning the facts of the case, concrete precedents, applicable customs, habits, common ideas, moral blameworthiness, and other logically pertinent considerations are consolidated and welded in generalizations."[31] Bingham rejected the contrary notion, that "law necessarily preexists, that it is something general and authoritative." He contended that this view was indefensible in logic or in a fair reading of historical experience; it was merely a manifestation of "the old superstitions"[32] and as such could produce "unwise decisions"[33] and was capable of causing damage to society's community interests.

"There is nothing authoritative in the existence of a rule or a principle," Bingham declared: "Courts produce concrete legal consequences," and the inherited rules should be regarded as valid if – and only if – they passed the pragmatic, essentially consequentialist, test as to what one predicted would be defensible "potential legal consequences."[34] Application of ordinary human intelligence, the analytical equipment and knowledge of the natural and physical sciences and of psychology, and predictive capacity (to ascertain most probable social consequences) were Bingham's prescription for analysis of the worth of a rule or principle.

This basic idea, which Bingham set forth in bold terms as a young scholar in his early years at Stanford, would later become a stock element in the rhetorical and conceptual arsenals of the legal realists in the 1930s: the imperative, as stated for example, by Felix Cohen in 1935, that "creative legal thought will more and more look behind the traditionally accepted principles 'justice' and 'reason' to appraise in ethical terms the social values at stake in any choice between two precedents."[35]

Asked to summarize his personal credo for a book that appeared in 1941, Bingham sounded the same themes with which he had thrown down the gauntlet three

---

[30] In this context, the term "pre-realist" evokes the continuing controversy among historians and legal scholars on basic issues of chronology and the proper classification of individuals with regard to legal realism. There is a fascination with the questions, Who specifically can be identified as the legal realists? And was realism in a defensible sense actually a "school"? In either case, when did the movement begin – and when did it end, if ever? (if indeed it was a "movement" or "school," rather than the term "legal realism" merely denoting no more than a congeries of loosely interrelated related legal theorists – and legal theories)? There is no need here to rehearse the debate of whether law and society studies represent a departure in fundamental ways from legal realism or instead (a view to which I adhere) are embedded in realism's legacy. For an insightful recent commentary, see Stewart Macaulay, "The New Versus the Old Legal Realism: Things Ain't What They Used To Be," *Wisconsin Law Review* (2005): 365–403.

[31] Bingham, "What Is the Law?" 14.

[32] Ibid., 17.

[33] Ibid., 18.

[34] Ibid., 22.

[35] Felix Cohen, "Transcendental Nonsense and the Functional Approach," *Columbia Law Review* 35 (1935): 809, 833; also in Fisher et al., eds., *American Legal Realism*, 218.

decades earlier.[36] "Systems of philosophy which put life and its purposes in a neat logically coordinated system," he wrote, were dedicated to "seek[ing] eternal truth" and as such should be seen as "interesting... exercises in dialectic," not as a valid way of stating what should be the law. He recognized that they could be influential, no matter how "illusory" in their philosophical foundation, but they could also be "on occasion distinctly pernicious." Bingham contended that historically such systems of law

> retarded seriously the development of a science of law founded on a wide and deep study of our very complicated, intensely interesting, and important field of professional efforts, and thereby have contributed to the persistence of bad government and human misfortunes. Indeed generally the highly artificial legal philosophies of Europe have been more concerned with elaboration and maintenance of systematized theory as an end in itself than with intimate knowledge of the facts of life and government and the improvement of society in its governmental phases.[37]

He admitted being resigned to the fact that legal usages were intractable – that "to try, in labored Hohfeldian fashion, to regiment the vocabulary of lawyers and jurists is almost as hopeless as to try to confine the blowing of the wind."[38] Yet still he remained, as he bluntly described himself, *"an American realist"* who wrote as "an iconoclast" dedicated to engaging in a mission of "advocacy, of opposing attack, of counterattack."[39]

When the academic firestorms of legal debate first broke out in the late 1920s and early 1930s, he was not an active player among the legal realists – although, as we have seen, his earlier contributions to realist thought became well recognized at that time. This is not to say, by any means, that he was inactive. He turned his attention to international law, and he participated in this arena with all the energy and reformist zealousness that he had brought to his earlier realist studies of domestic law and legal philosophy.

BINGHAM'S CAMPAIGN FOR OCEAN-LAW REFORM

It would have seemed unlikely when Bingham first established himself as a scholar at Stanford that twenty years later he would become a major figure in the American

---

[36] Joseph Walter Bingham, [untitled essay] in *My Philosophy of Law: Credos of Sixteen American Scholars* (Boston: Boston Law Book Company, 1941), 25.
[37] Ibid.
[38] Ibid., 11. Although he is easily lumped together with Hohfeld as an Austinian, Bingham in one of his major articles took specific issue with Austin's commitment to traditional usage of the concept of "law." It is "an essential error of Austin's work," Bingham wrote, "that it examines the paraphernalia of the law rather than its substance.... [H]is attempt to harmonize and unify led him into artificialities... [His] emphasis was so strongly laid on definition that the work does not approach a scientific exposition of the field of law and its elements." Bingham, *What Is the Law?* 3, note 4.
[39] Ibid., 7. Emphasis added.

academy in the field of international law. Bingham served during World War I in the War Trade Board and is said to have become interested there in international law, a field not then offered in the Stanford teaching curriculum but in which he began to conduct research.[40] He took a major part in the Harvard international law project, serving as the reporter for the project's study of the law of piracy, published in 1932.[41] Meanwhile he had also developed a specialty in water law at Stanford, and in 1934 he published an article contending for reform of California's riparian rights doctrine that was later influential with the state's high court.[42] He took time as well to do research for a major article of 1936 that set out a pragmatic, quintessentially realist, critique of the law of property rights in divorce cases involving conflicts of law – presenting an alternative approach that in fact was later adopted by the U.S. Supreme Court in a decision that overturned long-established doctrine.[43] In 1941, he would also publish a revision of an established case book on wills and inheritance.[44]

However, what came to interest Bingham most were the central issues in international law relating to the rights and duties of states in coastal and high seas areas of the oceans: issues of sovereignty, legitimacy of nation-state claims, and what he saw as the imperatives of technological innovation and scientific management in the rapidly changing arena of ocean resource use. Bingham asserted that these imperatives, especially with regard to the exploitation of ocean fisheries by ever larger fleets of ever more powerful vessels and gear, required an abandonment of customary norms and demanded a radical revision in the jurisprudential principles of ocean law. In the new arena of debate that emerged in the late 1930s, Bingham engaged these issues with the same level of energy, iconoclasm, and zest for polemical combat as he had shown in his earliest academic years. His objective now was to advance a reform campaign that would transform basic principles of coastal state rights and

---

[40] Kirkwood and Owens, "Brief History of the Stanford Law School," cited in note 9.

[41] [Joseph Walter Bingham, Reporter], *Draft Convention on Piracy* (Harvard University Law School, Research in International Law), in *American Journal of International Law* 26, Supplement (1932): 739–49. This report would later have an important influence on the project of the UN International Law Commission when it worked on codification of the law of the sea in the 1950s. Barry Hart Dubnev, *The Law of International Sea Piracy* (The Hague: Martinus Nijhoff, 1980), 37–93. A remarkably prescient aspect of the report was the attention it gave to the possibility of acts of terrorism or piracy "in or from the air," in light of the advances in aviation. Whether this was a contribution we can specifically identify with Bingham, the willingness to go beyond the traditional wisdom and historical definitions of piracy (confined to acts at sea) was certainly consistent with his intellectual style. See ibid., 52–64; and note 49.

[42] Bingham, "Some Suggestions Concerning the California Law of Riparian Rights," *California Law Review* 22 (1934): 251–76, proposing a procedural change that the California Supreme Court adopted in *Peabody v. City of Vallejo*, 2 Cal. 2nd, 351, 40 Pac. R. 2nd 486 (1935).

[43] Bingham, "The American Law Institute vs. The Supreme Court," cited earlier. The Supreme Court decision on "divisible divorce" that adopted his viewpoint was in the case of *Vanderbilt v. Vanderbilt*, 354 U.S. 416 (1957), discussed in Hancock, "Joseph Walter Bingham," 1011.

[44] Joseph Walter Bingham, *Cases and Materials on Wills, Descent and Administration*, by George P. Costigan (3rd edition, St. Paul: West Publishing Co., 1941). Years earlier Bingham had published as sole author and editor, *Estates of Decedents* (Chicago: LaSalle Extension University, 1913).

ocean law. In the course of his new involvements, it may be said Bingham carried "offshore" the cause of legal realism.

Just as Bingham had attacked classical formalism in law during his earlier years, the inherited formalist precepts of international law became his new target when he undertook his reformist campaign in the realm of ocean law. The specific issue on which he wrote was the law of territorial waters – the rules that prescribed the geographic distance and functional scope of coastal states' jurisdiction over ocean areas and marine resources off their shorelines. In particular, he offered a reconceptualization of the rights of coastal states to regulate offshore fishing that was conducted by vessels operating under foreign flags. At the time, in the dominant school of scholarship of international law, at least in the Anglo-American tradition, the "three-mile" rule of territorial waters was held virtually sacred.[45] This concept, which had come down in the tradition of Grotius since the seventeenth century, involved, among other things, the rule that beyond a fixed limit off the shores of coastal states the ocean's fishery resources comprised a commons that could not legitimately be claimed or controlled by any individual state. Although some coastal nations maintained a claim to ownership of the seabed or jurisdiction over fishing out to nine or even twelve miles beyond the shoreline, the United States and the United Kingdom had long adhered to the three-mile rule and contended for its universal application, as did other interested marine nations that accepted the rule as embodied in customary law.[46] With regard to ocean fisheries, the three-mile rule meant that, beyond that boundary line out to sea, the ships of any and all nations were free to engage in their harvest without controls by any nation other than their own flag nation. In practice, few nations exerted any kind of restrictions over the high-seas fishing activities of their nationals, either to target fishery species, the volume or method of catch, or, *en fin*, any consideration of sustainability and

---

[45] This can be said with reference to the standard Anglo-American legal literature up to the mid-1930s, although historically the three-mile limit had been made subject to exceptions by even the United States and the United Kingdom. In addition, it was not accepted universally, because many coastal states claimed up to nine or in some cases twelve miles for purposes of regulating fisheries or other activities, and (as noted in the text later) a few claimed full sovereignty (not just special jurisdiction for limited purposes) over territorial seas of more than six miles. See the standard historical and legal analysis by Stefan A. Riesenfeld, *Protection of Coastal Fisheries under International Law* (New York: Carnegie Endowment for International Peace, 1942); and also William E. Masterson, *Jurisdiction in Marginal Seas, with Special Reference to Smuggling* (New York: Macmillan, 1929); Sayre A. Swarztrauber, *The Three-Mile Limit of Territorial Seas* (Annapolis: Naval Institute Press, 1972); and the brief discussion in Douglas M. Johnston, *The International Law of Fisheries: A Framework for Policy-Oriented Inquiries* (New Haven: Yale University Press, 1965), 171–6.

[46] For the classic argument that the three-mile rule was "established international law," see Philip Jessup, *The Law of Territorial Waters and Maritime Jurisdiction* (New York: G. A. Jennings Co., 1927), chapter 1, passim. An authoritative work on ocean law, unique in the literature for its integration of legal development and related changes in technology, science, resource exploration, and public policies, is Lawrence Juda, *International Law and Ocean Use Management: The Evolution of Ocean Commerce* (London: Routledge, 1996).

conservation. Indeed, the ocean fisheries had long been regarded as inexhaustible, giving additional legitimacy to the three-mile rule and its variants.[47]

By the 1930s, however, it had become evident that marine fisheries could be depleted by overfishing in this traditional regime that was called – with significant rhetorical effect – the regime of "freedom of the seas." Steam-driven ships of ever larger scale and capability for distant and prolonged voyages, refrigeration of catches at sea, and diesel power were producing a dramatic rise in the volume of ocean fisheries harvested by the world's fishing fleets. Bilateral and multilateral international agreements were negotiated to deal with the overfishing threat, but these agreements applied to very few of the great stocks of commercial fish in the world's oceans. Hence by the mid-1930s, the rising scale of marine fishing harvests had become alarming to most fishery scientists and to government officials in the major maritime nations globally.[48]

Among the law writers in the field of international law, the dominant (though not universally accepted) view was that "freedom of the seas" and of the narrow territorial sea, as traditionally defined with regard to freedom to fish, navigation, or waste disposal, was a matter of "rule of law" established through customary practice (i.e., by dint of widespread acceptance by maritime states). As such, it was contended that the established rule would serve the interests of stability and peace: A clear rule demarcating the norms for behavior on the high seas was a deterrent to dangerous clashes of interest that could provoke the uses of force between maritime nations. The legal traditionalists did not oppose orderly processes for reform of the strict three-mile rule. Instead they contended that any revision of such a basic rule should be pursued only by treaties as part of a consensual process that would reshape the established universal customary law in international affairs. Self-interested, unilateral action to extend jurisdiction seaward was seen as menacing to the peace.[49]

---

[47] Harry N. Scheiber, "Ocean Governance and the Marine Fisheries Crisis: Two Decades of Innovation – and Frustration," *Virginia Environmental Law Journal* 20 (2001): 119–23.

[48] David Cushing, *Fisheries Resources of the Sea and their Management* (Oxford: Oxford University Press, 1975); F. S. Russell, *The Overfishing Problem* (Cambridge: Cambridge University Press, 1942). See also Harry N. Scheiber and Christopher J. Carr, "From Extended Jurisdiction to Privatization: International Law, Biology, and Economics in the Marine Fisheries Debates, 1937–1976," *Berkeley Journal of International Law* 14 (1998): 10–54.

[49] E.g, Philip C. Jessup, "The Pacific Coast Fisheries," *American Journal of International Law* 33 (1939): 134. Riesenfeld calculated that in the literature published during 1800–1899, of 113 acknowledged legal commentators on ocean law, 94 accepted the three mile (or "cannon-shot") rule as authoritative; but from 1900 to about 1939, of 114 commentators, only 61 regarded the rule as definitive as a matter of customary law. (*Coastal Fisheries*, 279.) Taking account of the nationality of each writer would, of course, be a useful indicator of bias in the aggregate numbers. Nonetheless, there is no question that Bingham was on firm scholarly ground in saying that the three-mile rule had been challenged in important ways, both in state practice and in learned commentary. Indeed, one of the central objectives of the Harvard project on the law of piracy for which Bingham served as rapporteur was to advance the concept of an "extraordinary basis of jurisdiction" in offshore waters for actions enforced against pirates (quoted in Dubner, *Law of International Sea Piracy*, 48.) The Harvard project went well beyond the traditional intellectual boundaries of ocean law discourse in foreseeing that piracy might

Bingham would launch a sustained campaign, in the realist vein, against these traditional views in international law. He would argue that customary international law had developed historically precisely as the common law had developed – as an ongoing process of change in which new technological, economic, and social imperatives had led to the adaptations in law and the acceptance of new doctrines – and that ocean law as it stood in the 1930s required the same kind of radical reforms as had successfully challenged the classical legalism of American domestic law.

Bingham's views came to prominence in a global debate of ocean fisheries questions that was the immediate result of a diplomatic confrontation that involved the United States, Canada, and Japan in the late 1930s. For the United States, the sudden appearance in 1937 and 1938 of Japanese-flag factory-ship fleets in the Bering Sea – an ocean area rich in salmon that had long been the exclusive domain of American fishing interests – made palpable the threat that the modernization and expansion of industrial fishing posed to both the fish resource itself and to the interests of coastal states. In this instance, the interest in question was a domestic salmon-fishing industry that been sustained by the operation of governmental fish hatcheries, the fishing fleet itself having been closely regulated by the U.S. government in an effort to maintain the salmon stocks on a sustainable basis. In addition, a pending Canadian-U.S. treaty regulating the two nations' Pacific salmon industries would be rendered ineffective if a third party (let alone one like Japan, employing large-scale factory vessels) should enter into the waters just outside the existing American and Canadian three-mile limits of jurisdiction.[50]

Inspired by the threat to American fishing interests represented by the Japanese governments' licensing of factory vessels to operate in Bristol Bay, the Institute of Pacific Relations (IPR) – an organization in which the Washington and Alaskan salmon industries had considerable influence – commissioned in 1936 a legal research project on the subject of the three-mile rule. The expectation was that such a study would suggest a reevaluation of the rule's appropriateness in light of the changes in marine fishing technology and would explore the possibilities for reform of international law. It was probably at the suggestion of Ray Lyman Wilbur, president of Stanford University and then a director of the IPR, that Professor Bingham was given the contract for this study. In any event, Bingham accepted the assignment, and he had the good fortune to engage as a research assistant a young German American immigrant scholar, Stefan A. Riesenfeld, who had studied law in Europe

one day, "with rapid advance in the arts of flying," take the form of action by "bands of malefactors" who would "engage in depredations in or from the air." (Quoted in ibid., 68.)

[50] In addition, the United States and Canada had put into effect a treaty by which they applied a joint regime of regulation to conserve and manage the halibut resources of the West Coast; they were still in the process of working out the bilateral agreement for regulation of the salmon fisheries of the two nations. In addition, the United States had invested millions in salmon hatcheries operations on salmon streams in Alaska. See, inter alia, Larry Leonard, *The International Regulation of Fisheries* (Washington, DC: Carnegie Endowment for International Peace, 1944).

and was then completing graduate studies at the University of California's School of Law in nearby Berkeley.[51]

For Bingham, the research assignment was an opportunity to examine through the lens of legal realism an intriguing and controversial issue in law and policy. For the U.S. Department of State (which may possibly have encouraged the IPR to undertake the project), it offered hope that scholarly support might become available to support the position it had taken in diplomatic protests to Japan against the recent incursions into the Bristol Bay.[52] In the 1937–8 confrontation, the State Department had indicated to Japan that the need to protect existing American fishing interests in the Bering Sea could justify an extraordinary departure from the rule limiting U.S. jurisdiction to only three miles offshore.[53]

The Bingham study was also seen as a possible source of academic support for President Franklin D. Roosevelt's personal view, which he expressed privately to the State Department lawyers: It might be desirable, Roosevelt suggested, for the United States to extend its offshore jurisdiction by presidential proclamation and thereby to "create a kind of marine refuge," well beyond three miles out to sea on Bristol Bay, so as to protect the American fishing interests; of course, there was no doubt that the Japanese would protest such a violation of the traditional "freedom of the seas."[54] As for Riesenfeld, the project developed into an opportunity for him to pursue the research question well beyond its immediate purposes; ultimately with Bingham's approval and support, Riesenfeld produced his great historical and jurisprudential treatise, *Protection of Coastal Fisheries under International Law*. The book was completed in 1939, but for reasons essentially political it was not published until 1942.[55]

[51] Interviews with the late Stefan A. Riesenfeld by the author, 1988, and later conversations on the subject with Prof. Riesenfeld.

[52] Riesenfeld stated that insiders at the time believed that the State Department had encouraged the commission by the IPR. (Ibid.) In the research for the present study, no documentation was found either in the IPR records or State Department archives to confirm that that this was so. The State Department records leave no doubt, however, that lawyers in the department were keenly interested in how the Bingham study would come out, and they referred to it often in their memoranda after its publication. Bingham wrote years later that he was first drawn into the project by his friend, the attorney Edward W. Allen of Seattle, who was a board member of IPR. Allen had been a fraternity brother of his at the University of Chicago and in the 1930s became a prominent learned commentator on international law, also serving as counsel to the salmon fishing and cannery industries of Alaska and Seattle. By the late 1930s, Allen was campaigning vigorously for a change in U.S. policy that would keep Japanese ships out of the Bristol Bay waters that were so important for American and Canadian salmon. (Bingham, *List of Writings*, 43–5. On Allen's role in this regard, see text at notes 74–76.)

[53] Harry N. Scheiber, "Origins of the Abstention Doctrine in Ocean Law: Japanese-U.S. Relations and the Pacific Fisheries, 1937–1958," *Ecology Law Quarterly* 16 (1989): 29–32.

[54] Franklin D. Roosevelt to R. W. Moore (Legal Counsel, Dept. of State), Nov. 21, 1937, in *Foreign Relations of the United States, 1937*, Vol. 4 (Washington, DC: U.S. Government Printing Office, 1954): 768–9.

[55] International law scholars in the traditionalist camp who served on the IPR board or as advisers were aghast at what they regarded as Riesenfeld's attack on "rule of law," and IPR asked Riesenfeld to accept publication with a preface by Philip Jessup or another senior scholar committed to the

While Riesenfeld continued working on what became his magisterial study, Bingham seized on their joint research findings to produce quickly a pamphlet-length study, *Report on the International Law of Pacific Coastal Fisheries*. It was published in 1938, with a subsidy from the Alaska salmon packers trade association, after the original sponsors at IPR backed off out of concern about its polemical character.[56] Bingham made no pretense as to the polemical purpose of his *Report*. He left the larger scholarly objectives to Riesenfeld. In a private letter, Bingham stated that he was convinced that the abandonment of the three-mile rule by the United States was "inevitable" and hence saw no point in making his report "discreet [or] purely technical"; in any case he was "opposed to pussy-footing."[57] In the report itself, he declared: "*It is a brief* and as a brief which seeks to influence others and to convert a Phalanx of American legal opinion saturated with traditional doctrine, it has been modeled for emphasis."[58] When his colleagues urged him to tone it down, out of concern that it would antagonize the Japanese government and would harm his standing in the law school world, he declined to change a word of the text.[59] He wrote out of a belief, Bingham asserted, that it was "of the utmost importance to the future peace and security of the United States" to see American interests on the Pacific Coast protected against the Japanese threat and other contingencies – and that such protection, so far as the fisheries were concerned, should be "extend[ed] as far from our Coast as efficiency demands."[60]

He stated that the law of territorial waters "is a remarkably fertile field for the development of adequate principles of law pertaining to natural resources which may be wasted by unrestrained exploitation." To fashion such principles required abandonment of the three-mile rule, which he dismissively referred to as "the Anglo-American doctrine" – a rule adopted as their own policy and championed in global affairs by the United Kingdom and the United States out of naked self-interest, even though it was contributing to a continuing situation of "chaotic problems of legal control of sea fisheries."[61] In responding to the claims of sacredness for the inherited canon of "freedom of the sea," Bingham used unrestrainedly scornful rhetoric, deploring "the comfortable conviction" that because a doctrine had been

---

"freedom of the seas" doctrine. Riesenfeld refused. When the United States entered the war in December 1941, however, the Riesenfeld position, regarded as aggressive vis-à-vis Japan, no longer seemed objectionable, and the Carnegie Endowment stepped in and agreed to publish Riesenfeld's study as a major book publication. (Information from the manuscript correspondence files in the IPR archived records, Special Collections, University of Washington Library, Seattle.).

[56] *Report on the International Law of Pacific Coastal* Fisheries (Palo Alto: Stanford University Press, 1938). The story of how IPR withdrew support and the intervention and subsidization by the packers is recalled by Bingham in Bingham, *List of Writings*, 49.

[57] Bingham to William Lockwood, June 7, 1939, copy in Allen Papers, University of Washington Library.

[58] Bingham, *Report on the International Law of Coastal Fisheries*, preface, v–vi. Emphasis added.

[59] Bingham, *List of Writings*, 49.

[60] Ibid., vi. His account is confirmed by correspondence in the IPR Papers, University of Washington Library. See note 55.

[61] Ibid., 9–10.

of long standing it should be "frozen" and perpetuated without regard to current realities and interests. In any event, to think that such a rule had "reached maturity" in a linear process that recognized rightful principles was "an academic delusion."[62]

At the May 1940 meeting of the American Society for International Law (ASIL), Bingham's position on the three-mile rule was the subject of a special panel session in which his principal critic was Professor Philip Jessup of Columbia Law School. There was no mystery as to how the debate would go: Jessup had just recently published his view that to extend jurisdiction unilaterally in the Bristol Bay area would aggravate the existing diplomatic confrontation of America with Japan, increasing the danger of armed conflict.[63] For his part, Bingham was already on record with regard to how the East Coast establishment in international law (no one in that category was more prominent than Jessup) was so "engrossed . . . with European and Atlantic events and problems [that] they often even today fail to realize the great importance of the Pacific Coast affairs for the future of the country." For this reason, their failure to respond to Japanese fishing in the Bering Sea resulted from their being locked into the traditional position that enshrined the three-mile rule.[64] The lines had already been drawn when the academic dignitaries gathered for the jousting at the ASIL panel.

Bingham opened the panel session by asserting that the inherited structure of international law had already been "shattered" by the "tides of change" of the twentieth century; therefore America's reliance on the "traditional tenets" of law – let alone reliance on the hope, to which Jessup clearly held fast, that the existing structure of international law offered the basis for peace among nations – must obviously be given up.[65] Once again deploying the familiar realist style and rhetoric, Bingham declaimed against the belief (held by "complacent conservatives – a vanished race today") in the benign nature of allegedly "definitive principles of justice established in tradition, existing independently of particular contending forces, economic, political and social."[66] In passages that underlined the convergence of *Realpolitik* precepts with those of American legal realism, he insisted that when confronted with "the stubborn realities of international affairs," every nation on earth would act in its own self-interest "with all the power which discretion permitted." He continued:

International law in most important particulars never has been impartially just and never has been stable, but always has been and always will be a product of the interplay of national interests, prejudices and pressures, and therefore has been unstable, uncertain and controversial; since some of the doctrines of the learned

---

[62] Ibid., 23.

[63] Jessup, "The Pacific Fisheries," 134–8. The ASIL panel is discussed briefly, in broad historical context, in Juda, *International Law*, 112–13.

[64] Bingham, *Report*, 49.

[65] American Society for International Law, *Proceedings*, 1940, 54–5.

[66] Ibid., 56.

are only the propaganda of powerful states more effectively advertised than the opposing propaganda of other states, any realistic, any intelligently hopeful efforts for improvement must start with recognition of these facts.[67]

With regard to the law of territorial waters in particular, Bingham declared that in this aspect "freedom of the seas" had come to mean a license for "destructive aggressions" against the fishery resources of the oceans beyond coastal jurisdictions. This trend toward destruction of marine fisheries could not prevail, he wrote, for "the irresistible tide of economic, political and social interests is running against the Anglo-American three-mile doctrine. It is doomed."[68] He praised the way in which the Supreme Court of the United States, faced with an unprecedented economic emergency and possible "social calamity" in the Depression, had "displayed its statesmanship" by reversing the long-honored constitutional doctrines that had proved so manifestly inadequate to the nation's urgent needs. Similar realism and flexibility were now required in international law of the oceans, Bingham declared; legal rules no longer serviceable or defensible had to be scrapped, just as "freedom of contract" and other such antiquated or perverse doctrines had been scrapped by the constitutional court.[69]

Jessup responded with a defense of the traditional concepts, objecting to what he said was Bingham's tendency to portray himself as "progressive" and those whom he opposed as "necessarily doctrinaire."[70] He did not deny the validity of Bingham's view that international law had always been "dynamic" and capable of responding gradually to new realities; indeed many rules had been modified in recent years or, as with regard to rules for high-seas transit of neutral flag ships in wartime, were obviously in need of modification. Yet he found misguided Bingham's analogy with the Supreme Court and its reversal of doctrine as applied to the New Deal's and the states' emergency measures. To be similarly legitimate, Jessup asserted, reform of international law should be accomplished through treaties and multilateral efforts more generally, not through the kind of purely self-interested unilateral actions that Bingham advocated.[71] Self-interest was invariably at play in international affairs, Jessup conceded; however, in the long run, he insisted that international affairs must be pursued in a manner that recognized that "a state's own interests are merely parts of the total interests of the society of nations."[72]

On the eve of America's entry into World War II, Bingham's legal views were cited widely by salmon-industry lawyers and lobbyists, who were pressing Congress to enact legislation extending jurisdiction out to sea as far as necessary to exclude foreign competitors ("intruders," as they invariably called Japanese and other potential new

[67] Ibid., 56.
[68] Ibid., 61–2.
[69] Ibid., 58–9, 62–3.
[70] Ibid., 64.
[71] Ibid., 62–6.
[72] Ibid., 66.

entrants to "their" fishing grounds).[73] One especially influential advocate was the prominent international lawyer Edward W. Allen, a close friend of Bingham's and counsel to the salmon industry, who in public speeches, scholarly journals, and trade publications stridently denounced the Japanese incursions and demanded action by the U.S. government.[74] When Allen sent to Roscoe Pound at Harvard a reprint of one of his articles making the case – invoking Bingham's views for support – that would justify unilateral U.S. action to exclude foreign fishing from Bristol Bay, Pound was quick to respond; he did not fail to take notice of the connection to legal realism in the debates of domestic law, especially Bingham's extreme view.[75] Pound regarded as unprincipled and dangerous the emergence of such an explicitly pragmatic, consequentialist position in the debate over ocean law. Pound's intriguing response to the Bingham–Allen view is well worth quoting in full, because it echoed his points of contention against Llewellyn in the famous exchanges on legal realism:

> I can well believe that you are quite right as to the necessity of adjusting the three mile limit doctrine to the fisheries situation in the Northwest. Perhaps with my eye on recent extravagant statements of those who would abandon all historical continuity in connection with law and the administration of justice, I [bear] down too hard. But the world seems to me to be suffering from a notion that when it suits the convenience of some power to repudiate what had been settled in international relations it is at liberty to do so, and I earnestly hope that the [Northwest fisheries] matter . . . can somehow be adjusted . . . without giving aid and comfort to those who hold that whatever can get by is justified because it gets by.[76]

From Jessup and others in the traditional camp came the same type of criticism, only given even sharper focus by the parallel controversy that was raging among international lawyers over what many of them condemned as President Roosevelt's unprincipled policies in violation (or at least a transparent evasion) of the Neutrality Acts by which Congress had sought to keep America clear of the hostilities gathering in Europe and Asia.[77] These critics argued that unilateral departures from the norms that had been articulated in international law were unacceptable, above all because

---

[73] In 1937 a bill had been introduced in the U.S. Senate to declare Bristol Bay within the continental shelf limits of the United States; hence, territorial waters and not open to foreign fishing operations. A variant approach debated in Congress later was for a declaration that the United States had a proprietary interest in the salmon stocks, and because they were thus declared to be "owned" by this country, they could not be fished by foreigners without U.S permission. See Jessup, "The Pacific Coast Fisheries," 136–8.

[74] See, e.g., Edward Allen, "Control of Fisheries beyond Three Miles," *Washington Law Review* 14 (1939): 94. See note 52 for Allen's key role in commissioning Bingham to write his 1938 report on fisheries and offshore jurisdiction.

[75] Cf. text at note 17 (regarding Llewellyn's own view of Bingham as perhaps extreme).

[76] Letter from Roscoe Pound to Edward W. Allen (September 19, 1939, Edward W. Allen Papers, University of Washington Library).

[77] For a review of the controversy in political and academic discourse over the Neutrality Acts, see Aaron X. Fellmeth, "A Divorce Waiting to Happen: Franklin Roosevelt and the Laws of Neutrality, 1935–1941," *Buffalo Journal of International Law* 3 (1996–7): 413–517.

such actions were destabilizing and fraught with the danger that the use of force would inevitably follow from such provocative policies.[78]

This then was the status of the confrontation between traditionalists and Bingham on the eve of America's entry into World War II. Bingham did not stand alone, however: By 1940, under heavy political pressure from the Pacific Coast, high-level U.S. diplomatic planners had begun to put together a strategy for a more aggressive policy on fisheries protection through a unilateral declaration of extended jurisdiction beyond three miles. However, this dramatic policy shift was also being impelled by the related opportunity for the United States to assure its complete future control over seabed petroleum resources that lay more than three miles offshore, out to the limit of the Continental Shelf.[79] As the war progressed and the magnitude of American hegemony in world affairs became increasingly evident, the State Department and the Department of the Interior moved in a coordinated way to achieve both objectives. They were parallel objectives, in that each of them required serious modification, if not to say abandonment, of the long-established U.S. position that held the three-mile limit as a centerpiece of its approach to ocean law and ocean diplomacy. The story has been told elsewhere as to how these debates culminated in September 1945 with issuance by the White House of what became known as the two "Truman Proclamations."[80] The better known of the two proclamations declared U.S. ownership of the seabed and its resources, most notably including petroleum deposits, out to the limits of the Continental Shelf.

The other proclamation, known as the "Truman Fisheries Proclamation," appeared to adopt in a robust version the realist premises and policy on coastal fishery waters that Bingham had advocated in his 1939 *Report*. President Truman declared that the United States was prepared to establish and control "conservation zones" as far out to sea as necessary beyond three miles to regulate fishing by both American and foreign vessels – and thereby to assure the sustainability of salmon and other valuable coastal fishery stocks. A supplementary letter issued the same day made explicit that the new policy was intended to protect the American-flag salmon fishing fleet in Bristol Bay and other coastal areas of the Northeast Pacific.[81]

This breakthrough in American policy was a moment of high triumph for Bingham and his allies in the fishing industry, in segments of the diplomatic policy planning community, in the academy, and among like-minded working international lawyers. However, it was a short-lived triumph, for as it turned out, the U.S. government never implemented the fisheries proclamation. Its main effect was ironic and in the end

---

[78] Jessup and other speakers, on the panel reported in ASIL *Proceedings*, 54 ff.

[79] Ann L. Hollick, *U.S. Foreign Policy and the Law of the Sea* (Princeton, NJ: Princeton University Press, 1981), 18–61.

[80] Ibid.; and D. C. Watt, "First Steps in the Enclosure of the Oceans," *Marine Policy* 3 (1979): 219–20 et passim.

[81] Proclamation No. 2668 (Sept. 28, 1945), *Federal Register*, 10 (1945): 12304, on which see Hollick, *U.S. Foreign Policy*, 47–61; and Scheiber, "Origins of the Abstention Doctrine," 34–35.

self-defeating. Together with the Continental Shelf proclamation, it served in fact to inspire similar declarations by Latin American governments, announcing extended offshore jurisdiction to protect their coastal fishing industries; in some instances, these states claimed actual ownership and full sovereignty over ocean areas far out to sea.[82]

Unlike the United States, which backed off from the policy that had been announced, the Latin American nations moved toward immediate implementation. This move was damaging, both immediately and potentially over time, to the distant-water American tuna fishing interests, and so the tuna industry leadership in southern California on the West Coast, a powerful group politically, pushed hard to head off any implementation of the Truman Fisheries Proclamation. Giving potent support to the tuna interests in their opposition was the U.S. Navy leadership. The Navy's concern was that if extended jurisdiction were to be declared by coastal nations globally, and jurisdiction well beyond three miles became accepted as customary international law, then the U.S. submarines and surface ships could be denied passage in strategically critical areas and Navy intelligence-gathering vessels would be kept far off the shores of hostile powers. In addition, an abiding opposition to implementation of the proclamation came from many State Department officers, who were concerned that it represented a protectionism, achieved through unilateral action, that undermined the larger U.S. postwar policy of fostering free access to natural resources and the building of institutions and precedents for multilateralism in global affairs.[83]

Many prominent international lawyers shared these concerns. Indeed, even some of the legal scholars who were sympathetic to Bingham's position responded to his writings on these issues from 1949 through the mid-1950s as being too extreme. These colleagues charged that Bingham was recklessly unmindful of the complexity of U.S. fishing interests in that he seemed to have no sympathy for the need of American tuna boats to fish in other nation's near-offshore waters. Some eminent figures in international law studies also believed that he was insensitive to the danger that the trend to offshore claims of special jurisdiction over fishing was already giving way to the outright claims to full sovereignty by some Latin American states on ocean

[82] David Joseph Attard, *The Exclusive Economic Zone in International Law* (New York: Oxford University Press, 1987), 1–20; cf. Garcia-Amador, "The Latin American Contribution to the Development of the Law of the Sea," *American Journal of International Law* 78 (1974): 33. For a perceptive contemporary analysis, see Richard Young, "Recent Developments with Respect to the Continental Shelf," *American Journal of International Law* 42 (1948): 849. See also note 84.

[83] Within the State Department, there were many top officers who were dogmatic on the three-mile rule, as reported by the insider Wilbert Chapman, who served for three years as chief fisheries officer in the department. However, Chapman later told the salmon industry lawyer and champion Edward Allen that the most effective source of pressure in this regard had come from the Department of Defense and the National Security Council, motivated by a concern to maintain U.S. naval strategy, as earlier stated in the text. (Letter from Chapman to Edward Allen, April 3, 1956, American Tunaboat Association Papers, Scripps Institution of Oceanography Archives, University of California, San Diego.)

areas twelve miles or even farther offshore. In addition, Bingham voiced criticisms of America's Cold War foreign policy more generally that alienated even formerly sympathetic international lawyers.[84]

This divergence of views among ocean law experts came to a head in 1956, when Bingham drafted a report for an Inter-American Bar Association meeting in which he likened the "awakened claims of national jurisdiction" by Latin American states (claims to full sovereignty over ocean zones 200 miles offshore) to the "bitter complaints of nationally awakened Asiatic peoples" and Pacific islanders with regard to U.S. nuclear tests in the Pacific. His fellow committee members representing the American bar, all of whom he had expected to join in this report – even his old ally, the Seattle lawyer Edward Allen – declined to sign it.[85]

[84] Ecuador, whose actions were particularly hostile to U.S. tuna fishing interests, stopped and held U.S. flagged fishing boats as far as 25 miles offshore in 1953–4, and Peru seized and detained five Onassis fleet Greek-flag whaling vessels 160 to 364 miles offshore in November 1954, holding them from release until stiff fines were paid. (Hollick, *U.S. Foreign Policy*, 87.) It is important to mention, however, that in his ocean law writings from 1938 to the 1950s, Bingham often advocated for the need to respect the interests of less developed coastal countries; they were short of resources and lacking in naval power, and for economic reasons they needed to extend their fisheries jurisdictional claims to considerable distances offshore. In 1939 he had urged the United States, as a powerful state whose example would win emulation, to lead the way in extending jurisdiction, because America had "a clearly just claim" in the Bering Sea case and could mobilize "skillful diplomatic support" of a new rule. (Bingham, *Report*, 41.) He wrote in 1952, "We live in a revolutionary age when the peace and welfare of the world urgently demand in international affairs cooperation and just recognition of the interests of small states as well as large." Joseph Walter Bingham, "Juridical Status of the Continental Shelf," *Southern California Law Review* 26 (1952): 8.
    Bingham later blended his concern for emerging nations with a bitter critique of U.S. policies in the Cold War – a phase of his career that can be mentioned only parenthetically here: He stated in his later memoir that since the end of World War II he had been largely ostracized by the American community of academic international lawyers for the beliefs he freely voiced concerning U.S. policies. In foreign affairs, Bingham wrote, the citizens were "illy [sic] informed and led, and have been incited to intolerance and hatred of necessary social, economic and political developments throughout the world. . . . The deaths and sufferings of millions of people all over the world is another consequence of our policies." He persisted in these criticisms during the period when anti-communist agitation, epitomized by Senator Joe McCarthy, was silencing so many critics. (Bingham, *List of Writings*, Postscript, 5–6.) Instead of pursuing humane and altruistic policies "[to] further the needs and possibilities of the masses of humanity," America had pursued an aggressive and arrogant course – "the most shocking development," he wrote, "in all my knowledge of history." (Ibid., at 86.) So far as I can learn, Bingham conveyed these ideas in meetings and conversations for the most part, not in formal writings. In any event, Bingham recalled, he had been denied salary raises and recognition by his own faculty at Stanford. The isolation he felt at home was in contrast to the continuing interest, as he recounted, in his participation in academic and policy discourses with his British and other European colleagues. (Ibid., at 66, and Postscript, 1–7.)
[85] Bingham, *List of Writings*, 107–8; and reports and quotations of Bingham's draft in letters of William W. Bishop, Jr., to Bingham, February 26, 1956, and March 16, 1956 (in the Chapman Papers, University of Washington Library). Bingham wrote later that he had been able to exert some influence with the Department of State during the Truman administration years, but that in the Eisenhower administration there was renewed dedication to the three-mile doctrine, and thereafter he received a more respectful hearing for his views in foreign countries than in his own. (Bingham, *List of Writings*, 63–6.) Actually the State Department's reversal of the three-mile doctrine began earlier. See text at notes 87–8.

One prominent critic, rather surprisingly, was William Bishop, who had led the legal staff in crafting the Truman Fisheries Proclamation policy when he was a State Department officer during the war. In the postwar years, Bishop parted ways with Bingham on the three-mile issue when they served together on the delegation representing the American bar at the 1956 meeting. Refusing to sign onto Bingham's draft report, Bishop complained that it "adopt[ed] the Latin-American line almost 100 per cent" and that it could be taken, in effect, as a brief for Latin American states that were seizing U.S. fishing vessels outside of the three-mile boundary. According to Bishop, Bingham had failed to discriminate between the legitimate protection of "historic" coastal fishing interests and simple self-aggrandizement as manifested by the Latin American governments' offshore version of a land grab.[86]

Bingham carried on his campaign in many forums nonetheless, but it proved to be a losing fight, at least in the short term. In the face of the aforementioned pressures, the State Department's chief fisheries officer, Wilbert McLeod Chapman, issued a formal statement in December 1948 – a little more than three years after issuance of the Truman Fisheries Proclamation – treating it as essentially inoperative and affirming America's renewed adherence to the three-mile rule.[87] The British Foreign Office planners, as did others dedicated to the three-mile rule in the face of new challenges – such as those from Iceland and Norway, nations that were then seeking to ban British trawlers from their coastal waters well beyond the traditional line – greeted Chapman's statement of policy as a gratifying announcement that the United States was abandoning its short-lived championing of "the Bingham doctrine."[88]

However, this reversal of U.S. policy came too late to save the traditional rule in international affairs, for once the "extended jurisdiction" genie had been let out of the bottle, getting it back in proved impossible.[89] In both national politics

[86] Letter from Bishop to Chapman, March 21, 1956, Chapman Papers, University of Washington Library; also, letter from Bishop to Bingham, Feb. 26, 1956, ibid.

[87] Wilbert M. Chapman, "U.S. Policy on High Seas Fisheries," *Department of State Bulletin* 20 (1949): 67–7. This policy paper declared that it would be U.S. policy to foster the development of scientific international fisheries management through bi- and multilateral agreements. Privately, Chapman told leaders of the fisheries industry on the West Coast that the Truman Proclamation was politically unworkable precisely because of its "broad sweeping implications – its new philosophy and its radical departure from holy precedent" on the matter of the three-mile limit. (Letter from Chapman to Montgomery Phister, Nov. 24, 1947, Chapman Papers); for analysis of Chapman's role in its political context, see Harry N. Scheiber, "Pacific Ocean Resources, Science and Law of the Sea: Wilbert M. Chapman and the Pacific Fisheries," *Ecology Law Quarterly* 13 (1986): 383, 455–61.

[88] The phrase was used explicitly, for example, by British Foreign Office officials in meetings with U.S. diplomatic planners, 1950–1. (See note 4 and accompanying text.) On one of the earliest of the dangerous post-1945 ocean conflicts over fishing in territorial waters, see Hannes Jónsson, *Friends in Conflict: The Anglo-Icelandic Cod Wars and the Law of the Sea* (London: C. Hurst, 1982).

[89] For reference in these terms to the Truman Proclamation and its unintended consequences, see Robert L. Friedheim, *Negotiating the New Ocean Regime* (Columbia: University of South Carolina Press, 1992) at 21.

and international relations, there was increasing pressure for extended fishery jurisdiction. This pressure came not only from nations whose fishing industries were
almost exclusively coastal but also from the coastal-fishing sectors of larger countries
(including the salmon industry of the United States itself) that had both coastal
and distant-water fleets. Also concerned to extend their claims to marine fisheries
far out beyond three miles offshore were many Third World coastal nations and
small island states, then emerging as assertive and vocal players in global diplomacy
during the postwar wave of decolonization. These proponents of extended jurisdiction, successfully forming effective coalitions as the issue moved into the United
Nations negotiations on ocean-law reform, gradually gained the upper hand in the
reconfigured international debate of ocean law.[90]

Still, Bingham's voice continued to be heard in the resultant international discourse as to how the territorial-waters issues should be resolved. In the public realm,
he served as a consultant to an international fisheries commission for the North
Pacific,[91] and he gave testimony before Congress with regard to regulation of fisheries and control of petroleum resources in offshore ocean areas.[92] In lively academic
exchanges on the law of territorial waters and fisheries that went on from 1945 to the
1980s, Bingham's best known contribution was an article published in 1952 entitled
"Juridical Status of the Continental Shelf."[93] He incorporated in this study several
long and key passages nearly verbatim from his 1940 ASIL panel presentation, but
now the context was entirely different: Whereas in 1940, his objective had been to
champion a reversal of U.S. policy and a new view of international law, in 1952 his
goal was to save a victory that seemed to be slipping away – that is, to contend, in
vain as it proved, for the immediate and vigorous implementation of the Truman
Fisheries Proclamation. Bingham still championed the proclamation as representing a salutary "revolutionary step" toward establishment of new, realistic principles
in ocean law.[94] The basic problem remained as it had been since the 1930s, Bingham
averred: It was the need to defend coastal fisheries against "piratical [sic] invasions
of coastal fisheries by large foreign organizations, resentful of any control over their

---

[90] Douglas M. Johnston, *The International Law of Fisheries: A Framework for Policy-Oriented Inquiries*
(New Haven: Yale University Press, 1965), 232–3, 332–44 and Hollick, *U.S. Foreign Policy*, passim.
Insofar as the United States resisted as long as it did, no doubt the principal influence on its policy
was the U.S. Navy's interest, as noted earlier (note 83).

[91] Hancock, "Memorial Resolution." (The commission in question was the International North Pacific
Fisheries Commission, established in 1953 in implementation of a Canadian-U.S.-Japanese fisheries
convention for the Northeast Pacific.)

[92] Testimony [on effects of the Truman Proclamation and on the continental shelf doctrine] in Hearings
on S. 1901 Before Senate committee on Interior and Insular Affairs, 83d Cong., 1st Sess. 438–43 (1953).

[93] Bingham, *Juridical Status of the Continental Shelf*, 4–20; see also his earlier article: Joseph Walter
Bingham, "The Continental Shelf and the Marginal Belt," *American Journal of International Law* 40
(1946): 173.

[94] Bingham, *Juridical Status of the Continental Shelf*, 6.

destructive methods and careless of the damage they cause to important sea food resources of coastal peoples."[95]

Assessing the long list of nations that had declared jurisdiction or even outright sovereignty over coastal waters out beyond three miles since 1945, Bingham conceded that some of their claims were "excessive and infringe[d] too far with insufficient reasons on the traditional doctrine of freedom of the seas."[96] For this seasoned pragmatist, however, it was the phrase "insufficient reasons" that held the key to the policy question: Extended jurisdiction would be justified only to protect "*true* coastal fisheries... and those fish which traditionally have been caught in commercial quantities only in shallow off-shore waters" (a concise description of the American salmon industry off Alaska's coast). However, jurisdiction beyond traditional limits offshore would not be justified "to cover the high seas species of fish which are caught principally in deep sea waters" (an equally concise description of the tuna fisheries, in which a dominant force internationally was the San Diego tuna fleet – whose leadership had successfully opposed since 1945 any active implementation of the Truman Proclamation).[97]

As one would expect, given Bingham's previous major writings, his argument turned in the end on a pragmatic standard: "New problems need new thinking." Barriers to rational change posed by adherence to "traditional juristic formulations," he contended, "must not be allowed to prevail."[98] The contemporary generation should not be held prisoner by the legacy of an irrelevant past. What he termed "democratic law" – that is, law that would be responsive to needs in the real world – must develop by acceptance of "competitive forces and varying conditions" in contemporary life. The alternative to such a rational course would be the same kind of

---

[95] Ibid., 8.

[96] Ibid., 9. The trend toward extended claims accelerated in the 1970s, as the UN meetings that led to the new convention were going forward. As of 1986, four years after signature of the convention, of 136 coastal states, 114 were claiming full territorial jurisdiction offshore from three to twelve nautical miles (89 of them at twelve miles). Ten states had extended their territorial sea claims to more than 12 miles, and fifteen claimed territorial sovereignty up to 100 miles. V.F. Tsarev, "Maritime Legislation of Coastal State and the 1982 UN Convention on the Law of the Sea," in *The Law of the Sea: What Lies Ahead?* 531n. (Law of the Sea Institute, 20th Annual Conference, Proceedings, Thomas A. Clingan, Jr., ed., n.d.). See generally William T. Burke, *The New International Law of Fisheries: UNCLOS 1982 and Beyond* (Oxford: Clarendon Press, 1994), for authoritative analysis, with historical background of modern ocean law.

[97] Emphasis added. It was ironic that the Japanese distant water tuna-fishing interests – which were now focused heavily on fishing tuna in high-seas waters off other nations' coasts, as the Japanese salmon fleet had been when threatening Bristol Bay in 1937–8 – were in the period from the mid-1950s to the 1990s an important ally of the U.S. tuna-fishing fleet interests in contending internationally for nonjurisdiction by any coastal state over "high migratory species," a category that consisted almost exclusively in commercial terms of tuna. See Harry N. Scheiber, "U.S. Policy, the Pacific Tuna Economy, and Ocean Law Innovation: The Post-World War II Era, 1945–1970," in *Bringing New Law To Ocean Waters*, eds. David C. Caron and Harry N. Scheiber (Leiden: Martinus Nijhoff, 2004), 29–54.

[98] Bingham, *Juridical Status of the Continental Shelf*, 19.

socially harmful applications of law as he had attacked nearly a half-century earlier in his condemnation of classical legal formalism. Bingham despised what he termed the legal conservatives'

> mechanistic adherence to traditional ill-digested generalities and slogans devised by theoreticians of an unscientific age of subsidized piracy, matchlocks, wood fires, and candlelight, wide-open spaces, and glorification of cruel aggressive force for self-profit – theoreticians who could have foreseen little of the technology, industries, social pressures, and dominant impulses of our crowded, complex, modern civilization.[99]

Bingham died in 1973, so that he could not savor the conclusion of the protracted negotiations that led to signature in 1982 of the United Nations Convention on the Law of the Sea (UNCLOS), codifying reforms on extended offshore jurisdiction that he had advocated for thirty-five years. However, he did witness late in his lifetime the enactment by Congress in 1966 of a unilateral extension of U.S. jurisdiction over fishing to a distance of twelve miles offshore.[100] Then in 1975, Congress legislated – in a bill signed reluctantly by President Gerald Ford, who would have preferred to stay America's hand until UN negotiations on the general treaty had been concluded – for unilateral creation of a 200-mile zone offshore that included full U.S. regulatory control over fishing by any nation.[101]

By validating the concept of extended fishery jurisdiction in an "Exclusive Economic Zone" (EEZ) out to 200 miles offshore of any coastal nation that wished to declare such a zone, the 1982 UNCLOS essentially made universal the extended jurisdiction policy. The UNCLOS represented a long-delayed triumph in international law of Bingham's positions on the question of fisheries protection through extended offshore jurisdiction. It also declared it to be an obligation of signatory nations to manage their fisheries in a sustainable manner within their EEZs and to support the objective of sustainability with regard to high-seas fisheries beyond the 200-mile lines. Here too, the arguments that Bingham and Riesenfeld had made forty-three years earlier resonated in the specific obligations that UNCLOS placed on coastal and distant-water fishing states. These two pioneers in carrying legal realism offshore had insisted from the start that unilateral action, such as they wanted the U.S. government to take, should be only the indispensable beginning for a process in organic international lawmaking that could bring the community of nations together to agree on new principles of sustainability and conservation of ocean resources.[102]

---

[99] Ibid., 20.

[100] Harry N. Scheiber and Christopher Carr, "Constitutionalism and the Territorial Sea: An Historical Study," *Territorial Sea Journal* 2 (1992): 67. The 1966 act referred to in the text is Public Law 89–658, 80 U.S. Stat. 908 (Oct. 14, 1966).

[101] Scheiber and Carr, "Constitutionalism," 68–70. The bill in question became known as the Magnuson Fishery Conservation and Management Act and in later amended form as the Magnuson-Stevens Act. (16 U.S.C. 1801=1882, April 13, 1976 as amended 1978–80, 1982–4, 1986–90, 1992–4, 1996, and 2006.)

[102] See Scheiber and Carr, "From Extended Jurisdiction to Privatization," 13–16.

And so this new – and in our day forgotten – variant of legal realism, in the tradition of the American movement of the 1920s and 1930s and infused with the DNA of Old World *Realpolitik,* had gone offshore successfully. By foreshadowing the general thrust and even charting the basic outlines of reform in a vital realm of international law, Joseph Walter Bingham had been at the storm center in this process, and his role in this transformation of international law was a large one. However, it is well to recall that Bingham's basic posture on international ocean law – concerning both what degree of respect was owed to tradition in the law and what objective imperatives required reforms – was derived from his position on jurisprudence at the very start of his career, when he had advocated so ardently the philosophy that later reached full flower with the legal realist school.

PART VI

Perspectives from Other Conceptual Worlds

20

Sociological Jurisprudence – Impossible but Necessary

The Case of Contractual Networks

Gunther Teubner

SOCIOLOGICAL JURISPRUDENCE – AN OXYMORON

"Network is not a legal concept."[1] If Richard Buxbaum's apodictic judgment is true, then lawyers have little to say about networks. Should they wish to make appropriate judgments when business networks, franchising arrangements, just-in-time-systems, or virtual enterprises do cross their paths, then they must consult social scientists, such as economists, organizational theorists, and sociologists. For better or for worse, they must engage in law, in action, and in sociological jurisprudence.

Lawrence Friedman would agree with such a realistic approach. Already in his first major monograph on contract law,[2] he explored the law in action rather than the law in the books.[3] In his later works[4] he demonstrated the responsiveness of the legal order to the manifold forces of economic, technological, and social change. From Friedman's perspective, the legal system functions largely as a dependent variable, with lawmakers responding to underlying developments in science, medicine, technology, economic organization, and shifting moral beliefs. In his recent book, *American Law in the Twentieth Century*, he states his case quite clearly: "The main theme of this book is that law is a product of society."[5]

Yet, "sociological jurisprudence" is a pipe dream. After a heated debate for almost a century, lawyers know that, logically speaking, it is an oxymoron – like a white raven. Practically speaking, it necessarily falters in the face of the normative closure of the legal system. This is a lesson we are correctly taught not only by traditional

---

[1] Buxbaum (1993).
[2] Friedman (1965).
[3] In his own words, "The working rules of contract are not necessarily the rules the casebooks talk about.... Business cannot go on without contracts; but it also cannot go on without trust, understanding, and common sense. The real world of contractual behavior was far more complex than the law books suggested." Friedman 385 (2002).
[4] See, e.g., Friedman (1985, 1990,1999a, 1999b).
[5] Friedman 517 (2002).

doctrine and by Max Weber's theory of formal legal rationality but also by advanced systems theory.[6]

However, Friedman remained a skeptic with regard to formal rationality and the autonomy of the legal system:

> My view, in brief, is that formal legal argument as such probably does not make much of a difference in the world.... I suspect that there was much less formal rationality, in fact, in the nineteenth century, in Germany and elsewhere, than Weber thought. He may have confused style with substance.... It seems perfectly obvious that social context determines what legal arguments will be used and which ones will strike judges and others as persuasive.[7]

In a later work, Friedman retains his skepticism:

> Perhaps law has a life of its own; but if so it is a very limited life. Law certainly has its own language. It has its customs and rituals. Every case... presented a legal issue; each one came wrapped in a cloak of technicality, the lawyer's own special ropes, strings, and bits of glue. But every case – and every statute, every administrative rule – also had a context, a background. And it is the background which made the problem seem like a problem in the first place – defined it, constructed it – and in the end, helps dictate, or influence, the way the system solved it (or failed to solve it).[8]

However, Friedman does not believe in going to history, sociology, or the economics of law to look for the correct answers. His legal heroes are neither Supreme Court judges and their formal legal arguments nor theoretical or empirical neighboring sciences as such. Instead Friedman suggests that we look to societal conflicts and struggles: His heroes are the individuals who advance these struggles to the courts and thereby change the legal system.

Against this background, I seek to support and simultaneously to undermine the claim for legal autonomy through concrete examples. My concrete observations are about new network phenomena, how they irritate the courts and provoke the judges to juridical adventures.[9] I raise the question of whether restrictions in the two common ways in which the law observes its social environment – judicial and legislative reality reconstructions – systematically preclude an adequate treatment of such new social phenomena. Does the law indeed need a third mode of observing so-called social reality? Business cooperation networks provide an example for the observation that this third approach cannot simply be secured through the social

---

[6] For legal doctrine, see, e.g., Pawlowski (1999). For formal legal rationality, see, e.g., Weber (1978); Luhmann (2004).

[7] Friedman 533 (1999b).

[8] Friedman 517 (2002).

[9] For a detailed analysis of networks from a legal and social science perspective, see Teubner (2008). Recently, two collective volumes develop an interdisciplinary perspective on the law of networks. See Grundmann (2010); Amstutz and Teubner (2009).

sciences, but is instead wholly dependent on a unique combination of legal doctrine and reflexive social practices. I describe this third way as an effort to irritate the legal system selectively with particular demands from its social environment. However, I still call it sociological jurisprudence, because this is the same form of necessary pipe dream that is represented by a legal policy analysis or by legal economics. Trying to move a couple of paces along this impossible but necessary third way, I demonstrate how the legal qualification of networks, in particular their legal conditions and their legal consequences, can be tackled through confrontation with nonlegal social reality constructs.

Thesis 1: It is a scientistic misconception of the law to believe that empirical results or theoretical insights from the social sciences can guide law to any significant degree. The decisive legal irritations are not supplied by interdisciplinary contact with social science disciplines *stricto sensu*, but with normatively loaded "reflexive practices" in various social fields. My example: The dramatic extension of liability throughout network systems is a judicial reaction to social perceptions of the risks posed by economic networks.

Thesis 2: The "translation" of reflexive social practices into legal doctrine is not a direct knowledge transfer from the social to the legal. Private law doctrine can only be persuaded to develop conceptual innovations by its own, internal, path-dependent evolutionary logic. My example: Network is not a legal concept. It is a social construct and its legal complement can only be reconstructed within the law, possibly by developing "relational contracts" into "connected contracts" (*Vertragsverbund*).

Thesis 3: One of the most important achievements of sociological jurisprudence is its ability to support law's contribution to the problem of how to deal with paradoxes within social practice. My example: Networks emerge when the environment confronts actors with paradoxical demands. Law reacts to such network paradoxes with a new legal concept of "double attribution."

PIERCING THE CONTRACTUAL VEIL IN DISTRIBUTION NETWORKS: THREE LEVELS OF LEGAL REALITY CONSTRUCTION

A Japanese car importer built up a dealer distribution system in Germany. The importer had only succeeded in gaining entry into the German market relatively late in the day and had difficulties in finding responsible dealers. As a consequence, the importer's marketing efforts were reliant on working relationships with dealers whose business credentials and solvency were not immediately apparent. The contracts stipulated that vehicles would remain the property of the importer up until full payment of the sales price. A customer took possession of a vehicle from a dealer, paying an initial installment on the sales price. The customer was given the vehicle, the keys, and the road license, but not the ownership papers, because according to the distribution contracts, they remained in trust until the full payment of the sales price. Under pressure from the dealer and his incorrect claim that full payment was necessary for the internal sales completion, the customer paid the remainder of the sales price without, however, receiving the vehicle's ownership papers. On the insolvency of the dealer, the importer demanded the return of the vehicle from the customer. The customer then claimed that the importer, as the central actor within the distribution system, was liable for the failure of the direct dealer to fulfil his legal obligations.

In a courageous judgment, the Karlsruhe Appeals Court (Oberlandesgericht) departed radically from contractual privity, a fundamental principle of German private law.[10] By "piercing the contractual veil," the court made the center directly liable, although there was no contractual link between the customer and center whatsoever. The court first confirmed the importer's demand for the return of property[11] and then rejected the customer's claim to the receipt of property in good faith on the basis that the customer's naiveté constituted gross negligence.[12] Employing a daring sleight of hand, however, the court then allowed a compensation claim against the importer. The court finally decided in favor of direct liability of the central distribution node, holding the importer responsible for the dealer's breach of legal obligations, notwithstanding the latter's independence.

However, the grounds for this decision are highly unconvincing. The judgment is an explosive mix of German law principles of organizational responsibility, of directors' liability, and of *respondeat superior* for the acts of individual agents. The quality of the judgment does not improve even if we make a clear distinction among the various grounds for liability. Either the court should have fundamentally changed at least one of these principles, explicitly distinguishing it from previous precedent, or it should have rejected piercing the contractual veil. Currently, precedent in German law would refute the court's finding that the construction of a business network with dealers of a dubious character constitutes organizational liability.[13] To date, organizational liability has only been applicable to authentic legal persons. In any case, its extension to other group phenomena remains anchored in the law of associations, and thus organizational liability has no application to simple contractual relationships.[14] By the same token, in such a case, breach of directors' liability is precluded by the conditions of the delictual general clause.[15] Equally, the escape hatch of *respondeat superior* is closed, because independent enterprises simply do not qualify as "agents" in tort law.[16] In view of these problems, it is little wonder that the Appeals Court cooked up a strange mixture of these three liability

---

[10] Karlsruhe 434 (1989).
[11] See § 985 of the German Civil Code (BGB).
[12] § 932(II) BGB and § 366 of the German Commercial Code (HGB).
[13] § 31 BGB. Cf. Palandt § 31, 7 (2010).
[14] Roth 435 (1989).
[15] § 823(I) BGB.
[16] § 831 BGB. Cf. Palandt § 831, 3 (2010). Several authors urge the courts to overrule this old principle. See Roth n. 14 (1989); Bräutigam 133 (1994); Pasderski 174 (1998).

forms and thus neatly evaded the questions of whether and, if yes, how it wished to overrule precedent by piercing the contractual veil of a business network that is constituted by bipolar contracts.

"The soundest judgment with the dullest opinion": Is this judgment best summed up by this cruel phrase? Certainly, the result is plausible and the justification weak. However, the judgment is not simply wrong. Rather the court was called on to tackle something that cannot be addressed within the concepts of contract and tort – the network phenomenon. In the last several decades, a massive increase in contractual networks has confronted the law with the troublesome implications of an evolutionary trend, which it cannot as a whole decode using its own analytical tools. Independent business units commit themselves to closely interconnected cooperation networks and undermine thereby the distinction between market and hierarchy and that between contract, torts, and corporation. Even if distribution systems were organized under the law of corporations and labor law, we would still be confronted by the liability problem, but it would no longer be an issue of piercing liability, neither would it violate the principle of contractual privity. The dealer's behavior would simply be imputed to the manufacturer/primary dealer, according to established rules of principal/agent law,[17] on the basis of the contractual obligations of the corporation. By contrast, if the distribution was organized among independent business units in a competitive market, then relationships with the external partners of the distribution system could not give rise to piercing liability. In conclusion then, establishing a network between independent enterprises causes judicial irritation. An integrated distribution system that, on the one hand, entails more than simple market relationships, but, on the other, does not create any true organizational relationships, forces judges to pierce the contractual veil, but at the same time causes them huge difficulties when they attempt to justify this decision.

"Judicial irritation" has a double significance.[18] Judges are irritated by networks and are provoked to respond to anomalies with piercing techniques that contradict the logic of their own system. In turn, judicial precedent on piercing irritates doctrine, which regards such seemingly equity-oriented ad hoc exceptions to privity of contract as a challenge to the workability of doctrinal concepts.[19] Is traditional doctrine in a position to qualify network phenomena such that simple equitable exceptions can be transformed into conceptually precise legal network rules? Or is the only source of help here "sociological jurisprudence"?

Approach 1: Casuistry

Even the most detailed case law analysis has little if any help to offer. The blinkered reality perspectives of courtroom proceedings prevent an appropriate recognition of

---

[17] § 278 BGB.

[18] For a concise analysis of judicial irritation in franchise law, see Joerges 21ff. (1991).

[19] For comprehensive discussion of piercing the corporate veil, see Rehbinder 69 ff. (1969); Rehbinder 496ff. (1997).

the trend to networking. Because the court's reality construction is founded in two-party proceedings, it necessarily dissects the complex relationships that multilateral networking establishes into bilateral claims and counterclaims. Working from the viewpoint of plaintiff or defendant, this reality construction can only take limited note of the overarching conflicts and risks that networks entail. In this perspective, any doctrinal approach seeking to generalize from case law can only but reproduce the claim and counterclaim culture and conclude by just balancing out the interests of the two parties.

As a consequence then, doctrine should decisively free itself from systematically limited judicial models that can only react to the irritations of networks with individual equitable corrections. These models are not to be criticized for the manner in which they demarcate conflict: "Rather, the reality construction entails the recognition of only two contrasting spheres of influence, represented either by the plaintiff or by the defendant. In this manner, courtroom proceedings are projected into the social order such that points of legal reference are in turn identified within the social order."[20] Such proceedings are fatal with regard to networks precisely because networks are distinguished by their extrapositional effects.

Approach 2: Political Lawmaking

Similarly, following policy-oriented trends within legal doctrine, it is not enough simply to adopt the reality constructs that emerge from the legislative process. Such a perspective entails too ready an acceptance of the worldviews of practitioners, who prepare and prestructure legislation. It can only implicate law within the uncontrolled balancing of interests that takes place in opportunistic reaction to transient social pressures and political preferences. Similarly, it is not enough to adopt a "legislative policies" perspective, because that means accepting the reality constructs of political parties and national and European political institutions, which likewise alienate "real" social conflicts through the filtering processes of power and consensus politics.[21] In network matters, legislative interventions are paradigmatic examples of political tunnel vision. European initiatives to free franchising from the strictures of competition law were selective responses to the highly effective lobbying activities of interest groups.[22] Similarly, in Germany, purchase money loans have been regulated from the exclusive perspective of consumer protection, even though they also raise comparable regulatory problems in other contexts.[23] Were doctrine nothing

---

[20] Luhmann 206 (1965).
[21] Here one is drawn into the dilemmatic juridification of "legislative policies." See Steindorff (1973).
[22] Shapiro 285ff. (1998).
[23] For an extensive analysis, see Peter Heermann (2009), The Status of Multilateral Synallagmas in the Law of Connected Contracts, in Marc Amstutz and Gunther Teubner, eds., *Contractual Networks: Legal Issues of Multilateral Cooperation*. Oxford: Hart Publishing.

but a systematic reproduction of interest groups' and legislators' policies, then it would only intensify existing inadequacies within the political reality constructs.

Approach 3: Reflexive Social Practices

Legal doctrine will only make a genuine contribution to the law of networks if and when it establishes, as opposed to case law and legislation, a third way of approaching the reality of change in economic organization. Today, this approach to reality is no longer possible through the "silent power" of autonomous legal conceptualization. Instead, what is needed is an explicit "structural coupling" of law with reflexive practices in different fields of society. All intensive cooperation notwithstanding, structural coupling does not merge social and legal practices, but rather ensures the autonomy of law.[24] However, at all costs, one must avoid the scientistic misconception, current within sociological jurisprudence and legal economics, that the law simply adopts social science conclusions.[25] This misconception is fed by the notion that the social sciences supply the empirical facts and the theoretical generalizations, from which follow the law's normative perspectives. Notwithstanding the significant role that scientific analysis may play in identifying the workings of networks, law needs to be far more concerned with the normative orientations in society that neutral sciences are simply not in a position to provide. Such orientations can only be found in the normatively loaded dogma within society; that is, in discourses in which social practices reflect on their own self-perceptions. Legal doctrine itself and the mother of all dogmas, theology, are organized as academic disciplines, but of course, they are not social sciences in the strict sense. They represent social practices of law and religion reflecting on themselves. The same holds true for other academic disciplines – at least for some of their subdisciplines – such as business management, economics, and political science, which do not as such form a part of the disinterested, value-neutral social-scientific search for truth. Instead, they are the manifestation of reflexive practices taking place in different social sectors. They make up part of what David Sciulli calls "collegial formations"; that is, the specific organizational forms of the professions and other norm-producing and deliberative institutions within society.[26] Social practices in the worlds of business, economy, and politics each create their own self-descriptions, which in turn inform and guide the underlying social practices.

In each discipline at least, an internal distinction must be made between scientific discourse and reflexive social practice. In the case of law, legal theory as reflexive counterpart to legal practice needs to be distinguished from legal sociology as a social-scientific observation of law.[27] Similarly, in the other social sciences we need

[24] On the structural coupling of legal theory and social sciences, see Luhmann supra n. 6, 496ff.
[25] Posner 761 (1987).
[26] Sciulli (1992).
[27] Luhmann supra n. 6, 53ff, 423ff.

to distinguish between discourses taking part in social practices and those taking part
in scientific observation of those social practices.

What we are looking for then is an autonomous legal reconstruction of normative social orientations, of orientations that law can glean in its interchange with
reflexive social practices. How do these orientations perceive the opportunities and
risks of the network revolution? This reconstruction gives us two advantages over the
common scientistic misconception. In enjoyable contrast to the normative poverty
of scientific analysis in its narrow sense, reflexive social practice provides us with a
plethora of normative perspectives – the famous *idées directrices* of social institutions,
the normative expectations, social demands, political rights, and utopian hopes of
individual participants within them, as well as principles gained in political conflicts
on the ground, which concern the institutions' overall social purposes and their contributions to different constituencies.[28] This is what social science in the strict sense
could never produce, much less legal doctrine create from within itself. At the same
time, however, the law, will, in juridifiying partial social rationalities, enforce its own
particularist–universal orientation above the particularist–universal orientations of
other forms of reflexive practice. For example, when it comes to structural corruption, law needs to distance itself from the results of social practices. Sociological
jurisprudence, currently cloaked in the mantle of scientific study, should thus in
fact be identified as a specifically legal mode of dealing with the collision between
different social rationalities.[29]

Business Studies

It is noteworthy that several legal studies on hybrid networks have now developed
a heightened sensitivity for business studies – in our words, for a reflexive social
practice that formulates the normative preconditions for business success. These
legal forays across the borders have proved successful, because they have discovered
opportunities and risks posed by hybrid networks and have allowed this material to
inform their legal solutions. Pioneering analyses of franchising made early detailed
reference to business studies and established their legal concepts in close proximity
to the organizational demands of franchising systems.[30] The resulting legal typology
maps interest conflicts onto different types of franchising (subordination, coordination, coalition, and federation), subjecting each type to a specific regulatory regime
(relational contract, partnership, and corporate groups). Risk analyses of new forms
of "systemic" dependence in just-in-time arrangements are based on detailed organizational studies that have unveiled, in particular, the importance of computer-based
integration as compared to merely contractual or corporate dependence and, via
analogy of the law of corporate groups, have drawn legal consequences.[31]

[28] These are phenomena that normative sociology focuses on. See Friedland and Alford 232 (1992);
Selznick (1992); Selznick et al. (1969); Fuller (1969).
[29] For an elaboration, see Teubner 149 (1997).
[30] Martinek 231ff. (1987).
[31] Nagel, Riess, and Theis 1506ff. (1989).

Legal Economics

Indeed, reference to reflexive social practices in business management has been fruitful, especially where legal concepts of network phenomena need to be developed according to the motivation of actors. Nonetheless, if the task is one of reconstructing the network revolution in its relevance for economy and society as a whole, then the business perspective is far too narrow. Empirical business studies tend to focus only on network effects on individual firms and fail to recognize general economic and social implications. Their normative viewpoint is similarly limited, because they concentrate on efficiency, effectiveness, and (occasionally) legitimacy of the individual network. This is a far too restricted basis for a legal appraisal of network opportunities and risks.

A step forward can be made here by taking into account reflexive theories of economic practice and, above all, ideas from transaction-cost theory, property rights theory, and economic institutionalism. Certainly, such theories conceive of themselves not as reflexive social practices, but as an integral part of the scientific knowledge system. However, pure scientific theorems, devoid of all preconceptions, would never handicap themselves with normatively loaded concepts and orientations, such as the *homo oeconomicus* or "economic efficiency." Taking normative orientations – particularly, efficiency concerns – as their starting point, legal studies of money transfer systems and other networks in the private sector are seeking to analyze and come to terms with the innovative yet highly controversial category of a "network contract."[32] Other studies on symbiotic contracts, inspired by institutional economics, have successfully demonstrated the efficiency gains of networking and consequently advocate their legal institutionalization.[33] Economic studies on network effects and their various legal implications are similarly profitable.[34]

Social Theory

However, if law is concerned with embedding business networks within their broader political and social context, it must engage in a legal reconstruction of sociological network theories.[35] If law is to develop "socially appropriate" legal concepts, the analysis of market networks must be broadened to take into account reflexive practices of other social environments. We are concerned here, all cognitive hurdles notwithstanding, with legal reconstruction of the normativity inherent to social practice. As for networks, social-theory-informed legal forays into status-based and contractual relationships within franchising are particularly noteworthy, because they unveil the semi-autonomous status of network participants and attempt to give

---

[32] Rohe 66ff., 81ff. (1998); Möschel 211 (1986).
[33] Kirchner 226ff. (1996); Schanze 67, 89ff. (1991); Schanze 691 (1993);. For a fruitful legal-economic analysis of cooperation contracts, see Kulms 55ff., 240ff. (2000).
[34] Cafaggi (2008); Lemley and McGowan 479 (1998).
[35] The social embedding of economic interchange is the objective of economic sociology, which has a closer empathy with the analytical interests of legal scholarship than purely economic analyses have. See Smelser and Swedberg (1994).

them legal security.[36] For example, studies of standard term contract regulation for just-in-time contracts reveal the role that case law can play in the promotion of productive networks and in limiting institutional misuse.[37]

TRANSLATION PROBLEMS: NETWORKS
AS CONNECTED CONTRACTS

However, I repeat: "'Network' is not a legal concept." All joyous legal contact with reflexive social practices notwithstanding, legal arguments only begin where other reflexive theories end. The debate is over the appropriate form of regulation for business networks, virtual business, just-in-time systems, franchising chains, and other cooperative contracts. They are generally established through bilateral contracts, yet give rise to multilateral (legal) effects. Hybrid networks are remarkably disruptive social phenomena. They can neither be subsumed under the category of market nor under the category of organization. After a long period of indecision, sociologists and economists have responded to this confusion with theories characterizing networks as autonomous institutions, very different from the usual forms of economic coordination.[38] How is law to respond, however? As innovation-friendly lawyers suggest, should it declare networks or symbiotic contracts to be *sui generis* legal institutions sailing in the Bermuda Triangle between contracts, torts, and corporations?[39]

In my opinion the term "network" is not suited to play the role of a technical legal concept. Networks traverse private law concepts. Legally speaking, they can take the form of corporate, contractual, or tortious special relationships. For this reason alone, legal doctrine cannot simply adopt the term "network" as a legal concept. Yet, the disciplinary barriers are even higher. Current ideas about knowledge transfer are misleading. Law cannot simply accept social structures of networks at face value; for example, the social preconditions for intensive cooperation. Neither can it simply adopt particular elements within social-science definitions, such as the economic formula, "hybrid between market and hierarchy," or the sociological formula, "trust-based exchange system." Instead it must itself reconstruct anew the constitutive contours of the correlating legal definition out of its own path-dependent evolutionary logic.[40]

---

[36] Joerges supra n. 18, 17ff (1991).

[37] Casper 397ff. (2001); Casper 314 (1995).

[38] For an economic theory of networks most prominent, see Williamson 269 (1991); Williamson (1985). For a sociological theory of networks, see Powell 295 (1990).

[39] For symbiotic contracts as a third institution between contract and organization, see Schanze supra n. 33; Kirchner supra n. 33. For network contracts as an institution *sui* generis, see Möschel supra n. 32, Rohe supra n. 32.

[40] For a particularly clear distinction between social system and legal system and their evolutionary dynamics, see Amstutz 309 (2009).

However, any attempt to subsume networks simply under traditional private law concepts is doomed to failure.[41] First, company law is inappropriate for market networks, because pooling of resources and joint decision making do not suit the decentralized network structure. Second, given the radical individualism of single nodes in networks, contract law is indeed the correct systematic arena, but needs to be considerably transformed to accommodate the opportunities and risks of market networks. Third, an independent legal category of a "network contract," which is based on traditional law of agency, is not appropriate for the decision structure of business networks. It follows that doctrinal qualifications of networks need be based on the development of an "organizational contract law" – the law of "controrgs," if you like – that recognizes their hybrid nature through the inclusion of organizational (i.e., not only relational but also multilateral) elements within the contract.[42] Here, one needs to exploit the developmental logic of a rudimentary but already established form of organizational contract law. In German law the notion of *Vertragsverbund* (connected contracts) has been developed – a doctrine that is ripe for further evolution in the network sphere. To quote a doctrinal authority from Germany,

> The notion of connected contracts is used to describe any plurality of contracts which refer to each other within either bilateral or multilateral relationships, whose interconnection gives rise to direct legal effects (of a genetic, functional or conditional nature), whether these simply result in an effect of one contract to the other (or others), or whether one can also observe mutual effects.[43]

It is the "economic unity" of several bipolar contracts that is determinative for the connected contracts. However, this concept also entails a strange paradox that time and again gives rise to harsh critique of the entire construction: Multiple contracts are directed to a single economic goal, which can only be achieved if all contracts are performed, but which is again also entirely dependent on the legal independence of each of the contracts. Legally speaking, this results in the strained formula that each and every contract is legally distinct but also builds an economic unity on which the law can focus.

However, the critique that this is all quite arbitrary[44] is wrong. Instead, to understand the mystery of connected contracts, we must make productive use of this "unbearable contradiction." The undeniable contradiction found within the notion of the "economic unity of distinct contracts" should not simply be regarded as a yet to be corrected logical mistake within doctrinal reasoning, but is instead itself the exact juridical correlate of the social reality of hybrids, the bedrock for their

---

[41] For more details, see Teubner supra n. 9, ch. 2.
[42] For a special law of "controrgs" (i.e., an "organizational contract law" for networks), see Teubner 115 (2009a); (2009b); Teubner supra n. 9, ch. 3; Teubner 231ff. (1993b) ; Teubner 129ff. (1991).
[43] Gernhuber 710 (1989). See also Larenz and Wolf 431 (2004); Esser and Schmidt 214 (1995).
[44] Wolf 62ff. (1978).

productivity, and the source of those risks to which the law must find appropriate responses.[45]

THE ROLE OF LAW IN SOCIAL DE-PARADOXIFICATION PROCESSES

This contradiction is absolutely central to networks. Private law must respond with sensitivity to the *coincidentia oppositorum* manifest within networks. The main thesis is as follows: Certain economic developments expose actors to a double-bind situation, which they react to with the aid of an internally contradictory network structure. The double-bind situation typical for networks arises where (1) the social environment makes ambivalent, contradictory, or paradoxical demands of business entities to which they must respond; (2) such demands are so central to business survival that they cannot be simply ignored; and (3) their explicit thematization is highly problematical.[46] The institutional answer to these problems is neither a contract nor organization, but a hybrid network, because this construct allows for the transformation of external incompatibilities into internally manageable contradictions. In turn, private law needs to respond in two ways with innovative doctrinal concepts: On the one hand, it normalizes and stabilizes network-specific contradictions; on the other, it combats various consequences of these contradictions.

Hybrid constructions within the triangle of contract, organization, and network facilitate escape from the double-bind situation. They constitute institutional arrangements that make network logic, as opposed to simple contractual or organizational logic, resistant to contradictory social environmental demands. More precisely, hybrids react to paradoxical situations (in their broadest sense) that threaten the operational capacities of actors. They do so through their ambivalence (A is or is not A), their contradictory nature (A is not A), or their paradoxical character (A because not A).[47] Generally speaking, there are two modes of escape from such imbroglios. The one is repressive, suppressing contradictions by admitting only one of the contradictory instructions and dismissing the other. The other is constructive, seeking to make paradoxes fruitful to the degree that it establishes a more complex representation

---

45 The relationship of network building to contradictory external demands made on business is the focus for many social science analyses, albeit dealing with different aspects of the problem. See Hirsch-Kreinsen 107 (2002); Luhmann 407ff. (2000); Buxbaum supra n. 1, 701; Cameron and Quinn 1 (1988).

46 On the paradoxical double-bind situation, see Bateson (1972); Watzlawick, Beavin, and Jackson, ch. 6 (1967).

47 Paradoxes, in their narrowest sense, denote situations such as "A because not A." In a wider rhetorical sense, paradoxes include ambivalence and contradictions that inhibit thinking within a given framework. Social science and law are best served by the wider definition that encompasses inhibition effects, as well as the potential to overcome them. For a general pragmatic perspective on contradictions and paradoxes, see Gumbrecht and Pfeiffer, ch. 6 (1991); Watzlawick et al., supra n. 46, ch. 6. On the legal treatment of paradoxes, see Suber (1990); Fletcher 1263 (1985).

of the world. This second approach is what is meant by "morphogenesis," which Krippendorff suggested for dealing with paradox:

> Unless one is able to escape a paradoxical situation which is what Whitehead and Russell achieved with the theory of logical types, paradoxes paralyze an observer and may lead either to a collapse of the construction of his or her world, or to a growth in complexity in his or her representation of this world. It is the latter case which could be characterized as morphogenesis.[48]

If in a double-bind situation people choose contractual arrangements, they tend to repress one of the two contradictory messages. If they choose integrated hierarchical organizations they repress the other message. Under certain conditions, however, hybrid arrangements provide for an institutional environment in which paradoxical communication is not repressed; it is not only tolerated but also invited, institutionally facilitated, and sometimes turned productive. Hybrids as a highly ambiguous combination of networks with contracts and organizations seem to be the result of a subtle interplay between different and mutually contradicting logics of action.

In the particular context of hybrid networks, the double bind stems from the imposition of environmental demands on actors to simultaneously obey different and contradictory operational imperatives. Some of these demands derive directly from contradictory economic pressures. Others result from a collision between economic requirements, on the one hand, and scientific, cultural, medical, and political principles, on the other.

Contradictory demands can be traced to economic trends that have increasingly overburdened individual firms and have forced them to engage in networking: "trends such as increased technological complexity, increased pressure on productivity and costs, as well as simultaneous market demands for a high degree of flexibility."[49] Empirical studies on intracompany cooperation have systematically researched the particular contradictions to which firms are exposed. Increasingly, the market demands "flexible specialization"; after the demise of standardized mass production, the demand is for "client-specific mass production." This goal gives rise to a barely surmountable contradiction between flexibility and efficiency. The trend in production is toward "systemic rationalization." This optimization standard cloaks a contradiction between complexity and reliability. Similarly, business is required to follow the goal of "decentralized self-direction," laying itself open to a contradiction between the autonomy of and oversight over decentralized business units. Business is then left with the question of whether it can choose only one organizational

---

[48] Krippendorff 51ff. (1984). On paradox and morphogenesis in social systems, see Luhmann 133 (1990). On exemplary reactions to the paradoxical demands of just-in-time systems, see Eisenhardt and Westcott 169, 191 (1988).

[49] Hirsch-Kreinsen supra n. 45, 107.

structure or whether it must seek out the far harder path of combination, fusion, and trade-offs.[50]

Networks are confronted with the problem of how to translate contradictory demands into internal structures, such that operational burdens are sustainable.[51] The determinative innovation of networks is that they transform external contradictions into a tense but sustainable "double orientation" within the operational system. One and the same operation is exposed both to individual network node orientations and to the collective orientation of the network, and it is simultaneously constrained and liberated by the demand that it must find a balance in each context.[52]

In contrast to contracts or organizations, which exhibit either an individual or a collective orientation, networks have created a double social orientation for individual operations. Each operation within the hybrid must simultaneously meet both the normative demands that stem from bilateral relations between individual actors and of those that stem from the network as a whole. The result is a remarkable degree of self-regulation within networks. This feature furnishes the key explanation for the conclusion of economists that networks and nodes engage in a specific form of profit sharing, distinguishable from forms of profit sharing found within other social contexts.[53] Although the law of corporations first attributes profit to the corporation and then oversees its distribution to members, networks provide for a simultaneous distribution to the net and its nodes. All transactions profit both the network and individual actors.[54] This type of profit sharing acts as a constraint, because all transactions must pass the double test. At the same time, however, it acts as an incentive, because all network gains are always related to individual gain.[55]

LEGAL CONDITIONS: DUAL CONSTITUTION
OF CONNECTED CONTRACTS

How is the law to respond to this transformation of external contradictions into an internal – simultaneously individual and collective – orientation? Law cannot just map network structures onto its concepts. In the face of the network irritation it has to find its own answers: in terms of legal facts through dual constitution of connected contracts and in terms of legal consequences through a selective double attribution to individual contractual partners and to the network as a whole.

---

[50] Semlinger 313ff. (1993).
[51] Hirsch-Kreinsen supra n. 45, 120; Semlinger supra n. 50, 332.
[52] On the key concept of "double attribution," see Teubner 324ff. (2002); Teubner (1993b) supra n. 42, 119ff. For double attribution from a social science perspective, see Windeler 194ff., 224 (2001); Littmann and Jansen 69ff. (2000). For double attribution in the law of networks, see Supiot 135 (2000); Collins 248ff. (1999).
[53] Dnes 136ff. (1991); Brickley and Dark 411ff. (1987).
[54] Dnes supra n. 53, 136ff.
[55] Norton 202ff. (1998); see also, Klein and Saft 349ff. (1985).

Any attempt to reconstruct the legal conditions for a business network must pay due regard to the internal evolution of doctrine. It is for this reason that the legal concept of "connected contracts," which has now been incorporated into the German Civil Code,[56] is so attractive for networks. Its particular characteristics derive from the legal logic of synallagmatic contracts.[57] To date, in German law, the major object of the law of connected contracts has been the purchase money loan. Moving away from its peculiarities in an attempt to develop a more general legal concept of connected contracts that also encompasses business networks, we can extrapolate from both case law and recent legislative advances to define three legal conditions.[58] Together, these three conditions constitute the surplus value of the dual constitution of the connected contracts as against a simple mass of disconnected bilateral contracts within a market:

1. reciprocal reference of bilateral contracts to one another, either found within the document and/or distilled from contractual practice ("multilaterality")
2. a contractual reference to the overall project of the connected contracts ("relational purpose")
3. a close and significant cooperative relationship among the participants within the multilateral relation ("economic unity")[59]

Does this mean that business networks are simply made up of a multitude of bilateral contracts? Is their only distinguishing characteristic that a relational agreement should be added to more commonplace agreements? No, rather what lurks beneath the three legal conditions is the social specificity of networking, which cannot as such be captured within legal categories. As I noted earlier, sociological jurisprudence is an oxymoron, and network is not a legal concept. There is a good reason why lawyers work with mysterious formulations in this area, such as "purposive nexus," "unity despite division," "accessory acts," *causa consumendi*.

Seen from the distance of systems theory, the entire matter can be understood as a difference between two closed systems, between social practices and legal doctrine. From the sociological standpoint, it is the network's specificity that causes a contractual system to observe its environment in a somewhat unusual manner. Usually, contracts focus their observations on markets and market conditions, in particular market prices, and adapt their decisions and internal structures to them. The network situation differs from this "normality": Where simple market observation no longer suffices, the system redirects its observation away from general market conditions and observes other contractual systems within the market and orients itself in

---

[56] § 358 BGB (*Verbundene Verträge*).
[57] Gernhuber supra n. 43, 710ff.
[58] For a restatement of doctrine and jurisprudence of connected contracts, see Habersack § 358, 26ff., 36ff (2007).
[59] For a more detailed account, see Teubner supra n. 9, ch. 3.

line with changes here rather than changes within the market.[60] Systems thus use networking to attempt to establish a symbiotic relationship with other systems, such that they can gain greater control over their environment. The fusion within such hybrid networking does not make a unity out of individual contracts; rather each contract remains autonomous in relation to its own function and its contributions to the environment.[61] Thus the relation between contracts becomes a mutual observation between two separate contracts, each of which autonomously pursues its own project, but adapts itself to each other through internal reflection.[62] It is simply not possible for this sociological picture of reciprocal reflection to appear on the screens of the law. Instead what we see on these screens are the three legal conditions of the connected contracts mentioned earlier – mutual referencing of contracts, relational purpose, and cooperative relationship – that establish the legal connectedness of the contracts.

If this is true for the legal construction of networks, then classical contract law needs to undergo considerable modification. In contractual networks, a heteronomous private order superimposes its demands on autonomous bilateral contracts. The reference of one contract to another entails the inclusive acceptance by the contractual partners of a foreign private order. Each bilateral contract must submit to a coherent overall system that needs to be respected. In practice, contractual conclusion is more or less reduced to a simple decision to enter into a homogeneous private order. Reference to other contracts is similar in nature to regard for standard contract terms, for customs of the market, or for social and technical norms. All in all, the bilateral contracts are caught in the institutional logic of networks: entry as a bilateral access to a multilateral order, trust-based interaction, decentralized coordination of a quasi-organization, and orientation of individual operations to the network purpose.

Taken together, the three conditions reconstruct the legal equivalent of a non-contractual "spontaneous social order" that comes out of a multiplicity of bilateral contracts. This is the proprium of social networks reconstructed in law as connected contracts. However, in marked contrast to Hayek's spontaneous order, the discovery processes of competitive markets – networking and cooperation, rather than market and competition – are the sources of spontaneous order.[63] Within such spontaneous orders, the stability of the relationship between legally independent units is deduced from beyond bipolar provisions.[64] "Beyond" bipolar provisions – this is the core of

---

[60] Luhmann supra n. 45, 407ff.

[61] Teubner (2002) supra note 52330; Castells 187 (2000).

[62] Amstutz supra n. 40.

[63] On spontaneous ordering in competitive markets and legal evolution, see Cooter 447ff. (1994); Vanberg 79ff. (1986); Hayek 72ff. (1973). On the important distinction between different types of spontaneous order, especially between markets and relational contracts, see Gordon 453 (1994). For a transposition of these ideas on contractual networks in the franchising and the construction business, see Heldt 137 (2009).

[64] Windeler supra n. 52, 240.

the argument. Various social coordination mechanisms of a noncontractual nature – reciprocal observation, anticipatory adaptation, cooperation, trust, self-binding, responsibility, negotiation, and stable relationships[65] – constitute the overarching order of networking and stamp the network's character on each bilateral contractual relationship.

LEGAL CONSEQUENCES: SELECTIVE DOUBLE ATTRIBUTION TO CONTRACT PARTIES AND TO THE NETWORK

What holds true in relation to the legal conditions of the network as connected contracts also holds true for its legal consequences. The double orientation in networks that is the result of a subtle interplay between contradictory logics of action must also find its resonance within the law.[66] This is true both for internal relations between participants within the network and its external relations. The appropriate legal response is a selective (!) double attribution of network acts to the contract parties and to the network, varying according to different structural contradictions within the network.

First Contradiction: Bilateral Exchange versus Multilateral Association

There is a first – should we say the standard – constellation of hybrid networks in which they appear as the result of contradictory demands from the market. Economic transactions, especially when they deal with knowledge-based products, are simultaneously exposed to the contradictory demands of bilateral exchange and multilateral relations.[67] An important explanation for the contradictory nature of behavioral expectations is the uncertainty of economic actors about future market development. Despite their antagonistic interests, this uncertainty forces the parties to engage in long-term exchange contracts to develop closely coordinated behavioral patterns, be they constructed along hierarchical or heterarchical lines.[68]

The traditional solution to such a collision between operational logics was a simple either-or decision. The suggestion made in the literature that we should qualify networks either as exchange contracts or as a corporation derives from this tradition. The result is the well-known rigid separation between market and hierarchies supported by similarly rigid rules of antitrust law, contract law, and corporation

---

[65] For discussion on the mechanisms and effects of such nonmarket spontaneous orders, see Sydow and Windeler 1ff., 12ff. (1998); Windeler supra n. 52, 240ff.; Gordon supra n. 63, 459.

[66] "Resonance" is not deployed here as a metaphor, but instead forms an important element within the theory of structural coupling. For the resonance of social problems within the law, see Luhmann supra n. 6, ch. 10.

[67] On contradictory environmental demands as a network-building impetus, see the sources in supra n. 45. In addition, see Sydow and Windeler supra n. 65, 6ff.

[68] Kulms supra n. 35, 227ff.

law. However, the enforced dichotomy between market/organization or between contract/corporation censors a more productive solution. Each institutional answer, market or hierarchy, contract or organization, represses the paradox. Each favors predominantly one of the contradictory orientations while pushing the other into the darkness of informality where it is sometimes discovered by subversive sociologists interested in the dark side of formal institutions.

The various routes out of these conflicts, which we characterized earlier as "morphogenesis," converge within the specific institutional logic of networks. The relevant concept within organizational theory is "detotalization." To react to external paradoxes, the network must give up its monolithic unity and recreate external diversity within its own institutions and functions. In such a process, antagonistic relationships (in this case, bilateral exchange and multilateral cooperation) are nurtured with one and the same partner – which cannot but prove to be a paradox should sectoral and temporal differentiations be ignored or "totalized."[69] Empirical studies have demonstrated that this internal division and recombination of exchange and cooperation are in fact possible on the ground. Within successful business networks, actors have been able simultaneously to maintain the logic of exchange within contractual sectors, such as logistics, quality, quantity, and pricing, and combine it with trust-based cooperation within relational sectors such as R&D and joint planning and construction.[70] Detotalization strategies thus aim to instutionalize new internal differences within a business totality that is indelibly marked by contradictions. The notion of "detotalization" internalizes external contradictions, legitimates them as simple tensions, and contributes to their contextual resolution through internal differences.

In stark contrast to the duties of good faith governing exchange contracts on the one side and to duties of loyalty to the association on the other, the legal category that is best suited to capture the network logic, to give it institutional support, and to compensate for some of its negative implications is surely the duty of loyalty to the network. This duty is distinguished by its double orientation within one formula to both network and contract: It explicitly adopts the contradiction between individual and collective elements within the network.[71]

The primary achievement of this duty is the internal translation of externally imposed insoluble contradictions into manageable conflicts between different levels and subsystems within the network and between nodes, relations, the center, and the network in its entirety.[72] The duty of loyalty therefore fulfills the following task in law: to create internal differentiations between various temporal, social, and

---

[69] Neuberger (2000) 207ff.
[70] Bieber 111–140 (1992).
[71] For a detailed discussion of these duties in franchising and construction contracts, see Heldt supra n. 63.
[72] Semlinger supra n. 50, 332.

functional sectors that translate initially contradictory demands into clear, contextually determined expectations.

The legal formula is thus as follows: to distinguish situations in which an intensified duty of loyalty to the network exists from situations in which only the contractual duty of good faith will apply, albeit that each obligation must be modified with reference to the other. The legal task is one of distinguishing between contractual good faith and duty of loyalty to the network.[73] At the same time, however, care must be taken to ensure that this duty of loyalty to the network is not simply equated with the duty of loyalty within corporation law, but is rather, for its part, given a decentralized bias. Such differences clearly educe from the repeatedly discussed distinction between a network and a collective: the pervasive combination of autonomy and association. This combination is better served by a contractual, legislative, and judicial apportionment of duties of loyalty – in contrast to resource pooling within a single hand or a legal person – that takes over the task of the context-dependent fine tuning of autonomy and association.[74]

Second Contradiction: Competition versus Cooperation

Here we are concerned with a second typical constellation in which hybrid networks evolve as an answer to external contradictions. Especially in the case of knowledge-based products, economic decisions are subject not only to the tensions between bilateral exchange and multilateral organization but also to the conflict between competition and cooperation.[75] Paradoxical commands given simultaneously to network participants are "cooperate with one another!" and "compete against one another!" Knowledge-oriented production gives rise to a contradiction between two fundamental forms of social experience. Within competition, individual goals can only be achieved at the cost of another, whereas within cooperation, individual goals are wholly compatible with those of others. This justifies the usual practice of institutionalizing a strict distinction between the two: market or organization.

Recent business studies nevertheless suggest that it is possible to conceive of alternatives to the rigid institutional separation of competition and cooperation, and indeed these alternatives do work in practice. The increased incidence of hybrid networks can be seen as a refined reaction to the contradictory demands of cooperation and competition.[76] "Coopetition" is the new magic formula that promises that competitive advantages will flow out of the combination of cooperation and competition that manages to combine organization and contract with network

---

[73] See the discussion of franchising cases. See Böhner 153 (2009).
[74] See Kulms supra n. 35, 231, 261.
[75] For the cooperation–competition conflict, see Semlinger 141ff.; Littmann and Jansen supra n. 52, 64ff.; Sydow 279–314 (1999).
[76] See, in particular, Jarillo (1993); Neuberger, supra n. 69, 207ff.

elements.[77] Coopetition would then constitute a social model that would allow, no, even demand, that competitors be congruent with cooperation partners.

One should nonetheless keep a certain distance from such purely combinatory approaches and emphasize "reentry" effects in this context. A simple mixture of competitive and cooperative behavioral patterns does not provide an easy exit out of paradoxical oscillation. In the technical sense defined by Spencer Brown, reentry has nothing to do with ending the division between the two sides of an either-or decision.[78] On the contrary, the distinction between competition and cooperation must not be ended and must instead be strictly maintained and institutionalized in a legal form. At the same time, this same distinction makes a second appearance. Now, however, it is reintroduced to one side of the institutional divide and once again institutionalized within it.

Mixed competition–cooperation forms only cease to be ideological, in the sense that they simply pursue only one orientation under the semantic cloak of "combination," if and when they are subject to reentry conditions. By the same token, neither do they simply squander the gains of each social model that only become apparent by virtue of their institutional separation. Instead, and insofar as reentry secures the stable identity of the distinction, they can maximize such advantages. However, this seems possible only under three conditions:

(1) sustainable institutionalization of market competition through the conclusion of parallel and distinct bilateral contracts (i.e., exactly not by the creation of a unitary organization)
(2) institutionalization of the reentry of the cooperation–competition distinction within the system of contracts, such that market competition is overlain by a sphere of operational cooperation
(3) situationally defined internal demarcation between operational spheres

Any attempt to institutionalize hybrids legally must pay due regard to such complications. It is exactly this complex of questions to which private law has yet to find a response. We are faced here with the difficult question of whether legal obligations can be established at all between network participants who are not contractually bound to one another. The problem is whether legal sanctions exist for the incorrect behavior of a participant within a delivery chain or a system of networked contracts.[79] The legal postulate of a mutual contractual liability of noncontractual partners within the network is becoming increasingly pressing because of the growth of network relations within the provision of goods and services. The privity of contract principle notwithstanding, arguments of fairness and prevention demand restitutionary liability in such cases. The liability of strangers to the bilateral contract within the network for damages is the consequence.

[77] Littmann and Jansen supra n. 52, 64ff.
[78] Brown 56ff., 69ff. (1972).
[79] Rohe supra n. 32, 98; Picker 101ff. (1987); Möschel supra n. 32, 187ff.

Third Contradiction: Unitas Multiplex

In a third constellation, hybrid networks appear as a response to contradictions within the attribution of social action. Who in the positive sense benefits from success and profit, and who in the negative sense suffers loss and liability – individual or collective actors? Is the network simply a trust-based relationship between individual actors, or does it form an independent collective, making its appearance as a new actor that becomes in itself a point of attribution of action and responsibility?[80] In this case too, the traditional approach of a strict division between contract and organization found both in sociological theory and in legal doctrine supplies inappropriate solutions. Social practice within hybrid networks has, however, identified its own solution: double attribution. This attribution technique is one of the most important characteristics of hybrid networks, facilitating the distinction between simple attribution to individual actors in the case of the contract and attribution to collective actors in the case of the organization. One and the same economic transaction is doubly attributed: to individual actors as network nodes and to the overall network.

However, this new form of attribution gives rise to new risks that in turn demand a new legal form of network responsibility to external actors that is distinguishable both from individual liability and from the collective liability of organizations. Although the "piercing of the contractual veil" proves its worth as a general formulation to establish network liability, a distinction must be made between two typical situations (i.e., between centralized and decentralized networks). Various hybrid networks are so centralized and the autonomy of their nodes so limited that they are little more than hierarchical organizations in contractual clothing. Such networks are just a strategic effort to evade the imperative provision of law. Empirical data confirm the suspicion that companies deploy disaggregation strategies to avoid the application of tort and labor law.

In the case of decentralized networks, we return to our example of the marketing of private automobiles. Although the external liability of the network and not just that of its individual nodes should be legally guaranteed, the piercing of the contractual veil should not result in unitary collective liability. Rather, the appropriate form of liability is a decentralized, multiple, and collective combination of network liability and the liability of nodes that have in fact participated within the operation under scrutiny.[81] In contrast to comprehensive collective liability in the case of formal organizations, this approach leads to a reindividualization of collective liability within networks. Analogous to the well-known concept of "market share liability,"

---

[80] For networks as mere relations between individual actors and not as collective actors, see Tacke 317 (2000); Heydebrand (1999). For networks as collective actors, however, under specified conditions, see Windeler supra n. 52, 225ff.; Castells supra n. 61, 177ff., 187, 209, 214; Sydow and Windeler 265 (1998); Teubner 54ff. (1993a); Teubner supra n. 42, 203ff. For a solomonic solution, see Luhmann supra n. 45, 408: Networks will "become social systems of their own, once they constitute clear boundaries and a history of recursive events on which trust will be based."

[81] For a discussion of external network liability, see Teubner supra n. 9, Ch. 6; Cafaggi supra n. 35; King 417 (2005); Emerson 609 (1992).

one might make use of the notion of "network share liability," a form of liability
that is particularly significant in situations where the root cause of damage cannot
be traced back to individual nodes but only to the network itself. Such cases do
not involve a traditional collective actor whose assets might serve as the object of
liability claims. Nonetheless, the network does serve as a point of reference for the
attribution of liability and as the springboard for the reindividualization of liability
among individual nodes. Such a reindividualization is to be promoted particularly
in cases where the individual contribution of nodes to damage can no longer be
clearly distinguished. In such a situation, liability could be met through the pro
rata liability of participating nodes, calculated in accordance with their degree of
participation within the network.

Fourth Contradiction: Intersystemic Networks

A final conflict between different operational logics becomes apparent within a fourth
constellation of hybrids. In the effort to promote technological transformation, the
state provides extensive grants to joint research projects between particular industrial
branches and independent research institutions. This results in a loosely organized
network of close relationships among the relevant industries, participating research
institutions, and public authorities that have an interest in such cooperation. The
network is charged with the pursuit of successful innovation. However, its attitude
to transaction costs is as irrational and extravagant as a series of UN conferences.

This is a conflict between different social rationalities that again disturbs institutional arrangements. Participating actors demand to be allowed to behave in
accordance with different and contradictory behavioral logics. The case of public–
private research networks would require rational actors to observe three mutually
incompatible categorical imperatives. In this case, hybrid networks appear as manna
from heaven, being exactly tailored to bridge multiple contradictory rationalities.
They facilitate mutual interference between rationalities without the imposition of
hierarchical order.

Can a legal concept of network respond to such demands? In the case of mixed
network regimes, the simple evolution of legal norms to support the transaction costs,
advantages, and efficiency gains of networks, as opposed to contractual or corporate
arrangements, is clearly not enough. In reality, such networks only offend against
the imperatives of transaction-cost minimization and allocative efficiency. Nonetheless they are successful innovators. Therefore, in this case of mixed public–private
regimes, the role of legal concepts of the network is far more one of developing principles of institutional autonomy, establishing fundamental rights, securing procedural
fairness, ensuring the rule of law, and fostering political responsibility.[82]

This points to one of the central tasks of a law of hybrid networks. In contrast
to traditional legal concepts, such as "contractual purposes" or "business interest,"

[82] See Abegg 255 (2009).

this task involves the evolution of a legally applicable concept of "network interest." As a counterpoint to instrumental autonomy, I call this the legally secured "reflexive autonomy" of individual subunits within the network. Within integrated organizations, be they private concerns, public corporations, or mixed form, rules on organizational procedure are always oriented in line with the common purpose. The character of this common goal is determinative in the case of a decentralization or delegation of functions. Decentralized units are afforded the freedom to use their local knowledge to chose the appropriate concrete means of pursuing the common aims of the entire organization or, legally speaking, the business interest.

This is entirely different within intersystemic networks. Legal norms must not merely afford network nodes a heightened degree of protection for their autonomy. Instead they must supply a different form of protection in that, despite centralization, they must guarantee reflexive capacities; that is, the capacity of nodes to balance out (of network relations) their own independent concept of their social function and contribution to their environment. Within intersystemic networks of scientific knowledge, politics, and the economy, this leads us in the direction of a quasi-constitutional guarantee for scientific freedom in the face of political and economic inter-references within the borders of a mixed network. This idea is in fact generalizable. In contrast to the case of companies, in which legal guarantees of the autonomy of subsidiaries protect the profit interests of the parts against the whole and vice versa, we are required, in the case of intersystemic networks, to respect the institutional integrity of health, education, journalism, technology, and art, not only within a decentral (not simply decentralized) structure of autonomous nodes but also within the inclusive network. Although it still makes sense to conceive of a common company interest in the form of procedural and material legal norms within corporation law, the network interest can only be created out of the depths of the compatibility of autonomous network participants.

REFERENCES

Abegg, Andreas (2009). Legislation and Self-Regulation of Hybrid Networks at the Intersection between Governmental Administration and Economic Self-Organization, in Marc Amstutz and Gunther Teubner, eds., *Contractual Networks: Legal Issues of Multilateral Cooperation*. Oxford: Hart Publishing.

Amstutz, Marc (2009). The Constitution of Contractual Networks, in Marc Amstutz and Gunther Teubner, eds., *Contractual Networks: Legal Issues of Multilateral Cooperation*. Oxford: Hart Publishing.

Amstutz, Marc and Gunther Teubner, eds. (2009). *Contractual Networks: Legal Issues of Multilateral Cooperation*. Oxford: Hart Publishing.

Bateson, Gregory (1972). *Steps to an Ecology of Mind*. New York: Ballantine.

Bieber, Daniel (1992) Systemische Rationalisierung und Produktionsnetzwerke, in Thomas Malsch and Ulrich Mill, eds., *ArBYTE: Modernisierung der Industriesoziologie?* Berlin: 1992.

Böhner, Reinhard (2009). Profit Sharing within the Network: Duty to Transfer Network Benefits, in Marc Amstutz and Gunther Teubner, eds., *Contractual Networks: Legal Issues of Multilateral Cooperation*. Oxford: Hart Publishing.

Bräutigam, Peter (1994). *Deliktische Außenhaftung im Franchising*. Baden-Baden: Nomos.

Brickley, James and Frederick Dark (1987). The Choice of the Organizational Form: The Case of Franchising, 18 *Journal of Financial Economics* 401.

Brown, George Spencer (1972). *Laws of Form*. New York: Julian.

Buxbaum, Richard (1993). Is "Network" a Legal Concept? 149 *Journal of Institutional and Theoretical Economics* 698.

Cafaggi, Fabrizio, (2008). Contractual Networks and the Small Business Act: Towards European Principles? 2008/15 *EUI Working Paper LAW*.

Cameron, Kim and Robert Quinn (1988). Organizational Paradox and Transformation, in Kim Cameron and Robert Quinn, eds., *Paradox and Transformation: Towards a Theory of Change in Organization and Management*. Cambridge, MA: Ballinger.

Casper, Steve (1995). How Public Law Influences Decentralized Supplier Network Organization: The Case of BMW and Audi, *WZB-Discussion Paper FS I*.

———. (2001). The Legal Framework for Corporate Governance: Explaining the Development of Contract Law in Germany and the United States, in Peter Hall and David Soskice, eds., *Varieties of Capitalism: The Institutional Foundations of Comparative Advantage*. Oxford: Oxford University.

Castells, Manuel (2000). *The Rise of the Network Society*. Oxford: Basil Blackwell.

Collins, Hugh (1999). *Regulating Contracts*. Oxford: Oxford University.

Cooter, Robert (1994). Decentralized Law for a Complex Economy, 23 *International Review of Law and Economics* 443.

Dnes, Antony (1991). The Economic Analysis of Franchising and its Regulation, in Christian Joerges, ed., *Franchising and the Law: Theoretical and Comparative Approaches in Europe and the United States*. Baden Baden: Nomos.

Eisenhardt, Kathleen and Brian Westcott (1988). Paradoxical Demands and the Creation of Excellence: The Case of Just-in-Time Manufacturing, in Kim Cameron and Robert Quinn, eds., *Paradox and Transformation: Towards a Theory of Change in Organization and Management*. Cambridge, MA: Ballinger.

Emerson, Robert W. (1992). Franchisors' Liability When Franchisees Are Apparent Agents, 20 *Hofstra Law Review* 609.

Esser, Josef and Mike Schmidt (1995). *Schuldrecht: Ein Lehrbuch. Allgemeiner Teil I 1*. 8th ed., Heidelberg: Müller.

Fletcher, George (1985). Paradoxes in Legal Thought, 85 *Columbia Law Review* 1263.

Friedman, Lawrence (1965). *Contract Law in America: A Social and Economic Case Study*. Madison: University of Wisconsin.

———. (1985). *Total Justice*. New York: Russell Sage Foundation.

———. (1990). *The Republic of Choice: Law, Authority and Culture*. Cambridge: Harvard University Press.

———. (1999a). *The Horizontal Society*. New Haven: Yale University Press.

———. (1999b). Taking Law and Society Seriously, 74 *Chicago-Kent Law Review* 529.

———. (2002). *American Law in the Twentieth Century*. New Haven: Yale University Press.

Friedland, Roger and Robert Alford (1992). Bringing Society Back In: Symbols, Practices, and Institutional Contradictions, in Paul DiMaggio and Walter Powell, eds., *The New Institutionalism*. Chicago: Chicago University Press.

Fuller, Lon (1969). *The Morality of Law*. New Haven: Yale University Press.

Gernhuber, Joachim (1989). *Das Schuldverhältnis: Begründung und Änderung, Pflichten und Strukturen, Drittwirkungen.* Tübingen: Mohr & Siebeck.

Gordon, Robert (1994). Hayek and Cooter on Custom and Reason, 23 *Southwestern University Law Review* 453.

Grundmann, Stefan, ed. (2010). *From Exchange to Cooperation: Networks and Long-Term Relationships in European Contract Law.* Amsterdam: Kluwer.

Gumbrecht, Hans Ulrich and Ludwig Pfeiffer, eds. (1991). *Paradoxien, Dissonanzen, Zusammenbrüche: Situationen offener Epistemologie.* Frankfurt: Suhrkamp.

Habersack, Matthias (2007) *Münchener Kommentar zum Bürgerlichen Gesetzbuch.* München: Beck.

Hayek, Friedrich (1973). *Law, Legislation and Liberty. Volume 1: Rules and Order.* London: Routledge & Paul.

Heermann, Peter (2009). The Status of Multilateral Synallagmas in the Law of Connected Contracts, in Marc Amstutz and Gunther Teubner, eds., *Contractual Networks: Legal Issues of Multilateral Cooperation.* Oxford: Hart Publishing.

Heldt, Cordula (2009). Internal Relations and Semi-spontaneous Order: The Case of Franchising and Construction Contracts, in Marc Amstutz and Gunther Teubner, eds., *Contractual Networks: Legal Issues of Multilateral Cooperation.* Oxford: Hart Publishing.

Heydebrand, Wolf (1999). *The Network Metaphor as Key to the Analysis of Complex Production and Service Relation in a Global Economy.* Stuttgart: Akademie für Technikfolgenabschätzung in Baden-Württemberg.

Hirsch-Kreinsen, Hartmut (2002). Unternehmensnetzwerke – revisited, 31 *Zeitschrift für Soziologie* 106.

Jarillo, Jose (1993). *Strategic Networks: Creating the Borderless Organization.* Oxford: Oxford University Press.

Joerges, Christian (1991). Status and Contract in Franchising Law, in Christian Joerges, ed., *Franchising and the Law: Theoretical and Comparative Approaches in Europe and the United States.* Baden-Baden: Nomos.

King, Joseph H. (2005). Limiting the Vicarious Liability of Franchisors for the Torts of Their Franchisees, 62 *Washington and Lee Law Review* 417.

Kirchner, Christian (1996). Symbiotic Arrangements as a Challenge to Antitrust, 152 *Journal of Institutional and Theoretical Economics* 226.

Klein, Benjamin and Lester F. Saft (1985). The Law and Economics of Franchise Tying Contracts, 28 *Journal of Law and Economics* 345.

Krippendorff, Klaus (1984). Paradox and Information, in Brenda Dervin and Melvin Voigt, eds., 5 *Progress in Communication Sciences.* Norwood: Ablex.

Kulms, Rainer (2000). *Schuldrechtliche Organisationsverträge in der Unternehmenskooperation.* Baden-Baden: Nomos.

Larenz, Karl and Manfred Wolf (2004). *Allgemeiner Teil des Bürgerlichen Rechts.* 9th ed. München: Beck.

Lemley, Mark and David McGowan (1998). Legal Implications of Network Economic Effects, 86 *California Law Review* 479.

Littmann, Peter and Stephan Jansen (2000). *Oszillodox: Virtualisierung – die permanente Neuerfindung der Organisation.* Stuttgart: Klett.

Luhmann, Niklas (1965). *Grundrechte als Institution: Ein Beitrag zur politischen Soziologie.* Berlin: Duncker & Humblot.

———. (1990). Sthenography, 7 *Stanford Literature Review* 133.

———. (2000). *Organisation und Entscheidung.* Opladen: Westdeutscher.

———. (2004). *Law as a Social System.* Oxford: Oxford University Press.

Martinek, Michael (1987). *Franchising: Grundlagen der zivil- und wettbewerbsrechtichen Behandlung der vertraglichen Gruppenkooperation beim Absatz von Waren und Dienstleistungen.* Heidelberg: Decker & Schenck.

Möschel, Wernhard (1986). Dogmatische Strukturen des bargeldlosen Zahlungsverkehrs, 186 *Archiv für die civilistische Praxis* 211.

Nagel, Bernhard, Birgit Riess, and Gisela Theis (1989). Der faktische Just-in-Time-Konzern: Unternehmensübergreifende Rationalisierungskonzepte und Konzernrecht am Beispiel der Automobilindustrie, 42 *Der Betrieb* 1505.

————. (1990). *Just-in-Time-Strategien: Arbeitsbeziehungen, Gestaltungspotentiale, Mitbestimmung.* Düsseldorf: Hans-Böckler-Stiftung.

Neuberger, Oswald (2000). Dilemmata und Paradoxa im Managementprozess in: Georg Schreyögg, ed., *Funktionswandel im Management: Wege jenseits der Ordnung* Berlin: Duncker & Humblot.

Norton, Seth (1988). An Empirical Look at Franchising as an Organisational Form, 61 *Journal of Business* 197.

OLG Karlsruhe (1989). 2 *Neue Zeitschrift für Verkehrsrecht* 434.

Palandt, Otto, ed., *Bürgerliches Gesetzbuch*, München: Beck.

Pasderski, Edgar (1998). *Die Außenhaftung des Franchisegebers.* Aachen: Mainz.

Pawlowski, Hans-Martin (1999). *Methodenlehre für Juristen: Theorie der Norm und des Gesetzes. Ein Lehrbuch.* Heidelberg: C. F. Müller.

Picker, Eduard (1987). Vertragliche und deliktische Schadenshaftung: Überlegungen zu einer Neustrukturierung der Haftungssysteme, 42 *Juristenzeitung* 1041.

Posner, Richard (1987). The Decline of Law as an Autonomous Discipline: 1982–1987, 100 *Harvard Law Review* 761.

Powell, Walter (1990). Neither Market nor Hierarchy: Network Forms of Organization, 12 *Research in Organizational Behavior* 295.

Rehbinder, Eckhard (1969). *Konzernaußenrecht und allgemeines Privatrecht: Eine rechtsvergleichende Untersuchung nach deutschem und amerikanischem Recht.* Bad Homburg: Gehlen.

————. (1997). Neues zum Durchgriff unter besonderer Berücksichtigung der höchstrichterlichen Rechtsprechung, in Eckhard Rehbinder and Heinz-Deter Assman, eds., *Wirtschafts- und Medienrecht in der offenen Demokrative: Freundesgabe für Friedrich Kübler*, Heidelberg: C. F. Müller.

Rohe, Mathias (1998). *Netzverträge: Rechtsprobleme komplexer Vertragsverbindungen.* Tübingen: Mohr & Siebeck.

Roth, Herbert (1989). Anmerkung zu OLG Karlsruhe, 2 *Neue Zeitschrift für Verkehrsrecht* 435.

Schanze, Erich (1991). Symbiotic Contracts: Exploring Long-Term Agency Structures Between Contract and Corporation, in Christian Joerges, ed., *Franchising and the Law: Theoretical and Comparative Approaches in Europe and the United States.* Baden-Baden: Nomos.

————. (1993). Symbiotic Arrangements, 149 *Journal of Institutional and Theoretical Economics* 691.

Sciulli, David (1992). *Theory of Societal Constitutionalism.* Cambridge: Cambridge University Press.

————. (2001). *Corporate Power in Civil Society: An Application of Societal Constitutionalism.* New York: New York University Press.

Selznick, Philip (1992). *The Moral Commonwealth: Social Theory and the Promise of Community.* Berkeley: University of California.

Selznick, Philip et al. (1969). *Law, Society and Industrial Justice*. New York: Russell Sage Foundation.

Semlinger, Klaus (1993). Effizienz und Autonomie in Zulieferungsnetzwerken: Zum strategischen Gehalt von Kooperation, in Wolfgang Staehle and Jörg Sydow, eds., 3 *Managementforschung*. Berlin: de Gruyter.

———. (2000). Kooperation und Konkurrenz in japanischen Netzwerkbeziehungen, in Jörg Sydow and Arnold Windeler, eds., *Steuerung von Netzwerken*. Opladen: Westdeutscher.

Shapiro, Martin (1998). Globalization and Freedom of Contract, in Harry Scheiber, ed., *The State and Freedom of Contract*. Stanford, CA: Stanford University Press.

Smelser, Neil and Richard Swedberg, eds. (1994). *The Handbook of Economic Sociology*. Princeton, NJ: Princeton University.

Steindorff, Ernst (1973). Politik des Gesetzes als Auslegungsmasstab im Wirtschaftsrecht, in Gottard Paulus, ed., *Festschrift für Karl Larenz*. München: Beck.

Suber, Peter (1990). *The Paradox of Self-Amendment: A Study of Logic, Law, Omnipotence and Change*. New York: Lang and available at http://www.earlham.edu/~peters/writing/psa/index.htm.

Supiot, Alain (2000). Les nouveaux visages de la subordination, 63 *Droit Social* 131.

Sydow, Jörg (1999). *Management von Netzwerkorganisationen*. Wiesbaden: Westdeutscher.

Sydow, Jörg and Arnold Windeler. (1998). Organizing and Evaluating Interfirm Networks, 9 *Organization Science. Special Issue: Managing Partnership and Strategic Alliances* 265.

Tacke, Veronika (2000). Netzwerk und Adresse, 6 *Soziale Systeme* 291.

Teubner, Gunther. (1991). Beyond Contract and Organization? The External Liability of Franchising Systems in German Law, in Christian Joerges, ed., *Franchising and the Law: Theoretical and Comparative Approaches in Europe and the United States*. Baden-Baden: Nomos.

———. (1993a). The Many-Headed Hydra: Networks as Higher-Order Collective Actors, in Joseph McCahery, Sol Picciotto, and Colin Scott, eds., *Corporate Control and Accountability*. Oxford: Clarendon Press.

———. (1993b). Piercing the Contractual Veil: The Social Responsibility of Contractual Networks, in Thomas Wilhelmson, ed., *Perspectives of Critical Contract Law*. Dartmouth: Aldershot.

———. (1997). Altera Pars Audiatur: Law in the Collision of Discourses, in Richard Rawlings, ed., *Law, Society and Economy*. Oxford: Clarendon.

———. (2002). Hybrid Laws: Constitutionalizing Private Governance Networks, in Robert Kagan, Martin Krygier, and Kenneth Winston, eds., *Legality and Community: On the Intellectual Legacy of Philip Selznick*. Berkeley: Berkeley Public Policy.

———. (2008). *Netzwerk als Vertragsverbund: Virtuelle Unternehmen, Franchising, Just in Time in sozialwissenschaftlicher und juristischer Sicht*. Baden-Baden: Nomos. (*Networks as Connected Contracts*. Available at http://ssrn.com/abstract=1233545.

———. (2009a). "And if I by Beelzebub Cast out Devils, . . . ": An Essay on the Diabolics of Network Failure, 10 *German Law Journal*, Special Issue: *The Law of the Network Society: A Tribute to Karl-Heinz Ladeur*, 115; also available at http://www.germanlawjournal.com/index.php?pageID=11&artID=1099, and in Grundmann, Stefan, ed. (2010). *From Exchange to Cooperation: Networks and Long-Term Relationships in European Contract Law*. Amsterdam; Kluwer.

———. (2009b). Coincidentia Oppositorum: Hybrid Networks beyond Contract and Organisation, in Marc Amstutz and Gunther Teubner, eds., *Contractual Networks: Legal Issues of Multilateral Cooperation*. Oxford: Hart Publishing.

Vanberg, Viktor (1986). Spontaneous Market Order and Social Rules: A Critical Examination of F. A. Hayek's Theory of Cultural Evolution, 2 *Economics and Philosophy* 75.

Watzlawick, Paul, Janet Beavin, and Don Jackson (1967). *Pragmatics of Human Communication: A Study of Interactional Patterns, Pathologies, and Paradoxes*. New York: W.W. Norton & Co.

Weber, Max (1978). *Economy and Society*. Berkeley: University of California.

Williamson, Oliver (1985). *The Economic Institutions of Capitalism: Firms, Markets, Relational Contracting*. New York: Free Press.

———. (1991). Comparative Economic Organization: The Analysis of Discrete Structural Alternatives, 36 *Administrative Science Quarterly* 269.

Windeler, Arnold (2001). *Unternehmungsnetzwerke: Konstitution und Strukturation*. Wiesbaden: Westdeutscher.

Wolf, Ernst (1978). *Lehrbuch des Schuldrechts. Zweiter Band: Besonderer Teil*. Köln: Heymanns.

21

How American Legal Academics' Positions on Economic-Efficiency Analysis, Moral Philosophy, and Valid Legal Argument Disserve Law and Society Empirical Research

Richard S. Markovits

Lawrence Friedman's work is certainly not atheoretical. However, the hallmark both of his scholarship and of the law and society movement to whose development he has made such a great contribution is the recognition that for a theory to be valuable it must explain or predict specified facts.

American law professors have long recognized that success as a transaction lawyer or litigator often depends at least as much on knowledge of the facts of the situation or case as on doctrinal knowledge or skill in legal argument. However, until fairly recently, these academics have done little empirical research themselves; instead they have made scholarly choices that implicitly assume that such research has little bearing on the academic questions their research investigates. Yet over the past two decades, American law professors have revised upward their assessment of the contribution that law and society empirical research can make to legal scholarship. This reassessment is manifest in (1) a vast increase in the amount of such empirical research that American law faculties conduct, (2) the fact that the plenary session of the 2006 Annual Meeting of the Association of American Law Schools was devoted to "Empirical Research: What Should We Study and How Should We Study It?" and (3) the decision of the Cornell, New York University, and University of Texas law schools to sponsor a series of annual conferences on empirical legal studies.

Although this good news is certainly worth celebrating, it is not my focus in this chapter. I focus instead on some coincident bad news: In the relevant fields in which I work (welfare economics, moral theory, and jurisprudence), the vast majority of American law professors continue to subscribe to (in my view, incorrect) positions that disserve law and society empiricism by denying its relevance to some issues whose study it could inform, by ignoring some determinants of relevant phenomena

© 2010 RICHARD S. MARKOVITS. Shortly after my wife Inga and I arrived in Stanford in 1967, we were befriended by Lawrence and Leah Friedman. For forty years, we have been entertained, educated, and supported by them. I am delighted to contribute to this collection in honor of Lawrence's work.

that law and society scholars would be well placed to measure, and by misspecifying some such parameters and the relevance of those parameters.

This chapter has six sections. The first four exemplify the claims I have just made. The fifth addresses the reasons why law and society scholars may be reluctant to engage in the empirical research that my moral and jurisprudential conclusions imply would be valuable for them to do – viz., the reasons that lead them to reject my moral and jurisprudential conclusions. The sixth delineates five additional implications of my economic-efficiency, moral philosophy, and jurisprudence conclusions for law and society empirical research.

WELFARE ECONOMICS AND THE PREDICTION OF ECONOMIC EFFICIENCY

American law professors who do law and economics often analyze the effect of a private choice or public policy on economic efficiency; that is, on the difference between the equivalent-dollar gains that private choices or public policies confer on their beneficiaries and the equivalent-dollar losses they impose on their victims where (roughly speaking) the equivalent-dollar sums in question are, respectively, the number of dollars the beneficiaries would have to receive to make them as well off as the policy would make them and the number of dollars the victims would have to lose to be left as poorly off as the policy would leave them. Unfortunately, like virtually all economists working outside law schools, these scholars use an approach to economic-efficiency assessment that fails to pay appropriate attention to many relevant facts, some of which law and society scholars would be well placed to supply. More specifically, these legal academics base their economic-efficiency assessments on the assumption that the fact that the economy will contain no economic inefficiency if seven so-called Pareto optimal conditions[1] are fulfilled implies that any tendency of a choice or policy to decrease the number and/or magnitude of the Pareto imperfections in a still-Pareto-imperfect economy will cause it to increase economic efficiency on that account. For current purposes, it is important to note that this approach assumes that one can assess the economic efficiency of a choice or policy that will decrease some type of Pareto imperfection that is its target without paying attention to the other Pareto imperfections in the system (i.e., without collecting data on those imperfections). This assumption is mistaken for reasons that were demonstrated by a theory that economists call the general theory of second best.[2]

[1] The seven Pareto-optimal conditions are no imperfections in seller competition, no imperfections in buyer competition, no externalities, no taxes on the margin of income, all actors have all the information they require to make the decision that is in their interest (broadly defined; that is, are "sovereign"), all actors maximize, and no misallocation is caused by buyer surplus (the difference between the price a buyer could break even by paying for some good and the price he or she had to pay for it).

[2] See Lipsey and Lancaster (1956) for the first formal statement of this theory.

According to the general theory of second best, given a series of conditions whose fulfillment guarantees the achievement of an optimum, if one or more of these conditions cannot be or will not be fulfilled (henceforth "if one or more imperfections will remain in the system"), there is no general reason to believe that fulfilling or more closely approximating the remaining conditions (henceforth "reducing the number or magnitude of the imperfections in the system") will bring you closer to the optimum than fulfilling or more closely approximating fewer of the remaining conditions. In other words, second-best theory demonstrates that, once one imperfection is present in the system, one cannot assume without further argument that reducing the number and/or magnitude of the other imperfections in the system *will even tend to yield an improvement*. The intuitive explanation for this conclusion is straightforward. Unless one can make an argument to the contrary, one must assume that the imperfections one can eliminate are as likely to counteract as to compound the effects of the imperfections that will remain in the system.

The general theory of second best applies to the pursuit of all types of optima. When the optimum in question is maximum economic efficiency, the relevant imperfections are the Pareto imperfections previously noted, and second-best theory's conclusion is as follows: Once one or more Pareto imperfections will remain in the system regardless of whether the choice/policy under scrutiny is made/adopted, one cannot assume without further argument that the fact that the choice or policy in question will reduce the number and/or magnitude of the Pareto imperfections in the system, implies that it will even tend on that account to increase economic efficiency.

I have developed a protocol for analyzing the economic efficiency of a private choice or public policy that responds appropriately to the general theory of second best. This approach (1) delineates a variety of kinds of economic inefficiency that are analytically useful to distinguish; (2) analyzes the different ways in which the various types of Pareto imperfections the economy contains and indeed the different imperfections of each type the economy contains interact to cause each of these various kinds of economic inefficiency; (3) considers the cost, probable imperfectness, and value of the various theoretical analyses one could execute that would be relevant to economic-efficiency assessment; and (4) considers the cost, probable inaccuracy, and the value of the various types of empirical data that would bear on the economic efficiency of the private choice or public policy being scrutinized. The details of this approach do not matter here. What does matter is that, although law and society scholars are not well placed to measure the imperfections in seller and buyer competition, the externalities, and the taxes on the margin of income that contemporary economic-efficiency analysts ignore, some law and society scholars do have considerable expertise in (1) determining such things as when and the extent to which buyers, producers, potential injurers, and potential accident-and-pollution-loss victims will make mistakes from their own perspective because they misvalue products or inputs, misestimate the cost of various production-process options, fail to identify the accident-or-pollution-loss avoidance moves that are available to them, misestimate the costs and/or benefits of the avoidance moves they do identify, or simply do their maths wrong and (2) measuring buyer surplus. The failure of law school professors who execute economic-efficiency analyses to note the relevance of these latter types of Pareto imperfections therefore does a disservice to law and society empiricism.

MORAL THEORY AND ALLEGEDLY EXTERNAL-TO-LAW EVALUATIONS OF THE JUSTNESS OF PARTICULAR ADJUDICATIVE DECISIONS, LEGAL DOCTRINES, OR LEGAL INSTITUTIONS OR PROCEDURES

For reasons that the section on the general-jurisprudence legal-positivist protocol partially explains, the vast majority of contemporary American law professors and legal scholars reject the claim that considerations of justice affect the answer to any legal-rights claim that is correct as a matter of law in the United States; that is, they reject the claim that justice arguments are valid legal arguments.[3] Nevertheless, many contemporary American legal scholars analyze what they denominate (admittedly, for some, for purely rhetorical reasons) the justness of a particular adjudicative decision, legal doctrine, law, or legal institution or procedure. This section argues that the legal academics in question and the moral philosophers on whom they rely take positions on the nature of the concept of justice and sometimes the proper way to determine whether a given society has justice commitments and, if it does, the identity of the moral norm it is committed to instantiating in the service of justice that militate against law and society empiricists' contributing to the relevant analysis.

The legal academics to whom I am referring subscribe to one of the four following positions on the nature of justice:

(1) the moral-skeptic position that justice convictions (and all other sorts of moral positions) are essentially tastes, like preferences for chocolate ice cream

(2) the moral-relativist position that claims that (a) moral "preferences" are essentially different from other sorts of tastes but fails to distinguish between justice commitments (which I claim are societally imposed in those societies that have such commitments) and moral-ought commitments (which I claim are made individually) and that (b) no moral value can be demonstrated to be "objectively" superior to the others

---

3 In my usage, an argument is "legally valid" in a given society if, in that society, the argument is supposed to be relevant to the answer to those individual legal-rights questions to which it relates that is correct as a matter of law. I use the expression "a society's valid legal argument practice" to refer not only to the set of arguments that are legally valid within it but also to the relationship between the individual types of arguments that are legally valid (or various combination of those legally valid arguments) and the answer to those individual legal-rights questions to which they relate that is correct as a matter of law in the society in question.

(3) the foundationalist position that one can identify an objectively true and therefore universally applicable concept of justice through pure conceptual analysis; for example

    (A) the "foundationalist" position (with a lower-case "f") that one can derive such a concept from the concept of "the moral"

    (B) the Aristotelian position that one can derive such a concept from the concept of "human flourishing"

    (C) the Kantian position that one can derive such a concept from the concept of "human freedom"

    (D) the natural law position that one can derive such a concept from an understanding of human nature

(4) the "Gallup poll" position that justice commitments are societal commitments that focus on concrete issues and exist if and only if, over a requisitely long period of time, the overwhelming majority of the members of the society in question did express or would have expressed that conviction when asked their opinions on the concrete issue in question in something like a Gallup poll[4]

Although these four positions on the nature of justice and/or the appropriate way to determine a given society's justice commitment (which I am asserting without systematic empirical support are collectively dominant in the American legal academy) differ substantially, they all militate against law and society empiricists' making as important a contribution as I think they can make to the identification of the abstract conception of justice that particular societies that have justice commitments are committed to instantiating in the service of their respective conceptions of justice. Moral skepticism does so by denying the importance of justice analyses. Moral relativism does so by failing to distinguish personal moral convictions from the moral commitments of societies. Foundationalism does so by denying that different societies can have different justice commitments and by implying that empirical analysis has nothing to contribute to the identification of the conception of justice that binds a particular society. Finally, the Gallup poll position does so – despite the fact that it acknowledges (indeed, emphasizes) the relevance of empirical analysis to the determination of a society's justice commitments – by misspecifying the relevant empirical inquiry (by denying that the goal of the relevant empirical analysis is to ascertain the abstract moral norm to which a society is committed rather than the society's possibly unreflective, possibly inconsistent consensi on concrete issues and relatedly by failing to recognize that, to the extent that the protocol for identifying a

---

[4] For a contemporary articulation of this position, see Mr. Justice Scalia's opinion in *Lawrence v. Texas*, 123 S. Ct. 2472, 2494–95 (2003) (Scalia, J., dissenting). For a detailed critique of this position and its implications for the ability of foreign and American discussions of foreign moral and constitutional commitments to inform analyses of American legal-rights claims, see R. Markovits (2004). I should note that proponents of this position have not given serious consideration to the moral status of the kind of concrete (often unreflective) consensi that Gallup polls can reveal.

given society's justice commitments includes interviews with society members, the interviews will resemble Socratic dialogues more than Gallup polls).

I now outline the empirical protocols that I think one must use to discover (1) whether a given society has any justice (moral rights) commitments and (2) the moral norm (henceforth moral principle) that a society that has such commitments is committed to instantiating in the service of its conception of justice. Not all societies have justice commitments. Indeed, not even all societies that have moral integrity – that have moral commitments and fulfill them to some hard-to-specify, requisite extent – have justice commitments. In particular, one can distinguish at least four types of societies that do not have justice commitments: (1) moral-goal-based societies, which are committed to instantiating a (defensible) moral norm but do not draw a strong distinction between what morally ought to be done and what justice requires (what its members and/or government are morally obligated to do)[5]; (2) amoral societies – societies whose members and governments either base individual choices on decision criteria that are neither moral nor immoral or make their decisions on an ad hoc basis, shifting among decision standards that may individually be moral for no principled reason at all but not for an inherently immoral reason; (3) immoral societies – societies whose governmental and individual member conduct conforms to a decision standard that is objectively immoral; and (4) religious societies, which draw a strong distinction between an actor's religious duty and what he or she thinks morally ought to be done and are committed to the position that religious duties trump personal moral convictions. In standard terminology, the type of society that does have justice commitments – that draws a strong distinction between the just and the good (between the choices that their individual members, participants, and governments are societally morally obligated to make and the choices that individuals believe morally ought to be made from some personally chosen moral perspective) and that is committed to instantiating the just over the good when it favors different decisions – is called a rights-based society: If such a society fulfills its moral rights commitments to a requisite extent, it is called a rights-based society of moral integrity.

The empirical protocol for determining whether a given society is a rights-based society can easily be derived from the preceding taxonomy. To make this determination, one must observe the prescriptive moral claims that the members and governments of the society in question make, the arguments they make for and against these claims, the way in which these arguments and claims are evaluated by different individuals, and the way in which the relevant private individuals and state officials behave to see (1) whether they draw a strong distinction between moral-rights claims and moral-ought claims by (a) distinguishing these two types of claims linguistically; (b) using different arguments when asserting, defending, and evaluating

---

[5] For a discussion of the distinction between moral-ought and moral-rights analyses, see R. Markovits 346–8 (2008).

these two types of claims; and (c) sometimes concluding that individuals are morally obligated to behave in a way in which the evaluator believes they morally-ought not behave or that individuals have no moral obligation to behave in the way that the evaluator believes they morally-ought to behave – and (2) whether they believe that moral-rights conclusions trump moral-ought conclusions when the two favor different decisions or courses of conduct.

The second empirical protocol that is relevant in the current context is designed to identify the moral principle that a given rights-based society is committed to instantiating – the moral norm from which it is committed to deriving its justice (moral-rights and moral-obligations) conclusions. More specifically, this protocol seeks to determine the moral norm that best "discounted fits" the prescriptive-moral conduct, discourse, and perceptions of the relevant society's members and governments where the discount in question reflects the fact that the damage that a given nonfit does to the candidacy of a particular moral norm for the society's "basic moral principle" title will be reduced if the nonfit can be explained in one or more relevant ways.[6] The "fit" component of the relevant protocol examines how well various basic-moral-principle-title candidates fit the following facts about the society in question: (1) the moral-rights claims that were made and not made by its members, participants, and governments; (2) the arguments that were made and not made in support of the claims in question by both the disputants and those who evaluated their claims; (3) the conclusions that were reached about the claims in question; (4) how close the "cases" – enquoted because the vast majority of relevant data relate to disputes in which legal-rights claims are not being contested – were perceived to be; (5) how certain people were about the resolution of each claim that was correct; and (6) the extent to which the members and governments of the society in question fulfilled the moral obligations they would have if the relevant candidate for the "basic moral principle" title were their society's basic moral principle. The "explicability of nonfits" component of the relevant protocol focuses on the extent to which the nonfits of the candidates in question can be explained by (1) the greater power of the nonfits' beneficiaries, (2) the presence of monetary or social transaction costs that made it unattractive for parties to pursue justified moral-rights

---

[6] The use of these "best fit" and "explicability of nonfit" criteria was first proposed by Ronald Dworkin. However, Dworkin also proposed that a third, "best light" criterion – the moral attractiveness of a "basic moral principle" candidate – be used as well to identify a society's basic moral principle. See Dworkin 94, 97, 120, 215, 256 (1986). I reject this "best light" criterion because it collapses the distinction between moral-rights analysis and moral-ought analysis, which I think is critical for understanding both the prescriptive-moral practices of rights-based societies and legitimate and valid legal argument in such societies. (In my usage, the use of a particular argument to determine the answer to a legal-rights question that is correct as a matter of law in a given society can be "legitimate" or "illegitimate" only if the society in question is a society of moral integrity. In such a society, the use of an argument for this purpose is "legitimate" if and only if that use is consistent with the relevant society's moral commitments.) For a detailed analysis of the relationship between my positions and Dworkin's, see R. Markovits 91–109 (1998).

claims or defend unjustified moral-rights claims made against them or made it attractive for parties to pursue unjustified moral-rights claims or defend justified moral-rights claims made against them, (3) the fact that the individuals in question did not adequately consider the beliefs they expressed or the conduct in which they engaged, (4) conceptual errors that the relevant actors did make or might very well have made (e.g., confusing two senses of a relevant word), and (5) empirical errors that were made or may have been made by relevant actors. Although some elements of the explicability-of-nonfits component of the protocol I have just described involve conceptual analysis and empirical speculation, both this second component and the protocol as a whole primarily require fact finding of a conventional sort.

To reprise, regardless of whether they think that justice arguments are valid legal arguments, American legal academics who are interested in assessing the (moral) desirability of an adjudicative decision, legal doctrine, law, or legal institution or procedure frequently base their evaluations (or at least their moral rhetoric) on some conception of justice. However, virtually all the relevant academics subscribe to a conception of the abstract concept "justice" and, in some cases, support a related approach to ascertaining a given society's justice commitments that militates against the law and society movement's making valuable contributions by providing information that illuminates particular societies' justice commitments. It does so (1) by denying the importance of justice (and often any other moral concept), (2) by failing to note that justice commitments may be societal rather than individual, (3) by denying the relevance of empirical research to the determination of the abstract content of any applicable conception of justice, and/or (4) by misspecifying the empirical study that one should execute to determine a given society's justice commitments. In addition to substantiating these claims, this section has prepared the way for law and society empirical studies that can reveal the justice commitments of a particular society by delineating (philosophically informed) empirical protocols for determining (1) whether a given society has a justice commitment and (2) if it does, the identity of the moral norm it is committed to instantiating in the service of its conception of justice.

THE RELEVANCE OF EXTERNAL-PREFERENCE-DERIVED GAINS AND LOSSES TO THE ECONOMIC EFFICIENCY, JUSTNESS, OR MORAL DESIRABILITY (JUSTICE CONSIDERATIONS ASIDE) OF THE DECISIONS THAT GENERATED THEM

"External preferences"[7] are preferences that one individual has for or against one or more other individuals' having resources or opportunities. An individual can value

---

[7] The expression "external preference" comes from Dworkin 234–8 (1978). Some law and economics scholars use the expression "disinterested preferences" instead of the expression "external preferences." See Adler and Posner 269, 281–2 (2001).

or disvalue in itself the effect of a private choice, public decision, or natural event on others for any one of a number of reasons: because the relevant others are loved ones, friends, family members, co-religionists, or fellow-members of some other group with which he or she identifies; because the individual believes that justice requires that others have particular amounts of resources or particular opportunities or that they be punished or disadvantaged in some way; because he or she supports some non-justice-related distributive norm that indicates that one or more others should have particular amounts of resources or particular opportunities for reasons that may or may not be related to any choices they made; because the individual is prejudiced against particular individuals or the members of some group; or because denying some individuals resources or opportunities or subjecting them to painful or disadvantageous experiences satisfies his or her sadistic tastes. This section argues that (1) the common belief of those law and economics scholars who teach in law schools (indeed, of economists in general) that external-preference-derived equivalent-dollar gains and losses should be excluded from economic-efficiency calculations and (2) the contention of some philosophers on whom many legal academics rely that both justice analyses and analyses of what morally ought to be done, moral-rights considerations aside, should ignore all external-preference-derived gains and losses disserve empiricism by denying the value of empirical studies on the basis and extent of external preferences that some law and society scholars would be well placed to execute.

The Law and Economics Arguments for Excluding All External-Preference-Derived Equivalent-Dollar Gains and Losses from Economic-Efficiency Calculations

Economists and law and economics scholars make two arguments for excluding external-preference-generated equivalent-dollar gains and losses from economic-efficiency calculations.[8] First, they argue that such effects should be ignored because they cannot be measured acceptably accurately acceptably cheaply. Second, they argue that such effects should be disregarded because it would be immoral to let them influence the choices or policies under review. Neither of these arguments is persuasive.

Thus, although it will be difficult to estimate the magnitude of external-preference-derived equivalent-dollar gains and losses when relevant actors do not have to put their money where their avowals are, I do not think that economic-efficiency calculations that are based on the assumption that external-preference-derived net equivalent-dollar effects are zero will be more accurate than ones that incorporate regrettably crude calculations of such net equivalent-dollar effects. Economists who disagree with this conclusion sometimes try to bolster their position by suggesting

[8] See, e.g., Adler and Posner (2001).

that it will be more costly and less feasible to estimate a choice's external-preference-derived net equivalent-dollar effects acceptably accurately than to generate acceptably accurate estimates of the other, conventional components of its economic efficiency. I have two responses to this suggestion. First, even if one could estimate the conventional components of a choice's economic efficiency acceptably accurately more cheaply than one can estimate the choice's external-preference-derived net equivalent-dollar effects, that fact would not imply the infeasibility, economic inefficiency, or moral unattractiveness of taking the choice's external-preference-derived effects into account when estimating its economic efficiency. Second, because the economists in question all ignore the general theory of second best, they massively underestimate the cost of generating acceptably accurate estimates of the economic efficiency of a choice, external-preference-derived consequences aside, and concomitantly the extent to which it is relatively cheaper to estimate acceptably accurately the net non-external-preference-derived equivalent-dollar effect of a choice than its net external-preference-derived equivalent-dollar impact.

Economists also argue that all external-preference-derived equivalent-dollar gains and losses should be excluded from economic-efficiency calculations because it is immoral to take morally bad external preferences into consideration when generating economic-efficiency conclusions. This argument fails on two accounts.

First, it fails because it assumes inaccurately that all external preferences are morally bad. External preferences that manifest their holder's commitment to society's morally defensible conception of justice or to his or her own morally defensible personal convictions about how resources and opportunities should be distributed are clearly not "morally bad." Nor, I would argue, are external preferences that reflect their holder's love for, friendship for, sympathy with, or empathy with particular others.

Second, even if all external preferences were morally bad, the claim that external-preference-derived equivalent-dollar gains and losses should be excluded from economic-efficiency calculations would fail because it is inconsistent with the nature of economic efficiency. Economic efficiency is not a moral concept, nor is it a good in itself. Moreover, the economic efficiency of a choice is totally irrelevant to its moral desirability from many normative perspectives and has only limited relevance to its desirability from those (utilitarian) perspectives that make it somewhat salient. This objection to excluding external-preference-derived equivalent-dollar gains and losses from economic-efficiency calculations is not sterilely definitional. The alleged moral justification for excluding such gains and losses from economic-efficiency calculations is objectionable because it sends the wrong message about the moral relevance of economic-efficiency conclusions – a message that confirms the false assumptions of many economists and law and economics scholars that (1) economic efficiency is a value in itself and/or (2) economically efficient choices are always just and morally desirable, justice considerations aside.[9]

It would be very useful for economic-efficiency analysts to report to the prescriptive-moral evaluators to whom they are supplying economic-efficiency information any data they have, not only on the magnitude of the external-preference-derived effects that their economic-efficiency calculations incorporate, but also on the substance of the preferences that underlie each of the effects in question (because the latter information might affect the normative significance of the external-preference-generated equivalent-dollar gains and losses in question). However, there are at least three "nondefinitional" reasons why providing such information is superior to excluding external-preference-derived equivalent-dollar gains and losses from economic-efficiency calculations (in effect, to giving a zero weight to such gains and losses). First, in some instances, a protocol that gives zero weight to such dollar gains does not produce the morally appropriate overall evaluation of the choice that generates them. Thus, in those instances in which a morally bad external preference critically affected the choice that was made, the morally bad preference in question will render the relevant choice unjust (moral-rights-violative) as opposed to "not more attractive" than it would be in its absence (as the exclusion would imply). In other circumstances, the appropriate way to deal with bad preference-derived equivalent-dollar gains is to attach a negative rather than a zero weight to them. Second, in my judgment, the concept of economic efficiency should not be defined to exclude bad preference-derived equivalent-dollar effects because economists are not trained to make and are inept at making the moral judgments such a definition would require them to make. Third, even if economists would do as good a job of determining the moral status of relevant preferences as would the people who are authorized to make the choices under consideration or the agents to whom these principals delegate this authority, economists should not exclude bad preference-derived effects from economic-efficiency calculations because doing so allocates to them decision-making power that has been assigned elsewhere. Although the "costs" of the usurpation of power that an unauthorized decision to exclude external-preference-derived equivalent-dollar effects entails will be mitigated to the extent that the economists who make economic-efficiency calculations that reflect such exclusions reveal what they have done, any definition of "economic efficiency" that excludes external-preference-derived and bad preference-derived equivalent-dollar effects will tend to be undesirable because it will tend to increase the extent to which economists exercise unauthorized power (which is bad in itself in a liberal, rights-based society).

[9] For my own analysis of the (limited) prescriptive-moral relevance of economic-efficiency conclusions and my critiques of the various arguments that economists and law and economics scholars have made for their conclusion that economic efficiency has far more descriptive-moral relevance than I believe it has, see Markovits (2008), chs. 5 & 6.

The Egalitarian Objection to Counting External-Preference-Derived Gains
and Losses in Any Prescriptive-Moral Evaluation

Some egalitarian philosophers make a different argument for their conclusion that all types of prescriptive-moral analyses should ignore external-preference-derived gains and losses. In particular, some egalitarians including Ronald Dworkin[10] argue that counting external preferences for or against someone's having resources or opportunities is morally unacceptable because it is inegalitarian in that it counts the relevant individual's benefits more than once or less than once. Thus, according to Dworkin, any protocol for evaluating a policy that counts in its favor the external-preference-derived benefits a policy generates when it benefits someone other than its direct beneficiary because the former individual values in itself the direct beneficiary's gain, is unacceptably inegalitarian because that protocol counts the direct beneficiary's benefits or utility more than once – once on his account and again because of the benefit it yields others who value his obtaining a benefit. I do not think that such a protocol entails double-counting that is inconsistent with egalitarianism. I would say that the utility of the direct beneficiary is counted only once in itself, although the fact that the direct beneficiary experienced a gain is also relevant indirectly to the extent that others value his experiencing that gain. In my judgment, it is no more inegalitarian or morally improper for some other reason to count such indirect consequences of a direct beneficiary's gain than it would be to count the utility gains the initial benefit generated by inducing the direct beneficiary to make a consumption choice that generated lower external costs than the choice he would have made had his real income or wealth not been increased. Of course, this conclusion is perfectly compatible with my previous statements that (1) the fact that a choice was critically affected by its indulging some of its supporters' prejudices or sadistic preferences renders it rights-violative (in a liberal, rights-based society) and (2) from some moral-ought value perspectives, the fact that certain equivalent-dollar gains derive from prejudices, sadism, or unjustifiable preferences for the choice's direct beneficiaries' obtaining benefits will warrant their being given no weight or even a negative weight in any analysis of what morally ought to be done.

In short, I believe that external-preference-derived equivalent-dollar gains and losses should be fully counted in economic-efficiency calculations and should be identified, measured, and considered in justice and moral-ought analyses. I therefore think that the economists, law and economics scholars, and philosophers who have argued that external-preference-derived effects should be ignored in economic-efficiency and prescriptive-moral analyses have done a disservice to law and society empiricism by denying the relevance of data on external preferences that law and society scholars could supply.

[10] See Dworkin 234–8 (1978).

THE GENERAL-JURISPRUDENCE LEGAL-POSITIVIST PROTOCOL FOR IDENTIFYING THE CONTENT AND STRUCTURE OF VALID LEGAL ARGUMENT IN ANY SOCIETY AND THE SPECIFIC-JURISPRUDENCE LEGAL-POSITIVIST CONCLUSIONS ABOUT VALID LEGAL ARGUMENT IN THE UNITED STATES

The General-Jurisprudence Legal-Positivist Protocol for Identifying the Content and Structure of Valid Legal Argument in Any Society

General-jurisprudence legal positivists are analysts of the concept of law who subscribe to a particular position on (1) the protocol one should use to determine whether any system of social control and/or dispute resolution (an admittedly inadequate description) should be characterized as a *legal* system and, relatedly, (2) the protocol one should use (a) to identify the set of arguments that are legally valid in any legal system and (b) to determine the relationship between the individual modes or mode variants of argument that are legally valid in any given legal system and the answer to any individual legal-rights question that is uniquely correct as a matter of law in the legal system in question or the answers to any individual legal-rights questions that are not incorrect as a matter of law in the legal system in question. I acknowledge that this subsection's account of general-jurisprudence legal positivism is contestable not only (1) because I have less expertise in legal positivism than many others do but also (2) because even those legal positivists who have substantial philosophical sophistication disagree on issues that are central to the argument of this chapter,[11] and (3) I am in practice using the term "legal positivism" to include the jurisprudential positions not only of the legal-philosopher legal positivists but also of the large number of American legal scholars who are not legal philosophers but who consider themselves to be legal positivists because they agree with the legal positivists' conclusions about the appropriate way to identify the structure and content of valid legal argument in any legal system.

From the perspective of this chapter, the critical feature of general-jurisprudence legal positivism is the position it takes on the protocol one must use to identify the content and structure of valid legal argument in any society that has a legal system. I start my account of this position by quoting Leslie Green's succinct

[11] Thus, Hart and Raz disagree about whether in some legal systems morality can be a source of valid legal argument. In particular, although Hart and Raz agree that the statement that a given society has a legal system does not imply that the substance of its laws can be morally defended (conforms either to the society's moral commitments [in their words, to the society's (moral) "customs"] or to some "morally defensible" conception of justice), Hart believes that the legal systems of some societies do and certainly can recognize their (moral) customs or some defensible conception of justice as a source of valid law, whereas Raz appears to believe that morality cannot be an independent source of valid law in any legal system. See Hart 189–202 (1961) and Raz 45–52 (1979).

formulation, then offer two friendly elaborations, and finally offer a criticism. According to Green,[12]

> The ultimate criterion of validity in a legal system is neither a legal norm nor a presupposed norm, but a social rule that exists only because it is *practiced* . . . by officials . . . [– a rule to which they actually appeal] in arguments about what standards they are bound to apply.[13]

My two friendly elaborations both relate to the protocol that, I suspect, legal positivists believe one should use to identify the content and structure of valid legal argument in any society that has a legal system:

(1) The term "officials" should be read to include not only (a) judges but also (b) lawyers when arguing before adjudicators, doing legal planning, giving clients advice about the legality of their past conduct or current legal entitlements, and evaluating the legal correctness of the legal conclusions that government officials reached and the legal validity of the arguments these officials used to justify those legal conclusions (either because lawyers are officers of the court or because their practice reflects their informed understanding of the sorts of considerations the society's official adjudicators deem legally relevant) and (c) the considered conclusions of executive branch government officials about their official legal obligations and authorizations, the legal correctness of legal conclusions that judges and other officials have reached, and the legal validity of the arguments such other officials used to justify their legal conclusions.

(2) In addition, for a source or an argument that is based on the source to be legally valid, it must be used to some hard-to-specify, requisite extent by relevant judges, lawyers, and/or executive branch officials.

My criticism relates to the following question: If a source (source-related type of legal argument) plays a critical role in the explanation of a requisitely significant set

---

[12] I suspect that many law and society readers will assume that the official practices that the legal positivists have in mind consist solely of the constitution-creating acts of the drafters and/or ratifiers of any written constitution the relevant society has and the regular-legislation-creating acts of the society's de facto legislators (some of whose members may be in a separate branch of government but whose members may in any event include officials who are organizationally in the society's executive branch [who promulgate legislation in the form of Executive Orders or regulations whose creation involves the exercise of strong discretion] and/or in the society's judicial branch [though even in common law systems, in which judicial decisions (precedents) have general legal force, there is disagreement about whether judges are authorized to make as opposed to apply the law, about the identity of the courts whose decisions have at least some legal force on particular other courts, about the strength of the legal force of "binding" precedents, about whether the element of prior judicial decisions that has legal force is their holdings as opposed to their dicta, and (relatedly) about how narrowly the holding of a case should be deemed to be]). However, I am confident that the legal positivists would agree that the relevant practices include not only such acts but also the positions that a society's officials have taken on the structure and content of valid legal argument in it both by making legal arguments and by commenting on the validity of the legal arguments made by others.

[13] Green 3–4 (2003).

of relevant conclusions reached by judges, lawyers, and/or executive branch officials of the society in question that best fits or best discounted-fits those conclusions, should that fact legally validate the source or source-related argument even if the source has not been cited (the argument has not been explicitly made) requisitely often by adjudicators, lawyers, and executive branch officials as a legal justification for the conclusions they reached? Legal positivists appear to answer this question in the negative. I think the answer should be "yes."

Assuming that legal positivists answer the question just posed in the negative, the general-jurisprudence legal-positivist positions on which I wish to focus are the following:

(1) To identify the set of argument types (modes and mode variants of argument) that are relevant to the determination of the answer to a legal-rights question that is correct as a matter of law (that are "valid" legal arguments) in any legal system, one must identify the general modes and mode variants of argument that have been explicitly used for this purpose to a hard-to-specify, requisite extent

(A) by the relevant society's judges when questioning lawyers at legal argument and writing opinions to explain the conclusions they have reached about the answer to individual legal-rights questions that is correct as a matter of law and

(B) by the relevant society's lawyers and other officials.

(2) To determine the relationship between the various individual types of argument that are valid in any legal system and the answer to any legal-rights question that is correct as a matter of law in that system (i.e., the structure of legal argument in any legal system), one must determine the structure that best "discounted fits" (my elaboration) the relevant practices of the society's adjudicators, lawyers, and other officials.

How does this general-jurisprudence legal-positivist account of valid legal argument differ from mine, and how (if mine is correct) does the general-jurisprudence legal-positivist position on the protocol one should use to identify the content and structure of valid legal argument in any society undercut the contribution that law and society-type empirical legal studies can make? Fundamentally, I reject the legal-positivist (implicit) claim that in all moral types of societies the legal validity of any mode of argument depends exclusively on the legal practice of its official adjudicators (and, I suspect, lawyers and other officials). In particular, I believe that, in both moral-rights-based and moral-goal-based societies of moral integrity, arguments that derive the concrete implications of the moral norm the society in question is committed to instantiating are valid legal arguments even if the society's adjudicators, lawyers, and other officials have not explicitly (or even implicitly) recognized them as such when executing the indicated analyses to the extent that legal positivists would require them to have done for the arguments to have been validated by practice.

Indeed, I believe that in societies of moral integrity such moral arguments are not just valid legal arguments but are (with the exceptions noted later[14]) the dominant mode of valid legal argument in a sense in which I describe later in this section and in more detail in the next.

I have two arguments for this conclusion. The first derives from the following moral axiom: For a society that purports to have moral commitments to be a society of moral integrity, its legal-argument practice and the conclusions it reaches about particular legal-rights claims must be consistent with its moral commitments. I believe that this moral axiom implies that arguments that seek to establish the concrete moral corollaries of the moral norm that any particular society of moral integrity is committed to instantiating are not only valid legal arguments in the society in question but (with the exceptions previously noted) are also the dominant mode of legal argument in that society in that they operate not only directly but also (with those exceptions) indirectly to determine the validity and valid argumentative force of the other modes and mode variants of argument that are sometimes made in adjudicatory settings in that society, or if I am right, more generally when analyzing the answer to a legal-rights question that is correct as a matter of law in that society. In failing to acknowledge this "moral reality," general-jurisprudence legal positivism misspecifies the empirical protocol one should use to identify the arguments that are legally valid in any society of moral integrity and the way in which those arguments that are legally valid interact to determine the answer to any legal-rights question that is correct as a matter of law in any such society by failing to acknowledge that the two protocols delineated earlier for determining, respectively, the moral type of any society and the moral norm that a particular society of moral integrity is committed to instantiating are relevant to the identification of valid legal argument in any society of moral integrity.

My second argument for the legal validity of arguments that derive the concrete corollaries of whatever moral norm a particular societiy of moral integrity is committed to instantiating also rejects the general-jurisprudence legal-positivist protocol for identifying any society's set of valid legal argument types. This argument asserts that the set of law-focused data that is relevant to the identification of the set of arguments that are legally valid in a society of moral integrity includes not just the law-related counterparts of the non-law-focused facts that the earlier section on moral theory and external-to-law evaluations indicated are relevant to identifying a society's moral type and basic moral commitment but also the best account that can be given of (1) the choices judges (lawyers, other officials, members/citizens) made when the question at issue was the legal validity of various alternative approaches to interpreting certain types of texts, the legal validity of broad-gauged or

---

[14] The exceptions are textual and historical arguments that relate to constitutional provisions that are inconsistent with the society's moral commitments but whose concrete entailments were understood by the constitution's ratifiers at the time of ratification.

narrow-gauged historical arguments in particular contexts, the legal validity of certain types of prudential arguments (about the legal relevance of certain sorts of consequences of particular decisions), and the legal validity of different variants of the legal practices of precedent and statutory construction and (2) the legal-rights conclusions that the society's judges (lawyers, other officials, members/citizens) reached. In addition, I believe that, when the society in question is moral-rights-based, the relevant law-focused data include data on the relevant society's judges', lawyers', other officials', and members'/citizens' considered positions on such matters as the moral integrity of their society, the connection between the answer to any legal-rights question that arises in their society that is correct as a matter of law and their society's moral commitments, the legitimate role of judges in their society, and the moral and constitutional permissibility of ex post facto legislation in their society.

I want to anticipate one critique of my conclusion that legal positivists have erred in failing to recognize that arguments that derive the concrete corollaries of the moral norm that any society of moral integrity is committed to instantiating are generically valid legal arguments in such societies even if their official adjudicators, lawyers, and other officials do not explicitly (or implicitly) acknowledge this fact – viz., the argument that the substitution of my position for the legal-positivist position would make a difference in a null set of societies because the failure of a society's legal officials to take account of the relevant moral arguments in the way that I argue their society's commitments obligate them to do establishes that their society is not a society of moral integrity. I would reject this argument even if the society's legal officials were not "appropriately" influenced by the relevant moral arguments, despite their failure to acknowledge that influence explicitly. Here is my counterargument:

(1) For a society to have moral integrity, its members and government need not always live up to its commitments.

(2) The failure of a society's legal officials to explicitly refer to (or even to be influenced appropriately by) the relevant moral arguments to the extent that legal positivists claim they must be for the arguments to be legally valid may not constitute a sufficient violation of the society's (alleged) commitments to warrant the conclusion that it is not a society of moral integrity (regardless of whether the damage that the failures in question do to the society's integrity is reduced by their relevant explicability).

Obviously, my argument against this critique will be more forceful to the extent that the relevant moral arguments do play a critical role in the best fitting or best discounted-fitting explanation that can be given of the society's relevant adjudicatory conclusions even if the adjudicators, lawyers, and other officials in question never explicitly acknowledged the relevance of these arguments.

If my position on this issue is correct, the general-jurisprudence legal-positivist protocol for identifying the content and structure of valid legal argument in any

society undercuts law and society-type empirical legal studies by denying the relevance of many facts that do affect the content and structure of valid legal argument
in some moral types of societies – in particular, in moral-rights-based and moral-goal-
based societies of moral integrity. Thus, if I am right in maintaining that arguments
that derive the concrete corollaries of the moral norm that moral-rights-based societies are committed to instantiating in the service of their conception of justice
(in my terms, arguments of moral principle) and arguments that derive the concrete corollaries of the moral norm that moral-goal-based societies are committed to
instantiating in the service of their conception of the good are generically valid legal
arguments in such societies – indeed (with the exceptions I noted) are the "dominant" mode of valid legal argument in such societies (in a sense that I elaborate on
later) – general-jurisprudence legal positivism disserves empiricism by denying that
(1) studies that execute the empirical protocols described in the earlier section on
moral theory and external-to-law evaluations for determining whether a given society
is moral-rights-based and for identifying the moral norm that any given society of this
type is committed to instantiating in the service of justice, (2) studies that execute the
counterpart empirical protocols I could delineate for determining whether a given
society is moral-goal-based and for identifying the moral norm that any given society
of this type is committed to instantiating in the service of its conception of the good,
and (3) empirical investigations of the various additional law-focused facts that this
part claimed are relevant to the identification of valid legal argument in societies of
moral integrity are relevant to the analysis of the answers to legal-rights claims that
are either correct or at least not incorrect as a matter of law in societies of moral
integrity.

The Specific-Jurisprudence Legal-Positivist Conclusions about the Valid Legal Argument Practice of the United States

By far the most sophisticated and best informed legal-positivist analysis of valid legal
argument in the United States is Philip Bobbitt's study of valid U.S.-Constitutional
law legal argument.[15] I focus on Bobbitt's conclusions not only because of the
high quality of his work but also because of the wide acceptance it has enjoyed in
American legal academia. Bobbitt's conclusions can be summarized by the following
four propositions:

(1) The set of arguments that are legally valid in the United States includes
    different variants of textual argument, different variants of historical argu-
    ment (including both broad-gauged and narrow-gauged historical argument),

---

[15] See Bobbitt (1982, 1992). Although, to my knowledge, Bobbitt has never defined himself as a legal
     positivist, the practice-protocol he uses to identify the structure and content of valid Constitutional-law
     legal argument in the United States is the protocol Green (2003) (subsequently) claimed to be the
     legal-positivist protocol.

structural arguments (about the point of our government or various critical features of its institutional design), different variants of arguments that focus on particular legal practices (such as the practice of precedent or the canons of statutory construction), prudential arguments of different sorts (which focus on various types of consequences that particular legal conclusions would have), and what he denominates "ethical arguments" (arguments that derive the concrete corollaries of an important element of the American governmental *ethos* – viz., the American commitment to limited government).

(2) None of the individual modes or mode variants of argument that is legally valid dominates the others, and no combination of the individual modes or mode variants of argument that is legally valid dominates the remaining modes or mode variants of valid legal argument.

(3) An answer can be given to an individual legal-rights question that is uniquely correct as a matter of law if and only if all modes and mode variants that are legally valid favor that answer.

(4) In all other cases, some answers to particular legal-rights questions may be wrong as a matter of law (viz., those that are disfavored by all modes and mode variants of argument that are legally valid), but there will be no uniquely correct answer to the legal-rights question at issue (all the other answers will simply be "not wrong"), and the judge will have to exercise strong discretion (legislate) to pick the "not-wrong" answer that he or she thinks is best.

In my view, this account of valid constitutional law legal argument in the United States (which can be easily generalized to cover all other fields of law) militates against law and society-type empirical research by implying that one variant of such research – namely, research into the United States' moral type and specific moral commitments – is less legally relevant than I believe it to be. More particularly, Bobbitt's account undercuts such research in two ways:

(1) by denying that the class of arguments I denominate "arguments of (liberal) moral principle" are generically valid legal arguments in the United States – see proposition (1) in the preceding paragraph.

(2) by denying that any valid mode of legal argument (or any subset of the modes of legal argument that are valid) dominates the other modes of valid legal argument in the sense in which I claim "arguments of liberal moral principle" dominate the other modes of actual and valid legal argument in the United States – see proposition (2) in the preceding paragraph.

I now (1) explain my claim that Bobbitt's list of the modes of legal argument that are valid in the United States does not include arguments of liberal moral principle as a class and (2) elaborate on the ways in which arguments of liberal moral principle dominate the other modes of legal argument that U.S. judges, lawyers, nonadjudicatory officials, and society members/citizens use that legal positivists claim to be legally valid.

I start with the first of these two issues. I believe that an analysis that follows the protocols that the earlier section on moral theory and external-to-law evaluations delineated would reveal that the United States is a liberal, rights-based state (i.e., a rights-based state whose concrete moral-rights commitments derive from a more abstract commitment to placing a lexically highest value on those creatures for whom the society is responsible who have the relevant neurological prerequisites having and seizing the opportunity to lead lives of moral integrity [by taking their moral obligations seriously and by taking seriously as well the dialectical task of choosing a conception of the good and leading a life that is consonant with that choice]). Slightly more operationally, I believe that the United States' basic moral commitment is to treat all such creatures with appropriate, equal respect and to show equal, appropriate (in the case of governments) or appropriate (in the case of nongovernmental actors) concern for them as well, in part for their welfare in the sense in which economists understand that term but preeminently for their having and seizing a meaningful opportunity to lead a life of moral integrity. I also believe that, in combination with this empirical finding, the moral axiom that, for a society to have moral integrity, its legal argument practice and the legal-rights conclusions it reaches must be consistent with its moral commitments implies that in the United States, arguments of liberal moral principle are generically valid legal arguments. Bobbitt does not agree. Admittedly, Bobbitt's list of valid modes of legal argument does include many modes at least some of whose concrete exemplars are explicitly moral or implicitly derive from moral concerns. Thus, the variant of Bobbitt's category of prudential arguments that focuses on whether a particular interpretation of a Constitutional or statutory provision will achieve the provision's object will be moral when that object is implementing some moral norm; structural arguments will be moral to the extent that the relevant structural features are moral-objective-related, and textual arguments will be moral to the extent that the relevant text makes reference to some moral norm. However, because many U.S. Constitutional and statutory provisions that are designed to obtain morally defensible goals are not designed to instantiate what I take to be the United States' liberal commitments, these variants of prudential argument will not always or even usually be arguments of moral principle; because Bobbitt does not seem to accept the claim that the U.S. government's basic commitment is to instantiate a liberal (or any other) conception of justice (perhaps because he does not believe that the United States is committed to instantiating a liberal or any other conception of justice), his category "structural argument" does not include what I denominate "arguments of moral principle"; and because, relatedly, Bobbitt does not seem to think that the various moral concepts to which the text of the original U.S. Constitution and the various amendments to it refer derive from a particular U.S. justice commitment, textual arguments that focus on such moral language also cannot be described as arguments of moral principle

in my terms. Bobbitt's implicit rejection of my claim that arguments of moral principle are generically legally valid in the United States is most clearly manifest in his
treatment of the mode of argument he denominates "ethical argument." Although
(if the relevant society is a society of moral integrity) the ethos of the people on
which this mode of argument focuses could be defined to refer to the moral norm
the society in question is committed to instantiating in the service of its commitment to a particular conception of the just or the good, Bobbitt defines it much
more narrowly to refer to a particular element of the U.S. population's position on
government – namely, the American people's commitment to limited government –
and firmly rejects my claim that this position is a corollary of a more general liberal
commitment whose prioritization of individuals' having and seizing the opportunity
to develop and conform their lives to a personally chosen conception of the good
implies inter alia that government should be limited both more specifically in being
prohibited from adopting or arguing for a particular conception of the good and
more generally in being prohibited from controlling people in ways that militate
against their feeling responsible for the lives they lead and having the knowledge,
skill, and emotional capacity to take their lives morally seriously.

The gap that Bobbitt's rejection of my conclusion that arguments of liberal moral
principle are (generically) valid legal arguments in the United States creates between
his and my account of valid legal argument in the U.S. is made much bigger by my
conclusions that (1) the United States is a moral-rights-based society of (admittedly
imperfect) moral integrity and that (2) arguments that concretize the implications
of the moral norm that any such society is committed to instantiating in the service
of its conception of justice are not only valid legal arguments in such societies but
are the dominant mode of legal argument in such societies. More specifically, in my
judgment, in the United States, arguments of liberal moral principle dominate the
other modes of legal argument that judges, lawyers, nonadjudicatory officials, and
society members/citizens make by determining (with the two exceptions delineated
in footnote 14[16]) their validity (the variants of them that are valid), the appropriate
way to execute those of them that are valid, and the argumentative force of those
modes of legal argument that are valid. Thus, on my account, in liberal, rights-
based states such as the United States, arguments of moral principle imply the legal
invalidity of prudential arguments that focus on whether the society's members and

---

[16] In my judgment, at present, the only provisions of the Constitution of the United States that might be
morally illegitimate are those that respectively give each state two senators and provide for the election
of the President through the electoral college. See, respectively, the Constitution of the United States,
Art. I, Sec. 3 and Art. II, Secs. 2–4 (1789). Both these provisions may be inconsistent with our society's
commitment to treating its members with equal, appropriate respect and showing equal, appropriate
(in the case of government) or appropriate (in the case of nongovernmental actors) concern for them
as well by giving each competent, trustworthy member of the society an equal role (in some hard-to-
define sense) in determining the laws that will govern him or her. For arguments that these provisions
really do have substantial effects and cannot be justicized by their historical origins, see Baker and
Dinkin (1997), Levinson (2006).

participants would obey what would otherwise be the correct legal decision, on whether the police and lower courts would enforce that decision, on whether that decision would provoke a violent reaction or induce people to violate the law more generally, and on whether that decision would reduce the extent to which the courts can protect moral-rights-related interests by leading the legislature to pass court-packing or jurisdiction-reducing legislation. Similarly, on my account, in liberal, rights-based societies in which arguments of judicial precedent are valid, arguments of liberal moral principle imply the invalidity of precedent practices that follow precedent(s) that were wrong when originally created or were rendered inapposite by subsequent changes in relevant social realities (except to the extent that following such precedents can be justiced by the reasonable choice of nongovernmental actors to rely on them). More positively, in such societies, liberal moral principles or ineliminable attributes of the concept of a moral position control

(1) the interpretation and application of texts that refer to such normative concepts as equal protection, privileges and immunities, unenumerated rights, freedom of religion, good faith, unconscionable conduct, and negligence

(2) the choice between broad-gauged and narrow-gauged historical argument (imply, for example, that if the question is whether legislation that allows heterosexual sexual acts but criminalizes comparable homosexual sexual acts violates equal protection, the appropriate historical inquiry is the broad-gauged inquiry into the way in which the society in question has responded to the interests that individuals have in engaging in the relevant type of sexual conduct and in preventing society participants from doing so, rather than the narrow-gauged inquiry into whether the relevant homosexual sexual conduct was prohibited by some states at the time the Fourteenth Amendment was drafted and ratified)

(3) the analysis of the point of the U.S. government – viz., to secure liberal moral rights

In any event, my justice-promoting-legalist (qualified-liberal-legalist) position on valid legal argument in the United States can be summarized by the following five propositions. In the United States,

(1) Arguments of liberal moral principle are generically valid legal arguments.

(2) Arguments of liberal moral principle dominate all the other modes and mode variants of argument that are used to determine the answers to individual legal-rights questions that are uniquely correct as a matter of law, except for textual and historical arguments that relate to provisions in the U.S. Constitution that are inconsistent with its moral commitment whose concrete implications were understood by its ratifiers at the time of ratification.

(3) Therefore, with the above two exceptions, even those types of textual, historical, structural, precedent-and-canon-of-statutory-construction-based, and

prudential legal arguments that have been used by relevant actors sufficiently often to be considered valid by specific-jurisprudence legal positivists whose use is inconsistent with the society's moral commitments (is "illegitimate" in my sense) are legally invalid.

(4) Those variants of the above modes of argument whose use to determine the answer to any individual legal-rights question that is uniquely correct as a matter of law is consistent with the United States' liberal moral commitments are legally valid.

(5) Every individual legal-rights question has an answer that is uniquely correct as a matter of law – either the answer that is required by the United States' liberal moral commitments or the answer that is favored by a relevant illegitimate Constitutional provision whose concrete implications were understood by the Constitution's ratifiers at the time of ratification or (when the legal right does not derive from a moral right) the answer that is favored on balance by the other modes of legal argument that are valid in the United States.

I want to close this discussion by summarizing why Bobbitt and I disagree about valid legal argument in the United States. Primarily, our disagreement reflects Bobbitt's implicit rejection of either or both of my conclusions that the United States is a (liberal) rights-based society of moral integrity and the moral axiom that, for a society to have moral integrity, its legal argument practice and its legal-rights conclusions must be consistent with its moral commitments. Secondarily, I suspect that our disagreement reflects four other disagreements I have with Bobbitt that would cause me to conclude that arguments of liberal moral principle were legally valid in the United States even if I agreed with the emphasis that legal positivists place on legal practice. The first is my disagreement with what I infer Bobbitt's estimate must be of the frequency with which American judges and lawyers explicitly use arguments of liberal moral principle to generate legal-rights conclusions. Although I offer no empirical evidence to support my view that U.S. judges and lawyers have explicitly used such arguments sufficiently often for them to satisfy the legal-positivist practice requirement, I assert that both in much of the nineteenth century and (after a partial but significant hiatus) increasingly in the last fifty years American lawyers and judges have made explicit use of what I call arguments of moral principle (as contrasted with arguments about what morally ought to be done) in their briefs, oral arguments, and opinions in both state and federal courts and (in the case of lawyers) when providing legal advice to clients not only in moral-rights-related constitutional law cases and situations but also in moral-rights-related common law cases and situations for such arguments to satisfy the legal-positivist practice criterion for legal validity. The second disagreement in question focuses on whether the failure of a mode of legal argument to be explicitly used sufficiently often to be legally validated by this practice should be deemed decisive when that failure is explicable in some "exonerating" way. I believe that it should not be. Bobbitt's conclusion seems to me to imply that it should be. This disagreement is salient because, to the extent that arguments of moral principle were articulated less often in the fifty years after 1905 than legal positivism would require for them to be legally valid, that fact can be substantially explained by the failure of the American legal community to draw the correct lesson from *Lochner v. New York*.[17] Rather than concluding that (1) the *Lochner* majority took the valid approach to analyzing the constitutionality of the wages-and-hours legislation whose constitutionality was at issue by examining the consistency of such legislation with the moral commitments of American society but reached the wrong conclusion about the constitutionality of the relevant statute[18] because it mistakenly found that those commitments were libertarian and not (as I believe) liberal and (2) the appropriate response to this mistake is to be more sophisticated and systematic when attempting to identify the American rights-based society's basic moral principle, some American judges, lawyers, and legal academics responded by concluding that neither the courts, nor Constitutional-law scholars, nor anyone else should consider moral principles at all when determining the answer to any legal-rights question that is correct as a matter of law in the United States; therefore they resolved not to make or be influenced by arguments of moral principle, and many more (who realized that the previous response would convert legal analysis into an arcane procedure disconnected from the moral issues raised by the disputes under consideration) concluded that, although their analyses of moral-rights-related legal rights would have to take arguments of moral principle into account, it would be prudent to conceal that fact whenever it was possible to do so. My third disagreement with Bobbitt that would critically affect our conclusions about the legal validity of arguments of moral principle even if I agreed with the legal positivists' emphasis on practice relates to their insistence that legal arguments can be validated by practice only if they are *explicitly* used. I believe that the relevant practice should be defined to include both Constitutional law[19] and common law[20] legal-rights conclusions that are best explained by arguments of moral principle when neither the lawyers involved in the cases nor the judges who made the decisions in question explicitly used such arguments. My fourth disagreement with Bobbitt and the legal positivists that would critically affect our conclusions about

---

[17] 198 U.S. 405 (1905).

[18] In fact, the *Lochner* Court's conclusion that the wages-and-hours legislation it reviewed was unconstitutional may have been correct for a different reason from the one the Court cited: The legislation may have violated the equal protection clause in that it may have been passed to protect long-time American residents against competition from greenhorns, who were willing to work longer hours for lower wages.

[19] For a discussion of many cases whose conclusions are better explained by arguments of liberal moral principle than by the arguments the courts and participating attorneys made for the conclusions in question, see R. Markovits (1998), chs. 3–4.

[20] For a discussion of important contract law and tort law doctrines that are better explained by arguments of liberal moral principle than by the arguments that the courts that developed them made for them, see (respectively) D. Markovits (2004) and R. Markovits (2006).

the legal validity of arguments of moral principle even if I agreed with the legal positivists' emphasis on practice is that, unlike them, I would say that the relevant practice should include not just the legal arguments explicitly made and conclusions reached about concrete Constitutional and common law legal-rights issues but also the arguments made and conclusions reached about such issues as the following: (1) Is the United States a society of moral integrity, (2) is the resolution of any legal-rights claim that is correct as a matter of law in the United States supposed to be consistent with the country's moral-rights commitments, (3) are American judges authorized solely to find the law, not to make the law, and (4) is ex post facto legislation morally impermissible and unconstitutional.[21]

For current purposes, the relevant point is that, if I am right and Bobbitt and the legal positivists who agree with him are wrong about the structure and content of valid legal argument in societies of moral integrity, law and society empiricists can make a substantial contribution both to the analysis of the structure and content of legal argument in societies of moral intergrity and to the analysis of specific legal-rights claims in such societies by executing the philosophically informed but still essentially empirical protocols I have delineated for determining the moral type of any society and the moral norm that any society that has moral integrity is

---

[21] Before closing this discussion, I want to respond to two objections that several general-jurisprudence legal positivists who are also specific-jurisprudence legal positivists have made to the claim that some moral norms are generically inside the law. The first is that this claim is inconsistent with the fact that judges often contend that the law constrains them to reach legal conclusions that they do not like in the sense that they think that the law should respond to the transactions or behaviors in question differently from the way it does. I believe that in virtually all such instances the judges in question are operating in rights-based societies and are regretting the fact that the law is inconsistent with the conception of the good to which they personally subscribe. To the extent that this conjecture is correct, the fact on which this specific-jurisprudence legal-positivist rejoinder focuses is irrelevant to my claim. The second of these two objections is that the position I am taking sacrifices an important advantage of the specific-jurisprudence legal-positivist position that law and morals are separate – viz., that it enables observers to criticize the law on moral grounds. I have two responses to this objection. First, even if it were true, it would have no relevance to the truth-value of the separation claim. Second, I see no connection between the separation claim and the ability of observers to criticize legislation or legal rulings on moral grounds. The belief that the moral commitments of a rights-based society of moral integrity are generically inside its law does not preclude or even militate against the believer's criticizing those components of his or her society's law that are not moral-rights-based on the ground that they instantiate a personal ultimate value that he or she finds less morally attractive than some alternative or on the ground that the law or judicial ruling in question was designed to achieve a goal that cannot be morally defended (because the goal was immoral or amoral, because the goal was to secure the parochial interests of its supporters when this is improper, or because the law or ruling in question was reprehensibly mistaken). Nor does a belief that law and morals are not separate in the sense that specific-jurisprudence legal positivists claim they are preclude the believer from morally criticizing those components of his or her society's law that do instantiate its moral-rights commitments on the ground that he or she finds these commitments less morally attractive than some alternative set of moral commitments a society could have. In fact, the position I am taking creates an additional basis for criticizing a rights-based society's law on moral grounds – viz., that some component of its law is inconsistent with the society's own moral commitments. In short, not only is the second objection to my claim that some moral norms are generically inside the law of certain moral types of societies irrelevant to my claim's truth-value, it is itself based on assertions that are mistaken.

committed to instantiating. Concomitantly, if I am right, both Bobbitt and those contemporary American legal academics who subscribe to his conclusions about valid legal argument in the United States do a great disservice to law and society empiricism by rejecting the claim that it can contribute to legal scholarship (and practice) in these ways.

A BARRIER TO LAW AND SOCIETY SCHOLARS DOING SOME OF THE TYPES OF EMPIRICAL RESEARCH MY POSITIONS IMPLY WOULD BE VALUABLE FOR THEM TO EXECUTE: THEIR REJECTION OF THE MORAL AND JURISPRUDENTIAL CONCLUSIONS THAT UNDERLIE MY CONCLUSION THAT SUCH RESEARCH WOULD BE VALUABLE

This section is included at the editors' request. I add it somewhat reluctantly both (1) because it involves my attributing to law and society scholars positions that I have heard them express orally but cannot document with citations to published materials and (2) because – given space limitations – I can do no more than sketch why I find those scholars' arguments against my conclusions either misguided or unpersuasive although relevant.

The concern that motivates this section is that law and society scholars will be unlikely to do the philosophically informed empirical research into the moral type of particular societies and the specific normative commitments of those societies that have moral integrity[22] – research that I think has important implications for the structure and content of valid legal argument in the societies in question – because they doubt (1) the coherence of many of what I take to be the coherent moral norms to which societies can be committed, (2) the operationability or practicability of the empirical protocols that I argue can reveal the moral type and (when relevant) specific moral commitments of particular societies, (3) the claim that any actual society is a society of moral integrity (i.e., conforms its choices sufficiently to a morally defensible evaluative criterion to deserve this characterization), (4) the conclusion that legal argument is capable of generating answers that are correct as a matter of law to any legal-rights claim or to any such claim whose answer is either contestable or socially contested, (5) my specific claim that the United States is a liberal, rights-based state of (imperfect but decreasingly imperfect) moral integrity and has always been such a society, and (6) my specific claims about the structure and content of valid legal argument in the United States and the existence of answers

---

[22] Admittedly, law and society empiricists may also be reluctant to do the kind of research into human errors, buyer surplus, and external preferences that I think is relevant to the determination of the economic efficiency, justness, and moral desirability (justice considerations aside) of many private and public choices, but any reluctance they have to investigate these issues will reflect nothing more than their lack of experience with these parameters.

to all legal-rights questions in the United States that are uniquely correct as a matter of law.

Like most economists,[23] many law and society scholars doubt the coherence of the various non-utilitarian moral norms (liberalism, libertarianism, equal-utility egalitarianism, equal-resource egalitarianism, equal-opportunity egalitaranisms of different sorts) to which I argue particular societies can be committed. (Indeed, unlike economists and with good reason, many law and society scholars also doubt the coherence of utilitarianism.) In my experience, those law and society scholars who take this position do so for the same reason that leads economists to characterize all such normative language as "mumbo-jumbo" – the fact that at least some of the concrete implications of these norms cannot be determined uncontroversially. I find the economists' underlying premise that concepts whose extensions are contestable have no substantive meaning inconsistent with the practice and belief of philosophers, lawyers, historians, many types of social scientists, and ordinary-language speakers (and, for this reason, bizarre). In any event, I certainly think that the work I have done on the abstract definition and concrete constitutional-law-related and tort-law-related implications of liberalism[24] refutes the claim that, at least as defined by me, this norm is incoherent.

I suspect that some law and society scholars will also reject the empirical protocols outlined in the earlier section on moral theory and allegedly external-to-law evaluations on the ground that they contain gaps that cannot be filled in nonarbitrarily (gaps that relate to the metric for determining which candidate for a rights-based society's "basic moral principle" title best discounted-fits relevant facts) and/or on the ground that the Socratic dialogues in which the protocols require the investigator to engage will inevitably bias his or her findings. I believe that many of these gaps can be filled in nonarbitrarily and that the differences in the permissible ways of filling in those gaps that cannot be filled in nonarbitrarily are unlikely to affect the analyst's conclusion about the identity of a relevant society's basic moral principle in a way that critically influences any moral-rights conclusion.[25] Moreover, although I agree that leaders of Socratic dialogues can guide their collocutors in ways that bias the leaders' findings, I think this outcome can be prevented.

Law and society scholars also tend to doubt that the governments and members of any society behave sufficiently consistently with any conception of justice or the good for the society to be a rights-based or goal-based society of moral integrity. I think that, at least in part, these scholars' rejection of my contrary position can be attributed to four mistakes they tend to make. First, some of these scholars are too demanding – that is, they assume that the governments and individuals in question must conform their behaviors with a defensible conception of justice or the good to

---

[23] See, e.g., Kaplow and Shavell (2001).
[24] See, respectively, R. Markovits (1998, 2006).
[25] For a discussion of these issues, see R. Markovits 23–34 (1998).

a greater extent than I believe is necessary for their society to have moral integrity. Second, some of these scholars place too much weight on the fact that most private actors and government officials are unable (1) to articulate the moral norms their society commits them to instantiating and/or their personally chosen conception of the good or (2) to explain any such norm's concrete implications. I place less weight on these realities and more weight on my experience that individuals who are unable to do these things on their own can identify the norm of justice that underlies their fairness conclusions as well as the conception of the good that underlies their respective conclusions about what morally ought to be done when moral-rights conclusions are not determinative and can concretize any such norm's concrete implications when induced to engage in Socratic dialogues that focus on these issues. Third, and relatedly, some law and society scholars put too much weight on the admitted reality that the individual answers that individuals give to Gallup-poll-type questionnaires (in effect) about questions of justice or the good often focus on facts whose moral significance is dubious or are inconsistent from any normative perspective. The relevant fact is the defensibility and consistency of the relevant parties' considered moral judgments, not the defensibility and consistency of their unreflective responses to a Gallup-type poll. Fourth, like political liberals, some law and society scholars misinterpret the significance of the fact that the members of individual countries subscribe to a wide variety of values. In my judgment, this dissensus is a dissensus on the "good," which is compatible with and may even support rather than refute my conclusion that the societies in question are liberal, rights-based societies of moral integrity, because dissensus on the good should not be surprising in a liberal, rights-based society, which by definition values most highly individuals' making up their own minds about the good.

I also disagree with the belief of many if not most law and society scholars that legal argument cannot generate an answer that is uniquely correct as a matter of law to any legal-rights question or (less encompassingly) to any legal-rights question whose answer is contestable or perhaps just socially contested. Some law and society scholars believe that this conclusion is required by the ineliminable imprecision of language. I reject this argument (which critical legal studies adherents also use) because I think it fails to take account of the wide variety of contextual factors that inform the correct interpretation of texts or oral pronouncements. Some law and society scholars justify this conclusion by citing the inconsistency of relevant legal practices (which led some early legal realists to reach the same conclusion[26]). I reject this argument because it fails to take account of the fact that, in societies of moral integrity, arguments that generate conclusions from the moral norm the society in question is committed to instantiating dominate the other modes of argument that it uses in adjudicatory contexts. Some law and society scholars believe that the fact that the answer to a legal-rights question is contestable (in the sense that

[26] See, e.g., Cohen (1935), Radin (1930). For a modern article in the same vein, see Quinn (1999).

individuals of requisite skill and knowledge can disagree in good faith about the answer that is correct after making appropriate efforts to resolve the relevant issue) itself demonstrates that no answer to the relevant question is correct as a matter of law. I reject this contention: Although scientific debates may be different from moral or legal debates in this regard, the fact that skilled, assiduous economists disagree about the magnitude of the monetary multiplier at some point in time is perfectly consistent with the multiplier's having a particular value at that time. Indeed, although I recognize that this reality is not decisive, my rejection of this law and society position is also supported by the fact that skilled people who disagree in good faith about the answer to a legal-rights question that is correct as a matter of law believe that their respective answers are correct as a matter of law. More positively, I reject the "no internal-to-law right answer" claim because I believe that the valid legal argument protocols I have delineated for societies of moral integrity can generate answers to individual legal-rights claims of all sorts that are uniquely correct as a matter of law.

Law and society scholars clearly do have good reasons to reject my conclusion that the United States is and has always been a liberal, rights-based society of (imperfect) moral integrity: inter alia, (1) the institution of slavery; (2) the historical and continuing practice of racial, ethnic, gender, and religious discrimination; and (3) the historical and continuing failure of the American governments to provide its members with the various resources and experiences (nutrition, housing, medical care, formal education, emotional nurturing, freedom from parental domination, and exposure to alternative lifestyles and conceptions of the good) that contribute significantly to their ability to take their lives morally seriously.[27]

Even if I had no space constraints, I would not be able to counter this objection noncontestably. Here is an outline of what I would argue:

(1) To be a liberal, rights-based society of moral integrity, a society's members' and governments' conduct and perceptions must not fit the implications of liberalism perfectly – they must only discounted-fit those implications to a hard-to-specify, requisite extent.

(2) With some obvious exceptions – the provisions that relate to slavery, give each state two senators, and delineate the method for selecting the President – the U.S. Constitution manifests the values of the (liberal) Enlightenment.

(3) The conduct and perceptions of America's members and governments fit the full range of liberalism's implications better than many seem to suppose, better than they fit any other account of its commitments, and increasingly better through time.[28]

---

[27] For a more complete list of the concrete obligations of the government of a liberal, rights-based State (which the U.S. government has fulfilled imperfectly), see R. Markovits 55–6 (1998).

[28] See R. Markovits (1998), chs. 3–4, R. Markovits (2004), and D. Markovits (2004).

424 American Legal Academics' Theoretical Positions and Empirical Research

(4) The damage done to my characterization of the United States by the institution of slavery is at least somewhat reduced by (a) the fact that, rightly or wrongly, the majority of Founding Fathers found the Constitution's de facto acceptance of slavery a morally dubious compromise necessary to secure rights more generally (a fact manifest in the Constitution's failure to use the word "slavery"), (b) the allegedly empirical "justifications" that supporters of slavery offered for the continuance of the practice, and (c) the continuing widespread moral opposition to slavery in the country up until its prohibition.

(5) The damage done to my characterization of the U.S. government's failure to provide the society's members with the resources and experiences that would contribute to their having a meaningful opportunity to lead a life of moral integrity is at least somewhat reduced by (a) financial and organizational constraints that limited the ability of early governments to perform this function, (b) the belief that the ability of individuals to settle on land in the "West" provided them with the opportunity to obtain the wherewithal to lead a life of moral integrity, (c) the fact that from its earliest days the central government did engage in significant redistributions to some people who were perceived to be in difficult straits through no fault of their own,[29] (d) the increasing protections that, starting with the Progressive era, the American government offered people deemed vulnerable, (e) the more general efforts to redistribute income to women and children that began with the Progressive era, and (F) the broader redistributive efforts that the New Deal initiated.

Although I readily acknowledge the force of the objections I just attempted to counter to my conclusion that the United States is and has always been a liberal, rights-based society of moral integrity, I reject as misguided the claim that this conclusion is defeated by the admitted reality that the value orientation of the output of the U.S. legislative and judicial branches has often not been liberal and has changed over time. In particular, I reject this claim for the following four reasons: (1) some of the relevant value choices and value shifts relate to moral-ought values rather than justice-norms; (2) some of the relevant value shifts reflect variations in American legislators' and judges' perceptions of the United States' basic moral principle; (3) some of the relevant value choices reflect decisions by American officials that violate their Constitutional obligations; and (4) some of the alleged value shifts are mischaracterized as such – that is, they reflect changes in the society's understanding of the concrete corollaries of its basic moral principle (e.g., its realization at the time of the New Deal that those who suffer unemployment and impoverishment during economic downturns are not morally responsible for their plights but should be analogized to victims of natural disasters to whom the American central government has from its inception offered assistance).

[29] See, e.g., Landis (Dauber) (1998, 2005) on natural disaster relief and Collins (2008) on war widow pensions.

Like most specific-jurisprudence legal positivists, law and society scholars also reject my claim that arguments of liberal moral principle are the dominant mode of valid legal argument in the United States and my related conclusion that answers that are uniquely correct as a matter of law can be given to all legal-rights questions in America. In part, these scholars reject this claim and conclusion because they reject its premise that the United States is a society of moral integrity. I have already outlined my response to this objection, whose relevance I do not doubt. In part, they reject this claim and conclusion because the value orientation of the society's judicial output has changed over time. Even if my valid legal argument claim and right-answer conclusion does depend on the United States' basic moral commitment's not varying over time,[30] such changes in value orientations would not defeat my valid legal argument claim and right-answer conclusion for the same reasons that they do not defeat my conclusion that the United States is and has always been a liberal, rights-based society. In part, law and society scholars reject my claim about valid legal argument in the United States and my related right-answer hypothesis for the same actual legal practice reasons that the specific-jurisprudence legal positivists reject them – namely, because judges, lawyers, and other public officials do not use arguments of moral principle sufficiently often for them to be valid, much less for them to be the dominant mode of valid legal argument in America. I reject this law and society argument for the same reasons that I rejected its legal-positivist counterpart.

In short, although I understand why law and society scholars may doubt the value of implementing my protocols for identifying the moral type of any society and the moral commitments of any society that has such commitments, I am not persuaded by the facts and arguments that cause these scholars to have such doubts.

FIVE ADDITIONAL IMPLICATIONS FOR LAW AND SOCIETY EMPIRICAL RESEARCH OF THE POSITIONS I TAKE ON ECONOMIC-EFFICIENCY ANALYSIS, MORAL ANALYSIS, AND/OR VALID LEGAL ARGUMENT

First, my conclusion about valid legal argument in the United States has implications for political science research that attempts to explain Supreme Court Constitutional law decisions on the basis of the attitudes of the deciding justices. Most such research[31] is premised on the assumption that the decisions the Court reaches in

---

[30] They might not: My account of valid legal argument in the United States and my argument for the existence of answers that are uniquely correct as a matter of law to all legal-rights questions in America at any point in time might not have to be revised in any significant way if one could devise a protocol for determining the substance and timing of any change in the society's basic moral principle (although if such changes took place, they would cause the answers to some legal-rights questions that are correct as a matter of law to vary through time).

[31] See, e.g., Segal and Spaeth (1993).

Constitutional law cases could not be driven by valid legal argument because valid legal argument is not capable of generating answers to the Constitutional rights issues on whose resolution these scholars focus that is correct as a matter of law. Although I do not doubt that the decisions of individual Supreme Court justices are influenced by their personal ultimate values, the political consensus of the time, the spankings their grandfathers received, and various other aspects of their psychological and professional histories and aspirations (in part because these things may influence their perception of our society's moral commitments and their conclusions about those commitments' concrete corollaries), my conclusions about valid legal argument in the United States persuade me that such argument has far more to do with the relevant judicial outcomes than these scholars assume. In my experience, the accounts of valid legal argument that these scholars provide to support their conclusion that it is incapable of generating answers that are uniquely correct as a matter of law to the Constitutional right questions on which the relevant scholars are focusing are wooden to the extreme. For example, assume that there are three types of valid legal argument in the United States – "plain meaning" textual argument that takes no account of the moral commitments of the society; arguments about framers'/ratifiers' intent that assume that the relevant intent relates to these actors' expectations about how the Constitutional provision in question would be applied to particular concrete issues rather than to the proximate goal, conception of the good, or conception of justice it was designed to implement; and arguments from precedent in which the practice's valid variant is assumed to be unrelated to the society's moral commitments – and that the valid decision protocol is either simplistically linguistic or instructs the decision makers to strike an ad hoc balance between individual rights and the interests of society that ignores the fact that the only type of societal interest that can justicize overriding an individual's rights-related interest (an individual's prima facie moral right) is the interest of society in securing weightier net rights-related interests of others as well as the fact that the weight assigned to any rights-related interest that is implicated by a governmental choice should be derived from the United States' basic liberal commitment.

I hasten to add that, even if I am right, the kinds of attitudinal studies these scholars execute could shed light on the actual functioning of individual justices and the Supreme Court as a whole. Regardless of whether some argument or fact is relevant to the determination of the answer to a legal-rights question that is correct as a matter of law in a given society or that is consistent with that society's moral commitments, it may be interesting and useful to learn that the argument or fact in question has influenced the way particular judges or courts have resolved one or more legal issues (although it may be difficult to establish the causal connection from correlations, and the significance of any causal connection may depend on how and why the relevant argument or fact did influence the judge or court in question).

Second, (1) the standard distinction I adopt between the just and the good; (2) my claim that different conceptions of justice and different conceptions of the good are morally defensible; (3) my claim that some societies do and some societies do not have moral integrity; (4) the partially related reality that some legislation is designed to instantiate the relevant society's conception of justice, some is designed to promote the society's or a particular conception of the good, some is designed to serve the parochial interests of its supporters, and some is simply mistaken; (5) my claim that answers that are correct as a matter of law can be given to many legal-rights questions in all societies that have legal systems and to virtually all legal-rights questions in societies of moral integrity; and (6) the partially related reality that some judicial rulings are correct as a matter of law and consistent with the relevant society's moral commitments, some are correct as a matter of law and inconsistent with the society's moral commitments, some are correct or incorrect as a matter of law in a society that has no moral commitments, some are "not incorrect" responses to legal-rights questions that have no answer that is uniquely correct as a matter of law, and some are mistaken (and promulgated for a variety of reasons) suggest a variety of ways in which existing research on the extent to which the members of different societies respect law and consider themselves to have a duty to obey the law could be supplemented. In particular, I think it would be illuminating to examine whether or the extent to which any individual or group differences that are identified reflect differences in the relevant individuals' beliefs about whether

(1) their society is a society of moral integrity
(2) the legislation that creates the legal prohibition or command is justice-promoting, "good-promoting," parochial, or mistaken
(3) in appropriate instances, whether the respondent supports the conception of justice or of the good the relevant legislation was designed to instantiate or, in the case of parochial legislation, has an external preference for its beneficiaries' obtaining a gain in the circumstances in question
(4) the judicial ruling that creates the legal prohibition or command is correct as a matter of law, is neither correct nor incorrect as a matter of law, or is incorrect as a matter of law, and, in this last case, on the reason the deciding court made the mistake in question[32]

Third, the economic-efficiency-analysis conclusion I have reached, the standard distinction between the just and the good, and the list I have provided of morally defensible moral norms should be of use to law and society scholars who execute historical studies of the outputs of particular courts or legislatures, at least to the extent that these scholars offer conclusions about the economic efficiency, justness, or moral desirability (moral-rights considerations aside) of those institutions' decisions or processes.

Fourth, my conclusions about the structure and content of valid legal arguments in societies of moral integrity – specifically, conclusions that arguments that derive

---

[32] For some related suggestions, see Tyler and Mitchell (1994) and Franck (1990).

the concrete implications of the moral norms such societies are committed to instantiating are the dominant mode of legal argument in such societies and that arguments
that derive the concrete implications of the conception of the good that underlies
non-rights-based legislation and constitutional provisions in rights-based societies are
relevant to their interpretation – has implications for the meaning of the proposition
that judges should be "apolitical"; these implications call into question any claim
that, properly understood, this role-norm significantly contributes to the failure of
judges in liberal democracies whose executive and legislative branches have been
seized by illiberal forces that did not relevantly alter the country's constitution to
oppose the new regime's violation of liberal rights.[33]

Fifth and finally, these jurisprudential conclusions also suggest that observers of
the discourse in law school classes should be more attentive to the possibility that what
appears to be instruction in arcane legal doctrine is really morally grounded.[34] In
my view, at least when the legal-right claim under consideration is moral-right-based
(as I believe most if not all common law claims are), the applicable legal doctrine
will usually be closely connected to the relevant society's moral commitments.
Although American law teachers may never articulate this point – indeed may not
even recognize it – their instruction manifests it.

CONCLUSION

One of the hallmarks of the law and society movement and of Lawrence Friedman's
scholarship is the attention they give to the facts. This chapter argues that the positions to which (it alleges) most contemporary American legal academics subscribe
on economic-efficiency analysis, various moral issues, and valid legal argument disserve law and society empiricism by incorrectly denying the relevance of empirical
studies that law and society scholars could execute to the resolution of important
issues related to the structure and content of valid and legitimate legal argument
and the legally correct resolution of concrete legal-rights questions by ignoring significant determinants of particular phenomena in which lawyers are interested and
that law and society scholars are well placed to investigate, by misspecifying other
determinants of the phenomena that law and society scholars could study, by failing
to reveal the way in which the determinants whose relevance the relevant scholars
do recognize affect the phenomena in question, and/or by misspecifying the way in
which legal analysts should use the data with which law and society scholars could
supply them. More positively, the chapter outlines the welfare economics, moral,
and jurisprudential positions I think are correct and delineates how these positions
serve law and society empiricism by identifying important empirical projects that law
and society scholars seem well placed to execute, suggesting some additional issues
that law and society studies of particular topics could usefully investigate, enabling

[33] See, e.g., Hilbink (2007).
[34] See, e.g., Mertz (2007).

law and society scholars who are trying to give an account of the output of particular legal systems or institutions to improve their economic-efficiency conclusions and normative characterizations, and calling into question various arguments that some law and society scholars use to oppose the claims that particular actual societies can be said to have moral integrity and that the valid legal argument practice of particular societies can generate answers to individual legal-rights questions that are correct as a matter of law.

REFERENCES

Adler, Matthew and Eric Posner (2001). Implementing Cost-Benefit Analysis When Preferences Are Distorted, in Matthew Adler and Eric Posner, eds., *Cost-Benefit Analysis: Economic, Legal, and Philosophical Perspectives*. Chicago: University of Chicago Press Journals.

Baker, Lynn and Samuel Dinkin (1997). The Senate: An Institution Whose Time Has Gone, 13 *J. L. & Pol.* 21.

Bobbitt, Philip (1982). *Constitutional Fate*. Oxford: Oxford University Press.

———. (1992). *Constitutional Interpretation*. Oxford: Oxford University Press.

Cohen, Felix (1935). Transcendental Nonsense and the Functional Approach, 35 *Cal. L. Rev.* 809.

Collins, Kristin A. (2008). "Let the Government Become Their Guardians": Administrative Law, Social Provision, and the Legal Construction of the Family in the Early Nineteenth Century (unpublished manuscript).

(Dauber), Michele Landis (1998). "Let Me Next Time Be 'Tried by Fire'": Disaster Relief and the Origins of the American Welfare State 1789–1874, 92 *Nw. U.L. Rev.* 967.

———. (2005). The Sympathetic State, 23 *L. & Hist. Rev.* 245.

Dworkin, Ronald (1978). *Taking Rights Seriously*. Cambridge, MA: Harvard University Press.

———. (1986). *Law's Empire*. Cambridge, MA: Harvard University Press.

Franck, Thomas M. (1990). *The Power of Legitimacy among Nations*. Oxford: Oxford University Press.

Green, Leslie (2003). Legal Positivism, in Penelope A. Bullock and Joseph Raz, eds., *Stanford Encyclopedia of Philosophy (an online publication)*, citing H. L. A. Hart, *The Concept of Law* 116 (2nd ed., 1994). Oxford: Oxford University Press.

Hart, H. L. A. (1961). *The Concept of Law*. Oxford: Oxford University Press.

Hilbink, Lisa (2007). *Judges beyond Politics in Democracy and Dictatorship: Lessons From Chile*. Cambridge: Cambridge University Press.

Kaplow, Louis and Steven Shavell (2001). Fairness versus Welfare, 114 *Harv. L. Rev.* 961.

Levinson, Sanford (2006). *Our Undemocratic Constitution*. Oxford: Oxford University Press.

Lipsey, R. G. and Kelvin Lancaster (1956). The General Theory of Second Best, 24 *Rev. Econ. Stud.* 11.

Markovits, Daniel (2004). Contract and Collaboration, 113 *Yale L.J.* 1417.

Markovits, Richard S. (1998). *Matters of Principle: Legitimate Legal Argument and Constitutional Interpretation*. New York: New York University Press.

———. (2004). Learning from the Foreigners: A Response to Professor Levinson's and Justice Scalia's Professional Moral Parochialism, 39 *Tex. J. of Int'l Law* 367.

———. (2006). Liberalism and Tort Law: On the Content of the Corrective-Justice-Securing Tort Law of a Liberal, Rights-Based Society, 2006 *Ill. L. Rev* 243.

———. (2008). *Truth or Economics: On the Definition, Prediction, and Relevance of Economic Efficiency*. New Haven: Yale University Press.

Mertz, Elizabeth (2007). *The Language of Law School: Learning to Think Like a Lawyer.* Oxford: Oxford University Press.

Quinn, Michael Sean (1999). Argument and Authority in Common Law Advocacy and Adjudication: An Irreducible Pluralism of Principles, 74 *Chi.-Kent L. Rev.* 655.

Radin, Max. (1930). Statutory Interpretation, 43 *Harv. L. Rev.* 863.

Raz, Joseph (1979). *The Authority of Law.* Oxford: Oxford University Press.

Segal, Jeffrey and Harold Spaeth (1993). *The Supreme Court and the Attitudinal Model.* Cambridge: Cambridge University Press.

Tyler, Tom R. and Gregory Mitchell (1994). Legitimacy and the Empowerment of Discretionary Legal Authority: The United States Supreme Court and Abortion Rights, 43 *Duke L.J.*

Index

CPSIA information can be obtained at www.ICGtesting.com
Printed in the USA
BVOW03s1252161014

371092BV00008B/93/P